BRAM FISCHER

"Stephen Clingman's passionate study of Afrikaner dissident Bram Fischer brings to light a . . . figure who was one of the founding fathers of the liberation struggle and a close comrade and friend of Mandela's." — Washington Post Book World

"The publication of Stephen Clingman's biography of Bram Fischer is a long overdue tribute to a most remarkable man. . . .The result is both inspired and inspiring." — The Sowetan

"This book on Fischer is like a crowbar. One can almost hear how the old, heavy and stiff beams of wood crack as they are prised away with every chapter you read. . . . [Clingman] handles the subject with a respect that does not shy away from the question marks. . . . The book allows Bram Fischer to live as a person." — Beeld

"I simply urge readers to get hold of it and read it – for its telling of the story of an extraordinary South African and for its insight into the history of struggle and counter-struggle for the meaning of being South African." — Sunday Times (Johannesburg)

Bram Fischer

AFRIKANER REVOLUTIONARY

Stephen Clingman

UNIVERSITY OF MASSACHUSETTS PRESS

Amherst

Second impression 1998

Copyright © 1998 Stephen Clingman

Published 1998 in Southern Africa
by David Philip Publishers
208 Werdmuller Centre, Claremont 7700, South Africa
and Mayibuye Books, University of the Western Cape, Bellville, Cape

Mayibuye Literature and History Series, No. 86

Published 1998 in the United States and Canada
by the University of Massachusetts Press
Box 429, Amherst, MA 01004

Printed in South Africa by National Book Printers, Drukkery Street,
Goodwood, Cape Town

LC 97-39287

ISBN 0-86486-318-7 (David Philip)
ISBN 1-55849-135-X (University of Massachusetts Press)

Library of Congress Cataloging-in-Publication Data

Clingman Stephen.
  Bram Fischer: Afrikaner revolutionary / Stephen Clingman.
    p. cm.
  Includes bibliographical references and index.
  ISBN 1-55849-135-X (alk. paper)
    1. Fischer, Bram, 1908–1975. 2. Communists—South Africa—
Biography. 3. South Africa—Politics and government—1948–
4. Apartheid—South Africa. I. Title.
HX450.5.A8C58 1998
322.4'4'092—dc21
[B]
                                              97-39287
                                              CIP

For Ruth and Ilse
who remembered and hoped

In memory of Paul Fischer
who would have seen it too

For Lorraine and Arthur Chaskalson
the clearest vision of justice and trust

For Moira, Amelia and Rebecca
who allowed their lives to be caught up with this

CONTENTS

Illustrations between pages 244 & 245

ACKNOWLEDGEMENTS

Working on this book has taken a long time, during which I have been grateful for the patience, support and assistance of a good number of individuals and institutions. I would like to acknowledge them here.

For support early on, and throughout the course of this book, I am deeply grateful to Joel Joffe, who at crucial moments ensured that I was able to travel and undertake research that might otherwise have been impossible. Both he and Arthur Chaskalson were in at the birth of this project, and I dare say without their encouragement I would never have begun it, let alone completed it. To these two Lorraine Chaskalson added her friendship, care and trust, crucial ingredients at all times.

As to those who are, so to speak, both inside and outside this book, I must, first and foremost, thank Ruth and Ilse Fischer. They took me on when all they knew about me was that I shared a birthday with their father, Bram. Over many years and many interviews they bore with me when I pushed them further than I had a right to go. Always open, forthcoming and generous, they kept their humour, they shared material without reservation, they answered questions of detail right up to the last minute. In the Fischer way, too, they opened their houses and shared their hospitality, not only with me but also my family. I am happy that through these years I have come to know them; my only hope is that they will feel it was worth all the trouble! Similarly, I must record my thanks to Drs Paul and Gustav Fischer, who were equally forthcoming and hospitable (they were known to my elder daughter – younger at the time – as the 'Doctors Fishes'). Sadly, Paul has since died, but the help he and Gus afforded me was invaluable.

Others have provided an underlying moral and practical support: Tom Karis, who has been behind the project throughout, and was one of the few who told me to 'take my time'; Nadine Gordimer, whose own interest in Bram Fischer is so marked; George Bizos, who helped arrange key interviews; Baruch Hirson, who was extremely generous both with his time and his contacts; Kwame Anthony Appiah, who supported the book from early on; and Caryl Phillips, who provided essential encouragement towards the end.

At successive institutions I benefited from the help of particular individuals. The Ford Foundation funded a fellowship at the Southern African Research Program (Yale University), admirably run by Leonard Thompson and Jeffrey Butler, with the wonderful assistance of Pamela Baldwin. At the African Studies Institute at the University of the Witwatersrand I was honoured to come into the collegial circle of Charles van Onselen and Tim Couzens. At the Society for the Humanities at Cornell University, I am grateful to Dominick La Capra and his assistants Mary Ahl and Agnes Sirrine. A fellowship at the Woodrow Wilson International Center for Scholars in Washington, D.C. provided an especially pleasurable and productive year, for which my thanks go to Charles Blitzer, Ann Sheffield, James Morris and their colleagues. Last but not least in the institutional vein, I am grateful to the University of Massachusetts, Amherst, and particularly to Lee Edwards for her support, as well as to my colleagues in the English Department, where no one so much as batted an eyelid when faced with my obscure, long-lasting, and apparently anti-disciplinary obsession. I cannot think of a friendlier environment in which to have worked.

At these institutions I have also been indebted to individual librarians, whose expert and amiable help made my work that much easier: Moore Crossey at Yale University; Mrs Anna Cunningham and her successor, Michele Pickover, at the University of the Witwatersrand; Zdenek David at the Wilson Center. At the South African Library in Cape Town I am grateful for assistance to Petre le Roux, and to Herschel Miller (who, pleasantly, also happens to be my brother-in-law).

At David Philip Publishers I would like to give especial mention to Russell Martin, who provided patient and attentive editorial work, conquering long distance by e-mail; at the University of Massachusetts Press Bruce Wilcox bestowed his characteristic care and dedication. My thanks must also go out to the many people I interviewed for the book, who gave of their time and information, or otherwise shared valuable material; while I cannot mention them all here (they are noted in my Bibliography), I am particularly grateful to Mary Benson and Hugh Lewin. One of the highlights of this book lay in corresponding with some of Bram's contemporaries, whose remembrances – whether small, large or sometimes complicated – were always thoughtful and helpful: my thanks are due to Sir Geoffrey Cox, Errol Harris, C.J. Johnson, Arthur Keppel-Jones and Sir Laurens van der Post.

I then have a list of friends and colleagues who have helped me in various ways, from doing the odd bit of research, to answering the vaguest of questions, to providing support both direct and distant. I shall mention them by geographical location (if I have left anyone out, I shall simply have to beg for-giveness). In England: James Simpson, and Stan and Barbara Trapido. In New Haven, a collection of friends around the Southern African Research Program during the year I was there: Neil Lazarus, Barbara Harmel, Mike and Mary Savage. In Johannesburg: Dr Phyllis Lewsen (who has provided such long-lasting support, as well as a good reading of an early draft), Phil Bonner, Matthew Chaskalson, Peter Delius, David Dison, Isabel Hofmeyr, Karen Lazar, Irwin Manoim, Santu Mofokeng. In Cape Town, and elsewhere in South Africa: Guy Berger, Nick and Pippa Visser, Stephen Watson. At Cornell: Chris Waterman. At the Woodrow Wilson Center: David Chandler, Michael Dunn (for willing and accurate research assistance), Laura Engelstein, Alice Freifeld, Mark Kinkead-Weekes, Renato Mazzolini, Bob Moeller, Anatoly Naiman. At the University of Massachusetts, and the Five-College area: Agha Shahid Ali, Margo Culley, Vince DiMarco, Anne Halley, Mzamo Mangaliso, Peggy O'Brien, Kathy Swaim, Don Weber, Michael Wolff. Those whose help has in various ways crossed geographical boundaries include Jim Campbell, Bob Edgar, David Everatt, Denis Hirson and Michael Reder. I would also be remiss if I did not mention those who have offered us hospitality during a peripatetic and sometimes hectic existence over the years: Geoff Budlender, Jules Chametzky and Anne Halley, Stan and Val Clingman, Paul and Bernice Looney, Mark and Brenda Schneider, Pat and Raymond Tucker, James Young and Lori Friedman.

Finally, I would like to mention especially the support of my family, both extended and narrow, over the years in which this book was written. To my parents, Reg and Madge Clingman, and my mother's sisters, Hilda Cohen and Sheila Lurie; to my cousin David Rosettenstein, who alternated the provision of physical sustenance with a readiness to answer the most abstruse of legal questions; to my brother Paul; to my wife Moira, and daughters Amelia and Rebecca: as I am of you, so is this book yours too.

Amherst,
September 1997.

Hence they are in error who censure Euripides just because he follows this principle in his plays, many of which end unhappily. It is, as we have said, the right ending.

– Aristotle, The Poetics

IN THE DESERT

c. 1880s

A life begins long before it starts, emerging from other lives before return-ing to them again. When it emerges it does so out of a current of time that long preceded it and continues on its way with scarcely a ripple long after. Though it has its own inner time, its own inner dimension and volume, when it emerges and takes shape it does so against the pressure, resistance and influ-ence of a surrounding history and ethos. It enters into the flow of this time, wafted this way and that, driven by it, sometimes altering its direction, match-ing as best it can its inner being to the demands of the time outside it. Both dimensions are real, inner and outer, and together they form the matrix that makes the path and trajectory of a life.

When we write a life, the book is not the life. Yet it must correspond to its essentials, its inner and outer dimensions. How to reach into those currents, extracting and understanding their forms? It may be impossible, yet it remains the objective, unless we fall too willingly into a play of self-deception and revelation. This is a biography and must rely on the facts; impression must be based on observation, interpretation on evidence. Yet it must also delve into those deeper currents. This account is predicated on the idea that even in telling the life of a political figure, through as political a history as South Africa's in the past century, the journey will be neither adequate nor meaning-ful if it does not integrate the outer and inner life. Nor, for that matter, will it understand the politics.

This means, among other things, hearing voices: those multiple and varied voices that enter into the self and provide the ground for its own re-articula-tion and identity. We must delve back in time and space to hear them, to see their presence in the identity they helped fashion, and the way the life both absorbed and transformed them, turning them into a different kind of utter-ance in the world. We must find those layers, as in a personal archaeology – competing, superimposed, fractured, intersecting – that underlie the visible landscape, that give it its inner shape and deeper modulations. We have to understand, in its broadest sense, a culture and its own modulation in a family, as both are entered into by the individual. We have to understand, in all of this, the inner and underlying and surrounding narratives that guide our lives in their encounter with the world.

We also have to understand how hard, and how crucial, it is to change them. It is a task that faces South Africa, transforming the reality of its past into a vision of the future. On a larger scale, in a world needing so much to imagine other possibilities beyond conflict and division, it remains no less necessary. How to build on and transform the identity as it is lived may be the hardest thing of all. This is the story of one individual who, born to expectations of prominence if not greatness, gave that expectation a new definition and language in the medium of his own life. In that respect, Bram Fischer's story is a story for our times, in all its complexity, fallibility and eminence.

I know why the writers of old called on the muses: how necessary, even when dealing with fact. A life begins long before it starts; a book may start in an unexpected place.

———

Once there was a man who came from another country, who lived in the African desert.

The year was 1882 or 1883, and the man's name was Bernsmann. He was a Rhenish missionary, and he lived in German South West Africa (present-day Namibia), in a small outpost called Otjimbingue. Some time during that year – whether it was 1882 or 1883 – he wrote back to his headquarters in Berlin, and asked them to send him a wife.

Just a few years earlier, in 1880, his first wife, named Emilie, had died. It had not been an easy time. Shortly before then, Otjimbingue had been in the midst of war, and the mission station had been attacked by the Zwartboois. Emilie had just given birth to twins. The eldest of the five children, Emmy, was not yet four when her mother died.

Bernsmann was himself not a well man. A visiting missionary remembered seeing him standing by his wife's grave, profoundly moved and alone. He could not maintain both his work and his home, and was in some anguish as to what to do. Finally he decided to entrust one of the recently born twins to a missionary couple in the Cape, and send the other back to Germany to be cared for. At the station an Herero woman named Annie took care of the remaining children, but even then things were too much for Bernsmann. In his solitude he wanted a wife.

In Germany a woman came to know of his letter, and agreed to go out to Africa to be married. She remembered Bernsmann from the time when he'd been a soldier in the Franco-Prussian War and she had seen him in uniform. She had also, it seems, been at the same mission school in 1872 and 1873.

So one afternoon in early March 1883, Bernsmann set off on the journey to meet his second wife. Together with his three daughters he said farewell to his small and beloved congregation in Otjimbingue, and the ox-wagon convoy departed. There were problems along the way. The oxen disappeared one morning, and one little girl (not Bernsmann's) had her dress catch fire – though it was quickly put out.

Bernsmann had travelled this way before, in the opposite direction. When he first arrived in South West Africa, on his way to Otjimbingue, the wagons had become stuck in the drifts, and he and a companion had continued on foot. There, at midday under the glare of the sun, he had played his trumpet, striding out into the desert. Because of the heat, he and his companion had walked on at night, under a full moon for guidance. As it was the very end of December, Bernsmann felt that he had walked from one year into another. At that time it was Emilie's arrival he was awaiting . . .

Now, after three weeks, they reached Walvis Bay. Bernsmann preached in the Dutch church, and drank champagne to celebrate the Kaiser's birthday. There were reports of new skirmishes and raids, by the Zwartboois and Nama. 'May God soon make an end of this thievery,' Bernsmann wrote in his journal, 'under which uncounted ones suffer from war.'

On Friday 13 April, the small family, together with Annie, boarded ship in Walvis Bay, bound for Cape Town. Towards evening, as they came out of the Bay, the waves grew higher, making them seasick, and Annie became inconsolable. She begged Bernsmann with all her heart to let her off the ship when it docked in Sandwich Harbour. She was so terrified, she said, that they might as well throw her into the sea as make her carry on any further. This caused Bernsmann great sorrow, because (as he wrote) Annie had been a mother to his children for a year; but she was steadfast in her conviction, and so he relented. In Sandwich Harbour they found two men from Walvis Bay (searching, so they said, for a stolen cat) who were prepared, for the sum of a pound, to take Annie back with them. 'So then I released her in God's name,' wrote Bernsmann. 'The parting was very hard for me, and Emmy cried. God keep her safely in good hands. The last we saw of her was as she walked off with her two companions, along the beach in the direction of Walvis Bay.'

By June Bernsmann was in Cape Town, waiting for his second wife, visiting friends and counting the days away as they passed. When he heard that the Warwick Castle had arrived at the docks, he rushed as fast he could to the harbour to meet it.

'My heart', he wrote, 'beat in my chest. Soon we were on the quay, exactly where the ship had put in.' But they could not see who was waiting on deck, nor could they go on board before the ship was properly moored. Finally, his bride appeared on deck, and there, holding her by the hand, was little Auguste, the twin who had been sent back to Germany, and who had now returned home with her new mother. 'Our hearts quickly found one another,' wrote Bernsmann of his new bride, and they went on to the mission school in Stellenbosch where, as the story goes, the new couple fell deeply in love, and were married within the week.

Bernsmann wrote: 'Yes, I love my little Charlotte with all my heart, and she has given all her love to me and the children. So we are very happy with one another, and I am richly comforted for the loss of my blessed Emilie.' But there was still the question of what to do with the other twin. 'I would very gladly – and my Lotte too – ', wrote Bernsmann, 'have her back, so that the twins would remain together, except that Brother and Sister Reinhardt are nearly inconsolable at the thought that they must once again be without her. And so my Lotte and I, albeit with heavy hearts, have decided before the Lord to leave her with them in this faraway place. Only later, if it is possible, she will go to the same school as her brothers and sisters . . .'

Later, Emmy, the eldest child, went to the mission school in Stellenbosch, as a boarder. Every year she made that same long trip, from Otjimbingue to Walvis Bay, then by sea to Cape Town, and at the end of the year all the way back. Later still she married a man with the name of Krige, in South Africa, and had four children. One of these was called Susanna Johanna (the second name for her aunt, the twin who had remained behind at the mission school), but everyone knew her as Molly.

It was Molly Krige who married Bram Fischer in 1937, but not before she had revisited the country of her mother's memory, and had put Bram off for some (seemingly endless) years . . .

This is a story that came out of the desert, blown by chance in the summer of 1985 into a garden in Johannesburg, where I was talking to Ruth and Ilse Fischer's Aunt Pauline. She was their mother Molly's sister, and she was telling me about their grandfather, an account supplemented later by his journals and other sources. It is a story that does not immediately concern Bram Fischer, but since then I have come to understand it as the overture: not obviously, not directly, but for that very reason as well. It comes out of the legendary past – as history does, in its sharper delineations – and it also becomes the basis for a human geography: this is the bedrock from which the carved figures take their breath and step into life.

Why did it continue to resonate in this way? First, because it shows how utterly different and alien the past is, how we have to search into it as into another form of life. But then also because it seems in some respects so familiar, with its recognisable dramatis personae, its basic, poignant and brooding realities. Though this was not Bram Fischer's own story, or even that of his own ancestors, none the less it formed the broader history of which he was a part. It was that history, with all its aliennesses and strangenesses, all its familiar and recognisable voices, which he would have to bring with him into the future, that became his definition of redemption. If he was to succeed he would have to do it both by understanding and by challenge; by being part of, yet refusing to participate; by widening the range of inclusion of this story; by knowing the relationship between past and future, and sensing how the gap between them is bridged.

There are other issues that resonate. This is a story of Europe and Africa, their juxtaposition and seemingly ineradicable divide. There are journeys, fast and slow, across the sands of the present towards some half-intimated destination. There are prejudice and preformed images, but also unexpected human contact and the glimpse of recognition. There are the twins – connection, and its sibling, separation – and solitude, death and endurance: how these are lived and re-lived. There are families, narrow, extended and metaphoric: what it means to belong to the family of humanity. There is the question of how to bring that family together again: whether it is possible from such a past; what kind of imagination and life can make it happen.

Ultimately, it is because this story is about finding a home, which turns out to mean how one defines oneself. It becomes a story of identity – of how that, in its origins, transformations and destination, becomes inseparable from the journey it undertakes. It begins over a century ago, and will take us towards the next century.

CHAPTER 1

FATHERS AND SONS

꩜

1850 – 1913

As for Bram Fischer's paternal grandfather, Abraham Fischer – Oupa Abraham – his journey began elsewhere, and followed different routes.

> Firbank
> 27th November 1907.
>
> My Dear Abraham,
>
> My heart is so full on this auspicious day that I feel I must write and tell you, besides my hearty congratulations, how proud I am of my worthy son on attaining this great appointment of *Prime Minister* of Orangia which you love so much and for which place you have done so much in times past and will I am convinced do your utmost in the future with God's help and blessing. May he give you health and strength to carry out this big work your people have entrusted to you.
>
> As we cannot be with you to day we will have to satisfy ourselves by looking at *your portrait* on the dining room chimney *gaily decorated* by *Maggie* with a *wreath* of *Orange* and *Green*. Give my fond love to dear Ada and tell her I shall write to her next – and with much love to yourself.
>
> I remain ever
> Your affectionate Mother Aunt
> H. Denyssen.

How such a letter came to be written on such an auspicious occasion by someone who called herself a 'mother aunt' is itself a matter of some interest. The Fischer line that led to Abraham traced back two centuries to a Johannes Fischer who had come to the Cape to serve in the artillery of the Dutch East India Company. Three generations later his descendant, one Johannes Jacobus George Fischer, married Catharina Anna Brink; Abraham was their younger son, born at Green Point, in Cape Town, on 9 April 1850.

The Fischers owned a farm called Klein Bottelarij near Stellenbosch, but as Abraham's father was a younger son and would not inherit the family patrimony, he went into government service in Cape Town instead. When Abraham was eleven, however, his father died, and there was an immediate crisis for the family. A woman with children could not survive on her own, and so, according to the custom in such circumstances, Catharina moved in with relatives. Her sister had married another Abraham – this time an Abraham Denyssen – and they absorbed the bereaved family into their home.

It must have been a particularly difficult time for the young Abraham. At that same age – eleven – he left his primary school, Tot Nut van 't Algemeen, and entered the South African College. There, apparently during an initiation accident, his right eye was so badly damaged that it had to be removed. Through these events the consolations of his new home must have been all the more important to him, and in fact Abraham became extremely close to his mother's sister: to the end of his life he would speak with veneration of how much he owed her. As for her, she doted on him, invariably calling him 'my worthy son'. So that was how someone could be both a mother and an aunt – the Mrs Denyssen who wrote to Abraham Fischer with such love and pride when he became Prime Minister of the Orange River Colony.

A young boy who loses a father at that age may develop the will-power to make his way in the world, assume the mantle of his destiny, and prove his worth to those who have shown loyalty to him. Certainly Abraham was sur-rounded by loyalty, not least on the part of his 'mother aunt' – and if the name revealed an understated and intimate humour, it also suggested a doubled maternal doting and interest. It is tempting to search for (and find) continu-ities, and much of Abraham's own life became the stuff of legend to his descen-dants, a family that nurtured and protected its memories. Yet it was as much in its form as in its content that his life became significant: loyalty became a guiding principle for the Fischers; 'family', in both its immediate and extended senses, a guiding if implicit metaphor for the obligations they felt; a certain maternal concern an intrinsic aspect of their engagement with others; a gentle humour one measure of their magnetic effect.

At the South African College Abraham Fischer studied law. Members of each succeeding generation, down to Bram Fischer's children, attended SACS (in its later incarnation as the University of Cape Town), and both Bram and his father Percy became lawyers. Bram went on to study at New College, Oxford, whereas Percy had been a student at Trinity Hall, Cambridge, which seems fitting in retrospect, since he was both son and father in this dynastic triad.

When Abraham returned from England he left Cape Town for Grahams-town, and then in 1872 moved on to Kimberley, where diamonds were just being discovered. The Fischers who remained at Stellenbosch apparently thought this a dubious undertaking, but Abraham seems to have been unafraid of new territory. There, in 1873, he married Ada Robertson of Fauresmith in the Free State; her parents were both Scots immigrants, and her father a doctor. In 1875 the couple moved to Bloemfontein, and founded the farm Hillandale, just outside the town. There, on 22 March 1878, Bram's father Percy was born.

In Bloemfontein Abraham practised law, and was drawn to politics. He became elected to the Volksraad and then, in 1896, was appointed by President M.T. Steyn to the Executive Council of the Orange Free State. Bloemfontein was a small town in an agrarian Boer republic in the hinterland of South Africa, President Steyn its leader sentimentally revered among the white populace. There, in times filled with gathering drama, Abraham Fischer found himself in the midst of conflicting forces.

⁂

Abraham was an inveterate letter writer, as befitted the setting of his life, his culture and his station. His official duties required a wide correspondence, but he wrote multitudes of personal letters as well, especially to his son Percy when the latter left home, first to attend school at SACS, and then when he went on to Cambridge. The letters gave an inner view of Abraham's world, and the ethos which in various ways he handed on.

There was nothing Abraham liked better than tramping for miles over 'Hill and Dale', as he called the farm in his letters to Percy – the name no doubt congenial to Ada with her Scots heritage, the walks a regular Sunday venture for her husband. Abraham watered the orange trees, or observed with attention the large and subtle differentiations of grasses and shrubbery and birds. He described for Percy how, across veld still untamed, he watched with mild amusement as his dog Pickle barked at the 'Spring bucks'. On other occasions there were 'Spring buck hunts', to which the eminent men of the Free State were invited, President Steyn among them. Above all it was trees that Abraham Fischer loved, and he planted willows and *karees* on his farm, a gesture of belonging and habitation, as if their rooting in the soil were an expression of his own.

Abraham Fischer did well, in time acquiring a town residence, Fern Lodge. He also renovated the Hillandale house, now with a private dressing-room for himself, a new 'west back wing', and two dams on either side of the garden wall to which pipes from the kloof brought water. He had a croquet lawn laid out, and there were numbers of servants to cater to all aspects of the household – a groundsman, a cook, a housemaid, and a 'third white girl' for general help, as well as the regular black farm labourers of the South African landscape. It was an elegant, patrician, paradoxically urbane life for a farm. At Christmas the Fischers would host lunch for two dozen or more, at the height of the South African summer in the open air under the almond trees. In October 1898, when Abraham and Ada celebrated their silver wedding anniversary, they entertained almost a hundred guests. Two enormous tarpaulins were stretched over tables set between the almond, fig and orange trees, decorated with coloured flags along the sides. The guests brought gifts of silver, and chief among them was a magnificent table centrepiece from President Steyn and his wife. Some of those assembled played tennis on the 'tennis ground', now a permanent part of the lawns, since tennis was all the rage in Bloemfontein.

Abraham told Percy, away in Cambridge at the time, that those expecting a religious ceremony at the anniversary must have been disappointed. For he himself was evidently of his world, but not entirely conventional. Abraham Fischer was not a Boer patriarch weighed down by the Bible as well as his beard: for him his customary walks on the veld on Sunday were a more meaningful ritual than anything the Dutch Reformed Church had to offer. He was, in his own way, a man of the world secure in providing a suitably broadening experience for his son. He took his place among the elite of Bloemfontein, made up of professional, commercial and political families such as the Reitzes, the Steyns, the Frasers and the Fichardts, some of whom were as likely to gather for a reading from Shakespeare as an address from any *dominee*. Nor was their sense of identity bound up entirely in language: Abraham had married a Scotswoman; the Fichardts were a mixture of German, Dutch and Welsh ancestry; and Ada Fischer and Mrs Steyn conversed together in their native English. They were as a group perhaps as differentiated from the country farmers who soon came to represent the iconic image of the Boer as they were from the styles of Europe they imitated. But that did not mean there was no local nationalism. Dutch, Scots, Welsh, German, English as they were, there was still a fierce attachment to their Republic, once held by the British, now independent, but threatened at the turn of the century once again. Abraham Fischer felt this too, notwithstanding the fact that he wrote to Percy in Cambridge in English.

<hr />

Percy was not Abraham and Ada's first child. His brother, Harry, older by three and a half years, had been born when the couple were still in Fauresmith, before they moved to Hillandale. He had also preceded Percy at Cambridge; in this much their experience was alike. Yet it appears that Harry took no degree, in itself a sign that there were differences between the two sons that came to matter to Abraham, especially as time passed.

In everything that Abraham wrote to Percy, their quiet friendship was apparent. When Percy first went off to SACS, Abraham told him how much he missed his 'Confidential Secretary & co Tramper' on his Sunday walks (a routine that Percy later handed on to his own children, on that same farm). Every now and then, Abraham wrote, he would still when 'in gedachte' [lost in thought; Abraham used Dutch for the colloquial intimacies] go into Percy's room with the notion that he was still there. But when he wrote to Percy about Harry a different tone of voice frequently entered in. Sometimes Abraham was amused: 'Harry is at the moment out on the verandah dividing his time between puffs of horrid boer tobacco & singing at the top of his voice, snatches of "The Last Rose of Summer" – .' Yet more often he could not conceal a current of anxiety, in the main about Harry's work habits, for Abraham suspected him strongly of being pleasure-loving and workshy. When President Steyn took an interest in Harry, taking him onto his farm, Abraham told Percy he hoped that Harry might learn an object lesson 'of what hard work & *system* can do combined of course with knowledge & experience.' He confided to Percy the specific nature of his concern: 'young lady visitors & parties in town do interfere a good deal with satisfactory farming, & I dare say that Harry will see this himself after a bit, at least I hope so for his sake.'

Every letter that Abraham wrote to Percy about Harry was also an implicit injunction to Percy, of what examples he should follow, and what to avoid. For along with his intimate indulgence, Abraham was never reticent on matters either of advice or of ambition, and was always clear on exactly what he expected of Percy, even from early on. 'If you only knew how proud I felt of my little son,' he wrote when Percy was but ten years old, 'when I saw all the big fellows of the class and heard his name called "first," you wd try and always take the lead.' And if Percy enjoyed some particular achievement, Abraham could not resist telling him, in his characteristic phrasing, just 'how proud of Johnny' he was.

When Percy left for Cambridge at the end of August 1897, Abraham said goodbye to him at the Bloemfontein railway station, and then, in his way, went home to write him a long letter which Percy would receive on board ship in Cape Town and read in the open hours at sea on his way to England. He told Percy, with true feeling, how empty Hillandale felt as he 'fossicked' around on his own. He wanted to avoid preaching, but could not resist: 'For the rest, & as to advice I don't believe in sermonising, if a young man is going to make up his mind to keep straight & to work honestly he will do so without being preached at, and if he means the other thing advice will be equally wasted. – You have given me your word as you did before, you kept it then & I believe you now & implicitly trust you, so warnings and reminders would be out of place. If you should, however, have any worry or get into any scrape don't forget that it will always be best at once to consult your "stern parent" in his other capacity of your best friend?'

Abraham's parental respect wrapped Percy in a fine web of trust and gentle conscience, so much more effective than admonition. It was not simply a matter of manipulation, but emotion both suppressed and revealed. As Percy left for England, Abraham extended advice for every occasion: to make friends not only with South Africans, but with people of different views, thoughts and notions; not to start with a prejudice, but to give the new life a fair trial; to take a share in the fun and sociability of his college; to join the Union and take part in debates; to keep in touch (as he put it) 'with *ladies*' society'. Abraham's hopes were enlightened ones, for the complete experience that his son should enjoy in England, but when Percy did badly at his initial exams, Abraham's understanding had an undisguised edge of exhortation: 'I don't think your place of 13th in the lot so bad after all. But the higher the better & as you take it in the right spirit, that is to try & do better next time, you have our best wishes for better luck at the next trial. Maybe a shot for *"first"* & make us more than proud of Johnny.' When, far from home, Percy turned twenty-one, Abraham reeled him in with the obligations of responsibility even as he welcomed him to independence: 'you are now arriving at man's estate & the principles you start with are likely to be the guiding ones through life: – try & avoid in the present creating causes for vain regrets in the future. But I am preaching when I only meant to send my loving congratulations . . . '

Abraham fussed, Abraham worried, but there was at least a mollifying self-awareness of his incapacity to do otherwise. There was also a wry, dry sense of humour. 'Old Philips the butcher tried to commit suicide on Friday,' Abraham told Percy, 'but he was not as good at his own throat as he had been at that of hundreds of sheep before, consequently he is recovering.' He wrote to Percy about the drought, but thought it had to end soon: 'I can't think Providence intended us to end our existence as involuntarily manufactured biltong [the dried, spiced meat beloved of the Boers].'

If Sunday mornings were spent walking on the veld, Sunday evenings were, religiously, Abraham's time for letter writing when, in his contemplative mood, he would recreate the colorations of the natural world around him and the human preoccupations, both large and small, it contained. As the years passed, Percy became increasingly his confidant, on matters personal, familial and political. Abraham passed on not only information but also a *style*, handed down from grandfather, to son, to grandson. Bram, like his father and his Oupa Abraham before him, had the same human concern and fussiness, the same restraint and engagement, the same enlightenment and primness, the same humour, the same drive to succeed, the same feel for family and sense of responsibility, the same need to win people over, the same propensity to write letters. Across three generations they all even had the same handwriting. A life begins long before it starts.

In October 1898, when Abraham Fischer was describing his and Ada's silver wedding anniversary, he wrote to Percy: 'Some twenty odd traps of all kinds made the outspan place look quite like a commando.' There were other signs of a change in the air. Earlier, Abraham had told Percy that Harry had been to his first *wapenschaauing* [armed parade], looking fierce enough to repel a dozen raids single-handed.

Raids were not out of the question. Just a few years before, in December 1895, Dr Leander Starr Jameson had led his ill-advised expedition against the Zuid-Afrikaansche Republiek (South African Republic, or ZAR) to the north, and common understanding was that he had done so with the connivance of Joseph Chamberlain, Colonial Secretary in Britain. Through the nineteenth century British imperial designs had waxed and waned, now intent on control over the two Boer Republics, later content to cede relative measures of independence. But in 1886 gold was discovered in the small encampment that later became Johannesburg, and that made all the difference. With the backing of Rhodes (who dreamed of a map coloured British red from Cape to Cairo) and Chamberlain (who with the unadorned brazenness of the powerful later denied all, and was cleared by a British parliamentary committee), as well as the imperfect support of the Johannesburg mining magnates (the so-called Randlords), Dr Jameson launched his raid, but was captured ignominiously.

The embarrassment that followed neither solved the problem nor curbed Britain's aims. The Randlords bristled under the corruption and incompetence of the ZAR's ramshackle state; the *uitlanders* [foreigners, mostly English] who had settled there now required fourteen years' residence to obtain the vote; and Britain still retained a nominal 'suzerainty' over the Republic which it attempted with increasing determination to enforce. Chamberlain, along with his new High Commissioner for the Cape, Sir Alfred Milner, turned up the pressure, obsessed with gaining control of the goldfields and the state to which they were so inconveniently attached.

It was in these circumstances that Abraham Fischer found himself in demand, and at every step of the way he wrote to Percy in Cambridge, imparting the details. Early in 1897 there were conferences in Pretoria. By October that year the ZAR were sending emissaries to Abraham at Hillandale: their State Secretary, Leyds, was retiring, and they wanted Abraham to take his place, both to engineer reform within the Republic and to stave off the British. But Abraham had no inclination to undertake what he saw as an 'Augean task.' He told Percy that 'concessions and jobbery' were rife in the ZAR, and he even feared that President Kruger had been, as he put it, 'tampered with'. 'Oom Paul', he wrote, 'has got some queer folk about him who *do* get him to do & say queer things occasionally.' By May 1898 the ZAR was almost desperate to obtain Abraham's services, and he told Percy of the 'combined forces of Volksraad, Executive & packs of telegrams . . . President Kruger personally poured in wires asking me to reconsider & not to disappoint & wired to President Steyn to back him & to urge the welfare of South Africa &c &c &c: however, I stuck to my guns, the storm has blown over & here I am & here I will remain . . . I am told the market (shares) boomed when I was elected & slumped when I declined, complimentary but probably untrue . . . '

If Abraham had few illusions about the state of affairs in the ZAR, he had even fewer about the avidity of British imperialism. 'It is unfortunate, but a fact,' he wrote in March 1899 to John X. Merriman, the veteran Cape parliamentarian with whom he was now closely linked in efforts to avert war, 'that we do not trust the motives or the policy of those who are just now responsible for the "safeguarding" (?) of British *Imperial* as distinguished from the Colonial or South African interests in this part of the world.' (For Abraham, whose love was for indigenous trees, the distinction between the 'imperial' and the 'colonial' was between outsiders greedy for gain and those who belonged to South Africa.) In June of that year Merriman invited him down to Cape Town to meet General Butler, Milner's deputy, and a man much more kindly disposed towards the Republics. Afterwards Merriman remembered that Abraham had said, 'almost with tears in his eyes', that if Butler and not Milner were in charge he would bring Kruger down to Cape Town to meet him, and that everything could be settled easily.

At that time Abraham was travelling up and down the country, called in to mediate on all sides. At the end of May he was one of the principal negotiators at the Bloemfontein Conference, working in close contact with Milner, an association he found distasteful but unavoidable. The most he could hope for, he told Percy, was that common sense would show Milner the absurdity of war. If Milner came only as Chamberlain's mouthpiece, to dictate terms, then nothing could save them. The 'Africander' (as Abraham spelled the term) would stand firm on the principles that Britain had no right to interfere in the domestic concerns of the ZAR, and that the idea of 'suzerainty' contained undefined and undefinable assumptions of authority. To Abraham's lawyerly eye these points were self-evident, and in writing to Percy he dwelt with some relish on the attendant ironies. Chamberlain had at last conceded that any Englishman who obtained the franchise in the ZAR would thereby cease to be a British subject. 'Now can England go to war to unmake so many hundreds or thousands of Englishmen? Or to help Englishmen in their endeavours to cease to remain English?'

But that was not, as Abraham well knew, what Chamberlain wanted. As for Milner, Abraham commented to Percy (much like Mark Antony invoking the virtues of Brutus after the assassination of Caesar) that it was difficult 'to deal with so honest and honourable a diplomat and statesman'. Milner had said he wanted peace, and for the sake of diplomacy one was compelled to pretend to believe him. The simple fact was that there was no choice; the horrors of war were too awful to leave any stone unturned because of unscrupulous scoundrels.

In June Abraham went up to Pretoria with a Cape plan for the ZAR franchise, but Chamberlain made an inflammatory speech in Birmingham which entirely undid his efforts. By early September, in the gathering crisis, Abraham's time was no longer his own. Chamberlain had rejected the ZAR's latest offer, and the latter, he told Percy, were about to reply in 'blood and thunder style'. Abraham sent wires to Pretoria, advising them not to oblige Chamberlain by losing their heads. Then it was up by overnight train to Pretoria, where endless drafts and dispatches followed on Chamberlain's demand for a joint commission on the franchise. Then back to Bloemfontein, where he reported to President Steyn. Then back to Hillandale, where he told a surprised Ada just where he had been in the interim; and then, as always, he wrote to Percy.

It was 'banja laat' [very late], and he was 'banja moeg' [very tired], he told Percy; otherwise he would have put in a few anecdotes about Oom Paul. Once or twice he had already done this, describing a 'very seedy' President Kruger attending 'his Executive meeting in his drawing room tricked up in an overcoaty looking dressing gown & a pink flannel night cap: characteristic but not beautiful to behold'.

When Abraham wrote that it was 'banja laat' and that he was 'banja moeg', his Dutch phrasing was altering recognisably into an indigenous and creolised Afrikaans. Like his changing language, the war that he was trying to avoid might have made a Boer out of Abraham, whose sons had begun their lives with the most English (or Scottish) of names.

On 17 September he wrote to Percy that the beginning of the end was at hand. Chamberlain's latest demand required the ZAR to surrender part of its independence and admit Britain's suzerainty and paramountcy. This had been refused, and now war was inevitable. Percy would know very soon from the newspapers, wrote Abraham, whether they were in for 'the most iniquitous attack ever made on a peaceful community by liberty-loving, fair play England or not . . . ' 'Judas Iscariot', he added, 'will have to look to his laurels now that Joseph Chamberlain is on the job.'

Two weeks later Abraham told Percy that he was stealing stray moments to write before the mails shut down. British troops were massing on the borders of the Free State and the Transvaal, and in both Republics the burghers had been mobilised. Abraham sent Percy copies of documents and a manifesto which he was to attempt to publish in the *Manchester Guardian* or *Daily Chronicle* in case of war. Although Percy's desire was to return home and take up arms, his father advised him to remain in Cambridge and continue with his studies: 'in that way you will soonest & best be able to help your country and me.' Abraham made plans for his continuing financial needs, and told him how his brother Harry had ridden off to join his commando.

For Abraham it may have been something of a relief that one of his children was out of harm's way, but to Percy it was absolutely galling (as his sons remarked later) that he should have been incapacitated in so helpless a manner. Provided for by Abraham, he must have felt like a kept man in Cambridge, suffering the particular indignity of being stuck as a student in the enemy country, while his father and elder brother went off heroically to war. He must have seemed to himself still on the wrong side of adulthood, now identified with national destiny. As Abraham vividly described for him the solidarity and sense of consecration in the Free State Volksraad, the contrasts could not have been more exacting: 'The spirit & unanimity is something wonderful: the closing scene in the Raad which had its session in secret was most stirring. There was no bounce or 'groot praat' [boasting] but quiet determination, & the spontaneous & unmistakeable enthusiasm with which the members (you know what a sedate lot they usually are) burst out into the Volkslied [national anthem] was something to remember. They were all most cheerful learning that the best had been done to avert war & that they were unjustly being dragged into it. The members were most hearty in their thanks to me & "Onze Abram" [Our Abram] came in for a lot of undeserved praise . . . '

Engraved like a photograph on the mind, some moments can become iconic in themselves. Here was an image of national apotheosis, illuminated with the radiance of heroic faith and gallantry, as well as humble acceptance of whatever the future might bring. And near its centre was Abraham Fischer, caught in the hearts of those who surrounded him as 'Onze Abram'. Abraham Fischer remained in family memory as a peacemaker, for whom war between South Africans was an ultimate evil. Sixty-six years later his grandson Bram would speak directly of his fear of the same horror, though the war he wished to avoid was not between Boer and Briton but between black and white.

Yet for both grandfather and grandson there was a certain resolve. It was rumoured that Abraham Fischer had drafted the ultimatum which the ZAR delivered to the British, demanding the withdrawal of their troops from the border. When the ultimatum was rejected the Boers attacked, and war began on 12 October 1899.

Abraham's last letter to Percy from Hillandale was dated '4 Febry /00'. On 13 March 1900 he stepped on board ship at Delagoa Bay in Portuguese East Africa as one of a three-man delegation dispatched by the Republics to solicit intervention and support from overseas powers.

At first the war went well for the Boers. In the east they invaded Natal and laid siege to Ladysmith; in the west they surrounded Kimberley and Mafeking; in the south commandos invaded the Cape Colony, recruiting Afrikaner sympathisers as they went. Following the devastating British losses at Stormberg, Magersfontein and Colenso, the news of a dilapidated army of farmers dressed in their homespun clothes defeating the uniformed might of the British Empire cast untold gloom in England and equal elation in the Republics. In Abraham's letters to Percy, sent by diverse and devious routes, he was satisfied to the point of exhilaration. The whole of northern Natal had been taken, he reported, and the town of Colenso 'brilliantly evacuated by the British' (Abraham was scathing on the standard style of English newspaper accounts). The Boers had lost just one hundred dead compared with the enemy's five thousand; Pretoria was swollen with prisoners; and the Republics had seized top-secret military dispatches. No doubt Abraham hoped that Percy might use these details to counteract British propaganda, even in some small way.

At Hillandale, Abraham told Percy, they were well and cheerful and, above all, hopeful. Ada Fischer was looking after the farm and baking biscuits for the commandos, as were many of the Bloemfontein women. Harry had been occupied in blowing up the Modder River bridge, and had even been involved in an attack on 'the much advertised armoured train'; now he was involved in the siege of Kimberley. At last Abraham sounded proud of Harry: 'He seems to have found his proper vocation. All who have seen him speak of him with the greatest praise: he is always bright & keeping up the spirit of his friends & companions and the first to volunteer for work any day or night. At least,' Abraham added, 'so they tell me.'

Abraham was also in the field, on tour with President Steyn to Natal where, he told Percy, he himself had made a close acquaintance with British artillery. At Colesberg and Tugela he made speeches to the assembled commandos, interviewed the *krijgsofficieren*, and moved among the common soldiers, finding out their needs. Abraham described men who were supposed to be invalids, some aged seventy or more, who would not hear of being considered sick or old. Their spirit, pluck and confidence, he wrote, and their absolute faith that God was with them, would put life into an Egyptian mummy. He gave their simple and quiet colloquial greetings to one another: 'Hoe gaat dit?' [How are things?]; 'heeltemaal goed' [altogether fine]; and 'nee, net fluks' [no, just right]. Abraham's own terms of speech owed a good deal to the Victorian tones of the Empire he was fighting: 'I did expect the burgers of the SAR & OFS to make a good & brave stand for their independence, but those are weak adjectives to express what they have really done & are doing. They have dumbfounded me: it is simply grand!'

It could not last. In the war's later guerrilla phase the British moved up the line of rail from the Cape, cordoning off successive areas with fences guarded by blockhouses, making sweeps to trap the commandos, destroying Boer houses and farmlands as they went. Women and children were taken into the world's first concentration camps where, because of disease and malnutrition, the rate of death approached some 344 per thousand. It was an Englishwoman, Emily Hobhouse, who gained the everlasting affection of the Boers by publicising the scandal, though she paid little attention to the African families also put into camps, where, by the end of the war, some 372 per thousand were dying.

Already in March 1900 the British were on the outskirts of Bloemfontein, and on the 13th they marched in. It was on that very day that Abraham Fischer, spirited out earlier, went on board ship with his delegation. They travelled to Holland, Germany, France, Italy, the United States and Imperial Russia, and that was how Abraham became the first Fischer to visit

St Petersburg. Thirty-two years later his grandson did the same, when the city was called Leningrad.

⚬⚬⚬

For the duration of the war, Abraham remained chiefly in Holland, at The Hague, where he was joined by his wife Ada, by Percy (after he had completed his degree at Cambridge) and by Harry, who had been taken prisoner of war by the British and was expatriated overseas. Also in Holland, though in more dismaying circumstances, was President Steyn, taken grievously ill in the field in South Africa, and evacuated to Europe for medical treatment.

A war of attrition had its results. Farms and farmland were destroyed; the Boer commandos could no longer feed themselves or their horses; Africans were occupying deserted white property. In the ZAR and Free State there were *bittereinders* [bitter-enders] who refused to give in, but the delegates called to Vereeniging in May 1902 to discuss surrender realised they could not hold out in the long term. Yet when the Boers signed the Treaty of Vereeniging on 31 May 1902, the after-effects rippled through the century. Many of those whose farms or livelihood had been destroyed by war streamed to the towns – mainly the mining fields of the Witwatersrand – where they formed a new underclass of poor whites. There they would feel threatened on two fronts – by British supremacy in economic and political life, and by Africans driven to the towns for similar reasons, with whom they now jostled in competition as a labour force. It was a powerful matrix, as time went on, for the generation of a renewed Afrikaner nationalism.

If a life can begin before it starts, a war continues long after it ends, and certainly the Boer War lived on in the imagination. Those left in the countryside, as well as those uprooted to the towns, nurtured memories of heroism and betrayal. Educated Boer opinion saw the links between imperialism, economic greed and exploitation. For all, the deaths of the women and children in the concentration camps scarred the future with unhealing themes of sweet grievance and bitter nostalgia.

In these circumstances the Fischers fared better than most. Even before leaving South Africa, Abraham, in his guise as astute businessman, had taken precautions so that if Hillandale were confiscated 'no one will lose thereby'. Now, immediately after the war, he remained stuck in London, unable to return home, and so he sent Percy on ahead with strict instructions. The British had indeed commandeered Hillandale as a supply depot; now they wanted to charge Abraham for 'improvements'. Percy's brief was to resist mightily, and also to charge the British rent from the time that they had taken over Hillandale and Abraham's town residence, Fern Lodge. But Abraham's resources must have been drained to some extent, for Percy was also to explore the sale of Fern Lodge, Abraham's offices in town and, if he could obtain the right price, Hillandale itself.

Returning home must have been somewhat dreamlike. In March 1904 Abraham Fischer, at last back in South Africa, wrote to President Steyn, still in Europe, describing life under British administration, mocking the tones of English superiority to make the point: 'Our beloved "masters" walk deeper and deeper into the mud. Once again the finances are in a hopeless mess. But ah they ah are ah teaching the ah stupid Boahrs how ah to ah rule ah country with ah ahbility & ah economy &c &c om maar niets to zeggen van [to say nothing of] "incapacity and corruption." Ja het is ah! akelig!! [Yes, it is ah! awful!!]'

But after the extended drama of war and defeat, self-government was not long in arriving. The Liberal Party in Britain had, throughout the war, been deeply critical of the brutality of its conduct, and now, when it came to power in 1906, granted to the Republics what they had fought so tragically to achieve, albeit within the orbit of British Empire. In the Transvaal, Generals Louis Botha and Jan Smuts led their party, Het Volk [The People], on a platform not only of nationalism but also, more realistically, of reconciliation with Britain and with English-speakers in South Africa. In the election of February 1907 Het Volk won a clear majority, and Botha became Prime Minister. In November in the Orange River Colony (as it had been named after the British annexation), its sister party, the Orangia Unie, won all but eight of the thirty-eight seats.

That was how its leader, Abraham Fischer, became the first (and only) Prime Minister of the Orange River Colony. That was when Mrs Denyssen, his mother aunt, wrote her letter overflowing with congratulation and love, and when her daughter Maggie wreathed Abraham's portrait in orange and green. And that was when, just a few months later, Abraham's grandson, Abram Fischer, was born on 23 April 1908.

⁂

On 13 March 1900, the day that Oupa Abraham left by ship from Delagoa Bay, and the day that the British army marched into Bloemfontein, Mrs Margaret Marquard was keeping up her correspondence from the Dutch Reformed parsonage in Winburg in the Free State. Once or twice in the preceding months Abraham had stopped off there, giving details of the war's developments as he rested on his travels. Now, as the enemy soldiers marched into the capital, Mrs Marquard gave an account of their approach, as relayed by the telegraphist in Bloemfontein. 'Now I see two English officers going through the streets,' had come the message. 'They say a deputation has just gone out to surrender the town' – and that was all he could send before the wires were cut.

On that same day in Bloemfontein, a group of British soldiers came up to a finely appointed house called Kayalami. There an Englishwoman, Miss Nakie Smith, was waiting at the gate with a double-barrelled shotgun in her hand. She informed the soldiers straightforwardly that the first who dared to pass through would have his head blown off in short order. As the story went, the soldiers turned round and disappeared.

Miss Nakie (pronounced 'Nah-kie') Smith worked as a governess for the Fichardt family. She had been born in 1845, so that on the day she turned the English soldiers away, she was no less than fifty-five years old. Her employer, Gustav Adolf Fichardt, had sought her out in England to take care of his daughters (his sons would go to school while the girls stayed at home). Fichardt himself had come out from Germany as an immigrant, to join his brother who had begun work as a missionary but had then opened a supply store in the fledgling Bloemfontein. In time Gustav came to run the store himself, and G.A. Fichardt's became one of the notable institutions of the town, and he the head of one of its leading families. In 1868 he married Caroline Beck, whose ancestry was Welsh on one side, and German, English, Dutch and French Huguenot on the other, so that when their own children were born, their identity was an extraordinary composite – European, but belonging to no European country. Instead that country was becoming, ingrained, South Africa.

They had four boys and two girls. The elder daughter, Maude Geraldene (nick-named Mollie), was born on 8 September 1877, and the younger, Ella Cecil, on 1 January 1884. Maude married Dr Bidwell, also an Englishman, but whose allegiance in the crisis of war had lain with the Boer Republic. And it was Ella Fichardt who married Percy Fischer, Abraham's son, on 12 April 1907. It was a marriage of two elite families, for the Fichardts were extremely wealthy. In the aftermath of the war their home had beautiful gardens, with a tennis court, lawns and trees, where the two daughters entertained their entourages, and at least some of those invited felt a little intimidated by the lavish surroundings.

When Percy and Ella's first child was born they called him Abram – after his grandfather Abraham, but with the biblical shift of name in reverse. And yet, in one of Abraham's finest moments, he had, as he had written to Percy, been called by his compatriots 'Onze Abram'. The abbreviation of the name into a more familial Afrikaans perhaps captured, especially for Percy, the illuminated nature of that moment when humble men, accepting their destiny, had taken on the might of Empire – a moment filled with an aura of self-revelation and identity that Percy *could only imagine when he had been so distant in England. Abram Fischer was named in that sense for a place and a belonging and a home, a renewed birth as well as continuity with the past.*

From the first Percy and Ella called him 'Bram' (pronounced 'Braam'), the further contraction tendering intimations and affections of its own. His grandfather was Prime Minister; his father, returned from Cambridge, was practising law and lecturing at the local college; his mother came from one of Bloemfontein's most prominent families. Unlike his father or his grandfather, he himself was the first-born, arrived in the wake of historic events when new beginnings and rededications were being affirmed. Because of the nature of those events, resistance was in his heritage as much as the idea and reality of leadership, an unusual and double legacy. But as much as he would have to learn from that heritage, there was a good deal that he would have to forget, and some of this was embodied in other aspects of his grandfather's life.

In power, as Prime Minister, Abraham Fischer evinced contradictions that were for their time only half paradoxical. To his white constituents – the larger 'family' that had suffered so much – he opened his heart and was the essence of solicitous concern. He wrote individually to men stranded by recession in isolated rural hotels and boarding-houses on the impossibility of finding them employment, and handed on specific names to a commission set up on poor whites. A woman whose son had had an accident sent Abraham money so that he could invest it in shares for her; he replied courteously but regretfully that he was not a 'speculator', and directed her to the market in Johannesburg.

But Abraham's humanism – and apparently his ethics – met their limits as soon as they confronted the realm beyond the confines of the white world. Even before the war this had been all too apparent as Abraham's defence of Republican liberty was enmeshed with a thoroughgoing racism. When Britain had, as part of its claims against Kruger, insisted on certain provisos on the rights of Cape 'coloureds' and Indians from Natal, Abraham had written scathingly to Percy: 'Fancy the might of Great Britain upholding the Cape Malaaier [Malay] and the stinking Coolie . . . It ought to be impossible to set white man against white man to further a few millionaires & please a couple of disappointed statesmen.' It was the voice of a populism at once radical, patrician and nationalist, and after the war it had by no means abated. When in 1908 the Native Vigilance Association of Bethlehem sent a petition to the Governor protesting against the treatment of Africans in the Orange River

Colony – by common account the worst treatment in South Africa – in response Abraham Fischer could muster only the weight of a righteous indignation. Such petitions, he replied, contained merely vile and impudent insinuations fomented by agitators from elsewhere. Africans in the Colony were 'entirely contented', and as for the laws which governed their lives, these were necessary to counteract 'the natural tendency of natives generally to lead lives of idleness resulting in evils amongst which it would seem that latterly would have to be included the one of harbouring and raising a class of native agitators'.

It was the voice of Abraham's successors of fifty and sixty years later, of prime ministers Verwoerd and Vorster, always certain that Africans were 'lazy' and unfitted for civilised life, always convinced that despite these disabilities they were 'content', and that any agitation persuading them to the contrary came by definition from outside. (Verwoerd and Vorster were also, with some irony, convinced that it was people such as Bram Fischer who were responsible for that 'agitation'.) But Abraham's response also represented the voice of his time. In 1905 the Lagden Commission, appointed by Milner to establish an agreed 'native policy' for the whole of southern Africa, had reported that the sole justification for the presence of blacks in the urban areas was 'to minister to the needs of the white man'. It was this consensus that established the basis for the unification of South Africa in 1910, under which the rights and interests of Africans were disregarded almost entirely. Abraham Fischer played a prominent role at the National Convention which set up the terms for the Union. As for his views on the African franchise (eventually only Africans in the Cape could continue to enjoy a limited entitlement), J.X. Merriman had described these with gentle understatement as 'difficile'. Given his history and also his views, it was quite fitting that when General Louis Botha, as leader of the South African Party, formed his first Union cabinet in May 1910, he wrote to Abraham Fischer inviting him to be a member.

In August 1909 Abraham Fischer was in London for a succession of conferences on the forthcoming Union. White-bearded, and with his one eye declining in strength, he still had a wry view of the foibles and fallibilities of the eminent, and reported his observations to Percy, at home in South Africa. Abraham and Ada had been invited to Buckingham Palace, where he had found 'Royalty . . . very affable and very "unconsuming."' Ada, with Lord Milner to one side of her, had for her part managed to keep the latter at a distance. 'I almost pitied the man,' Abraham wrote, 'he seemed so out of it.'

As for the young Winston Churchill, Abraham remarked that he spoke indistinctly, and wondered how he carried his audiences with him. Lord Asquith, the Prime Minister, was a strong man, but Abraham said his reputation for 'taking a bit more than is good for him' appeared to be not undeserved.

However, it was someone else's penchant for taking a little too much than was good for him that disturbed Abraham more directly. For at the very same time that he was proceeding around London attending to high matters of state, he was also absorbed in taking care of his elder son, Harry. Harry was in England together with his parents, and Harry, it seems, had a drinking problem. Thinking matters through in his correspondence with Percy, Abraham enumerated the various solutions he had entertained. One was to rehabilitate Harry by getting him a job, but confidential advice held that if his difficulties once became known, employment would be entirely beyond him. Abraham had also threatened him with an inebriates' home in Wales if he didn't reform – in response to which Harry had made various undertakings, saying that he wanted to find a job, that he would never return to South Africa (though he later did). Describing all this to Percy, Abraham wrote frankly that Harry's previous history did not give much reason for hope.

In memory Harry came down as the black sheep of the family, though the story of his drinking became sufficiently suppressed for Percy's children to know (or say) nothing about it. But for a black sheep to exist there also has to be a white one. Percy was now Abraham's confidant in every respect: he had followed in his father's profession, he had the requisite discipline, propriety and interests. And of course that line was being extended. In the very same breath that Abraham wrote about Harry's shortcomings, he spoke with delight of how well Percy's family was doing, and of his pride in his new grandson 'Brahm' (as he suddenly misspelled it), now but a year and a half old.

In the years immediately following Union, pressures were building in South Africa that left their imprint on the remainder of the century. The white-owned mines needed black labour in large numbers and at cheap rates; white farmers clamoured to prise away whatever claims Africans had to a hold on the land. The momentous result was the Natives' Land Act of 1913, which permitted blacks ownership rights in only some 12 per cent of South Africa, and curbed the widespread practice of labour tenancy. After its enactment Sol Plaatje, founding member of the South African Native National Congress (later the ANC), travelled the country, detailing the misery he found as, overnight, Africans were made 'pariahs in the land of their birth'. On farm after farm families were evicted, and trailed the roads searching for somewhere to live and work, now impossible to find. For some time in the Union cabinet Abraham Fischer was Minister of Lands, and although the Act was passed after his tenure, Plaatje well remembered him making a speech to the voters of Bethlehem: 'What is it you want?' Abraham had asked. 'We have passed all the coolie laws and all the kaffir laws. The "Free" State [the quotation marks were Plaatje's, always derisory] and all her colour laws have been adopted by Parliament. What more can the government do for you?' In Plaatje's account Abraham was clearly under pressure, but also clearly willing to accede.

The 'coolie laws' Abraham referred to were the extraordinarily severe restrictions on Indians, who were not allowed to own property, farm or trade in the Free State, or even to sojourn overnight if passing through. These laws had existed before the war; after Union they remained in force for the Free State. Indeed, Abraham Fischer made no secret of the fact that his preference as far as Indians were concerned was for their repatriation. In 1909 he assured a con-stituent that the Union would be 'the death blow to Asiatic aspirations and agitations' in South Africa. Later, as Minister of the Interior, he took up an Immigration Bill which set out to restrict the right of entry to South Africa for Indians, and had the reputation of being even less conciliatory in that regard than his predecessor Smuts had been. His chief antagonist in the matter was Mohandas Gandhi, just then in South Africa absorbing the experience of discrimination at first hand, and in response developing the strategies of resis-tance that would change the shape of the twentieth century.

Plaatje and Gandhi: the one an inspirational figure for the African National Congress in its resistance to apartheid; the other for resistance to colonial hegemony worldwide. Abraham's grandson Bram in time aligned him-self with their traditions, but Abraham Fischer opposed them both. When the Immigration Bill was ultimately passed, Gandhi undertook his most celebrated *satyagraha* campaign of active civil disobedience in South Africa. And after Abraham passed away, Gandhi's journal, *Indian Opinion*, in a special souvenir 'Golden Number' commemorating the years of passive resistance in South Africa, showed a photograph of 'The Late Mr Abraham Fischer' and gave a suitably wry tribute to his ministerial initiatives in the very year that he died.

Yet Abraham Fischer's efforts both as Minister of Lands and Minister of the Interior did not mean that he remained exclusively a hero to his people. This could not be a history of 'families', large or small, if it did not contain any schisms. The fact was that General Botha's Union government could not sus-tain the contradictory tensions within it. On one side of the white political spectrum was the Unionist opposition, whose aim was to achieve closer ties with Britain – the 'jingoes' of the pre-Boer War era, who had a broad base of English-speaking support. On the other was a modernising Afrikaner nationalism, led by the ambitious General Hertzog, questing for increasing independence. In between remained Botha and his deputy, Smuts, attempting to forge unity between English and Afrikaner, and to fend off by judicious accession the demands of the mine-owners, all under the banner of reconciliation, and within the realm of Empire. It was to prove a hopeless task.

In December 1912 Hertzog toured the country presenting a series of speeches that broke what unity there was in the South African Party apart. At Smithfield, his constituency in the Free State, he declared that only one person had the right to be 'boss' in South Africa, 'namely the Afrikaner', and he derided the Unionists as 'foreign fortune-seekers'. (To be fair, by the term 'Afrikaner' Hertzog meant all those South Africans, whether English- or Afrikaans-speaking, who owed their primary allegiance to the country and not the King.) A week later, at De Wildt in the Transvaal, he insisted that imperialism was acceptable only in so far as it was of service to South Africa; conciliation and loyalty, he added, were idle words that deceived no one. The resulting furore exploded Botha's cabinet. When Hertzog refused to resign, Botha did so himself. The Governor-General then asked Botha to form a new cabinet, which he did, leaving Hertzog out.

Eyes were turned on Abraham Fischer. The question was whether he would enter Botha's second cabinet, as invited, or stay out on principle. The loyalties were undoubtedly straining. If Abraham went in he would be accused of betraying both Hertzog and the Free State, and the larger Afrikaner nationalism they represented. But if he stayed out, the South African Party would split and the government undoubtedly fall. In Bloemfontein, Percy – now deeply anxious over this crisis affecting his father in his declining years – scurried around gathering opinions and advice, sending flurries of telegrams to Abraham. He spoke to Ramsbottom, former Treasurer in Abraham's Orange River Colony government, in which Hertzog had also served. Based on that experience Ramsbottom took a dim view of Hertzog's all too fallible and fractious nature, which, even if he promised not to fight (remarked Ramsbottom), would make him do so. Percy, considering the practical as well as philosophical issues, offered his father his own advice: 'In, with Hertzog's blessing, otherwise out.'

That was what Abraham believed he had. On 20 December 1912 he wrote to Percy that a long talk with Hertzog had 'once more proved how well he can rise above personal considerations'. Hertzog had assured Abraham that if he rejoined Botha's cabinet he 'would go with his full blessing'. Not only that, but Hertzog had even appeared to be contrite, thanking Abraham for a lesson in tact from which he would profit. Abraham told Percy that even old President Steyn, contacted by wire, had agreed; and so Abraham had informed Botha he would rejoin the government (having also indicated that it was wrong to exclude Hertzog in the first place). He was under no illusions that his troubles were over, especially in the Free State. 'But I feel satisfied', he told Percy, 'I have done the right thing, whether it is crowned with success or not. I think one good thing is certain, Hertzog & I came out of this stauncher friends than ever.'

But Abraham was seldom more deceived than this, and perhaps was just too trusting to see it. For on the question of his entry into the cabinet Hertzog turned against him, and by March, April and May of the following year Percy's letters both to his mother and to his father told something of the story. Hertzog, remarked Percy bitterly, had lost all perspective, all sight of anything except his great 'ego'. His attitude towards Abraham was childish and contemptible: Hertzog was thinking of Hertzog and nothing else. Percy told Abraham how he had been to see President Steyn at his farm Onze Rust; Steyn had taken the view that interested parties had been carrying tales of intrigue to Hertzog. But when Percy had allowed himself the remark that the President should know by now what kind of man his father was, Steyn seemed to take it to heart, and said he did not need to be reminded.

By June 1913 there was a formal vote of no confidence in Abraham Fischer at a district committee meeting of the South African Party at Bethlehem in the Free State, on the ground that he had joined Botha's cabinet 'without the approval of President Steyn and General Hertzog'. This impression Hertzog, despite his undertakings to Abraham, had done little to correct. Abraham remained hurt, but dignified. 'Esteemed General,' he had written to Hertzog in May, 'It only grieves me to have seen, shortly after my arrival in Cape Town in January, that you were systematically avoiding me and that a cooling was evident on your part which in no respect was or is shared on mine.'

What Hertzog was really about was splitting the South African Party, and in this respect it did him no harm to have Abraham Fischer as a convenient foil – the ageing collaborator with Botha whose time had passed – to boost his own status and sustain his own momentum. In January 1914 he and his followers broke away from the SAP and launched the National Party, dedicated to the cause of Afrikaner nationalism. In the general election of 1915 the National Party won sixteen of the seventeen seats in the Free State, and the party founded in this crucible was on its way to governing the life of South Africa for a substantial part of the century. Old Abraham Fischer had, ironically, played a significant part in the act.

Percy tried to cheer his father up. On Abraham's last birthday in April 1913, he took him back in time in his memory: 'Much love to Mother & yourself & a birthday kiss even if it can't be given at an ungodly hour of the morning in bed as in days of yore.' He told Abraham he had been to see President Steyn with a Miss Brink, who had been a friend of Mrs Denyssen's daughter Maggie, and who still thought of Abraham as 'young Mr Fischer'. As the revolt among Abraham's constituents gathered strength, he wrote to his father saying, 'Just tell them all to go to Jericho, and come for a walk on the farm.' But after the vote of no confidence Abraham Fischer began to withdraw from politics, brokenhearted. He went to England, and returned home ailing. In his last days General Botha came down from the Transvaal specially to be with him. Abraham Fischer died on 16 November 1913, and that afternoon all the public buildings in Bloemfontein were closed.

Hillandale had already been sold, though a portion of it, named Bergendal (its exact translation into Afrikaans), was retained by Percy.

If there are certain histories in the air, certain examples, gestures, styles, ways of being in the world, what did Abraham Fischer bequeath to his grandson Bram, five years old when he died?

There was a measure of steely canniness, but also a certain naivete and willingness to believe the best. There was a tempered resolve, but also a deep impulse to reconciliation, negotiation and peace. There was a readiness to commit oneself to the unknown of historic faith and obligation, and a politics of conviction and principle – but also to some degree of self-deception. There was an unfortunate propensity towards underestimating the opposition, but an insistence on dignity and grace, no matter what the circumstances. An easy charm and courtesy did not disguise a thoroughgoing anti-imperialism, and a withering regard for 'jingoes' and unprincipled 'capitalists'; but there were also the visceral impulses of an instinctive racism. As for the idea of a larger South African 'family' of which he was a part, Abraham's definition would have to undergo substantial change. Though identity is a matter of identification as much as it is bred in the bone, this makes every political struggle no less personal.

And what did Abraham leave to the son who survived him? Here there was a further reversal. For Percy, having once expressed 'such a personal feeling against Hertzog' because of his treatment of Abraham, soon became a follower of the man who had betrayed his father. Indeed, whenever the family visited Cape Town, Percy made a point of stopping in to see the General.

Perhaps it was Hertzog's anti-imperialism that won him over; perhaps he came to agree that Botha and Smuts were the real traitors in their submission to the interests of the mine-owners and Empire. (Bram's sister Ada, named after her grandmother, once cut General Botha on the street in Cape Town, to the delight of Ella Fischer.) But it was the impact of global events, along with their local reverberations, both major and minor, that sealed things for Percy, turning not only him but his son Bram into a nationalist.

CHAPTER 2

A FARM IN AFRICA

1914 – c. 1928

On 28 June 1914, in Sarajevo, the Serbian nationalist Princip fired the shot that killed Archduke Franz Ferdinand, heir apparent to the imperial throne of Austria–Hungary, sending the nations of Europe trundling towards their seemingly unstoppable confrontation.

South Africa, at some distance, soon found itself swept up. The British government requested Botha and Smuts to invade German South West Africa, and with some reluctance they agreed. On 4 September the Union parliament voted to join the war against Germany, but with memories of recent history still fermenting this was not an entirely popular decision among South African whites. Hertzog and the National Party followed a cautious line, not soliciting resistance, but opposing the war and any invasion of German territory. But some of the old Boer War generals went further; after an initial hesitation Beyers, Maritz, De la Rey and De Wet – the last two in particular heroes of the struggle against the British – gravitated towards open revolt. Beyers, head of the Citizen Force, resigned his commission; Maritz, military commander in the north-western Cape, went over with his troops to the Germans. Emotional meetings in rural areas of the Transvaal and Free State whipped up memories of the concentration camps, fostering the illusion that this was the opportunity to seize back a Republican destiny that had so recently been betrayed.

What came to be known as the Afrikaner Rebellion of 1914 took hold in pockets across the country, but as Botha and Smuts held firm it was not a revolt that could be sustained for very long. De la Rey, travelling with Beyers to a meeting in Potchefstroom, was killed at a roadblock just south of Johannesburg (set up – at least as the event was later presented – to trap the notorious Foster Gang, just then terrorising the town with its criminal activities). Beyers ended up drowning in the Vaal River, Maritz escaped to South West Africa, while De Wet's small force was defeated and his son killed. Botha, calling up the Union troops, made sure for symbolic reasons that it was mainly Afrikaners who put down this uprising among their brethren. Numbers of rebels were arrested, and there was one martyr, Jopie Fourie, executed at Pretoria Local Prison, which Bram Fischer later came to know well.

Percy Fischer's sons remembered with a certain humour his role in the Rebellion, although there was no doubting his earnest intent. Percy had been confined in England all through the previous historic drama; moreover, the allegiance of his father had recently been called into question. Like that generation of Englishmen who were born too young for the First World War and searched for causes right through the thirties, Percy now believed his moment had come, and together with some companions organised an ambulance to aid the rebels. In the tradition of his father this was at least a gesture of conscience and healing as well as of resistance, but either way it was of little benefit. The story was that the ambulance got as far out of Bloemfontein as Senekal, then fell into a ditch, by which time the Rebellion was over.

But that did not end Percy Fischer's involvement. As the rebels were imprisoned and put on trial, in his capacity as advocate rather than ambulance driver, Percy took up their defence. Years later his son Bram recalled his coming home from work in an absolute fury, threatening to burn his legal robes in disgust at the strict sentences being handed out by one of the local judges. But his advocacy carried its own price among the legal fraternity of Bloemfontein, for whom a professional association with a supporter of the Rebellion became something of an embarrassment. So, rather suddenly, Percy began to lose work: attorneys declined to send him briefs, and his fellow advocates shunned him. Hard times meant that Percy was forced to rent out the family home in Reitz Street in Bloemfontein, and he and Ella and the children moved out to Bergendal, the section of the Hillandale farm he had inherited from Abraham.

Emotions were running high as the whole family rallied round the rebels. Ella Fischer and her sister Maude were among a group of women who visited the Bloemfontein prison, taking flowers and food. Maude's husband, Dr Bidwell (now district surgeon), gave the prisoners medical attention, and once, when he came to examine General De Wet, found him arranging roses brought by Maude. Ella, on her visits, took along the children, who were evidently absorbing the intense mood of the moment. On one occasion, as they were leaving, Bram's younger brother Paul (who was about two at the time) threw a stone at a window of the prison and managed to break one of the panes. When a burly warder with a moustache came out wagging his finger, Paul managed to extrude the only words he knew in English, which happened to be (he said later) 'Good shot!'

As for Bram, some of his earliest memories were of those visits. There he received a present from one of the prisoners, a chameleon carved out of wood, with parts that moved and a pencilled dedication in Dutch: 'Made by [there was a name, but decades later it was illegible], Kommandant, Kroonstad, Kroonstad Rebels in the prison at Bloemfontein, 15 May 1915.' Bram, who had just turned seven at the time, never lost it. Many years later, when he himself came out of prison to stay at his brother Paul's house in Bloemfontein, that carved toy was still in his family's possession.

The idea of rebellion, therefore, and of acting according to conscience, was not foreign to the Fischer family, for all their eminence. Indeed, if Ella Fischer tendered any regrets they were, as she once put it, that De Wet had not gone straight through and taken Pretoria. Later, though, when she began to have doubts about the course that her son Bram's life had followed, she had to be reminded of these feelings. It was Maude's daughter Connie, who had also visited the rebels in prison, who reminded her what her own husband had done during the Rebellion.

After Bram's birth in 1908, siblings arrived with some regularity. His sister, Ada Cecil Fischer, was born in March 1910; then followed Paul Martheunis Steyn Fischer (his middle names in honour of the old President) in December 1912, Pieter Ulrich Fischer in August 1913, and Gustav Fichardt Fischer in January 1916, when the family was already living at Bergendal. The names rehearsed the lineages of family in both the immediate and extended senses.

The farmhouse that the Fischers moved out to was the exact opposite of the Reitz Street house which they had inhabited in town. That house had been given the name 'Harmonie', and there Percy and Ella had begun to construct an environment in keeping with the appellation. Ella in particular could look back to the salubrious surroundings from which she had come, and both to a certain graceful tradition. But on the farm they had to live in what was little more than a *pondokkie* – a small shack with four tiny rooms, comprising a kitchen, a living-room, and two bedrooms. To begin with, the younger boys slept in the outbuildings, while Ella and Ada shared a room, and Percy and Bram did the same. Later Bram moved out to join his brothers, though in summer all the sons would sleep out on the *stoep* in the open air.

It is not too far-fetched to say that for the young Bram – and for the older Bram later – the idea of rebellion was linked to his own closeness to the veld, to the South African landscape and its sensory mappings. Because, for the children, that period on the farm, far from being a hardship, was a most glorious adventure in which they thoroughly revelled. There, on their own, or with their cousins Joan and Connie (their Aunt Maude's daughters, who were with them so often they were virtually like sisters), they would go swimming or boating on the dam, or ranging over the farm, walking or riding on horseback. A favourite spot was the *kloofie*, a dry river-cleft that would fill up with pools of water when it rained, and where the children would swim. If they were daring there was Malmanskop, where it was rumoured that a madman had lived. Sometimes on summer nights, if Ella was in the mood, she would take them out in an old flat-bottomed boat on the dam and tell them ghost stories. They fought the Boer War all over again, playing a game called 'TTA', which stood for 'twelve thousand army', meaning the British: the children were the Boer guerrillas, and the TTA (recalled Bram's cousin Connie) was 'a dear little old governess', half-blind but very sporting, who walked about the garden while the children pursued her. At home, old Nakie Smith, once Ella's governess, now at the age of nearly seventy attendant on the children, read to them from her favourite Charles Dickens and told stories of how the British soldiers in Bloemfontein had ripped out the pages of his fattest novels to use as stuffing for pillows.

Bram's love for Bergendal – whose every stone, remarked his daughters, he knew – was reinforced by the Sunday routines that his Oupa Abraham had initiated with Percy. Abraham, it seems, fully abandoned the Calvinism of his youth in later life, and Percy had no religious inclinations. Only Ella was different, though she liked to go to church (observed her niece Connie) chiefly because it was the only place where she could find some quiet. Early on, the family came to an arrangement: every other Sunday the children would attend church with their mother; but punctuating this on the weeks in-between, Percy would take them out on the veld, pointing out the wildlife, the birds, the plants and the trees. Fairly soon the Sundays in church were dropped, and walks on the veld became an alternative ritual, embarked on with a relish and sense of meaning that in later years Bram reproduced for his own children. Whenever they went to visit Percy and Ella on the farm, Bram would take them out riding or walking, showing them the landscape his father had shown him, and the indigenous trees both at Bergendal and Hillandale – *karees, witstinkhout,* and *olienhout* – that Percy and Abraham had planted.

For schooling they went (brothers as well as sister) to the local establishment for girls, Oranjemeisiesskool, being driven off in the mornings in Percy's old Model 'A' Ford, with one of the children opening the gates down the rutted gravel road as they went. This was not such an unusual arrangement: many boys' schools started classes for pupils only at the age of ten or eleven, and the Fischers favoured Oranjemeisies because it had been founded by President Steyn, offering instruction in Dutch as well as English. At any rate, there were at least enough boys at Oranjemeisies to play soccer against the boys from Eunice, the other girls' school in Bloemfontein. Even at that age, Percy and Ella ensured that their children were fastidious about their studies. Once, when there was a torrential downpour, Bram, Joan and Connie (who would get a lift in the car every morning from Percy) were the only three children who went in. A teacher took them to see the waters flooding away down the town *sloot*.

During these years Joan, Connie, Bram, Ada and Paul were all but inseparable. Connie remembered enjoying the most marvellous childhood. She and Paul shared a birthday (she exactly seven years older), and Bram's and Joan's birthdays were very close. The Fischers tended to concoct a big fuss for family events, and so there were always lavish celebrations. Moreover, despite their reduced circumstances, they had not forgotten the decorous ways of their origins. On Christmas Day, just as in Oupa Abraham's time, there would be a sumptuous feast outdoors under the gum trees, with a turkey and all the family silver and appurtenances. One year, at Maude's house, she dressed up as Father Christmas and came down the roof with a sack of gifts slung over her shoulder.

For holidays – which seem not, during these years, to have been interrupted – they would travel by car, taking some seven to nine days to reach the Cape, driving on gravel roads all the way. (They also brought a small black child along to sit on the running board and open the gates.) There was a taste for the new and exploratory, especially when it involved unusual realms of South African geography: Percy and his family were among the first holiday-makers at Plettenberg Bay, later a pounding resort, but then just a remote and austere, if stunningly beautiful, whaling station. In other years Ella, together with Maude and all the children, travelled to Natal, picking up cousins on the Bidwell side along the way. From Mount Edgecombe the molecular family of three mothers and ten children would trek five miles by wagon to the beachhouse they rented for a month. Every few days a Zulu servant would have to jog that five miles to the station – and then back – to get bread, but no one among the white family would have given the matter a second thought.

Everything happened around the dinner table. For one thing, a linguistic flexibility was required. Percy, who had written to his father in English, now spoke in Afrikaans with his children; they, in turn, conversed in English with their mother, who with a German father and Welsh mother had no Afrikaans. No doubt the dual-language policy was deliberate as well as necessary, fostering a new kind of white South African identity, as well as making the children more prepared for the world they would inhabit. But what sometimes surprised visitors was the high-speed energy of speech, as both languages flew back and forth. In later years Bram's brothers could remember the family's exact placing around the table simply by recalling who spoke English to the left and Afrikaans to the right, or vice versa.

What also surprised visitors was the reach of the repartee, which included a fair amount of ribbing, even – in a generally authoritarian culture – by the children of the parents. Percy bore some of the responsibility for this, for balancing his political certainties with his juristic habits, he prescribed an open mind on every question, and indulged in a degree of playfulness. If one of the children presented a particular point of view, he would for the sake of argument take up a contrary position, and all topics were open for discussion. One of Percy's especial gifts was the ability to take children seriously without patronising them, with a combination of genuine interest and good humour. His own interests ranged from geography to astronomy, and he was apt to engage any passing child in a discussion of either – or simply on what they were thinking.

This intellectual openness applied also to his own certainties. Bram's youngest brother Gus remembered his father once remarking ruefully that there were two systems of law in South Africa: in a recent case a white man had been let off with a warning for shooting a black man who had stolen a sheep, while in another a black man who had stolen a sheep from a white farmer had been sentenced to seven years' imprisonment. In the 1930s, as Afrikaner nationalism was building towards its future ascendancy, Percy, though still a convinced nationalist, was also (partly under the influence of Bram) a member of the Left Book Club, and his children remembered seeing and reading the distinctive red books around the house. If this was a national-ist household, in other words, it was not the usual kind, and there was a habit of intellectual play and inquiry which meant that options and opinions were never entirely closed. Percy seems to have believed that reason would produce reliable conclusions, and it was a principle his eldest son absorbed, even if the conclusions he drew were markedly different from anything his father might have predicted.

If Percy provided the questioning, Ella too was something of a surprise. At first, considering her background, living at Bergendal was a strain. During her youth she had been as protected as a rare flower; now she was obliged to *grow* flowers to sell at the Bloemfontein railway station. She would be up more or less before dawn, not only to attend to the children, both the infants and those who had to be readied for school, but also to prepare flowers and vegetables for the market. During the day there were children to care for again, at home and then back from school. To be sure there were servants (the Fischers would have had to be extremely poor to do without them), but Ella often ended the day exhausted. Nor did she have any experience of farming: once when the dam wall was leaking and looked about to give way from the rain, she followed the advice of a column in the *Farmer's Weekly* and drove the oxen across it to compact it, but they all fell into the mud and had to be extracted.

Ella was not much more than five feet tall, yet her personality controlled the household with a quiet but insistent pertinacity, especially when it came to matters of family and its obligations and responsibilities. For Ella was the most *familievas* of them all – loyal to her loved ones no matter what, and promoting that loyalty in turn. She was in her way a natural archivist, gathering mementoes and treasures ranging from everyone's last letter to family-trees and trinkets. Even a lock of Bram's hair as a baby, as well as the numbers from his rugby jersey, found their way into her boxes. Later, back at Harmonie, the walls of her room were lined with photographs until it looked like some cavernous museum.

Ella could, with the presumptions of her background, be a snob, but she could also achieve the unexpected. Once, wearing a long black dress and riding a donkey, she went up Mont-aux-Sources in the Drakensberg, and slept the night in a cave. If anything defined her it was a deep magnetism for the idea of a humane *culture*, which for her meant a developed sense of enlightened mutuality, revealed in matters of tone and gesture as well as positive action. She promoted this within the family, but also more widely, taking on something of a public role. From early on she was a member of the Oranjevrouevereeniging [Orange Women's Union], which President Steyn had founded in the wake of the Boer War to help reconstitute women's lives. At the Oranjemeisiesskool she founded a 'mothercraft centre', where young women would learn domestic skills by taking care of orphaned babies. Later, in 1928, she was a member of the Flag Commission, attempting to design a new South African flag. Despite her short stature, Ella could be fierce (or, somewhat more deliberately, *appear* to be fierce): if ever she announced that she was 'putting on her bonnet' it meant that someone – usually a tradesman who had charged too much or delivered imperfect goods – was in trouble. But she also had personable traditions of her own: she would ring a bell to call the birds for feeding, or rap with a stone in the fishpond for the fish. Later, Bram's family did exactly the same, as did his children after that.

Together, Percy and Ella modelled their vision of an ideal world for their children. It was a world that was confident, cultivated, playful, adventurous and, most of all, secure, with its own idiosyncratic patterns of ceremony and insistence. Bram's Aunt Maude provided complementary textures of her own. Her house was called 'Vrede' [Peace], and this was in keeping with the philosophy she, as a remarkably gentle person, embodied as well as propounded. (When she came down the roof as Father Christmas, it was Paul Fischer who noticed how small and delicate her hands were.) In later years Maude built an outdoor 'peace room' for her grandchildren and great-nephews and -nieces, with pastel-coloured books she herself had made lining the walls, honouring the world's great men and women of peace (among them the same Gandhi who had so exasperated Oupa Abraham). She was also deeply moved by the South African landscape and, when Bram, Joan and Connie were young, wrote a play entitled *Breath of the Veld* (in which nature appeared as a spirit) for them all to perform.

In some ways nothing could have been more distant from the hard world of politics Bram Fischer entered; yet there was a connection. Later on, the imperative of peace was for him almost more important than that of revolution: indeed, in his view, this was what only revolution could ensure in South Africa. And of course, in a larger sense, the spirit of the veld never left him. In the 1960s, when his own rebellion of conscience made him face the most complicated of choices, there was never any real possibility that he would leave South Africa, the ground of his past and his future. On the run from the police he wrote to Connie, telling her how much he was thinking of the farm, and how much he longed to see it again.

To be rooted in a place: Bram Fischer took trees from Bergendal and replanted them in his garden in Johannesburg. From the world of his youth he took the courteous and confident charm that bore for all who came to know him the imprint of an essentially alluring presence. Like his father, he could talk with anyone, high or low, child or adult. Like his mother, his loyalties were firm. From it all – the resonances of an almost bodily memory – came the vision of a world that was not yet, but could be perfect.

※

Like his father and grandfather before him (and almost certainly at the insistence of his mother), Bram Fischer took to correspondence early on. Whenever his parents were away – and with or without the looming presence of a governess behind him – he would write and tell them how his days had gone. At the age of eight he told of a visit to his Uncle Harry, who had shot a rabbit, while he himself had bagged a meerkat. The following year he told of going to the football with his brother Paul, to see Old Greys playing the 'Collegens' [Collegians]: 'After that the old rugbie Crocks played the old soca crocks soca. Then the same people played rugbie.' Or, he went with his cousin Theunie Fichardt to the vlakte [flats] to shoot doves; but the wind was too strong, and besides there were no doves to be seen. Or he was taken to the circus, where they saw Dick Turpin's ride to York – but only up to the part where the horse died. Bram wrote in a mixture of Dutch and Afrikaans, and signed all his letters 'Met een grote soen, van Bram' – 'With a big kiss, from Bram'.

He was reading improving children's books – Force and Right, and Love and Duty (somewhat presentient titles), and 'The Little Gipsy' in Little Wide Awake, and he told his parents about his successes at school. A hundred out of a hundred for his sums, only a few mistakes in his English dictation and none in his geography; in Dutch he'd come top of the class. At cricket he had scored fifty runs not out, and he was playing lots of tennis with Joan and Connie. He and Ada were working hard at their French lessons and German (a few words to his father in the latter), and he was practising his music every day. They'd extended the dining-room table and were playing ping-pong. Gus (his youngest brother) was very sweet, 'and if you ask him where Mommy is then he says gone'. It was the same phrasing – the same family joke – that later his own daughters used.

In these years Bram watched the first aeroplanes arrive in Bloemfontein, circling over the farm. He went to the bioscope, where he saw silent films and the burlesque offerings of a comic-Italian music-hall artist: 'Andante, andante, fortissimo and pickled-tomatio.' He watched the Bloemfontein motor-bike race, and rowed on the dam, pretending to be a message-bearer in war. He and Ada, with whom he loved reading, would sometimes tease the others ('Paul said his was a fishboat, so we held our noses'), but it was usually tempered with affection: 'I made a nice sabre, and tied it with wire round my waist. Gus was eating some cake, and I said I would kill him if he didn't give me the cake. He got scared and just gave me the cake, but then I laughed and gave him a kiss, and gave back the cake.' He was a dutiful child: 'Tell Daddy that I couldn't write to him yesterday, because Auntie Maudie wrote to me and I had to reply.' Bram began to write to his father in Afrikaans and his mother in English, but by way of balance would end his letters to her 'Slaap gerus', and to Percy 'Goodnight'. Often it was still a mixture: 'Miss Ehrlich het my nie fair gemerk nie . . . ' [Miss Ehrlich did not mark me fairly . . .].

He was also beginning to take charge, as he revealed to his mother in September 1920: 'This morning the little ones & the little kaffers saw a snake in the waenhuis [cart shed]. I don't know whether [it] is true or just imagination. But at any rate you needn't be afraid because I have given orders that they are not to go near the place.' He had also (he told his father) given instructions for the pit to be dug and the ploughing to begin. He'd been looking for nests. He had seen a rabbit but didn't shoot it. The dam was full from the rain. He'd been milking the cows. The peach trees were magnificent, so full of beautiful blossoms. They were counting the days till their *mother and father came home. From eight to twelve, with undeniable sweetness, Bram was growing into the ambivalences of South African authority.*

There were other sides to this story.

For one thing there was more than a hint (observed Connie) that under all the success and pleasure Bram was subject to a certain amount of pressure in his life. He was the eldest, the bearer of the lineage that Abraham and Percy had embodied before him, and it was clear that his parents expected a great deal. Even when he was playing casual games, his cousins could perceive his palpable urgency to win. With barely articulated awareness at the time, but with greater clarity in retrospect, they also sensed a certain anxiety and self-doubt, as if, under the pressures he experienced, Bram felt a doubled need to live up to expectations.

There was another complication whose effects were felt deeply, if for the moment unconsciously, for all of the children. When they were young, they played with the black children on the farm without any sense of differentiation, and in later years Bram had occasion to remember this with some nostalgia as well as bemusement. Ella would sometimes chide them for rolling about in the cattle kraal with their black friends, but that was as far as the limitation went. Yet as they grew into their allotted roles, the weight of a white South African racial consciousness settled in. Once, when Bram was about fourteen, he demurred at having to sit in the back seat of the car next to a black woman, asking Ada to do so instead. Evidently, race and sex lines could not be crossed simultaneously, especially at an age of adolescent transition.

The other children had their own experiences. Gus remembered his confusion on first seeing a black man wearing a pair of glasses – for him this was almost a contradiction in terms, since spectacles could be worn only by 'whites'. When Paul was about fourteen he was engaged in a tug of war over a gate with an older black boy, Jerry Saila, who worked on the farm. Suddenly Paul's grasp slipped, and the gate swung back and hit Jerry in the face. When the blood emerged Paul remembered vividly being overcome with two intense and simultaneous emotions: genuine regret that Jerry had been hurt, and utter surprise that his blood was also red.

These were small matters, but they revealed a whole universe behind them. What was truly amazing was how quickly the innocent and (apparently) indiscriminate apprehensions of youth could transform into the rigid constraints of conformity. Percy and Ella's culture was easy and graceful, but it also assumed the limits it staked out. All this would take unusual awareness and will-power to change. Perhaps a good thing, then, that Bram had also been born to persistence, responsibility and thoughtfulness.

※※

The Fischers moved back into Bloemfontein about 1922, though they still retained the farm. The passions surrounding the Rebellion had died down, and Percy was again doing well in his profession. In 1926 Harmonie, in Reitz Street, was enlarged, now provided with a swimming pool and tennis court; there was also a sunken area of the garden covered by a pergola of luxuriantly scented and interweaving wistaria overhead, the mark of Ella's design. The Fischers were once again part of the Bloemfontein elite, and for many who entered their home it seemed to be a charmed enclosure.

During these years Bram had moved from Oranjemeisiesskool to Grey Primary School, and then on to Grey College. The college had been founded by Sir George Grey in the nineteenth century as an all-white boarding and day school, drawing its pupils from far and wide in the Free State, and offering instruction (in separate sections) in both English and Afrikaans. It had its fair share of famous – and infamous – pupils: Laurens (later Sir Laurens) van der Post, the Jungian searcher and writer, was a contemporary of Bram's; so too was Robey Leibbrandt, who went to Germany and was later captured during the war after being landed on the coast of South West Africa as a Nazi agent and spy. Also there with Bram was Joel Mervis, whose father had settled in Kroonstad as a Jewish immigrant from Lithuania, and (speaking Yiddish and Afrikaans) had fought for the Boers during the Boer War. Though Mervis first trained as a lawyer, he later became editor of the *Sunday Times* – and one of South Africa's leading humorists. And there was of course Bram Fischer himself, who took up his place in the Afrikaans section of the school.

There he began to impress his contemporaries with his personal and academic talents, developing a wide-ranging respect. Even the schoolmasters, recalled Joel Mervis (who was in the English-speaking section of the school), addressed him with an almost deferential tone of voice. This was partly because of his background, the equivalent of some local royal family. But, remarked Mervis, even if Bram had come from Timbuktu he would soon have established himself with his easy dignity and charm. In Mervis's eyes Bram was simply 'a marvellous individual', modest and unassuming for all the admiration that came his way, 'almost too good to be true', 'an absolute model'. Like both his parents, Bram was short (never more than five feet eight inches at full stretch), and at that stage of his life remarkably slight: he had a light touch, but the respect he created appeared to be substantial.

Fortunately, because otherwise his virtues would have been utterly cloying, he also had a certain vitality and irreverence, which derived in part, again, from his family. Though he was under age, Percy taught him to drive his car, and Bram, who had a certain feel for speed, took it off to go camping. Later he – and, it appears, even Ada – were given motor-bikes, and Bram would trail off on the gravel roads around Bergendal. He became editor of the school journal, and wrote to his mother for a definition of a journalist to put in, 'something, you know, about a poor beggar with no inspiration and a lot of self-pity'. Whenever Percy or Ella were away from home his letters took up again, always with a degree of whimsy. To Ella he described one of the household (Percy himself, or one of his brothers) at practice on the violin: 'Herr Paganini (snr) is hard at work at the present moment. He is searching and searching – in vain – for 5ths, and making an unholy din . . . ' He told of a gory book lent to him by Aunt Maude, called *The Cruciform Mark*, in which he expected none of the characters to be left alive by the end, as, after experiencing the most terrible dreams, they were all dying quietly with a red cruciform mark at the back of their necks. 'The man who tells the story is also having dreams now so I think the story will end with his funeral – .'

But underneath it all was an intensity of focus, the same will to achieve that his cousins Joan and Connie had observed. Bram began to take his tennis more seriously, and in his final year at school became junior tennis champion of the Free State. Despite his frailty – in his final year at Grey he weighed no more than 125 pounds – he played scrum-half at rugby, regularly for the school second team and sometimes for the first. Often his cousin Theunie Fichardt played alongside him at fly-half; many years later, in his professional capacity as a radiologist, Fichardt had to take care of Bram in a very different setting.

Bram was a member of the first cricket team, but gave it up in his final term in order (he claimed) to concentrate on his matric examinations. This caused some scorn among his team-mates, who believed Bram's father had ordered him to do it, and that Bram had simply obeyed. This was one instance, remarked Joel Mervis, in which he was 'too good to be true'. But Bram may well have made the change out of conviction. There was his drive to succeed, and it had always bothered him that he had never been far and away the best in his class (in his junior matric he had been awarded a bursary of £7 for coming second). But if this was the opportunity to establish his pre-eminence, it didn't quite turn out in the way he desired. Although he achieved a first-class pass (one of two boys in the school to do so) and came first, he received distinctions in only one or two subjects. When his Aunt Maude and his cousins went to congratulate him, instead of celebration they found (recalled Connie) an air of unexpected gloom in the family – not only on Bram's part, but also on Percy and Ella's – and for Maude it was sad confirmation of the parental pressure she suspected. But it was also apparent that Bram had ingested deeply the immense drive to achievement; later he told Connie that coming first in his matric had been a 'Pyrrhic victory'.

When Bram looked back on his school years, however, it was not his results that stood out, but the fact that he had come under the long-lasting influence and guidance of Leo Marquard. Once again there was a connection of a kind, for Leo was the son of that same Margaret Marquard who had hosted Abraham Fischer on his travels during the Boer War. Now he was the history master at Grey, and to Bram his most valued teacher. Leo Marquard had won a Rhodes Scholarship to Oxford from 1920 to 1923, and was just then in the first enthusiastic flush of his return. He had founded the National Union of South African Students (NUSAS) on the model of the National Union of Students in Britain, and still managed to be NUSAS president, despite the fact that he was no longer a student. In later years he was the author of *The Peoples of South Africa* and (under a pseudonym) *The Black Man's Burden*, which, as its title suggested, constituted something of a challenge to prevailing suppositions. For most of his life Marquard never moved much further left than liberal, and at Grey had to be careful to edit political discussion in the classroom; but none the less he always managed to engender an air of thought and inquiry which his pupils remembered with veneration.

Bram had no doubt that he benefited enormously. Some forty to fifty years later – in circumstances that were very much changed – he thought back nostalgically on his introduction to what he called the 'magic circle' established at Grey by Leo Marquard and his wife Nell. He remembered how Leo had given his pupils roneoed copies of the Sand River Convention of 1852 (under which Britain had recognised the independence of the Orange Free State), sending them home to determine what lay 'behind' it and making Bram, for one, feel like a real researcher. He remembered afternoon teas at Leo and Nell's, where he would meet visitors to Bloemfontein, some of whom had come from overseas to research issues of race in South Africa. According to Bram, in all his ten years at school and nine at university, he had come across only three teachers who had taught him how to think: one was Eric Walker, Professor of History at the University of Cape Town; another was an (unidentified) venerable going under the obscure nickname of 'Burglar Bill'; but the one that really mattered to him was Leo Marquard.

Together with a colleague, Leo took his pupils on camping trips to study, read and converse. He was that rare kind of teacher who involved his students in his current ideas and work (Joel Mervis was his NUSAS secretary for a while). In class, pushing the limits of the permissible, he would point out that white South Africa's prosperity depended not only on its own genius, but more directly on a permanent, cheap supply of black labour. Outside of class, Bram was clearly close to him – not only in sustained discussion, but also playing tennis with Leo and his brother Dawie, winning local doubles championships. For all these reasons and more, Bram in later life regarded Leo as his mentor, though the two retained their ideological differences to the end – Leo Marquard was never, and never could be, a communist. But that did not mean that his influence was all-encompassing, or even that he wooed Bram away from nationalism. In this, as in everything else, Bram Fischer's approach was initially more guarded and more deliberate, less a matter of instinctive insight or impulse than of methodical examination and conscientious thought.

On the contrary, during these years at high school Bram was in some respects an increasingly confirmed nationalist. There is the story (which became almost apocryphal) that he once refused to wear cadet uniform at school and take part in drilling because of its associations with British imperialism. His brothers later discounted the story on the ground that participation in cadets was not compulsory anyway (though the rules may have changed by the time they were faced with it). Yet Bram himself told the story to his daughters – adding, that on the day of his rebellion he was wearing his cadet uniform under his school clothes, just in case.

Yet his objections were real, and his opposition sometimes went further. In 1925, Bram's final year at school, the Prince of Wales visited South Africa, and came to Bloemfontein – still an outrage to some of those whose memories reached back a quarter of a century. Grey College was meant to participate in his welcome, but the Prince's arrival was due to coincide with a long weekend when the pupils would be away. The headmaster, J. Murray Meiring, whom Bram along with many others normally considered an amiable and enlightened man, offered the boys an alternative weekend holiday if they would stay and greet the Prince – and the result was an unprecedented ruckus. This was not only because the pupils wanted their holiday, but also because they objected to participating in a stage-managed imperial extravaganza. Each student was to receive a trophy decorated with the Prince's face, and also a quarter pound of chocolates. 'I think they're completely mad,' Bram wrote to his parents, who were away at the time in Cape Town. Classes were disrupted, and there was talk of a strike. Together with two other pupils, Bram went to see Meiring. Eventually the headmaster backed down, and the pupils were given permission to miss the Prince's reception.

In this regard, Bram's sentiments were very much in keeping with those of his parents. 'I hope you were all well out of the way,' wrote Ella after the royal visitor had departed. 'It can give one such a sore heartache (at least it did me down here) to see him treading his Imperial way through our country. I don't mind the English and SAP's honouring their Prince, but I'd rather not witness it.' This of course was something Bram managed not to do. 'We were all very thrilled,' he wrote laconically of the Prince's arrival, 'but did not have a chance of seeing him as we spent a lovely lazy day out at Auntie Maudie's.' Bram had taken his first political action, and it was, characteristically, against imperialism: it was an early indication that he would find it quite logical, as an Afrikaner, to be a communist.

In later years Bram saw this decade – the 1920s – as the crucial one when Afrikaners, extrapolating from their own experience and analysis of oppression, might have made common cause with South African blacks, just then developing the impetus towards their own political struggle. If the students at Grey were threatening a strike, there would have been sufficient examples both locally and nationally, ranging from St Petersburg in 1917, to the Rand Revolt of white mineworkers in Johannesburg in 1922, to the burgeoning growth of the black Industrial and Commercial Workers' Union, developing its own traditions of militancy. But the shift into a new mental and political framework was not one that Bram himself was yet prepared to make, and the forms of his subversion were still sanctioned by more familiar versions of tradition and authority.

For now it was his nationalism that he did not conceal. One night in 1924, he accompanied his cousin Connie to Market Street in Bloemfontein to hear – along with an increasingly voluble gathering – the results of the general election of that year as they were announced. Hertzog, as leader of the National Party, had established an electoral pact with the white Labour Party, which, representing in the main English-speaking white workers from the Rand, sought to protect their privileges against the claims of black workers. That night in Bloemfontein every time news of a Nationalist or Labourite victory was proclaimed, there were enthusiastic roars of approval from the crowd, and Bram and Connie cheered along with them (despite, remarked Connie later, some misgivings about Labour). The result of the election was historic. For the first time since Union in 1910 the South African Party government fell, and Hertzog's so-called Pact government – dominantly Nationalist – was in power.

Notwithstanding Bram's misgivings about Labour as a foreign and essentially suspect phenomenon, the election in itself might have been a clue. For here was an alliance between an anti-imperial nationalism and a party that propounded a form of socialism (albeit firmly constrained within the white world), and it unified, however evanescently, English-speakers and Afrikaners. Later Bram would search for a model that would be more universal in its purview, anti-imperialist as well as socialist, and holding out the promise, beyond any boundaries of race, of uniting all of South Africa's people. For the moment, however, the only thing that shocked Connie was when Bram took her aside to tell her he was an atheist.

When Bram left school at the end of 1925, he was in two minds about his future career. There was the beckoning prospect of law, and it was a persuasive possibility, the legacy of his father and grandfather. Yet, with the experience of Bergendal behind him, and the attachment to the land which it had strengthened, there was an aspect of Bram that very strongly wanted to be a farmer. This notion must have been alarming to Percy and Ella, although they gave no obvious indication. As for Bram, in a self-consciously methodical manner he kept a notebook, writing down the pros and cons of his options. He was in any case due to go to the University of Cape Town, and so it was arranged that during the long summer vacation beforehand he would work for six weeks on a fruit farm in the Tulbagh district. (Maude's opinion was that Percy and Ella had deliberately arranged this in order to push Bram, by aversion, into law.)

When Bram left for the Cape early in 1926 he found it quite alien and rather stiff, full of people (as he put it to his parents) speaking atrocious Afrikaans, who gave the impression that they had been too weak to participate in the Great Trek. Mr Nellmapius, who owned the farm on which he was to work, gave him advice on whether he should attend university or an agricultural college. University was preferable, considered Nellmapius, because farming could be learned on the job. And Bram did learn, starting at five in the morning and working fourteen hours a day, picking grapes for sultanas or wine. Yet it was not only the arts of farming he absorbed, but also, at first hand, South Africa's characteristic labour practices. He told his parents how, supervising coloured children of thirteen and fourteen years old, he felt sorry for them as they carried their heavy baskets for such long hours, especially since most of them were no older than his own brothers. He was also introduced to the 'tot' system, whereby the adult coloured workers would be paid in daily rations of wine in lieu of part of their wages. On some farms this happened six times a day, though at Nellmapius's only twice. The 'tot' system was a form of addictive enslavement, and although Bram did not see it in exactly those terms, he did say it would be almost impossible to retain coloured workers without offering 'tots'.

As it turned out, he entered into a discussion with his parents on questions of labour and race, provoked in part by events in Bloemfontein. For in Waaihoek, the segregated location that housed Bloemfontein's black workers, there were threats of a strike against low wages. The workers wanted 6s 6d a day, wrote Ella to Bram, her understanding and latitude combined with a certain moralism, 'which would be impossible from our point of view, tho' perhaps not unreasonable from theirs'. She conveyed an ethos of urgency and danger: churches had been closed, there were gatherings and processions, and township representatives were meeting the Bloemfontein town council. Ella had made arrangements for her domestic servants to sleep in or stay at Bergendal, 'so I trust', she wrote with a sense of personal priorities as well as human concern, 'we shall not be servantless.' Police strength had been increased to a hundred, but Ella hoped that force could be avoided.

Ella's commentary revealed how closely her habits of grace and civility were linked to a larger context of complacency and privilege. In Bram's case, for the moment, it went further, as on the farm he felt impelled to participate in another attraction of the day, the 'scientific' evaluation of other (and usually 'lower') races. He told his parents he had been drawn to the coloureds – not physically or emotionally, but intellectually. The subject was altogether a study in itself, he wrote to his father. The coloureds were 'naturally terribly uncultivated and filthy'; there wasn't one out of thirty men on the farm 'who had the least character in his face'. But still Bram found them 'pathetic': 'Lower than the kaffer from the moral point of view, nonetheless you can insult them greatly by calling them kaffers, and they are naturally proud of their rights, such as their admission into a canteen. But what struck me as their strong point was their sense of humour . . . ' On the question of race relations he was emphatic: 'It seems to me that people down here, where the kaffer question is taken to be at its most serious, just don't understand how far the matter has already proceeded with us [in the Free State] with the black man.'

Bram was nearly eighteen, and some of this could be attributed to the unsubtleties of a youth repeating the standard nostrums of his culture, as well as the generalities of the crude sociology to which he was drawn. And yet, he had used every available motif in the repertoire of racial stereotypes, from ideas of natural and moral hierarchies among races, to physiognomic theories holding that racial morality was apparent in bodily features, to specific slurs against the coloureds because of their mixed race. In reply, Bram's mother was genially condescending. She agreed that the coloureds were worth studying, all the way from their 'very real sense of humour through all the shades of pathos' to what she termed the 'tragedy of their origins'. On this she recommended that Bram read Sarah Gertrude Millin's *God's Step-Children*, which had then just appeared, and which she said gave 'a wonderful picture of the coloured man'. In retrospect, *God's Step-Children* appears to be a viciously racist novel, with many of the same pseudo-scientific classifications that Bram had found so persuasive. But when that novel first appeared, it was warmly received worldwide as a compelling and sensitive study, by H.L. Mencken and Eleanor Roosevelt among others.

Bram and his family were obviously not alone in their failings, but given this sheer weight of convention, any transformation in his sense both of self and of other would have to be a matter of assiduously conscientious attention.

By March 1926 Bram was at the University of Cape Town where, after the juvenile horrors of initiation (which for him included drinking a mixture of water and mustard, and having the hair on his legs burned off), he began to enjoy the independence and liberation of campus life. Despite the fact that he was living cheaply (reckoning with meticulous pride that his night-time cocoa cost him less than twopence a cup), he soon settled into an enjoyable social round, hiving off with friends to dances, concerts, the opera, picnics and walks. Climbing on Table Mountain he took in the beauties of Cape Town; on the shores of the Indian and Atlantic oceans he swam in its impeccable seas. Later in the year he went on a camping trip to Saldanha Bay, where a university friend (son of a local magistrate) secretly arranged for Bram and his companion to be arrested and imprisoned for the night. When Percy heard of this he was furious, telling Bram he should never have surrendered without insisting on seeing a warrant or knowing the reason for his detention. In later years, when warrants no longer became necessary in South Africa, Bram might well have wished that prison were always just the consequence of a practical joke, and equally temporary.

Bram's academic life wasn't always as pleasant as his various social engagements, especially as he struggled along in mathematics. But he was enthusiastic about economics (his intended major), took nearly as well to history, and somewhat less so to Latin (which he would need for law in South Africa, with its Roman–Dutch basis). In his tennis he was surprisingly successful early on, and an elated telegram to his parents the day before his eighteenth birthday in 1926 announced that he had just become the UCT champion. In a letter to Percy and Ella that followed he explained that when he stepped on court for the final round he had had no idea of how to take on his opponent: 'so I decided to chuck away the first set – as it was a five-set match – in finding out. I came to the decision to play on his backhand & take the net when he was leading 5–1 and I won in three straight sets 8–6, 6–4, 6–3. Really he was very sporting, though, and it was a jolly nice match,' added Bram, but his evident glee as well as the deliberate method he described indicated to his parents, if to no one else, the canniness that lurked under his charm.

In rugby Bram played for the Under 19A team – again a measure of his all-round achievement – but his participation in these traditional arenas of male conflict and camaraderie was not entirely predictable: for the final game of the season he was tempted to opt out to visit a flower show, something for which his walks on Bergendal had prepared him. Perhaps the only surprise of that year – given his atheism – was that he attended confirmation classes. This was almost certainly at the insistence of Ella, to whom he wrote that he was complying 'to get it over'. (Bram's younger brothers remarked later that they all took confirmation to please their mother.) Ella sent him a Bible for the purpose, and Bram took to it seriously, telling his mother that he was doing his best to study all the points with which he was in disagreement. It was a characteristic gesture, reflecting an instinctive openness as well as persistent rationalism, and there was also an impulse to inclusivity: Bram told Ella that there was much good in the Bible if only one could delve past the layers of convention and formula that had been built up around the Christian religion. With an unusual sincerity he really was looking to absorb the best that could be offered from every direction, and later on never lost his respect for the fundamental aspiration to universal brotherhood that Christianity, in its most impressive visions, offered. It was merely that later Bram felt that aspiration had been superseded by a more highly evolved and more rational form.

As for the temptations of contemporary politics, Cape Town was the ideal place to be, because of the proximity of parliament. Bram attended debates on what he called the 'Colour Bar Bill' (almost certainly the Coloured Persons' Rights Bill) which Hertzog was promulgating that year in combination with three other Bills (the Representation of Natives Bill, the Native Council Bill, and the Native Land Bill) to restrict even further the African and coloured franchise, and to keep South Africa what Hertzog later termed 'a white man's land'. At the time the whole of South Africa was in ferment over these Bills, which, along with legislation already passed in mining and industry, were intended to restructure the social and economic landscape in the form of a more strictly regulated racial segregation and inequity. Inside parliament Bram was intrigued by the way Hertzog castigated Smuts in the debate on the franchise, but he also went outside the building to observe a large crowd of coloureds who were sending in a deputation to protest against the proposed eradication of their vote. Later that evening there was a demonstration on the Parade, and Bram was there to listen – probably, he told Percy and Ella, the only white person in the crowd.

As his presence at the demonstration testified, Bram was doing his best to take in all sides of the issues of the day. He was evidently fascinated by the whole field of race relations and politics, coming to see it – as did many others – as *the* issue of the future. Bram went to lectures on 'native education'; he saw Hertzog address a Labour rally; in his economics course he was studying what was conventionally termed the 'native question'. To some extent his mind was opening up: he wrote to Percy and Ella that the Colour Bar Bill had 'clearly brought their disprivilege to the attention of coloureds', but there he might have been objecting to the vitriolic manner of the debate as much as its content. In the Debating Society at UCT, which he joined, he spoke in favour of (white) women's suffrage (which did not yet exist in South Africa), winning the motion by a majority of ten. But when Dr Malan (who later led the National Party to victory in 1948) spoke of '*die heiligdom van die Afrikaanse volkslewe*' (with its strictly untranslatable compounds roughly meaning 'the holiness of the life of the Afrikaner people'), it was still the melodramatic and sentimental rhetoric of nationalism that moved him. Bram thought Malan's words 'magnificent', and for him the large idea that evidently mattered was still the heady one that each people had its own national destiny to fulfil – and perhaps the corollary that the separate 'nations' of South Africa should fulfil those destinies separately.

In many ways Bram was being groomed for a future that could have been his. When he went to parliament he was invited to lunch by family acquaintances who told him all the gossip and inside political stories. He visited Ouma Steyn, the old President's wife, on a number of occasions; he spent a weekend at the Prime Minister's residence at Groote Schuur talking to Mrs Hertzog, who told him how she had been taken off to a concentration camp during the Boer War. He met Colonel Creswell, leader of the Labour Party and Hertzog's partner in government, as well as Havenga, future leader of the Afrikaner Party, which joined with Malan's National Party in the apartheid government of 1948; Mrs Havenga sent her love to Ella Fischer, whom she apparently knew well. Like his grandfather and father before him, Bram was being nurtured in the bosom of the Afrikaner family in power, absorbing its innermost gestures and myths, with the expectation that he would in time reproduce them.

Moreover, Cape Town invited a reconnection with his own family and its history. Virtually every Sunday Bram would go out to Sea Point to visit his godmother, Auntie Maggie (Mrs Denyssen's daughter) – a direct link, for him, with Oupa Abraham. Auntie Maggie took him to see the house in which his grandfather had been born, and another called Hillandale from which, Bram wrote to his brother Paul, the farm had taken its name. At the funeral of an ex-student from Grey who had died climbing Table Mountain, Bram came across his Oupa Abraham's grave, finding it both simple and inspiring. As much as the present consumed him, he was linking up with his beginnings, and could not get enough of the stories Auntie Maggie told him of the past.

In December 1926 another telegram arrived home giving Percy and Ella the results of Bram's first-year examinations. Suitably, he had achieved a first in economics, and second-class passes in his three other subjects. Yet Bram had decided that, instead of returning to UCT the following year, he would come back to Bloemfontein and attend Grey University College (then part of the national university-college system in South Africa). This wasn't entirely because Bram was homesick, but he had a more pressing reason. Surprisingly for someone whose instincts were so avowedly anti-imperialist, he had decided to try for a Rhodes Scholarship to Oxford, and the fact was that while he would have a fairly good chance applying from the Cape, the competition from the Free State would be much weaker. Once again there was a rather pragmatic, not to say calculating, attitude behind the strategy, designed to give the best chance of success. And whatever doubts there were about the ideological provenance of the Rhodes, it would give Bram the opportunity of travelling like his grandfather and father to Europe, broadening his experience, and deriving from it an inestimable prestige at a time when a number of Afrikaner leaders of the future were establishing their credentials by studying abroad. Leo Marquard was averse to the move back to Bloemfontein as part of this design, but after some correspondence both with him and his father, Bram made up his mind and returned.

Later he would lament the move, largely because the educational and political atmosphere of Grey was so much more constrained than the relatively enlightened world of UCT. And yet there was one aspect he never regretted, for once back in Bloemfontein Bram entered again into the 'magic circle' of Leo and Nell Marquard. Paradoxically it was precisely the established path of eminence and prestige opening up before him that they helped him question; or at least, indirectly, they helped him to see it in another way. In later years the one characteristic that defined Bram Fischer for those who came to know him was his integrity: ideas for him were little more than worthless if they were neither consistent nor put into action in life. At that time Bram's mind and life were both still in flux; he was making his way in the world, feeling out its shape, establishing a view in which he yearned perhaps more than anything else for coherence. What the Marquards invited was a form of enactment that ultimately made him think deeply about what coherence meant.

The Marquards drew Bram into local projects they were undertaking both for and with Africans, and from various points of view – over and above his affection for Leo and Nell – it made sense for him to participate. His mother Ella would have recognised in such activities the idea of 'good works', as well as the *noblesse oblige* that accompanied social privilege; from his father came the pattern of probing one's ideas from different angles. Bram was still a nationalist, but to him this did not imply an amoral or immoral distancing from other people. On the contrary, for him a true nationalism in South Africa involved a knowledge and understanding of other people and their own legiti-mate needs. If there are different versions of nationalism, Bram Fischer's was one he was still testing and extending.

Through the Marquards Bram became involved in adult education for Africans – in the same Waaihoek location in which, just a few years earlier, strikes had been threatened. Some forty and fifty years later, as Bram wrote from prison to Leo and then, after Leo died, to Nell, he remembered sitting there on windy, cold nights in winter (the name 'Waaihoek' literally meant 'Windy Corner') with dust blowing into the old building where they taught. Where Bram's attitude just a few years earlier had been one of glib condescen-sion, it could hardly survive unchanged in such circumstances. It was also at Leo's instigation that Bram became a member of the Bloemfontein Joint Council of Europeans and Africans, which, as part of the wider Joint Council movement in South Africa, served as a forum where whites and blacks (usually teachers or ministers) would meet to discuss issues of common con-cern. The Joint Council was by no means a radical institution (its effect was, on the contrary, to defuse tensions through discussion and mollification), but later Bram would tell the Marquards that he regarded this shift as his 'real break through', not only because it gave him the opportunity to meet Africans on a different basis, but more particularly because of one specific incident on the council that he saw as a critical turning-point in his life.

There, at his very first meeting, Leo introduced him to the others, and

Bram had to shake hands for the first time as an adult with a black man. In the normal course of events this would not have been a matter of much significance, but all the years of sensory indoctrination had done their work, and Bram found himself suddenly overcome by an instinctive feeling of revulsion which he had to force himself to suppress. Many years later, describing the event to Leo from prison, the moment of that handshake was still vivid in his mind, as Bram recalled too the difference from his early years as a child on the farm with his black friends: 'I can still sense the act of will that it required from one who had grown up on the farm with little Loel and Golokwaan as his only playmates, but who in the space of a few years had drifted completely into the normal S. African attitude.'

For someone else this incident, unsettling as it was, might have been dismissed out of hand, or else proved so disturbing that it would never have been repeated. But for Bram, coming now to define himself by the integrity and need for consistency that marked him, it prompted a depth of self-inspection he had never before undertaken. Such racial responses may be embarrassing, but Bram was aware enough to understand that something was deeply wrong. Indeed, it was such a significant moment for him that more than thirty years later he spoke of it in his speech from the dock in his trial, just before he was sentenced to life imprisonment for opposing the racism he had.on that earlier occasion embodied. 'Could I really, I felt, my Lord, as a white adult, touch the hand of a black man in friendship?' Yet it was following on this incident, Bram revealed, that he had begun to look inward, wondering whether the fault underlying his reaction lay not in the black man whose hand he had shaken, but in himself: 'What became abundantly clear . . . was that it was I who had changed, and not the black man . . . despite my growing interest in his problems. I had developed . . . an antagonism for which I could find no rational basis whatsoever.'

Bram had grown into a place and an attitude prepared for him; his unconscious response was deeply embedded in the world he inhabited. Therefore, in order to change that response, both for himself and for others, he would have to change the world that had engendered it. Perhaps, thinking back to his early years with Loel and Golokwaan on the farm at Bergendal, the deep and shaming ambiguities of his attachment to the land became evident. To win that attachment and make it genuine he would have to become a different kind of being, part of a much larger South African family, part of a different definition of its landscape. Everything else that happened in Bram Fischer's life developed from this moment of personal crisis, and the obligations and commitments that followed.

'The result of all this', as he remembered it in his speech from the dock, 'was that in the succeeding years when some of us tried to run literacy classes in the old Waaihoek location in Bloemfontein I came to understand that colour prejudice was a wholly irrational phenomenon, and that true human friendship could extend across the colour bar once the initial prejudice was overcome. And that I think, my Lord, was lesson number one on my way to the Communist Party, a Party which has always refused to accept any colour bar, which has always stood firm on the belief – a belief itself two thousand years old – of the eventual brotherhood of all men.'

CHAPTER 3

LOVE AND LETTERS

When Bram returned from Cape Town at the beginning of 1927, he moved in again with his parents at Harmonie in Reitz Street, and took up at Grey University College where he had left off at UCT. In later years Bram expressed himself critical of the way universities reproduced rather than challenged the received wisdom of their day, feeling from that point of view (since at the time he himself had undertaken no radical appraisals) that his time at university had been wasted. In more conventional terms, however, his return could not have been more auspicious. Bram took his BA with distinction in economics and history in 1928, and then began a part-time law degree at Grey while simultaneously working as registrar in the Supreme Court of the Orange Free State to the Judge-President, Sir Etienne de Villiers. This was the suitable start to his career that Percy and Ella would have desired.

Nor was his life as uncritical or uninvolved as it might later have seemed, especially under the varied aspects of Leo Marquard's tutelage. In July 1927 Bram attended a council meeting of NUSAS in Durban, where he pronounced himself (to his parents) exhilarated by the discussion and activity, and by Marquard's direction of the proceedings. Moreover, the council (no doubt at Marquard's instigation) had appointed him a member – not as a university representative, but as one of five additional delegates elected by the council itself. Such persons, he told his parents, were normally given specially designated tasks. In addition, he had been asked to be editor of *The NUSAS* magazine and, with Leo's encouragement, had accepted. 'Of course it was all his work,' wrote Bram.

The fact was that Marquard had an extraordinarily special feeling for Bram, in the way that teachers have for some pupils. Their friendship was a close and personal one, with its own unconditional respect, and in that sense Bram was never simply Marquard's protégé. But at the same time it is probably true that for Marquard Bram represented a specific kind of hope. With his own Afrikaner background (Marquard's father, a *dominee*, had died when he was eight, and he had been apprenticed to a carpenter), he had a sure view of the realities of South Africa's past; yet with his broader perspective he had a clear sense of the dangers and responsibilities of its future. For him it was an urgent need that in South Africa's intense racial climate men and women of insight be cultivated to provide the necessary wisdom and guidance. If this was to some extent an elitist view, it was at the same time practical and engaged, and Marquard was himself never less than wholly involved in the pursuit of a South African enlightenment. From that perspective Bram must have seemed to him something of a model in the making. He had the requisite courtesy, the humour, the openness of spirit and firmness of purpose; with his family background he also had the credentials to speak to and for Afrikaners, and – with the right guidance – to persuade them to speak to Africans. To be sure, Bram held firm positions (just then opposed to Marquard's ideologically), but these might be all the more reliable as, under considered testing and self-inspection, they changed. As for Bram, the example of Marquard's own respect for his moral and ideological differences, combined with his always personable attempts at persuasion by example, provided a model the ex-pupil was more than ready to absorb.

Bram took to his various tasks with a will, and developed the patterns that characterised his working habits for the rest of his life. At that time his brother Paul had taken to rising early – about 4.30 a.m. – and not infrequently would see Bram coming into the house just as he was on his way out. Bram would snatch a few hours' sleep, take a shower, eat his breakfast, and then shoot off to lectures or editing The NUSAS. As a magazine The NUSAS embodied no special vitality, and came under criticism for its dry and enervated style, but it did allow scope for new kinds of thinking. As editor, and taking up his earlier theme, Bram wrote on the need for women to be given the franchise in South Africa (this came, for white women, in 1931), and for a transformation in both personal and social relations that would allow them not only to enjoy independence, but assume their full responsibilities in society. In part, in writing this way, Bram may well have had his mother in mind, especially the scandal that someone of her talents did not have the vote; but also, in talking of a fundamental alteration in personal and social relations, he was suggesting a form of fulfilment and liberation for women of which Ella, with her traditionalism, might not have approved. There were other kinds of thoughts in the air. The NUSAS representative at a meeting of the Confédération Internationale des Étudiants (CIE) in Geneva drew pertinent conclusions from observing the exclusion of Jews from certain student organisations in Europe, and suggested that it was time for NUSAS to admit African students into its ranks.

This was one of the most inspiring dimensions of NUSAS activity – its international connections. It had indirect links with the International Students' Service, which had begun as a relief organisation in the wake of the First World War, and now promoted international and interracial relationships among students (Albert Einstein was one of its patrons). It was also directly affiliated to the CIE, based in Geneva as a kind of student League of Nations (open, too, to the same kind of nationalist posturings and wheelings and dealings as the parent body). NUSAS arranged tours for South African students to Europe and the United States, and there were CIE tours in return to South Africa. It meant that people of one kind or another were always arriving – among them J. Merle Davis, director of the Department of Social and Industrial Research in Geneva, who through the connection with Marquard paid Bram a visit.

It also meant that Bram was absorbing some of the dominant impulses and idealisms of his time. In one of his editorials he wrote fervently of the need for students to work for world peace: 'We, as students, have so much in common with students of every other nationality that we should undoubtedly be able to advance very far along the road to peace, that we should be able to succeed where others have failed.' His Aunt Maude would have approved, but if in a global perspective Bram wrote as an 'internationalist', in the South African setting it was still as a nationalist that he did so. This was revealed most intriguingly in the NUSAS parliaments in which he participated. These had been instituted by Marquard along the lines of the NUS parliaments in Britain, where student leaders would come together and argue the politics of the day, form the equivalent of national student governments and pass mock legislation, all along party lines, as in the real institution. It appears that the first such parliament had coincided with the NUSAS council meeting in Durban in 1927, and it may have been this that so excited Bram's interest.

In this arena 1929 saw the pinnacle of his power – and defeat. By January of that year Bram was busily at work as the student leader of the National Party. Later it turned out that Leo Marquard had attempted to persuade him to form a new party, to break out of the predictable South African Party–National Party mould, but Bram still wanted, as he put it afterwards, to follow a more 'patriotic' line. He travelled and wrote letters, trying to gain agreement on policies, and even consulted with some of South Africa's real political leaders as to the course he should follow. As the student parliament approached in July, he prepared a spirited speech proposing to abolish the King's veto on South African legislation – a change he said (in tones his Oupa Abraham would have recognised) that would 'alarm some of our jingoistic friends' – and to bring to an end the authority of the Privy Council in London as the final court of appeal in South African cases. (Later in life Bram would have reason to be pleased that the Privy Council's jurisdiction still extended as far as Rhodesia, but in 1929 its attractions weren't so obvious.) In these policies Bram was following an orthodox Nationalist line, favouring an enhanced South African independence. Indeed, he was able to press for them with even more fervour and candour than Hertzog, constrained as the latter was by the limits of the 'real' political world. As Bram put it, his party was making a national claim, but he was also at pains to point out that in this South African nationalism he saw no division between English-speakers and Afrikaners.

In that parliament of 1929, the National Party was able to form a government, and Bram, as its leader, became 'prime minister', an achievement which Marquard might have felt augured the real position in due course. When the Bill to abolish the King's veto and the jurisdiction of the Privy Council came up, it was adopted with the support of the Progressive Party (a group of Nationalist divergents from the University of Stellenbosch), and Bram had won his first victory. But his defeat followed just as quickly, over a proposed Industrial Bank. The Nationalists' Labour allies were prepared to support the Bill if the bank were termed a 'State Bank', with the specific aim of eliminating private enterprise, but this the Nationalists were not prepared to countenance. So Labour voted against the Bill, as did the Progressives, and the National Party lost by 33 votes to 32. Bram's government had to resign, and the South African Party took over.

The student parliament was both serious and superficial, with erratic swings of the ideological pendulum and the kind of politicking that imitated the real South African parliament all too closely. Thus, as the *Rand Daily Mail* reported, when the South African Party proposed a £7000 grant to set up a 'native agricultural school', Bram pounced on it, 'clawing it from several angles, and chiefly from the remarkable angle that it was not really liberal'. Meanwhile the Progressives declared the SAPs were lambs in power and lions out of it, while the National Party opposed SAP legislation they themselves had initiated when in power the day before. Much of the discussion, observed the *Rand Daily Mail*, was as sterile as that in the genuine institution.

꧁꧂

For Bram it was a period of ideological and political flux. By 1929 Hertzog had been re-energised in putting forward the 'Native Bills' he had introduced in 1926, whose main aim was to remove Africans in the Cape from the common voters' roll and establish representation for blacks throughout the country by a limited number of whites in parliament. Writing an editorial in *The NUSAS* in 1928, Bram hoped that the Bills would pass in a spirit of co-operation between the SAP and NP; but he also took them as a sign of universal acceptance of the need to give Africans the franchise in some form, almost a 'revolution', as he put it, in public opinion. Hertzog fought the 1929 general election (successfully) by raising the spectre of the '*swart gevaar*' [black peril] against which only the National Party could defend white South Africa. Yet by this time Bram, after his experience on the Joint Council, had realised that the *gevaar*, if it existed, lay somewhat more deeply within himself.

His continuing activities, on the Joint Council, in the literacy classes and elsewhere, would have reinforced his personal and political metamorphosis. One forum that drew his attention, at least for a while, was the Bantu Study Circles set up by NUSAS at various universities. There was much to be questioned regarding these circles – not least the assumption, emanating in part from an era of unselfconscious anthropological investigation, that so-called Bantu culture was simply there in a more or less passive way to be 'studied'. Yet what engrossed the circles at this time – as it did virtually everyone else – was the 'native question', and in this guise Bram attended a Conference on Equality in Pretoria in 1928. There he encountered at first hand some of the rough-and-ready approximations the idea of 'equality' might undergo, especially when it came to the intersections of culture, race and gender. One of the African speakers remarked that if whites were afraid of being overwhelmed by black voters they could balance things by giving the franchise to white women: 'the African woman doesn't want it.'

On the Joint Council (of which Bram was secretary by 1930) there was a good deal of practical work in addition to regular discussion. The Bloemfontein council (composed of an equal number of white and black men) initiated action on issues ranging from the ill-treatment of blacks in the post office to major problems regarding infant mortality, welfare, wages and housing. There were notable visitors: on one occasion they were joined by Sol Plaatje, who had reason to remember Abraham Fischer with such regret. As the new decade turned and the Depression set in, the Joint Council of necessity became absorbed in a series of more urgent questions. Blacks were being driven from the farms, poor whites were again streaming to the towns, and concern about poverty in general prompted two great social investigations – the Carnegie Commission on Poor Whites, and the Native Economic Commission (1930–2), which toured the country gathering evidence (later largely ignored) on the situation of Africans. In Bloemfontein Bram was on a subcommittee of the Joint Council which gathered information for submission to the Native Economic Commission, and he led it after Leo Marquard left for

England to undertake research for a book on the franchise in colonial settings. In February 1931 the Joint Council submitted its memorandum to the commission, and Bram, as its representative, testified at the hearings in Bloemfontein.

The memorandum spoke with a quiet passion against the accumulated administrative wisdom of thirty years and more: 'Finally the time has come to realise that native locations cannot be regarded merely as reservoirs of labour for European commerce and industry. They have come to stay and are growing rapidly.' In his evidence, Bram was subjected to questioning by the chairman of the commission, who wondered whether the Joint Council was against the idea of limiting the influx of blacks to the locations, and whether they would allow a free play of economic forces. 'Well, we discussed that fully,' Bram responded, 'and we came to the conclusion that it was more dangerous to the country as a whole to restrict the free flow of labour.' Was it true then, came the question, that the Joint Council was against segregation? 'That is so undoubtedly,' said Bram. Was that the *considered* opinion of the council? asked the chairman. 'We have not taken any resolution on that,' replied Bram, 'but judging from all the subsidiary resolutions, I think I can speak with a fair amount of confidence and say that we do not believe in segregation at all.'

Certainly Bram did not have all the answers. In reply to a question from an Afrikaans Senator (it took a Nationalist to undercut someone just emerging from the same quarter), Bram was forced to admit that it would not do any good to give Africans the same security of tenure in the countryside as they enjoyed in the towns, since they hardly enjoyed any security anywhere in South Africa. But the key point was that in saying that he – along with the Joint Council – did not believe in segregation, Bram had moved beyond the primary credo of Afrikaner nationalism, that blacks and whites in South Africa had to be separated. There was a view of Africans in his presentation that saw them not as units of labour but as participants in the making of South Africa whose humanity and rights had to be recognised. Indeed, in challenging the established conventions, Bram was contravening the codes not only of nationalism, but also of liberalism as it was propounded at the time by luminaries such as Edgar Brookes, who favoured segregation in order to protect African culture. In offering his presentation, Bram was just short of twenty-three years, facing the authority of a parliamentary commission, and speaking with a quiet respect and confidence that in the circumstances can only be regarded as remarkable.

In order to present his testimony Bram had, along with others, traversed the white and black sections of Bloemfontein, gathering evidence from employers and employees on the minimum wage, leasehold property rights, the relative value of skilled black labour as against unskilled white (strong opinion from employers in favour of the former), and the rise in unemployment – all the unending but crucial details of human suffering. At a black burial society, where he arrived on his own, there was suspicion of this sudden white intrusion, and he had to return with a black colleague to assure his good faith. He was learning in a practical way the exacting intricacies of interaction between black and white in South Africa, where much of the emotional terrain was uncharted and the protocols unsteady and uncertain. And yet, he was clearly being *pushed* by that dialogue and, as his testimony evidenced, had the courage to go where it led him.

The Joint Council movement was in many respects meliorist and reform-minded; at the same time, as in the declarations against segregation and the cruel use of black locations as 'labour reservoirs', it allowed for straightforward convictions that flew in the face of the established beliefs and practices of white government. Nor did this go unnoticed. Dr A.B. Xuma, prominent leader of the African National Congress and its future president-general, spoke with approval of people such as 'Messrs Fischer and Marquard' who through their night school and Joint Council (Bloemfontein's, he said, was 'one of the best') had shown a devotion to the cause of the African 'which can hardly be excelled, and is worthy of emulation by all'.

It was already a different world for Bram, the terror of his handshake perhaps now receding. In the same year that he testified before the Native Economic Commission, he responded in a private letter to 'yet another' attack on NUSAS for being too internationalist and 'anti-Afrikaanse tradisies en sedes' [anti-Afrikaner traditions and customs]. 'If there's one thing that really annoys me,' wrote Bram, 'it's when the blasted blackcoated and stiffcollared crowd start howling down the one idea in the world that gives one some hope – a scientific internationalism. I wouldn't mind so much if it were decent criticism, but they can't think further than giving a telephone number in Afrikaans.' It is just possible that in talking of 'scientific internationalism' Bram was drawing on Marxist and Bolshevik theory, for which each of those words would have had a specific resonance. It is also conceivable that it was the Bantu Study Circles – and the anthropology of the day – that stood behind the phrase, on the basis that a true internationalism required a thorough understanding of other 'nations'. Either way, where the boundaries of ideology are seldom fixed and permanent, it is likely that this was later one of the appeals of communism for Bram, in its proclaimed understanding of the problem of 'nationalities'. For, in true dialectical fashion, communism professed both to protect and preserve national identity and at the same time to transcend it in the name of something larger – just the combination, emerging through these years, which Bram would have wanted and needed, and which would have seemed so logical to him.

As Bram derided the propensity of Nationalists to insist on the official (and daily) use of Afrikaans, it is intriguing that his personal letter was so much more fiery than anything he would have allowed himself in public. The letter was addressed to a young woman he had met named Molly Krige.

⁂

On a moonlit summer's night in January 1931 something was declared in the cemetery in Bethlehem in the Orange Free State. According to Bram's celebration of the event one year later (what he might have thought of as his first anniversary), this was the night Molly Krige had said to him, 'I suppose I might as well leap.' The leap was of course into love, and later the story became the matter of family legend, retold in routines of mild comedy and allegation. On that night, apparently, Molly wouldn't state her allegiance unequivocally and, to distract Bram, dropped her handkerchief so that it blew away in the wind; he had to go chasing after it over the graves (and then refused to return it). As for Molly (this was true, and not legend), she was by no means alarmed by graves; on the contrary, cemeteries were among her favourite places, and that was why she and Bram had come.

The morning after, Bram was ecstatic. 'I love you. I love you. I love you,' he wrote to Molly from the Grand Hotel ('The Home for Comfort') in Ladybrand, where he was travelling on circuit as registrar with the Judge-President of the Free State. He added (the antic tone matched by a certain gravity), 'This sounds like the beginning of a Circuit Court. I wish I could make it the beginning of many happy years for you. But I've been terribly afraid today.' For, he told Molly, when someone heard what she had told him the night before, it was easy to imagine that all one's troubles would disappear. But the opposite was also possible. 'Molly, and now I'm feeling terrible. Were you sure of what you said? And even if you were, haven't I taken on much too big a thing? . . . My only consolation, Molly, is that I've never met a man who would be your equal. All would be merely . . . beggarmen without the secret of turning themselves into princes, seeking a princess.'

Just how serious Molly had been was open to question; it would be some time before Bram (or she herself) was quite sure. But for Bram there could be no doubt: once his faith was given he kept to it with an unwavering if often anxious loyalty. His letter to her of that morning (in love, in play, in concern) was representative of the many hundreds that followed over the next seven years, as in an extended courtship of time and distance Bram and Molly wrote to one another, both in South Africa and across countries and continents. Like some biblical Jacob labouring his seven years to win Rachel, everything Bram did had Molly Krige as its ultimate end. His need for her became caught up with his desire for a larger coherence in his life, and he sought the two together in the underlying rhythms of his journeys.

⚜

Bram first met Molly in 1927 at the Ramblers Club in Bloemfontein, where she had come as a member of the women's hockey team from the Transvaal University College in Pretoria during one of the regular Intervarsities against Grey. The men played rugby, the women hockey, and Bram was most likely a member of the rugby team. They were introduced by a mutual friend, Elodie de la Harpe from the farm Lusthof in the Golden Gate area of the eastern Free State, who had been at school with Bram's sister Ada. At first Bram and Molly paid little attention to each another, although Bram did notice at the time (as he recalled later) that her eyes were 'very very blue'.

After Molly's mother, Emmy Bernsmann, had left Otjimbingue and completed her education at the mission school in Stellenbosch, she had worked as a teacher in Britstown, and then in Bethal during the Boer War. There she was sent to a concentration camp, but was quickly released on account of her German nationality. As the story went, she had first met her future husband, one P.S. 'Tottie' Krige, in a strawberry field in Stellenbosch, and then again in Bethal. The 'Tottie' was sign of a tedious racial humour, for his hair was quite crinkly, and he therefore looked like a coloured or 'Hottentot' – in Afrikaans 'Hotnot', and so 'Tottie' – but it seems to have become a name he accepted as his own.

The Kriges, like the Fischers, had their own standing as a family: they traced their ancestry back a few hundred years in South Africa, and boasted among their extended number the poet and translator Uys Krige, who was about Molly's age. 'Tottie' Krige had been General Smuts's aide-de-camp during the First World War, and his sister Isie was married to the general. It was hard to be more auspicious than that, and yet the family had nothing like the weight and wealth of the Fischers. 'Tottie' worked as a land surveyor, and the Kriges lived on a smallholding in Silverton, near Pretoria, where they tended their own vines and mealies. There was seldom any money to spare, but Molly had strong memories of how her mother – the missionary Bernsmann's daughter and a devout Christian – would never turn a beggar away from the door without food. That was essential to Molly's character as well: she could never pass a beggar in the street without giving something.

Molly was born on 23 February 1908, and so she was exactly two months older than Bram. Her given names were Susanna Johanna, but 'Molly' seemed to suit her much better, and it was as good as a permanent appellation. From her early years she had a spirited vitality and energy, balanced in moments (if one could catch it) with a deeper inwardness and contemplation. When she was five she found herself expelled from Sunday school: she thought her voice was terrible, and refused to sing, simply mouthing the words. When the teacher caught her and threatened that if she didn't comply she wouldn't go to Heaven, the young Molly's retort was that she would rather not go to Heaven if what you had to do there was sing. So she suffered her excommunication, but it meant that while the other children sat in strict Calvinist concentration every Sunday, she was able to play outside on the swings, where she could indulge her own thoughts under the freedom of the clouds and the sky.

At the farm school she attended two teachers had the care of everyone from Grade One to Standard Five (ages of about six to twelve), all within one large and ill-equipped room. Molly was bright and advanced quickly, so that she matriculated from high school at the age of sixteen. She went to Pretoria Girls' High, an English school in the colonial tradition, although the Kriges spoke Afrikaans at home. Molly was talented and energetic at sports – hockey and gymnastics – and in her final year became a prefect, but despite the authority the school setting wasn't entirely able to tame her. One day she skipped school to watch a rugby match, and as a consequence had her prefect's badge confiscated. (Some years later the school principal told her she'd been obliged officially to do this, but secretly thought the whole enterprise rather sweet.) According to her close friend Herleve Clapham, whose first name Molly always punned affectionately as 'Liefie' [Lovey], Molly 'didn't give a damn' about such things. She always had a feel for the underdog, said Herleve, and never lost her irreverent spirit, but at the same time it was always Molly to whom her friends came for advice.

After school she wanted to be a veterinarian, but because there was no money for a professional degree, Molly decided to become a teacher instead. Later she said (in a way that managed at the same time to be both self-ironising and buoyant) that her choices were based on completely flimsy foundations – that she had changed course (and courses) with every new boyfriend, just so they would approve. For Molly and her friends it was an era of unselfconscious fun and games, of carefree vitality and almost methodical innocence. At Lusthof, with its breathtaking scenery of the Basutoland mountains, there was Elodie; in Pretoria, Herleve and Marie 'Ikki' Bosman (who took her nickname from her boyfriend's decrepit motor-bike, anointed Ichabod for 'the glory hath departed' – later the car Bram used to visit Molly also seems to have become an 'Ichabod'). Molly and her friends went swimming and camping together, or visiting Elodie at Lusthof, exchanging boyfriends as easily as they breathed. It was a liberty and pleasure linked to the landscape, a free and easy life without responsibilities.

Molly took her first job, teaching at the Housecraft School in Bethlehem in the Free State, and that was where Bram came across her again, remembering her blue eyes at the Ramblers Club, travelling now as registrar on circuit court with Sir Etienne de Villiers.

⚜

As Bram recalled two years later, he first 'fell' for Molly in May 1930. While the circuit court routes were being arranged he began to do his utmost to make sure that he was always assigned the sessions in Bethlehem. His mind was constantly ticking over with schemes to see Molly, ranging (as she chided him) from touring near Bethlehem with a tennis team to becoming travelling secretary for any stray religious society in Bloemfontein. Bram would borrow his father's Standard motor car (the drive took four and a half hours), or concoct plans with his friend Nick de Villiers, former tennis partner at high school, now co-contender for the Rhodes Scholarship and fellow clerk in the Supreme Court. Nick had an aunt in Bethlehem, and they would drive there, ostensibly to see her; thereafter the phrase 'Nick se Auntie' [Nick's Aunt] became a standing joke among the Fischer siblings as they ragged Bram. One midnight, as Bram was changing trains in Kroonstad on his way home from seeing Molly, he unexpectedly met his brother Paul, who was travelling with the Grey Amateur Dramatic Society. The response of both was identical: 'What the hell are you doing here?'

Bram's life with the Judge-President was not always as elevated as might have been expected. He would write to his mother while the court was in session, with (he reported) both counsels, the interpreter and the witness all shouting at the same time just in front of him. After the day's hearings in each successive town (usually after ingesting more boiled mutton for supper than Bram could fairly tolerate), he and the Judge-President would set off from whatever drab hotel accommodated them to the cinema, often taking in two films in a row. The Judge-President – who went universally under the obscure nickname of 'Oeffie', and whom Bram referred to as 'Oeffie, J.P.' – was by turns a rather morose and elated individual, apt to lie on his back in a park whistling for all the world to hear, following and discarding the latest health diets, and always fascinated by cars. On one occasion in June 1930, after Sir Etienne had smashed his car in an accident, Bram had to go on his hands and knees in the streets of Bloemfontein, inspecting the engines and undersides of prospective replacement models, and shouting reports to the Judge-President doing the same across the way. There were times, said Bram, when he couldn't stand him.

All this was while Bram was absorbed in his NUSAS work and on the Joint Council, and it was a lighter side of his life. Together with some friends he lit a fire in the wastepaper basket in his office and cooked sausages. One night he and Nick and some others ended up with female company at one o'clock in the morning in an encounter with a milk cart on the streets of Bloemfontein. When the Rector of Grey banned a dance for the visiting CIE students (after some wild jamboree of their own), Bram and his coterie roped in the female students from the women's hostel for an alternative event. One weekend he and his friend Beck de Villiers (who later married his sister Ada) rode out on Beck's motor-bike to Thaba Nchu and spent the night on the mountain.

This would have captured Molly's imagination because it met her spirit exactly. At the Housecraft School her life was much lonelier and more restricted than Bram's (later she felt she had been collecting 'green mould' in Bethlehem), but she found ways of providing her own invigoration. Molly was captain of the hockey team, swam in the Bethlehem dam, took walks at midnight; once she slept the night in the cemetery with a fellow teacher, a Miss Malan. She loved water of every kind, and revelled in walking or running in the rain ('by hurrying a bit,' she wrote to Bram, 'we still managed to get decently wet'); when she was a safe enough distance from school she liked nothing better than taking her shoes off, just for the pleasure of the mud between her toes. When the men's hockey team was short of players, Molly filled in; they didn't like it, she told Bram, because every time they swore they had to apologise. Herleve Clapham's brother Stratford (who was a pilot and one of her suitors) dropped bouquets of flowers for her from an aeroplane over the Housecraft fields.

She was an unlikely authority figure as a teacher. 'I feel neither clean nor godly tonight,' she wrote one evening to Bram. 'A few misguided pupils asked me to precede them in a prayer meeting. I could not do it and fled to my room. But they followed, and I was irresistibly reminded of the mountain coming to Mahomet. I evaded them by hiding under the bed where I collected incredible quantities of dust, also two spiders and a book I mislaid last week.' When two travelling secretaries of the Students' Christian Association arrived and unctuously asked the pupils to pray for the 'unredeemed members of staff' (by which Molly was sure they meant her and Miss Malan), she took comic revenge. 'We kept them awake the better part of that Friday night by playing hockey in my room. They slept in the one immediately below mine and ought to have heard enough to keep them praying for weeks.' No wonder the schoolgirls loved her. On her birthday they covered her chair and table at breakfast with flowers, and did the same in her classroom.

Molly started a garden in Bethlehem. Her eyes were blue, her favourite colour was blue, she planted blue flowers, and she loved the blue mountains that she and Bram saw on the road from Bethlehem to Bloemfontein. Seven years later Bram remembered that holding her hand for the first time was like 'a continuous electric shock'.

⁂

It was the great game of courtship, played under contemporary rules.

According to Molly's friend Liefie, the idea was to live as fully and even flagrantly as possible; the horror was the idea of marriage and being tied down at some stage. That wasn't Bram's horror: he became attached to the notion of marrying Molly as soon as possible, but even so there was an abiding sense of lightness and fun. Bram and Molly wrote and spoke constantly of 'play' – with one another and with others – and it seems to have had a literal, frolicking meaning. Bram would encourage Molly to visit him in Bloemfontein, saying she couldn't keep going home for visits: 'think of your family.' Or he would threaten to fall in love with Ikki or Elodie or any random female, and Molly would chaff him in return: 'You know, Braam,' (she insistently misspelled his name, and he liked it that way) 'you'll just have to fall in love with Elodie to cheer her up a bit . . . She herself suggested falling in love as a cure for her fit of depression – not with you, of course, but I think that if she's really feeling life is a nuisance she won't be too particular . . . '

With the patrician assurance of his family behind him, Bram's letters – as he and Molly wrote every few days – had the personable presence of a speaking voice. He had a natural way with words, wrote easily at length, and even under fervent emotions managed to create the feel of a spontaneous yet polished composition. He wrote to Molly teasingly, in the form of a legal minute: 'something undefinable was lacking among the gold and russet shades of the Kloof this morning. The general impression of the Court seems to have been that it was "blue." ' In his ecstatic letter the morning after Molly's 'leap' in the cemetery, he was quite prepared to dwell on the mystery of what had happened: 'I can't appreciate it yet and at present it does not seem as if I ever will. I'd love to hear you tell me again. It all seems so unreal tonight. All I can remember is your face. You looked so wonderful – that is what I wanted to tell you on the way to the cemetery.' For Easter 1931 Bram and Molly went to Lusthof, with its breathtaking views, and later Bram re-created it in his memory: 'I'd like to take you riding . . . where we can watch the sunset on the Malutis. Winter will be near by then. The willows will be brown and gold and the smoke from the native villages will be hanging very low . . . '

Yet if all this was designed to capture Molly, something within her refused to be enveloped too easily. Constantly Bram invited her to Harmonie, and even his parents and Ada would become involved – Bram's father offering personally to drive her back to Bethlehem. But invariably she would offer some excuse, or reserve the right to leave early if she came. She told Bram she didn't want to 'worry' his family, and thought they were inviting her just to be charitable to him. He retorted that she had Victorian scruples, which, in response, she didn't deny, saying it meant only the little common sense she still had. Where Bram was open and exposed she was much more careful and secretive, and for all Bram's tolerance it pained him. When Molly at last consented to come for a weekend, Bram had to beg her to tell him something about her life: 'Please Molly, and I promise not to mention it again. What would you feel like if all you knew about me was that I lived in Bloemfontein and worked in an office?'

As this little exchange indicated, the balance of power in their relationship worked more than one way. In part Molly's resistance came out of her sense of 'play', but it did not come entirely out of strength. She told Bram that writing was a kind of murder for her, and that she would spend about six hours beforehand in miserable anticipation. 'If this is too long,' she wrote in one of the brief communications that so exasperated and tantalised Bram, 'don't hesitate to let me know. I can say even more things I don't mean, in fewer words.' Her letters appeared cavalier, even wilful at times, but this may have been because of a need for self-protection. Just after her 'leap' in the cemetery, when Bram wrote that he would love to hear her words again, she demurred: 'Braam, please don't ask me to say things again. Some streak of perversity in me makes me doubt everything I say often and then I feel I have to change my mind . . . I'm not talking nonsense when I say I don't want people to know me well.' Molly claimed that one reason she never wrote serious letters – as Bram begged her to do – was that she couldn't believe anyone would have the slightest interest in what she had to say; she also confessed that this was just an excuse to conceal her laziness. She would try to put Bram off directly, saying she was always falling in and out of love with people, and destroying their happiness; as for herself, she claimed that she was much too frivolous to get hurt. But that was belied by her (sometimes evident) lack of confidence, as well as her need to defend her feelings, which like her favourite colour were on occasion also 'blue'. Underlying her instinctive vitality was a more shadowed area in Molly, something under the brightness which she would only very carefully reveal, but it was a part of what drew Bram on.

He too, under his ease and singlemindedness, had his anxieties. 'I don't know why I get the blue funks when I've been away from you for some time,' he wrote. 'I think I'm always afraid that you'll suddenly discover one day what a terrible mistake you've made . . . ' But when he worried or was overly serious about something (for instance, that because of the Depression it might be ten years before he earned enough money to marry Molly) there was always her freshness and clarity to save him. 'Braam, I wish you wouldn't be so foolish,' she wrote in response. 'Do you really think that a couple of years either way is going to make any difference to me as long as I'm in love with you? If ever I "leap back" that won't have anything to do with it and even if I do change my mind – or you do – I'll never regret this glorious "game" – and besides – I'm quite serious now – I don't want to get married for the next 10 or 12 years – not even to you. So for Heaven's sake . . . please don't reproach yourself for anything while I'm perfectly happy.'

Despite the tugs of love and self-doubt, they had a text which captured the essence of the understanding between them. Like the 'leap' in the cemetery, this too derived from an actual event, which occurred, as Bram remembered it afterwards, on a chilly night some six miles from Bloemfontein 'when you said Ruth to me and seemed to be ever so small'. They were both fully aware of the biblical resonance: '"Whither thou goest I will go" for always,' wrote Bram to Molly, 'if for no other reason than simply because I can't do otherwise.' In all their travels, distances and journeyings this was something that never left them, and it was another reason why (much later) Bram would never leave South Africa.

In 1929 Percy Fischer was raised to the bench of the Supreme Court of the Orange Free State. Family history as well as his own talents had assured his success, and Judge-President De Villiers told Bram in passing that the Appeal Court had always held Percy to be among the foremost advocates at the Bar. When Mr Justice Fischer heard his first case on circuit in Fauresmith, Bram – who attended – wrote back enthusiastic mock-headlines to his mother: 'New Judge: Roaring Success / First Appearance Very Popular / Big Reception.'

Bram had his own successes, in the unexpected arena of rugby. In the winter of 1928, while he was in the final year of his BA at Grey, he was selected to play scrum-half against the All Blacks of New Zealand, then on tour in South

Africa. It was a mighty New Zealand team (decades later still legendary among aficionados) with enormous forwards who had the unnerving habit of pounding the opposition into the dust, and they had already beaten the Free State in the first match at Kroonstad. There were calls in the local papers for 'the brainy and clever Fischer whose play at the base of the scrum is a pleasure to watch', and so Bram found himself chosen for the second game. Yet despite his efforts – he was injured in a valorous attempt to prevent the New Zealanders scoring, and returned to the field with his head swathed in bandages, which he soon tore off in annoyance – the Free State lost. In fact Bram was being seriously considered as a candidate to play for South Africa, and over the next few years was urged on by a variety of people, including his father and the presidents of a number of provincial rugby unions, to go into all-out training. By 1931, however, it was clear to Bram that he had other priorities. He was in his final year of law, on circuit much of the time, and besides, as he wrote to Molly, 'there are no matches in Bethlehem'. Finally, he gave up competitive rugby altogether, which he told Molly made him feel five years older; but at least, as he put it, he wouldn't have to worry which leg to sit down on of a Saturday night.

Bram turned twenty-one on 23 April 1929, and Ella arranged a formal dinner and dance for him at Harmonie for something approaching a hundred guests. According to custom, there was a programme printed elegantly on cards listing the dances in sequence, and along with the simple pleasure of the event it may have appeared for all the world as if this were the coming out – with the taste and decorum appropriate to a well-established family – of a son from whom everything was to be expected. Certainly others saw it in that light. Ouma Steyn, who had outlasted the old President of the Free State by many years (and perhaps thinking back to those days), wrote a letter of congratulation and welcome: 'I know that Bram Fischer is going to play an honourable role in the history of South Africa.' It was a prophecy that was destined to be true, but not in a way that Mrs Steyn or anyone else at that party would have foreseen.

The following year others were able to join in the sense of expectation, for, as planned, Bram had applied for a Rhodes Scholarship from Grey, and in November 1930 heard he had been accepted. Leo Marquard, perhaps with thoughts of the Joint Council and NUSAS on his mind, wrote to Ella Fischer that he believed 'very firmly in Braam' (he also misspelled) 'and I know very well how much his three years overseas will mean to him and our country'. Nell Marquard wrote in similar vein: 'Leo and I are following and will follow Bram's career with much interest . . . I am sure he will profit greatly and be a credit to South Africa – and a help.' Only Molly provided her regular, less inflated tones. 'Congratulations,' she wrote when she heard the news. 'I'm really very glad, but when I try to say what I mean, it gets mixed or just sounds like sobstuff. But you've heard it so often by now that it doesn't really matter if I don't.' Her down-to-earth awkwardness may have come as a distinct relief after the weight of responsibility everyone was heaping on Bram's shoulders.

The scholarship was to New College at Oxford – Leo's old college, and again he must have played a role. In the normal course Bram would have taken it up in October 1931, but because he would finish his law degree only in November, he applied to postpone his arrival until January 1932, and with some reluctance New College agreed; in effect he would miss a term. Yet, as Bram's departure approached, he confessed to Molly that he had never done anything for which he felt less inclined. It was not only that he would have to leave her, but this was the beginning of the break-up of his family (his brother Paul was also leaving Bloemfontein to study medicine in Johannesburg). Ella Fischer had been ill in recent years (there was a shadow on her lung that later disappeared), and Bram was sure he could feel her sorrow through her words of encouragement. He would watch her eyes well with tears as she moved about the rooms at home. But Molly gave him calm advice, saying she was sure he would love Oxford, and the time would fly, and besides, his mother wouldn't mind so much if she thought he really wanted to go.

But even Molly was allowing herself to be more tender now. 'Please tell me again', she wrote in almost unheard-of fashion in November 1931, 'that you love me.' After Bram left she told him what she had kept secret for a while, that she had been fired from the Housecraft School. The given reasons were that she had been too 'opgeruimd' (which she translated as 'cheerful', but she might have said 'spirited'), that she took too great an interest in sports and not enough in the girls, and that she had said openly that she didn't like the school. Anyway, she wrote to Bram, it proved that she was neither wonderful nor clever, nor any of the delightful things he thought she was, and it would be far better if he simply forgot her. 'I don't suffer from an inferiority complex,' she told him (Bram always accused her of this), 'but I just know myself better than you do.'

Bram was set to leave on board the *Usaramo* – a ship of the German East Africa Line – travelling third-class from Cape Town. The night before his departure by train from Bloemfontein (he reported to Molly), he and Ella wandered around till about three in the morning drinking whisky and shedding tears. In Cape Town he met up with two students who would be travelling with him, went to visit his Auntie Maggie, changed £22 into gold for the trip (telling Ella he now needed a private detective for protection), noticed (for Molly) all the blue flowers he could, bought a small camera as a gift from his parents, and went to visit student friends from *Die Burger*, the Nationalist newspaper, before setting sail on 18 December.

He wrote a last letter to Molly from the shore:

Goodbye, Molly . . . You've given me the two most wonderful years I've ever had. I can always spend hours dreaming of all kinds of pictures – wet curls & you in pyjamas, moonlight & Ichabod, mountains and trees and bare toes. All my thanks & all my love.

And in the same letter he wrote:

Molly, will you write and tell me whenever you cry? And by the way, I still love you for ever – just in case I haven't told you before.
A.F.

On board Bram shared a four-berth cabin with his two companions. He felt some depression at leaving, but told Molly he soon slept it off. On the first evening out he talked to the nightwatch – 'an interesting young German Nazi' – and thereafter on occasion he and his friends discussed Hitler with the crew. It was a different world Bram was heading into, ominous but – without any knowledge of the future – also enthralling. He and his friends were learning German, talked politics and psychology long into the night, swam in a pool rigged up on the deck, listened to the ship's orchestra in the afternoons. On Christmas Eve there was a party, and Bram was given a hamper that Ella had sent in advance to the ship. As always, they were taking care of him.

When Percy had left for Cambridge, it had been Oupa Abraham who had written his letter of advice. Now it was Percy's turn, and before Bram left Bloemfontein (perhaps with memories of his own trip in his thoughts) Percy gave him a word on the seductions and perils of imperialism. Bram did not appear to need it; his only concern was that the overweening complacencies of Oxford and the Rhodes Scholarship would drive him into the acrimonious nationalism of Hertzog. On board he also read a letter of Ella's, she too repeating the patterns of so many years before. His mother spoke of the strange inarticulacies of deep feeling: if she hadn't proved how much she loved him in the twenty-three years of his life, she remarked, then nothing she might say now could do so. She wrote of how Bram had always lived up to the highest standards, and dwelt on maternal heritages of separation and loss. In previous generations mothers and grandmothers had always benefited from the consolations of prayer: her own mother's Bible had little notes marking the dates whenever children left home, with some little prayer or text affixed. Yet despite her own religious instincts, Ella told Bram she placed her own trust elsewhere: 'My faith in your safety and success is based on your own character & intelligence . . . I can't place your future trustfully in God's hands, because I believe it lies in your own.' When Bram arrived in England he replied that after the twenty-three years Ella had given him he should have absorbed enough of Harmonie to carry what was significant in it for the rest of his life.

Bram's brothers (whom he had left ten shillings apiece) and his sister also wrote their last letters for his departure. Ada mentioned bumping into an acquaintance who was terribly worried by Bram's 'socialistic tendencies'. For a nationalist this may have meant anything that wasn't nationalism, but Bram's changes were already beginning to be marked. As he crossed the seas from one country to another, all of this was mixed and merged in his life: nationalism behind him, socialism somewhere in front, all the external and internal voices of politics and family resonating inwardly. And of course there was Molly, with whom he lived in his letters. One thing he would learn in the intimacies of absence: to keep faith with a distant ideal, always somewhere over the horizon.

CHAPTER 4

ANOTHER COUNTRY

January 1931 – October 1934

T he boat stopped off at Las Palmas where, besides the local cathedral, Bram
went to see the brothels (he wrote about this not to his mother or to
Molly but only to his father, describing the experience very properly as 'nause-
ating' and 'a study in the bestiality of man'). Oxford at first was no more pre-
possessing, though for rather different reasons. When Bram arrived at four
o'clock on the afternoon of a bleak and cold winter's day and saw the age-
blackened high walls of New College, he felt (he told Molly) just as if he were
going to prison. The Fischers had a saying for such moments when life itself
seemed to take on the impending chill of an unutterable loneliness – '*my
hartjie word koud*' [my little heart is getting cold] – and it was precisely to avoid
this that Bram set off immediately for Edinburgh to watch a rugby international with friends.

Soon, however, rugby gave him additional cause for complaint, for turning
out for a match in the first week of his arrival (and, said Bram, with no one
within yards of him on the field) he twisted his knee and put it out. He tried
rest and massage, and even consulted 'a bonesetter' (the Fischers were assiduous when it came to consulting a full range of medical opinion), but finally
Stanley Osler – the future rugby Springbok, who had suffered a similar injury –
advised surgery, and Bram went into the Wingfield Hospital at the end of
February.

The surgeon was one of the most renowned in England, and soon enough,
Bram reported to Molly, he was propped up in bed with his cartilage in a
bottle beside him, his leg enveloped in a wire cage to support the blankets, and
various bits of paraphernalia to keep him comfortable. The hospital specialised
in cases of spinal tuberculosis (Ella was subjected to a few weeks of panic until
Bram reassured her that it wasn't contagious). Every day blustery Scots nurses,
whose constitutional cheeriness alternated with a reproving sense of discipline, wheeled the patients outside into the open air, where they stayed until
it began to rain. Bram was visited by a run of South African friends, as well as
by the Warden of New College, H.A.L. Fisher, who had been a member of
Lloyd George's cabinet. Oxford evidently took care of its students.

Bram had expected to be out of hospital within two weeks, but then complications set in. During the operation there had been some bleeding into the joint, with a consequent danger of infection, and the ligaments were in any case badly damaged. When Bram's younger brother Gus (who himself became an orthopaedic surgeon) found out in later years what had happened, he knew that Bram must have been in severe pain, but all that Bram would admit to were a few 'pale-cream fibs' to his parents about the state of his knee. It was the end of March before he could leave the hospital, as under massage and rigorous exercise his leg slowly began to unlock. C.K. Allen, the secretary of the Rhodes Trust, had invited him to Rhodes House to recuperate during the Easter vacation. There Bram found himself in luxurious surroundings, occupying a beautiful room, with a study, a telephone and the pleasure (which to Bram was a genuine one) of entertaining the Allens' young children early in the morning, much as his own parents had entertained him.

The Allens, like many others, were drawn to Bram, and in later years visited Percy and Ella in Bloemfontein. As for Bram, at Rhodes House he was in the very heart of Empire, but he did not seem to mind. His own well-placed background as well as personal talents provided the necessary courtesies and graces, a kind of easy communion with those who were his social equivalents, despite the cultural contrasts. Soon Bram was playing tennis for New College, and helped them win the intercollegiate cup, but his leg was never the same. From that time on he always thrust it out with a limp when he walked, which gave him intriguing problems and opportunities some thirty years later in quite different circumstances.

⁂

Life in Oxford began to take over.

Bram's rooms in New College were almost absurdly comfortable – he had a bedroom and sitting-room, with a fire, and later, with some money his parents sent, he rented a piano. For the obscure reason that he was over twenty-three, he did not have to attend college roll-call in the morning. He began to get used to English beer. Now and again the Fishers would invite him for dinner to meet some luminary (such as, on one occasion, the High Commissioner for Southern Rhodesia), or the Allens would host Rhodes dinners and dances. Slowly Bram began to take to his courses, focusing on Roman–Dutch law, but also attending lectures more widely, by Élie Halévy, the great historian of England, or G.D.H. Cole, the authority on Marx and Marxism. He became used to Oxford's idiosyncratic and charming customs – May morning, when the choir sang at dawn from Magdalen tower and the morris dancers took to the streets in their white clothes and bells; and 'beating the bounds', when the boundaries of Oxford's parishes were marked out by choirboys with sticks. Bram learned the usual Oxford lore, of ancient battles between town and gown, of disputes between colleges resulting in archaic (not to say surreal) commemorations.

So the unprepossessing aspect of his new life slowly lifted, and Bram could appreciate Oxford's beauty, especially in summer. He went punting on lazy evenings on the Cherwell, jaunted by car or motor-bike through the Cotswolds or up to Stratford-upon-Avon, cycled through the countryside to visit sundry pubs, walked along the Magdalen College pathways at twilight. And yet, for Bram, the air of a certain loneliness never left him while he was away. Oxford was 'a wretched hole', he told Molly a year after his arrival, and he didn't think he'd ever be truly happy there (this, he confessed, had much to do with her absence). To Bram the snow and slush of winter turning to spring reminded him of nothing so much as the kind of pallid and weak ice-cream one got at a church bazaar in the western Free State on a hot summer's day. 'Here,' he wrote to Molly in his first dark February, 'there's never any rain and there's never any sun and I know at Lusthof there are blue blue skies and every afternoon huge thunderclouds, so let's go and lie in the grass somewhere near Salpeterkrans and watch the krantz [cliff] slowly toppling over us as the clouds shift over to Basutoland.' In Oxford there was a part of Bram that never left the Free State: it was memories of Molly and South Africa that excited the fierce longing of his imagination.

Letters became an alternative form of reality, more than a question of duty, as Bram marked out time through their cycles. Again the language division was maintained: he wrote to his father and siblings in Afrikaans, to Molly and his mother in English. His letters to Molly were up to ten pages long, but they took three weeks to be delivered by sea; this meant that any particular exchange – question, answer, response – could take up to a month and a half. If there were any misapprehensions or misunderstandings they could take forever to clarify, but the extended dialogue also allowed other possibilities. It was Ella who mentioned it first, and then Bram took it up with Molly: there were things to be said in their letters that might never have been expressed in such depth in person.

At first it was still the wrench of their parting that consumed Bram and Molly. Sure enough, they continued to 'play' and tease one another, for instance on the anniversary of Molly's 'leap'. She claimed she had been bullied into it by Bram, and that the particular day never meant so much to her anyway, but a sudden cable from her marking the date told a different story:

'I think cemetery and a swim at midnight. Love Molly.' Though Molly's letters were lengthening, Bram still found them much too short and begged her for 'glimpses inside' of her thoughts. 'For nagging,' on the other hand she retorted, 'I have never come across anyone to beat you.' Molly acquired a short-haired fox terrier named David (to whom thereafter she remained immensely attached), and Bram wrote to the dog complaining that his mistress was running herself down (his usual theme of her sense of inferiority). Molly responded on David's behalf, saying that if *he* wrote such nonsense he could also quite easily fill ten pages. Bram asked Molly for photographs of herself at all ages, and filled his room with them, but told her that for the sake of decency when putting on his pyjamas in their sight, he always left his shirt on until he had pulled on his trousers.

The plan had always been that Molly would join Bram at some stage, preferably to go touring on the Continent during the summer, but that became an ever-fading hope. In 1932 Molly was occupied with a Higher Education Diploma at the University of Pretoria, and her father had an operation, which meant less money for a trip; in 1933 she took up work at a farm school in a place called Jachtfontein near Johannesburg (with the Depression in full swing she had to take whatever work was available); and by 1934 the prospect was already of Bram's return home. Time and distance multiplied one another, prompting ever-renewed fears of loss for Bram, and throughout the period overseas he lived a subjunctive life of dreams and yearning in his letters.

❧

As if to compensate, he explored the external world around him with a will. He tracked over old connections, beginning with his cousin Connie's relatives, the Bidwells, whom he visited near Cambridge; they were 'county' people, who dressed for dinner every night. (Bram was fond of them, but later remarked that there was nothing to choose between a ball in Cambridgeshire and one in Pampoenfontein [Pumpkin Fountain] except for the higher intellectual level of the latter.) In London there was his cousin Theunie Fichardt, now a medical student at Guy's. Theunie took him to see some operations in progress, which seemed to be quite permissible. Visiting London, Bram and his friends took digs in Gower Street, where Percy had stayed some thirty years before; in Cambridge he took photographs of Percy's old rooms in Trinity Hall. At Bram's first Rhodes dinner he was introduced to Sir Reginald Coupland, Professor of Imperial History, who had met Abraham Fischer in 1912, and Lord Lothian, who had come to know Abraham at the Union Convention in Durban. As always, Bram had a place and an identity already furnished for him.

He did the regular tourist rounds, from the Epsom Derby and Stonehenge to Westminster Abbey (a hideous building, but not bad as a national cemetery, he told Molly, who had that sort of interest), took in the opera, films, lunch at the House of Commons (with a connection of Leo Marquard's), the Inns of Court and the Kit Kat night club. He was also reading widely: Shakespeare ('ghastly', remarked Bram with some gumption) and Trevelyan's *History of England*, which he found fascinating (he evidently preferred his history in non-fictional form). In London he went to visit Laurens van der Post, and later sent Molly a copy of his first (and most political) novel, *In a Province*. From the Continent he brought back Radclyffe Hall's *The Well of Loneliness*, which, as he pointed out to Molly, was banned in England for its lesbian subject matter even while the populist and rabble-rousing *Daily Mail* and *Daily Express* (the Rothermere and Beaverbrook papers) were allowed to continue publication. As for *The Well of Loneliness*, Bram felt it was a book that should be read by everyone, 'not only for the particular problem it depicts, but because tolerance & sympathy there would mean tolerance & sympathy in many other respects'. Accordingly, he sent copies to both Molly and his parents, and Molly told him she enjoyed it.

As Bram's reference to the *Daily Mail* and *Daily Express* indicated, he was also swept up in the turmoil erupting through British life in the early 1930s, following on from the effects of the Depression. By January 1933, just short of halfway through his stay, there were three million unemployed; the gold standard had been abandoned, and the value of the pound had fallen by 25 per cent. Ramsay MacDonald's emergency National government had taken over, while hunger marchers walked from Jarrow to London (passing through Oxford on the way) and did battle with the police in Hyde Park. As Oswald Mosley formed his British Union of Fascists, Britain seemed to be dividing down the middle, the same lines of conflict appearing there as were developing elsewhere in Europe.

In these circumstances a whole generation of students at Oxford and Cambridge began to search for alternative ideologies to explain the present and point the way to a future which appeared to hold out the promise equally of apocalypse and redemption. The poet Stephen Spender wrote, 'Who live under the shadow of a war/ What can I do that matters?', and the war he was referring to could have been the First World War, the Second World War (which everyone expected) or, just a few years later, the Spanish Civil War, in which fascism and socialism entered into their first historic conflict. Though Oxford was a quieter arena than Cambridge – there were no Philbys or Macleans recruited to spy for the Soviet Union at the former – it was almost impossible not to be caught up in the atmosphere of epic choice and confrontation. Oswald Mosley arrived in Oxford to open a Fascist Club, while the October Club celebrated the promise of the Russian Revolution.

In this setting Bram was insatiate for news, regularly buying all three editions of the *Evening Standard* (a decent paper then, as he put it later) on any given day. He was also present for the famous debate at the Oxford Union when the motion was carried by 275 to 153 that 'This House will in no circumstances fight for its King and Country'. This had enraged the Conservative press, Bram reported home to Molly and his parents; Oxford students were being called 'slighters of the heroes of 1914' and 'sexual indeterminates'. Ex-members of the Union including Lord Stanley and Randolph Churchill – 'son of Winston,' Bram commented mildly, 'and a full-blooded small reactionary' – were trying to have the vote expunged from the records. But they would only make fools of themselves, thought Bram, because even Conservative members of the Union would oppose such interference.

Perhaps it was seeing conservatism in another country that consolidated the shift in Bram's thinking, suggesting the relativity and insularity of all appeals to national glory. There was now very little that would align him with overtly 'reactionary' politics in any form. On the contrary, he himself was being drawn – if not quite to the October Club (which he never mentioned) – then to the Labour Club, 'quite the most wideawake political club in Oxford,' he wrote to his parents. There Bram heard Sir Stafford Cripps, the Solicitor-General of the ex-Labour government, deliver an 'excellent' address on socialist planning. Cripps's son John was at Balliol, and Bram came to know him quite well: 'I seem to be falling among socialists with a vengeance,' he observed to Percy and Ella. Later he met Richard Crossman, then a young philosophy don at New College, afterwards a Labour MP and editor of *The God That Failed*, in which leading intellectuals of the West described their conversion to communism in the 1930s and consequent disillusionment – the early currents of which Bram was then living through.

There were some with Bram in Oxford who were convinced he became a communist there. This is unlikely in any formal sense, although he may have sounded at times like a communist. From one point of view the Labour Club was a fairly guarded halfway house for someone who had been an Afrikaner nationalist, although Stafford Cripps (if he it was who fired Bram's enthusiasm) was a leading member of the Socialist League, a left-wing grouping within the Labour Party. Most likely, though (if somewhat prosaically), it was the technical aspects of Cripps's discussion that caught Bram's imagination, since Cripps had been and would be involved in various dimensions of administration and planning, and Bram's interest appeared to be very much in social engineering. At any rate, it was still the search for an ideological home that was absorbing him, rather than the fact of having found one.

So much was apparent from another club to which he was anxiously awaiting election – hardly revolutionary but more decorous. This was the Ralegh Club, Bram informed Molly and his parents (he also advised them how to pronounce it: 'Rawley'), and its orientation was decidedly imperial. Bram wrote that it was '*the* club in Oxford', limiting its membership to a few persons from each Dominion and some from England and Ireland, and inviting the highest men of power to discuss matters of the Empire and world affairs. The club kept no minutes so that all its discussion could be kept off the record. Its presiding presence was Professor Coupland (again the connection with Oupa Abraham, as well as with Leo Marquard, who had known Coupland when he was at Oxford). While still on probation for membership Bram attended one of the Ralegh dinners, addressed by the Lord Chancellor and, as he remarked, a couple of secretaries of state. Ramsay MacDonald, the Prime Minister, would have been there but for an operation, 'so you can see', Bram wrote to Molly, 'what election would mean to me.'

Bram had been recommended to the Ralegh by Arthur Keppel-Jones, later the historian of South Africa, whom he had known from the University of Cape Town, and who had preceded him in the club. Waiting from May 1932 until October to hear the result, ultimately he received the news of his success with a sense of due self-deprecation and irony: 'Ek is nou lid van die Ralegh Club,' he wrote to his parents, 'en die Empaaier is dus gered' [I am now a member of the Ralegh Club, and the 'Empire' is consequently saved]. It was characteristic that despite the retrograde imperial aura, Bram was so eager to join. Perhaps it was his old desire for success, and election was truly one measure of his 'arrival' in Oxford; but also Bram would have had a genuine interest in high matters of state affecting millions of lives. In this confidential setting the grand panorama of international politics was heavily seductive, and the air would have been redolent with echoes of Oupa Abraham's exploits in a previous time. As always, there was an abiding, almost instinctive tact on his part that meant he could engage with others and learn from the encounter, no matter what the presiding ethos and presuppositions – even if fundamentally imperialist.

During Bram's membership he heard more than a few secretaries of state: he heard Lord Lytton of the Lytton Commission speak on the Japanese invasion of Manchuria, as well as Sir Herbert Stanley, the British High Commissioner in Southern Africa, talk on the three High Commission territories of

Swaziland, Basutoland and Bechuanaland, which South Africa kept threatening to ingest (it was a relief to hear a 'non-Union view on the Union', remarked Bram). Stanley was someone Bram himself invited, for in April 1933 he was elected secretary of the Ralegh Club, which meant that he automatically became president the following term. Bram claimed this was due to luck – that the club merely needed someone from South Africa to take a turn at its head, and that he'd simply been in the right place at the right time.

But there were others who were sure they knew better. In May Bram sent home a seating plan of a Ralegh dinner showing himself, as secretary, seated next to the Archbishop of York and one person away from Ramsay Mac-Donald, whom at last he had succeeded in meeting. He wrote that he wasn't entirely impressed with the Prime Minister: MacDonald had offered a ten-minute speech of wonderful sonority but (observed Bram) little meaning; the Archbishop, on the other hand, he lauded as 'brilliant'. Nakie Smith, who thirty-three years earlier had turned away the British soldiers at the gate, now poring over the seating plan out of the corner of her one serviceable eighty-eight-year-old eye, declared that both the Archbishop and Ramsay Mac-Donald could count themselves privileged to be in Bram's company.

But not everything had to do with Empire. For even while Bram was ensconced in these intimate surroundings he had already taken in other, more breathtaking vistas. Early in June 1932 he had written to Molly: 'I always have a sort of feeling that I should go and see Russia.'

❧

As Bram recounted it, the idea came on the spur of the moment when a friend burst into his rooms (Bram had just returned from a motoring tour with two companions) and suggested they all travel to Russia. But if the suggestion was spontaneous, the ground had already been prepared. Earlier Bram had been to London to consult with a visiting socialist from Bloemfontein who was on his way to the Soviet Union, but discovered that accompanying him on the trip would take too long. Now in a frenzy of enthusiasm he and his three friends careered up and down to London filling in forms and obtaining passport photographs, and were ready to leave within a week. Their permits arrived from Moscow shortly before they set sail.

Bram's companions were Tom Jarman (the one who had burst into his rooms, later Professor of History at Bristol) and two Rhodesians, Treadwell and J.M. 'Mac' Macdonald; on the trip they picked up a Rhodes Scholar from New Zealand, Geoffrey Cox, who later fought in and wrote a book about Spain. In a four-week journey (organised at a cost of just £30 by Intourist) they were to cover 6000 miles, from Leningrad down to Moscow, on to Nizhni Novgorod (Gorki), then by riverboat some 1700 miles down the Volga to Stalingrad, then on to Rostov on the Black Sea, by train through the granaries of the Ukraine to Kiev, and then back to Leningrad again. The prospect was heady, and Bram could not contain his anticipation, reading up on Russian conversational dictionaries, biographies of Lenin, and standard studies of Stalin's Five Year Plan. For at least part of the tour he and his friends expected to travel rough; they took a range of digestive and germicidal supplies including biscuits, Bovril, Ovaltine, cheese, Lysol, Keating's Powder and ('*not to be read aloud*', Bram wrote to his parents) toilet paper.

They sailed on 25 June from Hay's Wharf in the heart of London (just below London Bridge) in a small, 3000-ton Soviet ship, and as they set off all the Russians on board began singing. Life on the JAN. RUDZUTAK, SOVTOGFLOT (Bram wrote out the name for his parents and Molly in Cyrillic script) was by no means uncomfortable, with two-berth cabins and five-course meals, including plenty of fruit, strawberries and cream, pressed caviar, oil, onions and aniseed. For baths one had to apply to the ship's soviet, but Bram reported that he had no complaints because all his applications had been approved. Intourist was setting off on the right note.

As they sailed through the North Sea in the direction of Denmark the weather was balmy, and Bram spent his time reading and sunbathing. The clocks moved forward an hour a day, and in the height of midsummer it was still light enough almost to read at 1 a.m. Bram took in some of the life around him. On board were Russian families working in London travelling home on vacation, as well as a small number of tourists. There were also Americans venturing out to work in the USSR who were, observed Bram, 'more extremely communistic than the Russians themselves', although he felt they might have had good reason, for most of them had been unemployed for two years or more. He also noted, in uncharacteristically condescending tones, an 'old, fat podgy Cockney Jew' whom he had mistaken on the wharf for a cabby, but perhaps this opened his eyes to a world in which customary appearances turned into a different kind of reality. In the Kiel Canal, on their way into the Baltic, the whole shipboard sang 'The Red Flag' to a party of children singing German songs in another boat across the way.

After their arrival in Russia, Bram's letters home divided. To Molly he wrote of the hectic and sometimes comic experience of it all – of rushed and jumbled eighteen-hour days, with a final meal somewhere between 11 p.m. and 2 a.m., when he and his friends could finally stop and laugh about the behaviour of some of their companions (the Scotsman who earnestly insisted that at least Glasgow had a bigger football stadium than Moscow). But Bram spoke also of impressive museums and operas, and inspiring sport and physical culture clubs: 'If you have stopped loving me by the time I get back to Leningrad,' he advised Molly, 'I'll just stay here and become a Bolshevik! (With a long beard!)'

That was exactly what his mother was afraid of. When she thought of Bram so far away, Ella confided on his journey, 'my hartjie word sommer klein en koud' [my little heart gets quite small and cold]. Ever since her youth, she remarked, Russia had been associated in her mind with anarchists, persecution, wolves and priests; at the moment she felt it was the centre of attention for a 'sick and despondent world'. Bram's letters to her, although avoiding politics altogether, would not entirely have dispelled his mother's fears as he mentioned the Rembrandts in the Hermitage in Leningrad, or spoke with awe of the Kremlin. He described Red Square and Lenin's tomb lit up at night, with a simple red flag illuminated and fluttering in the breeze above all: an image to endure in the mind – both Ella's and Bram's.

Many years later Geoffrey (by then Sir Geoffrey) Cox commented that he and his friends had not understood much of what they saw during that visit. For in the summer of 1932 Stalin's programme of forced collectivisation was at its height. Bram and his companions noted little traffic in the streets, and the food, while good on the ship, was by now meagre and unappetising, even for tourists. On the steamer down the Volga masses of people (chiefly old men, women and children) fought to get on board, carrying huge bundles, and travelled on the lower decks in a seething and reeking tide of humanity. But the Intourist guides, offering the official account, said this was merely part of a shift of population following on the Five Year Plan. That too was how they accounted for the crowds (in reality fleeing from starvation and persecution) who filled every inch of the railway stations in the Ukraine. In a dusty street in Kuybyshev the visitors saw a long column of ragged and dirty peasants, with beards and bast leggings, being guarded by soldiers with red stars on their caps; but these, suggested the guides (more clearly embarrassed, for once), were kulaks who had rebelled against collectivisation.

Geoffrey Cox said that it was only when he returned to England and read Malcolm Muggeridge's description of the absolute starvation in the wake of an 'organised famine' that he began to comprehend what it all meant. Bram and his friends were not the only visitors to be deceived in Russia during these years; indeed, there was a steady stream of willing and often distinguished hopefuls arriving in the Soviet Union from the West, all ready to be beguiled. Bram and his small group, moreover, lacked any obvious explanation or independent point of reference for what they saw; for all they knew, the visible upheaval was one of the after-effects of the Civil War, and at the same time the scenes they absorbed had to be reconciled with all the other images that flooded in, some of which appeared to reflect extraordinary social achievements. Thus, though Bram wrote of travelling 'hard' on the trains, of dust pouring into the carriage until one could hardly see, of bugs creeping in and out of everywhere, of the way the mattresses provided by Intourist suddenly 'disappeared', his spirit was still largely buoyant. Partly to annoy Molly he dwelt teasingly on the trip from Kiev back to Leningrad when he spent a number of enchanting hours speaking German to a pretty Ukrainian girl while passing through a lake district under moonlight.

It was only to his father that he wrote seriously of politics, and he did so, as always, in Afrikaans. In a minutely scripted ten-page letter written after he had left, Bram tried hard to come to terms with what he had seen, dwelling mainly on social and economic issues. As much as his observations were descriptive, they gave some inkling of the thoughts revolving through his mind. The central point about Russia, Bram suggested, was that the opportunity for private profit had been eliminated; it was because of this alone that the Russians had achieved their successes in heavy industry – their machinery, power stations and dams. These would be impossible under capitalism, where any unexpected development could rock the whole system – precisely what caused its regular crises. (Bram evidently agreed with much of what he had been hearing and reading.) There could, he remarked tautologically, be no such thing as a Five Year Plan under capitalism.

In that light, wrote Bram, there could be no doubt of the advantages of communism. But then the essential question became whether one could achieve the same degree of incentive under communism as the profit motive provided. The Russians weren't concerned about this: every section of industry was organised into soviets, and these provided 'a watchful and critical eye' on whatever aspect of the industry affected them. But while this might lend something in the way of incentive, Bram doubted it would prove as effective as capitalism. As to the idea of communism itself, there was no question that for a huge number of people ('say 4,000,000') it was nothing other than a religion 'with Lenin as Christ', followed as fervently in Russia as the Reformation in Europe during its early years. The unbeliever might object that like any other religion it would gradually lose power until it became an instrument of abuse, but Bram felt that such an argument was not entirely convincing: to say that Christianity had been misused was not to say that it had never done any good (again Bram's openness and latitude), or that it had not helped develop the world (as always his measure of significance). Both the veneration he saw at Lenin's tomb and the communal spirit of the workers' clubs offered the strong impression of religious spirit and ritual.

They had been taken to see a state farm, which in its gargantuan magnitude appeared to be 'an eighth wonder of the world'. It had in excess of 200,000 acres under single management, some 8000 workers and their families settled in modern apartments, and 170 tractors; seed was sown by aeroplane and harvested on the same scale. But whether it would actually pay, Bram remarked, was another question, for private farming was being rigorously suppressed, and he knew that most of the harvests had failed. He was also aware of repression in other areas: the Communist Party, with its 'famed Gay-Pay-Oo' (OGPU, predecessor to the KGB), exercised total control. But, said Bram, according to communist philosophy this was a necessary historical stage, and taking into account both the ideals and the difficulties of the system one could see that it was 'the only method whereby a world communist existence can be brought into being'. (Bram, who would later suffer at the hands of a different secret police, was here prepared to concede its necessity.) He was not as impressed with Soviet cultural repression, under which, he observed, 'the whole of French art since 1870' was explained away as a function of the rise of the bourgeoisie. But no one he had encountered had felt this to be a problem, and there were marvellous opportunities for artistic and intellectual progress. In winter there were some fifty theatres and operas every evening in Moscow; the Meyerhold Theatre was attempting techniques unheard of elsewhere; film directors such as Eisenstein were at the forefront of their art.

Certainly there was poverty in the Soviet Union, Bram conceded, and a shortage of luxury goods, but if one thought of the poverty that existed in 1914, or what Russia had suffered during the Civil War, it would be hard to pin all the blame on Bolshevik policies. At the moment the USSR was living under the fear of war, and to Bram it was a justified fear. France was supplying Poland and Romania with arms; Japan was awaiting its opportunity in the East; English oil magnates had their rapacious fingers dangling over the Baku oilfields. If America were not so antagonistic to Japanese imperialism, war would have already broken out.

Bram's letter, in its extended account, was circumspect to a fault, and if he had made any great 'leap' into communism he obviously wasn't revealing it to his father – or to Molly, or anyone else. Geoffrey Cox recalled later that at no time on that trip – or subsequently at Oxford – did Bram give any impression that he had become a communist. Rather, as in this letter, his approach appears to have been methodical and conscientious, as he weighed up the various sides of the issues in his mind. By and large Bram was storing up images and impressions that later would come into play. And yet – as may frequently happen – it was precisely because of his *misinterpretation* that a leap of the imagination was permitted which provided its own insight and, in due course, gave Bram a South African reason to be affected by communism.

For in that same letter to his father Bram spent some time considering the peasants he and his friends had observed, but whose displacement and attitude they could not comprehend. He used the Afrikaans word 'kleinboer' [small farmer – but with some of the resonances of 'boer'] to describe them, and then made an unusual, not to say crude, comparison. 'If you see him [the "klein-boer"] along the Volga and in the trains and stations,' wrote Bram, 'or hear about him from American engineers, then you understand how great the task is the communists have undertaken, because between him and our kaffers there is, as far as I can see, no difference.' In Afrikaans the word 'kaffer' might have meant little more to Bram than 'native' would have in English, although his experience on the Joint Council (both general, and the handshake that had meant so much) should have begun to draw him away from what remained an offensive term. Yet Bram's other images, offered with lofty socio-logical distance, were equally skewed. The peasant was intrinsically conserva-tive, he wrote; naturally he knew little about machinery, had no feeling for an engine, and 'just like the kaffer' had no sense of time. In a station you might see so many people lying and sleeping, he told his father, that you could hardly move across the platform, and they would be waiting for a train that would only arrive in twelve or fourteen hours.

In a sense the misapprehension was staggering: Bram had no conception of just why Russian peasants might wait fourteen hours for a train, or look so wearied (and he might have had no idea of why South African blacks some-times appeared the same). Perhaps in using the word 'kaffer' or recycling these standard images he was merely speaking the language his father might have expected to hear, although that would hardly constitute justification. But in this moment of, at best, linguistic or conceptual compromise between son and father there was an unexpected shaft of potential enlightenment. For if one saw – not the Russian peasant as a 'kaffer' – but the South African black as a Russian peasant, then the Soviet Union, with its tremendous experiment of bringing its society under concentrated force into the twentieth century, might have seemed to offer something of a model. Under such a model Bram would, in the short term, have lost none of the cultural and social condescen-sion which *was* a part of his time, the elevated assumptions of European 'lead-ership'. But he would have seen South Africa as involving a problem of social engineering which had its equivalent in the Soviet Union. Paradoxically, as time went on, what Bram saw in the USSR would have enabled him to see South African problems through *less* than racial eyes, and more in terms of social stratification, culture, class and technology.

Other aspects of what he saw reinforced this, specifically on the question of nationalism. Bram wrote to his father of the more than a hundred nationalities in the Soviet Union; he himself had travelled through two Russian republics, a German-speaking republic, a Tartar and a Ukrainian. Culturally and linguistically these states were wholly independent of one another – and the communists had even gone further, reported Bram, establishing orthographies in some of the eastern republics which had no written language, in order to aid the development of a national identity. To his brother Piet he gave a clue about his thinking: 'It is wonderful how the Bolsheviks have overcome all the problems that we have in South Africa, where there are only two nations.'

Again this was generous rather than disingenuous. It was Stalin's great boast that the nationalities problem had been overcome in the USSR (he himself had been Commissar for Nationalities), and Bram appeared to have accepted the standard propaganda. Moreover, although his intention may have been pedagogic – using terms Piet would recognise while drawing him beyond them – in speaking of 'only two nations' (English and Afrikaans) in the South African setting, Bram revealed how far he was still content to think in primarily 'white' terms. In other words, he may have been in the Labour Club at Oxford, but nationalism was still part of the matrix of his mind. Yet that was exactly why the Soviet Union may have been so attractive: here was a country that seemed to have reconciled the principle of distinct nationalities with a living internationalism within its own borders. Identity (for instance, Afrikaner identity, if one drew the analogy) could be preserved and at the same time transcended in the more satisfying and ultimately more meaningful form of something larger.

It was in this way that Bram's perceptions as well as misperceptions in Russia geared him for a change that would emerge in the future. He seemed to have no idea that the state farm to which he had been taken was merely a showpiece. Despite his assessment that the OGPU had its own necessary *raison d'être* (and whether or not he understood that his entire Intourist trip probably took place under a presiding OGPU provenance), if someone had asked him how Stalin was exterminating his enemies on the Central Committee and Politburo at that very time, he might have had no idea as to what the question meant. Those peasants waiting for trains might have been moved by a more than abstract fatalism or have known more about the state of the world than Bram surmised. Even the person whose name adorned the boat on which he had arrived – Comrade Rudzutak – was later exterminated by Stalin.

But given the model of nationalities and the peasantry, it was as a South African – and as a Fischer, with all his sense of obligation and responsibility – that Bram later became a communist. Bram's views did not change when he read Malcolm Muggeridge as his friend Geoffrey Cox's did, but it was not just a question of relative credulity. In the Soviet Union, both then and as he looked back, he saw a way of dealing with South African problems and issues that he personally was confronting. He entered communism not only because of what he saw through the portals of its grand edifices and showpieces, but also because of what he managed to glimpse through the back door of his mind. And of course the demeaning aspects of his comments did not constitute his final word on issues of race: his perceptions would still be transformed by the new South African world to which his oblique insights in Russia had introduced him.

On their return to Leningrad, Bram and his friends found that their second-class berths home had been taken. So together with 'Mac' Macdonald (and probably now inured to hardship) he left by third-class instead, while the others stayed on for a few days. Reporting home to his mother from London, he declared that he was now out of the land of 'shaggy beards, bombs and baby killers', which he gathered had been her impression of Russia. At home his long letter to his father led to a terrific debate in the family about communism, and old Nakie wanted the letter to be published.

⁂

In April 1932 (just before Bram's birthday), Molly raised the question of having children. Bram replied that he wanted children, but that it had to depend on Molly, for, as he put it, 'having children is one of the most unjust things in the world – so much of the trouble and pain is cast on the mother, and the father only shares in the easy side of it all.' But, becoming more insistent now, and scarcely waiting for a reply, Molly was sure, and had a suggestion to put to Bram: 'I kept thinking of the words from "Ruth" about "thy God and my God" and then I thought that if ever we have a daughter I would love to call her Ruth. May I, or would you mind very much?' Bram, for his part, was certain. 'I can't tell you how much I love it and of course we'll call her Ruth – because she will be the symbol of our motto . . . It was in "Ruth" that we found that creed and we'll realize it in a new little Ruth.'

Just a few months later, when Bram wrote to Molly of his impending trip to Russia – and despite the fact that she had said she 'hated politics' – she replied to him in surprising form. 'You mustn't start worrying about things. Perhaps Russia will do you good. How did you know I was more or less a socialist?' Of course Molly may have been 'playing' yet again with Bram, but then, in a series of almost subconscious connections, she continued directly: 'Do you remember the afternoon you took me to a little native church in Bloemfontein? I never thanked you for taking me, but I'll never forget it. It was the first time I was absolutely sure I would never "leap back," but I didn't know then that I would all the time learn to love you more & more. Don't die when you're about 30 please . . .'

In her mind Bram's journey to Russia was connected with socialism, with an African church they had visited together, and with confirming her 'leap' into love. This was what their love gave Bram and Molly: a vision of enduring fidelity, and the intimation of an authentic belonging in South Africa. Love, socialism, a connection with each other, with the land and with black South Africans: this too could be another country.

⁕

It was Europe that intensified Bram's political education, both that year and the following. In the summer of 1932, just a few days after his return to London from Russia, he took off immediately for Riga in Latvia, where as a NUSAS delegate he was to attend a three-week congress of the CIE.

On the way he stopped off at The Hague, retracing some of Percy's and his grandfather Abraham's steps from the turn of the century. But en route to Berlin, where Bram was to link up with the English NUS delegates to Riga, he was nearly arrested for the second time in his life. Going to the bathroom on the train, he noticed a man coming out; inside was a woman's handbag, and when Bram emerged the woman returned and claimed that ten marks was missing from her purse. She refused to listen to his account and, when the train reached Charlottenburg, called in the police. Bram was hauled off to jail, and thence to a magistrate, where only his demands for a translator from the British legation as well as the assurances of a German dentist with whom he had struck up an acquaintance on the train gained him a quick exit (the police too had been quite unable to find any German money on him). The longer-term result was that he became good friends with the dentist, and went to stay with him in Berlin after his trip to Riga. As for Ella, she was quite prepared, reported Percy, to 'put on her hat' and come over to Germany to deal personally with the woman who had falsely accused her son.

In Riga Bram found himself among 'a welter of fine men and weak men, international politics and vodka'. Giving Molly a brief history of the CIE, he told her how it had descended into a *mélange* of political intrigue, a tedious assortment of national blocs and alignments (the French appeared to be particularly troublesome). Bram was the kind of person for whom such things, if unelevating, held their own fascination; and there were other aspects of his journey that moved his spirit, especially the cultural riches he was experiencing for the first time. In Holland it had been the Mauritshuis and Rijksmuseum (the Vermeers, Ter Borchs and Rembrandts); now, after Riga, he travelled on to Berlin, Dresden, Prague and Vienna, and each stop seemed to bring greater enthralment. In Berlin he saw ancient Egyptian sculpture, in Dresden Raphael's 'Sistine Madonna' at the Zwingerhaus, which ever after became for Bram a place of epic memorial in his mind. Prague was utterly entrancing, with its winding streets, courtyards, tunnels and arcades, its atmosphere of history and legend swathing Hradčany Castle, the St Vitus Cathedral, and the Charles Bridge across the Moldau. And finally it all seemed a preface to Vienna, the city of Gluck, Haydn, Mozart, Beethoven and Strauss, where Bram became enraptured by its culture in the widest sense. Not all of this had to do with music or art: Bram's pension was run by a woman who also operated a social colony for children where they had very few rules and, he observed to Molly, almost no clothes. Bram told his parents this was an attempt to rid the children of distinctions of class, wealth and religion, which he felt was entirely necessary given the prejudices of Europe – 'e.g., in the Nazi movement against the Jews'. He was taken out to see the workers' residences of the Karl Marx-Hof ('socialistic buildings $1\frac{1}{2}$ km long', as Bram described them to Molly), and both there and in the novel design of a Roman Catholic church he came alive to the possibility of a new aesthetic to match the old, in its beauty, strength and efficiency becoming 'the religion of today'. He found himself swept up by the general and unaffected intellectualism of the city – so different, he suggested to his parents, from Oxford.

With an introduction from Vienna he angled off to the Salzkammergut in the Austrian Alps, where at the Seeblick Hotel in Grundlsee (some fifty miles to the south-east of Salzburg) he reported to Molly on nudist and semi-nude swimmers, and a clinic held by Freud's disciple Adler for women with inhibitions. As Bram was thrust into the midst of 1930s Central European life – its high culture, its avant-garde, its habits of behaviour, thought and feeling – it was as if he were discovering a new cleanliness of the soul. There was psychoanalysis, politics and *körperkultur*; there were communists in abundance and now also Nazis. The atmosphere of poignant promise but also threat deepened a year later when he revisited these settings with his sister Ada.

Ada was with Bram the following year because in October 1932 she arrived in London to study social work at the London School of Economics. The fact was that she had been unhappy at home – somewhat lost and lacking a sense of direction – until she came under the wing of a Miss McKenzie, organising secretary of the National Council for Child Welfare, who had suggested over-seas study. It was a highly unusual move for a young South African woman to make on her own, not least because the LSE (founded by Sidney and Beatrice Webb) was the home of an institutionalised socialism in Britain. But once again the Fischers appeared unafraid of new boundaries, and it was as much with a sense of the need for her daughter's happiness as the opportunities for her career that Ella, who had experienced no formal schooling of her own, sent off her daughter. As it turned out, Ada never became a socialist (let alone a communist): following in her mother's footsteps she took up the more practical and conventional work of social welfare, which consumed her interest for the rest of her life.

But she and Bram had always been very close, and when Ada arrived in London he was overjoyed. 'Dear Sir & Madam,' he wrote to Percy and Ella, 'I beg to acknowledge receipt of our daughter and/or sister in sound condition, having been kept right side (i.e. thumbs) up during transit from Africa. Resilience unaffected and if possible improved.' Over the next two years he and Ada spent a good deal of time together, whether in London or Oxford, touring England, or visiting the Bidwells. At the end of 1932 Bram took Ada to Paris, and in the summer of 1933 they visited his old haunts in Central Europe.

Yet in 1933 the ethos on the Continent was very different from what it had been a year before: Hitler had come to power in Germany, and there was an ominous feeling in the air to which Bram was attuned from early on. As it hap-pened, the transformation in Europe was accompanied by a change of regime in South Africa. Smuts's South African Party and Hertzog's National Party had joined in a new coalition government, an alliance which in turn prompted threats of a right-wing nationalist split under the leadership of D.F. Malan, the long-term preface to the first apartheid government of 1948. Percy was evidently intrigued by the revival of nationalism in Europe as in South Africa, and he questioned Bram on the subject, but for Bram the parallels made his growing antipathy to nationalism only more marked. 'I believe firmly that the world's one hope of salvation lies in the suppression of . . . nationalism,' he wrote to his father, 'and if a person takes that point of view, it's difficult to generate much enthusiasm for the birth . . . of exactly that spirit in our own country.' When Percy asked Bram for information on the Nazis, he replied that with its ideal of going 'back to the pure German', Nazism was the expression of a 'cancerous nationalism . . . My own opinion is that the whole movement is hateful – but the difficulty is that the Germans will probably make a success of it.'

That July Bram had a chance to see these developments at first hand when he attended an International Students' Service conference in Bavaria, and heard Hitler's Chief of Staff, Captain Röhm, address the assembled delegates. Yet though he tried his best (in his incorporative way) to understand the Nazis, and told Ella he was becoming more sympathetic – even finding some of the German students he met charming and 'frightfully sincere' – the deeper logic of the situation was quite apparent. At the conference the German delegation left the hall as soon as the subject of refugee relief (mainly for German Jewish students) arose, and the issue was so contentious that the second half of the conference had to be removed to Switzerland.

Writing to Percy from Innsbruck afterwards – and in much the same way as he had written to him about communism from Russia the year before – Bram offered his father an account of Nazism, which he said had been the 'hauptsache' during the full ten days of the conference. Clearly he had paid attention to the German students who put their case with some passion, but just as clearly he had not been swayed. Once again nationalism was the code through which he interpreted what he saw. Behind all the suffering and injustice which the Germans had undergone in the previous fifteen years, Bram remarked, lay a new philosophy which put all the stress on 'nation': 'Everything must yield to the nation, the national culture and "volkstümlichkeit."' Bram told his father he called this a philosophy because that was what the Nazis called it, but his own opinion was rather less flattering: 'Personally, it's complete nonsense to me, the rationalisation of emotion and the consequence of the nebulous thought to which the German language is so suited. Who, for example, can give any precise meaning to "volkstümlichkeit," a word used to the point of tedium?' (Bram wrote perhaps with some embarrassment at his own earlier enthusiasm for similar convolutions in Afrikaans.) However it appeared, he told his father, 'here you have an emotional, untruthful account . . . which will allow nothing to stand in the path of nationalist striving. It is cruel – 5 days ago the law was finalised permitting the forced sterilisation of any unwanted element (the Jews) . . . '

Even so, remarked Bram, he wouldn't quarrel if there was anything more to be seen, but about 'the socialist side' (he meant of national socialism) one heard almost nothing. The German students stressed the issue if one went so far as to *question* them, claiming that the new spirit wouldn't, for instance, allow a landowner to assume his property existed purely for his personal enjoyment. But in practice, wrote Bram, there had been no law passed against the landowners, and the restrictions placed earlier on the large department stores had now been relaxed. As for the new industrial council, ostensibly representing the whole *volk*, it comprised only one individual who was a genuine worker and, for the rest, men of the calibre of Krupp. On the issue of concentration camps (about which Percy, with a view to the South African precedent, must have questioned him) Bram reported that he could give little information. 'The Germans laugh about them and say they are necessary'; but he had been in communication with an English journalist who (though somewhat emotional, Bram conceded) had been to see one and had written back with 'ugly stories'.

After the conference, and back at the Hotel Seeblick in Grundlsee with Ada, the debates continued day and night. For, as Bram wrote, the place was 'crammed with Socialists and Jews and consequently we have been discussing politics for some 14 hours a day'. And what politics they were, he told both Molly and his parents. South Africans imagined that they had seen too much of this particular form of amusement, but they didn't even know the bare rudiments. Here it was a case of bombs and machine guns. The Nazis were organising openly in Austria, while the socialists were banned and more or less worked underground. They were also armed, and if they hoped for anything it was that the Nazis would opt for open resistance; then the socialists might support the *Heimwehr* and even come to control it, bringing about a revolution. 'Meanwhile, with their centre in Prague, they've come to the conclusion that lawful methods cannot be used any further. From now on it is the "cell" method throughout the whole of Europe.' All the talk was of secret police and secret alliances, military might 'and ultimately a communist revolution'. But if the communists expected a revolution in six months or even a year, observed Bram, they were seriously deluded. The latest opinion was that the shortest possible life of the Hitler regime would be ten years, and what the future would bring no one could tell.

In all of this Bram's mind was almost dizzy with the intensity of it, even as his opinions were taking shape. In Vienna he was not above calling on 'Nazi friends' from his visit of the previous year, finding them genuine if deeply misguided. In his account to his father after the ISS conference he found himself drawn to, though not wholly swayed by, the communist account of Germany – that fascism in any form was capitalism's ultimate attempt, under the cover of nationalism, to retard the natural political development of the workers. But on the issue of nationalism his mind was now evidently firm. To Percy, who was still eager to preserve the idea of a 'true nationalism' as against the distortions of Nazism, Bram wrote that he didn't know what a 'true nationalism' might be. Either, he objected, one placed the importance of one's own country above all else – in which case one found oneself in a situation of tariff wars, financial wars, restrictions or even fascism – 'or you are internationalist in outlook, and strive for the actual scientific organisation of the whole world'.

'Internationalism' and 'scientific': the words had come up again, and now to Bram they were opposed to fascism and Nazism. Bram was not yet a communist and would not become one for a number of years; nor did he become a communist in Russia or Europe. Yet the shift was clearly beginning in his mind, and retrospectively, when he completed the transition, the logic of what he had seen would have had the power of an overwhelming argument sealed by the emotional force of personal experience. It was like a primal scene whose full significance rises only in retrospect to the surface. Here everything Bram had witnessed seemed to demonstrate that the ultimate historic struggle in Europe – and perhaps in the world – lay between Nazism and socialism. Later, back in South Africa, the analogy between fascism and Afrikaner nationalism – replete with its own racial ideology and brutality – offered its own compelling force. Surely in these circumstances only a committed socialism could oppose it, providing a long-term solution to the problems that nationalism, in its illusions and devious deceptions, could merely repress and exacerbate? If the recent history of Europe had proved anything, it had certainly been that.

Specific time-scales and experiences can make the most extraordinary difference: not everyone in South Africa chose the way Bram did, and there were other ways of opposing apartheid. But with his first-hand observation of Europe behind him, the South African scenario would have looked uncannily familiar with the passage of time. In fact, Bram was giving a prophetic description of the major contours of his future existence, along with its underground methods, 'cell' system, the secret police and alliances. True enough, the Hitler regime did not survive much beyond ten years; those who had resisted, who had gone underground, were vindicated both morally and historically. Every reason to think, then, that the apartheid regime of the National Party would not endure much longer when it came into power in 1948. Surely in South Africa, as in Europe, the right thing to do was to resist, to go underground if necessary, and finally, when all else had failed, to take up arms? The vivid memories, the heroic gaiety and vitality of those he had met at the conferences, as well as in Vienna and at Grundlsee – these too would have been stored in Bram's mind.

In February 1934 Bram heard the news that Dollfuss, the Austrian Chancellor, had attacked the socialist strongholds in Vienna in a pre-emptive move to mollify the Nazis. Where the Austrian Communist Party had gone underground, preparing for armed resistance, howitzers rained down on the tenement houses of the Ottakring and Karl Marx-Hof (which Bram had visited). There was machine-gun fire from corridor to corridor, and the wounded were concealed in the sewers; ultimately Dollfuss had the socialist leaders hanged. Some of those Bram had met and talked with through night and day were under serious threat; some of them were in danger of losing their lives. Vienna in 1934 represented for many in Britain a cataclysmic moment, when the future of Europe seemed in the balance. 'Vienna, Vienna, fallen in Vienna,' remembered Stephen Spender. Kim Philby, who was in the city during that year, found his life changed by the experience. None of it could be forgotten by Bram.

Later he himself was remembered. When he was on trial in South Africa in 1965, a woman named Marianne Mahler, who had met him and Ada at Grundlsee in 1933, saw an article on Bram in *The Observer* and wrote to him, deeply moved, with her best wishes. She wrote from London, where she was living; perhaps she had been one of the refugees the Nazis had been hounding. To her, too, the struggle Bram was waging may have seemed part of a history continuous with her own.

✥

When Bram returned to England after his first summer in Europe in 1932, he felt compelled to write Molly a letter of confession and trepidation. On his journey back from Salzburg a young woman from the university in Berlin had wanted him to stop off with her in Munich where they could register at a hotel as husband and wife. Bram had declined, but the experience prompted a disquisition on sex and what he called his 'whole philosophy'. The central question was whether it was possible to have a number of sexual relationships and still love only one person. For Bram there was no right or wrong abstractly considered; sex and love were not identical, and physical fidelity was not an absolute good: 'For me the only thing that is wrong is that which impedes the development of intellectual life on this planet.' He told Molly he had not actually put his sexual philosophy into practice – 'just why is difficult to say' – but he was sure that he could love her even if she had lived with other men, and said he really didn't mind whom she kissed.

It was one of Bram's revealing letters, and though he lived in sheer dread of Molly's reply (he begged her to call everything off by cable if it made her fall out of love), her response, when it arrived, showed that she knew him better than he did. She wasn't so shocked by his letter, she told him, because she already knew his wider views on morality: 'That was one of the reasons I loved you best – I mean that you didn't look for evil where there was none.' This was despite the fact that Molly disagreed with him 'that it would make no difference if I had lived with other men, as you so naively put it . . . I do think that you would mind very much and that you would have been far less tolerant yourself, if you had actually tried out your own philosophy. You're rather a dear you know. You have such "frightfully loose moral standards" and then you never do a thing to be ashamed of . . . It's such a delightful change from all the people who disapprove of all the things they have done themselves, when they find it in others.' But Molly did submit that overemphasis on intellectual attainment was the cause of 'most of the unhappiness in the world today': 'if we weren't so beastly proud of our wonderful capacity for thinking – which we share with none of the lower animals (except women, according to some men) we might spend some time in learning how to live instead of how to think.'

It was an exchange that suggested everything between Bram and Molly, both what connected and what divided them. She was, if anything, a more instinctive and livelier thinker than he was, while he would labour more deliberately, whether on issues of communism, Nazism or sex. Bram believed in the idea of a science of human interaction more than he could fashion such a science himself; he cherished the concept of intellectuality more than he would ever be a true intellectual. But where Molly's streak of imagination was accompanied by a healthy dose of irreverence, Bram was nothing if not responsible to the world. For him the liberty he believed in implied a philosophical weight and allegiance, and if it prevented him from being a philosopher in the freest sense of the term, then that was the burden of his virtue. An intellectualism untied to its larger implications would have been a contradiction in terms; and so Bram would continue to seek authenticity, with every ounce of energy he could muster.

This, in a sense beyond ideas or ideology, even beyond what he might have articulated directly, was what he meant by his 'whole philosophy'. It had to do with honesty, fidelity and integrity: if his ideas on sex had changed he had to confess as much to Molly, at the risk of ruining their relationship, even if nothing measurable had actually occurred. In a subsequent letter Bram promised her he would be 'as honest as it's possible for a human being to be'. That, for many, was what defined Bram Fischer – his honesty, loyalty and integrity: what led him, sometimes misled him, gave him his aura and direction, now ineffably drawn to the monumental drama being enacted before him.

※◎◎※

As for Molly, she really was kissing a number of people, though none of it was in earnest, and she told Bram all the details. In general, she had three boyfriends who kept advancing through the revolving door of her life: one was

Liefie's brother Stratford Clapham, but the most significant was Jan Hofmeyr, also from one of Pretoria's well-known families (which had sent a number of Rhodes Scholars to Oxford). In the main this was still part of the great game of flirtatious sociability, although for the men it may have been more serious. Molly took some delight in telling Bram how the three would, by turns, give vent to their jealousy and chivalrous restraint. Molly camped with friends, went to dances, played hockey – but all this was suddenly punctuated by a terrible accident in December 1932 at Lusthof in which Elodie de la Harpe's brother and his girlfriend were killed by lightning while riding up Mont-aux-Sources. Molly's brother Jimmy had been on the expedition, and Molly was called out immediately, as if a favourite daughter, to help lay out the bodies of the dead and attend to the grief of the living.

In the same month she heard that she had achieved a first for her education diploma, which she regarded as rather ridiculous since, as she remarked, she had not worked for it at all. After this there was a gap in her career, because a teaching post she had applied for in the Cape fell through amidst the uncertainties of the Depression. Then in April she took up her post at the farm school at Jachtfontein. Yet, though Molly resumed her normal carefree habits while waiting in Pretoria, cavorting with her friend Liefie again, perhaps the sudden shadow of the Lusthof accident as well as the loose ends of her life prompted a darker mood, registering most directly on the issue of boyfriends.

'I'm just dying to run away from silly men who think they like me,' she wrote to Bram, 'although it's my own fault that they think so. But men are such idiots that I can't resist the temptation to make them like me, even if it's only by contradicting them.' In the face of this confession (which may have concealed as much as it revealed) Bram praised Molly for being 'more honest with yourself than anybody I know'. But at the end of May 1933 came an unexpected crunch: Molly wrote to him to say that she was out of love. Jan Hofmeyr had been taking her out and had asked her to 'play' with him always. It suddenly struck her that she could, and now she didn't know what to think: 'You know, Braam, I don't think I really love anyone.' In a first letter on the subject Molly claimed that she expected to be a good mother, but an awful failure as a wife, and that all she really wanted was to have children. But in a second she wrote that even this was an unforgivable excuse: it was merely her inordinate vanity that allowed her to encourage different men to love her, without taking the consequences seriously, and now she would have to pay for her folly.

Molly's letters were written with hazardous timing, just as Bram was preparing for his final BA exams, although they probably arrived soon after he had finished. At first he received the news in a state of stunned silence, though the break was by no means complete. Later he told Molly that he had tried to imagine a world without her, losing himself in London or Cape Town or Johannesburg, or burying himself in African education just so that he would be tired enough to sleep: 'It would have worked eventually, of course – everything does.' As for Molly, it is not entirely clear what had happened: the vision Bram had offered of a 'native church' and an alternative life had disappeared in a flash as sudden as the lightning that killed the riders from Lusthof. Bram and Molly had been apart for some time, and such moments of doubt were to be expected. But some two weeks later all hope was restored: Molly had written to Bram to say that she was back in love. He received the news in absolute joy. 'I'm just alive again,' he replied, and told her she was the background to every single thing that he did.

As it turned out, during the short period of Molly's doubt Bram had done something special for her at her own prompting. She had been looking for a text of the Book of Ruth as a present for his birthday, but had been unable to find one, and said he would have to find one for her instead. Bram had scoured London and Oxford without success, and eventually resorted to having a booklet specially made up by the university printer, and bound by Maltby's in Oxford. Sending it on to Molly he apologised for the quality of the print and the wrong shade of blue of the binding: 'In the kindness of your heart,' he wrote, 'you will overlook some of these faults and accept for the deed the will which will go where you go and die where you die.' Thirty-one years later, when Molly had her own unforeseeable and terrible accident, it is quite likely that something did die within Bram.

⁂

When Bram declined his stopover at a hotel in Munich (he described the event as well to his parents), Ella remarked that she was so pleased he had turned down 'the little German student's offer of a night's hospitality'. She was all in favour of Bram trying out new experiences, she told him, but there were one or two for which one had to pay too high a price in self-respect. She confessed her snobbery to Bram, but comforted herself with the thought that there was 'a certain aristocracy of mind that attracts wherever it is to be found' and that counted most of all in life.

While Bram studied Nazism and communism, his mother's emphasis on a certain gentility of gesture and mien continued to serve as intimate supplement to his political education. Throughout his stay in England Ella sent him a steady stream of encouragement and advice that helped fashion in him the being that everyone recognised. In Bram's letters she always asked for the personal touch, which he in turn elicited from as well as imparted to others. (Geoffrey Cox recalled that in Oxford Bram always seemed more adult, more at ease with himself than anyone he knew.) When Bram's knee was injured Ella told him she was grateful that no one else had inflicted the damage, so that she could eliminate resentment from the many emotions the accident aroused. When Fichardt's store in Bloemfontein was threatened with closure because of the Depression, she remarked that its most precious assets were unassailable – the principles, public spirit and foundation of integrity on which it was built. All of this could not but infuse itself into the texture of Bram's response to the world. He told Molly that looking at one of her photographs, if he covered her eyebrows he could be looking at his mother.

They discussed politics, in a supernumerary way. In the lead-up to the coalition between the South African Party and the National Party Ella told Bram of the 'Mad-Hatter's Tea Party' that South African politics had become, with Tielman Roos leaving the bench to dance putative saviour to the country (it was the era of 'strong men'), while Hertzog cursed him as a traitor and Smuts could not provide leadership. When Bram remarked that the main emotion evoked by the Nationalist paper *Die Volksblad* (which his parents had been sending him) was a desire never to set foot in the country again, Ella asked him if the Europeans had done any better when it took their best brains to construct the disaster of the Versailles Treaty. She told Bram that if he ever went into politics he must preserve his sanity and know when to leave the lead to others. Her hope for his future, she advised, was not for him to be prime minister; she had lived too close to success, both political and financial, to place any undue value there. Instead she wanted Bram 'to live usefully & happily & so bring benefit to others & contentment to yourself'. It was a different version of a political vision.

It was at this time that Ella (without any formal education behind her) wrote a novel, entitled *Die Loutering van Petrus [The Sifting of Peter]*, first in English, and then translated laboriously by teams of people round a kitchen table into Afrikaans. It was an Afrikaans readership that Ella was targeting, for the tale the novel told – of a narrow-minded Calvinist minister who falls in love with an American woman and discovers his humanity through sin – was pointed towards cultural enlightenment. But it was also clear, when she sent the manuscript to Bram, that it was his response for which she was waiting. Bram told Molly that seeing his mother's hand and understanding on every page, he would need some time to say anything, but when he did it evidently went right to her heart: 'your response to the picture I painted', wrote Ella, 'means to me the real success of my work – the essential success that matters most to me.' Ella told Bram she had read and re-read every sentence of his assessment, alone in her room with his letter.

Ella's central idea was still embodied in the name of her home, Harmonie. She told Bram that when he and Ada took care of one another, it was that principle they were upholding. When Paul Fischer arrived in England at the end of 1933 (he had been ill during his medical studies in Johannesburg) and Bram and Ada took him to Paris, it was the same principle in action. Ella remarked that the secret in bringing up children was simply to be what one wanted them to be, but she also observed that this was a difficult enough task in itself. As South Africa, following England, abandoned the gold standard, she closed one of her letters to Bram with 'the same dear love that, unlike the gold, keeps its undeviating standard in a world of fluctuating values'.

So in the midst of political turmoil, both then and in the future, it was always 'harmony' that Bram was trying to sustain along with his other objectives, always the imprint of a gentle tact that guided his outward expression no matter what conviction or passion he felt within. Together with his dedication to a new world was this somewhat old-worldly loyalty of identity and style, and even as he tried to fashion another country in South Africa there was always the vision of a larger amity that would define it, to be achieved among all the branches of the national family as it had been in his own more intimate one. Unlikely and even unintelligible as it may have seemed to some, no matter what else communism meant to Bram – and it meant much in the way of economic and social theory – there was always this more private and human component, that all should receive and be able to offer a natural gentility of the spirit.

To some extent this was apparent when, on 16 December 1933, Bram stood up in the Restaurant Frascati in London to offer a speech. It was Dingaan's Day, anniversary of the Battle of Blood River in 1836, when a relative handful of Voortrekkers had defeated the might of the Zulu army, loyal to their king Dingane. Just at this time, in the 1930s, annual commemorations of the victory were becoming occasions for triumphal Afrikaner nationalist revivals dedicated to a future as glorious as the mythicised past. That year, in London, Bram's cousin Theunie Fichardt was in the chair, and the printed programme was emblazoned with the patriotic poem 'Afrikaners, Landgenote' [Afrikaners, Countrymen], enjoining participants to 'wees getrou aan volk en taal' [be true to *volk* and language]. There were folk and religious songs, addresses by Theunie and his wife (who had the unusual name of Etrechia), and then by Bram. But in these sentimental surroundings, Bram, who had witnessed the fire and ice of communism and Nazism in Europe, undertook the delicate task of guiding his listeners towards a somewhat altered perspective. Speaking both in Afrikaans and then in English he did it diplomatically in terms they would understand. He took the Great Trek as measuring the birth of Afrikaner nationalism, a moment that marked a complete break from the past. Now, bringing in the world of contemporary European as well as South African politics, he intimated that a different kind of nationalism was required, as well as a different kind of break. Bram's notes from the evening survive, and this is part of what he said:

'No one but an out and out national–socialist would regard nationalism as an end in itself . . . Nationalism is, if anything, a means to an end, and before we seek to further it we must have some idea of the end for which we are striving . . . As for the Great Trek, one stands amazed at the courage of men and women prepared to sacrifice . . . to start life again in the wholly unknown against overwhelming odds and untold dangers. Today we stand again before a parting of the ways. Time out of number we have heard Blood River referred to as bringing the boon of European civilization to Southern Africa. But one point of view I have never heard Dingaan's Day considered from is the point of view of Dingaan. In everyday life we drug our consciences and critical faculties to his successors. The time has come, if it is not already growing late, for an acute examination of this attitude . . . I would not attempt to minimise the tasks. Many ideas as to race and nationality have to be destroyed or modified. This will require a new attitude of mind – of all human qualities perhaps the most difficult to attain . . . In September 1935 it will be a hundred years since Van Rensburg and Trichardt crossed the Orange . . . Now another great effort is needed, but it must be integrating this time, and draw together not only the two different European races, but see to it that these two advance together with our vast black population . . . '

When Bram used the word 'integrating', he may well have meant the opposite of 'segregating'. As he finished, a number of people congratulated him and an old Senator from South Africa remarked, 'Dammit, Fischer, I didn't want to think after dinner, and you made us all think.' Bram (writing as always on politics to his father) noted that Ada had been satisfied with the speech, and he hoped that Percy would have approved of the mildness of his tone. It was a small matter, in an out-of-the-way place, but for Bram it was his instinctive way of establishing the transformation he was seeking, to win people over by consent and thoughtfulness.

Bram wrote his finals for the BA in law in June 1933, working furiously to prepare himself for six days of examinations, morning and afternoon, under a system that drove everyone to the edges of their stamina and sanity as much as their knowledge. Both Percy and Ella had advised him that exams were not all-important (they were 'just one little incident in a busy interesting career', remarked Ella), and throughout his time in Oxford Bram had viewed his education in the widest sense, so that his travels in Europe and his first-hand experience of its history would be incorporated in that larger definition. Still, he had missed a term by arriving late, and then virtually another when his knee was injured, and now he tried desperately to make up for lost time. Bram told his parents that on the Friday night in the middle of it all he had been in a cold sweat and couldn't sleep at all. Finally, when the results were announced he heard that he had a viva (an oral exam), which usually meant that the candidate was on the borderline between a first and second class. In the meantime Bram had most likely received Molly's letters both falling out of and then back in love, and – despite his relief at the latter – the effects could only have been unsettling. Tantalised as he may have been by the idea of a first, after the viva it turned out that he had in fact received a third, and Bram was devastated by the disappointment. This was not his preferred model of success, yet it may have convinced him that he was more suited to practical rather than academic life. At least after this, he remarked to his parents, he could work for the sake of working and not for a degree. At New College his 'moral tutor' (the don assigned to look after his well-being) wrote to him that only overwork could explain his results: 'About your ability and knowledge there is no question whatever of course.' Later Leo Marquard told Ella Fischer that at least Bram had been able to comfort himself with the thought that he too had got a third.

The Warden of Rhodes House, C.K. Allen, wrote directly to Percy to say that despite Bram's disappointing results he had gained a 'general, and perhaps indefinable, benefit' from his time abroad. More to the point, he was concerned that Bram make the best possible use of the final year of the Rhodes, if not studying for a BCL, then taking an MLitt in economics. But Bram, perhaps now disenchanted with student life, wanted either to return home as soon as he had finished his residence requirements in Oxford and take up law (seeing Molly at last would be an additional bonus), or else to do something practical to further his career, such as accounting at the LSE. But the Rhodes rules would not allow the latter, and Percy advised Bram strongly against initiating his career in South Africa while the Depression was still in force.

In the end Bram compromised, beginning a diploma in economics in

October 1933, studying (among others) Keynes, whose theories, he reported to his parents, attempted to eradicate cycles of depression 'in our capitalistic world'. With 'Mac' Macdonald of the Russia trip and Len Klatzow, another South African friend, he moved into a house in north Oxford; at the end of October he became president of the Ralegh Club for the term; and in November helped organise a conference on race and nationalism. For Tom Jarman (also of the Russia trip, now lecturing in Nottingham), he addressed a Workers' Education Association class on 'South Africa and Her Problems'. It all indicated where Bram was heading: race, capitalism and nationalism were the topics of the times as well as the ones most centrally on his mind, and lecturing to workers at the WEA defined the experience of much of the student left in the 1930s. Bram kept up his activity for the ISS, especially on student refugees from Germany, but was not above skipping yet another conference to hear Jascha Heifetz play the violin at a concert in London.

Early in 1934 Percy Fischer took long leave, and he and Ella came to visit Bram and Ada for an extended stay. During the Easter vacation they bought a car and travelled as far as Italy. There, in Siena (which Bram told Molly he found the most beautiful of all – 'quite the most mediaeval thing I've seen') there were no sidewalks, and driving was nearly impossible. Bram had been sorely tempted, he told Molly, to strike a blow for democracy and run over about twenty fascists. 'I presume they would all be fascists because in [the] recent election Mussolini received about 99% of the votes, so my chances of killing a democrat would be very small indeed.'

By July 1934 Bram's parents had left for home, and by August he was ready to do the same, to be followed some time after by Ada. A confidential report from C.K. Allen, which mysteriously made its way to Percy Fischer via the South African Department of Education, summed up his feelings about Bram and intimated that his real learning at Oxford had not been undertaken in the lecture theatre or library. Bram, wrote Allen, had been 'one of the most delightful of the Rhodes Scholars from any country, and a man who has won universal esteem and affection. I cannot help regretting that his academic performance was not more representative of his real quality, but I fully realize that, after previous university training, he did not come to Oxford primarily for academic experience, and he has certainly derived the fullest and most judicious advantage from it in all other ways. All who have been in touch with him view his departure with real regret.'

When Bram steamed out of Southampton on 19 August, he left in the same adventurous spirit in which he had spent his years in Europe. Professor Coupland knew the Governor of Nigeria, and so Bram (armed appropriately with a pith helmet of Percy's) planned to spend some three and a half weeks there on his way home, primarily to study 'native administration'. In the midst of his stay he wrote that the attempt to advance the Africans without breaking from the past was 'a sociological experiment as interesting as that of Russia'. Again there was the connection between Russia and Africa, but Bram wrote little more on the topic because soon enough he was home.

Before his departure, Molly had written to him to suggest that he find someone else to help get him used to South Africa again, but Bram had replied that this was impossible. 'For one thing,' he told Molly, 'I've never met anyone else who has not been over here who realizes that S. Africa may take some "getting used to."' At some level Bram understood that his experience had made him another person, and therefore it was to another country that he was returning.

On 16 October a telegram from Cape Town was delivered at Harmonie in Bloemfontein. 'Arrive Friday morning. Inform Town Council and Railway Band.' It had been just two months shy of three years.

CHAPTER 5

LAW AND MARRIAGE

October 1934 – August 1939

It wasn't entirely true that Bram's devotion to Molly had remained uninter-rupted at Oxford, for in the last few months of his stay he had become some-what captivated by a young Englishwoman named Eularia Baines. She came from a family of civil servants and university dons, and in June 1934 Bram described her to Molly as being 'quite as mad as you are – is a heathen and studies theology while her real line is in painting – so you can't blame me for falling in love with her'. Bram's cavalier tone indicated that there had been no serious lapse (he and Molly always teased each other about falling in love with other people), but over the next few months it may have become more real. His brothers remembered some story that he had become engaged to an Englishwoman in Oxford. (Paul apparently went so far as to write and con-gratulate her, and Gus recalled that Ella had asked the woman to learn Afrikaans for Bram's sake, which apparently put a damper on things – no doubt with Ella's approval.) Three years later Bram claimed that it was simply loneliness that had made him turn to Eularia in Oxford ('I know that on the evening I told her I was in love with her, I didn't feel at all in love,' he suggested to Molly), but also remembered vividly how by the time he was com-ing home on his return journey he had 'nearly ruined all the future'. Then, when he arrived in Cape Town he found a letter waiting for him from Eularia, but none from Molly, and the effect was depressing. It was a token of much of what Bram and Molly would go through – that the magnetism between them involved complex fields of divergence as well as attraction – before they finally cohered.

On Bram's return to Bloemfontein his brothers found him rather tense and dejected, staying on his own in a little house that Ella owned in Reed Street behind Harmonie, reading much of the time and pondering his future. When he left England he had written to his parents that he wished he belonged 'to that very jolly class who have their three years at Oxford and then just long to get back to S. Africa', but told them he was only beginning to get the most out of Europe. Once home, the contrasts must have been quite overwhelming. Both in England and on the Continent Bram had been in the hot cauldron of the most volatile international events and at the cold centre of discussion; now he was back in the staid town of his birth, and it must have seemed a falling away. His most pressing decision had to be what to make of his life and where to make it. With Percy a judge of the Free State Supreme Court, a career for Bram at the Bar in Bloemfontein looked the most natural of prospects: there his family lineage as well as wider connections would vastly accelerate his success and assure – if he desired it – a career very much like his father's and grandfather's. Yet at the same time, in such a setting it would be hard for him not to feel smothered in his father's shadow. There was also now increasingly the question of politics, whether (at the least) Bram would feel a mere reproduction of the habits and manners of previous generations might be adequate. Bram's youngest brother Gus remembered him telling Percy that, while he hoped his father didn't mind, he had become very left in his thinking, perhaps even – thought Gus – that he had come close to communism. Given what he had experienced and witnessed in Europe, Bloemfontein must have seemed unnervingly recognisable and rather unreal.

It was in these circumstances that Bram decided to take up his career in Johannesburg. Cape Town may have been an option, but Johannesburg was in South Africa's industrial (and therefore political) heartland, and its Bar would have been that much more alive notwithstanding the Depression; also, Cape Town could not offer Molly just thirty miles away in Pretoria. So early in January 1935 Bram arrived in Johannesburg and moved into a boarding-house run by a Mrs Kemp in Wellington Road, Parktown. He never felt quite at home there, rooming yet again after all the years in Oxford, along with the standard boarding-house décor and furniture. One of the rooms Bram occupied at Mrs Kemp's was directly next to the bathroom, so (he apprised his parents) along with being woken by the birds there were other early morning sounds for him to contemplate. But Mrs Kemp made him sandwiches to take to work, and he managed a polite friendliness towards his co-boarders, although he told Molly he seethed at some of them underneath.

He began work – or at least going to work – almost immediately. The Bar in Johannesburg was based in chambers, at that time in Corporation Buildings in Rissik Street. Bram occupied Room 103 (his name on the door, he reported, looking 'most attractive') and in the normal custom joined a group with other young advocates, mainly to share a secretary and save costs. On 10 January 1935 he received his call to the Bar: it was, he informed Percy and Ella, 'extremely satisfactory & in fact a great success. Everybody was agreed that no better oath was sworn than the two I took yesterday.' The following day all his office paraphernalia arrived from Bloemfontein – desk, bookcases and books –

and Bram told his father that he had set up his room in imitation of Percy's, with the Appellate Division reports lined up behind him where he could reach them by simply stretching out. 'So now', he wrote home, 'I have my room all in order & am just waiting for the briefs.'

He had much waiting to do, for life at the Bar was a hazardous one for junior advocates beginning their careers, especially during the Depression. Briefs were few and fees were low (one of Bram's colleagues told him that in his first year at the Bar he had earned just £32). In the face of such dismal prospects Bram's attitude remained cheerfully sardonic: 'What a life – what a profession,' he wrote home. 'No rest, streams of clients & briefs – and what a variety of cases' – but through much of 1935 he found himself dependent on subsidies from his father, writing to ask shamefacedly for money. Even as Bram began to receive more work it arrived in a wildly erratic manner, adding to his sense of insecurity.

He began, as all young advocates did, by 'devilling' – taking on assignments from senior advocates to gain experience, for little or no pay – and reading up on law and court procedures so that when work did appear he would be fully prepared. As always he was thorough to a fault – when he submitted a 'devil' for W.H. Ramsbottom, one of the leading advocates at the Bar, the latter advised him gently not to overdo it, but observed that his final success was assured if he always worked so hard. And there were reasons, apart from sheer conscientiousness, why Bram would speed along faster in his career than most of his contemporaries, as his superiors took him in and nurtured him with a certain sense of patrician recognition. Ramsbottom (whom everyone called 'Rammie') came from one of the old-established Free State families and was in fact the son of Dr Alfred Ramsbottom, who had been Treasurer in Abraham Fischer's Orange River Colony cabinet, as well as first Administrator of the Orange Free State Province (it was he whom Percy had consulted in Abraham's conflict with Hertzog). Oliver Schreiner, also one of the leading lights of the Bar, was son of the Cape Prime Minister W.P. Schreiner (who had worked both with and against Abraham Fischer at various stages of his career), as well as nephew to the novelist Olive Schreiner. Philip Millin, one of Bram's other mentors, was married to Sarah Gertrude Millin, whom, despite her far less generous approach on racial matters, some regarded as Olive Schreiner's successor. In short, there was a sense of familial aristocracy and shared history in this elevated stratum of the Bar and, with due regard to the legacy of Abraham as well as Percy's current position, Bram's lineage would have been held in equally lofty esteem. Pretty soon Bram was devilling for all the major advocates and, as the year progressed, even taking on some cases as junior with them.

Bram was breathless at his first genuine cases. His very first was a divorce, followed soon by a murder, both of which he took up *pro deo*. In the murder case he represented Philemon Maklakhani, accused of killing one 'Baby' Mataung, and did quite well for a novice, obtaining a much-reduced sentence for his client. 'It's over,' he reported to his parents in February 1935, 'and the ice is broken, and the Judge said my plea of self-defence was nonsense, and my accused got 4 years & 7 lashes and Mr Justice Maritz in sentencing the poor little devil said that he ought to be very grateful for "the very able defence" which I had put up.' Bram told how his cross-examination of the prosecution witnesses had been fine, but that his own client was another matter: 'I went thru' my introductory stuff & then said now tell me about the struggle & oh Lord, he broke loose altogether & told a fantastic story of how the other two had attacked him. I think I lost control there for 5 or 10 minutes, but it's devilish difficult trying to guide your own witness when he gets excited and you are afraid of appearing to hide something, and above all when he's speaking Shangaan through an interpreter . . . However, it's all in the day's run & it's good to have learned what one may expect.' In yet another *pro deo* case involving a fight, Bram came across his first policeman who was prepared to lie in the witness box. At first, remarked Bram, he had been scared, not having the confidence to force a policeman through his paces, but eventually he unravelled the dissimulation through his questioning and won acquittal for his client.

As time went on there was more variety – and some money. In March Bram wrote home to his parents in a state of approximate shock having received a cheque for £26 5s, which suddenly appeared on his desk from Tielman Roos (the very same whom Ella had despised for his political arrogance some years before). It meant appearing with him in a case involving corruption in town government, and though Bram was somewhat alarmed at the association (the indicted individuals were probably Roos's followers), the money was another thing: 'I just walk around in small circles & feel like vomiting,' Bram wrote to his parents. 'And I shan't have to draw on Pa for years again!' For all Ella's suspicions of Roos, these were overcome by her motherly archivist's pride. 'Junior to Tielman Roos,' she appended to a telegram from Bram advising of his travel plans for the case, ' – fee of £26. First important brief.'

Then in April Bram received what he described to Molly as his 'first really legal brief', acting as junior to Tilson Barry in a case involving gold law. As Bram explained it, gold law was the most complicated of all legal areas, and Tilson Barry was South Africa's leading expert in the field – so, he told her, 'Hold thumbs for me.' This might have been necessary for more than one reason, for Bram was now living among some of the more idiosyncratic, if not to say eccentric, characters of the Bar. He described to his younger brother Gus how Barry would nearly kill both of them driving home to discuss the case: 'By Jove,' Barry would say as he careered down the road, 'they must be angry with me for passing on the wrong side. By Jove this is the way to keep young!' Bram's colleague Jack Lewsen – also a former NUSAS 'prime minister' (for the SAP rather than the NP) and now a member of the same advocates' group as Bram – remembered other stories about Barry. With his passion for dog-racing, Barry would solicit bets on a Friday from junior members of the Bar, and return their winnings on the Monday. If they happened to object that Barry owed them nothing because the dog they bet on had lost, Barry's frequent retort was that the dog they had chosen had been such rubbish that he'd put the money on another one. Bram told Molly how he would have to trick Barry into accepting his legal opinions, but all in all the experience was invaluable, not only in working with one of the Bar's most brilliant individuals (again an aus-picious association, for Barry's brother Charles was on the bench), but because it was from this initial connection that Bram's own later expertise in mining and mineral law derived.

Yet things were uncertain enough that when, in July, Bram was offered a position with the Johannesburg municipality at £50 a month for three months, he was sorely tempted to take it. The job would at least provide a secure income for a while, but the disadvantage was that he would break the contacts he had established at the Bar, and would have to make them up again later. Bram's incentive to earn money as quickly as possible was simple in one respect: apart from the question of his independence, it would bring him that much closer to marrying Molly. It was for exactly this reason that she general-ly observed she had no desire for him to make too much too quickly, and when she agreed with him that the municipality job wasn't suitable, he jokingly voiced his suspicion that she might have hidden motives in holding off his earnings.

Bram walked the two miles to work in the morning, and then back in the evening again. To fill in between cases and bring in some money he took to correcting exam papers in accounting at the University of the Witwatersrand. As he became involved in the routine of a professional life (wobbly as it was), it began to produce its own satisfactions, even from early on. People spoke of the 'perfect day' at Oxford, he told his parents, but he had never achieved 'such a perfect day at Oxford as I have here'. Still, despite his pleasure and pro-pitious connections, he revealed an inner insecurity that belied the calm and easy exterior which everyone knew. One of Bram's cases involved a widow who, in mortal toil herself, was suing her ex-husband's estate and – just before she finally saved everyone enormous amounts of trouble by dying – matters were suddenly complicated when three separate wills were found. After one particularly trying day at this, Bram went to the theatre and had to leave the auditorium twice for a glass of milk. His digestion was always an index of the state of his nerves, and this was a sign of the ulcer that later developed. By November he was also acting in what he called (to Molly) his 'lunacy case', involving a man who believed he was wrongly institutionalised but who was, in fact, quite dangerous. On this Molly was cheerfully encouraging: 'Stop worrying about your lunatics. Your arguments will never go wrong. If you can persuade me against my will surely a few magistrates & judges ought to be easy.'

At last, after being a student for so long, Bram was in what he might have thought of as the 'real world', and he explored Johannesburg's offerings with his characteristic mix of interests. He attended an *Afrikaanse byeenkoms* [Afrikaans gathering], but found the occasion drearily awful. He had a passion for using his hands, and eventually took up carpentry; it was a pursuit that expressed at least something of his personality, combining the mental with the physical, the aesthetic with the practical, the pleasurable with the purposeful, shaping inert but responsive material towards some organised end. He attended displays of what he was still able to call 'kaffir dancing' (probably at one of the mines), as well as a beer club once a month with his colleagues. More than anything else it was the collegiality of the Bar that attracted him, the feeling of being part of the machinery of a world at work in collective and professional association.

Even so, he may not have been quite prepared for the rapidity – not to say vengeance – with which that collegiality approached *him*, as almost in some pre-assigned way he became ensconced among the Bar's elite social circle. Oliver Schreiner took him out for drinks at the Rand Club (the most exclusive club in Johannesburg), the Ramsbottoms invited him for dinner, Tilson Barry took him home – perilously in his car – to discuss cases. Bram also went to dinner at the Millins 'with two rather fascinating jewesses from the University', and then afterwards on to a film. 'Sarah did not go because she has something wrong with her eyes,' he told Percy and Ella; perhaps he knew of her insufferable insomnia and attendant hypochondria. Bram played tennis, as well as golf; he went dancing at the Country Club. If he was living in a degree of financial uncertainty, it was by no means an unpleasant life.

He was also being assimilated into the routines and rituals of the Bar. On one occasion Bram described for Molly a memorial for a member who had died – 'Rather a ghoulish proceeding when one . . . sees 70 men around one for most of whom similar speeches will be made at some time or other' – but there were of course happier occasions. Towards the end of 1935 there was a celebratory dinner in honour of Schreiner, Ramsbottom and two other advocates on the occasion of their taking 'silk' and becoming King's Counsel. Specially invited for the occasion to propose the toast to 'The Bar' was the Honorable Mr Justice P.U. Fischer; and with a sense of fitting symmetry the reply on behalf of the Bar was given by none other than Bram.

Nothing could have indicated more clearly how intimately he was being taken into the family of his profession, and with what pleasure and self-gratification that profession admitted him. Bram was a Rhodes Scholar, his vintage and pedigree were perfect, his manner was assured and gregarious, and all those who spoke to him gained the distinct impression that they meant something special in his life. Advocate I.A. ('Issy') Maisels, then just a few years his senior, remembered the common wisdom of the Bar that Bram would become 'a second Ramsbottom'. All too easily he could have allowed it to come true, living a full life of professional achievement and uncomplicated social privilege. But the common wisdom was both right and wrong.

⁂

There was something of a mystery about Bram, revealed more clearly at this time than any other. Outwardly, to his parents as to his colleagues, he sustained the image of a quiet but unmistakable buoyancy, never giving the least hint of doubt except through a quietly self-deprecating irony that somehow added to his attraction. Yet to Molly he revealed a vastly different interior life, full of anxiety and worry, sometimes of vast proportions. Writing with an unusual fervour Bram would speak of his certainty that Molly didn't care for him at all, or reveal his fear that he might become violent or go 'roaring mad' without her.

Faced with some of this Molly must have felt a little overwhelmed, now the object of Bram's deepest needs and anxieties. 'I always thought there would be some big principles in life to which love – if it conflicted with them, would have to give way,' he told her. 'And now it's all so different. I know there is nothing I would not give up for you.' But there were other reasons why Molly may have felt strained, and why Bram would have been anxious. In late 1934 Molly's mother had died, leaving her feeling lost and alienated at home. Bram wrote now of her recurring black moods and depression; sometimes (he said) he felt afraid even to speak in her presence, and she would hate him for telling her he loved her. Looking back later he believed that by the end of 1935 Molly was on the edge of a nervous breakdown, sleeping only four hours a night. Sometimes she stood up to Bram, telling him that if he was always going to be nervous of hurting her, then she too would become frightened and never say a word in case it wounded him. She accused Bram of being so 'hideously polite' (which captured something of his public character in its least flattering light) that she never knew whether to believe all the things he said. But if he was uncertain of himself, then she revealed anxieties to match his. 'I was quite sure until I received your letter', she wrote to Bram, 'that I spent the whole of the weekend before the last in unravelling the knots in *my* soul, while *you* watched patiently & then you turn around & tell me that you did the unravelling & I the watching. Tell me who is right, please.' Bram spoke of twists in himself, she told him, but she was much worse: 'It's I who will smash up everything between us, if one of us must break things.'

This was evidently not a relationship of airy nothings, but it was also the most difficult time between Bram and Molly. Nor would it have continued if there weren't a degree of happiness, especially as the year progressed. Molly called herself a 'barbarian' and Bram was delighted, telling her he was sure they need never grow up: it was her instinctive spark as well as her capacity for depth that he loved, revealed most of all when they 'played'. Molly invited Bram over for a weekend, but remarked that the house would be full: he could sleep with the other guests in her father's room, or with her brother on the stoep, or in the fowl-run, or with her if he wanted. Bram replied that he would naturally opt for the fowl-run. He ended some letters to her as her 'loving husband', and began some with the salutation 'Dear Swine'. It is possible that privately, towards the end of 1935, he may even have proposed. He called Molly 'little wife', and told her, 'I don't think I've ever felt more married than I do today, and I'm sure I never felt happier about it.' He wrote to Molly, 'Don't ever, ever go away from me or die.'

There was also the matter of sex, and here Bram and Molly (both now twenty-seven years old) were, within the constraints of their era, unsuperstitiously open. Bram, who freely told Molly that he hated 'stark indecency', indicated that there was a difference between that and the beauties of an honest sexuality. When Molly asked him if he minded that she didn't write 'nice and sensible' letters, his reply was direct: 'Of course I do like "nice" letters, but then I have a feeling that we attach different meanings to that much abused word. You see one of the nicest things I know is sleeping with you.' But Bram was also extremely careful on the tender borderlines that sex before marriage involved. 'Sweetheart,' he wrote to Molly after work one night from Johannesburg, 'I'm longing terribly for you tonight and I'm afraid it's a very "fleshly" longing. I really want to sleep with you . . . but I'm so terribly afraid of that longing at the same time. All that sort of thing belongs to a part of the emotions which one really can't hope to understand beforehand. There seem to be such delicate balances of feeling & such fine shades between supreme joy and tragedy that I become horribly frightened at times. If I were to cast aside restraint some day and you did not stop me, might I spoil everything for you? Can't we have a really long talk about it one of these days? – right out in the veld somewhere – one Sunday morning, I think.' It was on Sunday mornings on the veld that Abraham had walked with Percy, and Bram with his father. Now he and Molly had to work their way into sexual knowledge and confidence in a world in which this was not the norm, and they explored the available options. Molly's friend Liefie brought her a copy of Van de Velde's *Ideal Marriage*, which she in turn had borrowed from a friend whose mother had ordered it for her daughter from England, since it was unavailable in South Africa. Although in retrospect the book appears like the equivalent of some Cold War sex manual, their interest was an attempt at both science and liberation. Molly passed it on to Bram, and he studied it seriously. He always advised her tenderly to take it easy whenever she was 'unwell' (having her period).

In December 1935 Molly spent a week of the summer holidays with Bram and his family at Umtentweni on the south coast of Natal, near Port Shepstone. Percy and Ella were there, as were Bram's sister Ada with her husband-to-be, Beck, and Paul with his future wife Nancy. Staying in a house right up against the Indian Ocean they swam in the sea before breakfast or in the moonlight, went for trips by car, played golf or took walks among the trees. For Bram the week was little short of perfection, and after it was over and he had reluctantly taken Molly off to the station at Durban, the pangs of separation left him little short of lyrical. 'I don't think there's much salt left in the sea,' he wrote to Molly. 'It seems to have lost all its buoyancy. Hell take the myriad white horses dancing about on the terribly blue sea now.'

Ever since Bethlehem days Bram had loved nothing better than driving with Molly on the front seat close beside him, and on his return to Umtentweni from Durban it was just such memories the journey evoked. 'Oh darling, you would have loved the drive back,' he wrote to her afterwards, ' – the rain and the mist and then the feeling of sleepiness over the last 20 miles. My shoulder just ached to have you sleeping there . . . The funny part about it now is that I don't know whether I want to cry for loneliness or because I'm terribly happy. Things seem to have become so much more real during the last week. I can see many pictures of you – pictures of Lusthof, pictures at Silverton or Bethlehem. I used to think they were vivid, but now they seem to be rather pale and distant. Now when I think of you in the forest – your body speckled with sun and shade or pale under the grey clouds – or when I think of your eyes suddenly green and your soft hair against a sand dune, my pictures are warm and living. I can feel you as I said goodbye to you in the train. I can even put my head on your breasts. Oh sweetheart, please believe what I told you then that there is nothing but you in the world for me – nothing, nothing is worthwhile unless I can share it with you.'

≈≈◎≋≈

Before coming Molly had explained to Bram that she would stay in Umtentweni only for a week because she always felt the need to be free to leave places when she wanted. She would love Bram a thousand times more in one week (so she insisted) than she would in a whole month if she stayed that long. From Umtentweni she returned home to be with her father, keeping him company over Christmas, and then travelled down to the Cape to be with, among others, Jan Hofmeyr. But as much as Jan might have been looking forward to her arrival, this was meant to be the moment when Molly gave him the bad news.

For both Bram and Molly had struggled along with the enduring echoes of their earlier relationships – he with Eularia, and she with Jan Hofmeyr. Bram had continued to correspond with Eularia, but found it exceedingly difficult to tell her he had taken up with Molly again. ('I can't go on like this, just not writing,' he had confessed to Molly earlier in the year. 'And on the other hand I dread hurting her. Do you despise me a lot? You must tell me, you know.') On Molly's side the association with Jan had continued, and part of her was genuinely drawn to it. In response to Bram's confessions she wrote to him to say that she had suddenly and somewhat alarmingly felt very sure that he would be happier with Eularia than with her, 'just as I would probably be happier with Jan than with you, in a quieter way, though I know that I want to play with you & be with you more than anything else in the world.' Now her intentions were clear: she was going to tell Jan that she planned to marry Bram and that, as she put it, she would 'never be able to play with him again'.

But when she reached the Cape she once again found it extremely difficult to say anything without ruining the holiday for Jan and everyone else. Bram wrote (he said from experience) to tell Molly he understood, and managed almost heroically in his letter to divide himself in two in order to give her advice. He spoke first as an 'outsider', saying that she should not feel bad if she had to tell either him or Jan that she was going to marry the other. If she were to tell Jan, he knew it would hurt like hell, and that she would be very sorry for a while; he could almost wish, he said, that she had decided to tell him instead, and advised her not to postpone. 'But skattie' [little treasure – as Bram and Molly called one another] 'always remember that if, after this next fortnight, you feel that you would rather tell me than Jan, I love you enough now skattie not to worry you any more.'

All that was from the outside, remarked Bram; from the inside his view was different. 'I love you & love you & love you. I want you to live with me & I'd do anything to try and persuade you to live with me.' Eventually Molly summoned the courage and told Jan – and then told Bram that his response could not have been more delicate or kinder. She and Jan had laughed and cried together in the sweet camaraderie of goodbyes, and things were apparently settled. But if Bram now expected that his life with Molly would be one of uninterrupted proximity culminating fluently in marriage, it was a forlorn hope. For after all their time apart and the difficulties and triumph of re-establishing their relationship, further distances and postponements intervened. Only now, instead of Bram, it was Molly who, following the logic of her own inner needs, felt that she had to go away. It was to Namibia she went, the setting of her grandfather Bernsmann's journeys and her mother's childhood.

⁂

The possibility of Molly's going to Windhoek had arisen in 1935, but had fallen through; now in 1936, the idea revived. The Director of Education in South West Africa was looking for a teacher to initiate a domestic science project at one of the schools, and Molly was apparently the most qualified for his purposes. When Bram first heard of the idea he was horrified – and felt equally guilty for being so. He knew that when he had told Molly in Bethlehem of his Rhodes Scholarship, she had done everything she could to encourage him – but he felt incapable of returning the favour. Now that he and Molly were so close, and especially after the holiday at Umtentweni, he couldn't face the prospect of losing her again.

Molly told him that her leaving had nothing to do with him but with the need to find her own identity: 'It's not because I doubt your feelings towards me & it's not because I'm not sure that I love you – because I am & I know I'm going to marry you & be happy ever after no matter what you say about it – but darling, I'm so dreadfully unsure of myself in my dealings with myself . . . I know that sounds dreadful, but it's true. I have never yet found out who I am or what I am.' The recent death of Molly's mother must have had more than a little to do with this, if it was an inner peace she was seeking. In 1918, when she was ten, Molly had visited South West Africa with her mother, and memories of that trip had continued to echo in her mind. Now, after her mother's death, this would be a journey of solitary remembrance: she had to go away to find what was within, and she would do it in the spare absences of the desert.

In one of her letters to Bram Molly also mentioned what she termed, with perhaps subconscious resonance, her 'third reason', that if she were far away it would be easier for Jan to forget her. And later she confessed to Bram that even after her December decision she had continued to see Jan in Pretoria simply because she did not have the strength to stay away. Bram replied without irony: 'Thank you for telling me your third reason. I should have known, but of course, as usual, the important things always escape me. I am sorry I have caused so much trouble over the past few years.'

Yet if Molly was seeking her own identity, Bram came to realise that her departure was also good for his. Whereas he had felt mortified by the weakness of his initial, more possessive response, and knew that in previous undertakings he had always been the one to leave, slowly he came to understand that Molly's independence – induced for whatever reasons – would help bolster his own, as well as his confidence in their relationship. As the year progressed – though her absence was always a kind of bodily pain for him – he continued to feel stronger, and by July 1936 could write to her that he was convinced Windhoek was good for them both: 'we've now rather changed positions since March.'

⚜

Molly left in early April, on a four-day train trip via De Aar in the Karoo through what she termed 'gloriously uninteresting' scenery, until she reached Windhoek and the Hotel Metropole, whose cosy hospitality belied its rather dingy and run-down appearance. There at first she felt her solitude – 'I feel very sad and alone in the world,' she told Bram on the day of her arrival, 'and more than usually sure that I'll make a mess of my work' – but soon came alive to her new surroundings.

Immediately she found herself attracted to the Herero women, in their elegantly flowing German-print dresses and turbans, and confessed herself faintly amused by her discovery that (going on the average) every white person in South West Africa had some ten square miles to occupy. She walked round town, too timid at first to enter the beer gardens, though not afraid to go out horse riding to the local cemetery (her usual fascination) where she found the European section too prim for her taste, but the African graves mingled among the thorn trees far preferable. Molly wanted very much to visit Otjimbingue, which she had seen with her mother in 1918, but the closest she came was Okahandja (some forty miles north of Windhoek), which she told Bram used to be the Herero capital: 'There's a long avenue of trees down which they used to lead a missionary once a year & then kill him. Even now hundreds of Hereros make a pilgrimage to it once a year.' In Windhoek she found that most of the Germans were Nazi sympathisers, except for a family of refugees who Molly thought had some Jewish blood; she lost no time in befriending them.

At the school where Molly taught, she found herself straining at the leash. Along with domestic science she had to teach arithmetic, biology and physics (all in Afrikaans as well as English), and it wasn't easy in an environment that managed to be both ante- and pro-diluvian. (One disapproving colleague warned her that she was taking a risk mentioning evolution in her biology class, and the principal advised her that she really ought to be stricter.) But Molly's instincts were quite the opposite: what she really wanted to do was teach sex and baby care to the older pupils. Again, as at Bethlehem, her unconventionality and spontaneity had its results, and she became a favourite among the schoolgirls.

Predictably, Molly became surrounded by a group of young men. Dev Rademann was a South African Airways pilot who before landing would fly once around Windhoek by way of greeting the town every week; Eric Jenisch later married Molly's sister Pauline; Percy Niehaus was a lawyer who knew Bram. Certainly two of these and possibly all three were in love with Molly at one stage or another. Yet though she went out regularly with each of them and even admitted to kissing all three at various times, after a while she became sadder at her own popularity, and asked Bram whether she really did have a 'come hither' look about her. He replied that of course she did, but not in any obvious way: 'You're the sort of woman who immediately makes men think of doing great things and falling in love.'

But the fact was that Windhoek was a small and incestuous town, in which scandal always threatened beneath the surface, and everyone knew one another's secrets. Towards the end of the year, inevitably it caught up with Molly: relations between two of her men friends soured, people told stories about her, and she felt besieged on all fronts. Perhaps this wasn't the self she had gone out to Windhoek to find.

※⊛✧

In April 1936 chambers in Johannesburg moved to its new location in Kruis Street, and Bram was pleased to find himself in a roomier and airier office. In May he left Mrs Kemp's boarding-house to stay with his colleague Jack Lewsen while Jack's parents were away overseas. In August he bumped into Laurens van der Post, whose American publisher gave Bram a stack of magazines on physical culture and (of all things for Bram) 'true romance'. One day Bram's friend 'Mac' Macdonald from Oxford suddenly walked into his rooms. He told Bram that his fiancée Marguerite would soon be joining him in Johannesburg, but that they'd secretly been married for eighteen months. When finally the 'marriage' did occur, Bram (with hidden pangs in his heart, thinking of Molly) was one of three guests at the wedding.

All this time his career was progressing, if unpredictably from moment to moment. Some months he would feel rushed off his feet, while in others he would sit around vacantly waiting for briefs to come in. Some, when they did emerge, had to do with the human comedy of law. Bram described for his father one such case involving an application for a dairy licence in which he was acting as junior to Oliver Schreiner: 'We (a married woman), maintain *injuria* because, when we appeared before the City council, one of the opponents of our application . . . stepped over to us and lifted his leg like a dog.' In general the devils and opinions (which were paid) arrived along the same network: in October Bram felt he had set a record for a junior, with five opinions in a month, of which two were with Ramsbottom and Schreiner. Tilson Barry continued to coach him on the gold law, and Bram was absolutely delighted when Tilson adopted a devil of his without any changes, merely writing out the Latin terms in upper case for the typist to read. That was against professional custom, since a 'silk' was not supposed to 'intrude his devil upon the attorney', but the attorney did not seem to mind, as he was the one who (also against regulations) told Bram about it.

Arthur Chaskalson, who came to know Bram many years later, remarked that Bram was extraordinarily methodical as a lawyer, and always tremendously well prepared. He would carry wads of notes about him, written on stray pieces of paper and envelopes, so that nothing would be forgotten. In court he was quiet and gently spoken, and never wasted time. He had the ability, observed Chaskalson, to make people agree with him simply because they wanted to please him. Once, in an insurance case, a man who had been involved in an accident claimed that as a result he could not lift his hand. Bram, representing his opponents, first made sure the man was at ease, and then (lifting his own arm) asked him in a matter-of-fact way whether, just before the accident, he had been holding up his hand facing this way, or that. Genially, the man lifted up his hand to show Bram – and lost the suit, probably on the strength of it.

There were of course larger and more important cases. In February 1936 Bram acted as a junior in a boundary commission hearing, in which a number of the towns of Johannesburg's East Rand were squabbling over some farms in dispute. Bram wallowed in local ordinances and Public Health Acts until he felt he could recite them in his sleep and, together with his senior and whole phalanxes of attorneys, consulted with the president of the Chamber of Mines. All this made him feel it must be a significant case, but he told Molly he could also not help laughing up his sleeve at the grandiose goings on: 'I'm afraid I shall never make a really nice, pompous lawyer.' Later, in October the commission prompted a new investigation, and there was a moment of hope and despair when Bram was approached for the case and then dropped by what he termed the 'astigmatic municipality of Springs'. But then, equally surprisingly, he found himself taken up by the other side, in a team comprising Tilson Barry, Ramsbottom and a number of other leading lights. Bram sent a cryptically punned telegram to Molly, 'Hope springs eternal,' and she replied, 'Joy cometh in the morning.'

The case was a boon for Bram. Not only did he earn the unheard-of sum of £160, but he was also able to see the experts in his profession at close quarters. And his own repertoire was expanding. In September, in a culpable homicide case, he helped defend a motorist whose car had collided with a train at a level crossing, killing his passenger. The driver was found guilty, but there were extenuating circumstances, and so he was detained 'only until the rising of the court' – and Bram had made thirty guineas. Attorneys (no doubt with an observant view as to Bram's connections and rising prestige) began to send him briefs in his own right. When he was approached for his first mining case to run by himself – for West Rand Consolidated Mines over some property in dispute – Bram told his parents that gold law was 'the most interesting, pleasant and lucrative work I have yet come across'. This was something of a surprise, because to most advocates it was an absolute mystery in its complexity.

There was also an obvious oddity in a socialistically inclined future communist becoming an expert in gold law and representing the mining houses, the largest exploiters of black labour in South Africa. And for years afterwards, long after his communism was well known, Bram continued to work on a retainer for some of the biggest mining companies. From one point of view he had no choice, since the ethic of the Bar (following a kind of 'taxi-rank' principle) dictated that an advocate was not free to turn away cases unless he was too busy or unqualified. Yet there are ways of being busy or unqualified if there is a certain kind of work one does not wish to do, and so the pattern was significant. On the side of the mining houses it indicated the respect (and even affection) in which Bram was held, even by those to whom he was opposed politically. On his side, depending on one's perspective, it was evidence either of Bram's ideological confusion or of his ability to separate his legal from his political fascinations. In any event, he usually represented one mining house against another, and almost never represented any of them against their workers. Once qualified in the field there was the simple matter of his expertise which everyone wanted. Moreover, at this early stage there was one prominent incentive for him to become adept as soon as possible – so that he could make enough money to marry Molly. None the less, in this complicated if not wholly contradictory behaviour, Bram was evidence that the Communist Party of South Africa was able to sustain surprisingly bourgeois manifestations along with its radicalism – and not necessarily to its detriment.

Bram's need to increase his earnings meant that there was no work he turned down. Throughout this time he was still correcting exam papers, and he also took up lecturing – to individuals as well as through correspondence schools and the University of the Witwatersrand. Unlike his more puritanical grandfather (and again in some tension with his developing ideology) he dabbled on the stock exchange, and even tried to make some money for Percy. But there were other activities being folded into the mix. At the end of the year Bram was approached by J.D. Rheinallt-Jones, 'adviser' to the Institute of Race Relations, to act for the Barolong of Thaba Nchu before a commission delimiting land under the newly instituted Native Trust and Land Act. At first he was reluctant to take it on because Molly was returning on holiday at exactly the same time, and he suggested that the Barolong could obtain advice more cheaply in Bloemfontein. But they insisted, and so he went down. Ramsbottom told him later that he had heard from Rheinallt-Jones that not only the Barolong, but even the whites of the district, as well as the commission itself, had been extremely pleased with his work. Bram, reporting this to his parents, said it sounded too good to be true, but that perhaps his mother would be able to 'take it'. After the Thaba Nchu consultation, Oliver Schreiner, just then drawing Bram into the Institute of Race Relations in his own right, gave him a copy of Eric Walker's biography of his father, W.P. Schreiner: all the connections were being reinforced.

In 1936, among his other successes, Bram won the Bar bogey golf competition. He joined the 1926 Club ('a sort of Johannesburg Ralegh Club,' he informed Molly), and heard George Findlay, the Pretoria communist whose book on miscegenation claimed that some 600,000 of the so-called whites of South Africa had 'coloured' blood. Later, as he had of the Ralegh, Bram became secretary of the 1926 Club. Also at that time, along with other members of the Bar as well as Raymond Dart, the famed palaeontologist and finder of the Taung skull, Bram became intrigued by the Alexander Principle of psychophysical balance, just then arrived in Johannesburg. The Principle had evolutionary overtones, and deep down Bram was nothing if not interested in the evolution of humanity.

꒰꒱

In February 1937 Oliver Schreiner was raised to the bench, temporarily at first but with the assurance that his position would become permanent. He was a popular choice as judge, and Bram told Percy and Ella that the whole Bar was delighted – although there was great sympathy for Philip Millin, who had been passed over (and would be again later). Not least, Bram was pleased because Schreiner's promotion would create more space for what he called the 'junior juniors' when someone took silk in Schreiner's place. When, at Bram's request, Percy wrote to Schreiner to con- gratulate him, the latter replied with some words about Bram. 'Dear Fischer,' he wrote, 'You must discount a good deal of what Bram says because he is such a dear, good fellow that he thinks well of everyone. He is doing finely at the Bar and is most popular. Popularity is sometimes accompanied by an inability to adhere to unpopular views but Bram is not like that. He has any amount of firmness and receives as much respect as affection.'

In May and early June of that year Bram defended one Walter Nhlapo accused of shooting and killing a woman. It was an extremely difficult case, and in court Bram had some anxious moments. Three times Nhlapo changed his story in the witness box, and three times (Bram informed his parents) they managed to save him. Finally, at five o'clock in the evening, Bram won an acquittal, and the following day received a letter from Nhlapo expressing his heartfelt gratitude. 'Dear Sir, . . . Am I dreaming that I am a freeman from the bonds of the Devil? It seems I am dreaming, but all the same I am not. And for my freedom, how can I pay you for this deed you've done. God only knows, and He alone can repay you the fullest measures you deserve . . .'

A year earlier, in May 1936, it was a letter from a servant in Percy and Ella's household in Bloemfontein that Bram received, written in the following way: 'Dear Bass Bram, . . . Yours was handed and the contents of it clearley understood . . . Bass Abram I was very glad to hear that the biscuits were very nice, I can be glad if you will have them all not living [leaving] any crumb behind Bass Bram, then I'll know that they were really nice for you Bass Bram . . .' The letter, in its mix of the formal and the personal, was impregnated with the deferences of South African mas- ter–servant relationships, but that did not mean that it contained no genuine senti- ment, nor that Bram showed no respect in return.

From the high to the low he seemed to have a way, but how would one deal with all these things together, and separate the compromised from the authentic? Power, privilege and patronage in his life and his career, the eternal deference and gratitude of those beneath him: precisely because of his virtues and his opportunities, all these might have been Bram's without thinking. He had to find a way of refusing them. Or was it because they came too easily that he began to look for something else – a more equitable form of human relations that would permit as well as challenge both the self and those others with whom it engaged to become who they really had the potential of being?

⁂

Privately Bram and Molly were engaged, and every day in Windhoek Molly used to wear a ring she had from Bram, taking it off only for school. She told Bram that Ovambo men provided their wives with heavy anklets, in proportion to the value they placed on them, and that he ought to bear this in mind when choosing a wedding ring. She wrote early on that she would now marry him at any time: she said she couldn't live without the beauty and peace that sleeping with him brought, and they talked about their imagined Ruth as if she were about to arrive.

In the school vacation of June 1936 Molly returned home for just over two weeks. The plan was for the two to become formally engaged at that time. She gave Bram strict instructions: 'you're not to *ask* my father to marry me – I won't be bargained over. I mean if I say I'll marry you, we don't have to ask anyone else, we'll just tell them & there you are. I'll probably mention it to him quite casually myself. After all, skat, it's a very ordinary thing, isn't it?' Ordinary or not, Bram found himself in a state of nervous anticipation as Molly's train approached Johannesburg, having warned her not to expect too much from him when they met again. Somewhere around 8 July their engagement became official, and Molly wrote to Bram's parents in appreciation of the way they had accepted her: 'You don't know what you have taken into your midst, but thank you for being so cheerful about it.'

When Molly returned to Windhoek, along the same interminable route (with David for company), she told everyone that her engagement to Bram was only a 'business arrangement', though in a moment of weakness she couldn't resist telling the Administrator's wife how it had all begun, with 'Intervarsities & Bethlehem & Circuit Courts'. In Johannesburg Bram was all the more lonely for having been so close to Molly, but he was also more in favour of Windhoek than he had been, feeling the benefits of greater clarity and security in both their minds. In court Bram used to keep a handkerchief of Molly's in his pocket for good luck, and did so the day of Walter Nhlapo's acquittal. All in all his tone, throughout this time, was much more confident and optimistic than it had ever been.

In September Bram, scrounging his earnings together, flew to Windhoek to see Molly (she told him that for the ride to the cemetery alone the £30 airfare was worth it). It was his first long-distance flight, and a very bumpy one at that: Bram became increasingly squeamish, spending the last part of the journey sprawled on his back on the floor. By that stage he was the sole remaining passenger, and through a prior conspiracy between himself, the pilot and Molly, they managed to arrive thirty-five minutes early (they circled the aerodrome to allow her to get there at the same time). Once in Windhoek Bram told Percy and Ella just how much Molly had 'captured the whole town'. There were innumerable invitations: one night they took 'two of the nicest men who are in love with Molly, & their partners to a dinner and a dance'. At times, he told his parents, he 'rather wished Molly were not quite so well liked'.

Landing at Kimberley on his way home (a calmer experience this time), Bram was utterly amazed to see his brother Gus walk into the airport building. It was nothing exceptional: Gus had been down to view a motor race, and had decided to stop in. After Bram returned to Johannesburg, Molly told him it was lucky that she had gone away: 'I was thinking today that I would never have become engaged to you if I hadn't left Pretoria. Is that a dreadful thing to say? I would have gone on playing with Jan & anyone else who wanted to play with me & I would never have realised that I only wanted you.' Now, she said, she hardly ever thought of Jan, and didn't regret it.

⁂

At the end of 1936, when Molly returned home once again for another holiday with the Fischers at Umtentweni, Bram remarked that the change was extraordinary. As he told Percy and Ella, Molly was being restful again for the first time since her mother died. Percy felt a little more restful too: he had been trying out Bram's Alexander Principle of relaxation on the golf course and now felt so nonchalant that he could hardly hit the ball.

But that was still not the end of this tale of love and distance – for instead of Molly's quick return to Johannesburg and a wedding at the end of her year's contract in Windhoek, she was about to travel even further, this time into the heart of pre-war Europe.

⁂

In the event it was at Bram's insistence.

When Molly arrived back in Windhoek at the beginning of 1937 (overwhelmed at the sight of the yellow *dubbeltjie* flowers flooding the desert on the way in), the squabbling and scandal by which she was surrounded made her only the more anxious to return to Bram and get married. But then in February her father offered her £200 for a trip overseas. In contrast to Bram's reaction when Molly had first raised the idea of teaching in Windhoek, he was now delighted at the prospect of her going to Europe. Deep down the reason was clear: he wanted her to have something of the same vivid and exhilarating experiences which had so expanded his own horizons. He even offered, in the most tactful way possible, to lend money to a friend of Molly's whom she would be joining if that would help them meet up.

Ultimately she managed to reserve a berth on the German ship the *Njassa*, leaving from Walvis Bay at the end of March. On board in early April, she listened to a sermon in which the minister maintained that sooner or later one had to think back on the past, and it prompted her memories again: of her trip to South West Africa when she was ten; of searching during the past year – but being unable to find – the house she and her mother had stayed in. 'I can still never think of S. West', she told Bram, 'without a tightening somewhere.' Molly's emptiness had not entirely been filled: her tightening inside had to do with the mother she had lost, and the lost home from which she had come.

***

Some of these remembrances were contained in a twenty-eight page letter to Bram which Molly began during her journey at sea, and which became the place for a final confession. It wasn't simply the case, she told him, that men just happened to fall in love with her: the truth was that whenever she came across anyone attractive she would begin working, almost unconsciously, to ensure that result. It had been the same with Percy Niehaus, her chief suitor in Windhoek. She had quite often imagined that she loved him, although now she didn't miss him at all. 'I can't even ask you to forgive me,' she told Bram, 'as I'll do it all over again . . . I'm sorry you have such a faithless wife.'

But Bram was now distinctly nonplussed. Over the more than 6000 miles which their letters once again traversed, he told Molly that the only issue of importance was that she should not worry herself under any circumstances. In the course of their lives they would both be attracted to other people. He himself (as he told her in earlier letters) had in moments of urgency and despair kissed both Molly's friend Liefie and a certain Miss Read. The main thing was to be open and honest, and if something serious came along – well then, they would have to deal with it. It was only because he and Molly had such a lot of 'rough' that their 'smooth' would bring them such joy. Far better that, he suggested, than a merely unconscious acceptance of one another.

On the way up the coast the boat stopped off at Freetown where Molly picked frangipani and had tea with a party of African tennis players. (All went well until her South African companion, in a fit of racial excitation, burst out laughing.) At Las Palmas (where Bram had visited the brothels) they went to cabarets. Approaching England they saw the *Graf Zeppelin* fly overhead, and in Southampton Molly told Bram that she nearly went mad to see the daffodils and tulips in the tiny gardens. Then it was on via Le Havre and Antwerp to Hamburg. Molly had personal reasons for going to Germany, because some of her grandfather Bernsmann's children had returned there, and she now had aunts and uncles to visit.

She did much of what Bram had done, and in some respects more, travelling to Vienna and the Salzkammergut (by bicycle to Bram's haunts at Grundlsee, now perhaps emptied of both socialists and Jews), through the Tyrol and Bavaria, to Munich and Nuremberg. Along with an American couple in Munich she became involved in an argument with a group of people from an array of countries (Austria, Sweden, Czechoslovakia, Yugoslavia, Germany, Hungary), some of whom were overt Nazi supporters, and the others at least profoundly nationalistic. All of them were amazed when both Molly and the Americans said they wouldn't mind criticism of their governments; at the very least, she told Bram, they appeared to expect bloodshed. For his part, he was horrified at her temerity: 'Probably anti-Nazis have been shot in that very place & then you go & pull Adolf to bits in the very womb of his whole movement.' Though Bram found her account of the night in Munich and its low culture fascinating – as he put it, probably 'worth any number of Carmens' – he was eager for Molly to reach England as soon as possible: 'When the next war comes there won't be any time to get out of the other man's country.' He wanted Molly off what he called the 'dark Continent' of Europe.

But it was further in that Molly went. Her Aunt Paulina (Bernsmann's daughter) had returned to what was, before the First World War, the town of Bromberg in Germany; now, lying between Poznán and Gdansk, it was the Polish city of Bydgoszcz. On the way there Molly became embroiled in a remarkable fracas at the border because she lacked a visa on a day that happened to be a Polish holiday, but finally she was able to get through. All in all, she was revelling in her solitary freedom, enjoying the sensation, as she put it to Bram, of having an entire tramcar agitated that she wouldn't disembark at the right stop, or strange men ordering porters for her and telling her how much to tip. Bram wrote that she was so much better at looking after herself than he was that she would just have to humour him after they were married.

Ultimately Molly returned via Paris to spend more time in England – Bram had advised her to stay on an extra three weeks so that she could do so; he had waited five months, he said, and an extra one would hardly make any differ-ence. Here she tracked some of his steps to Oxford and the Bidwells in Cambridge. Thanking Bram for 'the lovely trip you gave me', she left on board the *Usambara* on 30 July, and on the way home a Scotsman called (inevitably) Jock, returning to service in the British South Africa Police at Fort Victoria in Rhodesia, fell in love with her.

⚜

At home Bram was preoccupied with Molly's impending return, penning let-ters ten or twelve pages long in minute handwriting which described in every last detail his preparations for their life together. At last, at the beginning of July he moved into 29 Westcliff Gardens, a block of flats high on the Johan-nesburg ridge overlooking the Zoo, with a view to the Magaliesberg range in the north. There among the packing cases and the debris, he was overjoyed after seven years to be in a place of his own, and couldn't wait for Molly to join him.

They discussed their approaching wedding, which for Molly was an extremely touchy subject. It had already been postponed at least twice, first to accommodate her trip to Europe, and then her extra three weeks in England. She had once told Bram she didn't want a church wedding, and would just as soon live in sin, and now they discussed the available options: a magistrates' court in Pretoria or Cape Town, or a ceremony in Bloemfontein, at Harmonie. Molly, not wishing to give Bram's parents any trouble (or using this excuse to circumnavigate more complex aversions of her own), was as sensitive on every issue as the most exposed nerve. At one point Bram remarked that she would come to Harmonie only if there was no cake, nothing to drink, and no wed-ding dress – and it was clear that he was only half joking. All in all, he was involved in the most delicate choreography of persuasion as he had to tell his parents what to promise her, or not to say. Though Bram was sure he knew what Molly wanted – an uncomplicated but beautiful wedding at Harmonie – he was also aware that to try and push her even slightly would produce exact-ly the opposite result. Somewhere hope began to fail that the wedding would ever take place. 'Tell me soon that it is going to happen,' he had written to Molly in February. 'I'm beginning to lose confidence a bit after 6 years.'

Sometime in late April or May Molly had dropped her final bombshell. She had been thinking about her independence, she told Bram, and felt the need to bring some money of her own to the marriage, and so, in short, she wanted to teach for two terms before any wedding. His reply was blunt: 'Dear heart, I'm going to be vulgar . . . This . . . is balls, sheer balls.' He argued all the points. They would both be thirty the following year, and halfway through their lives: 'that, as far as I am concerned, is half my life wasted already.' Both of them wanted Ruth very badly. Bram didn't want a trousseau, he just wanted Molly, and if she postponed again it might mean their wedding would never take place. If she really wanted to teach, she could do so *after* they were married. He threatened that if she wouldn't be persuaded, he would send her £50 a week for the rest of her trip so that she would have some money to bring. 'The truth of the matter', wrote Bram, 'is that I'm not going to let you postpone our wedding anymore, no matter what you say. For once I'm really going to put down my foot even at the risk of crashing everything, and by September 15th at the very latest you will be Mrs Fischer.'

He was nearly right.

It was on 18 September.

Bram met Molly on her arrival in Cape Town on 23 August, and the two of them had lunch with his Auntie Maggie at the Round House overlooking Camps Bay – Auntie Maggie, who was the link with his Oupa Abraham, and who, Bram said, now got Abraham and Percy and himself all mixed up in her mind.

And Molly in a way was connected with her grandfather and her mother. A husband waited for a wife who had left from South West Africa, now coming from Europe by ship to Cape Town. He went to the dockside, to see her come down on to the shore.

It was Ella who scripted the whole thing, although with editorial revisions. Bram, in jest, told his mother that Molly's latest plan in her quest for privacy was to hide all the guests behind trees and shrubs so that they wouldn't see either him or Molly. As for the *dominee*, he would be behind a hedge, but whether blindfolded or not, Bram couldn't say. Molly was more direct, advising Ella that she had compromised on a white dress, 'which I'm going to hate & we're going to be married, but I'm not going to listen to what the "predikant" says or mean anything I promise.' But she went down to Harmonie to help plan things, and when she came back her mind was more settled.

The 18th was a Saturday, and the wedding was in the morning. Ella's script included a carpet laid from Molly's door, over some steps towards a stone bench in the garden where the *dominee* was waiting. There was only a small number of guests (including Ouma Steyn, the old President's wife), and Liefie was Molly's bridesmaid. For a joke she and Bram's brother Paul played 'Tiptoe through the Tulips' on the gramophone, just before the wedding march. The ceremony was in the sunken part of the garden, under the pergola laced with wistaria which Ella had hastily supplemented after a storm the night before. As Bram put the ring on Molly's finger, the household servants, standing behind, sang in a choir; they had asked to do so, and the *dominee* had agreed.

After seven years, in a last letter to Molly just a few days before, Bram had written: 'Totsiens [Goodbye] little Mrs Fischer and love me for a little while longer if you possibly can – just stretch a point this once angel mine.'

⁂

On 14 August 1939 a hasty note came from Bram to his mother, who had come up from Bloemfontein to Johannesburg: 'Don't get to bed until I've seen you. Get rid of the youngsters as soon as you can. I've taken Moll to the home and things are beginning to happen.'

That was the night that Bram and Molly's daughter Ruth was born.

CHAPTER 6

JOINING UP

A Meditation: 1914 – 1945

In September 1914, just prior to the Afrikaner Rebellion (and some months before Percy Fischer set off with his ditch-destined ambulance), a group of socialists in Johannesburg formed the War on War League. Colin Wade, Sidney Bunting, David Ivon Jones, and P.R. Roux were members of the South African Labour Party, affiliated to the Socialist International, which had declared in its Basle resolutions that any coming war could only be imperialist in nature and should therefore be opposed by workers of all countries. The South African Labour Party (made up largely of British miners and artisans) had endorsed these principles but, when war actually arrived, became caught up (like much of the Socialist International) in a wave of patriotic fervour that drowned all cries for peace.

Struggling for control of the SALP, the War on War League published the *War on War Gazette* and argued its case on the basis of expediency as well as philosophy. Here was a perfect opportunity, its members proposed, to set up a natural alliance with Hertzog's followers, who as Afrikaner nationalists opposed the war, who on the basis of past experience opposed imperialism, and who as an exploited underclass had suffered under capitalism. 'Among the Dutch,' the *Gazette* suggested in March 1915, 'it is unquestionable that opposition to war, and especially to compulsory military service and the German S.W. Africa expedition, was one of the factors inspiring rebellion. But among the British and other European elements, too, it would have been strange, it would have been humiliating, if some such movement as the "War on War League" had not sprung into existence.'

The War on War League did not prevail within the Labour Party, which during the course of 1915 opted actively for a pro-war policy. At that the self-styled War on Warites seceded, setting up first the International League of the South African Labour Party and then, in a further split, the International Socialist League (SA). It was the ISL which, in the wake of the Russian Revolution, combined with other splinter parties of the left to become the dominant component of the Communist Party of South Africa, forming itself as a section of the Communist International in July 1921. How odd it might have appeared to Percy Fischer – or more fitting it might have seemed to his son, if some years later he considered it – to think that at the time of the Rebellion the only companions of the Afrikaner nationalists had been communists.

Across time there may have been other echoes that Bram would have recognised. In September 1939, when the Germans invaded Poland and the Second World War began, the CPSA, like the War on War League before it, opposed participation. This was mainly because of the Nazi–Soviet Pact, one of the strangest alliances of all time, given the historic enmity of fascism and communism. Yet in communist rhetoric it was a Pact whose necessity was explained in the same terms as had been argued just twenty-five years before. The coming conflict was an imperialist war, whose real aim was the destruction of the Soviet Union: Stalin was convinced the West would never resist Hitler, but rather planned to use Nazi Germany to overthrow the homeland of socialism. Support for the Pact was therefore (by a kind of somersaulting logic) resistance to both fascism and imperialism. At the least Stalin had bought himself time to build up the force that the USSR would require when the inevitable onslaught came. Far from being a measure of cynical treachery or calculation, therefore, and despite whatever internal anguish it caused, the Pact may have seemed to true believers worldwide – precisely because of the act of faith it demanded – like the most thoroughgoing principle.

When Percy Fischer joined the Afrikaner Rebellion, he had been moved by the memory of Abraham's role in the Boer War. In linking himself with the communist movement a quarter of a century later, Bram Fischer may have felt that he was reinforcing, but also transforming, a direct line of continuity, from Abraham, to Percy, to himself. Here the Boers and the rebels as well as the War on Warites and the communists were conjoined; here anti-imperialism was linked with anti-capitalism; here Afrikaners could at last ally with African and English-speaking comrades, breaking the barriers of South African division; here Bram, having joined with Molly, could connect all the varying and developing aspects of his life, and extend the traditions of his family into a new world in the making.

Bram joined up, in a number of ways. When an alliance between Hitler and Stalin might have caused the most revolted aversion (especially given his experiences in Europe), Bram was drawn towards the Communist Party because for him all things were resolved there, and this was the most logical and decent thing of all.

❧❧❧

In 1919, on the second anniversary of the Russian Revolution, General Hertzog was happy to address his followers on the inspiration that communism had provided for Afrikaner nationalism: 'Bolshevism, I say, is the will of the people to be free, to govern themselves, and not to be undermined by a foreign regime . . . If we say that we have the right to govern ourselves, and if we feel that it is our duty to see that it [Bolshevism] is properly fulfilled, then we are in fact Bolsheviks.'

It was a quotation that the Communist Party of South Africa loved to reproduce, especially in later years when the chief inspiration and objective of Afrikaner nationalism appeared to be the wholesale repression and destruction of communism. When Hertzog spoke those words it was before his own Pact of 1924 with the Labour Party; he was still in opposition to Smuts's government, and the revolutionary (not to mention anti-imperialist) legacy of the Bolsheviks must have had its attractions. But it was one indication of how, in these two decades between the wars, varying conceptual currents in South Africa were congruent as much as they diverged, with different groups drawing on the same sources even as they vied for semantic and ideological space. This wasn't only a South African phenomenon: in Italy fascism had developed out of (a distorted form of) socialism, while futurism was an aesthetic mode that Italian fascists and Russian communists pursued with equal enthusiasm. Such phenomena indicated how the private and public languages we speak mark the limits of our consciousness: those things we are free to choose to think about, and those which establish the very dimensions of our choosing, which may in themselves be unthinkable. It is this that marks the historic in our lives, as thought strains against the boundaries of its conception.

In South Africa it produced paradoxical results, as more than a degree of political expediency was folded into the mix. In the early 1920s Hertzog was prepared to support Clements Kadalie's Industrial and Commercial Workers' Union, the largest black workers' organisation the country had ever seen; and in the election of 1924 Kadalie was not averse to returning the favour. Two years later Kadalie, though inspired originally by the Bolshevik revolution, expelled communists from the ICU, ostensibly because they were corrupting the African nationalist nature of the union. Something similar occurred in the African National Congress when Josiah Gumede, its president, returned from the USSR declaring that he had seen the new Jerusalem; traditional chiefs, still prominent in the organisation, feared they might suffer the same fate as the Tsar if the communists took over, and Gumede was ousted. White liberals, for their part, felt that communism (as well as the capitalist tug on Africans to the cities) threatened the purity of African tradition, and so what individuals such as Ethelreda Lewis and Edgar Brookes came to support was the ideological oxymoron of a liberal segregationism. In this, as in their fairly thorough-going racial paternalism, they too participated in the mentality of their time.

In these circumstances it would have been surprising if the Communist Party had not evinced similar complexities and contradictions, as was illustrated *par excellence* during the Rand Revolt of 1922 when a strike by white miners developed into an all-out battle against the state. The cause of the miners was by no means self-evidently pure. In conditions where the mine-owners were attempting to cut costs by eliminating certain categories of jobs 'protected' for whites, and do away with differential pay scales, the white miners wished to preserve the benefits of their situation. As the conflict intensified and Smuts (in support of the Chamber of Mines) sent in aeroplanes to bomb the strikers in their hold-out in the Johannesburg area of Fordsburg, the communists felt they had to support this 'red revolt'. Yet when armed strike commandos (largely Afrikaner miners) took to reinforcing their sense of solidarity by attacking Africans in the street, the communist leadership was caught in a quandary. The Party called for the protection of white standards – and expressed the hope that African standards would rise similarly in future. Hence in part the idiosyncratic sign that appeared on a banner at the head of one of the strike commandos: 'Workers of the World Fight and Unite for a White South Africa!'

It was resentment against Smuts as well as questions of ideology that, in the wake of the strike's suppression, led the CPSA to support the alliance between Hertzog and the Labour Party in the election of 1924. Yet, as Smuts was defeated and the Pact government came to power (to the cheers of Bram and his cousin Connie in the market square of Bloemfontein), the futility of such a strategy became clear. The white workers now had all their desired job protections and pay differentials passed into law without any need of the Communist Party, and the new regime intensified segregationist practices to suit the prejudices and predilections of a reinvigorated Afrikaner nationalism.

It was in these circumstances that people such as Sidney Bunting became convinced that the true destiny of the CPSA had to depend on the mass of workers in South Africa, and that in order to propagate a true socialist revolution the Party therefore had to Africanise itself. At the time it was a breath-taking and unforeseen realisation, and the CPSA began the unprecedented work of becoming a multi-racial, multi-class, and multi-cultural organisation, then and long after the only party in South Africa to open its doors to members of all races. A new generation of enthusiasts – among them Eddie Roux and Willie Kalk – took to the new spirit with vigour. The Party newspaper, *The International*, became *The South African Worker* (later *Umsebenzi*), developing an expanding readership. The CPSA organised unions in trade and industry, and established a night school in Johannesburg, as did various left and liberal organisations at the time. Through these diverse routes a growing number of Africans joined the Party, some of whom Bram Fischer later came to know well. There was Edwin Mofutsanyana, from Witzieshoek in the eastern Free State, and his wife Josie Mpama; J.B. Marks, a teacher who had been to the Lenin School in Moscow; Johannes Nkosi, murdered along with others at a Dingaan's Day demonstration in Durban in 1930; Albert Nzula, the first black acting general secretary of the CPSA in the late 1920s; Moses Kotane, jack of all trades from the western Transvaal (who with his acute intelligence pestered his teachers with questions), later also general secretary of the Party. Here they met not only white comrades of British extraction, but also Jews from Eastern Europe such as Solly Sachs and (later) Eli Weinberg, as well as Afrikaners such as Gideon Botha, Danie du Plessis and Bram Fischer. It was in many ways a startling mixture.

But just as the CPSA discovered itself as an organisation based on the principles of class rather than nationalism, fate in the form of the Communist International made it change direction. In 1928, at its sixth congress in Moscow, the Comintern determined that the true task of the CPSA was to work towards the establishment of an 'Independent Native Republic' as the first stage 'towards a workers' and peasants' government'. From the outside this may have appeared a mild resolution, even in keeping with the Party's new Africanising priorities, but in South Africa the repercussions were gigantic. For the CPSA the new directive was retrogressive. The Party had struggled hard to become 'colour-blind'; it believed in a one-stage revolution in which both black and white workers would combine in the creation of a socialist state. Now, in effect, it was being instructed to work for a bourgeois 'national democratic' transformation, as the first element in what would become a two-stage revolution. Communist theory was being recast in racial rather than class terms, in the form of nationalist rather than proletarian identity.

Later generations of communist theorists in South Africa would consider that the shift in direction had been necessary. The idea of a 'one-stage' revolution, for all its radical attraction, simply ignored the complications of race; the true relations between 'national and class forces' had to be both understood and embodied in the liberation movement. And it was true that this formulation did come to underlie the strategy and tactics of the liberation movement in South Africa for much of the course of the century (the CPSA always with its eye on the second stage, the ANC and its other allies much more content with the first). But perhaps more important than the issues, or the debate they ignited at the time, was the fact that the matter was settled in Moscow. The edict came down – 'the national question, based on the agrarian question, lies at the foundation of the revolution in South Africa' – and the South African delegation of Sidney Bunting, his wife Rebecca, and Eddie Roux (all white, and therefore compromised in their initial opposition to a 'Native Republic') bowed down before the wisdom of their revolutionary superiors, as did, in due course, the CPSA as a whole.

It established a disquieting pattern for the immediate years ahead. In 1930 the executive committee of the Comintern changed direction sharply once again, now ordering that the CPSA no longer work with petit-bourgeois nationalist parties such as the ANC and ICU. This, in direct contrast to its previous resolution, could only have been the distant reflection of Stalin's methods of political consolidation as he identified first enemies on the left and then on the right and targeted them equally for elimination – but as such it found reinforcement within the CPSA. As a new leadership emerged in the Party under Douglas and Molly Wolton and their associate Lazar Bach, they learned their lesson only too well that in order to sharpen the class struggle (and one's own power) there is nothing so convenient as inventing a nemesis with whom all sins are associated. South Africa's Trotsky (as Bram Fischer's future comrades Jack and Ray Simons pointed out) became Sidney Bunting, though in this case it was the preposterously named right-wing deviation of 'Buntingism' that was denounced.

A form of sad burlesque this may have been, but in the new world of razor-eyed zealotry and ritual purges some of the old-timers were out of their depth. Stalwarts such as Bill Andrews (first general secretary of the Party), Solly Sachs, Bunting and others were anathematised and expelled. *Umsebenzi*, which had developed a growing African readership, became filled with endless theoretical disquisitions which fewer and fewer bothered to read. Then, in 1935 the Comintern changed direction yet again with its new policy of the united front, and this time it was Kotane's followers who were expelled, while he (along with Eddie Roux) was dropped from the Political Bureau. All of this was only resolved when a hearing was called in Moscow to unravel the intractable tangles of the Communist Party in South Africa. There Kotane argued against Lazar Bach and a certain Maurice Richter, and there – in a dark form of poetic justice – the expellers were expelled, as Bach, Richter and Richter's brother were accused by their Moscow judges of protecting followers of Trotsky, concealing their compromised social origins and other similar transgressions.

It is likely that the expulsions were in a permanent form. It appears that Bach died in a labour camp, though Willie Kalk, who like Molly Wolton had been to the Lenin School in Moscow, was convinced that both he and the Richter brothers were executed, and Jack and Ray Simons, in their account of this period, concur. A. Lerumo (the pseudonym of Bram Fischer's friend Michael Harmel) wrote somewhat benignly in his official history of the CPSA that Bach was 'unsuccessful' in putting his case before the Comintern, and that 'he never returned to South Africa'. Kalk, a confirmed 'Stalinite' as he himself put it, who mildly regretted the fact that in all revolutions innocent people die, remarked that Bach wasn't bad – 'He had his ideas.' It may be a question of timing as well as personality and zeal: Bach found death in the Communist Party; Bram Fischer and others like him, life.

Sidney Bunting died in 1936, now remembered in the era of the united front as a hero. Others, including Bill Andrews, were readmitted, though many, such as Eddie Roux, never returned. When Rowley Arenstein, later a comrade of Bram Fischer's, attempted to join the CPSA in Johannesburg in 1938, the Party was both so wary of outsiders and so self-decimated that it took him six months to be able to find it.

⁂

Meanwhile, with the ICU in tatters (it had tailed off in allegations of financial corruption), the ANC in a period of self-imposed docility, and the CPSA imploded, white South African politics followed its supremacist course without substantial challenge. Hertzog's victory in the election of 1929 had been followed by a period of social and political repression: an amended Riotous Assemblies Act entitled the Minister of Justice (Oswald Pirow, whom Bram would come to know well in a variety of contexts) to banish persons for inciting 'racial hostility', which set a certain precedent for later years. In 1933 came Hertzog's and Smuts's coalition government, and in 1934 their two parties merged into the United South African National Party (later known as the United Party), which in its consolidation seemed symbolic once again of the unification of white South Africa in its suppression of the black.

Nothing illustrated this more graphically than what became known as the 1936 Bills – Hertzog's legislation on land and the franchise whose beginnings Bram had witnessed in parliament in 1926, and which now (reduced to two Bills rather than the original four) was passed into law a decade later. The Natives' Representation Act removed Africans in the Cape from the common voters' roll, giving them a separate vote for a small number of white representatives in the House of Assembly and the Senate (the latter elected also by Africans throughout the country). It also provided for a Natives' Representative Council which, despite the lofty promise of its name, would be only partially elected and nothing more than advisory in its powers (a 'toy telephone', in Paul Mosaka's apt phrase). The Native Trust and Land Act increased (as promised) the amount of land granted under the Natives' Land Act of 1913, but fixed it at about 13 per cent of the country's total area, at which proportion it remained more or less for fifty years. Thus were Hertzog's longstanding ambitions of electoral and territorial segregation achieved, and although African opinion was outraged, this did not compensate for an essential political disarray. In 1935 an All-African Convention was called in Bloemfontein, representing some fifty-three organisations and a host of smaller groups, but it fizzled out in eventual compliance with the new provisions.

It was at this very time that Afrikaner nationalism was mobilising in increasing depth and scope. The Broederbond – the secret organisation which became notorious for its control of the inner sanctums of apartheid – set about establishing the dominance of Afrikaners, socially, politically and economically. A generation of Afrikaner intellectuals, the most prominent among them educated in Europe, traversed the borderlines between nationalism and fascism in their thinking, and came to see communism as the distinct enemy. 'If the worker is drawn away from our nation,' wrote Dr Nic Diederichs, one of the formative apartheid theoreticians, 'then we might as well write Ichabod on the door of our temple . . . There are forces at work in the bosom of the People [*volk*] which seek to unite our workers with the proletariat of other lands . . . The headquarters of this movement is in Moscow . . . In South Africa we believe that the Afrikaner worker is still the most reliable Afrikaner . . . There must be no division or schism between class and class. May the day break here as is the case in Italy and Germany, where the worker may comfort himself with the thought: "What I do here I do as a worker, but I do it in the service of my nation."'

For Bram and Molly and their circle, the name 'Ichabod' had been the matter of a pleasantly convivial joke, but for Diederichs it conveyed a gothic portent and national doom. Others caught up in this swooning mood included Dr H.F. Verwoerd, who had studied at Heidelberg and later became the principal architect of apartheid, as well as Albert Hertzog, son of the General, who had studied at Amsterdam, Leiden and Oxford, and was now attempting to establish trade unions specifically for Afrikaner workers. The ethos of looming crisis, angled back from Europe, gathered hold in South Africa. It was in the light of Bram's experience of the former, and his perception of real danger in the latter, that the question of personal choice became all the more pressing.

The strange thing was that these people all knew one another, and all felt the intensity of the times. Walter Sisulu, then a youthful leader in the ANC, remembered later that in the early 1940s Bram had invited Verwoerd out to lunch in order to convince him to become a socialist. Verwoerd, apparently, had considered the matter, but declined. When Bram was in Europe – so he recalled the story in prison years afterwards – he had come across Albert Hertzog, who deplored the fact that Bram had remained at Oxford, and warned him not to lose his Afrikaner identity. But in this epoch of ideological flux and contest, as the Hertzogs and Verwoerds withdrew into the fortress of nationalism and ethnicity, they could not understand that Bram was drawn to socialism precisely because it enabled him to remain an Afrikaner while envisioning a new and enlarged world of freedom.

In 1932, as Willie Kalk was returning to South Africa after his three-year stint at the Lenin School in Moscow, Bram was just beginning his tour of the Soviet Union with its Intourist (and perhaps OGPU) imprint. In 1935, as the CPSA was falling apart in internal division, he was arriving in Johannesburg to join the Bar. In 1936 and 1937, as he and Molly drew together across their hundreds and thousands of miles, the Hertzog Bills became law. By 1938, as war approached, Bram had more or less settled the questions of identity and ideology that lay within him, but his route, like his route towards Molly, was a circumambient one. It began, oddly enough, where he had left off when he went to Oxford, and where he had experienced his life-changing handshake: with the Joint Council movement.

⚜

The first attempted links between the Communist Party and the Joint Councils were abortive. In June 1923 a letter applying for membership of the Council was received from one Sidney Bunting at Communist Party head-quarters in Trades Hall in Johannesburg on notepaper emblazoned 'Workers of all Countries Unite!' Perhaps Bunting wasn't entirely surprised when he learned that the executive 'could not see its way' to put his name forward for election.

When Bram first arrived in Johannesburg it was perhaps logical, given his background with the Marquards in Bloemfontein, that he should have taken up with the Council yet again. It was for him a known forum, one of the few where whites and blacks interacted, and would have provided a sense of continuity with his previous life. But there were also aspects of his immediate world which might have provided additional inducement. One of the founding members of the Council in 1921 had been Oliver Schreiner (his name listed on the original constitution, as if this were distinction enough, as 'son of the Hon. W.P. Schreiner'), and in 1923 (just about the time that Sidney Bunting's application was being turned down) Bram's other mentor at the Bar, W.H. Ramsbottom, was admitted. In 1933 Schreiner was chair of the Joint Council, and in 1935 it was Ramsbottom: it is hard to believe that either or both did not have a hand in reintroducing Bram. His gravitation towards them might have been conscious or unconscious imitation – their decorous model of social obligation complementing a universally acknowledged professional standing – and from their point of view Bram would have been the most attractive of protégés, part of an ascendancy that would in this way be extended and reproduced. On the Council he also came to know and work with other luminaries in an essentially liberal constellation – Alfred Hoernlé, Professor of Philosophy at the University of the Witwatersrand; J.D. Rheinallt-Jones, 'adviser' to the Institute of Race Relations; Margaret Ballinger, soon to be a representative for Africans in parliament; and Alan Paton, then the warden of Diepkloof Reformatory, later the author of *Cry, the Beloved Country* and leader of the Liberal Party.

As might have been expected in this relatively confined setting, Bram found quick advancement, but its speed did not limit his pleasure. Just before his birthday in April 1936 he wrote to Molly with some pride that he had been elected to the Joint Council executive, and a year later he was appointed honorary treasurer (work which in the main seemed to involve endless chastisements to members to pay their subscriptions, and the balancing of inevitably short budgets through donations – usually from the various mining houses – which in their semi-miraculous exactitude somehow made everything work out down to the last penny). Much of the activity of the Council, aimed at improving life for Africans, would have been familiar from Bloemfontein days. Through endless minutes, memos and deputations the Council attempted to reduce the thousand and one humiliations to which Africans were subjected on a daily basis, whether it be at the post office or on the railways, and it campaigned ceaselessly for improvements in matters both minor and major: the provision of rest rooms for African women, service lifts for 'delivery boys', a more enlightened administration of the pass laws. The presiding assumption may have been of the steady increase of civility through vigilance, respectful challenge and education, but for every grain of sand removed from the oppressive mountain, it looked no less mountainous for that.

Bram played a role in some of these challenges. In August 1935, along with Ramsbottom, Margaret Ballinger and others, he was on a subcommittee that prepared a statement for the Departmental Committee on Natives in Urban Areas, which (when it was produced) sounded very much like Bram's testimony before the Native Economic Commission in Bloemfontein some years before: 'The Joint Council holds that the view that urban areas are exclusively European areas is erroneous because the towns are the product of the joint labours of Europeans and Non-Europeans, and it is too late in the day to repudiate the share of Natives and other Non-Europeans in the development of the towns.' In February 1937 Bram wrote a lengthy memorandum on behalf of the Council for a commission investigating the treatment of Africans by the police. Later that year he was part of a deputation to Pretoria after a particularly vicious round-up of poll-tax offenders, who had been whipped with canes and imprisoned under intolerable conditions. In much of this the liabilities of the Council, working closely with the system it opposed, were as obvious as its virtues – in the case of the poll-tax offenders, who were permitted to pay off their debts through employment in public works, a form of forced labour was substituted for criminalisation – but at least some otherwise wholly unmitigated disasters were partially redeemed.

Bram also became involved in the response to the 1936 Bills, to which the Council, despite its careful approach and sometimes mollifying tones, was thoroughly averse. The ideal of total segregation 'which alone could justify these Bills', declared the Council, was 'an unrealisable dream', and it expressed its deep concern at the 'grave embitterment of race relations' that would result. In January 1936 in Cape Town a conference of all the Joint Councils condemned the abolition of the Cape franchise as 'an unmerited and flagrant injustice to the Bantu race', and passed a unanimous resolution calling for the extension of a qualified franchise to Africans throughout the country. In Johannesburg Bram, together with Rheinallt-Jones, Ramsbottom, Schreiner and Hoernlé, spoke at informational meetings in Eastern and Western Native Townships, as well as in Alexandra Township, just north of the city. When approached by Alfred Hoernlé of the Institute of Race Relations, he prepared summaries and analyses of both the Representation and Land Bills and then, also for the Institute, provided an extended analysis of the Land Bill as it applied to the area of Thaba Nchu. (Bram's main purpose in writing his account was to discover the optimum forms of purchase, transfer and exchange that would maximise the seven and a quarter million morgen to which local Africans would be entitled.)

All of this carried on while he was initiating his career at the Bar, nervously assessing his prospects, learning gold law or avoiding traffic accidents with Tilson Barry, devilling for Schreiner and Ramsbottom, and sustaining his relationship with Molly. Strangely, although Bram was prepared to discuss his legal career and court experiences at length both with her and with his parents, this political side was barely ever mentioned. Perhaps it reflected his continuing uncertainties with Molly, or just his relative priorities (it was Molly's visit at the end of 1936 that made Bram less than willing to work for the Barolong in Thaba Nchu); perhaps it was only after he and Molly were married that his political direction became completely clear. But for the moment his engagement on the Council was evident enough to some, and was duly recognised as such. In February 1937 Bram was invited to become one of the two Joint Council representatives (one white, one black) on the executive of the Institute of Race Relations. The immediate reason for this was that Oliver Schreiner, though remaining on the executive, would no longer be representing the Joint Council, and Bram was to be the assigned replacement. Once again he seemed to be following a pre-ordained path within a pre-ordained network. In 1938 Ramsbottom, like Schreiner, became a judge, and if Bram had continued to follow his mentors perhaps a judgeship too would have been his.

Bram remained on the Joint Council and on the Institute of Race Relations into the war years, to participate in their myriad campaigns – whether on the abysmal treatment of Africans at the pass offices, on freehold title in the townships, on milk bars to provide milk for children, or on the 1941 Factories Bill, which further limited the rights and benefits of black workers. Yet there may have been a change of mood for him at this time. In the event neither the Joint Council nor the Institute of Race Relations could prevent the passage of the 1936 Bills, and as the legislation went through its final reformulations their opposition lost momentum and faltered. For all the defensive and recuperative work of the liberal organisations, and their undoubted moral commitment, the essential weakness of an endless reformism may have become increasingly apparent.

It was this that the Communist Party stressed in an even stronger form. Reporting on the Cape Town Joint Council conference of January 1936, *Umsebenzi* commented that its resolutions expressed the hatred of the Hertzog Bills felt 'by the whole Bantu race and by many Europeans' who were not blinded by colour prejudice. Yet, remarked *Umsebenzi*, the essential question was whether anyone paid any attention: 'Herein lies the weakness of the Joint Council movement. The Joint Councils are actually of service to the slave government of this country. They provide an outlet for those members of the

Bantu race who wish to let off steam, to utter their protest against intolerable injustice. The Councils are rather like a safety valve. They delude those who wish to protest against injustice, against colour bar legislation, into thinking that they are accomplishing something when they pass resolutions of protest, recommendations to this Government, etc. As regards the Europeans, too, the Joint Councils are useful to the exploiting class, whose aim is to maintain the Bantu in their present condition of semi-slavery and even to increase the severity of the exploitation in order to rake in more profits.' On the Joint Council, maintained *Umsebenzi*, advanced members of both races might protest to their hearts' content; the government, undisturbed by their eloquence, went on to frame yet more oppressive measures.

This was a standard, even predictable radical critique, some of which might have seemed unfair to Bram: his intention was not to be 'useful' to the exploiting class, and *Umsebenzi* could not have meant that it would have been better if no voices had been raised in protest. But as to the impotence that *Umsebenzi* pointed out, there was something in it that he might have felt to be true. Though the principles of Bram's white and African colleagues were impeccably worthy, neither the Joint Councils nor the Institute of Race Relations could be the locus of real opposition to a gathering segregation. Perhaps the very nature and form of those bodies softened the force of, as well as enabled, their principles. At any rate, as time went on, Bram's involvement with both the Council and the Institute diminished. In 1938 he attended only three of ten Joint Council meetings; in 1940 it was one of eleven. By May 1941 he was no longer treasurer of the Joint Council, and had resigned from its executive as well as that of the Institute of Race Relations. This was just one month before the Nazi invasion of the Soviet Union, which possibly sealed things for Bram once and for all.

Yet whether he joined the Communist Party when that invasion occurred or before, two points are clear. One is that if Bram was a member of the Party before the war, then he continued to work with liberals after he joined. The other is that if he did not become a member until after the Nazi invasion, this did not prevent him, within an essentially liberal constituency, from edging close to communism. Perhaps it was just a reflection of the reigning policy of the united front; perhaps it was Bram's sustained drive towards inclusivity. Or perhaps the divide was not as wide as *Umsebenzi* had proposed. In 1946 one of the new members of the Joint Council executive was Oliver Tambo, soon to set up law offices with Nelson Mandela, and there he did the same kind of necessary and impossible committee work that Bram Fischer had done before him.

There were other, more visceral dimensions to contend with.

> *YOU! BLADY BASTARD!*
> *I defy you to read this letter at your meeting publicly – I don't suppose that you have enough guts to do it – Am specially writing this in large letters and distinctly as an ignorant idiot like you may not be able to read it other-wise and I do want you to read this letter.*
> *I don't know yet – what you are – a bastard fool – Lunatic – Mampara or what – I shall write and tell you after your meeting and when I saw and heard you I may [?] be able to judge – but one thing I am certain and that is that* Y O U   A R E   A   B L A D Y   IGNORANT   GOD   DAMNED   F O O L *and that is putting it mildly.*
> > *Your statistics for instance*
> > A R E   A L L   B A L L S *!!!*

This, one of the less appetising documents of South African history, was a forgery, meant to have been sent to the South African National Democratic Movement by a Jewish correspondent. In fact it was a libel put out by the SANDM, in order to 'prove' the obscenity of the Jews, and stoke up anti-Semitic feeling. In the wake of Hitler's rise to power in Germany, such affronts were not rare. In Port Elizabeth an inflammatory document purportedly 'stolen' from a synagogue was read out at a meeting of the South African Gentile National Socialist Movement (later the South African National Party, otherwise known as the Greyshirts), where the audience punctuated the proceedings with shouts of 'Heil!' In the small town of Dalton a Nazi meeting was addressed by one Ray Rudman who spoke (for three and a half hours) of Jews as 'snakes' and 'filthy poisonous reptiles' and much else. In Cape Town, a pamphlet put out by one J.H.H. de Waal wondered, 'Who would waste a bullet on any Jew?' The 'leader-in-chief' of the Greyshirts was one Louis Weichardt, and the organ of his movement, Die Waarheid / The Truth, displayed his uni-formed presence below two stark swastikas as South Africa's putative Führer. The Greyshirt anthem began (unambivalently, if with imprecise scansion), 'Watch in the world the Swastika/ The sign of awakening nations!/ The Greyshirts march in South Africa/ To free us from Jewish exploitations!'

The Institute of Race Relations took a secret interest in these movements and collected whatever material it could – to the point of humouring its enthusiasts (one of them the appropriately named E. Sauerländer) in order to gather information. But though the Greyshirts were on the fringe, there was nothing humorous about them, as their influence spread wider and developed long-lasting echoes. Oswald Pirow, Hertzog's Minister of Justice, had formed his own quasi-fascist organisation, the

New Order. Dr D.F. Malan, leader of the National Party government in 1948, campaigned to set an embargo on Jewish immigration from Europe, and in 1939 Eric Louw, later Minister of Foreign Affairs, introduced a private member's Bill in parliament for the same purpose. In 1941 the Transvaal section of the National Party banned Jews from becoming members – a prohibition that lasted until 1951. B.J. Vorster, Prime Minister during the 1970s, was interned at Koffiefontein during the war for being a general in the Ossewabrandwag [Ox-wagon Sentinel], a pro-Nazi paramilitary movement. Later, during the 1960s, Dr Louis Weichardt, ex-Führer of the Greyshirts, became a National Party Senator, at the very time when the African National Congress, in conflict with an apartheid system ridden with this heritage, found itself fighting the most desperate struggle just to stay alive as an organisation.

In the 1930s there was behind-the-scenes contact between the Institute of Race Relations and the South African Jewish Board of Deputies. One outcome was an organisation called the Society of Jews and Christians, whose aim was to resist the fascist incursion into South Africa; its journal, Common Sense *(edited by Amelia Levy), published some of the earliest short stories of Nadine Gordimer and Doris Lessing. In 1939 Bram Fischer became a member of the society, along with his future comrade Brian Bunting (son of Sidney Bunting, who had been rejected by the Joint Council in 1923) and others such as J.D. Rheinallt-Jones, Alfred Hoernlé and Sarah Gertrude Millin. With some variation it was a familiar constituency, the expression of civil solidarity across a broad front. No matter what Bram's specific reasons were for joining the Communist Party, and no matter what the criss-crossing logics of such associations, there could be no doubt that the Nazi alternative was an enemy that needed every form of resistance, in South Africa as everywhere else.*

After Bram and Molly were married they took a lazy honeymoon, motoring by car via Aliwal North and Engcobo through the wild and beautiful approaches to Port St Johns, on the Indian Ocean in the Transkei. From there Molly, now more tranquil, wrote to Percy and Ella that if they 'really were behind the bushes at the same wedding' she was, they may have realised it was the loveliest one any bride could attend.

Back at 29 Westcliff Park by October, they settled into an unaccustomed routine after all the years apart. They had a new DKW car, bought as a wedding present from Percy for the princely sum of £183. Bram's cases took up again, and on occasion Molly came to his office in the evening while he worked, bringing her dog David for company. She teased Percy and Ella about his sustained anxiety, saying he wished for difficult work when it was easy, and easy work when it was difficult: 'Evidently no barrister is ever satisfied with the amount or kind of work he gets . . . I've learned just to wish for whatever Bram is wishing at the moment.' In March 1938 Bram defended a mine captain on a charge of negligence in the death underground of an African worker – one of the only times he acted directly against a mineworker's interests, though Bram was disappointed to lose the case. His name was now sometimes in the newspapers, the sign of an increasingly successful practice, and Molly boasted to his parents that whereas the leading junior at the Bar had argued only two appeals, Bram (with half the years of experience) had dealt with more of them than he could count.

Every now and then they were invited to Irene, near Pretoria, to see Molly's Aunt Isie and her husband, General Smuts. There Bram would be relieved when the General was in a talkative mood, discoursing on South African history and – his passion – mountain climbing. 'He struck me as a man of unbounded energy,' Bram wrote to Percy and Ella, 'but with a marked prejudice against the Blacks, though that may have been my imagination.' Ella would arrive at the flat for a visit, and depart leaving hidden bottles of whisky as gifts, for which Bram accused her of being 'a crook' and a 'very foolish woman'. The Afrikaans version of her novel, *Die Loutering van Petrus*, was at last being published, and received a favourable review in Bloemfontein's English newspaper, *The Friend*, but not in the Afrikaans *Volksblad*. Bram thought this entirely inevitable, and Molly asked Ella if she now expected to be ostracised by all the Free State *dominees*: 'It should be rather fun if you go round on circuit & the parsons looked straight through you while they shook hands with the Judge.' Bram remarked that the novel was 'more thoughtful than 99% of our Afrikaans books', but said that for him it was so much part of his mother that he was unable to judge it objectively: 'I become much too emotional when I read it.'

If Ella's aim in the novel was to develop a more broadminded and tolerant Afrikaner culture, she may have had the same intention in agreeing to address the Voortrekker memorialists passing through Bloemfontein in their ox-wagons en route to Pretoria for the centenary celebrations of 1938. In the event her speech was broadcast over the radio, but Bram, in Johannesburg, managed to miss it. He was having dinner at 'Mac' Macdonald's, and (as both he and Mac were without a radio) said they had all rushed down to the nearest café to hear it, but arrived only after his mother had spoken. This wasn't necessarily intentional: although the 1938 centenary marked one of the peaks of the decade's Afrikaner nationalist revival (with somewhat melodramatic scenes as the pilgrims in their iconic nineteenth-century dress passed by, town by town, to Pretoria), Bram was sure that Ella would not give a predictable account, and pronounced himself delighted at her invitation. So did Molly, though she teased again: 'We've already been picturing you in a "kappie" and an uncomfortable dress . . . But seriously, we're terribly thrilled.'

Soon Molly was pregnant with the child who would become Ruth, and reported that she was kicked about so much at certain times of the night that she fully expected a boy, or twins. 'All my friends think I'll have a son,' she told Percy and Ella. 'No one wants to let me have the daughter I've always wanted.' She began to prepare for the arrival, but all of this became more complicated because she and Bram were now also looking for a house, a hectic and often depressing search in which Bram and Molly could either find nothing in their range, or else made offers only to see them fall through. Bram was his usual conscientious if not obsessive self. Percy had offered financial help (he couldn't take it elsewhere, he had told Molly, 'owing to the lack of pockets in an angel's garb'), and Bram now discussed everything in the minutest detail with his father, how much he could afford, how much he would need to borrow, how soon he would pay it all back. Then, just at the right moment, good luck arrived, though of an oblique kind and tinged with sadness. Aunt Maggie, the daughter of Oupa Abraham's 'mother aunt' in Cape Town, died and left Bram £2200. He and Molly bought a plot in Oaklands, a new area opening up in the north-eastern suburbs of Johannesburg, and, with £1000 borrowed from Percy and a design by the architect Norman Eaton, began building in December 1938.

Exactly a week after Bram's birthday in 1939 they moved in, finding their way among the workmen who had not quite finished. (Bram roped in his brothers Gus and Piet for the move.) He and Molly planted seedlings they had been preparing (all Molly's favourite blue flowers for the garden), and later Bram's brother Paul brought in saplings of *witstinkhout* that had originated on Oupa Abraham's farm. Molly was concerned that plans for the house were getting out of hand (Percy and Ella had suggested wildly elaborate tea-cupboards with built-in taps in the dining-room) and, just before they moved in, made last-minute changes to the design of the porch. But then, as she put it, they had to get things right, because this was a house that had to last a lifetime. Bringing Molly's second dog, Ripple, from Pretoria to join David, they arrived. The address was 12 Beaumont Street, Oaklands. Because the area leading up to the front door needed to be levelled, they brought in prison labourers to remove the rocks.

At the time of the Munich Conference of September 1938, when Neville Chamberlain brought back his famous piece of white paper bearing Hitler's 'guarantee' of peace in Europe, Bram wrote to Percy and Ella that it looked as if the British and French were about to buy their security at the cost of selling out Czechoslovakia: 'I think they're going to be treated more shoddily by Chamberlain than we were by his father!' The Prime Minister of England was the son of Joseph Chamberlain, Oupa Abraham's ancient antagonist, and for Bram the hypocrisy and treachery of imperialism existed along an unbroken historical continuum. In the event the concessions made by Chamberlain and the French Prime Minister, Daladier, to Hitler's demands for the partition of Czechoslovakia became emblematic for him. A year later he read G.E.R. Gedye's *Fallen Bastions*, which catalogued in passionate detail the sequence of Allied betrayals leading up to the Second World War and suggested strongly that socialism was the only alternative to fascism. For years afterwards Bram recommended the book to others wishing to find out the truth of those years.

It was just at this time that Percy and Ella were about to find out something of that truth themselves, for during Percy's long leave in the first half of 1939 they did something utterly foolhardy or glorious (depending on one's perspective), undertaking an extended tour by boat to the Far East and Europe. Setting sail in January they stopped in at Zanzibar, Mombasa and the Seychelles on their way to Singapore, Shanghai and Hong Kong, where Japanese aggression was intensifying. Then they returned via Ceylon and Port Said towards a Europe under the gathering shadow of Hitler.

'Lots of love,' wrote Molly as they left, 'and don't get lost or killed in the wars.' Bram expatiated on the theme with a degree of sardonic emphasis. 'I am still trying to fathom why I should be blessed with a father and mother', he wrote to Percy and Ella, 'who in a comfortable middle age wish to visit all the centres of warfare & incendiarism & slaughter (during their vacation, mark you) in this year of Grace 1939. Of course if you hurry back from the East you may still be able to catch the tail end of the Spanish War by landing somewhere in Spain first, before going on into Europe for the major conflagration.' Yet there was also a certain pride at Percy and Ella's sheer daring, if not brazen perversity: '(as a secret)', conceded Bram, 'I am also glad that I have parents who in their comfortable middle age are not afraid of visiting Shanghai just when the Japanese are considering taking over complete military control in order to prevent all their puppet Chinese ministers from being murdered.'

Letters such as these gave clues about Bram's world-view, and he was more than prepared to elaborate as, half frantic with worry at certain moments while Percy and Ella sailed blithely on, he relayed to them the urgent news he feared they would otherwise not be able to obtain. 'Hitler marched into Czechoslovakia yesterday afternoon,' Bram wrote on 15 March, as the Germans (after the earlier Sudetenland concessions) now began their obliteration of the entire country, '& today his troops have occupied Prague . . . Chamberlain & Daladier are certainly not going to do anything & so in spite of all our guarantees to the Czechs there will be no war. Well, I suppose as we pass each crisis successfully we all grow a little older & less likely to be called out . . . but that is really all that can be said for this way of avoiding war. Perhaps it is the only realistic outlook. But when it comes that war will be so much the worse for us.'

The key, thought Bram, as he tried to digest the implications of a newly transforming world, was what was happening in Spain. Hitler and Mussolini, he suggested to his parents, would not make demands on the West until, with their help, Republican Spain had been finished off: 'But heaven knows what they won't demand once Spain capitulates. That they will do something towards the West I'm certain, because I am convinced that H. is not going to move against Russia yet, where he knows he will meet with immediate resistance and not with Chamberlain.' Bram's assessment of Chamberlain's vacillation was in tune with a good deal of public opinion, but his other emphases revealed an underlying tendency. The contrast, increasingly for Bram, was between Western connivance with Hitler and Soviet resolve, and in the forced pace of the moment his view was gravitating leftwards, if not explicitly towards the standard communist position.

Certainly this was the analysis emanating from Moscow and elsewhere – the expectation of Western betrayal linked both Stalinists and Trotskyists – that French and British imperialism would concede everything in Czechoslovakia and Poland to protect its own interests. Just five days before Hitler marched into Prague, Stalin had announced this at the eighteenth Party congress in Moscow: 'Britain and France . . . have rejected the policy of collective security, of collective resistance, and have taken up a policy of nonintervention, of neutrality . . . The policy of nonintervention means conniving at aggression, giving free rein to war.' And, as Stalin continued to argue, the real target in this would be the Soviet Union, to be destroyed into the bargain as the final trade-off for peace in the West. 'Just start war on the Bolsheviks,' as he put it succinctly, 'and everything will be all right.' It was this line of thinking that led him into the machinations of the Nazi–Soviet Pact, concluded with Hitler in August of that year. As for Bram, the fact that he expected more resolve from Stalin rather than Chamberlain was in the event somewhat ironic; yet if he was to follow the demanding logic of the Pact, then in tracking this continuing saga of betrayal and abandonment it was evident that his mind was being prepared. Years later he told Mary Benson (using the orthodox defence of the day) that Western governments had let the world down to the point where Stalin was forced into the Pact to play for time.

Meanwhile Bram did everything he could to make sure his parents did not find themselves caught up in the conflict. In Johannesburg he went to the 1926 Club to hear Oswald Pirow, who had been to Europe and met Hitler. (Pirow's assurances on the paired honesty of Hitler and Chamberlain, reported Bram, made him despair.) One of his friends from Oxford, Len Klatzow, was also visiting, and gave news of the successive crises in Britain. Somewhere in the midst of the frenzy and tension Bram found what respite and light relief he could. He told Percy and Ella about the cricket test between England and South Africa at Durban, played under 'timeless' rules, which had been called off after ten days without result when the visitors (on a score of 650 runs for five wickets in their second innings) had to catch their boat home. 'So much', wrote Bram, 'for timeless tests.'

But mainly he continued to plead with his parents to be careful, and espe-cially – after the invasion of Czechoslovakia – not to land in Italy and travel on to Germany as planned. In the wake of the invasion Bram reported that Chamberlain was now making more belligerent noises, even as Hitler made new demands on Poland. Bram's thought, following the model of past experi-ence, was that both Chamberlain and the Polish Foreign Minister would let him have his way. Yet the opposite was also possible, and at the end of March he warned Percy and Ella with an especial urgency and tenderness: 'Now darlings, if Poland does fight, France must come in & England will follow. The result will be that quite possibly within 24 hours of the start the whole of Europe will be in it. *So don't land at Genoa.*' With pressing communications such as these Bram succeeded in persuading Percy and Ella to land in England before deciding about the Continent ('I'm just praying', he wrote on 12 April, 'that this is a letter which will welcome you to England and not one which will never reach you because the Germans or Italians do not deliver letters to their concentration camps'), but even then reports of crises and conscription in Bri-tain made him nervous. The news arriving in South Africa, he told Percy and Ella, led one to believe that the whole world would blow up at any minute.

Through it all Bram mixed his exhortations with a certain humour and refusal to panic. Ultimately, Percy and Ella did travel on to Germany, where they remained from mid-May until about mid-June. Ella sent Bram and Molly a picturesque card from Baden-Baden which mentioned nothing about the Nazis or the war. To add to her idiosyncrasies, she appeared to be quite fond of the Germans, even in militarist mood. When Bram wrote to welcome them back as (surprisingly undamaged) they sailed into Cape Town in mid-July, it was with a mixture of relief and barely restrained emphasis on this point that he did so: 'When you read this (it will be read within three days) you will be safely in Table Bay, having escaped Japanese gunboats & mines, Italian submarines & German wars (Yes Ma, German wars, I insist, in spite of their nice agricultural plots and friendly natures!)' For Ella it was perhaps, thinking back to the Boer War, because the Germans were against Britain. As for Percy, he managed, in the Far East, to steal a cutting of a rare aloe to plant at Harmonie, and on his return was made Judge-President of the Free State.

⁂

In February 1939 Bram was appointed a lecturer in law at the University of the Witwatersrand. In that same month he began wearing his first pair of glasses, though he had been shortsighted at least since his Oxford days. In April he and Molly moved into 12 Beaumont Street, Oaklands, where they did live for something like a lifetime. On 14 August, after Molly had booked herself into the nursing home for the customary fourteen days, Ruth was born, a day before she was due. In September Molly reported that she would go into Ruth's room during the night just to see that she was still breathing, because she slept so quietly. One night Molly developed severe pain in one breast and a fever. Although she didn't tell Bram at the time, she couldn't take her mind off her mother's breast cancer; that was how her mother had died. When she recovered, Bram told Percy and Ella he knew what was important to him: 'I really don't care what happens in Europe.'

These then were the conjunctions: the house that in due course became a symbol of what Bram and Molly represented; the birth of their child Ruth, so long awaited; the war that seemed so inevitable. The future, the past and the present: it was a defining, clarifying time.

⁂

It is difficult to say exactly when Bram Fischer became a member of the Communist Party. The Party itself has no record, and if records were kept by the Security Police in Pretoria (shredded now, or unshredded) or in some archive in Moscow, I have not been able to trace them. Moreover, virtually everyone I have spoken to or corresponded with has given me a different account.

There were those with Bram at Oxford who believed he was a communist at the time; there was his brother Gus's recollection that Bram claimed to be close to communism when he returned to South Africa. Their other brother Paul recalled that when he was a medical student in Johannesburg in the

1930s Bram used to discuss communism with him and recommended the Marxist classics, which made him draw the obvious conclusions. According to some of Bram's early colleagues at the Bar, his communist sympathies were well known, as was the fact that he associated with communists. Yet there is a difference between being close to communism in one's mind, associating with communists, or even claiming to be one, and being a formal member of the Communist Party – and no one has been able to say with any certainty that Bram was a member at this early stage.

It is conceivable that he joined the Party at Oxford, and was a secret member on his return. This was, after all, the era of the Cambridge spies (Kim Philby's definitive experience had – in a manner akin to Bram's – been in Vienna in 1934), and suspicions remained long after about an equivalent Oxford circle. In the South African setting such things occurred, although this had less to do with espionage than infiltration: Hilda Watts (later Hilda Bernstein) came out to South Africa from England as a communist 'sleeper' to join the Labour League of Youth, and E.J. Burford, of the Labour Party, was also an underground member of the CPSA. Edwin Mofutsanyana, who appeared to have had some dealings with Bram in the 1930s in the formation of the African Mineworkers' Union, maintained that Bram joined the Party 'long before the war', and hinted that he might have been a secret member. Other of Bram's comrades said his sense of integrity would have precluded any such dissimulation – which may have been a naive view, since he was certainly capable of concealment later in his life. Yet the argument against the possibility probably rests on less dramatic grounds: it would hardly have been the practice of any underground member of the Party to make his sympathies for communism so evident, and it seems that Bram – whether to his fellow students, his father or his colleagues – made no bones about it.

According to George Bizos, who assisted Bram many years later when he prepared his speech from the dock, Bram's own account was that he 'considered himself' a member of the Party by 1938, and that Yusuf Dadoo (the militant leader of the Transvaal Indian Congress and future leader of the CPSA) had been the one to recruit him. The phrase 'considered himself' was perhaps a careful and flexible one, admitting the same doubts on a formal membership of the Party as might have applied a few years earlier. (Bizos thought the CPSA may not have been completely 'open' about membership until Hilda Watts established a certain legitimacy by winning a seat on the Johannesburg City Council in 1943.) But the 1938 date was Bram's own recollection, and it is supported by the views of people such as E.J. Burford, who indicated that Bram was known to him as a member by 1939.

Yet others have clouded these waters, or been equally certain about other dates. Issy Heymann remembered that when they were together in prison, Bram told him that he had come late into the Party, and wished it had been earlier. Ray Alexander, trade union organiser and Party member from Cape Town, had the clearest memory of meeting Bram for the first time on 30 or 31 October 1940 at the CPSA offices in Progress Buildings in Johannesburg. Bram had just been coming out of the lift, and Michael Harmel – clearly thrilled that Bram, with his auspicious Afrikaner background, should have joined the Party – introduced them. According to Ray Alexander (who seemed, when we discussed the matter, to have a memory that transfixed its distant target like an arrow), Bram was not at the annual conference of the CPSA in 1940, but did attend the one in Cape Town in April the following year; she felt, therefore, that he may have joined by the October that she met him. Yet Rowley Arenstein was sure that Bram joined in 1942, pointing out that he had good reason to know because he was a member of the Johannesburg secretariat, and Bram's application landed on his desk just before he was transferred to Durban. Sonia Bunting (Bram's comrade, married to Brian Bunting) was also sure it was 1942, because she remembered that she, Molly, Bram and Joe Slovo all joined during the same year. If this was true, however, it could not have been at exactly the same time, because Joe Slovo recalled that when he joined the Party in 1942, he found Bram already a member.

There are ways of joining a movement, of being 'recruited' at one moment and later on filling in an application, and in some ways it may make a difference. If Bram joined the Communist Party in 1938, then he was fully part of the ideological gymnastics that accompanied the Nazi–Soviet Pact of 1939. Inwardly, he would have faced the difficult task of overturning all the convictions he had voiced to his parents on the absolute need to resist Hitler, and the same would have been true if he became a member in 1940. Either then or in 1938 he would have joined in the face of the show trials of the 1930s in the Soviet Union – evidence of Stalin's unadorned power only underlined by the murder of Trotsky in 1940. If Bram became a member of the CPSA during these years, in other words, there was quite a lot that he would have had to swallow, and he would have been confronted unavoidably with the issue of personal and political compromise. But if he joined in 1942, then it might have seemed more legitimate, for after the German invasion of the Soviet Union in June 1941 all doubts were suspended and no explanations were required. As the Nazis crashed through the Russian defences, the USSR joined the historic fight against fascism, and at last Bram's hatred of Hitler would have found appropriate expression.

But if one has already joined in one's heart, then perhaps explanations are required after all. Bram's boyhood friend from Grey College, Joel Mervis, who had then just switched careers, from law to journalism, told the story of a dinner party he hosted, probably in 1940, or at least before the German invasion of Russia. The guest of honour was Malcolm Muggeridge, who had written to such effect on the horrors of collectivisation during the early 1930s (persuading Bram's friend Geoffrey Cox, but not Bram himself, of the excesses of Stalinism), and who was now visiting Johannesburg, staying at Mervis's house. At the dinner party, according to Mervis, Muggeridge and Bram had the equivalent of a three-hour stand-up debate on the question of Bram's commitment to Russia and his attitude to the war, while some thirty other guests looked on in silent and awed fascination. Bram's position was that, without giving any credit to Hitler, he was not prepared to fight any capitalist war. On the question of the show trials, he maintained that the accused had had a defence, that they had confessed, that all the rest was Western propaganda. It was the communist position of the day, and Mervis had no doubt that Bram was a communist. Later, when Germany invaded the Soviet Union, Bram was all for fighting the war.

On another level, therefore, it did not matter when he filled in his application. There is a temptation to think that all would be explained if one could fix the exact date when Bram Fischer joined the Communist Party: this would be the moment of conversion, commitment, rebirth. Without the knowledge (I felt this up to a certain stage as I tracked the information with an ever-increasing sense of need) there is a gap at the centre of this story. Yet, it may be more than simply making a virtue of necessity to suggest that the absence of certainty may lead towards a deeper understanding. Births are preceded by gestation, there is seldom an instantaneous conversion, commitments and ideologies are discontinuous or superimposed in the mind, and history for the individual as for society operates in layered components of time.

Bram worked with liberals even as he drew close to the Communist Party; he could (it appears) be as hard-line as anyone else on the capitalist war, even as he was content to represent the mining companies as a lawyer or use prison labour for his house. He was resolute about the evils of Nazism, yet believed that when his mother addressed Voortrekker nationalists she was enlarging the ambit and orbit of civilisation. Along with many others he was prepared to credit show trials, although justice was his passionate regard. Yet, if the world progressed by contraries, this was not all evidence simply of confusion or personal failing, the sense of moral consistency that emerges only too slowly and imprecisely. Bram was metaphysical to the extent that he believed in a perfectible world, earthly in that he knew it could be achieved only by means that were never quite perfect. History proceeded from what existed to the not-yet-quite imaginable, and along with the sense of conviction was the awareness of a path that dipped into and out of sight. Decades later Bram would say, in response to Stalin's revealed crimes, that communists now knew what dangers they had to avoid, but that this did not invalidate their fundamental direction or objective. Then, as in the case of the Nazi–Soviet Pact, it was his particular capacity for loyalty that would have locked him on track; after all, it was when times were difficult and vision obscured that one's faith and fidelity were required most of all. After Bram's period of 'conversion' to communism, it was not as if these complexities disappeared.

Molly remarked later to her daughter Ruth that after she and Bram were married they began to look at their surroundings in Johannesburg – Bram's colleagues collecting art, living their easeful existences at golf and country clubs – and knew that it wasn't for them. Joining up – all the aspects of their lives – gave them a wider meaning and larger sense of purpose. Johannesburg was still an alien city for both, but perhaps it could be made into the definition of a new kind of home. They were married now, in a new house, their daughter born, and after all their travelling may have been freed to think of other momentous horizons, in time as well as space. After Bram's experience in Europe, his perspective was insistently global as well as local; with the world in crisis he now gravitated towards his own confrontation with choice. Together the urgencies of that larger perspective as well as the dynamics of the South African setting reinforced a recognition already gathering towards realisation – that the search for peace and justice would have to take on radically new forms and implications. Bram had been born to leadership and responsibility; these were in the range and repertoire of his life's possibilities and expectations. It may have seemed like the historic epoch: it meant taking on a new world in every sense in which that could affect one's being.

So it did not matter whether Bram joined the Communist Party in 1938 or 1940 or 1942: he joined at all of these times, and – with all the complexity, vision and contradiction of such a commitment – continued to do so for the rest of his life.

⁂

There is a photograph of Bram Fischer on the Johannesburg district committee of the Communist Party, taken at the annual conference of 1945. In the picture he is standing, dressed in a white open-necked shirt, a jacket with wide lapels, and darker trousers; he is slight, hair short, features slender, wearing glasses with round lenses and thin metal frames; his head is peaked to the left, a confident smile turned slightly downwards. Bram is there among his comrades – Solomon Buirski, Issy Wolfson, Josie Mpama, Hilda Watts, Eli Weinberg, Yusuf Dadoo, Ben Mnisi, Michael Harmel, Danie du Plessis (chair of the committee and, like Bram, an Afrikaner). Though the photograph is a formal one, there is an intimacy about it, and each face has its own presence. Bram looks open: one would do things for him, never turn him away. The photograph shows a good moment, a look of modest triumph, belief and conviction: here is a band of comrades tied to one another by friendship and mutual care as much as by mission. The war is nearly over; fascism abroad is about to be vanquished, and at home the Party has never been stronger. Their eyes seem to say it: there is a long journey ahead, but they are ready for whatever comes their way.

CHAPTER 7

WAR AND PEACE

June 1941 – June 1950

W hen Bram heard the news of the German invasion of the Soviet Union on 22 June 1941, his response was exhilarated, full of the fear and excitement and adrenalin of the moment, still disbelieving of any slander against Russia, still imprinted with suspicion of the West. One week into the new conflict he wrote to his parents: 'It's very difficult to work in these days. We've borrowed a radio from Pauline [Molly's sister]. We hang on that all night & I spend the days talking or reading all the newsprint that's put out in the Transvaal. What a blow for the Russians to be dragged into this. Not that they were not expecting it. They were keyed up for it when I was there in 1932 & I'm sure they knew to the minute when it was coming. Hence I find something mildly humorous in Churchill's statement that he warned Stalin some months ago. Well the next few months will show. If Russia beats off this attack, I think it's more or less the end of capitalist Europe. God help us all if she doesn't. And she'll have to do it all on her own because there's no time to get any help to her. That is if anyone really wants to help her. If she holds over for 6 months I'm putting my money on a gradual dying out of the war in the west. However, some time we might have a full and uncensored discussion. For the moment it looks as if the Russians are being successful with the very tactics which they have practised for many years – using their plains for a war of real movement. If it comes off – watch for a Russian counter-offensive through the northern Balkans and Czechoslovakia where they'll get enormous support from the common people.'

Whether Bram was officially a member of the Communist Party or not, and no matter how much his views had been censored for the public mails, there could have been no doubt as to where his heart lay, or on his feeling that the history and future of the whole world was concentrated in this moment. Just over a month later his sense of justification was physically palpable: 'Well, six weeks of the real war are over. Has history ever in so short a time vindicated a much maligned nation. What about the Finnish War & the entry into Poland or Bessarabia now? Golly, those Russians must be fighting like tigers. I don't pretend to prophecy – how far the Germans will get – but that they will eventually be beaten by the Soviets is I think beyond any doubt. This victory may of course come sooner than any of us expect, but by jove, when it does come you'll see things moving faster than they've ever moved in the history of this jolly old world before. I'm looking forward to a nice long argument when we meet again. But just consider Stalin's statesmanship in the meanwhile. Two years ago he was facing the almost immediate attack by Germany, France & Chamberlain (America as a junior). Now, for the time being at any rate, he has England and Roosevelt on his side!'

For Bram the inner logic of Stalin's genius had been revealed, and the invasion had brought a wider vindication for the Communist Party. In September 1939, when South Africa followed Britain into the war (Smuts rather than Hertzog winning the vote in parliament and being appointed Prime Minister by the Governor-General), the Communist Party had been left in a lamentable and invidious position. Communists had claimed to be the most resolute opponents of fascism, but now there was the uncomfortable matter, rather difficult to ignore, of the Nazi–Soviet Pact. If the Party opposed the war, it would, by default, risk aligning itself with the pro-fascist Afrikaner nationalist forces. Yet how could it support a war in which an unfree South Africa would be venturing abroad to fight for freedom, in which black South Africans, subject to a form of fascism at home, were expected to die in the struggle against it overseas? An editorial in the *Transvaal Communist* just before the war had outlined this principle: 'If we are to fight for democracy we must have some kind of democracy to defend.' But if such formulations permitted the CPSA to maintain a posture of resistance in South Africa while keeping faith with the Soviet Union, it provided only lukewarm comfort at best. The African National Congress, representing the mass of the people whom the Communist Party claimed to speak for, gave its official support to the war.

Brittle rhetoric was the surface manifestation of an inner tenuousness. When the conflict began in September 1939, a Johannesburg district committee pamphlet suggested that 'Smuts had no hesitation in dragging the people of South Africa into this bloody war fought in the interests of the rival ruling classes of Britain and Germany for the right to exploit the oppressed colonial natives'. At the same time the CPSA attempted to convince Afrikaner nationalists that their natural allies were the blacks, because 'they had suffered the most under imperialism'. Pamphlets in Afrikaans spoke in lurid terms of the 'smeary, stinking condition of capitalism in its putrefaction', the origin of this and every other war. Added to the Party's problems were international embarrassments, when the Soviet Union occupied eastern Poland under the provisions of the Nazi–Soviet Pact, or invaded Finland, ostensibly to protect the approaches to Leningrad, and suffered severe losses in the process. The Party newspaper declared that Finland was the 'fifth column' of world reaction, explaining that the Soviet Union's only intention was 'to free the workers of Finland from their oppressors, the Finnish capitalists and landlords' – salvation it had already provided for the Poles. But given the Pact with the Nazis it could only sound like defensive (and unconvincing) pleading.

It is not easy to judge what was going on in the minds of individual members; probably there was no absolute bad faith involved. Communists, for whom the Soviet Union was as much *their* country as the one they happened to live in – the 'first fortress of the world's workers', as the phrase had it – were deeply concerned about its fate in a supremely hostile environment, surrounded, as they felt, by enemies on every side. It was taken for granted that no real news could be expected from the capitalist press, and even fashioning a sense of what was happening overseas was in these circumstances relatively difficult. There could also be no doubt about the Party's local commitment when someone such as Yusuf Dadoo, in his capacity as leader of the Non-European United Front, was prepared to risk prison for his impassioned and deeply felt appeals to Africans to resist the war overseas until they were granted the right to live as human beings in South Africa.

Still, when Hitler finally committed himself to Operation Barbarossa and his forces invaded the USSR in the early hours of 22 June, it must have come almost as a relief to many communists, as at last their ingrained anti-fascist instincts could find public expression. The turnabout was as swift as the German attack, and the anti-war policy of two years went into sudden reverse. 'ALL SUPPORT FOR SOVIET UNION', declared the *Guardian* newspaper of 26 June, 'DEFEND THE CAUSE OF LIBERTY, DEMOCRACY AND HUMAN DECENCY'. It went on to explain how circumstances now were quite different from what they had been before. Previously the war had been an imperialist conflict for the redivision of the world's markets, colonies and spheres of interest, but the Soviet Union was neither fascist nor imperialist. On the contrary, the defeat of the Soviet Union would be the greatest triumph that capitalism could achieve, while the victory of the Soviet Union would mean the destruction of fascism. The Communist Party of South Africa had no hesitation, the *Guardian* reported, 'in calling upon the people to stand by the Soviet Union'.

As for Bram, he became involved virtually immediately. In the first week after the invasion, on 24 June, he was invited to present a six-minute talk on Russia (whether because he had been there in 1932 and was therefore an 'expert', or as a representative of the Communist Party, is unclear) on the African Broadcasting Radio service. Despite some misgivings (he had been invited by the Information Office, which controlled and regulated the news) he agreed, and he and Molly sat up till midnight trying to concoct something which, he suggested to Percy and Ella, would not be 'too political but would give the correct impression'. Afterwards he claimed that during the broadcast the information officer had attacked Russia and that he had only been able to get across two of his points in diluted form, but Molly thought he sounded quite natural. Ella, listening in Bloemfontein, said she had not recognised his voice at all. It was after being on the radio that Bram made his concession to official propaganda, and borrowed a set from Molly's sister to hear all the news.

It was in the pages of the *Guardian*, the most articulate of the pro-Party news-papers, that South African communists followed the fate of the Soviet Union with a particular intensity. 'For fifteen weeks', the paper commented in October 1941, 'the two mightiest armies in the world have been locked in a deadly struggle. Soviet Russia, the land of socialism, faces fascism, the enemy of civilisation and human progress. On the plains of the Ukraine, before Leningrad, Smolensk, and Odessa, and every village of the great Soviet Territory, the people of Russia are fighting the battle of liberty, fraternity, and equality with a magnificent heroism which has aroused the admiration of the whole world.' The war, maintained the *Guardian*, was a choice between the fascist rule of terror and slavery and a life of peace, prosperity and freedom. As the Nazi army ground to a halt in the snows before Moscow at the end of the year, the gigantic battle – arousing memories of Napoleon's prodigious ambitions and abject demise in 1812 – proved, remarked the newspaper, 'the superior morale of the Red Army over the morale of the Nazi fascist brigands'. By January 1942, as after their early disastrous defeats the Russians fought back in the south-west, communists followed the push towards Kharkov, measuring every inch of the map along the way. As winter gave way to spring they awaited the 'zero hour', for 'the greatest battle of 1942, probably the greatest battle of world history'.

That battle was to take place around Stalingrad. By September 1942 the combat was on in full force as beleaguered Russian remnants withstood the German Sixth Army for three months before the the Soviet counter-offensive won its most crucial victory of the war. The predominant images were of an epic, desperate and monumental heroism, as the *Guardian* wrote of the mad recklessness of the German attacks and the courageous self-sacrifice of the Red Army forces. There was speculation on the roles of 'Generals Mud, Snow and Frost' as the winter approached, and vivid renditions of battles 'almost insane in their ferocity . . . a huge cauldron of fire and steel, and rivers of blood'. There were accounts of German air superiority overcome, of the flow of arms and ammunition provided under impossible circumstances by Russian industry, as well as tales of everyday heroes: of the tractor plant at Stalingrad that turned out two hundred tanks in the month when the battle was at its height, of German forces reaching the centre of the city only to be thrown back again, of hand-to-hand fighting from house to house. By February 1943, when the *Guardian* reported the annihilation of the last Nazi troops left straggling and desperate in Stalingrad, of the relief of Leningrad after a siege of eighteen months, of the new Red Army offensives opening up, the pride of its readers could only have been unalloyed.

For communists, Russian triumphs over the Nazis, who were unconquered everywhere else, proved the superiority of the Soviet system in everything ranging from its industrial planning to its military tactics and inner spiritual resources. Russia itself became the hero, embodied in the iconic figure of Stalin, of whom one could now buy fine-art photographs suitable for framing (6d, postage free) from the Johannesburg Party paper, *Inkululeko*. In December 1941, in the depths of the war, the Johannesburg district committee of the Communist Party sent a cable to Stalin, signed by Bram's friend Michael Harmel: 'Warmest greetings on your birthday', it read. 'May the heroic struggle of the USSR lead humanity to the final destruction of fascism.' The *Guardian* recounted every Soviet triumph, whether it be of the Russian airman who fell five miles without a parachute to land unhurt in deep snow, or the amazing operation performed by a Soviet surgeon to remove a live bomb lodged in the shoulder of a Red Army fighter. There were rallies and meetings on every occasion, and none more rousing than a special commemoration in Cape Town at the end of 1943 on the anniversary of the Battle of Stalingrad. 'Stalingrad,' proclaimed the flyers announcing the meeting, 'named after the beloved leader of the Soviet People . . . defended with the greatest devotion and heroism history has ever known.' It was the turning-point of the war, and to communists in South Africa as elsewhere it must have seemed a turning-point for the whole of humankind.

⁂

Unsurprisingly, after the invasion, the war lent the CPSA an unprecedented legitimacy. Previously the Party had been among the most identifiable and discredited opponents of participation, along with South African Nazis, Trotskyists and other assorted marginals, all of whom denounced one another quite freely, and some of whom were interned in alarming propinquity to one another as subversives. Now communists were able to present themselves as the most principled, vociferous proponents of an all-out battle against Germany, and new alliances made for new bedfellows. Even Smuts and his ministers had to acknowledge the titanic battles fought by the Soviet Union, while communists basked in the glory of having Churchill as ally of Stalin.

This unaccustomed authority became embodied in a zestful new culture of the left. The possibilities had for some years been exotic (only in South Africa could there be a talk by the Communist Party member J.B. Marks at the Cape Town Juedischer Arbeiter Klub under the Xhosa slogan 'Ikhaka laba Sebenzi' [Shield of the Workers]). In Johannesburg, institutions such as the Left Book Club (modelled on Victor Gollancz's organisation in England), the People's Bookshop (communist) and Vanguard Booksellers (Trotskyist) were venues for meeting and discussion. In 1939 the Left Book Club had suffered a crisis when Gollancz supported the war (causing the South African group to change its name to the Left Club), but with the German invasion it grew both in strength and popularity. As early as October 1941 the Club moved to new and enlarged premises, with a lounge for theatre performances and lectures, and even (boasted the opening-night notice) a maple floor for dancing. There was a women's committee, an artists' group, an architects' group, and regular adverts in the *Guardian* offered lunchtime 'lecturettes' on current news, on culture and the Red Army, on art in the USSR, as well as evenings of swing music or choral performances of working-class songs, which members (the club was free to soldiers) could enjoy with tea and soup at 3d a cup.

Other groups and institutions reinforced the feeling of a solidified front. The Friends of the Soviet Union (FSU) had been formed in the early 1930s as a broader alignment for the Communist Party; now it too began to flourish. Medical Aid for Russia (MAFR) – not so much an organisation as a campaign – mobilised across broad segments of South African society to provide assistance and supplies to the Soviet Union and its people, who – as MAFR promotional material proclaimed – had 'lifted the stature of the whole human race' through their bravery. Among its patrons was Colin Steyn, Smuts's Minister of Justice, and son of the old President alongside whom Abraham Fischer had fought.

What became both romantic and familiar through all of this was nothing less than the Soviet Union itself. In March 1942 Medical Aid for Russia held a civic week in Johannesburg, featuring a gala evening that was a thorough-going exercise in Russian acculturation and apotheosis. The food was Russian, the music was Russian, and so was the drama and dance presented by the Narodnayakomedia [People's Theatre]. Even the advertisements in the evening's printed programme were 'Russified': the OK Bazaars with a picture of a Russian market scene labelled BAZAAR in Cyrillic script; a Cossack dancing in boots for ABC Shoes; Edblo Inner Springs 'for the family', represented by *matriushki* figurines. The programme included statements from the Archbishop of Canterbury on the urgent need to come 'to the aid of our heroic ally' as well as from Churchill. Even King George VI was represented, notwithstanding the fact that the Bolsheviks had killed his second cousins Nicholas and Alexandra: 'I heartily welcome as an ally the great Union of Soviet Socialist Republics.' Smuts intoned on the miracle of the Soviet recovery, while Stalin (above a cartoon representation of himself about to eat a surprised Hitler sandwiched in a roll) declared that 'Hitlerite Germany must burst under the weight of its own crimes'.

As elsewhere in the world, it was, in the new climate, not entirely paradoxical to find Stalin keeping company with George VI and the Archbishop of Canterbury, while their combined enthusiasts ate *borscht*, hot meat pies and chicken soup. When the Friends of the Soviet Union celebrated the twenty-sixth anniversary of the USSR in Cape Town in 1943, the proceedings were framed by four anthems: 'Die Stem' (Afrikaner nationalist), 'Song of the Fatherland' (Soviet Union), 'The Internationale' (Communist Party) and 'God Save the King'. 'THEY HAVE SAVED THE WORLD', declared the programme. As both the FSU and MAFR held celebrations of Russian military victories, so too they presented reams of adulatory material on other triumphs – in Soviet medicine, social security, rights for women, children and the aged. There were films from Russia – 'Conquerors of the Arctic', 'In the Rear of the Enemy' and (towards the end of the war) 'Battle of Russia', with a foreword by Winston Churchill. The Unity and People's Theatres put on left-wing plays, while performances of Verdi, Beethoven and Dvořák's 'New World Symphony' established a progressive musical tradition, together with Shostakovich's most revered Seventh 'Heroic' Symphony, which (claimed the supporting material) was 'about the war, about the impact of the creative man and the destructive beast'. The Soviet Union had taken on gargantuan and quasi-mythic proportions.

In these circumstances the Communist Party's presence and prospects appeared dramatically altered. The *Guardian* saw its circulation rise from 2000 in 1937 to 22,000 at the end of 1941, to 42,000 by June 1943. CPSA membership, though still small, rose from 400 in April 1941 to 1500 by December 1943 – nearly a fourfold increase in two and a half years. Communist Party meetings became so plentiful that circulars were distributed on how to run a good one.

In this setting the CPSA felt able, and obliged, to campaign on a wide range of social and political issues. The Party tried to obtain the release of its members who had been interned (including E.J. Burford, on the remarkable ground that he had been a 'premature anti-fascist'). Along with the FSU and MAFR it argued for South Africa's diplomatic recognition of the Soviet Union, pointing out the hypocrisy that, whereas both Vichy France and Franco's Spain were officially recognised, though collaborators with the fascist powers, this had not been extended to South Africa's ally, the USSR. The gratifying result was the arrival of the first Soviet consul, M. Demianov, in Cape Town in January 1942. The Party campaigned on everything from African beer-brewing (work familiar to Bram on the Joint Council) to trade-union rights for blacks, who were excluded under the Industrial Conciliation Act from the category of 'employee' – and who deserved, maintained the Party, better treatment, given the sacrifices they were making both at home and abroad. It opposed the conscription of labour since there was no equivalent regulation of capitalist wealth, and appealed for a national health service on the ground that the primary cause of illness in South Africa was structurally induced poverty. The CPSA also campaigned to smash the black market (as merchants withheld goods to drive up prices, or sold privately at inflated rates), it worked for price controls, for rationing, for a Ministry of Food – and when all else failed (especially towards the end of the war), undertook 'food raids', seizing concealed or overexpensive produce and distributing it at the correct prices to the poor in the streets.

There wasn't agreement in the Party on every issue. Some, such as Yusuf Dadoo, were not entirely happy when the CPSA supported the war, and he and others felt the same way when the Party, in keeping with policies elsewhere in the West, declared a moratorium on encouraging strikes by workers. Yet the Communist Party exploited its strengths, which lay chiefly in combining its demands for an increased war effort – especially for the opening of a second front in the West to take the pressure off Russia – with all of its major political campaigns. The argument, in essence, was that South Africa could not pursue the war properly unless all of its human resources were freed. From the start of its involvement, the CPSA (like the ANC) called for the arming of African soldiers (images of South African blacks in the Western Desert armed with assegais as the Stukas rained down remain among the war's most desolate motifs), and argued that for the war to fulfil its proper aims it must be a people's war, with all that the phrase entailed. To this end the Communist Party put forward a 'Programme for Victory', calling for (among other things) equal treatment in the army for all South Africans, first priority to the production of war essentials, the abolition of the colour bar in industry, the suppression of Nazis and fifth columnists, more land for Africans, an end to pass laws as well as to segregation and police raids, and the extension of democratic rights to blacks.

For a brief moment it looked as if some of this might occur. At the height of the Japanese threat from the East, when it seemed that bombs might soon rain down on Cape Town, Smuts threatened to arm every African and coloured: 'Isolation has gone and I am afraid segregation has fallen on evil days too', he declared famously in 1942. This was a strange evil that produced such a good, but Smuts soon forgot his words. Yet, though the prospect of a Japanese invasion began to attract some who expected liberation by a non-European people, the Communist Party maintained its clarity on exactly who and what the enemy was. Even Yusuf Dadoo, originally ambivalent about the war, was insistent in his appeals: Japanese fascists would not liberate South Africa, and only a free South Africa could fight them fully and properly.

Thus it was that the Communist Party supported the Non-European United Front campaign against passes (led, once more, by Dadoo). And when the residents of Alexandra Township (just to the north-east of Johannesburg) refused to pay a one-penny increase in bus fares, and boycotted the transport system by walking the many miles to and from work in the city every day until they won their demanded concessions, they were given support by the Communist Party, and some of its members – including Bram Fischer – were involved.

⁂

What's going to happen after this war? Will South Africa become a Socialist country? If it does, how will the clash between the different races be handled? . . .

THIS IS A DIFFERENT SORT OF WAR. Men and women are beginning to see that wars come because the good and decent things in the world are not shared equally by all, that some nations are privileged, that some classes are privileged, that people of a certain colour are privileged, and that the only way in which these privileged people can be made to give up their favourable position is by force.

Everybody says: 'We can't go back to the old days. There must be a change.' But not everybody is sure just what sort of change is needed, and very few know how the change must be organised and who is to do the changing . . .

But we, the Communist Party of South Africa, say that we can show you how a new South Africa can be built, with peace and prosperity for everyone, black or white, Afrikaans or English, Christian or non-Christian.

The Communists have a plan. Study it carefully and you will find the answer to your questions.

There is nothing, perhaps, so externalised as a political pamphlet, but it can speak inwardly as well. This one, entitled 'Meet the Communists', established a kindly presence, as if it understood the personal difficulties of making a momentous change, but also as if nothing could be more evident than the logic and morality of its appeal.

. . . Communism is more than party politics. It is a way of life. It is a philosophy of life. We have to decide between Fascism and Communism . . . The Communist Party makes no reservation about the colour of a worker's skin . . . What about intermarriage? If prejudice is an inherent force it won't disappear under Socialism. But if it does disappear, who are we to decide such things for posterity? . . . Isn't this the right way? . . . Can Europeans go on for ever passing repressive and degrading laws? . . . Isn't this the way that makes you feel comfortable inside, that leaves no bitterness in the hearts of people? Isn't this what you mean when you talk of justice, liberty and freedom . . . ?

The communist stream of consciousness flowed persuasively, with its grand themes, perhaps its grand illusions. This was the crucial time for Bram, when his commitment was sealed in the steel of war, the fire of its passions, the thunder of its morality, the solvent of its hope, the light of its so self-evident, omniscient understanding.

During the early years of the war aspects of Bram's life carried on with a certain degree of normality. His career continued to develop as he took on a range of cases, whether acting as junior to Tilson Barry, or conducting his own work before the Supreme Court. On occasion he appeared before his old colleagues – Mr Justice Schreiner, who granted him an interdict on behalf of Johannesburg Consolidated Investments against a farmer who wanted to sell portions of his farm on which JCI held the mineral rights, or Mr Justice Ramsbottom, before whom he won a defamation case. Very little of his legal work was tinged politically (in one case before Schreiner a policeman – on behalf of fifteen others – sued to stop the proceedings of a Riots Enquiry Commission on the ground that it might prejudice his forthcoming trial, which Bram resisted successfully), and much of it was commercial. Bram represented the Wanderers Club, whose cricket grounds were being expropriated by the Railways, and ISCOR (the giant state steel corporation) in a water rights case against some farmers. Some of these associations made Molly feel rather uncomfortable (Bram's rationalisation, she advised Percy and Ella, was that he would charge a lot), but he too was aware of the ironies: 'Something wrong about a communist making money like this', he had written to Ella in July 1940. Whether this was a wry joke to his mother, his sense of political identity was fairly clear.

The recession which affected the legal world at the beginning of the war was balanced by the fact that numbers of barristers had gone off to fight, but either way it did not seem to matter for Bram as clients sought him out. 'The JCI still think Bram is Xmas', Molly wrote to Percy and Ella in September 1943, 'so we won't starve.' According to her, Bram's opinions were considered to be among the best at the Bar, and Molly's only complaint was that, in cases in which he acted as junior, his seniors made him do all the work and paid him only two-thirds of the fee. Yet the respect in which Bram was held was more than evident, from his peers as much as his clients. In December 1942 he was elected to the Johannesburg Bar Council for the first time, a body on which he then served without a break for the following ten years. Percy called it 'a wonderful sign of appreciation from your colleagues, especially with the number of votes you received'. On one of his many re-elections later in the decade, Molly pointed out to Percy and Ella that Bram had won the greatest number of votes among the juniors: 'I think it's rather nice, as everyone knows his politics & his convictions, & they're a conservative crowd at the Bar.' Despite Bram's unconcealed communist affiliations, he had a way of winning people's confidence and loyalty.

Yet, as events at the beginning of the war showed, his capacity for anxiety had not entirely disappeared. With a marked internal timing, in the weeks leading up to the German invasion of Russia the digestive problems Bram had experienced since his youth flared up again, and shortly after the invasion X-rays showed a duodenal ulcer. His stomach, Bram wrote to his parents a few months later, had been 'producing HCl on a commercial scale'. He took bicarbonate of soda, drank milk continuously, even tried – a suggested remedy – what was still called 'kaffir beer', a home-made sorghum brew which made their household (according to Molly) quite popular among the servants of the neighbourhood. Bram put on weight from all the milk, and discovered (he wrote, while bedridden early on) 'how strong a resemblance there [is] between steamed fish, boiled chicken, & blotting paper'. Later on he tried, with only temporary success, to give up cigarettes and alcohol.

Ulcers were a Fischer family trait (both Percy and Bram's brother Paul suffered terribly), but Bram's was decisive in one respect. Although in 1939 he had obviously not signed up for the army (nor had any of his brothers, in their case because of residual anti-British, Afrikaner nationalist feelings), with the

German invasion Bram volunteered immediately for conscription. But his ulcer – and developing high blood pressure – gave him no chance, and he was rejected on the grounds of his health.

⁂

Yet from that first radio broadcast Bram gave after the German invasion, he took to the war in other ways with an evidently increasing intensity, becoming swept up in all the activities of the left. In November 1941 he was a speaker at one of the large initiatory conferences of Medical Aid for Russia, along with Colin Steyn. 'Oom Colin', wrote Bram (he and Molly were always somewhat derisory about Steyn to Percy and Ella, who seemed not to mind, perhaps because Steyn was in league with Smuts) 'made a socialist speech & we had 103 organisations represented. We've already sent off £20,000 as you may have seen.' In May 1942 he and Molly helped set up a Soviet pavilion for a Liberty Cavalcade, and Bram made another speech. Roped in at the last minute, he performed at an FSU pageant in October, and only missed a massed rally – so large it overflowed from the Johannesburg City Hall – on the first anniversary of the German invasion because he was away on his ISCOR case.

The new legitimacy allowed many an ironic moment, as Molly noted to Percy and Ella at the end of August 1943: 'Your friend Oom Colin is speaking together with Madeley [leader of the Labour Party] & Demianov [the Soviet consul] – to celebrate the fall of Kharkov. Now don't say we're compromising.' After Stalingrad, Kharkov was the next major victory for the Red Army, and the celebration took place at the Left Club, where Bram and Molly were also heavily involved. According to a division of labour still gendered in its orientation, Molly was chiefly involved with catering and fitting out the new premises of the club, but her work was still substantial enough that when Bram was away in February 1943 he joked that he expected her to be interned if the Nationalists ever took over. At the Left Club Bram was again – a growing speciality for him – a speechmaker: he gave news reviews, he presided at anniversary celebrations of the Russian Revolution, he presented a series of lectures on 'Economic and Political Conditions in South Africa' which the *Guardian* (of course unprejudiced) was quite prepared to call 'brilliant'.

Early on Molly pointed out to Percy and Ella that 'the sort of speeches Bram and his pals make are never mentioned in the capitalistic press'. Yet, despite his inexperience and inveterate legal tendencies, she also thought that his style was improving: 'sometimes [he] even remembers that he's not addressing a learned judge.' Bram had been particularly proud, she reported, of his performance at a meeting in Krugersdorp, one of the most strongly nationalist of towns, where the last ten rows were occupied by Ossewabrandwag supporters who had booed all the previous speakers: 'When Bram's turn came he just ignored them & after a few minutes they all listened to him – even though his views couldn't have pleased them as he was telling them facts about the Soviet Union.' Bram's style, as always, was quiet and confiding, and his intention was to get people to think: when he spoke at the Library Theatre in Johannesburg on 'How the Soviet State is Run', the chair of the proceedings criticised him for not having enough 'sobstuff and fistbanging' – but, remarked Molly, the audience enjoyed it, and ended up asking for lists of books about Russia, an effect that would have pleased Bram exactly.

The sudden existence of large groupings of men in the army, together with the sense of idealism surrounding the war, provided an excellent forum for progressive constituencies to generate a following. (Leo Marquard, who had joined the Military College in 1940 and then helped establish the Army Education Services, was extremely effective in providing a liberal perspective.) In June 1942 Bram travelled down to Kimberley, to speak to soldiers about the Red Army and social services in the Soviet Union, and he was accompanied on that trip by Jessie McPherson, the future Labour Party mayor of Johannesburg, and Bettie du Toit, a young woman who, in her combination of fragility and verve, clearly fascinated him. She had been brought up in a Dutch Reformed Church orphanage, he told Percy and Ella, and her life's experiences included both domestic and factory labour, a jail sentence for participating in an illegal strike (she had refused on principle to pay a £2 fine), and a three-year sojourn in Moscow. As she was 'a pretty slight Afrikaans girl', remarked Bram, 'you can imagine that she goes down rather well with the audience.' To him she must have seemed the very type of what Afrikaners could become if they only dared.

In this line he too felt a special responsibility, and left no avenue unexplored in pursuing his innate belief that even the most ingrained Nationalists would be persuaded of the truth if they were simply presented with the facts. Late in the war he told Percy and Ella that he had established a contact on the *Vaderland* newspaper, and suggested his strategy in his plans to speak at the university in Bloemfontein: 'I promise not to raise the colour bar – I guarantee that it will be raised – unless they are absolute hooligans. I also guarantee to get them to listen to me on that.' In applying himself to an Afrikaner constituency, as he explained to his parents, he felt reinforced by no less a figure than Moses Kotane: 'Kotane, our general secretary, who [has] been here from Cape Town recently, puts forward an interesting thesis: In the last analysis the alliance required to abolish oppression in this country is an alliance between

Afrikaner & African!' In that light Bram was quite prepared, among his other duties, to speak at 'Afrikaner evenings' for the Communist Party (duly derided by the Nationalist *Volksblad*), working against the evident odds. But for those – Afrikaner or otherwise – who remained resistant in their allegiance to fascism, he also displayed a resolution that worked in tandem with his understated approach. Addressing a meeting of the radical soldiers' organisation, the Springbok Legion, he spoke unhistrionically of the conditions facing soldiers serving in the north, but also made sure to warn the 'fifth-columnists' (the Ossewabrandwag saboteurs and their cohorts) that their day of reckoning would come.

All of these commitments, together with Bram's legal practice, meant that he was often working at a staggering pace. In March 1942 he wrote to his parents that he had spent a mere two evenings at home in three weeks, and those only because he had skipped political meetings to prepare law cases for the next day. 'You'll notice, therefore,' he wrote, 'that I still put law before politics – but it means very concentrated work during the days.' By the end of 1944 the average day-in-the-life he described to Percy and Ella was little short of overwhelming: 'At Potchefstroom last night to address a soldiers' club, back at 12.30 – worked till 6.30 at office this evening. – After supper prepared a Water Court brief for Witbank for the end of the month & a speech for Boksburg for tomorrow evening. – Pretoria with a heavy application tomorrow & two big trials still on the programme this month. What fun. On top of that a serious situation may arise at any time at Alexandra because bus-fares are going to be raised for the Africans, so just hold thumbs for the end of the year.'

Molly was dizzied by his daily and weekly schedules, and expected him to crack up at any time. She told Percy and Ella that she and Ruth hardly ever saw him. Bram worked up to eighteen hours a day, six or seven days a week, though his health – paradoxically as time went on – seemed only to improve. With an amazing capacity to fulfil numbers of duties simultaneously, Bram would steal a few minutes to write to Percy and Ella as he kept Ruth company when she woke up coughing in the night and couldn't go back to sleep. Yet, as always, he did not allow his eminence, whether in law or – increasingly – in politics, to shield him from even the most mundane activities. All of his comrades later testified that Bram would take time from his hectic schedule to collect money for the *Guardian*. Violet Weinberg, who with her husband Eli was among Bram and Molly's closest friends, remembered the story of how, on one occasion, he had been soliciting contributions with an Indian comrade among the merchants of Market Street. The comrade would speak to the shop-owners in Gujarati, and the money would magically appear, but when

Bram found out the reason why, he was horrified: his comrade had been informing the shop-owners that Bram was the son of the Judge-President of the Free State, and would himself soon be a judge, that they would one day appear before him, and had therefore better pay up *now*. Bram had then insisted on talking to the merchants himself, and collected what was needed despite their lack of political interest, because (remarked Violet) 'the goodness shone out of Bram'.

It is no exaggeration to say that this was what being a communist meant to him: when it came to human interaction he brought to it an unswerving consistency of personal ethic and approach. Bram's other close comrades, Lionel ('Rusty') and Hilda Bernstein, observed that even though his political activities might have jeopardised his legal career, he never begged off any obligation, whether large or small. Together with Jessie McPherson Bram was an honorary treasurer (his Joint Council training) of Medical Aid for Russia; he was also Transvaal chairman of the National Food Council. Like others, he spoke on the City Hall steps of Johannesburg, facing the nationalist and sometimes fascist thugs; and later both he and Molly participated in food raids, despite their marginal legality. Violet Weinberg remembered Molly in an Indian store selling consignments of rice and sugar at the government price of 6d a pound, and giving the due proceeds to the owner. Joe Slovo had the clearest vision of Bram in the immediate aftermath of the war sitting on a pavement outside a shop, jemmy in hand, opening a box of Sunlight soap to sell to the people lining up.

In February and March 1943 Bram went to Maseru in Basutoland, where he was acting in the case of Constantinus Bereng Griffith Lerotoli versus Amelia Matsaba Seeiso Griffith, a complicated royal succession dispute. There, bored by the tedium of a colonial backwater, he found his spirit relieved by news of the Soviet successes at Rostov and Voroshilovgrad. At home Ruth, still not yet four, who saw her father intermittently at best, asked why he didn't sometimes come for a visit.

In July Bram took off by train for Bulawayo, on his way, via Ndola and Nkana, to Mufulira and Luanshya in the Copper Belt in Northern Rhodesia, on the border of the Belgian Congo. This time the trip was political in nature, and Bram was accompanied by his comrade Fred Zwarenstein, to spread word of the cause as widely as possible. He reported on his progress to Molly – on a winter school that enabled 'people out in the Bundu to keep up to date with the latest developments of science & philosophy', on being rushed through an endless round of meetings, talks, lunches and dinners where Bram gave what he called 'composite' speeches on anything from trade unions to democracy or religion in the USSR. It was also the African landscape that captivated him: antheaps twenty feet high at Luanshya; the Victoria Falls, where, Bram told Molly, he wanted to return and feel 'as free as the spray itself'; Nkana, where the 'golden atmosphere' reminded him of all the places he had been to with her – Bethlehem, Lusthof, the Cape.

At home, while he was in Maseru, Molly organised a fundraising dance for the Guardian at Beaumont Street (as time went on these became one of the major attractions of left-wing life in Johannesburg), and it was characteristic that she was prepared to do so without Bram's assistance. For, despite her modesty and reticence (to Percy and Ella she referred even to Bram's political activity as 'outside work'), Molly was also extremely busy. She participated in street collections for the Communist Party, and organised fêtes and jumble sales. (Once Bram, returning home, found one of his own coats among the assorted clothes, and gave Molly £5 to have it back.) She went out canvassing with Hilda Watts when the latter was standing for the Johannesburg City Council, and found that many were surprised to meet communists without knives, beards and red scarves: 'It seemed rather a shock to them that we were so ordinary & respectable,' she told Percy and Ella. Molly was responsible for procuring funding for some eighty post office workers on strike, helped in translating American strike plays (replete with New York slang) into Afrikaans, and followed up her special concern for the young. Along with Oliver Schreiner's wife she worked in African crèches, she established 'refuge homes' for African children, she gave a series of talks in municipal nursery schools to mothers ('all very poor and mostly Afrikaans') whom she helped set up co-operative clubs, to buy wholesale and double their purchasing power.

Bram and Molly both read detective novels as well as sentimental socialist-realist literature; they saw the requisite Russian films – 'Stalingrad', 'Guerrillas', 'Volga Volga' – and once in a rare while managed to steal off into the veld for a picnic. When Percy and Ella came to Johannesburg, Bram and Molly took them to the Left Club; Bram's brother Piet (later a Jehovah's Witness and Nationalist) made posters for the Left Club Theatre, and Ada helped with the catering when the new premises were opened. Ella even gave money to the Left Club, contributing (as she told Molly and Bram) to their 'various nefarious activities', though Molly was able to assure her that her name wouldn't be published as a donor. Just five months before old Nakie's hundredth birthday, Molly presented her with a subscription to the Guardian, and the paper ran an article on their oldest reader.

It was at this time, between Bram's visits to Basutoland and Rhodesia, when horizons both at home and abroad were expanding, that a universe of a different kind contracted and produced a new being in the world. Bram and Molly's second daughter, Ilse, was born on 16 June 1943, little more than three weeks before her father took off for the Copper Belt, and some three months after Molly had arranged *the* Guardian *dance, heavily pregnant. Whereas Ruth had been awaited so long, her name prepared years in advance, Ilse came into a household at the peak of its wartime activity, and Molly, in a degree of speculative uncertainty, referred to the new arrival as 'Ilse?' before her birth was registered. Amidst the pace and pulse and the tumult – the war and Russian triumphs, the speeches, the cavalcades and lectures, the dances and fundraising and strikes, the law cases and travel and translating – it appeared to be Ilse's destiny, as at her birth, to have much of her life crowded by politics.*

Bram and Molly did what they could to carve out an interior space.

Both before and after Ilse's birth, they described to Percy and Ella every aspect of their – first one, then two – daughters' development as they grew up. On holiday at the sea Ruth was persistent about climbing a gatepost some four and a half feet high; if anyone tried to help she would weep bitterly, climb down, and begin again. Or she would tightrope-walk along a veranda wall five feet off the ground. Molly would refuse to allow anyone to tell her to be careful, and the result (Bram told Percy and Ella) was that 'I just quietly walk into the back yard & pray'. When Ruth was nearly six she observed that if there were no poor people in the world her parents would not have to go out so often, and then she offered Molly one of her dolls to give away to the needy because, she said, she had another one.

As for Ilse, from early on Bram and Molly were convinced that she had a mind of her own: they called her a 'Robertson', after Oupa Abraham's wife, who had a family reputation for being something of a Tartar. 'When you ask her where Oupa or Ouma is,' Molly wrote when Ilse was two, 'she says "gone" with a wave of her hand as if it were entirely your fault if you are not in her scheme of life at the moment.' For a while Ilse's first language became Zulu because – given her parents' constant activity for the 'poor' – she was so often in the care of a servant. When the head of her nursery school wanted Ilse to do something, she would ask her own Zulu servant to translate. Some years later Molly described Ilse's will-power, how she would grit her teeth at swimming when other children would give up: 'Perhaps one day her perseverance will stand her in good stead,' she told Percy and Ella.

Despite their communist allegiance, Bram and Molly allowed a broad tolerance at home. They were atheist but, when Ruth came home from school unsure of how to position her hands when praying, they discussed with her the proper technique. They also adopted older traditions, stretching back to Harmonie and Hillandale, of early morning birthday tables laid out with *pakkies* [small parcels], to ensure the maximum anticipation and pleasure. Although, as Molly said, Percy and Ella did not see 'eye to eye' with them on politics, there was the closest possible relation between parents, grandparents and children. For Ella, as ever, the notion of 'family' was a category that superseded all the passing fancies of an ideological world, and Percy loved to indulge his special interest in the young. When Ruth turned seven he wrote to her (his technical skills on the typewriter rather atrocious, but his affectionate, teasing style just right): 'Consider that I am also seven years old, but just that a big 0 must come after it – then you are 7 and I 70. And a "0" is just a "0" and doesn't count.' Or, when she got chickenpox: 'What made you go and get chicken pocks. Why not a full-fledged Hen pocks or even a cockadoodledoo pocks? But a chicken. You could have done that in substandard one.'

Bram and Molly sometimes took the children by train to see their grandparents at Harmonie, where Ella, now in her sixties and gathering a certain physical substance around her short frame, provided an aura of mystery of her own. In her huge room (Ruth remembered) she had a brass bedstead topped with five mattresses – the children would clamber into Ella's bed to be read to. At Harmonie or at the farm, as a special treat they could explore the recesses of her jewellery box, or play with marvellous coloured blocks on her carpet. Though Ilse could hardly remember those early years at Harmonie, she was able to capture something of her grandmother's intimate authority: 'this . . . large lady in her large bed, with her little husband tucked away in a cubby-hole next door' – for Percy's room was much smaller than Ella's.

During the war years there were restrictions and shortages. Petrol was rationed (hence the railway trips to Harmonie), and even clothes were hard to come by. Bram and Molly took to growing their own vegetables, and later Ella sent parcels of cheese, canned food, butter and tea from Bloemfontein, which had a more plentiful supply. Yet Bram and Molly still managed to take the family on holidays – in winter to Umzumbe in Natal, and in summer to a rented house at the sea in Hermanus, followed by the annual Communist Party conference in Cape Town. At home Bram painted the roof, and he and Molly remodelled the garden with a new rockery, new lawn, a pergola, a Wendy house Bram made for the children, and new flower beds supplemented with nerines, harebells and haemanthus brought in from Harmonie and Bergendal. It was still a composite life, with its gestures towards the past as well as the future.

They also added on servants' quarters to the house, for there was a steady rotation of servants at Beaumont Street. There was a gardener, a maid and often a woman specially to take care of the children. Even when Bram and Molly went away on holiday, they took two or three servants with them. In this sense it was true that their revolutionary efforts depended on a steady supply of African labour at home, and there was no doubt that – in all the frenzy of their activity – life for Bram and Molly as communists was easier than it was for many others. But as time went on there was a closeness and sense of human commitment that only deepened. Matthias (or Tias) Mlambo, who worked in the garden, stayed with the family through the most difficult years and beyond. When Mary Mlambo – whom Bram said Ruth seemed to love more than she did her parents – was gravely ill and seemed set to die after a miscarriage, Bram and Molly were with her at her bedside in hospital. She recovered, and the relationship with the Mlambos endured – not only with Mary, but also with members of her family both close and extended. The strange mix of intimacy and inequity that characterised the nature of South African domestic labour may have encouraged a pattern familiar to many left and liberal homes, but it was accentuated at the Fischers. There was, remarked Ilse later, almost a feudal sense of mutual obligation.

In this regard Bram and Molly opened themselves up with an unusual liberty in every direction. Molly's friend Elodie de la Harpe came to stay when she was about to have her second child; so too did Bram's cousin Connie and her daughter Mollie when the latter was very ill with tuberculosis of the spine and needed medical treatment in Johannesburg. Liefie stayed when her brother Stratford (who had dropped flowers for Molly from his plane over Bethlehem) died young of cancer. Hilda Watts's mother and child moved in so that Hilda could campaign for the City Council without hindrance. When Bram's friend and colleague Johnny Kneen died in an airforce accident in Pretoria, Bram took over a case he had been running, and Johnny's wife Audrey and their daughter came to stay. When Audrey had an operation and called for her husband while coming out of the anaesthetic, it was Molly who was there at her bedside to be with her. Given the frenetic nature of things there was sometimes irritation at the continual flow of visitors, but Bram and Molly embodied traditional Afrikaner hospitality now inflected by an enlarged sense of responsibility.

It was in this spirit that the Fischers took in Nora Mlambo, Mary's niece, to be part of the household. Much was made of this later, as if it were somehow Bram Fischer's unholy communist 'experiment' to bring up a black child in a white family, or his intention by so doing to shake the foundations of the South African state. There is no doubt that it was in many respects a remarkable gesture for those times, especially for an Afrikaner: it was unheard of for whites deliberately to transgress the dividing lines of race, especially within the sacred confines of the home. But the reality of it was probably simpler than any grand political or symbolic scheme, for the fact was that Nora's mother (Mary's sister) had died, and the child needed to be taken care of. For the Fischers this was all that really counted. Ilse, who was about two at the time, already shared Mary as an alternate mother to Molly, and in this light it made sense that Nora, who was just a little older, could participate in the reverse direction. No doubt Bram and Molly considered the alternatives – they could have paid to have Nora looked after, or she could have lived with her aunt. Yet it is hard to say which was more decisive: the communist ethic, which decreed a universal equality, or the clear sense of human reciprocity which Bram and Molly brought to it.

Of course there were complications. Mary was in some way a 'servant' to her niece, who now lived in the house. Nora and Ilse shared a room, and later were in the same standard, although at different, segregated schools. When Ruth and Ilse's brother Paul was born, and Nora developed whooping cough, she and Ilse were packed off with Mary Mlambo to Molly's parents in Silverton, where they ate their meals together, but exiled on the stoep. (There it was a sign of Ilse's life that she was most uncomfortable on Thursdays – the regular servants' day off – when Mary would take Nora to the African location at Eersterus, and she had to eat in the dining-room alone with her grandparents.) Years later, after Percy died, when Ella came to stay at Beaumont Street, Bram and Molly would delicately ask Ilse to eat with Nora in the kitchen, because Ella simply could not tolerate anything else.

Bram and Molly's communism was a personal one. They would not have dreamed of upsetting an ageing grandmother just as they would not have allowed Nora to go unattended. In the heightened climate of a segregated South Africa their gesture might assume the proportions of scandal, but that was not the reason for undertaking it. For all concerned – not least, in this case, Nora – it was a commitment that involved complication, but complication was what South African life was about, and Bram and Molly showed themselves prepared to work through it. Perhaps it was because they were Afrikaners that this issue of identity came so close to their hearts: this was what becoming true South Africans would mean. Having devoted themselves to a communist ideal, they were prepared for its implications to course through their lives. They added to the creed they believed in by their capacity to extend themselves and to care.

Others were not in the same mood, as a pamphlet circulating in Johannesburg in 1942 indicated.

'*Alexandra*. VIGOROUS ACTION URGENTLY NEEDED! The North Eastern Districts Protection League Demands: The early abolition of Alexandra Township with its attendant dangers and evils, and the re-establishment of the inhabitants in healthy and congenial surroundings, for the betterment of the inhabitants themselves and the security of the community as a whole.' Photographs in the pamphlet, with suitably suggestive captions, conjured up an ominous picture: 'Conditions in Alexandra make for the savagery of the rat-pit in money matters'; 'Thick ooze, enriched with latrine seepage, creeps down this eroded gutter to the nearest donga'; 'Washing water for local and European laundry comes from slimy pools like this one, a few yards below the dead dog.' But though the NEDPL presented itself as friend to the 'hardworking, desperately poor' residents of the township, the Alexandra Vigilance and Protection Standholders Committee saw in the League a white group from the adjacent north-eastern suburbs of Johannesburg agitating for the extinction and expropriation of Alexandra.

Alexandra was one of those South African anomalies, like Newclare or Sophiatown to the west of Johannesburg, a place where blacks were fully entitled to own land and property in an otherwise white area. It had been founded as a white settlement in 1905 but, when that venture proved unsuccessful, was converted to an African and coloured township in 1912. Paradoxically, ownership rights were protected under the Natives' Land Act of 1913, which preserved these where they already existed, and since that time it had been governed by a succession of so-called Health Committees (appointed rather than elected), which attempted to cope with problems that were straightforwardly the outcome of a system of racial inequality. Because the area of Alexandra was limited, as time went on property prices rose. Owners could not afford to pay off their bonds, and rented out rooms to multiple families at a time. Funding was dependent on township taxes, and therefore minimal; sanitation was inadequate, disease rife, infant mortality running at up to 50 per cent in the first year of life. A medical report initiated towards the end of the war spoke of severe overcrowding in rooms where, in the brightest daylight outside, 'a torch was needed to identify the mass of huddled limbs'. Government commissions had reported on Alexandra *ad nauseam*, and in these circumstances a succession of Health Committees had broken down in disarray, often with the accumulated resentment of the township residents.

Bram became involved towards the end of 1941 when he was recommended for nomination to a reconstituted Alexandra Health Committee by the Department of Native Affairs. Why this government body should have been interested in him is unclear; perhaps it had to do with his credentials, then just still current, in working with Africans in the moderate environs of the Joint Council and the Institute of Race Relations. At any rate, the letter of nomination spoke of him as 'the son of Judge Fischer of the Orange Free State' and 'a man of ability [who] with his legal knowledge should prove a great asset'. Chair of the new committee was Alfred Hoernlé (again the liberal network), and the medical officer was Dr A.B. Xuma, president-general of the African National Congress. There were four appointed members and two elected Alexandra residents; Bram was acting chair whenever Hoernlé was away.

On the Health Committee – which he now added to the list of his other wartime activities – Bram would have been familiar with much of the work from his Joint Council experience. Here it was milk schemes, sanitary arrangements, housing construction and the like. Dr Xuma reported regularly on the incidence of enteric fever or tuberculosis. But chiefly the committee was concerned to resist the campaign for Alexandra's expropriation. There was a conference on the matter in Pretoria in 1942 (prior to which Bram's standing in the township was indirectly suggested: a public meeting voted to boycott the conference on the information – which turned out to be wrong – that Advocate Fischer had advised non-participation). Then, in January 1943, the Johannesburg City Council called for the abolition of Alexandra and the removal of its inhabitants. Hoernlé asked Bram for written comments, and then submitted his own forty-one-page memorandum which, while stressing the moral issues, also managed to call for stricter segregation between the township and the city. In a setting as heated as it was confused, the abolition campaign was held off.

But that did not solve the nightmarish conditions in the township, or the internecine conflict they promoted. The milk scheme the Health Committee proposed, Bram told Percy and Ella, was opposed by African dairymen and by a women's group which claimed it would impinge on their trading rights. Trying to introduce cheap, pasteurised milk into Alexandra, he remarked, produced 'periodic riots'. Hoernlé – a patrician and summary figure – was in continuous conflict with the Alexandra branch of the Transvaal African National Congress, with the Alexandra United Committee (which may have been linked to the Communist Party), and with the Alexandra Anti-Expropriation Fund Committee, whom he was not above informing on when they sent a deputation to the Minister of the Interior, Harry Lawrence, in Cape Town. Ultimately the endless stress became too much for him: Hoernlé resigned in June 1943 after a heart attack, and died soon after.

For Bram Alexandra was an introduction to a direct and dramatic political arena. His friend and colleague on the committee, the Johannesburg attorney Charlie Johnson, remembered one occasion when a large gathering of squatters suddenly invested the township's main square. The black members, recalled Johnson, 'not unnaturally wanted to bring out the machine guns' in order to protect their barely held rights, but were blocked by Bram and himself. It was then that Bram's particular skills for conciliation became apparent. He spoke to the squatter leaders and persuaded them to move to vacant land owned by the City Council (possibly, given the expropriation campaign, two targets addressed here at once). Bram could 'charm the birds out of the trees', observed Johnson; and the squatters packed up and left.

All this meant that when the Alexandra bus boycott of December 1944 took place, and men and women began streaming towards Johannesburg on foot, Bram was somewhere near the centre of things. To Percy and Ella he wrote: '12000 people have for four weeks religiously refused to use a bus, & Johnson & I have been dashing from one meeting to another: Min. for Native Affairs, City Council, bus owners &c &c.' Leo Marquard, directing the Army Education Services, and soon to be a lieutenant-colonel and MBE, visited Bram and Molly, and described the events in a letter to his wife Nell. Along the streets, he wrote, he had passed 'thousands of natives' walking back to the township. An emergency regulation had prohibited all meetings in and out of doors: 'But the communists (Bram, Berrangé & Co) discovered a flaw in this. Unfortunately, they communicated by telephone which was tapped, and the regulation was hastily redrafted, but not before a big meeting had been called. So then the communists had to avoid a clash with the police by calling the meeting off.' Vernon Berrangé was an advocate like Bram, and his future colleague in many a trial. In this tempestuous setting they were experiencing their first taste of the fact that those working for justice would have to deal with the police among their principal adversaries.

Bram was convinced, wrote Leo, that both the government and employers wanted a showdown, because Africans were learning to unite. But on this, as in other matters, Bram's imagination may have veered towards the apocalyptic, for in the end the boycotters won their concessions without violence or any dramatic confrontation. Molly, along with other whites (both liberal and communist), travelled along the bus route to give lifts to the walking workers, subjecting herself to the police harassment and car searches that ensued.

As for Bram, his contacts were inevitably widening, his legal and political background ever more valuable. He told his friend Mary Benson many years later that Dr Xuma, with whom he worked on the Alexandra Health Committee, had asked him to help draft the new ANC constitution of 1943. It was a constitution that was non-racial, and in doing away with certain feudal features in the ANC (above all, the Upper House of Chiefs), it simplified and democratised the organisation, clearing the way for more dramatic and radical developments later in the decade.

⋙⋘

The CPSA had its own innumerable pamphlets and flyers. One of them, produced in September 1945, showed a photograph of Ruth and Ilse Fischer, aged six and two. Both appeared neatly and prettily dressed, gazing sweetly upwards towards a floating soap bubble; Ruth had a bow in her hair, while a teacup placed on a table in front of the angelic-looking sisters suggested pristine innocence and domesticity. With their blonde hair and pure-white features, and the caption 'Beveilig Hulle Toekoms / Safeguard Their Future', the presentation looked for all the world like something one of the far-right Afrikaner nationalist organisations would have put out in the 1960s or 1970s to indicate its undying hostility to the threat of black rule.

But the purpose of this particular flyer was to announce that one Susanna Johanna Fischer was standing as the Communist Party representative for election to Ward 3 (Hospital/Braamfontein) on the Johannesburg City Council, and that she was 'Pledged to Fight for These Things for the Sake of the Children!' In 1943, at the height of the Stalingrad ascendancy, Hilda Watts's campaign for the Council had been successful, and in Cape Town Sam Kahn and Betty Radford (editor of the *Guardian*) had also been elected. Now the Party wanted to follow up these successes: in Johannesburg, alongside Molly, they offered three other candidates: Franz Boshoff, Issy Wolfson and Michael Harmel. As for the photograph of Ruth and Ilse, Bram conceded to Percy and Ella that it was evidence of rank exploitation, but remarked that the children seemed to be only mildly interested: 'I suppose one day we shall owe them an apology for having posted their picture to some 11,000 people.'

Molly had to win approval for her candidacy at a full branch meeting of the Party, and either the stormy incestuousness of left-wing politics or Bram's habitual nervousness had made him anxious in advance. He told Percy and Ella that he had been worried because he expected a critical if not 'hypo-critical audience', but the outcome was a great success: 'the strongest Non-European group promptly promised to assist with all our technical work', and Molly, though still shy, had spoken firmly and with charm. In her campaign Molly took up the theme of her flyer. 'Candidate Canvasses Children', pro-claimed an article in the *Sunday Times*, placed there with the help of Joel Mervis, who worked on the newspaper. It listed the demands Molly had ostensibly collected from a young group in Johannesburg's Joubert Park: a bicycle stand in the children's playground, and milk-bars or ice-cream counters where they could discuss affairs of the day such as (suggested the article) 'the rising price of toffee' and the 'abolition of Latin and Arithmetic'.

But Molly was quite serious about the issues she would address in a low-income city district: the fact that in her whole ward there wasn't one municipal nursery school, crèche or clinic; the 110 cases of typhoid attributed in a year to contaminated milk; the high cost of fruit and vegetables; and the overcrowding, high rents and malnutrition among the poor of the area. As her campaign progressed, she presided over street-corner meetings, went out canvassing three nights a week, and addressed a residents' gathering at a block of flats where rents had been raised. At the Children's Hospital, she told Percy and Ella, she had interviewed a matron who claimed to be an outright conservative, but agreed with most of her policy. If all this was unusual behaviour for a former schoolteacher filled with as much self-doubt as instinctive energy, Molly did not give much outward indication. Soon things were going so well, observed Bram, that his only fear was that she would be elected. Molly felt the same way: everyone had been so helpful, she remarked to Percy and Ella, that only a 'miracle' would keep her off the Council – adding that she would 'hate' to get on. The *Rand Daily Mail* reported that she and the United Party candidate were overshadowing the Nationalist and Labour Party campaigns, and even the United Party representative confessed his expectation that Molly might win.

In the event, when the vote took place in late October 1945, the result was rather different. For Molly lost and lost badly, coming fourth out of four, and polling only 461 votes to the United Party's winning 2387. Perhaps she had believed her own propaganda too easily; perhaps her United Party opponent had simply played her (and the electorate) along. At any rate, she was in good company: none of the Communist Party candidates had any success, and Michael Harmel even lost his deposit. Either way, Molly seemed to be genuinely relieved: 'It's very nice not to feel sick constantly,' she told Percy and Ella. 'I don't know why Bram doesn't change his profession as he assures me that he has the same nervous sick feeling all his life. It doesn't seem worthwhile & I'm sure he would be happier as a bricklayer.' She was also quite simply exhausted, for during the campaign she had been 'running one jumble sale, one dance & one raffle, and assisting with one fête, one Left Club & one straightforward collection'. And yet she was quite prepared to say the whole enterprise had been worth it: 'The work we do must have some effect in the long run & seeing that we are all convinced that what we are working for must come *or* that we all go up in an atomic bomb, we feel that either way we come out alright.'

The bomb Molly was thinking of had been presaged just two months earlier in Hiroshima and Nagasaki, and while its power had brought an end to the war (there was joy and relief in Johannesburg, as elsewhere), it also served notice to Stalin of the terms of the Cold War to come. On Victory in Japan Day in August, Bram and Molly had attended a number of celebration parties, one of which included (she informed Percy and Ella) a crowd of 'ex O.B.'s [Ossewabrandwag members] now Nationalists, who exhibit Bram & me as rather interesting specimens'. But she did not go on to surmise whether this was because they were regarded as victors or vanquished, shining lights whose faith had been vindicated or quaint moral and historical curiosities.

<hr/>

On 2 January 1945, after the annual Communist Party conference in Cape Town, Bram spoke alongside his comrades Hilda Watts and Jack Simons at the Muizenberg Pavilion on what the world would be like after the war. In March 1945, at the annual conference of the Johannesburg district committee, Bram was nominated to be chair. He declined, as did Yusuf Dadoo and Issy Wolfson, leaving the runoff to Danie du Plessis and Edwin Mofutsanyana, which Danie du Plessis duly won. Bram was then (re-)elected treasurer, his habitual occupation. It was at this conference that the formal photograph had been taken, out of which the district committee had looked with such readiness and hope.

In December 1945, again in Cape Town, Bram was elected onto the central committee of the CPSA. The annual conference discussed, among other matters, Palestine (no fixed policy) and trade unions (a resolution for the establishment of a non-racial national trade union), and was called by the Guardian 'the most stimulating in recent years'.

Jack Simons – then UCT lecturer and Party theoretician – recalled later that a special meeting of the central committee towards the end of the war predicted there would be a testing period ahead: 'We took it for granted that when the war was over, the temporary latitude given to us would come to an end.' There was an air of twilight as the world shifted. In November 1945 the Friends of the Soviet Union still celebrated the anniversary of the Russian Revolution, but there was a certain air of nostalgia, if not desperation, in its call to 'Remember Stalingrad' and the unity of just two years before. The Communist Party began to berate the United States for being on the brink of fascism; on the City Hall steps in Johannesburg Party meetings were still attacked by pro-Nazi thugs, while Smuts allowed the Greyshirts to go free.

In March 1946, just a week after Winston Churchill proclaimed in Fulton,

Missouri, that an 'iron curtain' had descended over Eastern Europe, the leader of the National Party, Dr D.F. Malan, cited the speech with approval in parliament, and asked when the government would deal with the communist menace, which he asserted had won over a majority of 'natives' in South Africa. Arthur Barlow, speaking for the government, replied that Malan's assessment was exaggerated, but that a number of prominent communists who led the 'natives' came from Afrikaner nationalist families – and he mentioned the name of Fischer directly.

Circumstances by no means changed overnight. In September 1946 the new Soviet consul-general, Mr Pavel Atroschenkov, arrived in Johannesburg to be greeted by the mayor, Mrs Jessie McPherson of the Labour Party, now also president of the Friends of the Soviet Union, with whom Bram had travelled to speak in Kimberley during the war. The Springbok Legion, the radical ex-servicemen's organisation, carried forward the momentum of previous years. But as the map of the world was being redrawn, so too were its internal contours, projections and expectations.

For Bram too, the view was relatively unclear. At the beginning of 1946 he told Percy and Ella that legal work was streaming in to such an extent that he wondered whether he would be able to devote any time to politics at all. By the end of the year, however, his path was more or less determined, for with the peace a new war was arriving in South Africa, and its advance signal was the African mineworkers' strike.

It was a strike that had been brewing for some time, for African miners remained among the most exploited workers in South Africa, even as they carved out the wealth that had supported the war. In the main they were migrant workers, housed under strict control in single-sex compounds, sleeping in concrete bunks in overcrowded rooms with barely space enough to move. During the war reduced rations meant that food was more inadequate than ever, and real wages had dropped over time (in 1946 black miners received the same £3 per month as their predecessors had been paid at the turn of the century).

The African Mineworkers' Union (AMU) had been revitalised since 1941 under the leadership of Gaur Radebe, James Majoro (a mining clerk who became secretary of the union), and J.B. Marks of the Communist Party, who became president of the AMU in 1944. Bram may have had a role in some of this, for Edwin Mofutsanyana indicated that he had brought Majoro to meet him in Johannesburg in the 1930s, when the union was being activated. Bram, recalled Mofutsanyana, had expressly asked him to find someone who could do the work (this was why Mofutsanyana thought Bram was already a member of the Party). But the union was hampered severely in its activities. War Measure 145 prohibited all strikes by Africans, and War Measure 1425 banned all meetings of more than twenty people on mine property, which made recruitment and organisation extremely difficult.

During the war the Communist Party had also been antipathetic to strikes, not wishing to support any activity that might jeopardise the defence of the Soviet Union or the later onslaught against the Nazis. However, the temper of the times was changing. In 1943 the government had rejected the recommendations of its own Lansdown Commission on a cost of living increase for miners (only a small increase in wages and overtime was granted), and now in the aftermath of the war the Communist Party too may have desired a test of strength. When, on 4 August 1946, the decision was taken at a mass meeting of miners in Market Square in Johannesburg to strike for a minimum wage of ten shillings per day, it was represented as a spontaneous and unanimous inspiration. Later, in 1990, Joe Slovo was prepared to say that the Communist Party had a primary role in instigating and organising the confrontation.

The deadline was set for 12 August, and when the strike took place it was the most momentous in South African history, far outweighing the Rand Revolt of 1922. Twelve mines were brought to a complete standstill, and nine others partially paralysed as upwards of 70,000 workers took part. The authorities also responded with extreme brutality: police surrounded and attacked men in their compounds, sealing them off from outside contact; when miners responded with sticks or stones, they used guns. A procession of 4000 miners marched towards Johannesburg, until charged and fired on by police. At the Nigel Mine workers embarked on a sit-down stoppage in the stopes, until they were driven up level by level by policemen with batons. For a while the stock exchange shimmered and quivered, as white newspapers blared headlines of panic. In Pretoria the Natives' Representative Council adjourned in disgust *sine die*, for it was as good as ignored by the government during the events.

When the strike was ultimately brought under control it had lasted five days, though in effect it was in force for only three. By the time it ended, 9 mineworkers had died, and 1248 were injured (these were the official, almost certainly underestimated figures). The Communist Party, for its part, also paid a price. While the strike was in progress the Johannesburg district committee had thrown itself into the mêlée with all the resources at its disposal – which in the main meant a small core of people working with frenzied and creative imagination as the confusion and resistance unfolded. Embroiled virtually around the clock, CPSA members copied leaflets, scaled fences, and threw flyers over walls, all to keep the isolated miners militant and abreast of the latest news. But J.B. Marks was arrested almost as soon as the strike began, and on 16 September the Johannesburg district committee headquarters were raided by the police. It was clear that a trial was to follow.

Bram had been in Johannesburg in the weeks leading up to the strike but, with an odd timing for anticlimax, was away on holiday with Molly and the children in the Kruger National Park when it occurred. (As he explained in his later testimony, he had clearly underestimated what was about to happen.) As soon as he heard the news he returned, arriving in Johannesburg on 14 September, but by the time he attended a meeting the following night, the strike was in effect over. When 'invited' to police headquarters at Marshall Square (that was how one was arrested in those days, remarked Ilse later) he complied, and though he could easily have pleaded his absence, he insisted on standing accused with his comrades on the district committee. For Bram it was once again a question of responsibility and integrity, but he wasn't the only one put on trial who had not been involved in the strike. Yusuf Dadoo was brought under escort from prison in Newcastle in Natal, where he was already convicted for his part in the passive resistance campaign opposing the so-called Ghetto Act, which delimited living areas allotted to Indians.

When Percy heard the news of Bram's arrest, he closed his court in Bloemfontein and rushed to Johannesburg to see if he could help. When Ella found out she instantly telephoned Molly, telling her not to worry because the Fischers had been through this sort of thing before. No doubt she was thinking of the Rebellion, when she and Percy and the children had suffered the consequences of their political convictions in their exile to Bergendal. Before that there had been the Boer War. The experience of being on the receiving end for political beliefs was a familiar and respectable one for the Fischer family.

<hr>

Danie du Plessis described for the *Guardian* what it was like to be an awaiting trial prisoner. 'You are led in through the main entrance down a narrow passage and into the reception room. This is a long narrow room with a cement floor, thick walls, a concrete ceiling and as cold as an ice chest . . . Here you find people stripped naked, no clothes and no boots on. They are standing in a row, and the warder shouts out the names one by one as he deals with them. Everyone is searched . . . ' Yusuf Dadoo, whom Du Plessis had seen standing in the reception room, said that during the day he had been stripped naked and had been given only a blanket to cover himself.

The trial began on 26 August, when fifty people – black, coloured, Indian and white, communists and others – appeared in the Johannesburg Magistrates' Court charged under the Riotous Assemblies Act. It was Bram's first political trial, and along with everyone else except Yusuf Dadoo he was granted bail, set for him at £100. At first the accused faced a whole barrage of allegations, including involvement in trade-union activity throughout South Africa, as well as Springbok Legion agitation against the Greyshirts – which was, given the circumstances, a somewhat ironic accusation.

The evidence turned on the course of the strike, as well as conditions the mineworkers faced in their daily lives. Mr Alfred Limebeer, secretary to the Chamber of Mines, testified that during the pre-strike period he had been instructed not to reply to any communication from the AMU regarding negotiations. It was the view of his committee, he indicated, that 'the intellect of the mine native is not comparable to that of the urban native, and . . . not suitable material for a trade union.' Senator Basner, African representative in parliament, spoke of unacceptable living conditions, and testified that he had specifically warned the Minister of Labour, Colin Steyn, that a strike was imminent unless something were done. Detective Sergeant Steyn described how police had opened fire at the Nigel Mine; after four workers had been trampled to death and one died of bullet wounds, the miners had 'volunteered', as he put it, to return to work.

During the course of the trial counsel for the defence announced that his clients were prepared to admit aiding and abetting a strike, without conceding any allegations under the Riotous Assemblies Act or the charge of incitement. Bram pleaded guilty along with the others. He was the only accused called as witness by the defence, no doubt with due consideration to the aura of his name as well as his own standing and experience in court. Entering the witness box, he attested that he was a practising lawyer and a member of the Communist Party: it was now an unambiguous statement of identity. Bram spoke of low wages, of food rations, of famine in the reserves, and suggested that the effect of these conditions had been more or less to compel the miners to contravene War Measure 145. He told the court that it was against Party principles to usurp the functions of any union, although it would lend its support and assistance when necessary. He testified that he had no knowledge of any conspiracy to manipulate the strike (the prosecution had presented certain letters which remained confusing and unclear) and said the idea of doing so horrified him: if there had been any conspiracy, it had been one organised against the mineworkers. No member of the Communist Party would recommend violence in the absence of negotiations, but in certain circumstances, remarked Bram, violence might be necessary. For his own part he had pleaded guilty not because he had done anything to assist the strike, but because, as a member of the Johannesburg executive, he felt bound to abide by its decisions and associate himself with the actions of the Party.

This was a serious stand for Bram to take. With Percy's experience of 1914 behind him, he knew the risks to his reputation and career, but in the circumstances he evidently felt that his allegiance made his choices clear. On 16 September sentence was passed on forty-five of the accused. The prosecution had asked the court to differentiate between those who were more responsible (being 'more intellectually advanced') and those who had merely distributed pamphlets, and the presiding magistrate was prepared to follow the distinction. Thirty-four were sentenced to £15 or three months' hard labour suspended for a year, and eleven (principally the Johannesburg district committee) to £50 or four months' hard labour suspended. But if there were risks for Bram as for the others, there was also a certain measure of glory. Among the letters Bram received during the trial was one from Leo Marquard, who wrote to him a satiric pastiche of colonial bravado: 'Well, Bram, keep a stiff upper lip, remember the old school tie, play the game you cads, Poona and the Hills, treat 'em rough, keep a straight bat, keep your eye on the ball, never kick a man except when he is down, tackle low, God Save the King, the ladies, God bless 'em; and, above all, try to remember what we taught you at school: if Smuts and Pirow are laid end to end, what else can you expect.' He ended the letter on the subject of police intervention – and perhaps, by abbreviation, on Smuts's United Party: 'if this document falls into the hands of any unauthorised person, and if such U.P. reads it, may his eyes blister and his toenails drop off.'

It was still possible to joke about the police, regarded in liberal and left-wing circles pretty much as heavy-limbed neanderthals, yet just a few days after sentence was passed the government gave earnest of its real intent. Harry Lawrence, the Minister of Justice, ordered police raids of Communist Party, trade union and *Guardian* offices throughout the country, as well as of the homes of left-wing individuals; large supplies of documents, papers and books were confiscated. The result was another trial, this time on charges of sedition against eight Cape Town members of the central committee. (Jack Simons remarked that in Cape Town they half suspected the Johannesburg members had pleaded guilty in order to focus attention elsewhere.) In the wake of the raids, Bram took a stand again, writing to *The Friend* in Bloemfontein (as usual addressing a constituency where he might have a particular effect), and this time his theme was the same as it had been in his earlier testimony. Industrial unrest could never be overcome by repression, he suggested, since the effect would only be to aggravate unrest. The miners had by no means required any 'agitators' to advise them what to do. Harry Lawrence's methods held out not the promise of industrial peace but, on the contrary, the threat of fascist methods.

Bram was involved distantly with the defence in the sedition case, which lasted through a desultory series of preparatory examinations and trials only to end in acquittals for all the accused just prior to the general election of 1948. As much as this denoted success for the Communist Party, however, there were more ominous and long-lasting effects. The National Party government, ushered in that same year, was able to use all the material seized in the 1946 raids to assist in tracking down its enemies, and as for Bram, he did in fact pay the personal price he may have suspected. According to Nelson Mandela, by 1946 the United Party government, in the person of Harry Lawrence (and possibly Bram's old family 'friend' Colin Steyn, or even his relation by marriage Jan Smuts), had plans to make Bram a judge. But after the mine-workers' strike and the trial – and no doubt after Bram's letter regarding Lawrence's 'fascist' methods – this was a possibility that receded for ever.

Yet there had also been some useful experience for later years. One of the prosecutors in the first round of the sedition trial was a young lawyer named Percy Yutar, whom Bram came to face in the Rivonia Trial of 1964.

One day in December 1947, when the Fischers were again on holiday at Hermanus in the Cape, they went on a drive that brought back a flood of memories for Bram, because it took in all the places he had been to in his youth. From Hermanus to Sir Lowry's Pass, to the Strand, then to Gordon's Bay and a swim 'in a sea like a mill-pond' under mountains flowing down into the ocean, then to the heights of Steenbras and a view of the whole of False Bay: describing it to his parents, Bram remembered his father's old Ford backing up Sir Lowry's Pass, the Buick burning its brakes near Caledon, visits to Vergelegen, climbs up the Steenbras Mountains. He told Percy and Ella it had been 'a day in a million'.

Earlier, in August, Bram and Molly's third child, Paul, had been born. At first there was some doubt about his name, for while Bram and Molly wanted to give him the initials 'P.U.' in honour of Percy, they realised that if they did that the combined initials of Ruth, Ilse and Paul would be 'R.I.P.', which didn't sound entirely auspicious. But it turned out that the nurses who took care of Molly had worked under Bram's brother Paul, and began calling the child 'little Paulie'. So the name stuck, and Paul was Paul Ulrich Fischer after all.

He was a small child to begin with, and then grew quickly into someone who tried *to saw the legs off chairs or through bricks. He had a wheeze, though, that wouldn't go away, except when he went to the sea. That year he was with Bram and Molly and his sisters, on that day to end all days at the Cape.*

On 26 May 1948 the National Party won the general election, with a minority of the votes cast (rural ballots were weighted to count for more than urban ones). For the United Party it was a tremendous shock. In the Free State the UP retained only one constituency out of thirteen; in the Transvaal even Jan Smuts lost his seat in parliament. *Die Vaderland*, whose headline was 'Triomf!', suggested that the '*volk*' had dealt with a 'deadly calm decisiveness', and the newspaper's cartoon showed the sun rising over a frozen landscape, with the caption 'The Sun Rises over South Africa!'

With that the National Party took power, and did not relinquish it for another forty-six years. Apartheid wasn't (except in name) an entirely new concept, but the government now pursued its segregationist policy with an accumulating ruthlessness. It eradicated racial mixing in whatever guise, from church to the distribution of land; it separated husbands from wives, lovers from one another. One of its chief targets was the Communist Party, now demonised as a sacrilegious and subversive conspiracy orchestrated from Moscow to sow national disaster and racial suicide. In this twilight the CPSA carried on with its speeches and anniversaries, even the occasional socialist-realist play, but no one could turn away the rising anxiety. Fascism, so recently defeated in Europe, appeared to be enjoying a macabre afterlife in South Africa, along with all the appurtenances of a discredited racial philo-sophy. As the sun rose for the Afrikaner nationalists, a chill descended upon everyone else.

In January 1949 Bram travelled with Molly, her brother Jimmy and her father to Spionkop, where 'Tottie' Krige had been wounded and left for dead during the Boer War. Mr Krige wanted to find the place he and the Pretoria men had stormed in their battle against imperialism, but in the dreamlike ter-rain of his memory the specific features of the landscape were unclear. In 1949 old Nakie Smith – who had come out to South Africa in the 1870s, who had turned the British soldiers away at gunpoint in Bloemfontein, who had lived through the Rebellion, and who had wanted to publish Bram's letter from the Soviet Union – died at the age of 104.

In 1950 the National Party government finalised the Bill that would become the Suppression of Communism Act. It provided for the liquidation of the Communist Party, and defined communism as, among other things, any attempt to bring about political, social or economic change through any unlawful act. In June of that year the central committee of the CPSA met in Cape Town to discuss the issue and its implications, and on 20 June Sam Kahn, Party member and Native Representative in the House of Assembly, rose to announce its decision in parliament. Kahn was a boisterous and tenacious interlocutor, who liked nothing better than a ringing diatribe aimed at fascist idiocy and malignance. But on that day he had solemn news to impart: 'Recognising that on the day the Suppression of Communism Bill becomes law, every one of our members, merely by virtue of their membership, may be liable to be imprisoned, without the option of a fine, for a maximum period of ten years, the Central Committee of the Communist Party has decided to dissolve the Party as from today.' It was almost exactly nine years to the day after the Nazi invasion of the Soviet Union.

CHAPTER 8

FAMILIES

June 1950 – July 1956

It was a full meeting of the central committee in June 1950 that decided on the dissolution. Bill Andrews was there, one of the founders of the Party in 1921, who had been through the Africanisation policies of that decade, the schisms of the 1930s (when he was both expelled and rehabilitated), the acrobatics of the Nazi–Soviet Pact, and the glories of the war, and he was one of two who now opposed the majority decision. The other was Michael Harmel, close friend of Bram, and widely credited as one of the pre-eminent theoreticians in the Party.

No doubt to these two it was unthinkable that a Communist Party with its sense of historic mission and incorruptible discipline should simply dissolve. Yet a majority of fifteen on the central committee, including Bram Fischer, Brian Bunting, Yusuf Dadoo, Sam Kahn, Moses Kotane, J.B. Marks, Edwin Mofutsanyana and Jack Simons, evidently thought otherwise. For not only was the Party fatally threatened by the Suppression of Communism Act, but it was singularly unsuited to transforming itself into any kind of underground organisation without extensive preparation. At every level the CPSA had operated openly and above board; everyone was known, everyone was vulnerable. Members who had joined (so the argument ran) had done so under the conditions and expectation of legality, but if those conditions were changed, should they now be subjected to risks to which they had not in the first place agreed? No one could predict with any degree of safety how a range of individuals recruited at different times, for different reasons and with different degrees of commitment, would stand up if the Party suddenly attempted to operate illegally. There might have been a time when an underground network could have been established, but that opportunity had now disappeared. Resignation from the Party (a kind of self-denunciation and ideological abnegation) was not an option: there seemed to be only one course open – the dissolution of the Party for the present.

Persuasive as these thoughts might have been, they did not diminish the extent to which the CPSA was proving itself a Communist Party of a special type. It was hardly in the best traditions of Bolshevism – enjoining the unblinking endurance of repression, exile and privation – that the earliest hint of trouble, however serious, should mean collapse. When the decision was relayed back to the regions, there was a good deal of dissent and dismay, as rank and file members felt abandoned, if not betrayed, by their leaders. The reasoning behind the decision struck many (as Rusty Bernstein put it) as 'eye-wash', a series of rationalisations drummed up by those who were themselves unprepared to risk going underground. In later years the Party itself declared the dissolution to have been subject to a bourgeois 'legalism': in accepting the legitimacy of the South African state and the premises of its laws, the political imperative of sustaining a revolutionary vanguard had been abandoned.

If there was a 'legalism', it must have borne the fingerprints of Bram Fischer, for it was the legal aspects of the crisis that he (along with Sam Kahn, the other lawyer on the committee) would have been called on specifically to address. Later Joe Slovo recollected accounts that Bram's views had played a 'significant' role in the discussion that day. Whenever the Communist Party admitted 'failure' in public it needed sacrificial figures (many, in private, appeared to blame Jack Simons, Harmel's competitor on the central commit-tee for intellectual leadership), though in this case the need for silence over-rode even that. There was inevitable speculation: perhaps the dissolution had been both a ruse and an opportunity – to clear the deadwood in the Party, after which it would be reconstituted in some other form. But the central commit-tee, suspecting that the government might wish to force an admission that the move had not been genuine, made no decision on this question. It kept no minutes of its discussion, and made no declaration on the future.

At that the Party hushed up all talk of dissent, and spoke only of universal acceptance. It closed ranks in its last act of obligatory unanimity as the CPSA dissolved.

***

When the Suppression of Communism Act was passed in 1950, it had tacit support in surprising quarters – not least within the African National Con-gress, just then undergoing its own transformation from an acquiescent reformism towards a greater militancy.

This development was largely due to the activities and energy of the ANC Youth League (ANCYL or CYL), established in 1944 under the leadership of Anton Lembede and a core group that included Nelson Mandela, Walter Sisulu and Oliver Tambo. These were all members of a younger generation who came from varied backgrounds: Lembede, a schoolteacher from a farm-labouring family in Natal; Sisulu, a migrant from the Transkei who had worked at everything from kitchens to gold mines to his own property agency; Mandela, the youth who had rebelled against the wardship of his patrician uncle in Thembuland and then experienced the sudden dip and acceleration of proletarian life in Johannesburg. But what they all held in common was a thoroughgoing dissatisfaction with the genuflectory political habits of their ANC elders, and they set out accordingly to work as a pressure group within the parent body. By 1949 the Youth League's insistence helped produce the ANC's new 'Programme of Action', in which for the first time the organisation declared itself prepared to use extra-parliamentary and extra-legal forms of mobilisation, including boycotts, strikes, civil disobedience, 'non-cooperation' and national stoppages of work.

The CYL also followed a resolutely African nationalist line, which made it wholly hostile towards communism. Anton Lembede was a charismatic figure and original thinker who – like his successors Robert Sobukwe and Steve Biko – pursued themes in Africanist philosophy; he was also entirely suspicious of white duplicities, especially on the part of those who claimed to be 'helping' the oppressed. From this point of view, for the CYL communism was yet one more foreign ideology foisted on blacks by whites, providing a misleading analysis of the African situation at best, and at worst another form of control. Africans who subscribed to communism were rejecting their own authentic form of liberation (a perspective which had been shared, ironically, by Afrikaner nationalists considering their own relation to communism), and the Communist Party was attempting to manipulate the ANC. Thus it was that the CYL moved the expulsion of all communists from the ANC; and in 1946, although in public the Youth League supported the mineworkers' strike, elsewhere it condemned the CPSA for engineering the stoppage for its own ends, and without proper regard for the people whose lives it was so callously jeopardising.

And so, as Nelson Mandela put it later, 'we were not unsympathetic to the banning of the Communist Party'. This was despite the fact that many realised (as did Mandela) that among the targets of the Suppression of Communism Act was the ANC itself. Moreover, when the Communist Party dissolved, the Youth League doubled its disdain, because to them the weak-kneed surrender merely proved the bad faith of the communists and their capacity for betrayal of the cause they claimed to support. When stayaways from work were called on May Day 1950 in solidarity with Moses Kotane, J.B. Marks and Yusuf Dadoo – all members of the Communist Party – as well as others who had been restricted under the Riotous Assemblies Act, the ANC was involved in all kinds of mixed response, which only underlined the ambiguities and rifts.

Yet there was another side to this that presaged a change in the relationship over time. When Nelson Mandela wrote an editorial for the CYL newspaper indicating his views on the Suppression of Communism Act, he was paid a private visit by Moses Kotane, who asked him, in essence, what he thought he was doing. Kotane put the case that the communists were allies of the ANC, fighting for the right of Africans to determine their own future – and Nelson Mandela, as he recalled it, found it hard to reply. Even in the depths of their worst suspicions, the Youth Leaguers could see that the CPSA was the only party of any substance that included white and black members and had white and black leaders. It also became significant to individuals such as Mandela and Sisulu that some of the most respected and militant leaders within the ANC were communists, such as Kotane and J.B. Marks. Kotane's credentials were impeccable, for he had, among other things, helped draft the 'Programme of Action' alongside Oliver Tambo. According to Walter Sisulu, Kotane had an almost universal respect, because his approach was resolutely non-ideological: Kotane could win over ANC leaders as diverse as the rather conservative Professor Z.K. Matthews and the deeply Christian Chief Albert Luthuli, as well as the Youth Leaguers themselves. Yusuf Dadoo, who had served time in prison, and who on one issue after another had proved his militancy and unswerving principles, also went out of his way to sustain contact with the CYL leaders, to talk, to question, to argue.

In this way a degree of personal connection was established that became persuasive, acting as a bridge for the CYL members towards whites and Indians, not to mention towards communists. In this Bram too played something of a role, although it was characteristically more reserved. Walter Sisulu remembered that Bram never tackled the Youth Leaguers directly, in the form of a Kotane or Dadoo, and yet the Youth Leaguers could see what Sisulu saw – that Kotane, Dadoo and Fischer were always close, deferring to one another, supporting one another in every discussion. No one could believe that Bram was intent on manipulation, and he always managed to leave a particular impression of candour and integrity. 'Even when we were still attacking the Communist Party,' remarked Nelson Mandela, 'I used to say that Bram is really exceptional . . . He was not really a communist. He was in that Party because there was no other Party that men like him could join.' This was a characterisation that Bram (had he known of it) might well have resented, but along with other evidence it had its effect. The idea seeped in slowly, recalled Mandela, that the ANC should not discriminate against people because of differing political ideas. As conditions intensified through the 1950s, and the atmosphere of a struggle took over, it became almost beside the point to ask questions about the ideological predispositions of one's allies. Walter Sisulu remembered that when the Communist Party was about to announce its underground existence in 1960, and Moses Kotane went to see Chief Luthuli, then president-general of the ANC, to inform him of the imminent event, Luthuli had offered only one main question in response. He asked Kotane whether this was the same party he had known before, with individuals such as Bram Fischer, Joe Slovo and Rusty Bernstein among its members, because it was only on those terms that he felt he could trust it.

The personal contacts, in other words, made a difference, and a general readiness to work across racial boundaries in the liberation movement was deepened. These people did not only represent political parties and ideological tendencies but, through their connections and constant interplay, their increasingly tactile knowledge of one another, were becoming something of a family network, with all the personal loyalties such relationships entailed. These were relationships, loyalties and connections that were to have long-lasting political and historical effects.

It was in this way that the subtle business of a mutual symbiosis took place, merging with an impulse towards unity that already existed. In 1947 Dr Xuma of the ANC, Dr Naicker of the Natal Indian Congress, and Yusuf Dadoo (also, in his professional capacity, a physician) of the Transvaal Indian Congress had signed their so-called Doctors Pact approving co-operation between their organisations. This commitment was reaffirmed by the ANC and NIC in 1949 in the wake of riots that had broken out between Africans and Indians in Natal. In 1950, as the enactment of the Suppression of Communism Act approached, the ANC and the South African Indian Congress combined yet again in declaring 26 June a 'National Day of Protest and Mourning'. The stay-aways from work they called for nation-wide materialised only unevenly, but both Walter Sisulu (now secretary-general of the ANC) and Nelson Mandela were involved in organising the protests for that day.

This was how 26 June became a significant day for the ANC as well as the Communist Party, and was henceforward celebrated annually as Freedom Day. It was also on Freedom Day two years later that the campaign began that was to give the ANC its very stamp and image for the next forty years. This was the so-called Defiance Campaign, proffered by the ANC in response to the white government's plans to celebrate the tercentenary of Jan van Riebeeck's founding of a settlement at the Cape. Walter Sisulu wrote a joint letter with Dr James Moroka (president-general of the ANC) to Prime Minister Malan

demanding the repeal of six 'unjust laws', including the pass laws, the Group
Areas Act and the Suppression of Communism Act, failing which batches of
disciplined volunteers would proceed systematically but non-violently to defy
these laws nation-wide. Malan dismissed the demand out of hand, as if he had
no choice in the matter (a letter from his secretary pointed out that the laws
were 'permanent and not man-made'), and so on 26 June 1952 the Defiance
Campaign began.

Volunteers contravened curfews, occupied segregated railway and post
office facilities, flouted location statutes, and refused to carry passes. Nelson
Mandela was the volunteer-in-chief, and he (unintentionally) and Sisulu
(intentionally) were arrested on the first day. In Natal, Luthuli was ordered by
the government to resign from the ANC or from his chieftainship, and refused
to do either. Marching against the police, defiers sang songs, chanted in call-
and-response form 'Afrika! Mayibuye!' [Africa! May it come back!], and gave
the ANC thumbs-up sign indicating that Africa would indeed return to its
rightful people, and they to it. The ethos of resistance was changing, as the
stirrings of a mass movement became apparent in all its potential. By its own
objective (the repeal of the laws) the Defiance Campaign was not ultimately
successful, nor did it end non-violently: the government introduced financially prohibitive and physically punitive penalties for defiance, and there were
riots in Port Elizabeth (initiated, claimed the ANC, by provocateurs). But by
the end of the campaign more than 8000 defiers had been arrested, and the
ANC's membership shot up, by some (perhaps inflated) accounts, to 100,000.

In the main it was Africans and Indians who defied the government (the
campaign had been inspired in part by Gandhi's legacy of *satyagraha*, which
had so inflamed old Abraham Fischer). Not many whites participated,
although there were a few such as Bettie du Toit, who had accompanied
Bram to Kimberley during the war, and who now, together with Patrick
Duncan (a liberal), Manilal Gandhi (the Mahatma's son, who first objected to
the campaign, then joined) and others, marched into the segregated confines
of Germiston location near Johannesburg in December. Communists by and
large were sceptical of the Gandhist nature of the campaign, but in its wake
were galvanised into action. In November 1952 there was a famous meeting in
Johannesburg, addressed by Walter Sisulu and Oliver Tambo among others,
that prefaced the birth of two new organisations. One was the South African
Congress of Democrats, founded in 1953, and committed (as the 'Congress'
appellation implied) to the objectives of the Defiance Campaign, as well as to
a broader alliance with the ANC, the South African Indian Congress, the
South African Coloured People's Congress and, in due course, the South

African Congress of Trade Unions. These were the racially defined but radiating spokes in the wheel (the image that was used at the time) of the Congress Alliance, and it was the Congress Alliance that was behind the other heroic moments in what was consciously seen as an heroic decade: the Congress of the People and the Freedom Charter; the women's demonstration against passes in Pretoria; the emblazoned unity of the Treason Trial. Also founded in 1953 was the Liberal Party, anti-communist, but also anti-apartheid in limited terms (it favoured the franchise for suitably 'qualified' Africans).

It was in this light that the 1950s became known as the era of multi-racialism. If the intent of the apartheid government was to prove some misguided point about God-given racial hierarchies and distinctions, then the anti-apartheid movement would show through its most intimate gestures as much as its wider institutional structures that not only were racial co-operation and harmony possible, but that the only kind of superiority there could be was moral. In a wider social and cultural sphere other energies reinforced the political, as racial boundaries were transgressed in everything from the jazz opera *King Kong*, which took Johannesburg by storm, to the drinking life of the shebeens of Sophiatown, glorified by an exuberant young generation of black writers on *Drum* magazine. Disrupting the weight of repression there was the sense of a force in the making equal and opposite to that of segregation.

Bram Fischer was a founding member of the Transvaal Congress of Democrats, which together with the Springbok Legion and the Democratic League of Cape Town fused in the South African Congress of Democrats. SACOD was suspected by the Liberal Party as well as by Africanists within the ANC of being a Communist Party front set up to control the Congress Alliance, and certainly there were grounds for the suspicion: many ex-communists joined the COD, since there was no other legal party that expressed their commitment to full-scale democracy. On the other hand, prominent members of the COD were by no means communist – Helen Joseph and the Rev. D.C. Thompson among them – and it is unlikely that people of the calibre of Mandela, Tambo and Sisulu, with their resolute Youth League background, would have succumbed very easily to any form of external control.

By 1953 (the same year as the COD was founded) the CPSA had indeed been reconstituted clandestinely as the South African Communist Party (the name shift may have been a 'legalism' of rebirth to equal that of the earlier dissolution, protecting those who had belonged to the old Party as much as it was intended to mark a new era). It took the decision that all its members, of whatever race, should work in and through the Congress organisations, as Kotane, Marks and Dadoo had done for many years. The formal idea was that in this capacity they should prove their worth and fervour by working for the objectives of these organisations, rather than directly for those of the Communist Party, which, when all was said and done, remained a separate body. It was perhaps a fine line, but given the CPSA's – and now the SACP's – illegality, it was apparently the only line that existed.

Mr J. de Villiers Louw, appointed under the terms of the Suppression of Communism Act the 'liquidator' of the CPSA, had in addition to his general duties of disposing of the Party's assets the task of compiling a 'list' of its 'office-bearers, officers, members or active supporters'. This list was to remain with the Minister of Justice, and individuals named on it would be subject to specific disabilities. They could be banned from certain areas, or prohibited from holding public office (as were Sam Kahn, Brian Bunting and Ray Alexander, successively ejected from parliament as Native Representatives, and Fred Carneson, who was removed from the Cape Provincial Council). They could not, with a certain heavy-handed irony, bring actions of slander for being called 'communist'. Attorneys could be prohibited from belonging to the Law Society (which meant they could not practise), and advocates excluded from the Bar Council (which would make practice extremely difficult). The Minister of Justice, however, had taken pains to assure ex-communists that he would use these powers only in cases of necessity.

Initial 'naming' letters were sent out soon after the Act came into force, and Bram appears to have received his early in September 1950. Molly sent it on to Percy for his inspection, and thanked him when he returned it: 'They're now tuppence a dozen – & the novelty has worn off for all but the people concerned.' Then, in the second half of 1951, further notice went out from the liquidator, inviting recipients to show cause why their names should not be placed on the final list. Forty individuals from the Johannesburg area, including Bram and many of those who were now his friends as well as comrades of some years – Yusuf Dadoo, Danie du Plessis, Rusty Bernstein, Moses Kotane, Eli Weinberg, Edwin Mofutsanyana, Michael Harmel, J.B. Marks, Joe Slovo and Harold Wolpe, among them – replied to the Minister of Justice that they refused to participate in any such process: 'You are attempting to silence us first, but ultimately all critics of your regime.' History, wrote the 'named', had shown that attempts to arrest human progress could not ultimately succeed: 'Your tyranny will not survive the judgement of the people.'

In the wake of the Party's dissolution the previous year it may have been a less than compelling statement, and the Minister of Justice, C.R. Swart, was evidently unimpressed. The communist letter was published in newspapers on 4 September, and final notices confirming the list were sent out just a few weeks later. Bram, along with many others, received one, but the full South African capacity for absurdity as well as complexity was revealed to him in a personal way shortly thereafter. For barely a month later, in November 1951, Bram received a second letter from C.R. Swart – who went under the fond appellation of 'Oom Blackie' [Uncle Blackie] to all who knew him in the Afrikaner nationalist fold. Bram knew him too, as did his family, because the Swarts were Free Staters, and 'Oom Blackie' was, like Percy and Bram, a lawyer; these people all knew one another. Now Swart was writing to Bram to congratulate him on his appointment as King's Counsel – approved, as all such appointments were, by the cabinet, and overseen by the Minister of Justice. Moreover, Swart's letter, though it bore the official Ministry of Justice insignia, was not a formal one: it was a personal letter, combining an undeniable brevity with an unexpected intimacy. 'Beste Braam' [Dear Braam – the usual misspelling], it opened, and continued in Afrikaans, 'I congratulate you on your admission to senior status as an advocate. I also wish you success in your further career at the Bar. With good wishes.' And it was signed C.R. Swart.

It appears that Bram had first been encouraged by colleagues to take silk as early as 1946 – which would have made him the youngest member of the Johannesburg Bar to do so – but had demurred at that stage. Now, perhaps feeling that his opportunity might disappear for ever, he had applied. As for Swart, he would not have had a great deal of choice in the matter, given the highly structured traditions of the South African judicial system, but evidently for him, as for other Nationalists, Bram was not entirely beyond redemption. This was not just a matter of polite deference to his background, but involved a real degree of personal admiration. (Nelson Mandela remarked that even B.J. Vorster, Swart's successor in the 1960s, whose repressive capacities made Swart look positively tame by comparison, had an unusual respect for Bram.) But numbers of people noted the irony of the appointment. 'The position of C.R.S[wart] who must officially congratulate you', wrote Leo Marquard, 'reminded me of the late George V when it was suggested he christen a new battleship the *Cromwell*.' Bram's Aunt Maude, in sending her congratulations, was upset only that Bram had been appointed a King's Counsel and not a 'P.C.' (presumably, People's Counsel): 'I was born under a Republican government, & hope to die under one!' A communist had been appointed King's Counsel by an anti-monarchical Nationalist: no one could have been satisfied. Bram's brother Paul addressed him as 'Geagte Edelagbare' – which meant 'Esteemed Honourable', or vice versa.

In writing to Bram, Swart had wished him luck only at the Bar and nowhere else; he may have been trying to suggest that Bram restrict himself accordingly. Bram's reply, which he put through at least two drafts, was also written in Afrikaans, and equally careful. 'Beste Oom Blackie,' the second draft began: 'It was friendly of you to congratulate me on my appointment as K.C. I value it highly. The disadvantage of the recognition is that if one does not succeed in the elevated status, the 'appointer' – the Minister – cannot be held responsible! But whether I succeed or not, I hope nevertheless that I shall always be able to exert myself to maintain the high traditions of our profession.'

In saying that he hoped that he would always 'be able to exert' himself in this way, Bram had crossed out 'we shall always try to maintain the high traditions of our profession'. In other words, he may have been suggesting (ever so indirectly) that he hoped he would always be *permitted*, or find it *possible*, to uphold what the profession – which was Oom Blackie's too, he reminded him – represented. Each, in his own way, was trying to remind the other to stick to the law. Years later, under Vorster's regime, when the rule of law was entirely abrogated, Bram's quest for justice became impossible in the form to which he now gave his allegiance.

In the meanwhile, he used his newly elevated status to accentuate that quest. In May 1952, when Solly Sachs, secretary of the Garment Workers' Union and one-time communist, defied his banning order by speaking at a public meeting, Bram defended him in court. In November and December of that year, when twenty Congress leaders, including Mandela and Sisulu, were put on trial under the Suppression of Communism Act for their activities in the Defiance Campaign, Bram was one of the lawyers who took up the defence, and he wrote affectionately to Percy and Ella about 'all my accused'. In 1954, when the Transvaal Law Society (the attorneys' organisation) applied to have Nelson Mandela struck off the roll because his activities in the Defiance Campaign 'did not conform to the standards of conduct expected from members of an honourable profession', Bram was instrumental in obtaining the services of Walter Pollock, a senior Queen's Counsel, who acted *pro amico* in winning the case with costs (which was unusual) for Mandela. The judge in the case happened to be Bram's old mentor Ramsbottom, and Nelson Mandela observed later that he was 'very good, and friendly'. The connection with Bram could not have done any harm.

The Defiance Campaign trial was an intriguing one. It was of course a heavily politicised affair, and the preparatory examination in Johannesburg was accompanied by mass demonstrations which Moroka and Dadoo had to calm down. Yet Moroka, a doctor whose flourishing practice in Thaba Nchu was renowned among whites as among blacks, became uneasy at the turn of events, and the police, perhaps sensing this, targeted him directly. According to Nelson Mandela they showed him sections of the Suppression of Communism Act providing for the confiscation of personal property in the event that it had been used in the commission of an offence, and pointed out that the other accused had little or no property to lose, but that Moroka stood to lose everything. It was in fact a false threat, since Moroka's property had not been used in the Defiance Campaign, but he became alarmed at the sudden possibility, as well as by the fact that some among the defence counsel for the twenty – including Bram – were listed communists. Accordingly, he opted to be represented by separate counsel, and during the trial asserted his own anti-communism with vigour. There was a danger that others would do exactly the same, concerned both by the communist lawyers and also by the presence of communists among the accused, but apparently Bram played a key role in talking to them and preserving what unity remained. 'He saw us through that trial,' recalled Mandela.

In effect Moroka had divided himself from his followers, and the resentment aroused by his actions had repercussions. He himself had been the candidate of the Youth Leaguers when he replaced Dr Xuma as president-general of the ANC in 1950. Now the Youth League dropped its support, and turned instead to the redoubtable Chief Luthuli, who was appointed president-general in elections immediately following the case. In a sense the CYL had been betrayed by one of its own ANC leaders, but the communists had proved their mettle and solidarity through the course of the trial. Once again the new relationship was cemented. As for the outcome of the case, the accused were found guilty of what the judge was prepared to call 'statutory communism' only, and not, as he put it, 'of what is commonly known as communism'. He accepted that the defendants had consistently advocated a peaceful campaign, and sentenced them to nine months' imprisonment, suspended for two years.

Bram heard of the verdict in Europe, where he thought the sentences 'wonderfully light – I've always said, please God to give us nationalist Judges', but also remarked that the convictions raised all sorts of problems for the future. Possibly Bram preferred 'nationalist Judges' in such matters because he believed that, being in the party of power, they might permit themselves some of the discretion of authority – or feel the need to prove their fairness – instead of merely following the ruthless intent of the law. As for the problems he foresaw, these must have had to do with the ominous category of 'statutory communism', which could cut a large swathe of accusation and guilt. In the event the Defiance Campaign case did indeed have echoes that would return. The name of the judge in the trial was Rumpff, and he was to be the presiding judge in the Treason Trial, where the two central questions were whether the Congress Alliance's record (from the time of the Defiance Campaign on) had been peaceful or violent, and whether the ANC was intrinsically linked to com-munism. There the stakes would be higher, the climate of accusation more shadowed, and Rumpff's role somewhat less salutary and more aggressive.

～～

Bram was in Europe when he heard the Defiance Campaign sentences, because at the end of November 1952 he was on his way to Vienna, to attend the Congress of the Peoples for Peace. Writing to Molly from London en route he gave her marvellous glimpses of his journey so far:

> It seems unbelievable and I'm still pinching myself to see if I'm awake. Tuesday Johannesburg. Wednesday, eleven o'clock tea at Nairobi and Tel Aviv at 10 p.m. Sandwiches and a beer with Naomi and her husband. Then the 'sightseeing' really started and I wish I could have had Ruth with me. We could have gone through her whole classical history together. Just as it became light, the lights of Athens twinkled below us . . . From Athens . . . a pale emerald sea . . . Italian villages . . . a clear view of Vesuvius . . . Naples like a toy city . . . St Peter's and the Coliseum in Rome . . . the Arno . . . Florence . . . Pisa clear as a miniature . . . the Jungfrau and the Matterhorn . . . So high that to get down to Zurich we had to circle down like the homing pigeons at Silverton. France . . . tea at Orly airfield and then the lights of Paris as we left . . . in moonlight above the clouds until we plunged down into thick fog at Heath Row . . .

Heading for Vienna, the city of art, music and resistance he had last seen in 1933, Bram must have reflected on some of the ironies of history, for the threat of fascism he had last seen there had now been vanquished in Europe, only to take stronger root in his own country. It was a comment on the world of 1952, Bram wrote to Molly after her own first letter to him, 'when one is glad the other has left [South Africa] safely'.

In the post-war world a peace congress had ambiguous overtones, for 'peace' had become a rallying cry in the new Cold War, as the East's rhetorical and ideological response to what it represented as the imperialist and militarist designs of the West. 'Peace' was a call that successfully aligned the support of

Western intellectuals and progressive movements with anti-colonial and anti-imperial struggles from Malaya to Korea, but if the tenor of this was orchestrated from Moscow, that did not mean there were no genuine believers. To Bram, with a sense of South African as well as recent European history, it would have made perfect sense that only just and democratic societies at peace with themselves could transcend the otherwise endless cycles of oppression and conflict. From his Oupa Abraham's efforts prior to the Boer War to the name ('Vrede') of his Aunt Maude's house, he may have felt that it was a cause he had been born for. It was in this light that when the Transvaal Peace Council was formed in 1951, he had been a founder member, and that was why he was now travelling, along with Alan Lipman, to Vienna as the council's representative.

In London he found himself in a world of post-war rationing and recovery, a startling contrast to the earlier environs and ethos he had known. The smells were the same as two decades earlier, he told Molly, though there were no napkins or menus for meals, and newspapers were minute. Bram revisited the digs in Gower Street where both he and Percy before him had stayed, but found them turned into a Ministry of Supply building. He saw the miraculous survival of St Paul's, with a bomb-flattened landscape around it. Chiefly Bram battled the fog, the worst in London for forty years, so bad that it turned his white nylon shirts black, and enveloped the hotel so completely that he could not see down the passage. Through the streets wandered shades as if strayed from the realms of Dante or T.S. Eliot, heading at night, suitably enough, for the Underground: 'Walking to the tube the visibility dropped to no more than 3 yards. Dark coughing figures would appear out of the gloom, & disappear as soon as they had passed . . . Several people joined us and then eventually we all reached the tube.' Bram was writing this to Molly and the children on holiday at Port St John's: from the infernal depths of fog to paradise and sun.

Although Bram was revitalised by the cultural life around him, it was evident that his political and aesthetic tastes had hardened from twenty years before. West End theatre he found bourgeois and neurotic, and even the stage charms of Peggy Ashcroft could not win him. He much preferred, he wrote, 'a real play about Malaya' at the socialist Unity Theatre (it showed, he told nine-year-old Ilse, 'how badly the people there are treated – even worse than in our own country'), or an East German film about the Krupps in the Second World War ('what is . . . interesting is to see films with a real message'). He went to an exhibition of Paul Hogarth's drawings of the poor in Greece, and felt at home meeting minor writers and Eastern Bloc attachés at left-wing parties.

Perhaps his patience had frayed just a little in the last six years, or else it was simply an overwhelming relief to gravitate towards an environment that validated his sense of belonging. Certainly it was in this spirit that Bram left London, via Zurich, for Vienna, where he arrived for the opening of the congress on 12 December. In the Western press the congress was derided: it had nothing like the number of participants claimed in advance, reported the *New York Times*, and the presiding suspicion was that the whole event was being choreographed by the Chinese, currently embroiled against the United States in Korea, or the Cominform. But to the enthusiastic delegates arriving in Vienna such allegations would have been virtually empty of meaning – emptied of the sense of a new world in the making. There Bram found himself amidst luminaries aplenty, including Diego Rivera, Emil Zatopek (the Czech long-distance runner), Ilya Ehrenburg (a staple at such events) and Jean-Paul Sartre, but it also pleased him that not all of the delegates were obviously 'left' – that there were some, such as Nitti, the liberal Italian parliamentarian, whose passion for peace helped create an affiliation of conviction surpassing ideology. This to Bram was the historical current he was seeking, the broad alliance of morality and conscience which was the only hope for a world needing radical transformation.

The congress turned on the central issue of the Korean War, and specifically on allegations by the Koreans that the Americans had been employing germ warfare. Of this Bram became convinced: after visiting a Chinese exhibition on the subject he told Molly it was 'sickening and conclusive', and ever after the motif of germ warfare as the utmost scandal against humanity and the logical outcome of rampant imperialism preyed heavily on his mind. There were stories from elsewhere as well, he reported, as 'one delegate after another . . . told us of the suffering of mankind – in Korea, Vietnam, Malaya, China, Algeria, Tunis, Morocco, &c &c'. As account after account was delivered, the cumulative testimony produced a rising well of feeling among the participants. Bram described to Molly how, after a Korean woman had spoken, delegates had wept in the hall, and then cheered her for ten minutes as she was lifted shoulder high. The Malayans, embarked on their own guerrilla struggle against the British, had received practically the same welcome. It was, remarked Bram, 'an emotional experience one does not have often in life'.

It was this kind of upswell that led to the collective passions of the final session, where ballots were taken on an 'Address to Peoples' and an 'Address to Governments': as the text of each was approved overwhelmingly, the results were read out to shouts and cheering and rolling waves of rhythmic applause. After Nitti made the farewell speech, the climactic response went on for twenty minutes, and Bram felt as if it would never end. To Percy and Ella he summed up the momentous effect as one of 'complete inspiration': 'At a Congress like this one really feels the enormous urge to peace of millions upon millions of people – people of all shades of religion, politics & colour. And not merely a passive urge but an active unselfish drive to act positively – to be vocal even at the risk, for many of the delegates, of real persecution on their return to their countries. In fact, I do not suppose that ever in history has such a Congress been assembled. Just try to imagine well over 70 nations represented by over 1600 delegates. Imagine Germans & French together, Americans & Koreans, French & Vietnamese, English & Malayans, to issue declarations that peace between them can be arranged . . . '

In his own way Bram had played a small part at the congress. It was to him that the minor honour had fallen of announcing the time of the final session (which, in the manner of such events, inevitably started some four hours late), and during one of the night sessions on easing international tensions he had spoken directly about South Africa: 'It is unspeakably cruel that because of their colour the black and brown people of our country should be condemned to dire poverty, to an infant mortality [rate] of 400 per 1,000, to illiteracy and to voicelessness in the affairs of state; should be deprived of the right to land, of freedom of speech, of movement and association . . . [S]uch a racial system constitutes the broad road to a full-blown fascist state with all its inherent dangers to peace.' Earlier Bram had told Molly that there had not been much self-criticism at the congress, apart from German speakers who accepted blame for the war, and one or two Frenchmen: 'Perhaps we'll be able to do that – certainly the English have not.' This, then, was Bram's acceptance of responsibility in South Africa – a personal characteristic translated into national and global terms, voiced in a hugely public forum. Voiced too was the danger of a South African fascism, which all of Bram's available analogies would have suggested, and hence his overwhelming urgency in opposing it in Vienna, where he had seen it launched two decades before.

There can be no doubt that the congress had burnt a personal inspiration into Bram's psyche, even though much of what happened there may have been formulaic and predictable – the vacuous poetry warning South Africa's Prime Minister Malan to 'beware', and proposing 'Death to the killers who enslave their native land!' There were the inevitable superficialities of a Cold War congress for peace to which, on occasion, Bram's own orthodox language and world-view succumbed: 'This time', he wrote to Percy and Ella, 'the war mongers and armament kings will dig their own graves.' All of this may have meant that it took a particular innocence – credulity as well as dedication – to find a home in such an ambivalent historical setting; and yet there had to be some virtue in dedicating oneself to work within as well as against irony, for peace and an end to armaments and war. How many other choices were there? Even as Bram felt the pinched isolation of repression in South Africa, here was the breath that could fill the spirit with a renewed sense of life, the sudden release of reassurance that one belonged to a larger conglomeration of what was right and good in the world.

Bram described everything for Ruth, Ilse and Paul, sending them postcards attuned to their individual interests. On Christmas Eve he wrote of seeing the old synagogue in Vienna, dating to the thirteenth century, now surviving the Nazi affliction. The base of the building was some feet below ground, and had steps leading down to the front door. The clock inside ran anticlockwise because of its Hebrew orientation, and in the cemetery the graves pre-dating 1400 revealed an archaic script on their stones. Bram had been shown around by the caretaker, an old man of seventy whose name also happened to be Fischer.

He also visited the city cathedral, with its medieval stained glass of resplendent colours, and a nearby street dating back a thousand years where alchemists had lived under King Rudolf of Bohemia in 1600. Later, on his way home, Bram stopped off in Oxford where he revisited New College, and was shown recently discovered old treasures – ash flooring more than 500 years old, Bishop Wykeham's crozier from the fourteenth century, the first Chinese bowl to reach England (during the reign of Henry VII). In London he met up with Sydney Kentridge, a young advocate at the Johannesburg Bar on holiday in England with his wife, and asked Molly, 'Do you think we'll ever be able to manage that?'

This was the other life that Bram might have lived. He was as entranced by the alchemy of the past as he was by the history of the future, but it was to the demands of the latter that, given his circumstances, he had to be dedicated.

Some clocks do have to run anticlockwise.

Bram left London on 25 January, and arrived back in South Africa some fifty hours later, having absorbed whatever peace a peace congress could give him.

In July 1954 it was Molly's turn to leave for London, and Bram and the children went to see her off. 'When eventually your plane sailed away,' wrote Bram, 'you took our hearts with you and left us with chattering teeth and sinking stomachs – or rather no stomachs at all. Also, our upper lips were not so stiff. Fortunately Paul bumped his head & had an excuse for a small cry.'

There was an air of mystery surrounding the departure. Bram gave Percy and Ella to believe that Molly was suffering from stress and overwork, that she had been 'in a flat spin' at home, and that on her journey overseas he wanted her 'to have a break, to see some theatre, ballet & enjoy herself'. But in inviting Percy to take her place on a holiday with him and the children in the game reserve, he had added specific instructions: 'As to Molly's trip, keep that quite to yourselves for the moment and don't even write to us about it. You can just say we have some extra accommodation in the Reserve.' Either Bram still trusted the mails for his own letter, or he must have sent it privately. As for Molly, before she left, she wrote a note to the Rev. D.C. Thompson, chair of the South African Society for Peace and Friendship with the Soviet Union – the old FSU, of which Molly was now secretary – to be mailed by Bram afterwards as a sign that she had left safely.

Molly was travelling to England, but wanted to go farther, to Eastern Europe and the USSR, and she was also tantalised by the hope of a trip to China, of which there had been some indication. Cryptic references on all these matters punctuated the letters between her and Bram. Bram advised Molly to discuss her 'other possible visit with V.' – this was most likely Vella Pillay, an Indian friend and left-wing contact in London, who had gone into exile from South Africa with his white wife – and to tell him 'precisely what happened here before you left and why it was thought it would be a good thing for you to go'. There was talk in both directions about 'Oliver' (perhaps Tambo) who 'appears to be a possibility now', and of his 'arrival' that never materialised. Molly wrote about collecting money in London, probably for the SASPFSU, and certainly for *New Age*, the latest successor in the *Guardian* line, each of whose journalistic reincarnations was systematically being banned by the government.

Given the South African Communist Party's recent reconstitution, it is hard to believe that Molly's trip did not have any clandestine purposes. If she was attempting to establish contacts, however, she found no assistance from any obvious quarters. Before leaving South Africa she had applied for a visa to the USSR through an agency known dimly as VOKS – the All-Soviet Society for Foreign Cultural Relations, an organisation almost certainly overseen by the KGB – and had been turned down. Given the experience, she felt there was no point in approaching them in London again. As for the response of VOKS (or the KGB), they may have had their reasons: it had been just a year since Stalin had died, and amidst the struggles for power in the Soviet Union there might well have been suspicions of any unacknowledged and unannounced new South African Communist Party. But even the British Society for Peace and Friendship with the Soviet Union didn't seem to carry much weight with the relevant authorities when Molly contacted them. And so she appeared to be stuck in London.

Ultimately it was the trip to China that opened things up, for Ruth First was already there, and through her Molly was sent an invitation to the fifth anniversary of the Chinese Revolution, to be celebrated on 1 October 1954. Where the Soviet bureaucrats had been dull and unhelpful, Molly found the Chinese by contrast delightful and efficient: she had her visa to China within a week and then, on the strength of this, was ultimately able to obtain a transit visa for the USSR. En route Molly was also to travel through East Germany, Poland and Czechoslovakia, under the auspices of the Women's International Democratic Federation in Berlin (she had obtained the endorsement of the Federation of South African Women to establish her credentials). In this way her initial plans for a holiday – or something more than that – of two months overseas turned into a journey of twice that duration.

Having visited the famous churchyard of Gray's 'Elegy' ('you know how I love cemeteries,' Molly reminded Bram), she left England by the third week in August for Bonn, where she met up with one of her German cousins (the Bernsmann connection), and saw the hotel where Chamberlain had stayed on one of his futile visits to Hitler in 1938. There Molly found the bourgeois ways of her West German relatives somewhat stifling, but as soon as she crossed to East Germany a new exhilaration entered in. Overnight, Molly told Bram, she became a 'delegation', and was showered with gifts; she soon perfected the technique 'of presenting at any institution the bouquet I had received at the previous place'. She laid chrysanthemums at the memorial to the Fallen Soviet Soldiers, produced a report on the Federation of South African Women, gave a radio talk to be broadcast in English, German, French and Spanish, and had lunch with the celebrated writer Stefan Heym, who enquired after Harry Bloom, just then trying to publish his own novel, *Transvaal Episode*, in which Bram appeared by name. Heym said Molly should tell Bloom that he '& all other artists are paid better than the Prime Minister'.

Molly travelled to Dresden, so destroyed in the war, but where for her the miracle of socialist revival was now marked by the reconstruction of Bram's beloved Zwingerhaus and the delicate restoration of its sculptures. She visited a home for child victims of the Korean War, where she received 'firm handshakes and hugs' and was requested to write in the visitors' book in Afrikaans. At a march-past of sportsmen she was placed on the podium and was announced, yet again, as a 'delegation from South Africa'. In short, Molly was being treated with the best care the East could give its own, but outweighing this in significance was always the attitude of the people she met: 'They all seemed so enthusiastic & certain they would succeed.' The pattern was sustained in Prague, where Molly was chaperoned by a personal attendant (coincidentally named Ilse) who did her best to cater to her every wish. Molly was becoming familiar with the *quid pro quo* – a report for the Friendship Society, a lecture replete with a university professor translating and applause that went on 'for about 5 minutes' – but confessed to Bram an inner uncertainty that belied her outward composure: 'I keep thinking about the remark that one must go through fire and come out steel not ashes. At the moment I feel much nearer ashes than I have ever felt before.' It was in Prague that her transit visa for the Soviet Union finally came through.

She travelled via Moscow (if there was Party work there it remained hidden) to Ulan Bator in the Gobi Desert where, aside from the camels dotted about and the cattle of a quite unknown breed, the brown scrub and brass aerodrome reminded her of home. From there she made her way to Peking – and so it was that on the fifth anniversary of the Chinese Revolution Molly Fischer found herself standing with numbers of other delegates on a podium just beneath Mao Tse-tung, watching the massed ranks of a four-hour parade in the Square of Heavenly Peace. She described it all in meticulous detail for Bram: the soldiers, sailors, pilots and parachutists flowing past in endless number, the cavalry and tanks in front, jets roaring overhead. There were processions of pioneers, with flowers, hoops and flags, and workers marching eighty abreast, all with the tools and models of their trade. Surveyors, geologists, prospectors and film-industry workers marched past, then labourers from the canning industry '& other factories, all with large charts showing production increases in the last five years'. There were red, purple and yellow balloons, some with slogans demanding the liberation of Taiwan; the peasants and civilians paraded, and minorities in national dress. Even the monks, nuns and Catholic priests had their place; for Molly the marchers looked like nothing so much as acres of Dutch tulips in colour. After two hours there was a merciful withdrawal for refreshments, and still the procession continued; finally the schoolchildren and students appeared, and then the athletes and dancers, and there were universal cheers for Mao. That night the fireworks and dancing went on until morning.

How far and how different from South Africa. And yet this was the promise of a world of unity and joy, renovation and peace to which Bram and Molly hoped they could belong. It was a prospect confirmed and enriched for Molly by her other experiences and observations – from an exquisite performance at the opera, where lovers were transformed after death into butterflies, to a session at the National Peoples' Congress, where of the 1226 deputies 11.99% ('please note, not 12%,' she wrote to Bram of the Chinese penchant for statistical accuracy) were women – the youngest a nineteen-year-old model worker who had invented a new spinning method. At the Peoples' Congress Molly found the atmosphere bright, constructive and serious – so different, she told Bram, from the South African parliament. Coddled by an interpreter who took care of her every slightest whim, she marvelled at the Forbidden City and the Temple of Heaven, and also visited the only prison in Peking, where two-thirds of the prisoners were 'political' (meaning a low percentage of criminals, Molly deduced with a self-revealing twist), and where conditions were apparently so enlightened that many of the prisoners refused to leave on completion of their sentences, and were paid a salary. At the university Molly met the principal, who – she told Bram – looked just like Percy, and was immensely proud of the fact that so many of his students and faculty were women.

She travelled on to other cities, in Shanghai looking out 'from the windows of my 6th floor luxurious hotel bedroom' on to a sea of red-tiled roofs and a river as busy as the Thames – sampans in the place of barges – down below. She visited a 'Children's Palace' in what had used to be the British Overseas Club, where bright young pioneers now welcomed their guests with handclapping and firm handshakes and performed folk-dancing on the lawn. In Nanking Molly inspected a 'National Sanitation Village Class I', converted from what had been the equivalent of an inhabited sewage dump to a clean village of whitewashed cottages and trees. Her interpreter had been one of the students who, during the 1952 Patriotic Sanitation Movement, had ventured out with chopsticks and a paper bag to dig for fly larvae, and 'like everyone else' had fulfilled her quota. Molly's every curiosity was satisfied: when she voiced an interest in Chinese legal proceedings, she was taken together with a French judge to a divorce court presided over by a woman.

Ultimately Molly returned via Hangchow and Peking to Moscow and London, where (after a brief visit to Stockholm on behalf of the Federation of South African Women) she left for home in the middle of November. Before her departure from China she had written formally to Tsai Chang, president of the All-China Democratic Women's Federation, the organisation whose guest she had been. In her letter Molly wrote of the part women now played in China, as doctors, lawyers, judges, factory directors, locomotive drivers, actresses, trade-union leaders and teachers. All of this was a truly wonderful achievement, she observed, 'when one remembers that five short years ago women were still subjugated by feudal laws and customs'. Women now had their needs taken care of; pregnancy was no longer something to be feared.

China's first National Congress had more women deputies than England's 'Mother of All Parliaments', which had only one woman member. 'To the visitor,' wrote Molly, 'the new China is a miracle . . . I can only humbly offer my thanks to the women of China and wish them still greater success in the tasks ahead of them. I say with them "Long Live World Peace."'

It truly was another world. Molly and Bram were not just fooled by what they saw and believed in. Yes, a prison had prisoners who wanted to stay on. But even if they knew they were being shown model scenes from luxury hotels, what they saw still represented in many ways the beginnings of a new and better life. Molly called her letter to the Chinese Federation a 'bread and butter' affair, but when Bram showed a copy of it to Joe Slovo in Johannesburg, Slovo read it and said, 'Good old Molly.'

When the South African Communist Party was reconstituted – after numbers of splinter groups had formed and dissolved – it was much thinned from previous years. The old Party, for all its revolutionary objectives, had been an open one, with local branches and district committees, even (at one time) interest groups for architects, artists and lawyers. Now its successor had to learn the difficult business of clandestine activity in every aspect of its operations. Drawing on the experience of underground organisations elsewhere, the Party opted for a cell system within a pyramid formation, in which one member of a small group would communicate upwards, and one down, and there was limited (if not zero) lateral contact. In theory no one knew the full membership of the Party, though many felt they could easily guess in particular cases.

To begin with, both the communists and the still-watchful Special Branch were amateurs, as they circled each other in a wary dance of mutual observation. SACP cells held meetings in motor cars, the open air, or safe or rented flats; those attending left home at different times, to avoid any obvious inferences. On the other side, the ubiquitous police Volkswagen which invariably tailed them (replete with two plain-clothes men in grey suits) was usually quite conspicuous, and could easily be shed. There was something of the air of a cops-and-robbers game, with codenames, car-switching and secret writing. Molly Fischer was in a women's group with Violet Weinberg, and their habitual meeting place would be in the public space of the Wilds in Johannesburg, where the whole cell would sit on a bench among the outcrops of rock and riotous flowers and do their knitting.

Surprisingly, the subterfuge was successful, despite the fact that the police knew all the old communists, frequently to the point of first-name familiarity. Yet as the assault of apartheid legislation strengthened (in 1953 the National Party won its second election with an enlarged majority), the sense of gathering siege deepened. Laws introduced in the space of a few years prohibited sexual relations across the colour line, reinforced the control of black labour in 'white' areas, standardised and extended the pass system, and – in the form of Verwoerd's Bantu Education Act – undertook to train Africans to fill 'certain forms of labour' only. When C.R. Swart introduced the Public Safety Act of 1953 (providing for the declaration of states of emergency, under which all normal laws would be suspended), Bram could only watch in dismay. He wrote to Percy and Ella that 'so-called European democrats have sold their souls and we have passed into a police state with barely a murmur from them'. Later he remarked that 'the turn of the tide will come. It's a pity everything today seems designed to make that turn into a tidal wave.'

Bram was now often witness to the new brutalism in the air, not least as he became involved in the campaign to defend Sophiatown, the mixed-race freehold township on the west of Johannesburg which, with its jazz, racy black journalism and drinking shebeens, had come to represent a vibrant cultural alternative to the racially pure rigor mortis of apartheid. The government planned to get rid of Sophiatown under its Western Areas Removal Scheme, and the ANC set up a campaign in its defence, joined in this by figures such as Father Trevor Huddleston of the Community of the Resurrection, whose striking cassocked presence helped define an unbending spirit of resistance. Bram, who often appeared on platforms in Sophiatown, was called out there urgently one Sunday, and afterwards sent a description to Percy and Ella: 'Can you picture the situation?' he asked them; '1200 delegates at a conference – a body of police breaking in to drag a leader off the platform – outside some 300 police armed with assegais, rifles with bayonets, & sten guns. I didn't see all this because by the time I got there it was all over, but I'm certain that if Father Huddleston had not been on the platform there would have been a bloodbath. By the time I got to the police station I saw the arms & ammunition being turned in again. God help the whites of this country within the next 10 years. Is it inevitable in history that at some stage or another a whole class commits suicide in a lunatic fashion?'

In events such as this Bram would always be called on in his capacity as lawyer, to safeguard rights, obtain bail, and provide general protection. The police, confronted by his arrival, still had a healthy regard for the authority represented by a King's Counsel, and could quite easily be intimidated as he came to the aid of ordinary black citizens. But he and Molly were now both themselves targets, as became evident when Bram returned from Vienna in January 1953, and took up the theme of peace with an increased urgency. He spoke at venue after venue, and his text was invariably the same. Peace, he would insist, depended not only upon governments but on the people, without whose consent war could not be waged. It was only this that could prevent the cataclysm of an approaching third world war, the war in Korea, or a war engendered by the policies of South Africa. When Bram opened a conference to form a Natal Peace Council in July, Chief Luthuli (under a ban that prohibited his appearance) sent a message of support: 'One is all the more grateful for men and women throughout the world who band themselves together to use all legitimate means to oppose these forces of evil.' When Bram chaired a youth rally in Johannesburg in August, to mark the opening of the World Youth and Student Festival in Bucharest, the speakers included Nelson Mandela and Ahmed Kathrada.

It was no surprise then that he drew increasing attention. On 20 August 1953, just two days before a conference to inaugurate the South African Peace Council (at which Bram was to have given the welcoming address), he was served with two notices under the Suppression of Communism Act, banning him from any gatherings for two years, from membership of the Congress of Democrats and the Peace Council, as well as (Molly informed Percy and Ella) fifteen other organisations of which he happened not even to be a member. Instead of the welcoming address, Bram beat the ban by recording a message to be played at the meeting. (This became, suddenly, a standard technique, as Nelson Mandela, Hilda Watts, Cecil Williams and Michael Harmel all made recordings about this time.) On tape Bram told his unseen audience that he had already given his response to C.R. Swart, that this attack would not prevent the march of the people towards peace. He also remarked that 'the real reply to Mr Swart will come not from me but from the determination of this congress to spread the work of peace throughout South Africa'. The conference resolved to send a deputation to the Minister of Justice urging him to lift the ban, and elected Bram one of its vice-presidents notwithstanding his restrictions.

Molly told Percy and Ella that Bram's tape-recorded speech had caused quite a stir among his colleagues at the Bar. As for the ban on meetings, she hoped it would at least give him a little more free time. But in the gathering alarm of this new era, the truth was that time was no longer 'free'. Beaumont Street had already been raided by the police in July 1953; and then in September 1954, while Molly was overseas, Bram arrived in chambers to find, as he put it, 'two thugs from the Special Branch' awaiting him. First they searched his office, and then accompanied him home, where they confiscated numbers of innocuous pamphlets and documents (of which, observed Bram, they already had copies). These were just two among the counted and uncounted, documented and undocumented raids Bram and Molly would experience in the years to come. In January 1955, just over a month after Molly had returned from China, Bram wrote a laconic note from Coffee Bay to his parents: 'Your daughter-in-law, incidentally, has been banned from all gatherings for five years and from about 3 dozen organizations.' The South African Society for Peace and Friendship with the Soviet Union also made a public announcement that its secretary, Mrs Molly Fischer, had been ordered by the Minister of Justice to resign her position. Along with many others they were now foxes to the police hounds: going off to the game reserve, Bram had earlier advised his parents that if he and Molly got lost, Percy and Ella should use a good tracing agent – 'such as C.R. Swart'.

<hr />

It may have been no wonder that under the cumulative pressure of this encirclement filial and fraternal loyalties intensified, that large questions sometimes remained unasked, that the world narrowed in other respects.

By 1953, shortly before Stalin died, there was in the Soviet Union and in a number of East European countries a fairly concerted campaign, putatively aimed against Zionism, but in effect broadly anti-Semitic. In Hungary the Jewish Minister of the Interior, Laszlo Rajk, was accused of being an American and Yugoslav agent, and shot. His communist pedigree extended all the way back to the Spanish Civil War, but under Stalin that in itself held its own liabilities. In Czechoslovakia it was Rudolf Slansky, the secretary-general of the Communist Party, who was found guilty of Zionist subversion in a trial featuring mainly Jewish defendants. In the Soviet Union a 'doctors' plot' was triumphantly revealed, a conspiracy ostensibly fomented by a group of doctors (most of them Jewish), who had allegedly succeeded in killing Zhdanov and Shcherbakov, and were now planning a similar fate for Stalin. Such 'revelations' were not necessarily the product of pure and cleanly controlled manipulation, but the paranoia generated by Stalinism produced its own incentives for terror and fatal games of power.

As it turned out, all the anathematised figures were later rehabilitated, but in the meantime communists in South Africa added their voices to the vengeful clamour. The newspaper *Advance* equated Zionism with Nazism, and spoke of its role in the conspiracy to wreck the Czechoslovakian economy. On this it quoted with approval a statement by the Czech President which overlaid traditional anti-Semitic assignations with a none-too-subtle ideological veneer: 'The investigation showed that a new channel of treason and espionage had been created. It was Zionism . . . Normally it would have been hard for a former banker, factory owner or even a rich peasant to get into the Communist Party, and he would never be able to hold a leading position. But with people of Jewish origin and Zionist inclinations we did not pay so much attention to their class origins . . . ' Bram Fischer, who could not believe in any betrayal by the world with which he was so passionately linked, defended that world with passion. In February 1953, soon after his return from Vienna, he addressed a fractious meeting at the Selborne Hall in Johannesburg, where in response to Jewish hecklers he insisted that charges of Soviet and East European anti-Semitism were 'a political hoax pulled on the world, a most monstrous lie and a deliberate attempt to poison international relations'. The world was once again seeing the use of such lies, he maintained, to inflame people for war.

As before, it was Bram's experience of Europe in the 1930s that lay behind his interpretation of the present, in particular the 'great lies' propounded by the Nazis to legitimise their political and territorial ambitions, or those drummed up by Western propaganda to delegitimise communism. Yet this was still far from Bram's finest moment, and perhaps the best that could be said was that his intense feelings about 'peace' had clouded all other issues. Bram was very far from any anti-Semitism in his private life, indeed he would have been revolted by it; but a different logic was gaining the ascendancy, and it had an air of beleaguerment about it. This was evident in the wake of Stalin's death, when Bram wrote to his parents, with his focus again on distortion and lies: 'The campaign to prove that everyone now wants to exhume Stalin and burn him at the stake is reaching the absolute limits of mendacity. It seems as if no journalist cares any more whether he is found lying or not: can you imagine Stalin ordering his soldiers not to fire at the enemy. That's one of the accusations, isn't it – in all these "unconfirmed" reports.' But many of those unconfirmed reports later turned out to be true: Stalin had indeed restrained his forces disastrously when the Germans invaded the Soviet Union in 1941 – and much else besides. The fact was, either the West and its capitalist press were lying, or else – and this was almost unthinkable for Bram in the circumstances – there was something of a lie at the heart of his beliefs. The very intensity of his emotions – and a certain fragility in his tone – indicated the stakes.

Was it possible to be fighting for the truth and the lie at the same time? Bram, who believed in history, might have confirmed the tragic view that this was – in the larger sense – not only possible but inevitable, but the personal implications, in this particular setting, were unacceptable. It may have been that South African communists were so overwhelmed by the urgency of a local cause, and so consumed in its dynamic, that international developments seemed strangely peripheral. As Rusty Bernstein put it many years later, if Soviet tanks were rolling into Budapest, the police were present in South African townships every day. Communists were so much under attack in South Africa that any criticism of communism in the global sphere appeared to them an integral part of the same malicious and ill-intentioned onslaught. It was true that many anti-apartheid South Africans – liberals, social democrats, independent Marxists and Trotskyists – held no brief for Stalinism, and proclaimed their views loudly and openly, but for communists the results would only be counterproductive. For those who had committed themselves to the Party as underground members, whose sense of identity was thoroughly wrapped up in the acute risk they were taking, the feeling of siege would have been only all the more profound, the intimate friendships and loyalties all the more binding.

That was why, on Stalin's death, Bram's cry from the heart revealed his increasingly vulnerable assurances, for Stalin had represented everything South African communists held dearly, and the drawing-in was as much psychological as political. 'When Stalin died,' wrote Sam Kahn in *Advance* in March 1953, 'the Russian earth shook with the sobbing of millions and was wet with the tears of mourning for the man etched deep in their hearts . . . In death he has joined Lenin as he did in life.' Others did not succumb to quite the same degree of sentimental melodrama, but still grasped at the only categories and words of safety at hand. Molly Fischer, marking the first anniversary of Stalin's death, wrote in her official capacity as secretary of the SASPFSU on the continuity of Soviet foreign policy: 'As every earnest student of Soviet affairs realises, policy-making in the USSR is not, and never has been, a matter of individual "dictatorship" but one of collective discussion.' That policy was, continued Molly, ever more now one of 'peace'.

This reflex was sustained in March 1956 when Khrushchev, addressing the twentieth Party congress in Moscow, detailed Stalin's crimes and defined the 'cult of personality'. The irony was that South African communists had no direct access to any information, least of all to communist information, for the Soviet consulate had been closed down by the South African government that February, and so all their links were cut. The SACP, like everyone else, had to rely on newspaper reports, and thus evolved the poignant and sadly comic choreography of its response. At first in *New Age* there was no comment whatsoever, except to note that there had been extensive coverage of the congress in the world press. Two weeks later *New Age* admitted that there had been some 'severe criticism' levelled by delegates. Finally, a month after the congress, it was left to Michael Harmel to put everything in perspective, redeeming Stalin in precisely the same terms in which he had been condemned. Stalin had rendered services of incalculable value, wrote Harmel. He had been foremost in the struggle against 'the Trotskyites, Bukharinites and other traitors and saboteurs' who had sought to undermine the Soviet Union and divert it from the course charted by Lenin; his name was indissolubly linked with the struggles of the Soviet people. But the image of his infallibility had undermined the democratic procedures of the Communist Party, allowing 'the Beria gang' to defy socialist law and accuse innocent people. Now the Soviet leadership had shown the strength of the communist system in its courageous act of self-criticism . . .

Since Bukharin and Trotsky were still evidently 'guilty', how would one now know who was 'innocent' under Stalin? The SACP was not alone in these frantic acts of recuperation: from Italy to France to Britain, the official line was the same. For communists everywhere there were complex combinations of acceptance and refusal, and this was certainly true of Bram Fischer. Bram was not among those, recalled Joe Slovo, who believed that the Khrushchev revelations were false, a deliberate ploy in a continuing power struggle. Nor, however, did the accusations undermine for him an assurance in the fundamental validity of communism and its self-corrective strengths – as others confirmed. Miriam Hepner, who knew Bram well at this time, remembered driving with him one day past the Wilds, and asking him about the allegations against Stalin. He looked absolutely crestfallen at her question, she recalled, as he acknowledged that the revelations were true, and there was 'genuine shock' on his face. And at the same time it was equally clear to her that his loyalty to the Soviet Union was 'unshakeable'. This was also Bram's theme in the wake of the Soviet invasion of Hungary in 1956. Myrtle Berman, in and out of the Communist Party with divided feelings of her own, remembered how Bram, in addressing a querulous underground cell, had listened carefully and respectfully to their concerns, but insisted on an overriding loyalty: for if one country in the socialist camp fell, he argued, it would be followed by all the others. Loyalty, acceptance, refusal, realpolitik: all these were superimposed upon one another.

There were no mass defections from the South African Communist Party, as there were in Britain and elsewhere after the Khrushchev revelations or the invasion of Hungary. From that point of view, what appeared as a matter of moral and intellectual rigidity may have had more to do with the realities of siege sustaining an improbable internal coherence, as the Party came through remarkably intact. Yet a certain doubt and doubleness must have entered in. Bram was a lawyer who believed in justice: when the news emerged of show trials, frame-ups, the rehabilitation of Laszlo Rajk, how exactly could these be reconciled with his life's commitment both in South Africa and abroad? When I spoke to a loyal Party member, who had remained in the SACP after 1956 (our discussion took place before the collapse of the Soviet Union in 1989 altered her political landscape yet again), she would talk about such matters only off the record. At the time of the Khrushchev revelations she had been walking with her daughter along a city street in Johannesburg when she saw the billboards announcing the news. All it took, she remembered, were the headlines, and their force hit home like a mental and physical blow. She knew in her heart what they meant. What communists had heard for so long, had perhaps half known and repressed, took hold as a deeply unsettling recognition.

In June 1953 *Advance* recorded the fact that in the United States Julius and Ethel Rosenberg had been executed in the electric chair as spies for the Soviet Union. There was the strong suggestion that witnesses against them had given false testimony in exchange for a deal with the prosecution. The Rosenbergs themselves had rejected a similar arrangement, refusing, they insisted, to compromise the truth of their innocence. Six appeals to the Supreme Court had been turned down without a review of the case. The Rosenbergs were also Jewish; they left two sons, aged six and ten. *Advance* showed a photograph of the bodies lying in state.

The Cold War was a war, for all the fact that it was 'cold'. In the United States there was McCarthyism, to match the doctors' plot in the Soviet Union. To Bram, whose suspicions of the Western press were not entirely misplaced, nothing that had happened in the Soviet Union would change his map of the world. There was no monopoly on mythology, whether of the public or personal kind.

Nor did Bram abandon the personal.

Bram's cousin Connie's daughter was named Mollie, after her grandmother Maude (nickname, 'Mollie'). It was the young Mollie who had been ill with tuberculosis of the spine when she and Connie stayed in Beaumont Street in the 1940s, and it was Maude, the older 'Mollie', who had constructed a 'peace room' for children, containing a rainbow bookshelf lined with books on the great men and women of peace. Also there on the shelves was a report Bram had sent from the Vienna peace congress, which had evidently met with his Aunt Maude's approval. The young Mollie's view was that her grandmother was a 'militant pacifist' – and this was the air she had breathed in as a child.

She had also turned to Bram for inspiration. Once she had seen Bram tip his hat to an African woman, a maid, and observed how the woman had drawn herself up in visible pleasure and renewed dignity; it had been a small and gentlemanly gesture, to be sure, but one which in the South African world had a much larger meaning. Later, after she left school, Mollie had come to Bram, troubled by issues of war and peace, and questions of means and ends. He, taking the concerns of an eighteen-year-old seriously, had written to her at length in two letters, friendly and confiding, directly and personally.

In his letters Bram agreed with the point Mollie had raised that wars were falsely glamorised, although he insisted that there had been some – such as the Boer War – in which a people had defended themselves heroically. In general, remarked Bram, glamour was invented by those who stood to gain from war, but this did not mean that violence or resistance was never necessary. In that regard, he suggested, he had to disagree with Mollie on the problem of means and ends. What if an airman were taking off on a mission to drop some germ-warfare weapon? (It was the example Bram had absorbed in Vienna.) What if Mollie had to decide whether she and her children should live as slaves or become free – even if this meant, Bram added, doing some plantation owners out of a few pounds 'without bloodshed'? In Mollie's philosophy classes at university she would be expected to swallow absolute rules, such as the idea that ends never justified the means; but this was a philosophy – as these examples showed – 'that is intended, and has been created, to preserve the existing state of affairs'. Those labelled 'rebel bandits' in Kenya, Malaya or Vietnam – as the Boers had been earlier in the century, Bram suggested – were to their own people 'fighters for liberty', representing 'the highest ideals of the brotherhood of man that have inspired men and women from the time of Christ to the modern world'. But in place of outdated ideas there was now a new kind of knowledge in the world, and it belonged to that class 'which seeks to change the whole of society into something new, something more suited to modern civilisation, something more humane and less cruel'.

Bram's letters were as revealing about himself as anything he communicated to Mollie Anderson. She commented that what she valued most about him was that he never proselytised, but tried in the gentlest possible way to open up her world – and it was true that on all these matters he begged her to read everything she could, and to make up her mind for herself. And yet, at the same time, it was clear that for Bram *the answers to his questions were, in their formulation, already given. There was no doubt that for him the ends he projected were the right ones, even if the means sometimes entailed their ambiguities.*

Every letter contains its own inner dialogue, and it is possible that – even as for Mollie, Bram both opened up and closed down certain options – he was trying to answer himself. Perhaps ultimately it did have to do with means and ends: a Stalin might become corrupt, a Laszlo Rajk be falsely accused, but imperfect methods did not necessarily make imperfect results in the long history of an unfolding perfection. Having set sail for that horizon, Bram was prepared to voyage in that ship.

Some years later, Mollie Anderson joined the Communist Party and, as it turned out, was put on trial with Bram. On one occasion, after she had been arrested and subjected to physical and mental torture, she suddenly had an overwhelming conception that it would be a good idea to line her interrogators up against a wall and shoot them. Yet in that very instant she realised that she could not do it, and moreover, she understood exactly why she couldn't: for this would be the final victory of her captors over her.

It may have been the resurrection of her own contemplation of means and ends, but she remembered that in that moment it was also Bram's inspiration she felt. Perhaps he had taught her after all to think for herself, in the gestures of his being as much as his words. It was by the image he held out of the human ideal that she measured her intentions: this too is part of a political struggle.

The night that Molly took off for Europe in 1954, her son Paul, then aged seven, wrote her a letter:

> Dear mommy
>   how are you? I hope you had a nice holiday I hope you will a lovely trip and I hope you see the falls and I hope it is nice in england and I do hope you see athens and it is nice I hope it is nice in the plain was it. I hope you have a nice sit in the plane was it nice and I hope you arrive there with out a crash
>   love from Paul

For the next four months Bram was single parent to the children at home. At Paul's birthday party he supervised a horde of boys tearing around the garden in an impromptu rugby match, and took them off to see a film called 'Under the Red Sea'. 'When we arrived at the Astra,' he wrote to Molly, 'most of us had to retire to the Gents. Half way thru' the most exciting part of the film, just when we were getting close to the really big sharks, half of us had to go out for a drink of water. Nonetheless, it was a great success.' Ruth's fifteenth birthday, a few days later, entailed its own complications, because Bram, working late the previous night, had forgotten to buy a cake. Slipping off early in the morning he persuaded a local bakery to transform a creation already prepared for one Michael into a cake for Ruth, because Michael's birthday was only the following Monday. Bram darted home by eight, jumped back into his pyjamas, and by half past he and the other children had set up Ruth's birthday 'table' in Bram and Molly's room. Though Ella had telephoned her earlier, in her half-wakefulness Ruth never knew the difference. Bram put it to Molly that the 'almighty' had been with him, but Paul felt that the bakery couldn't have been very good, because they appeared to have messed up Ruth's name on the cake.

During those months Bram's underground communism alternated with activities ranging from advising 'Sir E' (who could only have been the mining magnate Sir Ernest Oppenheimer) 'how to avoid death duties on the cool matter of £7 mill' to seeing Ruth through her confirmation – a ceremony, he told Molly, that was 'very charming if somewhat barbaric'. In order to make Ruth feel at one with her peers, Bram bought her a prayer book and Bible, and a necklace with a cross 'from Molly'. Though Ruth's apparent devotion was somewhat unsettling (this was not how she remembered it: she felt she had simply been unwilling to flout the conventions, and soon abandoned any formal religious impulse), Bram and Molly would never have dreamed of standing in her way: in relation to their children, as towards others, there was an innate respect for individual choice. At home Bram read to Paul adventure stories of southern Africa – Sir Percy FitzPatrick's *Jock of the Bushveld* and, oddly, Oswald Pirow's *Shangani*, which opened, in true New Order form, with the line 'History is made by leaders'. From the tales of King Arthur Bram read a description of Lady Guinevere, 'with golden tresses, deep blue eyes, and cheeks as pink as peaches' – to which Ilse, in attendance, and bored with stories she had heard many times before, added 'and a large orange nose'.

This was, in other words, a home which bordered on normality, but not in one respect – for the wheeze that had bothered Paul as a small child had never disappeared. Indeed, it had turned into a cough that wouldn't leave. Paul never grew as he should have: he was small and slight, with a large barrel chest. The first diagnosis was that he had a prolapsed bowel, and he was put on special diets. But early on, when Paul was not much more than two years old, Molly asked Bram's brother Paul (who had just returned to Bloemfontein from medical training in the United States) to examine him. When the older Paul saw his nephew he knew with some dread exactly what the problem was, for news of cystic fibrosis was just becoming well known in America, and little Paul showed all the symptoms. It was a recessive genetic disease that affected the exocrine glands in the body: the lungs would fill up with a sticky, immovable mucus; the pancreas did not produce enzymes responsible for the digestion of fats. If both parents were carriers there was a fifty per cent chance that a child would be a carrier, and a twenty-five per cent chance of manifesting the disease: Paul had been the unlucky one. On Bram's side of the family it must have come via Ella, for two of Connie's sister Joan's children were also victims of cystic fibrosis. For Paul the prognosis was blunt: life expectancy at that stage did not extend much beyond six years. This was the news that Bram's brother broke to Molly, and he wrote to the child's doctor in Johannesburg to inform her of his findings.

During these years Bram and Molly's letters to Percy and Ella were full of news about Paul. They described his 'little chronic cough' which, whenever he was truly sick, was as agonising to his parents as it was to him. Sometimes Paul coughed so hard that Bram and Molly thought his lungs would simply burst. Though antibiotics were becoming available, they were no help for the primary condition, and there was always the threat of pleurisy or bronchial pneumonia. Often the only solution was to let Paul's head hang over the edge of a bed and beat him on the back to loosen the mucus in his lungs. Then, when Paul was eight, there was a further setback sometimes associated with cystic fibrosis, as he developed diabetes. Bram and Molly gave him insulin injections; if one of them hurt him he would turn to the other parent to do it the next day. His physiological balance was extremely difficult to maintain, and he was constantly threatening either to faint away from too little sugar or to get out of control from too much insulin. There was the daily routine, at the age of eight and nine, of urine checks, diet calculations and the relentless coughing. At ten Paul had a major operation on the stomach for a cystic fibrosis complication.

Bram and Molly worked intensely hard for him. They took him to the sea, where his breathing was easier in the humidity and high pressure than at Johannesburg's drier and more rarefied elevations. They bought a 'nebuliser' machine that sprayed a saline solution to liquefy the mucus inside his lungs. Yet, although they tried every available remedy, and although Paul knew from early on about his condition, Bram and Molly never indulged either him or themselves in any unnecessary pity. Ella had diabetes as well, and when Paul heard the news about his own, he wrote to her matter-of-factly for company (wrapping himself around the difficult spelling):

Dear Ouma

Thank you for haveing us. I have diabetets. On Tuesday I went to Silverton and we swam and drew in the sand . . .

Everyone who knew Bram and Molly has testified to the resolute spirit with which they allowed Paul to be himself. If his life was to be short, so they reasoned, it might as well be fulfilled. At primary school Paul played soccer for the 'A' team, which meant five practices as well as a match every week. 'Poor scrap!' wrote Molly to Ella just after his eleventh birthday. 'He weighs 57 lbs & is the smallest & lightest boy in his class, but is prepared to fight & win [against] any boy . . . so we can't stop him playing games.' Paul sang in the school choir, and ran in a relay team at the school athletics competition; he needed rest, but was the only one who seemed not to know it. 'We're always so glad', wrote Molly, 'if he can just feel that he is not any different from other boys.' At the age of ten Paul travelled by train with Ilse to see Ella at the farm in Bloemfontein and, on the spur of the moment, decided to stay on and then return on his own. Bram and Molly felt it crucial to let him learn to take care of himself.

For a deeply ill child – indeed, for anyone – Paul had a bright and irrepressible spirit, with an acute sense of irony from early on. When he was seven Bram took him to a rugby match, where he persisted in asking in a loud and squeaky voice (to the amusement of everyone around him), 'Are they allowed to kill one another in this game? . . . Whose side is the referee on? . . . If a man gets hurt do all the players carry him off?' He could also, because of the demands of his body, be fractious – starting early on when he might refuse to go to school, fall in a fishpond, and end by calling his mother a 'bloody bugger' for making him put on dry clothes. Much later his rebellion – and irony – took on other forms as he insulted his parents' politics and would sometimes (to the acute embarrassment of company) talk about 'kaffirs' while pouring out wine in otherwise impeccable style. Irony perhaps came from a sense of mortality: even for a child, everything must have seemed fiercely doubled, as he strove to be normal and knew he was set apart.

In many ways Bram and Molly's emphases and tolerances, combined with Paul's will-power, worked. If his life expectancy was six years to begin with, and then ten, and then fifteen, Paul lived to the age of twenty-three, which at that time was virtually unprecedented. It was all the more miraculous given the pressured circumstances and headlong intensities surrounding the Fischers. When Arthur Chaskalson met Paul's ex-headmaster at St John's College in Johannesburg, in preparation for the speech he gave at Paul's funeral, he found out that the only official note the school had in his medical records was that he was 'allergic to starch'.

All the political parents in South Africa felt to some extent that they were sacrificing their children's lives for the sake of their own beliefs, but for Bram and Molly there was this additional, agonising dimension. In the late 1950s, when Bram's old friend Jack Lewsen was standing for the Johannesburg City Council as an independent liberal, and Molly broke her ban to serve at an election table with Jack's wife Phyllis, this was what she spoke about quietly: Paul. And yet part of Bram and Molly's insistence on normality lay in not sur-rendering their politics or beliefs, but making the inevitable mystery of Paul's fate integral to the determined struggle of their lives.

In March 1954 Bram and Molly began constructing a swimming pool at Beaumont Street. It may have been built, in the first instance, for Paul, so that he could exercise his lungs and body. (While Molly was away in Europe Bram told her that Paul could do a length underwater, which he meant to surprise her with when she returned.) Bram associated the pool, from the start, with a certain kind of luck, because a neighbour wanted the soil that had been dug up, and Bram did not have to pay to cart it away; as he said then, using his characteristic phrase, 'Ry met my' [Ride with me]. As soon as the pool was ready Bram became an insistent swimmer, for his family as much as for him-self. In the middle of winter in June, if the others refused to swim, he would threaten to turn it back into a compost heap – at which, Molly told Percy and Ella, 'we all fall in'. Somehow, for Bram, the pool was connected with his per-sonality. He would, recalled Anthony Eastwood (who later became his son-in-law), take an unhesitating, head-first somersault into its cold waters in the early mornings.

The pool was also connected with Bram and Molly's hospitality, their sense that there was a gracious and welcoming place for all – a sentiment disclosed as much by implicit demonstration as any overt expression. In that respect instinctive social gestures combined aspects of culture, personality and politics, but in private – as with their open-house policy in the 1940s – Bram and Molly revealed an ambiguity they never disclosed in public. First intimations of this came early on, as the relatively rare resource of a pool in Johannesburg in the 1950s made it an obvious attraction. When Molly was about to return home from Europe, Bram advised her that she might like to lie at the edge of a pool the whole of the first weekend she came back – but 'preferably not ours if you want quiet'. Later Molly confirmed the impression to Percy and Ella: the pool on a hot weekend looked much like the beach at Muizenberg in the Cape at the height of the season. Left-wing politics did not supersede residual colonial expectations: tea and beer flowed in startling quantities. 'It's all very interesting,' Molly told Percy and Ella, 'but sometimes I long for a rainy Sunday.'

Yet beyond functionality, or occasional exhaustion, the pool took on symbolic overtones, for all the political family came to swim, and it became the mirroring element of other possibilities. The Bernsteins, the Slovos, the Hodgsons would be regulars, but there were many others, of all colours, as well. In a world of apartheid's fetishisms the pool at Beaumont Street was in the most easy way multi-racial, so that its liquid absolutions would combine the amniotic with the amnesiac, and the scandal of varied skins immersed in the same lazy water could simply be forgotten. There, together in that pool, a new kind of South Africa could be represented, all the more outrageous to white puritanism for its refusal to be anything more than ordinary. Though the pool altered no obvious dispensations, stopped no removals of communities, gave voting rights to none, it became its own kind of enchanted domain. It meant a huge amount to people such as Paul and Adelaide Joseph, long-time stalwarts in the South African Indian Congress, not only because there were no public facilities for their family in Johannesburg, but because beyond patronage or condescension, the Fischer pool was such a good and reinforcing place to be. People came at all hours of the day and night, and were virtually never turned away. Marius Schoon remembered a rather drunken night-party in the 1960s which was disturbed only by Bram leaning out of an upper window and asking for a little less noise because he had a big case in the morning. 'That house was part of the struggle,' remarked Fred and Sarah Carneson many years later. Paul Joseph certainly felt so: at night he brought a comrade clandestinely in the country to the Fischers, in order to teach him how to swim.

<hr>

In this setting Ruth and Ilse, as the older children, had a highly unusual upbringing in South African terms, with its own specific complexities. Bram and Molly did their best to soften their experiences, not only – as in Ruth's case – on matters of religion, but in the more threatening realms of politics as well. Ruth remembered that during the 1948 election, when she asked her parents how they were voting, the reply was that they were communists, but that at school Ruth could tell her friends they were United Party if that would make her life any easier. Ruth was perhaps the more reticent one, Ilse from early on more feisty, though with her own questions and hidden dimensions. For her Bram was initially a distant and somewhat austere figure. Percy and

Ella had moved to a new house on a smaller section of the Bergendal farm called Diepwater, and that was where Ilse lost her first tooth; she remembered climbing a windpump there with tears streaming down her face – Bram following anxiously after – because she was frightened he would be angry when he saw the gaping hole in her mouth. Many years later she found a note from herself to Bram, which he had kept: 'Dear Bram. I hate you. Love Ilse.' Ilse remembered that she cried for the first eleven or twelve years of her life, although she said she was not necessarily miserable 'inside'. Later her fire was more obviously directed outwards, as she would object fiercely to racist language, or defend communism to her classmates as a fair share for all.

The children came to know their parents under the skin: Molly, like her own mother, would never pass a beggar in the street without giving something, or, if she was served before black customers waiting ahead of her in a shop, would become involved in an instant altercation with the shopkeeper, insisting that they be served first; Bram in such situations was more reserved, avoiding confrontation where possible. At home, however, he would offer his own more formal kind of political education, reading to Ruth from Maurice Cornforth, or enjoining Ilse to study the economics of Leo Huberman. Where Percy Fischer had ranged freely and more playfully in his discussions, with Bram there was the expectation of a certain seriousness and, most likely, of certain answers. Because of the enveloping securities and assurances Bram and Molly provided, it became difficult in this household to disagree – not so much because of any coercion, but because it was impossible to imagine other ways of seeing a problem. Ruth remembered herself as earnestly wanting to live up to Bram's expectations – perhaps the same kind of awe and distance that Ilse, initially, felt.

When Ruth and Ilse were small, Bram and Molly spoke Afrikaans to them at home and sent them to English-language schools – a variation on the bilingualism they themselves had experienced and on their habitually inclusive instincts when it came to matters of identity. When the government instituted its policy of Christian–National education, the threat that a family's home language would determine which school the children would have to attend altered their approach, and with more than a little regret Bram and Molly switched to English at home to prevent Ruth, Ilse and Paul from suffering the full rigours of Nationalist indoctrination. Later Ruth and Ilse went to a private high school, Kingsmead, and Paul the utterly colonial and anglophilic St John's: these were at least marginally more liberal schools, with – on occasion – the slightest hint of racial integration. Yet here was another anomaly to add to the list: the children of revolutionary communists attending the most elite of private institutions. Being communist did not mean a thoroughly revolutionised existence – but in the warping mirrors of South Africa it made an equivalently warped kind of sense. Ruth and Ilse also became conscious of all the other anomalies of their lives – that they had servants, for instance. But they also knew that their servants were paid more than the standard rate, and that in households such as theirs the ethos of familiarity and mutual fidelity was different from much of what they witnessed elsewhere.

To be the children of communists meant that a doubled awareness entered into everyday life. Early on Bram and Molly explained everything in the simplest terms to their children: that they did not approve of the government, and the government did not approve of them, and that was why they had been banned. As for their regular and hurried disappearances, to go to meetings, the children understood soon enough that it would be better if they just did not ask. Ruth, Ilse and Paul learned the paths of secrecy in the way that questions were absorbed and deflected; they both knew and did not know what was happening around them. Bram and Molly kept the reconstitution of the Communist Party from the children, but when parents come and parents go, and visitors arrive at the back door, it is easy to draw the obvious conclusions: Ruth felt in her bones that she knew the Communist Party still existed. There was the understanding that telephones were tapped, that some conversations would be held outside, that scraps of paper would sometimes float in the toilet bowl. Later, when Ilse's friends would drive round for a swim, their parents would receive calls from the police asking what their cars were doing parked at the Fischers. All children learn secrecy in relation to their parents, but this was a secrecy *with* and dispensed by the parents – a strange and almost incestuous kind of complicity.

They watched, with the pure regard of children, the visitors who came to stay, or to talk, or for dinner. Nelson Mandela would arrive, charming but somewhat formal and austere. Walter Sisulu, Ruth felt, was just like her grandfather Percy; he had an undeniable warmth, especially in relation to children, and they took to him with real affection. Moses Kotane was a frequent guest, as was Michael Harmel. Sometimes it all got a bit much: the odd guest would transfix the younger generation (brought up stringently when it came to matters of etiquette) with displays of bad table manners, or irritate by arriving for a drink and simply refusing to leave. Ruth and Ilse resented some of this: the fact that on a Sunday the guests would swan around the pool while Molly – notwithstanding her vision of female liberation in China – would be slaving away the whole day in the kitchen to provide refreshments. On such days, when Bram came down from his work he would be greeted with awe and veneration, but Molly appeared to be taken for granted – except by those (often younger) who came to talk to her for her sympathetic ear. Protectively, Ruth and Ilse felt that some of Bram's comrades took advantage of him, exploiting his idealisation of them or even (though they could hardly formulate this at the time) his own insecurities. But if they voiced any criticism, with his gentle insistence Bram would defend his political kin all the more. 'He had a tremendous loyalty to them all,' remarked Ilse. 'If you were with him politically he forgave most of everything.'

Ruth and Ilse called Bram 'Bram' and Molly 'Mommy' or 'Ma', a combination of distance and equality as well as intimacy. It was true that Bram could be somewhat prim and bourgeois for a communist: there was no make-up for the girls, no chewing gum or eating in the streets; at school events the girls would *wish* that Bram would not insist on speaking Afrikaans, or wear shorts in public. But he and Molly would also be utterly enveloping and protective, finding ways, despite all the tensions and collusions, of reassuring the children that they came first in their lives. On one occasion, when Ilse invited friends from school who would have been embarrassed by the multi-racialism of the pool, Bram found a way of explaining this to a family of Indians who were there, and inviting them to return another time – and he managed to do it all without any offence.

But what exhilarated Ruth and Ilse in these years were the *Guardian* dances and other jamborees, which continued despite the increasing restrictions and cramped features of life under an ever more militant apartheid. Long after the *Guardian* had been banned and reincarnated under its successive titles, annual fundraising dances remained a regular feature at Beaumont Street – by common consent, the natural and logical venue. There Bram and Molly would host upwards of two hundred people, with a marquee on the lawn, and dancing in the lounge and dining-room. In the aftermath Molly would describe for Percy and Ella the details of taking sandwiches out of the piano, and prising the last cigarette ends from the carpet. Like so much else at Beaumont Street, these dances became part of a mythic memory for those who ever after regarded themselves as fortunate to have been inside the charmed aureole of that setting. The police cars would be parked outside: inside there was another universe.

For Ruth and Ilse too, with their own family of friends – the children of Bram and Molly's comrades, or with the adults themselves – all doubts fell away at these dances, and another South Africa came to life in body, spirit, music and mind. Bram could still, despite everything, swoop them all up for a picnic on a Sunday. When the family went on holiday he insisted on opening the first sandwiches when they reached Booysens, just on the edge of Johannesburg. When they visited Percy and Ella on the farm, they would get up early for rusks and coffee, and then go out for a walk in the rising sun, or climb Malmanskop before breakfast. There they would ride horses out to Hillandale, where Bram showed Ruth the trees that his Oupa had planted, and where he had played as a child.

In March 1948, just before the National Party came into power, Percy Fischer retired as Judge-President of the Free State. The Bloemfontein Nationalist newspaper, *Die Volksblad*, acknowledged the event by intoning a sonorous appreciation of his career: 'It is often said that the degree of civilisation of a *volk* can be measured by the highest level attained by its Judiciary. If that is the case . . . then civilisation in our country has reached a very high level . . . The Afrikaner *volk* can be proud that such sons are born of its womb . . . '

But just a few years later, Percy severed the umbilical cord that linked him to the nationalist source, and it happened, suitably enough, over the independence of the judiciary. In 1951 the government introduced the Separate Representation of Voters Act, designed to remove coloureds in the Cape from the common voters' roll; it was the culmination of Hertzog's plan, the origins of which Bram had witnessed in parliament some twenty-five years before. Yet when the legislation failed to achieve a two-thirds majority at a joint sitting of both houses, as required by the constitution, the government decided to proceed in any case. When this was declared *ultra vires* by the Supreme Court, the government overcame the inconvenient obstacle by passing legislation declaring parliament to be the ultimate 'High Court' of the country. When this too was declared *ultra vires*, the government finally took the expedient of enlarging the Senate and packing it with its own party members (to facilitate a two-thirds majority), and enlarging the bench and filling it similarly. The legislation was duly passed in 1956, but somewhere along the way the flagrant gerrymandering with both the Supreme Court and the constitution became too much for Percy Fischer, and he resigned from the National Party.

Through the 1950s Percy's health was not good. In June 1956, while visiting Bram and Molly in Johannesburg, he suffered a stroke that left him partially paralysed. Returning to Bloemfontein he had to be boarded with a couple who looked after him, since Ella, wheelchair-bound by this stage, could not do so. His mind wandered, and he wasn't sure where he was; yet in April 1957 he and Ella still managed to celebrate their golden wedding anniversary together. Then, on 10 June 1957, he died. Ella wrote to Bram: 'somehow my main spring seems, for the time being, to have run down – & I find myself sitting with a book or a paper & not following a word of what I read.'

When Percy was up at Beaumont Street he was looked after by Bram and Molly's servant Tias and his counterpart from Diepwater, William, whom Ella had sent to Johannesburg for the purpose. Percy said they were the gentlest nurses he had ever had. Ella wrote: 'In my gratitude I must include Tias. What wonderful people they are. I am always so struck with their tact and gentleness. Tell Tias I say thank you from my heart.'

Bram and Molly's children still went down to the house at Diepwater to see Ella, and she still came up to Johannesburg. If Nora was there when she visited, Nora and Ilse still ate in the kitchen. Ella regretted that Bram's politics had taken him so far, yet, although she was aware of the bannings, restrictions and raids, she and Percy had never tried to dissuade him or Molly. Now, as before, the ties of family overrode all other considerations.

Molly's father died in July 1956, also after a stroke, and the whole of Silverton came to the funeral. For, as Bram wrote to Ella, Mr Krige had served on the *kerkraad* [church council] as *diaken* [deacon] or *ouderling* [elder] since approximately 1910, and had lived at Silverton since the year of Molly's birth.

Family upon family upon family. One of the Communist Party's underground codenames was – perhaps with felicitously subconscious resonance – 'The Family', and to Bram it would have meant something direct. At every level of the personal and the political, both in South Africa and across the globe, there were extraordinary intimacies, allegiances and contradictions. But Bram was determined to be loyal to all his families without betrayal, and it was the mark of what some considered his sublimity that he managed to embody that objective with a certain graceful ease in his life. Together with the dedication of others, the connections established in these years may have had some effect on the moral culture of South Africa and its future, a triumph which in the peaceful elections of 1994 was organised, in part, around the recognition of a national family.

Nelson Mandela said of Bram Fischer, 'He just emerged you know, and became a friend of mine.' He said, 'He was at peace with himself, and therefore at peace with the world and the people around him.' Bram did not have the political drive of a Joe Slovo, remarked Mandela, the kind that could make him force tough decisions through, or the calculation that is sometimes required. But, said Mandela, he was a diplomat, who received the support of everyone he worked with, and this was of crucial importance in a multi-racial movement.

And Nelson Mandela, coming to the house, judged very personally. 'You know, you assessed his attitude not from what he said but from the way he treated his workers. You know, he had a gardener, he had a lady who was working for him, and then he adopted a black child. Now those were the days when apartheid was at its worst . . . But he took that risk of adopting a black child. And the woman who worked for him . . . she regarded Bram as a brother, and she would be involved in his parties not just as a waiter but as a colleague, as a comrade. And then you saw what type of man Bram was.'

Walter Sisulu, who sometimes stayed on after late meetings, remembered Bram getting up for Paul when he coughed in the night. He said, 'Bram Fischer's children, they are like my children, and I knew the problems when his family was very ill. Bram was a very kind man. Nothing else tortured him as he was tortured by Paul's illness. And I was sleeping there and I would hear Bram running down to sit with Paul. And that touched me. So that when Paul finally died, it was like my own child had died.'

CHAPTER 9

LEGAL POLITICS

February 1948 – March 1961

I n June 1949 Bram Fischer received a letter from London, one of the odder
specimens ever to find its way into his collection. Handwritten in ornate
and emphatic flourishes, it read as follows:

Dear Fischer,

I venture to address you in this friendly way because I cannot think of
you, Hanson, and Vernon [Berrangé] as other than Friends, and further-
more I hate formality, that formidable obstacle to desirable human
relations. I write to offer you my thanks and gratitude in the part you
have played with Vernon & Hanson in making

Truth Triumphant

in the face of obstinate opposition associated with almost-devilish
means-whereby, arising on the one part from prejudiced ignorance and
on the other from hatred and malice. Those responsible for these manifestations should ere now have learned a lesson which one hopes may
prevent them from ever attempting to harm others by making unjust and
misleading charges. I will hope to see you here one day, and believe me a
hearty welcome awaits you . . . Again with my very best wishes and
thanks,

Yours very sincerely,
F. Matthias Alexander.

The writer of the letter was the inventor – or, as he may have put it, the
discoverer – of the Alexander Principle that had so intrigued Bram during the
1930s. Alexander was an idiosyncratic Australian who had worked out his
theories when, as an aspirant actor, he suffered from a chronic loss of voice on
stage. By studying himself in mirrors, and noting the habits of his physical
behaviour, he developed a method of 'inhibiting' patterns that were themselves constricting, thereby opening up a heightened psychophysical awareness and freedom. Alexander held that human beings should pay more
attention to the 'means-whereby' action was carried out (the reference in his

letter), and less to the ends such actions aimed at. A true self-awareness of this kind would aid in mental and physical health (and also produce more authentic and morally favourable ends). Teaching his technique in London, Alexander had assisted any number of patients abandoned to pain by the orthodox medical profession, and he developed a fairly large following. Enthusiasts included the novelist Aldous Huxley and the American educationist John Dewey.

In South Africa, his leading disciple was Irene Tasker, and it was she who had taught Bram and Molly, as well as other enthusiasts such as the palaeontologist Raymond Dart (who was still practising the Alexander Principle into his nineties, when I met him). But a certain Dr Ernst Jokl, a physician and physical educator who came to South Africa from Germany in 1933 and was now the physical education officer for the South African government, took exception to the technique. Encouraged by Dr Cluver, director of the South African Institute for Medical Research, he wrote an article for the journal *Volkskragte* [Manpower] in which he attacked the Alexander Principle as quackery.

From London, Alexander sued Jokl, Cluver and the editor of *Volkskragte* for libel. Oswald Pirow (ex-Minister of Justice, ex-leader of the authoritarian New Order) appeared for the defendants; Bram Fischer appeared as junior to Harold Hanson, KC for Alexander, and later they were joined by Vernon Berrangé. The brewing trial had the effect of refreshing Bram's interest in the technique, and once again he took lessons from Miss Tasker, along with Molly and Ruth. He was prepared to find all kinds of benefits, discovering how for years (he told Percy and Ella) he had spent his energy when writing in his foot muscles and left shoulder, and playing tennis 'principally with my neck!' Later his brothers Paul and Gus (both orthodox medical men) regarded all this as further evidence of what they termed Bram's 'gullibility', his preparedness to throw himself wholeheartedly into unproven philosophical systems, and there may have been something in the allegation. For Bram, however, the issues had more than simply personal overtones. In the aftermath of the war, here was an avatar of German 'science' overtly attempting to smother a method that was at least innovative and interesting and, like communism in more 'objective' dimensions, promised its own version of liberation from the constrictions of the past (not to mention some resolution of the problem of means and ends). It was at any rate intriguing how, in the apparatus surrounding the trial, left appeared ranged against right. In the realm of medical philosophy as in politics, it seemed the Pirows of the world were always on the opposing side.

The trial, which began in February 1948, caused an international stir. Both sides collected evidence from eminent figures and physicians in London (Lord Adrian and Sir Henry Dale for Jokl; Lord Lytton, Sir Stafford Cripps and Sir Arthur Sherrington for Alexander), and the proceedings were reported in, among other places, the *British Medical Journal*. Crowds flocked to the court, but Molly's description to Percy and Ella – of Pirow's junior reading evidence at a page every three and a half minutes, of Pirow himself and the judge (Bram's colleague Jack Clayden, recently promoted) both asleep, of Hanson away in his office while Bram took the occasional note – suggested there was less drama than had been expected. Finally, when the judgment came down, it was somewhat ambiguous. In Molly's words to Percy and Ella, Clayden had 'found Alexander a "quack" but not as bad a one as the article alleged', and therefore awarded him £1000 damages. Jokl took it on appeal, which caused Bram no end of anguish because the case had involved an immense amount of work, all of which he feared would have to be repeated. But Jokl lost decisively the following year.

It was this that produced Alexander's characteristic and embellished letter. 'Truth Triumphant': it was a fine and gratifying idea, but there is no indication whether, in the world of 1949, Bram found it quaint and touching or merely bizarre. Yet the trial, though an oddity, was a harbinger of a kind, where the legal and political began to be enmeshed, where Bram's team and Pirow's represented ideological as well as forensic alternatives, where the attention was increasingly international, where trials began to drag on for years. From that point of view it was a relatively congenial warm-up for what what would become a much more difficult struggle to make truth triumphant in the courts.

※◎◎◎※

Bram's politics were of course well known to his colleagues, but that did not lessen in any way their evident respect for him or their affection. In 1951, shortly before he was listed by C.R. Swart as a communist, he was elected to the Johannesburg Bar Council for the ninth consecutive year – a longer run than any other member of the council. Indeed, between 1942 and 1963 Bram served on the council for all except three of the twenty-one years (often elected with a substantial majority of the votes), and in 1961, even as the political world was exploding around him, he was appointed Bar Council chairman. As Molly had suggested earlier to Percy and Ella, 'I think that indicates that in spite of his politics the advocates don't think he's such a bad fellow.' Many years later this was still how he was remembered: his unassuming integrity in matters both private and public and the magnetic seductions of his personality were an unusual combination.

Other trials pointed the way. In 1956 Bram appeared before Mr Justice Ludorf, defending *The Star* newspaper against an action of libel. The fact that Ludorf was presiding represented another dimension of the new legal and political entanglements, for Ludorf had been on the executive of the Transvaal National Party, and had stood for parliament against Jan Smuts in 1943; he had also defended Bram's old schoolmate, the Nazi Robey Leibbrandt, in his trial for treason in 1942. Now, though he and Bram had been appointed silks at exactly the same time, Ludorf was very quickly a judge under the National Party regime, a sign of predilections to come. As to the libel case, it concerned the constitutional manipulations that had caused Percy Fischer to leave the National Party. *The Star* had alleged the equivalent of a 'party lottery' as party members had paid deposits of £20 to be considered for places in the enlarged Senate, in order to dismantle the coloured franchise. If selected, their salaries of £1400 would provide an impressive return on their initial investment, suggested *The Star,* and it offered the opinion that these candidates were volunteering 'at a handsome fee . . . to do the dirty work of the Nationalist government'. At first Bram argued his case on the grounds of fair comment, and on the legal principle that an allegation concerning a group could not form the basis for individual libel, but his mistake, as the trial progressed, was to maintain along with his witnesses that there was no personal imputation of dishonesty on anyone's behalf. Since this was precisely what the article had originally alleged, the case for libel in effect strengthened. Ludorf found for the plaintiffs, though he limited damages to £100 each.

There was too the famed 'ITC–UTC' case, which still brings a smile of amusement to those who remember it. This was a case about cigarettes, in which the International Tobacco Company and the United Tobacco Company were pitted against one another. ITC produced a cigarette called 'Max' and, with its slogan 'Men of the World Smoke Max', had turned it into the most popular brand among blacks – a highly lucrative achievement. UTC had then hired two African propagandists to promote its own cigarettes, but when more orthodox techniques proved unsuccessful, these two ventured upon the idea – and a novel method – of disparaging the competition. They went around to divers beerhalls in Johannesburg and left behind them various whispered rumours about 'Max': that it was the wrong cigarette for Africans to smoke, that ITC was the enemy of Africans and did not employ blacks, that 'Max' caused coughing and tuberculosis. The results were spectacular: in 1950 alone (the judge found) ITC experienced a drop in sales of 147.5 million cigarettes and at least 300 million per year thereafter. In a judgment running to some 80,000 words, Mr Justice Clayden (once again of the Alexander trial) awarded ITC £580,000 in damages – the highest amount ever given at that time in a Commonwealth court.

Once again Bram was on the losing side, but here the lessons were not so much political or strategic as gluteal. For when the case was decided in May 1954 it had lasted four years from first summons to judgment; there was evidence from some 150 witnesses, running to 10,000 pages; when Bram finally presented his part of the closing argument, based on approximately 4800 documents, it took him eleven hours to do so; but that was nothing compared with his colleague I.A. Maisels, QC, who argued for nine days. Notwithstanding the defeat, UTC were enamoured of Bram, to the extent of placing him on a retainer just in case they were also sued by Rembrandt cigarettes. This did not prevent Molly from bemoaning the destruction of family life as Bram worked regular hours from five o'clock in the morning until eleven at night. In the midst of it all, she fully expected that the trial would go on until all eternity, and that in years to come Bram would be wheeled into court, still haggling over the question of a few cigarettes.

The law is an arena whose performances oscillate quite easily from the comic to the tragic: comedy, because of the vanities and obsessions of human greed and folly, regularly revealed within its confines; tragedy, because of the element of fate, in which 'justice' can be deployed by the powerful and destinies decided by a glance. In that sense, Bram's legal trials over the years tended to shift from the comic to the tragic, though there were usually admixtures of both elements. Yet even the comic trials had their purposes. When Bram next stood up in court in a major case alongside Issy Maisels, it was in the Treason Trial – a trial which, in its own length, number of documents, combination of tediousness, farce and genuine drama, made the ITC–UTC case look as significant (or long-lasting) as a packet of cigarettes. At the same time the methods learned in earlier trials, the long hours, modes of referencing and argument, the work habits, were all none the less crucial, and the government would come to regret the disciplined intensities of the Johannesburg Bar.

Bram's preoccupation with trials of this magnitude explains – beyond the fact of his banning – why he was not even more active politically in the 1950s than he managed to be. Yet during these years the legal arena itself became a kind of politics, crucial to the very survival of the anti-apartheid movement. In this, Bram Fischer played nothing less than a central role. And if he took his law from his politics, there are indications that he also did the reverse. When Bram went underground a decade later, one of his codenames – perhaps with some ironic memory – was 'Max'. He also took the pseudonym of 'Mr Black', and although there may have been practical considerations at the time in the choice (for instance, taking the name of someone who had died for an identity), there is no telling whether for Bram there was some distant resonance of his major antagonist in the 1950s, 'Blackie' Swart.

✳

On the anniversary of Freedom Day in June 1955, Bram and Molly took Ruth and Ilse to a little *koppie* overlooking a soccer field in the African township of Kliptown, some fifteen miles from Johannesburg. Bram looked out at the scene arrayed in front of them and told Ruth and Ilse that it was an historic occasion.

They were viewing the scene rather than participating in it because both Bram and Molly were banned, and this was the site of the most momentous political gathering of the 1950s, the Congress of the People, which by definition now they could not attend. The idea for the congress had emerged some two years previously when Professor Z.K. Matthews, president of the Cape ANC, had made a specific proposal for a 'National Convention, a Congress of the People, representing all the people of this country, irrespective of race or colour, to draw up a Freedom Charter for a democratic South Africa of the future'. The concept of such a document had distant allusions to the Chartist movement of Britain in the nineteenth century, but the 'Congress' dimension imprinted it as an expression of the Congress Alliance: this was to be the event that signalled and initiated a renewed quest for full enfranchisement and social equality in South Africa.

The setting became all but mythologised in its memorialisations, evoking through its images of the promised land a humble heroism and vibrant dedication that had to resonate and inspire for the nearly forty years in the wilderness that followed: the bare platform in the veld with, above, a banner showing the freedom wheel of the Congress Alliance; the thousands of men and women (those whom the police had not, with their usual assiduity, held up at railway stations and roadblocks) streaming in from all parts of South Africa by train, car, lorry, bus and on foot; the enclosed strip of land where they gathered, marching and singing beneath ANC flags. There were stalls, a peace pavilion, pamphlets, slogans, and everywhere the ANC colours of black, green and gold. One group wore green shirts, yellow scarves and black trousers; one delegation marched in behind a brass band. There, as first among the acts of the congress, Piet Beyleveld – Afrikaner comrade of Bram's, and first president of the Congress of Democrats – conferred the title of *Isitwalandwe* (traditionally bestowed on military leaders) on Father Trevor Huddleston, Chief Luthuli and Yusuf Dadoo (the careful selection of the honoured, as always, stressing a multi-racial approach). There for two days delegates to the congress heard explained clause by clause a charter which declared, as first among its principles, that 'South Africa belongs to all who live in it, Black and White'. Other clauses called for the nationalisation of banks and mines, for universal suffrage, for equal rights, for equality before the law, for work and security, for 'the doors of learning and culture' to be opened, and for global 'peace and friendship'.

It was not only the delegates who attended the congress, however, for plain-clothes policemen were present throughout the proceedings. Then, at about 3.30 p.m. on the second day, with two more clauses of the charter to be announced, there was a wholesale invasion by police armed with sten guns. As they cordoned off the area and moved up onto the platform, the delegates, realising what was happening, began singing 'Nkosi Sikelel' iAfrika' as if to intone bodily the resonance and dignity of their resistance. The police announced that treason was suspected, and that every delegate's name would be taken; they confiscated every stray item, pamphlet and document they found, and the questioning went on by the light of hurricane lamps till well after dark. Yet while the police searched, those remaining within the cordoned area continued to dance and sing, and the brass band continued to play.

In the course of time a certain amount of controversy would surround the Freedom Charter, as both white liberals and Africanists within the ANC came to denounce it as a communist document produced through communist manipulation. Here again, as in other matters, the prevailing realities applied: communists were active in all the Congress organisations, but that did not necessarily imply a conspiracy – or, if there had been a conspiracy, effective control. And, though there was undoubtedly some manipulation – for instance, in the collection and 'translation' of the proposals gathered from ordinary people around the country prior to the congress into the formal state-ments of the charter – there was nothing much, beyond gestures towards socialism (nationalisation of banks and mines) and the catchwords of the era (peace and friendship), particularly communist about the final document. By and large the dominant impulse behind the Freedom Charter was the vision of a democratic and multi-racial South Africa, and it was in this spirit that it was ratified at a special conference of the ANC in March the following year. Other events reinforced the momentum, among them the gathering, in August 1956, of 20,000 women (mostly black, but led by a conspicuously multi-racial con-tingent) at the Union Buildings in Pretoria, to protest against the extension of the pass system to include black women. Once again Ruth Fischer was there to observe, taken by Molly to watch the multitudes of marchers going by.

In the wake of the Congress of the People, 'Blackie' Swart had announced in parliament that large-scale arrests for treason could be expected. At the end of 1956 he made good on his word. In the small hours of 5 December there were sharp raps on doors around the country, as in a carefully orchestrated operation 140 people were arrested; those in outlying regions were flown in to Johannesburg by military aeroplane. Bram and Molly – probably because they had not been part of the Congress of the People – were left alone, but long before the news broke that morning the telephone at the Fischers began ringing and would not stop. People were phoning Bram to tell him what had happened, and to ask for legal advice. Ruth – to whom it seemed that he was always the one that they called – had good reason to remember the details: she had a matriculation history exam to write that day at school, but this was a different, and deeply unsettling, kind of history in the making.

That afternoon *The Star* showed a photograph of Helen Joseph, already one of the stalwarts of the Congress of Democrats and the Federation of South African Women, smiling buoyantly in her trade-mark dark glasses behind the wire mesh of a police vehicle as she was taken off to the preliminary hearing at the Johannesburg Magistrates' Court, where spectators stood six deep at the doors and hung at the windows. That night Hilda and Rusty Bernstein went out with Joe Slovo and Ruth First to a movie, and felt quite strange still to be at large, unarrested among the general public – a feeling accentuated for Hilda because she was pregnant. But then in the succeeding days Rusty, Joe and Ruth were arrested, and everything felt oddly normal again. After the Congress of the People Ruth First had, with her characteristic flair, written up a stirring account for *New Age*, and had her notes seized by the police. These were later produced in court, and hence – with a certain Kafkaesque circularity – an account of the initial raid for treason became evidence of treason in the monumental Treason Trial that followed.

In all, an additional sixteen people had been arrested, to make a total of 156 accused (plus one commercial company). The prosecution announced that it expected a case of 'six to eight weeks', but the trial was to last for over four years.

≈⊗≈

Arthur Chaskalson, a young attorney in Johannesburg in the 1950s, remembered that on that first day of the preparatory examination for the Treason Trial, the Johannesburg Bar sent down its most senior advocates to lead the defence, among them Maurice Franks, Norman Rosenberg and I.A. Maisels. This in itself was something of a demonstration, indicating that the accused must be defended, and that no aspersions could or should be cast on those who defended them. In the lowering climate of treason evoked by the government, it was an early indication that there would be those at the Bar in Johannesburg whose loyalty to justice, and the courage it required, would not be lacking.

Yet if the assumptions behind this demonstration had less to do with politics than with a more traditional institutional insistence on the right of any accused to a fair trial, then the setting that confronted the advocates introduced another dimension to the proceedings. The first application in the examination had been to have the hearings moved, for reasons of space (there were so many accused), from the Magistrates' Court to the Drill Hall, a white-faced and red-roofed colonial-style military building on the north-east perimeter of the city area. It was the court arrangements established there that produced the second application of the case, as Maurice Franks, QC objected to what he saw in the most voluble terms: 'I invite your Worship's attention, Sir,' he told the presiding magistrate, 'to the scene which confronts you this morning. Your Worship confronts this unprecedented scene which we see before us today, the accused caged – as your Worship sees – caged, one might almost say – I am most anxious not to allow my indignation to get the better of the language I use – but I think I am justified in submitting to your Worship they appear before the Court caged like wild beasts and it is in these circumstances that in this South Africa of ours it is expected that a Preparatory Examination shall take its course.'

The prosecution, in its zeal to concoct an aura of conspiracy and danger, had indeed constructed a cage of scaffolding, wire mesh and grille to contain the 156 accused. But if this was a South African version of a show trial somewhat ineptly borrowed from other sources, it was one that was unlikely to succeed. Franks continued to object that if the conditions were not improved, giving the advocates proper access to their clients, the defence would withdraw in its entirety and take no further part in the proceedings. Emotions outside the court were as heated as those inside: a crowd of thousands, which had greeted the accused (conveyed to the Drill Hall in barred prison vehicles) with signs proclaiming 'We Stand by Our Leaders', now retaliated with stones and oranges when baton-charged by the police, and eventually there was shooting. Inside, counsel for the defence and the prosecution reached an accommodation: the cage would be modified but not removed altogether, and the examination would proceed.

The purpose of a preparatory examination was to determine whether there was proper cause for a trial: here the Crown (representing, with some political irony, the Queen as head of the South African state) would lay out the lines of its evidence and argument, and here the defence would gain its first sight of the accusations it would have to answer. It was with all due attention, therefore, that they heard the public prosecutor present his opening address. The case arose, the prosecutor suggested, from the activities 'of certain associations which are commonly called the National Liberation Movement, and this Movement consists mainly of the organisations, bodies, committees, councils and societies such as the African National Congress, the Indian Congress, the South African Congress of Democrats, the South African Congress of Trade Unions, the South African Coloured People's Organisation and the South African Congress of Mothers with the respective youth and women's sections, generally referred to as the Congress Movement or Congresses; and other organisations such as the South African Peace Council, the South African Society for Peace and Friendship with the Soviet Union, the Federation of South African Women, and various committees, such as the People's Peace Committee, the Liberation Committee, the New Youth Committee, the "Fighting Talk" Committee and others.'

It was a stunning array of organisations, ranging from the virtually unheard-of to the most familiar, including a number very close to Bram and Molly's hearts. Evidently the Crown wished to draw them all together under the allegation of some vast conspiracy, and as the prosecutor levelled the burden of his accusation, the exact nature of that supposed conspiracy emerged: 'The evidence will be that no alternative Government under the existing Constitution, that is the South Africa Act, by any other political party is acceptable to the Movement . . . The case of the high treason charge will be the incitement and preparation for the overthrow of the existing State by revolutionary methods involving violence and the establishment of [a] so-called People's Democracy on the basis of the Eastern European Communist Satellite States, and China.' It was, then, a conspiracy of the most sweeping proportions, involving not only the broadest swathe of the major extra-parliamentary organisations opposed to apartheid, but also an international communist dimension, and the use of violence.

The forum was a legal one, but the accusations political, and it was in political terms that Vernon Berrangé rose to reply for the defence. Berrangé was one of those idiosyncratic people found both in political organisations and in legal fraternities, except that he combined the two aspects in his singular personality. He had been a communist until he left the Party in the 1950s, yet his instinctive affiliations always drew him to cases such as this. He was a lean, aquiline man, who combined his radical passions with a penchant for high living, hunting and fast cars; and he was an absolute terror in cross-examination, ruthlessly trapping policemen in the travails of their own inconsistencies, to the point where he was universally feared by prosecutions.

It was in ringing terms that he proposed a defence. The accused and their organisations, he pointed out, had at all times striven to bring the various racial groups in South Africa together, to create harmony and co-operation. In the international setting they had worked for world peace and the settlement of disputes by negotiation. If such peaceful objectives and methods constituted treason, remarked Berrangé, 'then I can only say that my clients stand convicted'. But these were no ordinary accused, the kind one might find in any criminal court. Here were members of parliament, clergymen, lawyers, journalists, students, clerical workers and labourers, who came from all races but held one thing in common: 'Despite the fact – and this is important – that they have different and differing political affiliations, at least they believe in the brotherhood of man, and the desire to work . . . towards his ultimate freedom . . . The Defence will therefore contend', continued Berrangé, 'that this case arises out of a political plot of the type which characterised the period of the Inquisition and the Reichstag fire trial. We believe, that in the result, this trial will be answered in the right way by history.'

It was indeed a stirring account, drawing on European and Nazi iniquities and suggesting the obvious parallels. It was the basis for a political defence, and it was precisely this tone of majestic contempt and glorious assertion that Berrangé could provide. But it was not the right way to win the Treason Trial. For this was a trial that would be won not head-on by political argument or more distantly by history, but by an attorney named Michael Parkington, an advocate named I.A. Maisels, QC, and the team they led through one of the legal masterworks of the twentieth century.

⁂

The Treason Trial became famous for its archival malevolence, as if it were being conducted by some obsessed, if not paranoid, librarian attempting to catalogue the political universe. In all, at the preparatory examination, there were some 12,000 documents handed in by the Crown, ranging from Exhibit A.1, an ANC membership card belonging to R.M. Resha of 41 Birkett Street, Sophiatown, taken from him in a search of ANC offices on 27 September 1955, to the Freedom Charter, the constitution of the Congress of Democrats, notes on European history of the seventeenth century, the Vienna Settlement, the slave trade, the foreign policy of Castlereagh, the Polish–Saxon question of 1750, and – taken notoriously at the Congress of the People – signs advertising 'Soup with Meat' and 'Soup without Meat'.

As all the material was produced for the court, it soon became apparent that this would become a trial peculiarly elongated in time as well as elastic in concept. Police witnesses came to report on meetings and speeches, the kind that Berrangé could all too easily lead up the false trail of their own garbled accounts – that is, where those accounts were not virtually illiterate. As item after item was submitted, report after report given in, both sides in the case faced the nightmare of a trial without end. Oswald Pirow joined the Crown as its leader, attempting to shape more carefully the legal grounds for a treason case. Then, in December 1957, a year after the original arrests, the Attorney-General withdrew charges against sixty-five of the accused, for lack of specific evidence.

But at the end of January 1958, after closing arguments by Pirow and Berrangé, the magistrate dismissed an application by the defence for the discharge of the remaining ninety-two. 'The court's decision is that there is sufficient reason for putting all the accused on trial on the main charge of high treason, and [therefore] all the accused are committed on a charge of high treason.' Among the remaining accused were most of the major figures in the Congress movement, including Chief Albert Luthuli, Nelson Mandela, Walter Sisulu, Lilian Ngoyi, Helen Joseph, Z.K. Matthews, Moses Kotane and Joe Slovo, and the maximum penalty for treason in South Africa was death.

⁂

The defence team for the trial proper settled down by about May 1958. Whereas Berrangé had been the *de facto* leader in the preparatory, the new attorney, Michael Parkington, now assembled a different combination, with Issy Maisels in charge and Bram (the only other QC on the team) as his second-in-command. There were, in addition, as fine a group of advocates as could be gathered, including Sydney Kentridge and Charlie Nicholas, as well as a number of others who would all, in due course, become silks and, in some cases, judges.

In some respects the new arrangements were paradoxical if not directly anomalous. Maisels, like most of the other advocates for the defence, was not a 'political' lawyer, and undertook the case solely on the condition that he could run it as a legal and not political trial – an attitude which provoked some tension among the defendants, concerned that he would be able neither to understand nor represent what the case was really about. As for Parkington, he was originally a true-blue Tory Englishman who had won the Whehell Scholarship in international law at Cambridge – a distinction at that time held by only one other South African, General Smuts. He also loathed communists with some venom (particularly, for some reason, Ruth First), an oddity in a case in which the two alternative charges were framed under the Suppression of Communism Act. But, recalled Issy Maisels, Parkington absolutely loved Bram (perhaps one gentleman's recognition of another), and his were some of the key insights and much of the backroom work in configuring and structuring the trial.

Originally the accused elected to be tried by a judge and jury, but when the trial was set for Pretoria (not an auspicious location for a jury in a political case) they opted for a judge and two assessors. There was a flurry over this as well, because under this option the Minister of Justice was not entitled to appoint a special criminal court to which he would name the judges – as had occurred in the 1914 Rebellion, the 1922 Rand Revolt, and the Robey Leibbrandt trial. But that was no problem for 'Blackie' Swart: he merely changed the law, and established a special criminal court. Presiding would be Mr Justice Rumpff – who had officiated in the Defiance Campaign case, and acted for Pirow in 1947 when the latter was charged with incitement to commit public violence – together with Justices Ludorf and Kennedy, the latter a Natal judge who in 1957 had sentenced twenty-one Africans to death in a mass murder trial. The prospects for the defendants – at least in view of Swart's appointed bench – were not entirely promising.

The venue was to be the Old Synagogue in Pretoria, no longer a building of any religious import, but one taken over by the state for many political trials, then and to come. All the accused were on bail, and would travel daily from Johannesburg to Pretoria in a bus provided by the authorities. Most were unable to work, and lost their jobs; some, such as Helen Joseph, stood trial in the mornings, and worked in the late afternoons and evenings. By the time the proceedings finally ended, the accused had journeyed some 20,000 miles in their bus, almost once round the globe at its circumference, and so one might say in more than one sense that the trial returned them to where they began.

As for Bram, his life became thoroughly immersed in the ebb and flow of the trial. Though, like the other advocates, he emerged from time to time in order to take on some other life-giving case, this became the element of his existence, the medium into which his personal and political identity merged inextricably until 1961. His biography became the biography of the trial.

When the proceedings opened in August 1958, the defence began as they meant to continue, with an infernal harrying of the prosecution that started then and did not cease until the very end.

The first thing Maisels did was to apply for the recusal of both Justices Ludorf and Rumpff. The objection to Ludorf was twofold – that he was closely associated with the National Party, and that he had appeared for the police in a case which would now constitute part of the evidence he would have to hear. Ludorf rejected the former accusation, but accepted the latter, and disappeared from the case, to be replaced by Mr Justice Bekker, after one of the trial's innumerable adjournments. The application against Rumpff (which had its comic side) was based on the fact that 'Blackie' Swart, when faced with criticism of his initial selection of the judges, had maintained in parliament that Rumpff had nominated Ludorf. This, contended Maisels, was grounds for his recusal – but Rumpff rejected the application, saying that he had made no such nomination. The implication was that either he or the Minister of Justice was lying – and the defence, in accepting Rumpff's explanation, was prepared to concede it wasn't Rumpff.

Then Maisels began with his proper objective, embarking on a thunderous assault on the indictment. The Crown, he maintained in an address that lasted over nine hours, had not complied with the elementary rules of framing its allegations, in that the accused were not informed in clear and unmistakable terms what charges they had to meet. On the one hand the particulars supplied by the Crown disavowed the suggestion that the accused had acted in common agreement; yet on the other, the indictment alleged that they had acted with common purpose, under which agreement was implied. For evidence, the Crown appeared to be relying on the record of the preparatory examination, but this amounted to some forty volumes of 80,000 pages; against this the accused had the right to know exactly what charges they had to answer. Maisels dealt with the extensive use of the words 'and/or' in the indictment, showing that three paragraphs alone contained the words nineteen times. An attorney had calculated that when each of the charges in every paragraph was alternated with each of the others, the accused faced some 498,015 charges in all – to which the Crown had also added the words 'inter alia', which meant that the number of charges was infinite. 'Would it be unfair to say', Maisels enquired of the court, 'that the Crown appears to be a little uncertain on the terms of its conspiracy?'

Bram followed up for another four hours, on the two alternative counts under the Suppression of Communism Act. Again he insisted that the accused did not know exactly what offences they were alleged to have committed; there was an embarrassing lack of particularity in the charges, placing 'an intolerable burden' both on the court and on the accused. There followed discussion by other counsel on the nature of conspiracy, and of advocating communism, after which the judges quashed one of the alternative charges under the Suppression of Communism Act and ordered the Crown to supply further particulars on the other. When the prosecution was unable to comply, they withdrew the second alternative charge as well. If Pirow had expected to stage his opening accusations with an air of grand allegation and retribution, he was now very much on the receiving end.

The method was relentless, and had to be ruthless. Pirow, for the prosecution, replied to the defence's objections by maintaining that the Crown would rely solely on the question of conspiracy in the remaining charge of treason: 'The Crown', claimed Pirow, 'stands or falls by conspiracy. If the Crown fails to prove a conspiracy then all the accused go free.' But this too the defence was not prepared to accept. The accused, insisted Maisels, had to meet the charges as they were set out in the indictment, and not as Pirow chose to interpret them; if Pirow stood by his statement, then the indictment had to be put in a different form. 'The time has come', Maisels advised the judges, 'for the Crown to be put in its place.' Eventually, after offering concessions and amendments to the indictment, the Crown accepted the point, and Pirow rose to inform the court that the indictment was being withdrawn by the Attorney-General.

Ella Fischer was delighted, and wrote to Bram with a due sense of vindication: 'My dear old son – what a triumph for the defence, & what a victory . . . Does this mean the Crown starts all over again – or will the case just crumble? The Department of Justice & the prosecution must feel rather fools.' Ella had no special sympathy for communism, but she had monumental pride in her son (even at the age of fifty), and no tolerance at all for mendacity, whether in court or elsewhere.

<hr/>

As it turned out, this was not the last time that the prosecution felt rather fools, which meant also that the case did not crumble right away. A second indictment was presented in November 1958, and the government gave notice that there would be a separation of trials. Thirty of the accused were to be tried in January 1959, and the remaining sixty-one in April, all before the same judges. Again the prosecution's expectations on the timing as much as the outcome of the proceedings were as sanguine as they were deluded.

For it was at this stage, in the early running, that the outcome of the case was determined. Much of the customary focus on the political ethos of the period ignores the fact that the essential drama of the Treason Trial was a legal one. From that point of view, the initial brilliance of the defence was that in all their harrying, pestering and baiting, they succeeded in shaping a case they knew they could win. Thus, if the Crown had maintained the alternative charges under the Suppression of Communism Act – which required only proof of policies directed towards the establishment of an alternative form of government – there might well have been convictions, for it was not difficult to argue that this was what the accused had been trying to achieve. But it was precisely those charges that had been dropped, and in the second indictment there were crucial specifications that the prosecution would come to regret. Now the main burden of the charges was that the accused had 'wrongfully, unlawfully, and with hostile intent . . . conspired . . . to: (a) subvert, and overthrow, the State by violence, and to substitute therefor a Communist State or some other State; (b) make active preparation for the achievement of the objects set out in sub-paragraph (a) hereof'. In this, the very definition of communism which the prosecution adduced was a critical one: the defendants were charged with promoting 'Marxist–Leninist doctrine, inherent in which is the establishing of a Communist State by violence'. In other words, the Crown was alleging that violence was central to the concept of treason, and it accepted this as its definition of communism as well. It had its reasons for doing so: the government wished to prove to its own public and to the world at large that a much-maligned South Africa was faced with violent revolutionaries. But the paradox was that the defence could not have been more gratified, for it was precisely this definition that it had been at pains to drive the Crown towards all along. In essence, the defence felt it had every prospect of proving that the ANC and its allies were by no means violent movements, and that on those grounds it could overturn the charges.

Both in response to the first indictment, and now to the second (which the defence also applied to have quashed), this was what Maisels's team argued and refined. Nicholas, in what Sydney Kentridge called the most brilliant discussion on the point he had ever heard, argued from the legal authorities that treason in peacetime depended on 'hostile intent'. But the word 'hostile' came from *hostis* – an enemy; the definition had to involve violence, and this was what the Crown had to allege. On the nature of conspiracy, which the defence felt had not been adequately defined in the case, Maisels dissected the options with a surgeon's precise scalpel. If the accused were not charged with vicarious responsibility for one another's acts, then he suggested they were not properly conjoined for trial; but if they were charged in that way, then the indictment was bad in law for that reason, because it contravened basic principles of justice. Yet again he lambasted the prosecution on its inability to provide adequate particulars relating to the charges. Trengove (one of Pirow's assistants) had said it would take six months, and Pirow had said it was impossible. But six months was no answer, said Maisels: the Crown had had two and a half years: 'If it is impossible then the Crown has no case.'

The defence had tempted the prosecution with the idea of violence, and the prosecution had taken the bait. At one point Maisels asked Pirow why he had dropped the focus on everything else. 'You don't charge parking tickets,' came the reply. The response may have suggested a degree of hubris, but Pirow would have done well to take early warnings on what normally follows in its wake. In April the court pronounced itself convinced by the defence argument with regard to the alternative group of sixty-one accused, and quashed the indictment against them. But the case against the first thirty proceeded.

❧

When the trial resumed in August 1959 (merely a year after it had begun, and well into the third year after the original arrests), Pirow wasn't ready to present his opening argument, and applied for an adjournment. Rumpff, in a huff, ordered the proceedings to resume the next day. Molly – ever the chorus to Percy and Ella of Bram's adventures in court – managed to extract a certain wry pleasure. 'The defence lawyers are very amused', she wrote to Ella, 'to find that when Pirow's great moment came, he was unprepared.' She had already described the trial as 'a complete farce', and told Ella how Pirow was working up his case by holidaying on his farm in the Bushveld – at a cost of £25,000 to the taxpayer for his services.

The trial was like the baggiest monster of a nineteenth-century novel; the hard part, for the defence, was to keep an eye on its overall outline and, more than that, to become the secret author of its shape, even though they were not nominally in control. This meant a vigilance and an opportunism at every stage. In the absence of Pirow's address, the trial proceeded with the Crown presenting its documentary evidence (much diminished from the preparatory examination, but still an enormous hoard). But whereas, at the preparatory, much of this had simply been handed in to the court, now the defence, knowing that the judges would become exasperated, insisted that every item be read into the record. A newspaper described the resulting 'reading marathon', as the prosecution advocates took it in turns to read reports of ANC meetings at about 150 words a minute: 'The three Judges lean their foreheads on their fingers, and the 30 accused sit in a half doze . . . The only leavening comes from the Non-European gallery. Most of the ANC reports end with the exhortation: *"Mayebuye Afrika,"* and as the advocate reads the words there is a murmur, almost as if in benediction, of *"Mayebuye"* from the gallery.' Molly told Ella that the prosecution was reading documents in the order in which they

Bram Fischer as a young man

Abraham Fischer (De Zuid-Afrikaan, 19 August 1899)

Percy Fischer in his chambers

Family portrait: Bram, Ada and Ella Fischer

Bram at New College, Oxford, c. 1932 (Photo by courtesy of Arthur Keppel-Jones)

Kiev, July 1932. From right to left: Geoffrey Cox, Bram, Tom Jarman, Intourist guide, 'Mac' Macdonald, unknown (Photo by courtesy of Sir Geoffrey Cox)

Emmy Krige and Japie (standing) with Pauline, Jimmy and Molly seated in front

Pauline, 'Tottie' and Molly Krige

Molly before her marriage

Bram and Molly in their garden at
12 Beaumont Street, Oaklands

Ruth, Paul and Ilse with Sholto Cross

Johannesburg District Committee of the Communist Party, 1945. Seated (left to right): B. Mnisi, M. Harmel (secretary), D. du Plessis (chairman), J. Mpama, H. Watts. Standing: S. Buirski, A. Fischer, I. Wolfson, R. Fleet, E. Weinberg, W. Roberts, Y.M. Dadoo. Inset: E.T. Mofutsanyana

Molly in China, mid-1954

Bram Fischer, QC

Bram with the oldest Treason trialist,
Elias Moretsele

I.A. Maisels being lifted high after the
Treason Trial result, with Bram (left)

Last day of the Treason Trial, 29 March 1961. From left: the Harmels, Bram, Amina
Cachalia, Ruth First and Molly (Photo by Struan Robertson)

Lilliesleaf Farm, Rivonia, at the time of the police raid (University of the Witwatersrand, photos copied by Santu Mofokeng)

Below: Denis Goldberg and Walter Sisulu in disguise, photographed after their capture by the police

Bram and Vernon Berrangé at the time of the Rivonia Trial

Bram with Ilse and Paul on his departure for London in October 196

oel Joffe, Himie Bernadt
nd Bram on their way to
onsult with prisoners on
Robben Island after the
Rivonia Trial, 22 June
964 (Cape Times)

Bram, in his disguise, in
he grip of a security
oliceman as he is arrested
Die Transvaler, 12
November 1965)

Bram Fischer (Photo by Eli Weinberg, courtesy of the Mayibuye Centre, UWC)

had been seized, without any attempt to sort or organise them. When the judges pointed out that there was no reference to violence in any of them, 'Pirow just looks wise and says that everything will become clear later . . . Certainly in legal circles, Pirow has become a laughing stock.'

In order to facilitate matters, the defence announced that it was prepared to make certain admissions – among them that the ANC and its allies demanded 'a new and radically different form of government', and advocated universal suffrage and the abolition of racial discrimination – but Pirow kept insisting on the relevance of his documents. Mr Justice Kennedy remarked that if the prosecution intended to read all the documents *in extenso,* you've heard the old popular song – "Forever and Ever"?' At one stage Rumpff asked Pirow whether the criminal code said anything about 'the quantity of proof being dependent on the quantity of paper'. There was a dizzying maze of documentation, allegation, cross reference and insinuation, to the point where the central issue seemed to be an understanding of each document in relation to all the others. At times the proceedings represented an approximation of Kafka's *Trial* – the allegations unclear, the evidence obscure, the proceedings interminable, except that in this case the judges seemed as exasperated and confused as the accused.

Certainly, some of this was seductive for the prosecution, at least in so far as a characteristic left-wing political script coincided with the most vivid of right-wing nightmares. The prosecution read documents from the ANC, the Congress of Democrats and the Communist Party; they read accounts of Jean-Paul Sartre in Berlin, and the World Federation of Democratic Youth; they quoted *Fighting Talk* on the greatness of Stalin and the need to defend Hungary; there were supportive views on the Mau Mau in Kenya and resistance in Malaya, and quotes from *Liberation, Advance* and *New Age,* on China, the Taft–Hartley Bill and much else besides. It was this profusion of material together with a disarming incapacity for concealment on the part of the Congress Alliance that prompted Maisels to remark that if the ANC had been a cloak-and-dagger organisation, 'there may have been dagger, but no cloak'. If all the Crown had been trying to prove was a concerted attempt to establish an alternative form of government, it would have had more than a fighting chance. But, as it came to understand in due course, that opportunity had been discarded.

In the midst of this – and as if in symbolic enactment – Pirow died over one weekend (this was the same weekend that Ilse, on a picnic with her high-school friends, discovered the body of a murdered man at the Zoo Lake, a recreation spot in the northern suburbs of Johannesburg). When the court resumed on the Monday, among the memorials was an address, on behalf of the defence, by the communist Bram Fischer – a rather sweet South African irony. Molly informed Ella that the defence lawyers were somewhat regretful about Pirow: 'He was certainly more of a help to them than the Crown.' She also said that a small team of African witchdoctors had been visiting the trial with some regularity, and had forecast the week of Pirow's death; they were, however, distressed when a car accident involving Kennedy had proved minor, as they had been 'working on' him.

The prosecution ceased reading documents a few days after Pirow's demise, in the middle of October 1959.

❦

In court, Bram would have heard his name mentioned a number of times, not as the eminent barrister, but as a comrade of the accused. Once (when he wasn't there) it had to do with speeches regarding his banning that had been delivered at the conference launching the Congress of Democrats. (Molly's banning, too, was read into the record, as was her place on the executive of the COD.) There were accounts of Bram due to make his address to the National Peace Congress of 1953, and even recollections of his speeches as a communist on the City Hall steps after the war (a Detective Chief Constable Viviers, when asked whether he remembered any others besides Harmel, Watts and Bernstein at the City Hall, replied 'Advocate B. Fischer'). But the prosecution made no attempt to rope Bram into their accusations. They had enough trouble with their case, remarked Sydney Kentridge later, without trying to bring in the Communist Party or embarrass Bram.

In court Bram held a special position among the accused, for they felt that he not only represented them, but more importantly was *one* of them. Molly mentioned to Ella the opinion she had heard among the accused that the other lawyers could get them discharged because they were clever, but that Bram would get them discharged because he knew they were innocent. Bram understood what his comrades had been through, his beliefs were their beliefs, and it made a particular difference to them that he appreciated on a level beyond the legal exactly what the case was about. He was also, as so many came to appreciate, unofficial welfare officer of first resort for the defendants. Given that they had to be in court on a daily basis, and very few could hold down employment of any description, the trial was causing great hardship: families lived in poverty, marriages were under strain, children were going hungry. The Treason Trial Defence Fund, set up to deal with such problems (as well as to provide minimal payment for the defence), could not always cope adequately. Whenever a particular crisis emerged, it was always Bram who found a way of providing a solution, and he gave himself effortlessly and tirelessly to the task.

At home he and Molly regularly invited numbers of the accused for dinner, to meet white friends or colleagues from the Bar who did not normally encounter blacks on any level of equality. This was Bram's particular perspective, that personal contact and involvement would produce all kinds of beneficial results. On one occasion when both Chief Luthuli and Nelson Mandela were present, a discussion arose as to whether whites would accept majority rule. The white guests in general demurred, but – as Hilda and Rusty Bernstein recalled – it was the blacks who were more conciliatory and generous, feeling that everyone was open to reason – except perhaps Pirow. It was in moments such as this that whites who were in some imperfect way liberal came to meet and understand the black figures who had been mere names to them, and transform their own sense of the possible. As for the actual accused, their presence together in a trial of four years cemented the ties between them, transforming their various organisations into a unified movement.

In court Bram presented a diffident figure, a legal man, like his father, of the old school, gentlemanly, quiet, respectful and unassuming. Some of those whose lives depended on his acumen quite frankly considered him boring – but many who began by being unimpressed soon came to understand exactly what he was able, through his approach, to achieve. Ben Turok, sitting in the dock, realised how Bram's manner enabled him to advance the argument further than anyone might have suspected. Paul Joseph saw how much the judges respected Bram, and how his own quiet dignity lent an equal dignity to the cause of the accused. Helen Joseph, in her account of the trial, contrasted Bram's half-apologetic style with the vibrant flamboyance of Berrangé, which could electrify the air. But Bram too, she saw, could be equally relentless, winning the confidence and sympathy of a witness with his understated approach until he received just the admission or concession he was after.

In August and early September, as various policemen testified about the origins and provenance of the evidence they had confiscated, Bram showed the full potential of his self-deprecating and solicitous cross-examination. He spoke of the South African Peace Council 'putting forward its usual call for ending colonial wars'; concerning a peace gathering in Warsaw, he remarked to a Captain Buytendag, 'That, I think, is a sentiment which is frequently expressed by the Congresses, isn't it, that there is a possibility of different races living together peacefully?' and won the simple answer 'Yes'. When Rumpff observed that all organisations had their administrative difficulties, Bram commented that some – such as the Cape ANC – had such difficulties that they were incapable of forming revolutionary organisations. Time and again his sympathetic interest would gain the ready admission from policemen that although they had confiscated any number of documents, there were always many more left behind. In answer to one of Bram's questions, a Detective Sergeant Visser remembered almost ruefully, 'It was not really that the day had come to an end, but I had a small little Anglia to convey all these things, and it was just about packed full up to the roof' – but Visser was also prepared to acknowledge that he had confiscated only a twentieth to a thirtieth of the books that had been available on that raid. Later the defence would fashion a forceful dual argument on this issue, maintaining both that the police had taken too much, in that most of their documentation was irrelevant, and that they had taken too little, in so far as they had left behind, or did not cite, the vast mass of evidence that the Congress movements were essentially non-violent.

In Bram's questioning there was never any intimidation, never any coercion, and perhaps because of this policemen who may have been expecting the worst were quite ready to tell him all they knew. As he treated them with an unexpected respect, he invariably gained their honest reply. One of the clearest examples of this came in his cross-examination of a Special Branch policeman, Truter, on the policies of the Natal Indian Congress. First, Truter was prepared to agree that the NIC had been strongly influenced by Gandhi's non-violent principles. Then Bram cited a speech which mentioned a 'non-violent army' and 'non-violence':

FISCHER	Now, Mr Truter . . . what would you say about that in the various Congress campaigns in Natal?
TRUTER	As far as I know there was no violence at all.
FISCHER	I am not trying to lead you on this. What did people say about non-violence?
TRUTER	I don't think that any of the speakers ever advocated violence.
FISCHER	Leave that out for the moment. There may have been, and you may have heard an occasional violent speech, but did people speak about non-violence?
TRUTER	Yes, my Lord.
FISCHER	And did they do that frequently?
TRUTER	Yes, they spoke of non-violence frequently.
FISCHER	What I was asking you is whether they often spoke in that way?

TRUTER	Yes.
FISCHER	And moreover, did different people speak of that?
TRUTER	That is so, my Lord.
FISCHER	It was not only Dr Naicker?
TRUTER	Yes.
FISCHER	Or Mr Lawrence. There were others as well?
TRUTER	Yes, my Lord.
FISCHER	In fact, might it not be fair to say that one would have heard non-violence preached in one form or another from almost every platform?
TRUTER	I think it would be correct to say that.
FISCHER	Because I want to put this to you, because fundamentally that was the basis of all the campaigns that were conducted by the Congresses?
TRUTER	That is so.

This was Bram in his essence, in his quiet way obtaining exactly the answers he wanted, repeating some of his questions to maximum effect, heading towards his appointed culmination, which in the circumstances could not have been more significant: that the Congresses were peaceful organisations. Truter had been in the police force for twenty-six years, and Molly remarked to Ella that the older policemen were still at least prepared to tell the truth. Some of that may have had a lot to do with Bram, but as his performance here intimated, it would have been a mistake to identify the content of his method entirely with the form. For though the quietness and respect were genuine, underneath it all lay a maximum degree of preparation and as steely a feel for the jugular of a case as any of his companions. It was the old, disarmingly congenial tennis player coming out.

⁂

In order to prove the intrinsic connection between communism and violence (an argument that would have concerned Bram directly), the prosecution, now led by Advocate De Vos, produced its star witness, A.H. Murray, Professor of Philosophy at the University of Cape Town. He had already been introduced at the preparatory examination and rendered somewhat ridiculous by the defence (he had, at one point, identified his own writing as 'communist'), but that did not prevent the Crown from trying again.

As before, the harrying began from the start of his evidence, specifically on his status as an expert witness. When Murray began reading from notes, the defence objected immediately, wishing to clarify whether the notes were evidence and, if so, whether they should be handed in. Indeed, how much was Murray entitled to 'know' where he was not a first-hand witness on matters of fact? Some of the defence objections on this issue produced hilarious exchanges. Was the S.N. Khrushchev who had delivered a report of the central committee to the twentieth congress of the Communist Party of the Soviet Union the same Khrushchev who was leader of the USSR? Was a fact part of a theory (Welsh, for the defence) or a theory a fact (Rumpff)? When De Vos produced a document on the Seventh All-China Congress of Trade Unions, containing a speech by one Saillant on behalf of the World Federation of Trade Unions, the judges wanted to know how he could prove who Saillant was, and whether the document was evidence against the WFTU. De Vos replied as best he could: 'My Lord, in my submission, prima facie, that document is what it purports to be' – to which Rumpff replied as if in revelation to himself as much as anyone else, 'Is any document what it purports to be in this court?'

Molly commented to Ella that after two weeks Murray 'should be a broken man & completely discredited as a witness & an expert'. This had, in large part, to do with his litmus test for communism – the widespread presence of the word 'fascist' in communist discourse. Strictly speaking, according to Murray, the term could legitimately be applied only to a certain form of Italian corporatist state under Mussolini; otherwise its usage revealed a communist bent. Molly, in her running commentary to Ella, suggested an approximation of his method: 'Pointing to a cow: That animal has 4 legs; an elephant has 4 legs; therefore that animal is an elephant' – and the defence was no less quick to take advantage of the resulting absurdities. After a weekend's search by Parkington and his team through the university library in Johannesburg (acting on tip-offs from colleagues in Britain), Maisels came prepared with sources ranging from Roosevelt, to Churchill, to Clement Attlee, to Bertrand Russell, to Adlai Stevenson, to the United Party leader J.G.N. Strauss, to show that by Murray's definition their communism was plain. It was almost obligatory, as in the preparatory, to quote anonymously from Murray's own writings (minimal as they were, in the Afrikaans family magazine *Die Huisgenoot)* so that he could identify them as communist. Maisels pointed out that Oswald Mosley had called his movement the British Union of Fascists, and asked Murray whether that organisation had consisted of Italian emigrés. Regarding Goebbels, whom Churchill had identified as fascist, Maisels asked him whether he was Italian. 'Would you mind explaining to me', remarked Maisels at one point, 'how your mind works?' Finally, Maisels persuaded Murray to agree that 'the so-called extended use of fascist or fascism is in no way indicative or may not be in any way indicative . . . of communist belief' – to which Murray answered, 'Yes.'

But the defence was concerned also to establish that the ANC and its allies had impeccable credentials, which were by no means simply 'communist'. They quoted from the Universal Declaration of Human Rights to show how closely the Freedom Charter resembled it, as it did Pope Pius XI's encyclical *Quadragesimo Anno* of 1931 and Pope Leo XIII's *Rerum Novarum* of 1891. To this same end they cited the Paraguayan constitution, the Basic Law of the German Federal Republic, the Magna Carta, and the constitution of the United States; they even cited Bismarck on health. Kentridge persuaded Murray to agree that there was nothing in communist doctrine indicating that the external features of a people's democracy could emerge only through violence, or that the objectives of the Freedom Charter could be achieved only by violent methods. He remarked to Murray that his attitude reminded him of the leading official of the USSR who said that the Empire State Building reminded him of communism 'because everything reminds me of communism'.

By the end of Murray's testimony there wasn't much left, but Molly told Ella that his conceit as well as his ignorance meant that no one had much sympathy: 'For years he has been telling the police that perfectly innocent documents were communist doctrine. Without his advice there may never have been a trial – so he deserves everything he gets.' Yet here too the trial revealed one of its bitter-sweet twists, because the remarkable irony was that the judges believed Murray, and it was quite fortunate they did so. For it was Murray who gave them the definition that communism required violence, and that was the test they applied to the case. And because they were unable to find violence, they were also unable to find communism.

In later years Issy Maisels remembered the trial as 'absolutely endless. I can't tell you how terrible it was.' One liability for these eminent defence lawyers was that they could hardly take on any other cases, and there was a financial toll. As for Bram, he was absolutely delighted in March 1960 when a case involving mine property and flooding by water came his way, his old specialities. It was 'absolute heaven', he remarked to Ella, to be doing something other than treason.

By March 1960 whole cycles of life had come and gone at home. Ruth, who had completed her matriculation exams when the treason arrests were first carried out, was now a psychology student at the University of Cape Town, where Bram had preceded her thirty-five years before, and it was Ilse who was in her final year of school. Through these changes the one dimension of the Fischer household that had not altered was its openness. As always, people came to stay – Hilary Flegg, whose husband had helped finance the *Guardian*, and the Shanleys, who were among the original batch of trialists from Durban. Bram's instincts in regard to the latter family were characteristic, for when Hilary Flegg told Dorothy Shanley that she should bring only her youngest child, and Bram found the two of them at home, he jumped in the car right away to fetch the others. To him it was unthinkable that a mother should be separated from her children, and the pressure of the trial made no difference. As before, the Fischer home became – in Bram's easiest and most hospitable way – communist property. Ultimately Dorothy and her youngest stayed for a year. (As for Ilse, she took a great shine to Dorothy Shanley, who in contrast to Bram and Molly's primness wore bright-red lipstick, and took Ilse upstairs to try it on.)

By March 1960 the Crown was in the last stages of its evidence, and the defence was cross-examining the endless relay of policemen who had taken notes (usually unreliably in shorthand and completely waywardly in long-hand) at Congress meetings. Bram dealt with a Detective Masilela, whose first language was Sesotho, though he had taken notes in English on a speech delivered in Zulu. One extract read, 'I like to speak like a free man in this country in France . . . who serves seven years in gaol he did not know the people of China but I know you here.' Robert Resha, in a speech, was alleged to have said, 'You can only do that if you kill your brother', and there was some dispute as to whether the word was 'kill' or 'tell'. Kentridge asked for a court interpreter to listen to the words in Sesotho that followed, and they turned out to be, 'If you go and deliver the message to your friends . . . then they will be well informed.' Rumpff more or less threw out a Sergeant Isaac Sharp during Bram's cross-examination. Chiefly the defence managed to maintain the structure of its case. When the prosecution – which could also see what was happening – began to shift the ground of its allegations, arguing that the Congresses only appeared to be talking about peace, but were attempting to provoke the state into a violent conflagration, Bram would have none of it. The only hostile intent the Crown was entitled to find, he insisted, was not the intent to mislead, but an overt conspiracy to overthrow a system of government by violence. The judges accepted his definition, and the prosecution was once again stuck with its self-crippling indictment. These were the familiar lines of battle when the Crown case closed on 10 March, and the defence opened on the 14th with its first witness, Dr W.Z. Conco, deputy president of the ANC.

Exactly one week later, on 21 March 1960, at the African township of Sharpeville, just outside Vereeniging to the south-west of Johannesburg, there occurred one of the darkest moments in South African history. There the Pan Africanist Congress, formed when the Africanist segment of the ANC seceded in 1959, had called a demonstration in support of its anti-pass campaign. A crowd gathered at the police station, and though later evidence indicated that those present had been peaceful, the police opened fire: the best construction was that they had panicked, but the worst suspicions were more dire. Newspaper photographs showed the carnage, with bodies strewn on the ground in all the impossible poses of violent death; most had been shot in the back or side while trying to escape. When everything cleared it was found that 69 had been killed and 187 wounded, and nothing could have been more representative of the bare savagery of the South African system.

That very day at the Old Synagogue in Pretoria, the defence in the Treason Trial had called Chief Albert Luthuli as its second witness. It was while he was giving evidence on the non-violent policies of the ANC that the first reports of the Sharpeville massacre came through. In response to a question from Maisels, Luthuli counselled restraint and a peaceful approach on all sides, but because of the violent outbreak the whole trial had taken on a new and quite different perspective. There was more drama to follow. On 26 March, while still on bail, Luthuli burned his own pass, and urged other Africans to do the same. The following day the pass laws were suspended across the country (though this turned out to be only a temporary measure), and on the 28th, a week after the massacre, there was a nation-wide stay-at-home. Two days later, on the 30th in Cape Town, a young man of twenty-one named Philip Kgosana led a march of 30,000 from the townships of Langa and Nyanga into the city, almost reaching the Houses of Parliament. There he was promised a meeting with the Minister of Justice if the crowd dispersed, but when Kgosana returned later in the day for the meeting, he and his associates were arrested. That same day the government declared a State of Emergency and called out the Active Citizen Force; the police began massive roundups, and ultimately some 2000 political activists were taken into detention. On 8 April both the ANC and the PAC were declared illegal, and the following day a white man (later declared insane) attempted to assassinate Prime Minister Verwoerd at the Fiftieth Union Exposition in Johannesburg. It was a staggering two weeks, when revolution appeared to be imminent and, though turned back, its threat still quivered in the air. As the shock waves of Sharpeville continued to register, as an international outcry gathered force, as capital flowed out of the country by the hour, it was apparent that this was a turning-point for South Africa, and nothing would be the same again.

In Pretoria, on 30 March, there was consternation when Chief Luthuli, along with seventeen other defendants, did not appear in court. It turned out that he had been arrested at three o'clock that morning (and assaulted). Finally he was tracked down in prison and presented by the prosecution to a set of indignant judges, but by then Maisels wanted an adjournment of the trial. By declaring a State of Emergency, he maintained, the government had already cast judgment on the case, and produced a situation quite abnormal for the court; in addition, numbers of witnesses might have gone into hiding, or else be wary of giving evidence for fear of contravening the Emergency regulations. Maisels won one adjournment and then (when he refused to accept any assurances of an indemnity for witnesses from the Minister of Justice) another, but, on 26 April, the judges determined that the case must proceed. In response Maisels asked leave for the accused Duma Nokwe, secretary-general of the ANC (and the first African advocate in the Transvaal) to address the court. The latter informed the judges that in the light of their decision and the difficulties outlined by the defence, all the accused 'cancel their instructions to Counsel and have instructed them to withdraw from the case'. Maisels rose to reinforce the point: 'We accordingly have no further mandate and will consequently not trouble your Lordships any further.'

Much later Issy Maisels indicated that although the defence would have had genuine difficulties in continuing with the case (even gaining access to the defendants in prison was a problem), their withdrawal was a tactic, principally to delegitimise the trial. The idea was to provide maximum embarrassment for the proceedings in the larger court of public and world opinion, but of course there was a risk, for now the accused would have to defend themselves without the sustained legal vigilance and preparation their counsel could provide. But as to that, remarked Maisels, the defence team had complete confidence in both the integrity and intelligence of the defendants. It was a confidence that was more than justified. Now the Old Synagogue became setting to the most remarkable scenario of the accused being led in turn, as witnesses, by their co-accused, and cross-examined by the prosecution, and their resilience and stature were stunning. Luthuli was questioned by Advocate Trengove, for the Crown, on Robert Resha's apparent disposition towards violence, and rejected the idea that a leader's actions necessarily represented a whole policy: 'If Resha as a general departs, he departs as Resha. It has nothing to do with the African National Congress.' When Trengove put it to him that he never expected the white oppressor to accede peacefully to Congress demands, Luthuli was simple and superb: 'My Lords, I wouldn't be in Congress if I didn't expect that white South Africa would some day reconsider. That is my honest belief. When, my Lords, I cannot say.'

Helen Joseph also had to endure – in her case fierce and sustained interrogation by Rumpff, who evidently felt during this phase of the trial that the prosecution case would not be adequate without his particular assistance from the bench. Adding his weight to the cross-examination he questioned Joseph repeatedly and searchingly, sometimes on hypothetical issues, such as whether the existence of a ruthless fascist state would incline her to violent methods. Through all of this Helen Joseph survived undaunted in court, though it turned out afterwards that she had had something of a breakdown in prison. Later Rumpff's treatment of her (and others) became the substance of a second application by Bram for Rumpff's recusal, on the ground that his interventions had 'given rise to a reasonable fear in the minds of the accused that they [were] not obtaining a fair trial'. Helen Joseph wrote that the application required great courage in the face of such a rampant judge, and that the accused 'admired and loved' Bram more than ever for undertaking it. And it was true that it took someone like him to make it, who could with his combination of tact and quiet incorruptible clarity put the case with equal degrees of respect, honesty and determination. Rumpff turned down the application, but thereafter proved much more restrained, able to preside without succumbing ever again to the temptation of throwing his weight about as before, and the atmosphere in court became much improved.

⁂

As repression proved generally effective, the State of Emergency regulations were lifted slowly, and the defence returned to the case. Bram was back by 26 July. That August he undertook one of his most significant passages of work in court as an advocate, leading the evidence of Robert Resha, whose ANC membership card had been Exhibit A.1 when the preparatory examination had begun so long ago. Again it was no accident that Resha was given to Bram to examine, for much of the case would turn on his words, and they demanded a quiet, unclimactic exposition.

Resha's words, in fact, provided the core of the prosecution's allegations. He had been volunteer-in-chief in the campaign to resist the Sophiatown removals, and in November 1956 had given a speech at ANC headquarters that had caused the police no end of excitement. On that occasion the Special Branch had been secreted in a room upstairs from the ANC offices, busy with a tape recorder that refused to work; but as Resha's speech began, so did the machine, and the recording had been duly played in court. First Resha had told his audience that war had been declared, and that it was time for the ANC to take the offensive. Then he called for volunteers, and defined their nature: 'Volunteers are those people who do and die. Volunteers are those people who . . . when they are given leaflets to do they go out and distribute those leaflets . . . A volunteer is a person who is disciplined . . . When you are disciplined and you are told by the organisation not to be violent, you must not be violent. If you are a true volunteer and you are called upon to be violent, you must be absolutely violent, you must murder! Murder! That is all.'

On paper the words of what became known as the 'Murder, murder' speech were one thing, and could even be defended: Resha had given a conditional definition, and his argument was more about discipline than violence. But the atmosphere of the tape overrode all that, for with Resha's rising exhortation to an increasingly clamorous audience it was hard to put anything but an apocalyptic construction on the overall effect. It was Bram, then, who had to calm things down, and apply a different perspective.

He began by asking Resha about the Sophiatown removals, and the passions engendered by its deliberate destruction – to which Resha replied that Sophiatown now was 'in ruins . . . like a bombed city, my Lord'. Then Bram questioned him on the nature of ANC policy, and Resha responded that it was a policy of non-violence that he had both accepted and preached. Bram continued on the critical point:

FISCHER   Now I want to ask you whether you have ever departed from this policy in any of your speeches.

RESHA   I think I have.

FISCHER   Can you explain to the court why you have departed from it, if you have?

RESHA   My Lords, when I think of the brutal methods used by the government in imposing its inhuman policy on my people, I sometimes have grave doubts about the policy of non-violence. Sometimes it seems to me that if the government is prepared to use this force and violence in stifling every endeavour by my people to improve their lot and to attain some political rights, then sometimes I feel we too have the right to use this violence at times.

FISCHER   You would like to use violence at times? If you sit down and ponder what the policy should be, what is your conclusion?

RESHA   When I sit down calmly and consider the African National Congress policy, I realise that the only wise policy is the policy of non-violence.

Bram raised the key speech once more:

FISCHER   [Y]ou know by heart probably now the end of the much-debated speech in which you suggested that if a volunteer were ordered to murder he should 'murder, murder'?
RESHA   I think I know that speech by now.
FISCHER   Can you reconcile that with African National Congress policy?
RESHA   The example I used in that speech cannot be reconciled with the policy of the African National Congress.

It was an examination in which only a tone of calm and genuine engagement would do, and it appeared to have some effect. Later (as Issy Maisels remembered it), when Hoexter, for the prosecution, was cross-examining Professor Z.K. Matthews, he asked him what he thought of Resha's speech. 'Just words,' came the reply, and Hoexter said, 'You know, I think you are right.'

On 7 October 1960 Bram closed the case for the defence. Because the prosecution wasn't ready with its closing argument (Rumpff's patience tried yet once more), resumption was set for 7 November – the anniversary, Maisels reminded the court with his usual jocularity, of the Russian Revolution.

<hr/>

In relative terms the end was not far off, though with the endless self-perpetuations of the trial not many would have dared to make rash assumptions. First came the closing argument for the Crown which – with adjournments – went on for four months, and a fairly abysmal presentation it was. As De Vos began insisting that the Congress Alliance was a communist movement, acting according to a communist master plan to overthrow the state and replace it with a communist government, the patience of the judges ran out altogether. Rumpff and Bekker pointed out some of the deficiencies, not least that the prosecution had not proved that the policies of the ANC and its allies were derived from the Communist Party either in South Africa or in the Soviet Union, or indeed that the defendants had any knowledge of that. Rumpff asked for the argument on the defendants' knowledge of the connection between communism and violence, and De Vos replied that that section of his argument wasn't ready. Rumpff drew attention to the eight months since the Crown case had closed; Maisels drew attention to the four years since the trial had begun.

Good advocates make the law as much as judges do, outlining the basis and shape of a case, defining the central issues, and dealing with the wider ramifications of concept and content in a pre-emptive way. Poor advocates will not understand any of this, and will flounder – and they are liable to outrage a Rumpff: Sydney Kentridge remarked later that Rumpff was ruder to De Vos through the latter's closing argument than he had ever seen a judge be to counsel. It was with some desperation, then, that the prosecution did its best to blur the issues, particularly on the question of violence. When Trengove took up the argument he suggested that treason required only hostile intent – that one should treat the state as an enemy and attempt to overthrow it. Such a policy would be even more serious, he continued, if one truly believed the government was fascist, because then a violent clash would be more likely. But when asked by the judges what form of violence the Congresses envisaged, he was not able to give any indication.

It was this kind of slippage that the defence set out to demolish when Maisels at last opened argument at the beginning of March 1961. At best, he maintained, the prosecution case was now one of 'contingent retaliation' – that Congress policies would provoke violence by the state to which it would then respond – but this had not been covered in the indictment or in the pleadings. The case had to be proved as one of *conspiracy*, and therefore the Crown had to show that each and every one of the accused knew of and supported a policy of violent revolution. Why, if the conspiracy had been nation-wide, had the prosecution been unable to provide even one direct piece of evidence? Maisels reminded the court that when Trengove had been arguing he had suggested that there could be a case of treason without violence, and that Mr Justice Bekker had said that was not true under the current indictment. In recollection Bekker now intervened, as if in emphasis, 'He was wedded to violence', and Maisels replied, 'That is so, my Lord.'

The defence pounded the prosecution on issues of law. Nicholas succeeded Maisels on the connection between treason and conspiracy, which he argued required an agreement and nothing short of it, neither discussion nor intention. Kentridge followed with a devastating disquisition on the law of treason, which required two separate witnesses – each of whose testimony was independent and sufficient in itself – to prove each alleged overt act. Where more than one act of treason was alleged, each of these had to be proved by at least one (but not the same) independent witness; therefore, once again, a minimum of two witnesses was required. As Kentridge showed brilliantly, the permutations posed insuperable difficulties for the Crown, which had to satisfy these requirements, proving both conspiracy and adherence to it, with regard to each of the accused, twenty-seven co-conspirators, and twenty-five organisations, over the four years covered by the indictment – and in this they could only be regarded as having failed signally. It was at this point that the judges took unprecedented action, asking the prosecution to reply on the points of law raised by the defence, which the Crown (unprepared as usual) took up some days later. But they could do so only in the most dilatory fashion: if there was any variance between their argument and the indictment, they suggested, they would offer to amend the indictment. It was very much like the kind of discussion with which the trial had opened.

Molly, who had taken a rather dim view of the judges all along, now wrote to Ruth and Ilse (who had joined her sister at the University of Cape Town) to say that everything was suddenly looking rather hopeful. The defence had thrown in everything, she told them, to convince the court in favour of an acquittal, but this was not preventing Bram from preparing his own lengthy section of the argument, which he expected to take about three weeks. Yet even now, hopeful or not, it was clear that for some the price of the trial had been too high. Molly told Ruth and Ilse that there was an air of sadness about the court, for Elias Moretsele, the eldest of the defendants (known as Uncle Retse to all), had died after four years. 'One way of ending the trial would, I presume,' remarked Molly, 'be to go on until the accused died off one by one.'

When Bram took up his section of the argument, he had, Issy Maisels recalled later, the most difficult task – an analysis of the mammoth collection of facts, comprising all the evidence the prosecution had produced on Congress policies in all the various regions, including all the speeches. Bram had prepared with his usual methodical care, and began on 20 March. The record – mythologised outside the court almost instantly, as events unfolded – shows that after a series of interruptions from the judges, directing Bram to focus on specific issues, on 23 March they adjourned to consider whether there might be some aspects of the defence it would not be necessary to hear, in the interests of shortening the trial. When proceedings resumed the following Wednesday, on 29 March, it ended virtually unbelievably almost where it began, with the prosecution rising to indicate that if the court believed there was a variance between the allegations and the indictment, they would ask for leave to amend the indictment *yet again* to cure the defect.

But the judges, by then, were having none of it, and Rumpff announced to an Old Synagogue packed with spectators that they had reached a unanimous verdict. Ultimately their full reasons ran to hundreds of pages, but for now they offered an abbreviated judgment – which none the less took Rumpff some thirty minutes to read. Among the many points he covered were the critical ones. The judges had found no proof that the form of state envisaged in the Freedom Charter was 'a Communist state'. Whereas the issue of communism was relevant to the issue of violence, the prosecution had failed to show that the accused 'had personal knowledge of the Communist doctrine of violent revolution, or [had] propagated this doctrine as such'. Though some speeches by ANC leaders had tended towards violence, these had formed an insignificant proportion of the total number of speeches made, and Resha's speech in particular had contravened ANC policy 'not to become violent even in the face of provocation'. As to the question of 'contingent retaliation', this had not been covered in the indictment, nor was there sufficient evidence of any such policy. Finally, although the ANC and its allies had envisaged a fundamentally different kind of state from the one that existed, and had embarked on a programme of illegal methods to achieve it, the prosecution had 'failed to show that the African National Congress as a matter of policy intended to achieve this new State by violent means'. 'The accused are accordingly found not guilty', Rumpff concluded, 'and are discharged.'

It was how the defence had shaped the trial, and after four years the emotions were overwhelming. The accused and the spectators sang 'Nkosi Sikelel' iAfrika', and someone chanted a praise-song in Zulu for Maisels. People wept and embraced, and outside the court the discharged defendants raised Issy Maisels and Bram Fischer, beaming with the elation of it all, high above their shoulders.

⁂

'Liewe kinders,' Bram wrote to Ruth and Ilse on 1 April from the farm at Diepwater, where he and Molly had gone to visit Ella and recuperate: '[E]ven now it's hard to believe it's not some sort of April fool's day delusion. Ruth, do you remember when we used to go into town every morning at the end of 1957, and one day when we passed the Drill Hall we wondered how life was going to change when once the trial started? That was a long time ago & you, Ilse, were still in Standard VII. And now we've come to the end of that Chapter – a complete end too, because the court has found unanimously in our favour on the *facts* and not on the law and once that happens there is no appeal, for the Crown can only appeal on points of law. As a matter of fact that was one of the reasons we were jittery towards the end: both our law points went down so well that we were afraid we would win on one of them and possibly have to face an appeal, and have the whole thing drag out until 1962!'

Bram described the final stages for them – Kentridge's argument on treason witnesses, the Crown's unedifying reply, the defence team's uncertainty as to whether the judges, when they adjourned, were writing a judgment on the law, or had disagreed with them, or would want to hear them fully on the facts. Bram had settled in for a long disquisition, but then, shortly after he began on the longhand reports of speeches, the judges told him to focus on the short-hand accounts. He had rearranged his notes, and began on the Western Cape; the following day the judges intervened again, wishing him to discuss the Transvaal (where the most threatening speeches had occurred). Bram indicated that he wanted to deal with Natal and the Orange Free State first, and the judges listened for a while but 'by 9.45 would not listen any more and insisted on going North'. Bram had just begun when the judges intervened again, and asked what he had to say about one of the police witnesses, and then another. 'They said that would be all, and they would adjourn . . . That was the end. The rest you know . . . '

'Some of the congratulations', wrote Bram, 'have been most touching. Apart from the cables from overseas, what is much more heartwarming is the Africans who stop me in the corridor or in the street or in the court – men I don't seem to know at all who shake me by the hand & say thank you.' Writing to his family, Bram indicated yet again how much it meant in a moment of triumph and release such as this to be part of that larger 'family' to which his actions and his thoughts made him always committed.

⁂

Molly had also kept Ruth and Ilse informed on the last stages of the trial – how in the last week the defence had furiously shortened and redrafted its argument; how there had been a rising tempo of expectation; how proud they would have been of Bram, looking distinguished in court with his hair that he had at last consented to grow a little longer. All the accused agreed, she commented, that as soon as Bram began his argument the whole atmosphere had become more gentle and kindly, 'as if a sympathetic teacher were instructing an unruly class of small boys'. She told them how, when the trial was adjourned, everyone felt it could mean only one thing, and how the defence team had gone a little crazy with it all. Kentridge, 'the staid softspoken – oh so correct lawyer – danced a little jig & was heard to use bad words. Later he put some ice down Parkington's shirt & the champagne cork in his own ear!' Bram had had tea with the accused, and they had all felt stunned. 'Bram says he just feels quite empty.'

She had also written to Bram when it was all clearly over:

Home, Wednesday 22nd March.

Darling heart,

I was so proud of you today. You looked so distinguished with your long-cut greying hair, wearing your sober black. Now don't let the word 'sober' set you off imagining that I'm the very opposite. I admit that I have been terribly excited all evening since you phoned to say that rumour had that it won't be long now. Hilary was out at a cocktail-dinner farewell for Joe, so I told Paul that it wouldn't be long now, & then wrote to Ouma & Ruth & Ilse to tell them that it wouldn't be long now, and then I thought I had better write & tell *you* that it wouldn't be long now in case you hadn't realised the significance of it. Paul & I won't be quite so lonely any more.

Darling, the accused say you were wonderful; Leon [Levy] said that he was listening carefully for the 1st time in 4 yrs. Helen [Joseph] said she sometimes missed your 'pearls of wisdom', because you spoke away from the microphone & that made her very sad, but she realised it was important to take the bench into your confidence. Someone else said that from the time you took over, kindliness descended over the whole court!

I'm not underestimating the role played by the rest of your team, but I'm certain you've been the key pin & if we win well . . . ?

All my love for always,
M.

✣

The night the trial ended, there was a party at 12 Beaumont Street – a party to end all parties, like the abandoned *Guardian* jamborees of former years, but now with the particular intensities and recognitions of something to celebrate. Two car-loads of plain-clothes policemen came to watch, for yet again the easy multi-racial proclivities of the Fischer household constituted (to the police) a public provocation. Bram told Ruth and Ilse about it: 'The party of course was a huge success and completely chaotic. You may have read about the police hanging around – there must have been 20 of them. But as we gave them no excuse for coming in, that expedition too was a failure.'

Chief Luthuli, who won the Nobel Peace Prize in 1961, wrote that the 'grim pre-dawn raid' of four years before had transformed his movement. Though the arrests had been 'deliberately calculated to strike terror into hesitant minds and impress upon the entire nation the determination of the governing clique to stifle all opposition', the trial had by contrast forged unity among the defendants of all races. On this the Chief could not be more emphatic: 'In all humility I can say that if there is one thing which helped push our movement along non-racial lines, away from narrow, separative racialism, it is the Treason Trial which showed the depth of sincerity and devotion to a noble cause on the white side of the colour line.' Among others the Chief singled out for special mention 'the brilliant team of legal men who defended us so magnificently for so little financial reward'.

It was true. Though the ANC and its allies had been stymied by a trial that dragged on for so long, they had been transformed from a dispersed and somewhat disparate collectivity into a national movement centred round individuals who had used the four years to refine their policies and politics – and not least the policy of non-racialism. Not much is answered by history, but history was answered in this case by the accused, and by those who were prepared to put their careers and expertise on the line when the odds looked so daunting and so few would help. As Luthuli's words at the time intimated and even prophesied, once again there was a direct line between the Treason Trial and the non-racial vision of a free South Africa in later years.

❧

Perhaps the most positive twist in the trial was that the judicial system had actually worked. The state may have intended to strike terror among the populace, but then – and despite the doubts of Molly among many others – a legal momentum had taken over, and the government had found it impossible to interfere with the autonomy of the court while it lived up to its own traditions. This too was one of the particular mysteries (if not miracles) of the South African story – that even in much-thinned and reduced times echoes of this independence would endure, as would the readiness and commitment on the part of a small core of lawyers opposed to apartheid to take on the most difficult of political trials. Among this core the inspirational figure was undoubtedly Bram Fischer, who as in so many other areas of his life provided a personal bridge between the political and 'non-political' worlds, who in the combination of his magnetism and integrity provided the compelling model to be near.

There were of course other twists. One of those who had come to watch the preparatory examination was B.J. Vorster, member of the Bar and ex-leader of the Ossewabrandwag during the war. By the early 1960s he was Minister of Justice (and future Prime Minister after Verwoerd's assassination) and he no doubt drew his own conclusions from the trial: if his antagonists could not be crippled under the law, then it was clear that the law had to be changed, and there were always other methods of gaining evidence to be explored, beyond the clumsy and inconvenient attempts of shorthand and longhand reporters at public meetings.

When the accused were found not guilty of violent conspiracy, the irony was that virtually at that very stage the ANC and its allies were being driven towards an armed struggle, and the verdict of the trial was obsolete. Also, although the prosecution had attempted unsuccessfully to argue for a vicarious 'communism' on the part of the ANC, there was in fact an active Communist Party underground. In pamphlets distributed on 14 July 1960, during the State of Emergency, it had announced its existence. One of its chief representatives, a member of its central committee, was in court virtually every single day: Bram Fischer.

As long as legal methods make sense in the struggle for justice they will be used, and that was what Bram did in a formal and literal way during the Treason Trial. But when they become impossible or irrelevant, then different options will provide their own temptations – and dangers. In fact they were all already in a different world, and Bram and Molly knew it directly. Because when the State of Emergency was declared in March 1960, one of those detained by the police was Molly Fischer.

CHAPTER 10

EMERGENCY

30 March 1960 – October 1963

'It's all right dear, it's for me.'

In those first few hours of the State of Emergency on 30 March 1960, a few hundred people were arrested by the police, but neither Bram nor Molly was among them. Some of those taken in were detained illegally, as the Emergency had not as yet been properly proclaimed. Joe Slovo, among others, applied for a court order for his release, and won it, but Colonel Spengler of the Security Police (whose presence was also becoming increasingly familiar) merely delayed until the Emergency proclamations arrived, and then rearrested all those in his charge in terms of the Public Safety Act.

Others – very few – such as Ben Turok saw what was coming and went underground; Michael Harmel and the indomitable Ruth First escaped to Swaziland. Bram, involved in the Treason Trial, waited and fulfilled his usual role, assisting those who had been detained in the brief flurry of searches and court order applications that resulted. He fully expected to be arrested. A few nights later, when the doorbell rang at two o'clock in the morning, no one at the Fischer household was very surprised. Ilse heard it, and went to Bram and Molly, and Molly went downstairs to the door to give Bram some extra time, but then they heard her call up in a different tone: 'It's all right dear, it's for me.'

It was a calm and quiet response, as if this were a polite call from a neighbour in the middle of the day, but of course – the lights suddenly on in the house – it was the opposite of that. The Security Police allowed Molly upstairs to pack while they searched through the rest of the house. Bram could hardly believe they had let her up alone. Ilse remembered him urging Molly, 'They're obviously giving you the chance to get away – jump out of the window!' But Molly merely replied, 'Ag, don't be silly', and went down to be taken to jail for the first time in her life at the steady age of fifty-two. It was quite possible that the police had left her alone because Bram's intimidating position as an advocate still counted for something, and there were residual gestures of tact in arresting figures of such standing. But there was a new pressure in the air. Ilse couldn't remember whether it was on this occasion or later that one of the policemen said, 'Things have changed, you used to give us tea.' That was the madness of it: revolutionary white South Africans, being raided, used to fulfil the polite obligation of offering their visitors hospitality – as if to include their antagonists within the realm of their own morality, as if to show no personal hard feelings. That was when they had all been learning their way together; but after this, in the new circumstances, for little longer.

And then suddenly Molly was out of the door, still calm as she was taken away, but Bram, tense – both a husband and a lawyer – stood in the street and shouted futilely as the police car pulled away, 'If anything happens to her I'll hold you responsible!' Hilary Flegg (still staying at the Fischers) was up, and so was Nora. Very likely this was on 8 April, when the *Rand Daily Mail* reported that more than a hundred people, 'many of them named communists', had been arrested. At police headquarters at the Grays in Von Weilligh Street the reporter Raymond Louw saw two white women laughing and chatting as they were led through to the cells, but he, like everyone else under the new dispensation, was not at liberty to identify them. Perhaps one of them had been Molly, but who could tell. This was also the day that the ANC and PAC were declared illegal.

Ruth, at the University of Cape Town, had been swept up in some of the drama – and the trauma – surrounding the State of Emergency. At UCT, as elsewhere in the country, she remembered, the slogan was 'In 1963 we shall be free' – a manifestation, in part, of the rolling tide of independence coursing its way through the African continent, and the rising anticipation it encouraged, as if by sympathetic response, in South Africa. When Philip Kgosana's march of 30,000 had wound its way into Cape Town, Ruth had been there to watch, and felt the premonitory thrill of exhilaration: it seemed that the moment of liberation was imminent. Later Kgosana had visited Bram in Beaumont Street, and told him all about the march. Bram, with his usual impulse towards alliance rather than division, was less troubled by Kgosana's membership of the PAC, or the PAC's strident anti-communism, than he was by the opportunity that had been missed. With his usual tact he would not say anything directly to Kgosana, but afterwards he said it vehemently to Ilse: 'Why the hell did they turn around? You know they had it there, they could have done it . . . '

Almost on the eve of the Emergency Ruth had been out distributing pamphlets with her housemates and some other friends. Half of them (including Ruth) were lucky: they went to the coloured area of District Six and came back intact; but the others were not: their visit to an ostensibly 'safer' white suburb ended in their detention by the police. With a new feeling of exposure and vulnerability Ruth phoned Bram to ask for his advice – and then, a few days later, came the telephone call from him to tell her about Molly. For her protection Bram explained once more what they already knew, that the names of the detained could not be divulged. Ruth found herself suddenly so paralysed by the situation that it was days before she could even tell her housemates what had happened to her mother.

It was only on 6 May that the Minister of Justice released the names of the detained to parliament, to be reprinted in newspapers around the country. It was a whole swathe – at first some 1700, later more – of the known and un-known who had been arrested. Most of the latter were African – they made their sacrifices without any spotlight of general recognition or assurance that their families might have ready access to newspapers – but as Bram and those of his comrades who remained out of jail read through the columns it must have seemed like an onslaught on a whole way and web of life. More than that, so many were from the political family with whom Bram's life had become intimately bound up: Hymie Basner, Rusty and Hilda Bernstein, Harry Bloom, Brian and Sonia Bunting, Fred Carneson, Bettie du Toit, Issy and Anne Heymann, Ahmed Kathrada, Albert Luthuli, Nelson Mandela, J.B. Marks, Z.K. Matthews, Govan Mbeki, Duma Nokwe, Jack Simons, Walter Sisulu, Joe Slovo, Eli and Violet Weinberg, Harold Wolpe, and many, many more. And there, one among the multitudes in the small print of the columns, was 'S.J. Fischer'.

Once again the phone was ringing as people were picked up all around the country and husbands or wives called Bram to ask for help. Sometimes the Security Police, listening in over their wiretaps, would intervene and say in their heavy accents, 'Yew can't talk to him.' It was like being in a new uni-verse, with its own laws of time, space, perception and – most of all – power. It was how power worked: through fear, and premonition, and foreboding.

⁂

No one could be quite sure why it was Molly and not Bram who had been detained, though most likely the Treason Trial had a good deal to do with it. It would not have done, in the wake of the Sharpeville massacre, to have arrest-ed a member of the defence counsel in a political trial under the glare of inter-national scrutiny. Paradoxically, and not for the last time over the next few years, Bram's exposure in this regard was his best protection.

Even so, Molly's activities during the preceding period – at least those visible on the surface – barely rated her detention. Perhaps most visible of all had been her participation, as a teacher, in the campaign to resist the removal of Indians from Johannesburg. When the government attempted to apply pressure by closing down Indian public schools in the area of Fordsburg, the community responded by setting up the Central Indian High School on a private basis, with Michael Harmel as headmaster. There Molly, who had taught rural white children in Bethlehem, Jachtfontein and Windhoek, became a teacher again in very different circumstances. This particular experiment was related to a broader (and brief) campaign by the ANC to set up schools to resist the depredations of Bantu Education, and no one could doubt the Indian High School's general provenance. (One of Molly's co-teachers was Alfred Hutchinson, who absconded after the first indictment was withdrawn at the Treason Trial and took off with his white lover to Ghana.) Still, in and of itself it hardly constituted significant subversive activity, and it appears that Molly deliberately limited her overt political involvement during these years so that she could take care of Paul. (His condition, however, prompted her active interest in child welfare.) As for Molly's membership of the reconstituted Communist Party, the Special Branch had no evident knowledge of that. Perhaps in her case, as in that of many others, the police were merely working at short notice from old lists, rounding up, under pressure from the Minister of Justice, all the usual suspects.

That did not make life any easier at home while she was gone. From Cape Town on 11 April Ruth wrote, 'Are you all right still Bram?' In fact he was rather tense and under pressure, as the Treason Trial adjourned, then continued, and the defence made its difficult decision to withdraw from the case. Bram was also acting *pro amico* for Joe Slovo, who was now suing the police for his illegal arrest. (Because the names of detainees could not be revealed, the case was known as '*10020* vs *Col. Le Roux*'.) All the while Molly was detained, and Bram was trying to find out how she was, visiting her first at the Fort in Johannesburg and then, when the white women were moved in May, twice a week in Pretoria.

Things were if anything even harder for Ilse, now in her final year at school. Hilary Flegg had stayed on in the house, and in name at least took on the day-to-day management of things. Yet in effect much of the burden fell upon Ilse, and neither she nor Paul could resist the feeling that Hilary was now an interloper in their mother's place. Bram, in one of his censored and rationed letters to Molly, commented on how capably Ilse was doing – running the housekeeping, taking care of Nora, even looking after Hilary. Ilse herself, in her own letters, kept up a resolutely cheerful tone, telling Molly how she had searched all over Johannesburg for a birthday present for Bram, how she and Nora were practising their maths in doing all of Molly's accounts. But Ilse, who kept the machinery of domestic life running at home, cried at school – because that was where, she recalled later, she could let her emotions go. Her form mistress advised her to become a boarder, but perhaps knowing what it would mean for the others at home, Ilse declined. She was becoming used to a sense – almost an expected vocation – of responsibility that would become intimately familiar.

In jail, Molly's number was 417/60: it had to appear on all communication. In her first letters home (and to Ella) she too did her part to keep up a reassuring and resilient tone. She thanked Ilse for her foresight ('all we had for lunch on the day of the arrest were the things you packed, and we all blessed you sweet soul') and Nora for fixing up her skirt ('the standard of dress around here is pretty high'). In fact, Molly was in jail together with a strange mix of relatively prosperous women, some of whom were current and up-to-the-minute political activists, but many of whom hadn't been involved in anything of significance for years (those old police lists once again). Older colonial predispositions meant that their conditions, as befitted white women, were accordingly plush. Molly wrote of sheets, feather pillows, as many blankets as the women needed, and the fruit and food they were allowed to purchase. Their quarters (which had been the hospital section of the jail) were clean, they had hot and cold running water, hot baths once a day, and waterborne sewerage; the detainees could even get ironing done. Molly wrote of basking outside in the sun for hours at a time, and inside she evoked a boarding-school atmosphere, with French and maths classes as well as sundry lectures run by the women, chess and Scrabble, and large jigsaw puzzles. She was of course trying to cheer up her children: 'I've made friends with my mattress', she told Ilse and Paul, 'so I know how to snuggle down comfortably to sleep well.'

As Molly may well have suspected, all of this – cosied and prettied up for reassurance as it might have been – was some distance from the life of black detainees who were five or six to a bare crowded cell, slept with lice- and bug-infested blankets on the floor, and for their sanitary amenities had communal buckets covered with a cloth next to an open pail of drinking water. As many observed at the time, one might go to jail for opposing apartheid, but that did not stop apartheid from going to the jails. In a few years, though, white women too would be subjected to very different treatment. As in other respects, both sides in this burgeoning and swirling engagement were still playing under rules that would soon be out of date.

For the moment, however, morale was high as even the relatively apolitical detainees became swept up in a commonality of identity and purpose. When they were moved to Pretoria, the prospect of being taken even farther from their families made the women refuse to leave, and they had to be carried out bodily. Soon after their arrival there they wrote to the Minister of Justice, threatening a hunger strike unless they were released. The Minister refused, and the strike duly began on 13 May. All the women participated except for Helen Joseph, preparing for her ordeal as a witness in the Treason Trial, and Hannah Stanton, an English missionary who was about to be deported and who was advised to keep up her strength. The women drank water with glucose, but as the days dragged on they were barely able to leave their beds. The strike did not gain full support: the white men participated for a while in desultory fashion, while the black detainees – so undernourished by the apartheid jail regimen in any case – kept their solidarity more or less on a symbolic level.

Yet these white women led the way, and it was a threatening affair. Despite the censorship, news trickled out of the prisons, and Helen Suzman asked questions in parliament. By the end of nine days the authorities decided to break the women's spirit by dividing them, sending eight to the women's prison in Nylstroom in the eastern Transvaal. By now the women's personal and collective resources were meagre, and doctors, brought in, gave dire assessments. Bettie du Toit had become extremely ill, but was refusing to abandon the strike on her own – and so the women brought the strike to an end. But after that they always felt with due pride that they had proved something. It meant a great deal to those outside as well; Bram wrote glowingly to Molly in prison, 'All our love & good wishes & admiration.' Even after they had been released, the lessons offered by the women – beyond French and maths classes and lectures – lingered on. 'After the way you people demonstrated fearlessness', wrote Bram to Molly in January 1961, 'I don't think anyone should create the slightest impression that we do fear anything.'

For the first time Ruth and Ilse had to visit a parent in prison. For Ruth it felt more like some pre-acknowledged fulfilment than an overt shock: 'I knew in my bones from early on that sooner or later Ma and Bram would be in jail.' Seeing Molly was chaotic, with four or five sets of visitors clamouring through the wire partitions at the same time, but they (as did others) explored the limits of the possible, smuggling news in to Molly by wrapping flowers in the front page of the *Rand Daily Mail*. They remembered her instinctive resilience and brightness. On Ilse's birthday Molly managed to squeeze some violets from the prison garden to her through the mesh, and wrote a poem that began:

What gift for a dear teenage daughter,
Can a mother present her from gaol,
Where shopping is strictly 'verboten',
And strictures and censors prevail . . .

Like all the other detainees, Molly looked forward to these visits with a sense of nervous anticipation, in which excitement would be balanced by anxiety. She described how everyone would be up early on visiting days, washed, brushed and agog like children at their first party, and how afterwards they would all exchange family news and gossip. Yet no one could prevent or completely resist the currents of creeping depression that set in. Unlike a jail sentence, detention was by its nature indeterminate, and the stasis of the present stretched out into an unforeseeable future. As the first flourish of resistance ebbed, routine set in, and time slowed; wives thought of husbands, mothers of children. Some thought they would crack up, while others rallied round. As for Molly, Myrtle Berman (who had earlier bristled under what she regarded as Molly's surveillance of her communist orthodoxy, and was now one of her co-detainees) said she came through as lovely and delightful, her humour irrepressible and redeeming. Even for Molly, though, there was an undertow: towards the end of the hunger strike she confessed to Bram, 'I'm not as bonny as I used to be.'

This was not only – and quite understandably – because she was hungry, but she was also considering the advisability of a visit from Paul. Though Paul's stamina and singlemindedness remained startling, the general state of his health had continued on its riotous and erratic way. He had just begun high school now, at St John's, and the physical regime was so much more taxing. While his medical condition would have provided any excuse, it was not excuses he was after: Paul was in the 'A' cricket team, playing or practising five afternoons a week; he swam, and participated in athletics, cadets and the choir. 'I don't think he can stand the pace,' Molly had commented to Ella before her imprisonment, 'but he must just decide for himself.' Regularly Paul now used his 'nebuliser' machine, spraying a fine mist into his lungs, under air pressure. On holiday in January 1960 his uncle Paul had rigged up a tube that could be fitted to the car's spare tyre, to provide the necessary compression; so even there Paul lived strangely, surviving off spare wheels on the beach. To aid his breathing Molly and Bram were also thinking of importing a 'tent' machine from the United States, at a cost of some $580 – but as Molly wrote to Bram from that same holiday with the children, when Paul had one of his bad spells 'I always feel I would sell the house to get him relief for 24 hours'.

As Molly's comment that Paul 'must just decide for himself' suggested, she and Bram still regarded his sense of independence as having as absolute a value as his health. Yet there can be no doubt of the private anguish his condition must have caused his parents as it did him. Just some three weeks before she was detained, Molly described his regular routine to Ella: twice a day nebuliser inhalations; twice a day postural drainage of the lungs; twice a day antibiotics and vitamin pills; three times a day pancrex digestive pills. All this was over and above the daily insulin injections for his diabetes, and salt pills or biltong 'whenever we can persuade him to shove them down his throat'. Paul also needed to see an oculist, because the insulin was affecting his eyesight. 'I'm amazed', remarked Molly to Ella, 'that he is still fairly normal.'

And now Molly was in jail, unable to take care of Paul or oversee his routine. At first her thoughts might well have tended to despair and the dragging reproaches of guilt. Yet a certain indomitability was part of Molly's own bodily economy, and as for guilt – no matter what she may have felt deep inside – she and Bram had long decided that part of Paul's normality had to be the moral and political engagement of his parents. Soon there were reassuring signs: Molly learned how, with Ilse's assistance, Paul was administering his insulin injections by himself, and as far as anyone could tell other aspects of his personality appeared remarkably undented and undaunted by his mother's disappearance. Ilse described Paul's boyish and gory relish at the prospect of taking biology at school, with all the 'bones, skulls, dissected dog fish, tapeworms, etc.'. Paul himself wrote buoyantly, using the ready slang of his twelve years: 'Dear Mom, How are you there, 'cause we are just tit here in the cold weather.' As the winter came on he told Molly that he was wearing long trousers, that the rugby season had started, that he was planning to be confirmed. He described other pleasantries and diversions: 'We have been doing bum slides in the showers at school and you can't even see 4 feet when all the steam rises; it's the first time we've had hot showers at school . . . it's real tit.'

There were pictures he had drawn to accompany, of bum slides, and a family tree with everyone caricatured as birds and Bram a surprisingly recognisable 'Old Man'. Paul wrote, 'Tias and Katy and Nora and Hilary send their love. But Ilse and Bram and me and Ruth are more special and send more love and it's more better than the rest.' To which Molly could only reply, 'I loved getting special love from my family, so I send love to the household [but] the most special, specialest love to you.' In time Molly came to speak to some of the other women about her son. It wasn't that Ruth and Ilse weren't on her mind, recalled Hilda Bernstein, but she used to speak obsessively about Paul, about everything she and Bram had to do to keep him alive.

At first, children under sixteen were not allowed to visit detainees, ostensibly because of the distressing circumstances in which they would see their parents. Then in early May there was a general concession, and Paul was permitted a 'contact' visit with Molly. On that occasion, somewhat perversely, the son of the man who had refused to participate in cadets at school because of its imperialist associations sought advice from one of the prison warders guarding his mother on how to get the best shine out of his Sam Browne belt for cadets at St John's. But later, after the hunger strike, when Bram used his authority as an advocate to smuggle Paul in for a regular visit, and Paul saw his mother from his side of the bars across the few feet of space to her mesh screen, he found a deeper cause for his passion and rebellion. When the time came to leave he grabbed hold of the bars and with the fullness of his twelve years said, 'Nobody's going to take me away from here.'

One Saturday morning, in the middle of the hunger strike, there was a demonstration on the City Hall steps in Johannesburg – one of the last at that venue. While some thirty children ranging in age from eighteen months to seventeen years stood outside with placards reading 'We Want Our Parents', 'Why Must They Starve', and 'I Want My Mammy!', Ilse Fischer went inside with her friends Toni Bernstein and Mark Weinberg and a small deputation to request the mayor's help in obtaining the release of their parents. A crowd gathered outside, and overseas television crews arrived. Then the police raided, and arrested the children – at first, they said, under the Emergency regulations, but later they insisted they had merely taken the children into protective custody, as they appeared to be 'in need of attention'. According to the now ubiquitous rules of apartheid, the white children had the privilege of being taken off in a police car, while the black children were loaded into a pick-up van. When Ilse and her friends emerged from their meeting with the mayor and discovered what had occurred, they ran through the streets of Johannesburg to Marshall Square, where they searched from office to office until they found the detained children. At first they weren't allowed access, but they insisted that if the others deserved arrest, then so did they too. Some time later, according to the newspapers, 'a legal representative, father of one of the girls' (it was Bram) arrived, and the police – perhaps fearful of the gathering embarrassment – released the children within ten minutes.

The following day there was a party at Beaumont Street with cakes and ice-cream for all the children. Here Ilse and her friends told reporters intrigued by the whole event that they had conceived of the demonstration themselves.

It was certainly more than a stunt – these children knew their mothers were on hunger strike – but there was an undoubted element of strategy and coordination. The very next day in Cape Town Ruth headed a children's delegation to parliament which handed a petition to Jan Steytler, leader of the Progressive Party, for delivery to the Minister of Justice. If one of the aims was publicity, it certainly worked: there were photographs in all the papers of Ilse and her deputation with the mayor, of children leaving police headquarters at Marshall Square, of toddlers at Beaumont Street covered innocently in ice-cream, of Ruth and her company assembled outside parliament. Yet publicity could have adverse effects: Ilse received one phone call offering assistance – a good whipping with a *sjambok* – and later there was a death threat, all of which she had to absorb at the age of seventeen.

And there was a parting of the ways. In the Cape Nationalist paper *Die Burger* – where despite political divisions Bram had always felt he could visit old friends from his own nationalist days – the columnist 'Dawie' noted that at the head of the children's demonstrations in Johannesburg and Cape Town had appeared the Fischer daughters. 'Dawie' recited the family history, beginning with Abraham Fischer's role in the Boer War, and working all the way forward. Bram, he wrote, had been a youth 'dear to a man or woman's heart'; he had been bright, conscientious, finely cultivated and lovable, and on top of that an outstanding tennis and rugby player. But in Johannesburg 'Braam Fischer . . . became more and more left – or should I say liberalistic? – and that goes for his wife as well. Indeed, there developed a wide chasm between the political attitude of old Abraham Fischer and that of his grandson Braam. The apple fell far from the tree, at least as far as politics were concerned. What a shame!' To this Bernard Sachs, brother of the ex-communist and trade-unionist Solly Sachs and one-time radical in his own right, now editor of the *South African Jewish Times*, appended his own wry message in sending a copy to Bram: 'Dear Bra(a)m,' he wrote affectionately, 'You degenerate!'

Ruth wrote to Molly in prison about the article, commenting that Bram ought to feel complimented, in that it appeared to be written 'completely without malice but just a little sadness at the fate of one who might have been a great asset' to the *volk*. Yet it was evident now that divisions which once could be contained within the larger Afrikaner family were becoming more and more definitive and absolute. The more vehement of the Afrikaner nationalists increasingly began to regard Bram as apostate and irredeemable, a traitor to his people whose predilections were bluntly unintelligible, and whose lost promise could at best be regarded with nostalgia and dismay. The universe his children inhabited was the one they feared most of all, because it looked like the end of their world.

⁂

In Pretoria the women detainees refused to answer any questions put to them by the police until they knew what charges they faced. They also maintained that the threat of indefinite detention until they agreed to answer questions was a form of unfair pressure (in a few years such phrases would be meaningless). The commanding officer of the prison, Colonel J.J. Snyman, observed that the length of their detention and the separation from their families were the hardest aspects for the detainees, and that mothers were especially anxious about their children.

But after three months that detention was soon to be ended. One day towards the end of June Bram phoned Beaumont Street from work with the news that Sonia Bunting had been released, and told Ilse and Ruth (back from Cape Town for the winter vacation) that he would be home early. Then they received another call, this time from Pretoria, to say that Molly was being released and that they must come to pick her up. This was at about four or five in the afternoon, but in the event Bram did not return early because he had gone to see Sonia Bunting instead. Ruth and Ilse, half frantic, waited and waited; eventually, by the time they all made it to Pretoria it was 7 p.m., and there was Molly sitting on her suitcase inside the gate wondering why no one had come to fetch her. The only other detainee left by that stage was 'Aunt' Mary Moodley, a long-standing activist from Benoni, and the Fischers – as always – offered to take her home.

It was when they arrived there, down an alleyway in the township where Mary Moodley lived, that the full meaning of the moment overwhelmed them. The sound of ululation pulsed through the streets as people poured out of their houses to throw their arms around Mary Moodley and welcome her home. It was then, remembered Ruth and Ilse, that they all wept, in emotion at this demonstration of love, loss and acclamation. It was not for themselves that the Fischers wept, but for someone else. For the Fischers found it hard, if not inappropriate, to weep for themselves.

⁂

While Molly was isolated in Pretoria, things had reached a certain pitch in the household at Beaumont Street. When Hilary Flegg first arrived Molly had pronounced herself delighted, and told Ella how much she liked her. For her own part Hilary was equally enamoured, commenting to Bram's sister Ada, when Molly was in detention, on how wonderful the children were, and how her own nine-year-old daughter was doing her best to emulate them. Yet for Ilse and Paul there was a little too much of the *materfamilias* about Hilary. Bram also had his difficulties as, in a well-meaning but rather intrusive way, she tried to protect him from the demands of the world. One night it all came to a head when Hilary told an important caller – it may have been Issy Maisels – that he couldn't speak to Bram because his ulcer was playing up. That certainly wasn't Bram's or Molly's approach, and Bram's anger, multiplied by his politeness, was fiercely cold and silent as he stood there carving dinner. Hilary was weeping, as were Ilse and Nora, while Paul was cursing low and intensely under his breath that he wished Hilary Flegg would go away. No one told Molly about this except Ruth, who wrote obliquely from Cape Town about the tensions at home. Ultimately Hilary did leave, and when Molly returned home she was in some way relieved at the episode. Now if something happened to her, she remarked to Ruth and Ilse, Bram would not simply marry someone else.

There were other complications to attend to. Just two days before Molly had been arrested, she had received a call from Nora's convent school in Lydenburg to come and fetch her, for Nora was pregnant. (This was the reason Nora was at home the night Molly was detained.) Afterwards Molly said she had felt guilty in prison for not having told Nora about contraception; she had even thought of obtaining an abortion, but Nora had her dates wrong, and Molly didn't realise how early in the pregnancy she was. One year later Bram and Molly were in a sense 'grandparents': Nora's son Leslie had been born, and Molly told Ruth and Ilse how beautifully he had grown, and what 'a very bright little boy' he was. Molly paid for Nora to finish her schooling by correspondence, and Bram provided a motor-mechanics course for her husband. But from that time on Nora and the Fischers lived in different worlds, if they had not before. Nora had not only her own child to look after, but six more in her extended family (a matter which concerned Molly greatly); and Bram and Molly's own path was leading in a more ominous, all-consuming direction. Taking Nora in had in the first place been an act of spontaneous and natural humanity, but it may have underestimated the power of the South African situation to contain and disrupt even the most humane of reflexes.

Molly had been released along with some 1200 other detainees after Freedom Day on 26 June had passed without incident. The State of Emergency lasted only another two months. In the fragile pacifications imposed by a modernising machinery of repression, and especially in the wake of the tumultuous end to the Treason Trial in March 1961, Bram and Molly attempted a certain normality. They dropped Paul off with some friends to see Cliff Richard, just then in the country on tour, and sneaked off themselves to see 'Never on Sunday'. (Molly told Ruth and Ilse, apropos of the film, that Hilda Bernstein had asked Ivan Schermbrucker whether she was too old to go off to Greece to join the prostitutes: 'He assured her she was not,' wrote Molly, 'but that it wasn't necessary to go to Greece!') She described taking their dog Snoffie, who had just given birth, for walks, with her teats dragging from side to side on the ground, and people in cars laughing as they passed: 'Bram is contemplating calling in a plastic surgeon to restore her former beauty & I'm trying to design a bra to give her a lift up.'

But the tenor of life had changed. In January 1961, while Bram was in the last throes of the Treason Trial, he had written to Molly on holiday to say that he had been served with a new banning order for another five years: 'I suppose I should have anticipated it, but it came as quite a surprise.' (With his hackles tangibly rising and his customary certitude that self-evident iniquities should produce general outrage, he also commented that he favoured 'maximum publicity'.) One night in May Tias was attacked in his room and gashed so badly that Bram had to take him to hospital. Molly gave Ruth and Ilse a description of a more familiar occurrence earlier that same week: 'When there was a knock at the door at 4 a.m. on Wednesday, Hilary [who was back at Beaumont Street] & I held a council of war. The two young men at the door said they were stationed at Hillbrow so we took the precaution of phoning the police station there only to be told that they knew nothing about the men. We then had a conversation through the door, during which time the 22 yr. old special branch fellow (the other was a uniformed policeman) offered to bang down the door & he took out his revolver & threatened to shoot Snoffie!! . . . Just then the phone rang. It was the Colonel in charge at Hillbrow, who said he had checked up & the men were police, so we could safely let them in.' When they came in Molly and Hilary put on a mock show of having to restrain Snoffie (dragging teats and all) from staging a vicious attack. The police, for their part, confiscated some telegrams congratulating Bram on the Treason Trial success, a couple of *New Age* magazines, a photograph of Chief Luthuli, and some newspaper cuttings.

Molly's account, despite its determined ebullience, revealed the facts, of a twenty-two-year-old Special Branch man threatening to shoot a QC's dog, and a colonel, whose own authority was being superseded by the Security Police, reassuring Molly that she could let the men in 'safely'. Towards the end of May there was a burglary at Beaumont Street: a window was smashed by a brick, the telephone broken, and clothes taken. Bram, out driving, was stopped for speeding, and Molly paid the £2 fine for him without argument: 'These days', she wrote to Ruth and Ilse, 'we don't argue with the law.' The Minister of Justice, F.C. Erasmus, propagated new legislation allowing the Attorney-General to prohibit a court for twelve days from releasing an arrested person on bail.

The ethos of politics and the law – both of them Bram's province – was changing in front of everyone's eyes. Earlier that May Bram had already written to Ilse: 'Die gerugte van arrestasies kom nou natuurlik daagliks. Ek wonder wat gaan gebeur. Dis 'n interessante tydperk waarin ons lewe maar nie juis rusvol nie.' [Naturally, there are now daily rumours of arrests. I wonder what will happen. We are living in an interesting time, but not exactly restful.]

May 1961: the symbolic overtones of that month would certainly have struck Bram, over and above what was happening at Beaumont Street.

On 31 May South Africa became a Republic, and there were newsreels of Verwoerd, with whom Bram had once discussed socialism over lunch, impishly waving goodbye to a British Commonwealth which had refused to countenance an apartheid South Africa in its midst. There were new stamps, a new currency, new hierarchies. South Africa, freed from even the nominal restraints of the British yoke, was to be a white, Christian–National country, a *volksstaat*. On the racial front Verwoerd was developing his theory of grand apartheid, according to which blacks would gain their 'independence' in the Bantustans (later 'homelands'). The removals, the dumping of people now designated as 'surplus', gathered pace as whole communities were displaced. In the 'resettled' areas malnutrition became rampant, and children's bellies grew large in the dismal mockeries of kwashiorkor. Through all this the structures of profit and exploitation were only enhanced: cheap labour for the mines, for white farms and industry, a flow controlled by the 'reservoirs' of the homelands, as if men, women and children were water, a natural resource, merely to be used as required.

In February 1960 the British Prime Minister Harold Macmillan had said in a speech to the combined Houses of Parliament in Cape Town that the 'wind of change' was sweeping through Africa, as country after country gained its independence. Verwoerd, the Prime Minister of South Africa, maintained by way of response that there was 'a psychotic preoccupation with the rights, the liberties and privileges of non-white peoples' in the world, at the expense of due consideration for 'the rights and merits of white people'.

For Bram it would have been a time replete with ironies. Was this the

Republic for which his Oupa Abraham had fought, the true culmination of that historic struggle which had lasted sixty years if not a hundred? Was this Percy's Rebellion, Hertzog's nationalism; had the Afrikaners at last crowned their anti-imperial resistance with success?

In 1962 the General Law Amendment Act, otherwise known as the Sabotage Act, provided for twelve days' detention without trial, at the discretion of the police. In May 1963 this became ninety days' detention without trial, and later six months. Detainees had electrodes attached to their genitals, and their heads plunged into buckets of water. They slipped on soap, fell from windows, inexplicably bashed their heads against walls, and were found hanged by their own clothes. The first to die was Looksmart Solwandle Ngudle in September 1963, and the magistrate at the inquest determined that he had committed suicide by hanging: his death was not due to 'any act of or omission involving or amounting to an offence on the part of any person'. The police began to break the underground ANC and PAC; later, too, the SACP.

⁂

1961, in response.

Towards the end of March Nelson Mandela, taking advantage of a lapse in one banning order before the next was imposed, appeared at an All-In Conference in Pietermaritzburg and called for a national convention in South Africa before the Republic came into effect. After his appeal was ignored by the government; after the threatened nation-wide three-day strike to coincide with the inception of the Republic began to fail on the second day; after the might of the state helped it fail with invasions of the townships in armoured vehicles bought from Britain and spotlights shining down from helicopters before dawn: both before and after all this, minds began to shift in new directions.

Ironically, all the discussion on the compelling logic of violence at the Treason Trial may have assisted the change. Chief Albert Luthuli had written (and his words were quoted at the trial), 'who will deny that thirty years of my life have been spent knocking in vain, patiently, moderately and modestly at a closed and barred door?' Now that door appeared to be made of Verwoerd's favoured material, granite, and it was evident that no amount of peaceful persuasion, moral or rational, could move or mollify the white government. Not only were black South Africans excluded from any form of genuine consultation or representation in this new Republic, but their every effort at participation or negotiation had been spurned in the most brutal way. In these circumstances a new organisation, uMkhonto weSizwe [Spear of the Nation], was formed as an offshoot of the ANC and Communist Party to explore and then initiate an armed struggle. Although uMkhonto retained its own distinct structure and autonomy in order to protect its parent bodies, this could not conceal the reality that a conceptual and political boundary had been crossed.

In undertaking this transition, the ANC and SACP drew their inspiration from anti-colonial movements ranging from Latin America to Algeria to Vietnam, but they also hoped to channel a general drift towards violence in South Africa and give it political direction – as well as meet the competition of other movements. The PAC had developed its own offshoot called Poqo [We Alone], a populist and ideologically ragged movement that fomented random attacks against whites. Sabotage, as a tactic, was actually initiated by the National Committee for Liberation (later, the African Resistance Movement) – comprised in the main of liberals disillusioned with their own marginality, Communist Party dissidents and at least one Trotskyist – which had an especial penchant for attacking electricity pylons.

Then on the night of 15–16 December the first uMkhonto explosions were triggered at empty post office buildings, electrical installations, railway signals and the like. The date marked the anniversary of the Battle of Blood River – Dingaan's Day, the Day of the Covenant – the same anniversary Bram had marked in London in 1931 when he called for a new direction among Afrikaners, a different kind of Great Trek into the future. Thirty years later the selection of this same date by uMkhonto announced the renewal of an historic struggle: apart from the intention of provoking whites to reconsider the nature of their 'covenant', it served as a clarion call. The flyer distributed to herald the explosions proclaimed that 'the time comes in the life of any nation when there remain only two choices: submit or fight'. Even so, the targets were carefully selected: in this, the first stage of armed struggle, uMkhonto took care to avoid any loss of life.

Nelson Mandela went underground, travelling round the country, eluding the police to emerge here and there, a figure soon dubbed the 'Black Pimpernel'. Clandestinely in January 1962 he left the country for North and East Africa where he met major African statesmen, underwent military training in Algeria, and made arrangements for uMkhonto cadres to do the same. Both before his departure and after his return he stayed at (among other places) a farm called Lilliesleaf in Rivonia, just north of Johannesburg, where over a period of time the National High Command of uMkhonto became established.

It was in this setting that the Sabotage Act of 1962 – besides providing for detention without trial – made any attack on property open to a definition of sabotage, and therefore to a death sentence. (The onus in such cases would be on the accused to disprove any political intent, upon which the definition of sabotage rested.) Under the Act some 102 people (including Bram and Molly Fischer) were banned – numbers of them now for the third or fourth time – and these bans affected not only their political activities but also their private lives. Under the new provisions the banned could not attend any meetings or gatherings, nor could their words be reproduced or quoted in any form (later it became illegal to reproduce images or photographs of prisoners). Nor could they communicate with one another in any way – though husbands and wives could apply for exemption from this provision. There was also a new form of detention, house arrest, imposed not through the courts but by decree, which in effect confined its victims at home for up to twenty-four hours a day. As the government shut down the remaining left-wing newspapers (*Spark*, the last avatar of the *Guardian*, finally suppressed through the simple expedient of bans on all its writers and editors), and promulgated new censorship legislation aimed at political and cultural containment, all the pieces of a large-scale repressive policy began to be fitted one by one into place.

In August 1962, apparently acting on a tip-off, Detective Sergeant W.A. Vorster stopped a car at Howick in Natal. The driver was Cecil Williams, gay ex-schoolteacher, now theatre director, whom Ruth and Ilse Fischer remembered affectionately as one of the frequent – and more flamboyant – visitors at Beaumont Street. The passenger was dressed in the blue suit and peaked cap of a chauffeur, which was what he claimed to be, despite the fact that he wasn't driving. He called himself David Motsamayi, but in fact he was Nelson Mandela, captured now to police ecstasy after nearly two years underground. Later that year he was sentenced to five years' imprisonment for leaving South Africa illegally and for incitement to strike.

On 11 July 1963 a dry-cleaning van turned into the long driveway of Lilliesleaf Farm at Rivonia, and headed for the buildings hidden from the road by eucalyptus trees. When it stopped in front of the main building a squad of Special Branch men burst out and (according to later police narratives) invaded from all sides through windows and doors. The police maintained they had been acting on a tip-off, though others believed they had 'turned' an uMkhonto member under ninety days' detention. In either case the result was disastrous for those inside the building, for at Rivonia the police discovered a good number of the leading figures in the National High Command of the liberation movement, including Walter Sisulu, Govan Mbeki and Ahmed Kathrada. Later in the year Nelson Mandela was brought from prison to join the others as accused number one in what would henceforward be called the

Rivonia Trial. The main charge was sabotage, and the defence would be led by Bram Fischer, under the spotlight of the world.

⚜

Through all this the South African Communist Party contemplated its own future, and Bram, like many others, faced monumental personal and political choices. To begin with, during the Emergency, the Party had barely survived. Ben Turok, national secretary of the Congress of Democrats, who kept (he said) a bag packed for such occasions, left home at ten minutes' warning for a safe house in the suburbs of Johannesburg. There he was joined by Moses Kotane and Michael Harmel (after his return from Swaziland): these three came to constitute the effective hub of the SACP. Over the course of five months they moved to ten different houses. Others, including Yusuf Dadoo, Ruth First and Bram Fischer, would join them in their various locations for meetings and consultations.

In these circumstances the leadership of the Party faced a number of pre-occupations, the most immediately pressing of which was whether or not to announce publicly the existence of the SACP. Younger members of the Party especially had long called for this: in the 1950s the attendant conflict had produced what Joe Slovo remembered as some 'rough discussions'. Now, under the intensities of the Emergency, there was a more militant mood, and most of the reasons for remaining clandestine appeared to have fallen away. For one thing the ANC was also illegal: no need now to protect it from allegations of communism or manipulation by the Communist Party. (If the existence of the SACP had not been secret in the 1950s the outcome of the Treason Trial might well have been different.) For another, the ANC, being illegal, had publicly defied its own outlawing: could the Communist Party do any less? To many swept up in the dramatic currents of the moment it appeared to be a time of incipient revolution. Under these conditions, ran the argument, the Communist Party had an historic obligation to raise its own standard as the vanguard of socialism in the struggle. So it was that at an underground conference the decision was taken, and the SACP emerged in the midst of the Emergency, announcing its existence, appropriately enough, on Bastille Day, 1960.

As Ben Turok recalled these developments, Bram was somewhat tentative about the decision, concerned in the main about the possibility of a backlash by the state. To some of the more ready revolutionaries there appeared to be other anomalies about him. Whereas the underground triumvirate as it moved from house to house was preoccupied twenty-four hours a day with the tense necessities of the moment, and faced any number of risks on a continuous basis, Bram (remarked Turok) seemed somewhat 'absent' in this setting. He was, after all, still a practising advocate, still involved in the unreal 'real' world of chambers, consultations and esteem. He would bring a bottle of wine to meetings to make the lives of his co-conspirators feel a little more human for an evening: it seemed to them a gesture quaint and thoughtful, but almost from another time and place. Where the others were frenetic with issues of structure, strategy and tactics, Bram was concerned with individuals and their well-being. He had heard that someone was suffering; someone's wife needed help; money was needed for someone; someone had problems in prison. Bram, as always, spoke quietly and gently, and the others listened and even agreed, but it seemed to them a little beside the point. Only in later years – and not to all – would the virtues of a personal communism, melded for Bram out of all the disparate elements of his identity, become apparent.

Yet it was far from the case that he was taking no risks. On a number of occasions towards the end of the 1950s Bram had told his brother Gus that he knew he would end up in jail, and that the police were beginning to target him. (Both Gus and Bram's brother Paul came under police surveillance: Paul, for one spell, by an asthmatic eavesdropper breathing heavily over the wiretap, which prompted numbers of his friends to enquire anxiously after his health.) At this very time Bram's wife was in detention, he had two children at home (one of them often desperately ill), the Treason Trial was proceeding, and he was living a semi-clandestine life, a senior advocate at the Bar dodging police trackers and tails for every one of these meetings. How much easier it might have been in these circumstances to retreat into the 'unreal' world of normality, but it was characteristic of Bram that in the chaos surrounding his life the discipline of his concern would remain current: that he would remember the bottle of wine, the wives of those languishing in jails, the many who needed money. For Bram communism had to take care not only of structures and policies but also people: these were inseparables for him.

And there remained something of a personal flair. On one occasion during this period, as Turok recalled, Bram – that same senior advocate – smuggled a radio into prison hidden in a pair of socks. Under the delicacy was a daring that had its boyish aspects (almost as if he were still playing Boer War games on the farm) and, as the next few years would show, an obstinacy that would not give up.

❧

In 1962 the SACP produced the most considered and elaborate policy document in its history, 'The Road to South African Freedom', approved at the

Party's sixth and final underground conference inside the country. While Bram was an unlikely theorist (he played no greater role in the Programme than most of the others, said Joe Slovo), Ben Turok's account placed him together with Michael Harmel and Moses Kotane on a committee which consulted with some thirty Communist Party organisations overseas in its drafting. Evidence at Bram's trial was that sections of the draft were in his handwriting, and that he wrote the introduction, and some of this he was prepared to admit. George Bizos, who was a member of the defence team at that trial, went further, drawing the conclusion from his consultations with Bram that his contribution to the Programme had been significant, and that he had settled the final draft (an assessment sealed for Bizos by the Programme's insistent gestures towards broad alliances in South Africa, and his impression that its language was that of the advocate rather than the politician).

There were indeed elements of the Programme that reflected Bram's particular concerns – for instance on the imperative he stressed at his trial to avoid civil war as the ultimate disaster in South Africa. Yet key motifs were of a different kind, and most likely originated from other sources. One was the analysis of South Africa in terms of 'internal colonialism', or 'colonialism of a special type'. As the Programme put it: 'The indigenous population is subjected to extreme national oppression, poverty and exploitation, lack of all democratic rights and political domination by a group which does everything it can to emphasise and perpetuate its alien "European" character . . . Non-White South Africa is the colony of White South Africa itself.' The formulation had an instinctive plausibility and evocative purchase, not least in cultural terms, though later the theory would be challenged on political and economic grounds. Its chief advantage was to provide renewed legitimacy for SACP policy – not only through the implicit linkage with anti-colonial struggles elsewhere in a decolonising era, but more directly for the refreshed and more sophisticated account it permitted of the 'two-stage revolution' (dating back to the 'Native Republic' of 1928). Once again the 'national-democratic' revolution could be seen as the necessary counterpart of and precursor to socialist transformation, and the alliance with the ANC appear as the political and organisational embodiment of this dual perspective and teleology.

If the theory of internal colonialism outlined the unfolding strategy of the South African revolution, the most urgent tactic to be addressed was that of violence, now firmly on the agenda with the existence of uMkhonto. The SACP by no means discounted non-violent methods of opposing apartheid, maintained the Programme, and would continue to pursue them; nor did it approve of 'undisciplined acts of individual terror' (this an implicit rebuke to the PAC). But new circumstances meant that principles previously regarded as absolute had to be reconsidered. In language drifting, in the characteristic way of such things, to intonations of objective and historic necessity, the Programme announced a new readiness: 'The patience of the people is not endless . . . today they are left with no alternative but to defend themselves and hit back; to meet violence with violence.' The debate on this issue had begun, recalled Ben Turok, as early as 1960 at the prompting of Michael Harmel; yet it could have been no surprise that there was dissent. In Cape Town Jack Simons argued that nothing would be gained from violence in the current circumstances except more violence. In Durban Rowley Arenstein held that conditions in South Africa did not meet the primary conditions of a revolutionary situation, and that violence was therefore inappropriate. Others objected that the underground organisations were not equipped to initiate an armed struggle, and that the attempts that were ultimately made were top-heavy technologically and underweight politically. Given what ensued, all of these objections may have been correct.

Much of the impulse to violence must have been related to the pressures of the moment, the overweening truculence of the South African state, and the feeling that an inevitable conflict should be controlled and directed rather than merely let loose. There was at any rate a good deal of pressure from below to which a central committee meeting of the Party felt it was responding when it adopted the new policy. As for Bram, however, there were again specific anomalies. Most of his comrades had the impression that he tendered misgivings about the shift, and not only because of his outwardly gentle and tactful disposition. Walter Sisulu remembered that Bram was critical of the decision on violence as having been hasty (a feeling Sisulu intimated that reflected his own). Bram was especially concerned – as were others, said Nelson Mandela – that the campaign remain under political control rather than degenerate into a form of militarism. Joe Slovo remembered Bram's doubts as to whether, without experience, the underground movements could mount a campaign as well as avoid the expected counter-blows; and – voicing a theme that would become central for him – he was also anxious to avoid a step from which there could be little turning back for South Africa. A proposal was put forward – and Bram supported it – that before the first explosions on 16 December the government should be warned and given one last chance to change its policies. But this option was voted down as undermining the entire operation's prospects of success.

In practice Bram came to support the policy of violence. It may have been that for all his personal misgivings he was persuaded by the arguments of others. On the other hand there were historic precedents that would have struck him with a particular resonance and personal recognition. The Boer Republics had been forced to fight the British for their independence from a form of 'internal colonialism'. Bram's grandfather Abraham too had been a peacemaker with a marked aversion to the lasting effects of what (from one point of view) could be seen as a 'civil war'; in this setting he had attempted to bring opposing factions together, but when the inevitable arrived he had faced the consequences with courage and more than some personal risk. There was Percy Fischer's support for the rebels in 1914, and the consequences it had for Bram's life on the farm, where his sense of South African belonging had taken on its physical consecration. Yet for all the precepts of Party discipline and the personal antecedents on which, at various levels of awareness, Bram could draw, the inner reality of his situation was even more subtly textured and troublesome than this.

Bram's daughter Ruth said that he spoke to her over and over about the decision on violence, emphasising again and again that every alternative had been explored. She felt that in his very need to discuss the issue he was trying to convince himself, and that he had been persuaded of the necessity of violence by a majority position. In fact there was nothing about Bram's personal inclinations that could be considered in the abstract, separate from their larger context, for that context came right into the very matrix of his being. In a sense the two sides of Bram's life were at war with one another in the decision on violence: his identity, bred in the bone, as an Afrikaner, and his wider identification with South Africa's population at large. Nelson Mandela wrote many years later that Bram showed a level of courage and sacrifice 'that was in a class by itself': whereas he had fought only against injustice, Bram had had to fight against his own people. From that point of view one might say that Bram's situation was unlike his grandfather's, for in Abraham Fischer's moment of choice – though courage and definition were undoubtedly required – personal and national identity were united rather than divided.

Yet it was much more complex for Bram – and to some extent even Nelson Mandela's estimation of that complexity was inexact – because at issue for him was exactly who his people were. He had no wish to relinquish his identity as an Afrikaner: more than anything he wished to bring it to completion as truly South African. That too was what he desired for Afrikaners in general, that they should find fulfilment and self-identification within the larger context of South African belonging. But that was precisely what an incipient civil war threatened to disrupt in an irreversible way. Bram would have done everything he could to avoid this split: healing the division for him was, searingly, both a personal and political matter. The decision on violence marked a boundary from which there might be no returning, or a kind of historic fall that the future might prove incapable of redeeming. Bram's vision of reconciliation in which South Africans of all races discovered the logic of reciprocity and mutuality – a logic that was so self-evident and convincing to him – appeared in its essential fragility: perhaps that unity would never be found.

That was why for Bram the decision on violence was never simply a theoretical or tactical issue. Others might – and frequently did – consider it on an intellectual or philosophical plane, but for him it went to the core of his being. Yet for all this, once the decision was taken, that same core meant that he took absolute risks for a policy in which initially he had not wholly believed, and for which in the end he paid the absolute price. It was part of the instinctive morality of his choice that it would have been of no account to him that there were others who got away with less.

❧

The 1962 Programme was discussed at, among other places, Rivonia. Contrary to the popular image, Rivonia had never been planned as an uMkhonto headquarters, but had its origins as a Communist Party hide-out until a certain cumulative drift led to its use for other purposes. (Aspects of the financial transactions whereby the Lilliesleaf farm was purchased – ostensibly owned by Arthur Goldreich, fronting as a gentleman of leisure – were revealed at the Rivonia Trial, though not in their full communist guise.) Bram Fischer was never a member of uMkhonto weSizwe, though later, at his trial, he admitted to being acting chairman of the central committee of the SACP at this time. This meant, among other things, that he was deeply involved at Rivonia, attending meetings, discussing policy, drafting documents. He also oversaw a security committee entrusted with the details of Nelson Mandela's movements underground.

What of 11 July 1963 – the day of the Rivonia raid? 'He was not to be there that day,' remembered Walter Sisulu. 'There had been a meeting in which he was present, and he was not going to be there that day.' A degree of personal good fortune, in which Bram continued to sustain a resilient and nearly innocent faith, still obtained.

❧

It didn't obtain in quite the same way for Denis Goldberg who, at the age of thirty and with a background in engineering, was at Rivonia to investigate the production of explosives – hand grenades, land-mines, timers, detonators and so on. If he hadn't been so exhausted on the day of the raid, he would have been in Johannesburg looking for a forge in order to experiment with casting and recasting iron. As it turned out, he was reading in the lounge of the main house while a meeting convened in one of the outbuildings when the police burst in:

Oh God! And I looked up, and there was a guy whom I subsequently came to know as Warrant Officer Dirker, wearing a trilby and a raincoat, and his hand in one pocket. And this great big fat slob of a man, dancing on the balls of his feet, coming through a French window. And I had a notebook with notes in it, and I walked through to go to the loo to get rid of the notes, but they were coming through the door, and I was just caught there. And you kind of freeze . . . No matter how many times the cops have raided your house, and they must have done it a dozen times in Cape Town, they raided, they were there, and you kind of, your mind's working furiously . . . I tried to get to the loo, I should have bust my way through, sort of walked quickly, maybe they would have shot me, so maybe that's why I didn't, and they had dogs as well, coming in through the doors. So they asked me my name, and one of the names I had created for myself was Don Williams. So I said I was Don Williams, and I was going to be an irrigation equipment salesman, but I didn't have anything to back it up, no identity documents. I had another name, Charles Barnard as well, and we were trying to get a new I.D. card in that name . . . And then I thought, my God, if I use the name Williams, and I'm going to be arrested, I'll just disappear . . . So after a time I said my name was Goldberg and that I was from Cape Town. And they said that I was Arthur Goldreich, because at the time I had a beard and I looked something like him, I suppose – Jewish, both wearing beards and moustaches – that's enough for them. And they wouldn't believe me. Anyway that was it. You freeze. I tell you, when we were taken to the Fort that night, about five o'clock in the afternoon I reckon we got there, and it was a cold day, it really was cold, but I felt cold right through, as though I'd been in icy water for hours. I looked up over the battlements of the Fort, looking at the night sky, looking at the stars, really just to look at a night sky, I didn't know when I'd see one again, and one of the security policemen said, 'Ag, ou Denis, you'll never get over those walls', and he was right.

From the Fort in Johannesburg Goldberg was sent to Vereeniging prison where he did manage to jump over the walls, but the alarm was raised and he was brought down by guard dogs just yards from being clear. (His wife only discovered what had happened when his clothes came back for laundering, gashed and covered in blood.) Later, Bram asked him why he hadn't sent advance warning of his plans, so that someone could have met him – for Bram had been running a committee helping people to escape. As time went on during the life sentence he came to share with Goldberg, Denis would have to help Bram, but by then there was no chance of escape.

⋘⋙

When 'Dawie' commented in his column in *Die Burger* that Bram Fischer had become 'more and more left – or should I say liberalistic?', it was an index of the times when to be 'liberal' (with its intimations of licentiousness somehow worse than 'left', and used interchangeably with 'communist') was, for most whites, to be identified with the devil. In some cases this was explicit. Dr J.D. Vorster, moderator of the Dutch Reformed Church and brother of the Minister of Justice, B.J. Vorster, published a pamphlet entitled *Kommunisme Die Vuurrooi Draak* [Communism the Fire-Red Dragon] which identified the dread antagonist of white power: 'Communism is *the* anti-Christian force . . . It is the most evident foreshadowing of the Antichrist.' The atmosphere was lowering and vindictive as the Afrikaans newspapers and state-run radio (there was no television) joined in. For more than a year, since March 1962, the Minister of Justice had been preparing legislation to prohibit communist attorneys and advocates from practising law.

Yet for the moment – prior to the Rivonia arrests, and despite successive bans – somewhat incredibly, Bram's legal career continued in the modicum of safe space that remained. Perhaps unsurprisingly, his major cases had nothing immediately to do with politics. Up to May 1962 he was involved in what became known as the Kariba Arbitration in Southern Rhodesia, which arose from the creation of the Kariba Dam, covering some 2000 square miles of land, and necessitating the resettlement of 50,000 Tonga people as well as the evacuation of many thousands of animals ('Operation Noah'). There were insurance claims and allegations of damages, and the Rhodesia and Nyasaland Federal Power Board was involved. Bram's speciality was water rights and property, and he was called in, winning the case. Up in Salisbury he had dinner with Jack Clayden (he of the Alexander and ITC–UTC trials); and with Issy Maisels (who had been made a judge of the Rhodesian High Court) and his family, Bram enjoyed a Friday night sabbath, where he was touched to be included when they all rose for 'the Word'. With his feel for the atmosphere of Africa he wrote to Molly before dawn: 'The crows have started talking although there's no light in the sky yet.' Mary Benson, friend and writer, staying at the house in Beaumont Street, saw how Molly brightened, as she might have once at Bethlehem, when Bram's telephone calls came.

Rhodesia continued to occupy Bram's attention, for the Kariba hearing was followed by an appeal in the Federal Supreme Court in Salisbury towards the end of that year which – given its remarkably dry matter – became of unexpected importance in Bram's life. The case itself revolved round trademarks in a suit brought by Farbenfabriken Bayer Aktiengesellschaft in Germany against Bayer Pharma (Pty) Ltd, its former African subsidiary. Before the war the latter company had been entrusted with the familiar Bayer trademark, and during the war it had developed another. Now the German company claimed it owned both trademarks (as promised in a letter of 1939 by Bayer Pharma), as well as the company's trading 'goodwill' in the territory. The case was exceedingly dusty and complex, and turned on a number of points: whether the trademarks had been enemy property during the war, and should now be returned; whether 'goodwill' was property; whether, if so, Bayer had been building 'goodwill' for an enemy, which would, apparently, be intolerable; and whether (and this was decisive) the German company had no right to claim because the rights to enemy property during the war vested in the Custodian of Enemy Property or the Administrator of Rhodesia. The intricacies of international trading law favoured, in this instance, local priorities, and Bram won the case for Bayer Pharma. But the German company reserved the right of appeal to the highest authority. This, given specific dispensations within Rhodesia's colonial status, was the Privy Council in London: something for which in due course Bram would have reason to be particularly grateful.

All this continued while Bram's and Molly's lives were ever more restricted. Molly could now no longer see or speak to Violet Weinberg, because both were banned. (Molly and Violet had become particularly close, perhaps not least because Violet too had a son who suffered from a physical disability: Mark Weinberg, two years older than Ilse, had been thrown through the window in a motor-car accident at the age of five, and the head injuries he sustained had resulted in meningitis, which in turn led to deafness.) Ilse remembered this as a time when visitors began to come to the back door rather than the front. For a family that had defined itself by a gregarious sociability and comradeship, this was a dispiriting transition, and – preparing for all eventualities – Bram and Molly handed out their powers of attorney in a number of directions. From Rhodesia Bram lamented the fate of his friends and even (privately) allowed himself to resent the claims they were making on him: 'Michael [Harmel]'s tsorris [Yiddish for 'trouble'] – I think that's the word', and the fact that Molly was giving him free legal advice; also the loans that people were asking for, when he and Molly had given so much already. Molly was considering a visit to Bram in Rhodesia, but was concerned that her passport might be withdrawn: 'everyone is a bit jittery down here. There are so many rumours floating around, but no doubt our luck will hold as usual.' She commented on the degenerating public climate: 'One gets sicker & sicker as more & more people accept what is happening here as if it were inevitable.'

In Cape Town, where Ilse had joined Ruth at university, the two sisters pursued their own interests. These still revolved around the nucleus of Bram and Molly's meaning in their lives in ways that would never wholly alter. Bram had fixed on Ilse to be the political heir, ever since her performance in a school debate at the age of eleven had drawn the comment from a teacher that she had the makings of a public speaker. She too had grown up among an age-grade of political friends – the sons and daughters of Bram and Molly's comrades – and now at UCT was taking to economics, which fired Bram's hopes. This was not so much the case with Ruth, who had not had the benefit of that same kind of cohort, and now showed a much greater interest in the internal dimensions of human development, studying psychology. Bram, in his traditional Marxism, was sceptical, since for him human problems could in principle be solved only at the social level rather than the personal, and initially – as Ruth recalled – he had put his 'gentle kind of Bram-ish pressure' on her to postpone taking psychology until her second year. But Ruth's first act of rebellion was to take psychology from the start: in this she felt her inspiration came from Molly – not only because of her mother's understanding of people, but because of Molly's instinctive rebelliousness, which Ruth now applied to her father. In this way, within the family, an external form of politics was both replicated and inverted. Ruth felt that her psychological focus allowed her to see things about Bram that he himself suppressed – for instance, her estimation that he achieved more in the world because of the kind of person he was than because of the impersonal ideas he espoused. She was also particularly attuned to his high expectations, which could be enabling and dampening at the same time, and even – beneath the magnetic and sociable charm – the feelings of inadequacy she detected that made Bram never wholly confident in his own capacities. In that light he may have matched himself to an external history to prove himself in the ultimate and most demanding form.

And yet it was Paul, in his constant battle with mortality, whose entire existence resonated with the ambivalences of his familial environment. Molly described the scenario to Bram in Rhodesia of Paul playing the model host to guests at dinner, holding his own in conversation 'if somewhat in disparaging manner about our blacks'. Paul, whose parents could not save him from an early death, took it out on the objects of their political affections. What meaning could politics have in relation to his reality? Yet when Mary Benson – to whom Paul had taken when she stayed at Beaumont Street – gave him a copy of her book *The African Patriots*, on the struggle for freedom in South Africa, he devoured it right away. Perhaps if explanation came from someone else it might be more palatable. At last, Molly commented to Ilse, 'new ideas are penetrating which might make him less antagonistic towards his aging parents'.

If she were ten years younger, Molly told Ilse towards the end of 1963, she would have taken up medical research on cystic fibrosis. Some nights Paul would heave and splutter and vomit as if close to death, while at other times he was completely at peace, though the pattern of his treatment never changed. 'So we feel frustrated and helpless. Within the last week three people have suggested to me that I take Paul to 3 different quacks or miracle healers. The only cheerful note in the whole set up is that Paul is beginning to talk to his parents – I mean he even says "Hallo" & "good night."' At school Paul, with his own quirky brilliance, came home with 27 per cent in Afrikaans, twenty-second out of twenty-two in the subject, and Molly didn't know whether to ignore it or give him hell.

In all of this, there was still Bram's personal touch. When Ahmed Kathrada was under house arrest, and the bell rang on his birthday, he opened the door to find a bottle of Bols Brandy, and caught just a glimpse of Bram disappearing round the corner. (Even this showed not so much modesty as due consideration: Bram, banned, would not have wished to make Kathrada contravene the terms of his house arrest.) When Harold and AnnMarie Wolpe were going through a particularly difficult time in their lives (he avalanched as an attorney during the day with ANC and Poqo cases and at night with underground work for the Communist Party; she pregnant with their third child) and were thinking of leaving the country, it was to Bram that they went for advice. He would not tell them what to do, Harold Wolpe recalled, but in his characteristic way dwelt on what they had to offer. Bram, remarked Wolpe, had a capacity to take on the personal in an unharassed and unharassing way. 'He helped us clear our minds, and we stayed on . . . He was a very gentle character, with a deep feeling for people.' Marius Schoon, who spent as much time as he could at Beaumont Street, and who later smuggled the story of Bram's illness out of prison, said, 'No one taught me as much in as lasting a way as Bram and Molly did.' And he said, 'It wasn't only political things that I learned from Bram and Molly.'

About a week after the Rivonia arrests, Bram and Molly and all the children went camping with Eli Weinberg at a place called Mariepskop on the Blyde River – this despite the fact that the area was not really for camping, but belonged to the Forestry Department, with a radar installation at the top of a hill. One evening a couple of trucks came down with forestry men, and at first sight of the government vehicles and the uniforms, Bram – who had appeared relaxed just seconds before – took off precipitately into the bush. When he ambled back afterwards everyone laughed, but circumstances were evidently tense. This was the last holiday the Fischer family took together.

There were more than enough reasons for the tension, and also for Bram to be out of Johannesburg for a while, for in the aftermath of Rivonia events had moved quickly. One of the first things Bram had been obliged to do was dispose of a car. Denis Goldberg had been driving two vehicles, and one of them, registered at Rivonia, had been left in the suburb of Mountain View at a cottage belonging to a couple called Kreel. This particular cottage was becoming useful as a safe haven, but if the car were found it would be a dead giveaway. And so Bram Fischer, sworn officer of the court, fifty-eight with high blood pressure and a record of ulcers, went like some common criminal with a companion to the cottage, opened the garage door (they may have had to force it), wheeled out the car, coasted it downhill, and then drove it miles away to dump it.

A sense of crisis had been endemic since the day of the raid for all those associated with the underground headquarters. Dave Kitson was one of them: he was on the logistics committee of uMkhonto weSizwe, and that Friday was ill in bed with the flu. Like Denis Goldberg he was an engineer, and he was some ten years younger than Bram; the two had first met in 1953 when Kitson was a student on a scholarship in Oxford and Bram was passing through on his return from the Vienna peace congress. When Kitson first arrived back in Johannesburg he had (on Bram's recommendation) rented a house owned by Ella Fischer and recently vacated by Bram's brother Piet.

Now Kitson lived in Shipstone Lane in the small suburb of Victoria, and that morning Arthur Goldreich had arrived to take him to a meeting of the logistics committee scheduled for later in the day at Rivonia. Though Goldreich was the nominal owner of Lilliesleaf Farm, the property had in fact been bought for the SACP by a man named Vivian Ezra, who then 'rented' it out to Goldreich; the rent was meant to go back to the Party. But Goldreich (so Kitson said) had not been paying his dues, and Ezra was complaining. When Goldreich said he would speak to Bram about it this was first confirmation, for Kitson, that Bram was involved in the Rivonia dealings. Goldreich was also upset with Kitson – in part because he was sick and would not be able to attend the meeting, but primarily because he usually brought another member of the committee, Lionel Gay, and now couldn't remember Gay's exact address. That was Gay's good luck, as the flu was Kitson's. When Goldreich arrived home at his 'own' farm later in the day, he was met by the police expectantly awaiting further arrivals, and arrested along with the others.

The next morning Kitson went to do some shopping and saw the newspaper placards announcing the raid. Being an impulsive sort of man, his first thought (which he afterwards admitted was somewhat harebrained) was to round up a force of the hundreds of uMkhonto cadres he knew must be in and around Johannesburg and mount an attack on the Pretoria prison before the police knew who their captives were. The problem, though, was that Kitson didn't know how to contact the members – until he remembered that Goldreich, in discussing Vivian Ezra, had mentioned Bram. So he went round to Beaumont Street – one of the back-door visitors that Ilse recalled – and found Bram, as he put it, 'full of sherry'. The fact was that Bram's comrades and associates of many years had been captured, and his movement was in danger of being wholly destroyed; for all Bram's inner strength, remarked Kitson, he was an emotional man. Kitson unveiled his idea to Bram, and said he wanted to contact Harold Wolpe, who he believed would have the necessary information. But Bram said that other arrangements had been made for Wolpe, and found a way – despite or because of the sherry – to tell Kitson that his idea for an attack on Pretoria should be reconsidered.

Later that same Saturday, however, Bram came rushing over to Kitson's house in Shipstone Lane in evident alarm: the connection with Vivian Ezra, which Kitson had mentioned earlier in passing, had set off a delayed trigger in his mind. Before the State of Emergency, the Communist Party had classified its members: 'A' were those already in jail; 'B' were exposed or known to the police; 'C' were somewhat more protected; and 'D' were meant to be wholly unknown and under cover. But during the Emergency some of those who knew the identity of the D's had been detained, which was an obvious risk as far as security was concerned, and so an alternative plan was devised. The list of D's had been entrusted to Vivian Ezra, who was himself quite deeply under cover: he had been given the job of memorising all their names and addresses – all the people who were, in a sense, the most valuable members of the Party. But at the same time another section of the SACP, in ignorance of these arrangements, had set up the dealings whereby Ezra purchased Lilliesleaf Farm – and he himself had not mentioned the doubling-up to anyone. This had the makings of a momentous calamity, as Bram now realised with such awful urgency: if the Rivonia line were traced to Ezra, and he were taken in, the Communist Party stood to lose every most hidden member on its list. Bram told Kitson that they had to get Ezra out of the country with all possible speed, and they began to set up an escape committee to do so.

According to Kitson, the route taken by Ezra was later used by Harold Wolpe and Arthur Goldreich. Among Wolpe's other capacities as an attorney, he had originally (with great reluctance) handled the transactions for Lilliesleaf Farm; as he remarked later, it was a clumsy operation, involving large amounts of cash and lines that could lead directly back to himself and Ezra. In addition, Wolpe had also prepared an uMkhonto disciplinary code, and (as he put it) his fingerprints were all over the place at Rivonia. It was therefore with an immediacy equal to Bram's that, as soon as news of the raid emerged, Molly Fischer appeared at Wolpe's house. He thought she had come to give him the address of a party to be held that night, but, looking extremely pale, she showed him a copy of *Die Transvaler* instead, listing the names of all those arrested. The first imperative was to track people down and warn them, which was by no means an easy task. Then Wolpe took off for Hartbeespoort Dam, nestling in the Magaliesberg to the north of Johannesburg, where his brother-in-law, Jimmy Kantor, had a cottage – and there Bram and Ivan Schermbrucker came to see him, to discuss his prospects. They told him that it was impossible to maintain him underground, and that there was as yet no organisation to arrange an escape: he would have to do it on his own. But trying to cross in inevitably amateurish fashion from the northern Transvaal into Bechuanaland, Wolpe was apprehended and taken into custody by the police.

Back at Marshall Square in Johannesburg he found Arthur Goldreich, as well as two other comrades, Abdulhai Jassat and Mosie Moolla. From there the four of them engineered one of South Africa's most famous escapes. With advance approval for the plan (quite possibly from Bram) they suborned a sympathetic young warder who needed money, and after one aborted attempt, some abysmal disorganisation on the outside, and a degree of spectacular luck, Wolpe and Goldreich ended up in that same cottage owned by the Kreels. There they lay low through one of the biggest manhunts ever mounted in South Africa. Bram came to visit them a number of times, now part of a fully fledged escape committee, also comprising Ivan Schermbrucker, Hilda Bernstein and (in his prior connection) Dave Kitson. Bram, said Harold Wolpe, was absolutely thrilled that they had escaped from jail; now the problem was to get them out of the country. Eventually the two were driven out in the boot of a Ford Fairlane, hiding under a heavy tarpaulin the six or seven hours it took to get to Swaziland. From there they flew to Bechuanaland disguised as priests (Bob Connolly's 'Breakfast Quip' cartoon in the *Rand Daily Mail* showed two clean-shaven, dog-collared priests walking down a street with passers-by agog. The caption read, 'The way people are staring – you'd think they had never seen two parsons before!') From Bechuanaland their escape was so well publicised, however, that their route was effectively blown for future use. The warder who had assisted them confessed within hours, and was sentenced to six years in prison.

Bram had become used to taking risks, but this was now on an altogether different plane. In the 1950s he and Joe Slovo had frequently met for 'consultations' in one another's offices to discuss Party matters. (There Slovo had seen another side of the impeccable Bram everyone knew in public, as he sometimes swore volubly after putting down the phone to some niggling or irritating question.) Now the same kind of clandestine operation took place with Hilda Bernstein: Bram took her on one occasion to a colleague's rooms to which he had the key, and which would not be bugged by the police. When Hilda objected that the man might return, Bram insisted he was on holiday; but the colleague did return, and Bram put on his charm to make some excuse. This only made Hilda all the more anxious: Bram, she felt, was becoming singleminded to the point of recklessness. She also felt that under his gentle exterior there was a core of steel running right down the centre of Bram. If so, he would have to use it.

⁂

When Molly was detained during the Emergency in 1960, it affected Ella Fischer deeply: 'I can't sleep at night thinking of Molly', she wrote to Bram, '& wondering how she is & wishing I could pack a hamper for her. I can so well imagine how you all feel. Please give her my love & tell her how constantly she is in my thoughts.' She told him that Ada had begun sending food parcels to detainees, and that she herself wanted to be involved, but found it impossible at her age.

In these years Ella was still filled with pride at Bram's cases, wishing his father and grandfather could have followed it all. After the Republic was declared she was confused as to what to call him: 'Are you S.A. [*Staats-advokaat*], S.C. [State Counsel] – or Q.C.? I wish you'd tell me!' She thought the world was going a little mad, and wondered if all the international incidents (the Cuban missile crisis had just come and gone) weren't engineered to feed the press and the munitions works: 'I wonder, too, if, without the wireless, my parents had a more peaceful life when all they had to expect was a spear from Naval Hill.' Ella still used commas to mark real pauses in her sentences as in her life. There was an evocation in her that never entirely left Bram, of a consistency and constancy, and an old-worldly presence and pace.

In 1963 she chided him that on Sundays at the pool Molly worked too hard while he gave out legal advice *pro deo* to anyone who required it in such comfortable surroundings. Paul resented it, she said, and she did too, because of the imposition. Ella had seen what happened on Sundays at Beaumont Street because she had been up to Johannesburg for radiography treatment. At the end of 1962 her sister, Bram's Aunt Maude, had passed away, and now Ella herself was ill: she had cancer, suffered a stroke, and spent her time in and out of hospital. Eventually she died in Johannesburg in 1964, in the midst of the Rivonia Trial proceedings. At the funeral Bram and Molly, under the strain of everything else in their lives, and still determinedly atheist, allowed a rendition of the Lord's Prayer as a gesture. Others afterwards said the obvious, that it was a good thing Ella did not survive to see everything that followed.

⁂

In August 1963, just less than a month after the Rivonia raid, Molly wrote to Ilse in Cape Town, telling her that she and Tias had gone berserk in the garden, to make it easier to manage '& also more saleable if that becomes necessary – but don't talk about the latter. We're working on the basis of not spending a penny, but only using such stuff as we already have.' She told Ilse that she wasn't up to the physical labour of twenty years ago, but 'I find hard manual work keeps me from thinking about unpleasant things'.

A month later she told Ilse that Paul was better but tired. 'He's so like Bram – they drive themselves mercilessly. Who cares that he comes 2nd in Latin, Physics & Maths (according to his fortnightly reports). I'd much rather he went to bed early.' She described how their garden gate had been stolen and then dumped at one of their neighbours, but didn't even mention the possibility of police harassment: 'Probably just some venturesome teenagers having an evening out – but what a nuisance.' A month later the news was that Ruth, who had gone for a year to England at the beginning of 1963 (Bram had encouraged her, saying she might never get another chance, and also to postpone her Master's degree in psychology), had become engaged to Anthony Eastwood, once a student with her at the University of Cape Town, whom Bram and Molly had never met. The Eastwoods were from Rhodesia, and Anthony's parents were coming down from Salisbury for a visit. Molly hoped they would bring pictures: 'It would be pleasant to recognise my future son-in-law should I meet him in the street.' Anthony's father had been chair of the Friends of the Soviet Union in Bulawayo during the war, and in 1963 had just left Roy Welensky's cabinet, and so there should have been much in common – but after their arrival Molly told Ilse about the interminable chatter they had had to endure: 'The Hon. W.H. Eastwood C.B.E.!! Poor Ruth.'

She also discussed the life that she and Bram were leading. 'Bram is still working himself to death. The enclosed cutting shows you part of his work. Heaven knows how he manages it. He is carrying most of the burden of the Rivonia Trial & lots of other people's burdens too. I mean everyone comes to him for comfort & advice – so if we both turn into alcoholics you'll know the reason why.' Molly was doing some teaching at the Hope Home, an institution for physically handicapped children, but her heart wasn't in it. Bram hadn't been pleased that she had taken it up, but, as she remarked, 'I may need a job, so it's as well to start now.'

Just two days before the Rivonia Trial began she was in touch with Ilse once again. 'I have no excuse for not writing sooner. Life is just too depressing. Esmé Goldberg [Denis's wife] was arrested at our swimming pool & Heaven only knows how they knew she was here. I took her mother-in-law to Marshall Square today to say goodbye to her. They're taking her back to Cape Town, probably to Bellville. Quite a number of us are going to Pretoria tomorrow where the trial of some of the 90-Day detainees is due to start, but will most probably only be remanded to a later date.

'We had a letter from Ruth today. She and two friends have had a most interesting trip on the continent, but she's rather depressed about work & says that she thinks of coming home towards the end of the year, depending on what our plans are. Poor dear she doesn't realise that we don't "plan," but only live from day to day.'

Molly wrote, 'Alles sal regkom – Jy sal sien.' It was Paul Kruger's old phrase, from the days of Abraham Fischer and the Boer Republics: 'Everything will come right – You'll see.'

CHAPTER 11

INTO THE DARK

October 1963 – 4 July 1964

On 20 April 1964, Abram Fischer, QC rose to address the court before Mr
Justice Quartus de Wet, Judge-President of the Transvaal, in the Palace
of Justice in Pretoria. 'May it please your Lordship. My Lord, your Lordship
will have realised, from the cross-examination of the State witnesses, that
there are certain important parts of the State evidence which will be admitted
by the accused. Your Lordship will also have realised, from the cross-examination, that there are certain equally important parts of that evidence which will
be denied, and which we shall maintain are false.

'I wish to mention some of the more important allegations of the State
which will be placed in issue, and which I think ought properly to be stated by
the Defence, before it leads its evidence.'

Seven of those on trial had been arrested at Lilliesleaf Farm on the day of
the Rivonia raid: they were Walter Sisulu, Denis Goldberg, Govan Mbeki,
Ahmed Kathrada, Rusty Bernstein and Raymond Mhlaba. Elias Motsoaledi
and Andrew Mlangeni had been arrested later; so too had Jimmy Kantor who,
as Harold Wolpe's brother-in-law, was put on trial in retribution (many suspected) for Wolpe's escape. Nelson Mandela was brought from Robben Island,
where he was serving his five-year sentence, to join the others. This was the
Rivonia Trial, and Bram was leading the defence.

Bram spoke quietly, in his characteristic manner, about the accused. Where
a histrionic prosecution, in its opening argument as well as its examination of
witnesses, had cast blurred and dramatic allegations about a wholesale conspiracy to wreak terror and havoc, it was necessary to set clear lines, to assert in
dignified tone as much as content the true nature of the struggle for freedom in
South Africa – and to do this not only for the sake of this trial but for the
many others that might follow. At stake were the lives of the accused and, in
that respect, the very future of the movement they led. No trial in which Bram
had appeared had come close to equalling the significance of this one; in none
had his own life been so involved with those of the men he was defending. Yet
the style of his defence had to remain the same: he spoke without a glimmer of
unnecessary emotion, extending his customary respect for the judicial pro-

ceedings of which he was a part (if not for the power the law represented). All had to be offered with a self-possessed stature and clarity.

Bram indicated first of all that the defence would deny that Goldberg, Kathrada, Bernstein and Mhlaba were members of the National High Command of uMkhonto weSizwe, or even members of uMkhonto at all. The second point at issue, he remarked, was whether uMkhonto weSizwe was a section of the African National Congress: 'Here the Defence will seek to show that the leaders both of *Umkhonto* and of the African National Congress, for sound valid reasons which will be explained to your Lordship, endeavoured to keep these two organisations entirely distinct. They did not always succeed in this, for reasons which will also be explained, but we will suggest that the object of keeping the two organisations separate was always kept in mind, and every effort was made to achieve that object.'

The third allegation the defence would contest was that the ANC was a tool of the Communist Party: 'The Defence evidence will deny this emphatically, my Lord. It will show that the African National Congress is a broad national movement embracing all classes of Africans within its ranks, and having the aim of achieving equal political rights for all South Africans . . . [T]he evidence will show how *Umkhonto weSizwe* was formed, and that it was formed in order to undertake sabotage only when it was considered that no other method remained for the achievement of political rights.'

All this, Bram contended, was relevant for the fourth point the defence would dispute:

That Umkhonto had adopted a military plan called Operation Mayibuye and intended to embark upon guerrilla warfare during 1963, or had decided to embark upon guerrilla warfare.

BY THE COURT: Will that be denied?

MR FISCHER: That will be denied. Here the evidence will show that while preparations for guerrilla warfare were being made from as early as 1962, no plan was ever adopted, and the evidence will show why it was hoped throughout that such a step could be avoided.

In regard particularly to the last issue, the Court will be asked to have regard to the motives, the character and political background of the men in charge of *Umkhonto weSizwe* and its operations. In other words, to have regard, amongst other things, to the tradition of non-violence of the African National Congress, to have regard to the reasons which led these men to resort to sabotage in an effort to achieve their political objectives and why, in the light of these facts, they are to be believed when they say why Operation Mayibuye had not been adopted, and that they would not have adopted it while there was some chance, however remote, of having their objectives achieved by the combination of mass political struggle and sabotage.

There was a pause while the judge finished taking notes, and then Bram continued: 'The Defence case will commence with a statement from the dock by Accused no. 1, who personally took part in the establishment of *Umkhonto*, and who will be able to inform the Court of the beginnings of that organisation, and of its history up to August, when he was arrested.'

Accused number one was Nelson Mandela.

⁂

The Rivonia Trial had opened in the worst of circumstances. After the police raid some nine months before, the atmosphere in the country had grown tangibly more hostile, to the point of being downright poisonous for the accused. They had been held under the ninety-day detention provisions: no one had had access to them nor they to anyone else – indeed, no one even knew for a fact exactly who was to be put in the dock. In the normal course prisoners who had been charged and were awaiting trial enjoyed certain protections, among them that public comment on a forthcoming case was prohibited by law. But those detained at Rivonia had not been charged, and a generalised clamour on the radio and in most of the newspapers offered daily homage to police ingenuity in cracking the 'conspiracy', all the while whipping up public hysteria as to the guilt of the detained. The police, for their part, felt no hesitation in proclaiming that their aim was to break the leadership of the ANC and the Communist Party.

Even finding lawyers prepared to join a defence team appeared to be no easy task in these circumstances, though many simply assumed that Bram would be involved in the case. Nelson Mandela said that he would naturally have thought of Bram in any legal crisis, and may even have suggested his participation. However, seeking out lawyers was only part of the problem: there was also a juridical choreography to observe that compounded matters appreciably. The normal procedure required that clients approach an attorney, who in turn would brief an advocate. But in this case, as no one was certain exactly who the 'clients' were, and since there were no attorneys in sight willing or able to take on the case, matters had to proceed the other way round. Because of the entangled political and legal dynamics, even some of those in the defence team or directly involved in assembling it weren't fully apprised of how it happened.

This is what seems to have occurred. Arthur Chaskalson, a young advocat with a growing reputation for his brilliance, had in the 1950s been articled a an attorney to Charlie Johnson – Bram's old colleague from the Alexandr Health Committee days. Once Johnson had sent him into Bram's room where, recalled Arthur, he was immediately drawn by Bram's personal magnet ism. For some reason he had also been with him on the day the Treason trial ists were given bail (this had been granted on a sliding racial scale, which dre an acerbic comment from Bram on the true nature of South African justice) Now in the lead-up to the Rivonia Trial he was once again with Bram i chambers, and offered him any assistance should he need it. Later Bram aske him if he knew of any likely attorney for the case, since Harold Wolpe, th obvious choice in such matters (but now an escaped prisoner), was no longe an eligible candidate.

Arthur mentioned his friend Joel Joffe, with whom he had been at uni versity. Joel had also been an advocate, and he and Arthur had collaborate on a PAC case in which the accused had been charged with the rather enter prising plan of raiding the outdoor suppliers, ME Stores, for arms and ammuni tion. Joel, in nearly terminal disgust at the South African situation, had the been on the verge of emigrating to Australia when he was asked a favour fror a different direction. After Jimmy Kantor was arrested, his legal practice wa on the verge of disintegration; Kantor's family approached Joel and asked hir whether he would step in as caretaker until his departure. Joffe, who – sai Arthur Chaskalson – had 'certain saintly qualities', agreed and left the Bar fc the Side-bar, where he became an attorney once again. Now Chaskalson wa suggesting him for the Rivonia Trial. The three of them – Arthur, Joel an Bram – accordingly had lunch one day, and Joffe agreed to take on the case Bram said he would send Hilda Bernstein around to see him; as wife of one c the detainees, she would be in a legitimate position to obtain his services.

Hilda Bernstein understood it from a different angle. She remembered tha she and Bram discussed the whole matter of the trial one day, and that whil they had no trouble establishing potential advocates, there were no likel attorneys to be had. They went through the names over and over again unti finally Bram said she should approach Joel Joffe; this she did, and then she an Joel, considering the matter, 'chose' Bram to lead the case. Hilda had no ide of what Joel knew, and the same was true in reverse: that, apparently, was ho things had to be.

There were two other members of the team. One was George Bizos, also young advocate, who had escaped from Greece in a boat with his father durin the Nazi occupation, and whom Vernon Berrangé had taken on as somethin of a protégé. Where Chaskalson had the tall leanness and inner attention of a genial hawk, Bizos, with his rotund form and gregariously expansive manner, had, in his few short years at the Johannesburg Bar, taken on more political trials than virtually anyone else. (His reason for doing so, he indicated later, was simply that he was a 'democrat' – and the merest glint in his eye suggested it was a natural enough phenomenon for anyone with an ancient Greek heritage to live up to.) Bizos's first association with Bram had been when the latter invited him to assist Berrangé in defending Eli Weinberg, who (though banned) had photographed a meeting in Freedom Square in Sophiatown from the roof of an adjacent shack. The successful argument, which Bizos developed, was to suggest that Weinberg had not contravened his restriction by being present at the meeting but, on the contrary, had been 'conspicuously absent'.

The final member of Bram's team was none other than Berrangé himself, then in London, but Bram called on him urgently to return. They needed Berrangé, remarked Chaskalson, for the qualities he had shown during the Treason Trial. In a case in which witnesses would be produced who had been subjected to ninety days' detention (frequently in solitary confinement), and in which the police were more than likely to introduce pliant distortions to the truth, Berrangé's job would be to cross-examine as only he could – to pursue and then trap the prosecution in the curved mirrors of its own construction. Also, as Joel Joffe observed, Berrangé's experience in the hard-boiled and tough-skinned world of the criminal courts would be invaluable in a trial with its ugly aspects. Bram, whose judicial predispositions remained comparatively naive, was never made for that as a lawyer.

It was a trial which changed the lives of the cohort of young men who had the courage and the presence to undertake it. When Joel Joffe, for his pains, had his passport confiscated by the South African government, and the Australians denied him entry to their country, he went instead to Britain with a few shillings in his pocket, and there became extremely successful – and a guest of Nelson Mandela's, for a defence team reunion, when Mandela became President of South Africa. Over the course of three decades George Bizos and Arthur Chaskalson participated in many political trials – frequently conducted under even darker conditions of autocracy than those that affected the Rivonia proceedings – from many of which they emerged with some margin of humanity and justice redeemed. Ultimately all of them – Joffe, Chaskalson, Bizos – had that rare experience of an historical vindication they had never asked for, living to see the justice they had defended established in the eyes of the world, and a new beginning in South Africa. They had all been transformed by their connection with the accused, and with Bram. Of them all it was only Bram who never had that experience, who never came back.

⚜

Bram was reluctant to go into the trial. The younger members of the team were baffled by this, but all he offered by way of explanation was that he had too much work and other commitments. At first they suspected a professional issue: Bram had been involved politically with the accused, and there was the question, in legal ethics, of whether one should be engaged in the defence of people with whom one has been associated in the activities with which they are charged. Bram, the revolutionary, had an unusual vulnerability in such matters of loyalty to his profession as to his comrades. It fell to his junior members to convince him, and George Bizos gave the credit to Arthur Chaskalson for arguing forcefully. Those on trial had done no more for their cause and their beliefs, insisted Arthur, than the Afrikaners had in the 1914 Rebellion; only an Afrikaner of Bram's standing could convince an Afrikaner judge of that. It was crucial for him to be in the trial, especially because of the threat of death sentences.

Later his team came to understand another dimension to his initial misgivings. For Bram's involvement at Rivonia meant that he had been observed by a number of people, including the black workers at the farmhouse who were now to be called as prosecution witnesses. Any one of them, asked to identify any individual in the courtroom they had seen at Lilliesleaf, could have turned to Bram and pointed him out. For Bram to enter into the trial was in that regard an enormous, even life-threatening risk – and it was for this reason that when Rusty Bernstein first heard that he would be leading the defence he turned to his co-accused and said, 'He deserves the Victoria Cross.' That was also the reason why, during the opening stages of the trial, when most of the farmworkers were called to give evidence, Bram managed to be out of court, engaged in an arbitration which he freely admitted was 'hopeless', but which had the advantage of keeping him busy elsewhere. Without Bram, George Bizos and Arthur Chaskalson suddenly had to cover their inexperience and take on cross-examination in the biggest case of their lives.

Bram faced the risk without discussing it or confiding in anyone. On one occasion Arthur Chaskalson and Joel Joffe went over to Pretoria to examine some of the documents seized at Rivonia but not handed in by the prosecution as evidence – and saw that a number of them were in Bram's handwriting. It was then that they began to realise the extent of his involvement. The fact that the state did not use the documents against Bram at that stage may have indicated an unwillingness to prosecute him; on the other hand, they may not have known whose writing it was. During one session in court a handwriting expert was presented, to testify as to the authorship of certain documents. The prosecutor produced one item, handed a copy to Bram as leader of the defence, and gave the original to the expert – who identified the writing as Harold Wolpe's, although in fact it was Bram's. Bram had inspected the document without so much as a flicker of an eyelid, and then handed it on to the rest of his team, who read it aghast and amazed.

Walter Sisulu remarked that everyone knew Bram would be arrested sooner or later, and that the police were just biding their time. Nelson Mandela's assessment was that everyone knew about the handwriting, because every now and again the prosecutor would say with some emphasis, 'There is a document here, my Lord, which is in somebody else's handwriting . . . ', and then leave it at that. Yet, in these circumstances, Bram's presence at the centre of the trial provided his only immunity. That was how he explained it to Ruth when she came back from London to be married to Anthony Eastwood in December 1963. He told her there was evidence in the trial in his handwriting, but because of the international attention he felt he was safe for a while. The leader of the defence could not simply be arrested – not when the accused were on trial for their lives, under the observation of the world. And so Bram bought time in the only available space, unexpectedly in the heart of the labyrinth.

Ultimately there could be no doubt of his participation, for this was much more than a legal proceeding. The accused were Bram's friends as well as his comrades, and their lives and their movement were at stake. They were on trial for what he himself believed in, and so he was going to be there.

<hr>

The very nature of the trial did not improve any prospects for success. In contrast to the Treason Trial, government legislation now provided for political cases to be run as summary proceedings, without a preparatory examination; so a defence had no preliminary idea of how the case was to be conducted, or even which witnesses might appear. In addition, many of those witnesses would have been held in solitary confinement for up to ninety days – mental torture in itself, to which frequently the physical variety had been added. Also, in so far as 'intent' became a significant criterion under the Sabotage Act, the onus was not entirely on the state to prove guilt, but to some extent on the accused to prove innocence. The Treason Trial had evinced its own peculiarities, but at least it had been run under recognisable rules. Now fundamental rules had been altered, as the defence would have to scurry to deal with the sudden appearance of unknown witnesses and their inevitable distortions.

Indeed with the Rivonia Trial the defence did not even know when it was to begin. That was the handiwork of the prosecutor in the case, Dr Percy Yutar, about whom a number of speculative narratives circulated to explain his loyalty to the government. Whatever the reason, it was a loyalty that few could doubt. As soon as the case was under way Yutar moved into an office of the Grays, headquarters of the Security Police, and there did his best to thwart every legitimate need of the defence. On 7 October Joel Joffe phoned Yutar because he had heard a rumour that the trial was to open the following day, which Yutar confirmed. As though it weren't bad enough that a defence should have to glean such basic information about a major trial in this way, when Joffe, Bizos and Chaskalson arrived at the Palace of Justice in Pretoria the next morning they discovered that nothing was happening. They weren't alone in their chagrin: even the Attorney-General of the Transvaal, who had arrived with similar expectations, was bitter that Yutar and the Security Police had managed, between them, to keep him too in the dark.

Yet that morning the three defence lawyers had their first meeting with the accused, in Pretoria Local Prison. Among them was Nelson Mandela, looking hollow-cheeked and underweight, dressed in the prison clothes of Robben Island – ill-shaped shorts, badly made sandals and an open-necked khaki shirt – all to confirm him, surmised Joffe, as the South African version of a black 'boy' and not the respected leader of his people. Consultations in prison with the accused had to be conducted in something approaching an obscure if not wholly arcane ritual. The working assumption was that both the defence and the accused were under continual surveillance, and that any conversations were bugged. Methods of circumvention, invented for the purpose, took on both spontaneous and systematic forms. One was the use of gestures: Nelson Mandela always referred to Bram with a tilt of the head and a lowering of the hand as 'the short one'. The lawyers and defendants also wrote the key words – whether names, dates or concepts – of any given sentence on pieces of paper, burning these in ashtrays at the end of each daily session. This form of sub-terfuge allowed for a certain amount of disinformation, as well as some comic relief at the jailers' expense. On one celebrated occasion, when the warders had become visibly distressed at the burning of papers, Captain Swanepoel of the Security Police came to observe the proceedings through the door of the consultation room. Govan Mbeki, noticing his presence, wrote on a slip of paper, 'It's so nice to have Lieutenant Swanepoel with us again' (deliberately downgrading the captain's rank). Joel Joffe made a show of studying the message intently, whispered conspiratorially with the others, and then prepared to light the paper, fumbling for matches. At this Swanepoel, unable to contain himself, rushed in, claiming that he had left the ashtray he always used in the room, and dashed out clutching both ashtray and paper – not to return for some time, after he had read its contents. Bram was a little too dignified to participate in such pranks, said the others, but allowed himself to be amused at the results.

Even at Beaumont Street, where preparation for the case carried on after hours, and sometimes under high pressure past midnight, the defence team followed systematic precautions. In daylight they would work for preference outside, to avoid bugging devices inside the house. At night they would turn on a radio to block out their speech, or use the prison technique of slips of paper, or – if there was some really important matter – step outside for discussion. Bram, besides leading the defence, was also arranging for its funding, writing innumerable letters overseas: this was a small team for such a big trial, though they were being paid the lawyer's equivalent of a pittance. The other members of the team were aware of how extremely hard he was working – not only on the trial, for there was always a steady stream of people to the front door (and no doubt to the back). They were all continually aware of Molly's presence – sitting on the floor clipping newspaper reports, looking up legal references, bringing tea or something to eat, touching hands for a moment with Bram. If the two of them had stopped to consider it, it was a long way from those early days at Bethlehem.

Yutar's big moment in court arrived when the trial finally opened on 9 October 1963, two days after the date he had originally confirmed for Joffe. The whole of Pretoria was teeming with police for the South African political trial of the century, as a convoy brought the accused from prison to the Palace of Justice, and a crowd packed the galleries inside. Yutar had given out copies of the indictment to the press in exchange (Joffe suspected) for the interviews and front-page spreads that garlanded the newspapers, but even on the morning of the trial he refused to give one to the defence. As soon as it was produced in court, however, Bram rose to request an adjournment so that the defence could prepare its case. Yutar, who had appeared with his opening address done up all decoratively in a ribbon, opposed, urging that the trial proceed for the sake of the witnesses. 'I fear for their safety!' he pronounced with hand aloft and a voice which in moments of (all too ready) melodrama was apt to rise to a rather alarming squeak. But Mr Justice De Wet granted a three-week postponement.

Bram devoted those three weeks to a thorough consideration of the indictment. It turned out – in a form reminiscent of the Treason Trial – to be a shoddy piece of work, suffering from many of the same defects. In all, the accused were charged with two counts of sabotage (alleging some 193 separate contraventions) under the Sabotage Act, a third charge under the Suppression of Communism Act, and a fourth which had to do with the financing of their activities. Most alarming was the lack of specific and detailed allegations. When the defence, in assessing the document, asked the prosecution for further information – what particular acts each of the accused was purported to have committed – Yutar's characteristic written response was either that 'These facts are unknown' or 'These facts are peculiarly within the knowledge of the accused'. It was a strange set-up, to say the least. The implicit logic, as Joel Joffe suggested, was that the accused were guilty and therefore knew what crimes they had committed: the prosecution had no obligation to tell them.

When the trial resumed and the defendants appeared in court, each in turn emerged from the dark stairwell of the cells below, faced the public gallery, gave the ANC salute – right fist clenched, thumb up – and declared, 'Amandla!' [Power!], to which the reply from the galleries came 'Ngawethu!' [It is ours!]. Bram's first move, following the precedents of six years before, was to apply for the indictment to be quashed. He pointed out the generality, obscurity and even contradictory nature of the document – for instance, that some of the alleged acts of sabotage had been committed before the Sabotage Act existed, and therefore could not be charged retroactively. Nelson Mandela alone had been charged with 156 acts of sabotage committed while he was in prison. The first accused was listed as the National High Command, which in legal terms was an absurdity. Most damning was the lack of particularity: if the prosecution knew who had committed specific acts of sabotage it should say so, or otherwise release the accused. With an unusual emotion Bram suggested that the state appeared to have decided that the accused were guilty, and that there was no point in a legitimate defence: this alone could explain its response to repeated requests for particulars.

The situation was beginning to look uneasy for Percy Yutar. After a second attack by George Lowen – representing Jimmy Kantor – he attempted to defend his indictment. The defence argument, he claimed, was not a sincere one, and as earnest of his own good intent he offered them a copy of his opening address, which he maintained would provide all the necessary particulars. But an address is not an indictment, nor can it be submitted in court as a document, and the judge did not even allow Bram to object before batting down the proposal. Yutar then began to list all the evils of which the accused were ostensibly guilty, but this did not constitute an answer to the defence objections to the indictment. He began to appeal to the judge, indicating that he would reformulate the charges – as good as an admission of defeat. It was deeply embarrassing, given Yutar's assiduous advance publicity, a spectacle of an unexpected kind, and his performance turned into a Dickensian self-parody of obsequiousness: 'I would earnestly beg your Lordship, nay crave your Lordship not to squash [he meant "quash"] the indictment, but to order that the State does what it undertakes to do, that is to supply further particulars. And I undertake to do this a week from today.' Justice De Wet, unmoved, quashed the indictment.

Technically the prisoners were free, but within moments Captain Swanepoel (of the paper-and-ashtray joke) had come down to the dock, thumped each of the accused on the back, and rearrested them on the same charges. Still, this was a victory of sorts – not only, as in the Treason Trial, to improve the prospects of the defence, but also so that the pitch of hysteria surrounding the case would die down. An adjournment would allow crucial time for international opinion to be mobilised, and everyone felt that at least some of the wind had been taken from the prosecution's sails.

When the trial resumed towards the end of November 1963, the second indictment was more adequately framed, but suffered from many of the faults of the first. Bram, objecting on many of the same grounds, attempted to have it quashed once again, but this time the judge was unimpressed. He evidently wanted the case to go ahead without any further delays, and Bram could not credit the difference. In his view the second indictment, like the first, was defective, and therefore ought to have been rejected. While quite prepared to sustain his own revolutionary activity both outside and, to some extent, within the trial, Bram felt that the courts had, so to speak, their own laws as far as actual judicial proceedings were concerned, sacrosanct from the intrusions of politics. In some ways, it appeared, he didn't understand the relationship at all.

❦

Later Molly wrote to Ilse that the evidence in the trial was 'ghastly. I can hardly bear to read it – so I don't know how the accused can bear to listen to it.' At the end of one Sunday in November, just before the trial resumed, she wrote to Ruth and Ilse that 'Life is absolutely fascinating if one is strong enough to take it', and gave an account of her previous twelve to sixteen hours. First Stanley Uys, the well-known newspaper reporter, had arrived for breakfast. Then Molly had fetched the Slovo children (their mother, Ruth First, was in her fourth month of solitary confinement, omitted from the

Rivonia Trial, Bram believed, only so that a white woman would not be given the death sentence) and served tea to the Berrangés. Then reporters from the BBC and *Daily Telegraph* had come, after which there was lunch for Bram, Paul and the children, as well as three unexpected guests. In between, some swimmers appeared, and then, at 2.30, four lawyers for a consultation on the Looksmart Ngudle inquest. These were followed at 3.30 by the defence team to work on the Rivonia Trial, and then Harold Hanson and his junior turned up – they were representing Jimmy Kantor. After that Molly had to dash to the airport to meet a '6′ 4″ English M.P. and advocate' who was arriving as an observer to the trial. In between there were 'more swimmers – more teas – more drinks', while the English observer stayed to dinner and Stanley Uys pitched up once again. In addition, during the day, there had been the 'odd half dozen people who came to see Bram urgently "for literally two minutes."'

Through all this Katie, Bram and Molly's servant, had been off duty since the previous day, and Molly had had to do everything on her own. 'Now', she wrote, 'I've stacked the supper dishes for Katie for tomorrow's penance and it's after 9 p.m. & I haven't done the Sunday Times crossword puzzle yet . . . All this is just to prove to you that Johannesburg is as interesting a place to live in as anywhere in the world. Only sometimes I'm prepared to settle for a little peace in London or Timbuctoo. Dallas Texas may be a little too exciting even for us.'

Anthony Eastwood, who was due to marry Ruth, and who met Molly for the first time in December 1963, challenged the idea that she and Bram were the perfect married couple. He remembered that Molly looked somewhat depressed at the time, a little alien from the world even as the world buzzed around her husband. Pat Davidson – daughter of Molly's schoolgirl friend Herleve Yates, and staying in the Fischer household – noticed something similar. She recalled that whereas Bram was preoccupied and busy, would arrive home, have supper, snatch a glance at the newspaper, and head upstairs to work, Molly's days seemed to have entered into a kind of stasis. Banned, cut off from her customary activity, she spent ages doing the crossword every day. She was nervous and anxious, and – remarked Pat – a little lonely. Certainly there was enough to be depressed about at the time.

⁂

Bram's life had its own secret drama.

UMkhonto weSizwe had been all but destroyed at Rivonia, and it was necessary to reconstitute it, even if in minimal form: this occurred while the

Rivonia Trial proceeded. A new National High Command was established: Wilton Mkwayi was seconded from the ANC, and Dave Kitson from the Communist Party; they were joined by a comrade called Chiba. Following precepts all the more stringent now, each of them had to cease active membership within his home organisation, but at the same time there had to be links. Accordingly, Bram Fischer became Dave Kitson's liaison with the Communist Party, and they kept up regular contact. Bram would meet Kitson at the top of Nugget Street, and there they would converse in the Greek cafés of Hillbrow; alternatively they met at a flat Bram managed to 'borrow' while the man who owned it was out. Bram brought Kitson money in large amounts, smuggled in from overseas, and fairly soon, Kitson recalled, they had reactivated the uMkhonto structures, with some 600 members in the Transvaal alone, as well as acquiring cars, vans and other equipment.

Bram also brought along exhibits from the trial, now a repository that was proving surprisingly useful. For handed in among all the documents were maps of likely targets for sabotage, as well as plans for blowing them up – and Bram gave them to Kitson to pore over. Perhaps, given the machinations of the prosecution, Bram took the dry view that documents, once submitted as exhibits, were in the public domain; or he may have been able, to this extent, to separate his various commitments and responsibilities in competing areas of his life. Still, there was a certain flagrancy, if not an outright contradiction of his normal fealty to the ethics of the court. Bram was not so naive after all: with the trial on in full force, and under the fierce onslaught of the state, there was no need to retain an absolute purity; legal imperatives had been subordinated to the political – a boundary crossing of another kind. As long as the trial proceeded there was a moratorium on all sabotage activity (it was crucial to avoid any provocation that might reinforce the possibility of death sentences), and other organisations observed the moratorium as well. But as soon as it ended the new leadership clearly had it in mind to re-initiate their campaign. Even some of the accused, remarked Kitson, relayed suggestions via Bram of what to blow up and how.

Plans converged and radiated in various directions. In Cape Town there was a man called Watson who had been a captain in the Royal Engineers; he was teaching the African Resistance Movement how to make delayed action bombs (he had even, with a degree of detailed imagination, imported plastic explosives in the false bottoms of crates). In some respects the ARM and uMkhonto were in competition, but there were also connections between them, as well as abortive attempts to merge the two organisations. One of the people whom Watson instructed was Sholto Cross; he had become Ilse

Fischer's boyfriend, as well as a friend of the family. At Bram's instigation, Kitson would meet Cross at various places in Johannesburg, and take him off to Lionel Gay, uMkhonto's expert in such matters and himself an accomplished technician, to pass on the skills he had learned.

There was now, in a more accentuated form, the issue of what to do with people who, whether by fact or suspicion, were regarded as traitors. One such was Patrick Mthembu, who had occupied the cell next to Looksmart Ngudle when he was killed, and apparently took the implicit warning to heart. He had directed the Johannesburg regional committee of uMkhonto, and was now a witness in the Rivonia Trial. It caused complicated dynamics in court: Bram told Kitson how he would be cross-examining Mthembu when at any point the latter might have said, 'But you know about this, Bram, because you were at the meeting.' Yet Mthembu never did, though he revealed much to implicate the accused. From that point of view betrayal was seldom a simple phenomenon, riven through as it was with prior loyalties and the spontaneous instincts of the desperate. This was something uMkhonto may well have understood, but the new leadership felt that traitors ought to be executed, and even established a hit squad for that purpose. At the same time, they recognised the need for political guidance, and so Dave Kitson approached Bram for the Communist Party perspective. Bram was horrified: it wasn't just the moral dimension that troubled him – which, given his earlier doubts about violence in general, would have affected him deeply – but any executions, he told Kitson, would virtually guarantee death sentences at the Rivonia Trial, and had to be avoided at all costs.

And so there were no executions. Three weeks after Mthembu was released he was re-detained by the police, despite the indemnity he had been granted. Betrayal worked in many directions, and some lost themselves at the heart of it. After that Mthembu was produced as a peripatetic witness at trials around the country; several years later he was killed, almost certainly by uMkhonto weSizwe. That was what civil war meant, tearing identities apart limb from limb, taking people into territory they never thought to go.

⁂

The prosecution in the Rivonia Trial relied centrally on a document found in the Lilliesleaf raid, entitled 'Operation Mayibuye'. Though only nine pages long, it was an extraordinary – and extraordinarily revealing – piece of work, invoking the need for guerrilla warfare in South Africa. It outlined all kinds of fanciful plans, including the landing of soldiers by sea or air, guerrilla forces of 7000 dispersed in groups countrywide, and a sustained supply of arms to meet their needs. Bram's own feeling was that much of this was politically suspect and wholly impractical, and at his trial later he described the plan as 'an entirely unrealistic brainchild of some youthful and adventurous imagination'. He also indicated that when 'Operation Mayibuye' was first presented to the central committee of the SACP, the committee had, after discussion, rejected it completely. But for the prosecution now it was a godsend, for it appeared to show that all uMkhonto's pretensions to safeguard life in South Africa were nothing more than mere camouflage, concealing its preparations for a full-scale war in South Africa.

According to Nelson Mandela there was some debate among the accused as to whether or not 'Operation Mayibuye' had been adopted by uMkhonto weSizwe. Govan Mbeki, who apparently helped draft the document with Joe Slovo, felt that it had been approved, while the others (consistent with Bram's understanding) demurred. Yet it represented the issue to which, in the main, the defence had to respond, and early on in consultation with the accused they determined their strategy. Unlike the Treason Trial, there was in this case no chance at all of an acquittal – at least for the chief accused, though for Bernstein, Kathrada and, most of all, Kantor (who was indeed freed during the proceedings) there seemed some hope. Rather, the question was how to avoid death sentences, particularly for the most threatened, Mandela, Sisulu and Mbeki. In this the tactical strength of George Bizos came to the fore. He argued that it was imperative to give the judge a reason not to impose death sentences, and that the way to do it was to prove that 'Operation Mayibuye' had been discussed but never adopted. Given the dispute on the matter there were at least grounds for such a contention, and Bram decided to make it the centre point of the defence.

Other aspects of the strategy were more direct. There would be no attempt by the accused to deny responsibility for their actions; rather they would take every opportunity to explain their case, and to discriminate the truth from the falsity. The trial had been set up as a political forum, and that, in a fitting reversal, was how the defendants would use it, not only describing but also defining the nature of their struggle. Percy Yutar never quite understood this: he fully expected the accused to attempt to squirm out of their guilt while he hunted and trapped them in their inconsistencies. From that point of view he wholly misjudged their stature and political commitment, as well as the nature of their defence. When they were first required to plead, each of the accused followed Nelson Mandela's example by standing up and saying, 'I plead not guilty. It is the government who should be in the dock.'

Yutar had called his witnesses, among them the dramatically entitled 'Mr

X', Bruno Mtolo (his name kept secret for safety), who had been an uMkhonto operative in Natal. Mtolo's evidence was damaging, for he had a remarkable memory and spoke much of the truth, thereby establishing a certain credibility upon which more inventive flourishes could be based. Other witnesses were more predictable, in particular Sergeant Dirker, a rather large, unintelligent man with a Hitler moustache, who was becoming a regular feature of life for many allied with those in the dock. Dirker had been the one to arrest Denis Goldberg, and now the prosecution wanted to use him to settle Rusty Bernstein's guilt. In this, however, it miscalculated badly, for Dirker testified that during the raid he had raised the bonnet of Bernstein's car, and felt the engine, which was cold. This, according to the prosecution, could only mean that Bernstein must have been at the farm for some hours (for it would take so long for an engine to cool down), and had attended the meeting in progress. But under Vernon Berrangé's customarily surgical questioning it emerged that Bernstein's car had an alarm that would sound if the bonnet were raised. Even more decisively, Berrangé proved that Bernstein had, according to the terms of his house arrest, signed in with the police at Marshall Square an hour before the raid occurred. If time and distance were calculated, he could therefore have arrived at Lilliesleaf only a few minutes before the police, just as he claimed – and the engine of his car could not have been cold.

The defence strategy was determined in discussion and debate. Early on they decided that Nelson Mandela should not give evidence as a witness, but instead should address the court from the dock. This meant that his testimony, unchallenged by the prosecution, would be less convincing in judicial terms, but it was a desirable option for a number of reasons. In Mandela's earlier appearance in 1962 he had made a point of not recognising the authority of the white court, and had conducted his own defence; now he did not wish to confer any legitimacy previously withheld by appearing as a witness. More importantly, it was necessary for at least one of the accused to outline, without any attack or maligning from Yutar, just what the commitment of those in the dock was about, and there could be no one better to do it than Mandela. He would speak, as George Bizos put it, 'in a loud and clear voice', unapologetic and openly. This was a Socratic defence, an apologia of a different kind: Bizos, once again with his Greek background, had a special feel for the classical resonance. Everyone knew what this would be about – in a literal sense it would be the speech of Mandela's life.

The lawyers worked with Mandela, and in the meantime managed to fool the prosecution once again. As if they were preparing for Mandela's evidence, they began to bring in the records of the Treason Trial. Because all their movements were reported to the prosecution, pretty soon the multiple and vast volumes of the Treason record began to pile up on Yutar's desk as well, as he worked on his anticipated cross-examination. And so finally the day came on 20 April when Bram opened the case for the defence, pointing out what the accused would admit and what they would deny, and then calling on Nelson Mandela to make his statement. At this Yutar, seeing his long-awaited opportunity disappear, leaped up in confusion and dismay. 'My Lord! My Lord!' he appealed to Mr Justice De Wet, 'I think you should warn the accused that what he says from the dock has far less weight than if he submitted himself to cross-examination!' The judge – who from the time of the débâcle over the first indictment had habitually referred to Yutar as 'Mr' instead of 'Dr' – pointed out drily that Mandela was attended by experienced counsel and probably had no need of Yutar's assistance.

Nelson Mandela entered the dock and, by the time he left, had spoken for five hours, reading from his prepared statement. He began with his childhood, recalling how as a boy he had listened to tales of the historic African leaders Dingane, Bambatha, Hintsa and Makanda. He gave a history of the ANC and its attachment to the principles of non-violence, explaining why it was necessary for uMkhonto to be a separate organisation. He discussed the reasons for sabotage – that it was a decision arrived at only after the last peaceful attempts of the ANC had been spurned. He outlined four stages of violence – sabotage, guerrilla warfare, terrorism and open revolution – and said that uMkhonto had been determined to test the first stage fully before taking a decision on any of the others. He stressed that orders had been given to all uMkhonto members to guard against any injury to life. He told of how he himself had received military training in North Africa, but only so that in the event of guerrilla warfare he could fight alongside his people and share the hazards they faced. He discussed carefully the activities at Rivonia, denying that the ANC was dominated by the Communist Party, or that he himself was a communist. He spoke of the reasons why the struggle for freedom was necessary, commenting on the realities of African poverty in South Africa, the inequities in health, education and employment. White South Africans, he observed, tended to regard Africans as a separate breed, forgetting that they were people with families of their own: 'they do not realise that we have emotions – that we fall in love like white people do; that we want to be with our wives and children like white people want to be with theirs; that we want to earn enough money to support our families properly, to feed and clothe them and send them to a school.' He spoke about the pass laws.

'Above all,' he said, 'we want equal political rights.' Political division, based on colour, was entirely artificial, and when it disappeared so would the domination of one colour group by another. 'This then is what the ANC is fighting. Our struggle is a truly national one. It is a struggle of the African people, inspired by our own suffering and our own experience. It is a struggle for the right to live.'

For those five hours in court there was a commanding quietness of attention while Mandela continued to read. Then, coming to an end, he put down his notes, looked up directly at the judge, and spoke in the most absolute silence around him: 'During my lifetime I have dedicated my life to the struggle of the African people. I have fought against white domination, and I have fought against black domination. I have cherished the ideal of a democratic and free society in which all persons live together in harmony and with equal opportunities. It is an ideal which I hope to live for, and to see realised. But my Lord, if need be, it is an ideal for which I am prepared to die.'

Before his final sentence Mandela had dropped his voice very low. As Joel Joffe remembered it, the silence lasted some thirty seconds after Mandela sat down before anyone even audibly took a breath. Some in the gallery began to weep.

Mr Justice De Wet, who would have his own monumental choices to make in the trial, turned to Bram and said, to the defence ears almost gently, 'You may call your next witness.'

Bram called Walter Sisulu.

☙❦❧

Nelson Mandela wrote later that Bram had not wanted him to deliver that final paragraph of his speech, under the presumption that if he did so he might as well walk outside to be hanged. Mandela felt that he was likely to be hanged in any case, and so at least ought to have the benefit of saying what he thought, but Bram's caution was testimony to his own priorities, that the saving of lives superseded everything else.

There was intense debate among the defence team as to whether to call any of the other accused as witnesses. Joel Joffe and Arthur Chaskalson argued against, holding that all Yutar needed to do was concentrate on the evidence and the question of violence to make his case impregnable. George Bizos, however, supported active testimony, on the ground that it would be so much harder for a judge to hand down death sentences to people who had been in the dock in front of him, debating, talking, coming alive. He also had a strong hunch – which turned out to be correct – that Yutar would not be able to resist the temptation of a political dispute, and that in such an arena the defendants would more than have his measure. Bram, in his way, listened to all the discussion (pro and con, ingrained from Percy's days) and then, the day before the defence opened, decided the matter (recalled Bizos) under a tree in the garden at Beaumont Street: the accused would go into the witness box.

Anthony Eastwood had commented at one point after the trial began on how impressive he found Walter Sisulu; Bram had agreed and said that was why Sisulu would give evidence. As events turned out, the contest between Sisulu and Yutar was one of the most remarkable ever seen in a South African court. Sisulu had been born to a peasant family; his formal schooling had extended only as far as one year beyond the primary level and he had largely educated himself; he had behind him the black everyman's experience of a steady rotation of jobs. Yutar, for his part, held a doctorate of laws, and was the most qualified prosecutor in South Africa. It seemed an unequal match. But, over a period of six days of testimony while – against all precedent and custom – Sisulu was kept secluded not only from counsel but also from his co-accused, he proved his impeccable legal and political reflexes. Consistently and carefully he refused to incriminate anyone not already accused or else safely overseas, and on this front turned away Yutar's incessant badgering. When Yutar harried him on a particular letter naming him secretary-general of the ANC after he had been banned, Sisulu insisted on his right to a proper response: 'If you'll just give me a chance to explain,' he told Yutar. 'You're not going to handle me like that, just getting it out of me. Let me explain the position.' At one point, when Yutar doubted that blacks in South Africa were persecuted, Sisulu allowed his emotions to rise: 'I have been persecuted by the police. If there is a man who has been persecuted it is myself. In 1962 I was arrested six times. I know the position in this country . . . I wish *you* were an African and knew the position.' By the time six days had passed, Yutar had been so sidetracked in attempting to demonstrate that the ANC misrepresented the lot of the African people that he quite forgot to ask Sisulu what the meeting on the day of the raid had been about, and whether uMkhonto had adopted 'Operation Mayibuye'.

Govan Mbeki, taking his turn on the witness stand, simply refused to answer certain questions, saying he didn't feel like it, or that he was tired at the end of the day – and Mr Justice De Wet, peculiarly, allowed him the indulgence. (Threats of contempt of court held little significance in the circumstances.) He also described movingly how, in the 1930s, poor Afrikaners suffering through the Depression had come to his father for food and clothing. Bram, with a special feel for the connection, allowed the recollection to continue. Like Sisulu, Denis Goldberg was also kept isolated during his evidence, but Bram found ways to encourage him, standing nearby during adjournments and commenting to the others in a loud stage whisper, 'Denis's evidence is very good, isn't it?'

When Rusty Bernstein took the stand, Yutar's priorities became somewhat tangled, for Bernstein had written a letter to his sister in which he complained about Yutar's conduct of the case. The offending item had been intercepted by the Security Police, who had passed it on to Yutar; now Yutar (ignoring the small matter of how he had come by the information) wanted revenge, and interrogated Bernstein at length on the letter. He also took the opportunity to cast aspersions in Bram's direction, focusing on an article Bernstein had written in 1953, entitled 'I Think of Bram Fischer' (this had been at the time of Bram's first banning). Yutar wanted to know who had been the secretary-general of the Communist Party, but Bernstein refused to reply. 'Well, since you are unable to answer that question,' commented Yutar, 'perhaps we may conclude that it was the gentleman referred to in the exhibit before you.'

Over and above the dubious logic of the inference, this was a stark contravention of the protocols of judicial respect normally afforded an opposing counsel. Yutar's local skirmishes, however, usually meant larger losses. By the time Bernstein left the stand Yutar had forgotten to ask him what he was doing at Rivonia, and suddenly Bernstein's prospects began to look rather promising.

⁂

On 20 May Yutar arrived for his closing argument with bound copies (replete with gold lettering) of his address, and gave five sets of these to the press. In his argument he raised allegations of murder – which had never been charged – without let or hindrance from the judge; in caricature fashion he poured scorn on the accused, drawing up a mock government cabinet to which he said they aspired (if he knew who the leader of the Communist Party was, he remarked, he would automatically name him president of the revolutionary movement); he asserted that the defendants had planned a general uprising for 26 May 1963 – some weeks before they had been arrested; he maintained that the people of South Africa owed a debt of gratitude to the police, without whose actions the country would be embroiled in a bloody and savage civil war.

In response the defence argument – with the training now of some years in these matters – was both methodical and meticulous. Chaskalson dealt incisively with the police evidence, bringing down the number of legally proven acts of sabotage from the alleged 193 to 12, none of which had involved any injury to life. Bram set out to argue the two crucial issues that the ANC and uMkhonto were distinct organisations, and that uMkhonto had not adopted any plans for guerrilla warfare. On both counts, exactly as in the Treason Trial, the judge stopped him in mid-flight, accepting the points. Bram, who had prepared for months, was taken aback, but these were vital successes, both for this trial and for others in future. Berrangé responded to Yutar's sarcastic attacks on the accused (which they had, he indicated, with their customary dignity chosen to ignore, though Yutar's manner did not represent 'the best traditions in which prosecutions are conducted in this country'), and argued the case for the acquittal of Bernstein, Kathrada and Mhlaba.

On Thursday, 11 June, in a decision lasting barely a few minutes, the judge found seven of the accused guilty on all four charges; Kathrada was found guilty on one charge; and Bernstein was acquitted. Sentence was set for the next morning at ten. There was barely time for any elation for Rusty Bernstein; as expected, he was rearrested immediately, this time on charges of contravening his banning order on the day of the Rivonia raid.

The accused, and the defence, went away to await what the following morning would bring. As at the start of the trial, the one and only issue was whether or not there would be death sentences. There were some reasons for hope. During the course of Yutar's concluding argument, when he had raised the allegation of guerrilla warfare, Mr Justice De Wet had for once intervened: 'Dr Yutar, you do concede that you failed to prove guerrilla warfare was ever decided upon, do you not?' – and Yutar, stunned, had conceded. It was after a similar exchange during Walter Sisulu's cross-examination that Bram had confided a restrained optimism to Denis Goldberg: he couldn't explain why, he told him, but just had a feeling there would be no death sentences. Even at the beginning of the trial there had been some encouragement. Early one morning in October 1963 Bram had arrived at George Bizos's house. George, also an early riser, was watering his renowned vegetable garden at dawn. Bram had a copy of the *Rand Daily Mail* in his hand, the headline of which announced that the Security Council of the United Nations had called for the release of the Rivonia trialists. Bram knew George was going over to see the accused later that day: 'Take this to Pretoria,' he told George. 'They daren't hang them after this' – and then, with even deeper passion – 'they daren't hang them!'

As it turned out there were more direct indications, though not everyone knew of them. Harold Hanson, always a blustery and impressive advocate, had been arguing bail for Jimmy Kantor early in the trial, and became embroiled in a blow-up with the judge. When the newspapers reported his remarks the next day, Hanson denied to his colleagues that he had said anything of the kind, but they reminded him diplomatically that he had. 'Oh,' said Hanson. 'Can't say that to a judge' – and he had disappeared to apologise. Now he was due to argue mitigation in the case, and went again to see Mr Justice De Wet before he did so. When he returned he said to Arthur Chaskalson, 'He's not going to impose the death sentence.' Chaskalson asked, 'How do you know?' Hanson swore him to secrecy, and then said, 'I asked him.' Hanson had enquired whether De Wet was considering the death penalty, because if he was it might affect the nature of his argument. And De Wet had simply said, 'No.'

George Bizos found out from another source. He was at a party the week before the verdict, and there had seen Minford, the British consul-general. Minford had said to him, 'George, there won't be a death sentence, and Rusty Bernstein will be acquitted.' Bizos told Bram, who asked him how he knew. Bizos said, 'Minford was drunk, and swore me to secrecy.'

⚜

Still, there was no assurance for the accused, and they returned overnight to wait. Nelson Mandela had already decided that if he were sentenced to death he would not appeal; Sisulu and Mbeki were similarly resolved. They weren't hopeful of the outcome. Earlier one of Mandela's warders had asked him what sentence he expected, and Mandela – just to gain some consolation – had replied, 'Well, I am sure they're going to hang us.' The warder agreed. Walter Sisulu was also sure they would die. In other trials around the country young schoolboys were facing twenty years in prison for relatively minor offences, whereas he and the others had been planning a revolution. How could there not be death sentences? Sisulu's wife Albertina, who had led a crowd singing 'Nkosi Sikelel' iAfrika' outside the Palace of Justice before the convictions were announced, came to see Walter on that last day, and then cried through the night because of his certainty. Nelson Mandela even prepared a speech in case they were sentenced to death.

The next morning, Friday, 12 June, there were roadblocks all the way from Johannesburg to Pretoria, and policemen thronged the court, even taking up the seats of the defence team. Outside, a contingent of white students from the University of Pretoria stood ready to confront supporters of the accused; Elias Motsoaledi's wife could hardly gain entrance. It began with pleas in mitigation of sentence, and Harold Hanson called Alan Paton, author of Cry, the Beloved Country, to give evidence. Later Paton claimed that he had appeared in the Rivonia Trial despite knowing that he was being used by Bram Fischer; but, according to others who were there at the time, that was not how it appeared. Paton was leader of the Liberal Party and in a profound sense anti-communist, yet when he and Bram met they evinced an immediate and instinctive respect for one another. The defence had approached a number of people to appeal for clemency, but given the climate most had refused. Paton, to his enduring credit, asked just one question: 'Are their lives at stake?' When the answer came in the affirmative, he had just as quickly agreed to testify.

After Paton's testimony, however, Yutar did the unthinkable. He had the right to cross-examine any witness, but it was a privilege almost never exercised when someone was pleading for clemency. Paton was speaking – courageously in the circumstances – from the deepest of human sympathies, but Yutar decided to question him – and he did it, as he said, 'to unmask this gentleman'. He embarked on a vicious attack on Paton as a fellow-traveller of the Communist Party, his objective apparently sheer humiliation. After this – especially given the judge's evident lack of interest in the clemency plea – the defence decided to call no further witnesses. There remained only Harold Hanson, and he gave a moving and encompassing account, rehearsing how Africans had been denied all legal forms of expression, and how the Afrikaners themselves, in their own struggle for freedom, had resorted to many of the same methods as the accused. He pointed out that the South African courts had traditionally shown leniency in such cases, for it was not only the effects of a crime which had repercussions, but perhaps more importantly those of a sentence.

The judge was visibly unimpressed. Denis Goldberg watched him lean back, the breathing chest under the robes and the white-fronted dicky arcing up and down in accentuated impatience. Then he nodded to the accused to rise for sentencing, leaned forward and began to read from a slip of paper, wanting to get it over with. He was not convinced, remarked Mr Justice De Wet, that the motives of the accused were as altruistic as claimed. People who organised a revolution usually took over the government, and personal ambition could not be excluded as a motive. The crime of which the accused had been convicted was in essence one of high treason, but the state had decided not to charge it in that form.

'Bearing this in mind, and giving the matter very serious consideration, I have decided not to impose the supreme penalty which in a case like this would usually be the proper penalty for the crime. But consistent with my duty, that is the only leniency which I can show.

'The sentence in the case of all the accused will be one of life imprisonment. In the case of the accused who have been convicted on more than one count, these counts will be taken together for the purpose of sentence.'

And that was all. Nelson Mandela allowed himself a smile. Many years later Walter Sisulu recalled the relief that made him feel almost as if he were being discharged. But the acoustics in the Palace of Justice were so poor that many in the galleries had not heard the judge's words. Denis Goldberg's mother, still in the anxiety of unknowing, leaned down towards her son and said, 'What did he say? What did he say?'

And Denis said, 'Life! Isn't life wonderful!'

⁂

The accused disappeared down the black ink of the stairwell one last time. Bram's juniors shook hands silently with him, sensing in the awe of the moment that this might be his last trial. That Friday evening there was a small party for the defence, and Vernon Berrangé said, 'Well, I think we saved their lives.' It was part of the truth: international pressure had also contributed its own compelling force. But Bram and his team had played a significant role in saving the men who one day would return to do the same for their country.

The police and prison authorities had promised that the accused would remain in Pretoria for consultation with the defence on the question of an appeal. But next morning the newspapers reported that the black prisoners had been flown off secretly in the night to Cape Town, on their way to begin their sentences on Robben Island. Only Denis Goldberg remained. If they had all stayed in Pretoria, that was where Bram would have consulted with them, probably over the weekend. If there were thirty minutes', even ten seconds' difference in the universe, then everything in the whole world would be different.

⁂

Elizabeth Lewin was a young woman from the Eastern Cape, now running the Johannesburg headquarters of the Defence and Aid Fund. There she was concerned with the immensely difficult job of tracking down and seeing to the needs of political prisoners and their dependants. She was a member of the Liberal Party, and in the process of being divorced from Hugh Lewin, soon to be arrested in the police breakup of the ARM. Through her contact with Ivan Schermbrucker, Liz had come to know Bram and Molly, and developed a passionate affection for them. In fact it was Liz Lewin who, because of her Liberal Party credentials, had acted as go-between in approaching Alan Paton to plead in mitigation in the Rivonia Trial.

On the final day of the trial she was in the Defence and Aid office. Two African women were there, but seemed reluctant to say what they wanted. Then the phone rang with news of the sentences, and Liz gave a whoop of delight. When she told the women what it was about, they too showed their obvious pleasure. Then they told Liz what they wanted: they were the wives of two PAC men who had been hanged, and they had come to find out how they might retrieve the bodies.

The next day, Saturday 13th, Bram, Molly and Liz set out for Cape Town by car. At that point Bram knew his immunity was over, and it was advisable to be out of town for a while; in any case, this would be his and Molly's first holiday since the start of the trial. There was also a more personal reason for the journey, for Ilse, born in 1943, would be twenty-one on 16 June, and Bram and Molly wanted to be with her for the celebration. As for Liz, she felt that Bram and Molly were taking her along in order to sound her out on possible membership of the Communist Party. Bram, with a mixture of sentimentality and efficiency, took along all kinds of papers which would be safely away from Beaumont Street, but which he might have thought better to destroy.

They left at about lunchtime, a highveld winter's afternoon, in Bram and Molly's grey Mercedes-Benz. Bram was tired after the tension of the trial, and Molly drove while he rested in the back. After all the pent-up emotions, the prevailing mood was one of release and elation at the sentences, and the three joked and chatted as they drove. Between Kroonstad and Winburg in the Free State, as dusk began to fall at about 6.30 p.m., they switched around: Bram took over the driving, and though Liz offered to sit in the back, Molly said she preferred to do so because she wanted to rest. She took up her place behind Bram, so that Liz could turn easily to talk to her. Bram was going pretty fast – his usual seventy miles an hour or so – and the twilight was staining down from the sky when suddenly he said, 'There's a cow in the road.' A cow was crossing from left to right, but Bram didn't brake at that point. Then a motor-cycle came towards them out of the dusk, and startled the cow, which stepped back towards the path of the Mercedes. It was then that Bram braked, and turned the car to the left.

They were at a place called Koolspruit, just south of Ventersburg, and at the side of the road – as the road bridged above it – was a deep pool of water. It was the oddest thing, for the Free State is normally dry, and in the middle of winter there is no water about, but this was a pool some twenty or thirty feet deep that always seemed to be there. As Bram pulled the car over, it angled off the road, down the incline at the side of the bridge. Liz remembered their hitting a small willow on the way down and had an impression of Molly bouncing up behind, because she had been turned to talk to her. The whole thing seemed to be happening slowly, almost as if the car were under control. There was a fence that they went over or through. It was dark, but there was the sense of a river ahead. And then the car stopped, and there was the sound of settling or whooshing. It felt to Liz as if they had come to a stop at the bottom.

And we thought we'd landed on sand, just river sand. And I tried to open the door, and I said, 'Bram I can't open my door', and he said, 'I can't either. Don't worry, I'll open the window and I'll come round and open the doors.' And he started to open his window. And – I think I was in shock – I started to open my window, because that's what he was doing. And he got out. And then I could see that there was water. But we thought, oh, we're on the bottom of the river.

We had on our heavy winter clothes, because it was cold. So he got out, and I got out – scrambled out the window. And I realised I couldn't stand.

Jesus, then you know, we realised . . . but we still thought . . . We couldn't see anything . . . The car lights were still half shining, so we could see some reflection off the roof, the cement of the bridge. And it was very narrow . . . A pool . . . But we seemed to be very close to the bank on this side, and I thought, well, if we can pull this down on the bank, then it'll settle and we'll be able to get Molly out.

And I called. And Molly was on my side of the car. I remember thinking, if I can open the door from the outside – you see we still didn't know how deep the water was – even if she can't open it from the inside, we'll be able to get her out. And I said to Bram, 'I can't swim, and I can't open the door', and he said, 'Don't worry, I'm coming round.'

And then I thought, if we can pull the car down on the bank . . . I pulled down on an exhaust pipe and got a hand burn because I was pulling on it. And then the car disappeared.

And the bank was very steep right there and very difficult. And I said to Bram, 'I'm getting out to stop a car.' And he said, 'Yes, go stop a car.' And he went on swimming and diving and trying to find her.

The whole event had taken but two or three minutes. Liz went up to the road. There had been a car ahead of them whose occupants had seen what had happened and came back immediately to help. They went down to Bram, and dived with him there; he even dived from the top of the bridge to get depth. Eventually they had to pull him out of the water: he wouldn't leave, swimming around in his heavy winter clothes.

They drove Bram and Liz to the hospital in Winburg. Even in that state Bram was conscious of the danger of an encounter with the police, and gave his diary to Liz for safekeeping. He was in a terrible state of shock. In the hospital he couldn't sit still, but would stand, draw in breath, and then start pacing and pacing. Yet still, in his way, he spoke to the family who had helped him, and discovered that they were on their way to Bloemfontein to visit a young niece in hospital. Bram asked them who the paediatrician was – and the reply came, 'Dr Paul Fischer.' Later this family, dyed-in-the-wool Afrikaner nationalists, came to Beaumont Street and brought flowers of condolence as if it had been someone they knew who had died.

In Bloemfontein Paul Fischer got a phone call from Bram, saying that he'd had a terrible accident and Molly had drowned. At first he thought it was a bad joke, or that Bram was drunk, because one could not drown in the Free State in winter, but then Bram explained. So Paul drove up to Winburg to fetch him. He wanted to take him back to Bloemfontein, but Bram was thinking of his own son Paul who, in his final year at school, had stayed home to study. (He was at Beaumont Street with the historian Rodney Davenport, who had also agreed – but after the Paton débâcle was not called – to plead in mitigation at the trial.) Bram felt he had to go back to give Paul the news. So they drove up together, Bram and Paul and Liz Lewin. It was a freezing cold night. Even on the way to the hospital Bram had said it was his fault, that he shouldn't have been driving so fast. Liz Lewin felt her own guilt, that she had been in the front of the car and survived while Bram's wife had died.

In Johannesburg Joel Joffe phoned Pat Davidson, the daughter of Molly's old friend Liefie, who had left Beaumont Street a few weeks before. He wanted her to go to the house, to be there when Paul was told. But when she arrived it was Paul who had already heard, who ran out to tell her. In Cape Town Ilse had no phone, so someone contacted Leo Marquard, who went out to her house in Claremont to find her. Bram telephoned Ruth in London. At first the operator told him there would be a twenty-four-hour delay, but when he told her the reason, he was given a special call. It came through on the Sunday morning. Ruth was up early, and the operator said the call was from Johannesburg for Anthony Eastwood – and it was then, said Ruth, that she started shaking. She woke up Anthony, and Bram told him, and then he told her. Ruth nearly fainted.

Ilse flew up to Johannesburg early on that Sunday; Ruth arrived the following day. Tuesday was Ilse's twenty-first birthday. It almost never snows in Johannesburg, but on the following night it did. They woke up on Thursday to the most beautiful snow in the garden. That night in Johannesburg it snowed.

※✿❀

Whither thou goest I shall go. It had been Bram and Molly's first avowal of personal belief.

A car goes into a pool of water and a life is ended. For one person time stops, for another it goes on for ever. The light from that scene travels outwards, and is travelling still. It will continue for ever, and there are stars in the universe where that scene has still not yet arrived.

It will never end. In Bram's mind it would not go away.

∞

He wandered round the house, and could not settle down. The night of Molly's death he would not take the whisky his brother Paul tried to give him. It was his son Paul who took over, who told Bram it was time to go to bed, who made sure that everything was all right.

The next day someone came round, the usual thing – someone involved in a trial – and even in that state Bram helped him. But still he would suddenly get up and roam about the house, saying, 'My arme vrou' – 'My poor wife.' People poured in, Africans and Indians, and out of respect sat there silently. Bram's old comrade Issy Heymann arrived to help, dealing with everyone. As usual at Beaumont Street, there was tea and cake for all, round the clock, Tias and Katie taking over. Everyone who came said that outwardly Bram was amazingly strong, consoling others where he himself should be consoled. But when he saw Arthur Chaskalson's wife Lorraine, who had become very close to Molly, he just wept on her shoulders.

Bram's brother Paul left for Bloemfontein again on the Sunday: he had his practice to attend to, and also he was to identify Molly's body in Winburg. When he did so, he noticed that there was a bruise above her eye, and the doctor who carried out the post-mortem told him there had not been much fluid in her lungs. It was quite possible, since there had been no seat-belt in the back of the car, that she had been knocked unconscious in the tumble down the slope and had not been aware of what happened. Otherwise, as everyone agreed, she was fitter and more agile than Bram, and would have been out of the window before him. At any rate, it was some consolation to think that she had not been conscious when she drowned.

Before Paul left, Bram asked him another favour: if the police had salvaged the car and retrieved his things, there was a small box of tissues he should rescue. Paul went for the identification with his other brother Piet, whom Bram would not take into his confidence in the same way – for Piet, who had been through a succession of jobs, was gravitating politically to the right, and also eventually became a Jehovah's Witness. So Paul said nothing to Piet but, after he had identified the body, went over to where Bram and Molly's luggage had been placed, and took away the box of tissues. No one asked him any questions; he simply walked out. Later he dried the box and took out the tissues, and there, on the very bottom, was a map with a pattern of dots. Paul remembered thinking they must be sabotage targets, but he also noticed that not one of the dots was in a city. He took the map back to Bram.

The news devastated Bram and Molly's friends and comrades. After the accident Bram had thought of phoning the Bernsteins, but resisted because he knew that Rusty had been given bail and that it was his first night out of prison – evidence to them of the depth of his thought for others. He did call Ivan Schermbrucker, who at three o'clock in the morning phoned Eli Weinberg. Eli, banning order and all, put on his dressing gown and went up to the Fischer house. Ivan, also banned, went to tell the Bernsteins early the next morning, and sat in their bedroom and cried.

The cremation was held a week after the Rivonia Trial ended. Bram and the children had originally thought of a small gathering for the family, but Ruth and Ilse remembered that it was their Indian friends in particular who said no, that Molly belonged to everyone. Hundreds of people arrived, and the whole of Molly's family – despite strains over her communism – were there. Bram had no wish for a religious ceremony but just before the end handed his brother Paul a slip of paper asking him to recite the Lord's Prayer for the sake of Molly's brothers and sister.

An Afrikaner nationalist came to see Bram, someone he had known from Oxford. He had connections in government, and he took Paul Fischer aside. 'Tell Bram to get out,' he told him. 'They're chasing him, they're chasing him hard, and they're going to catch him.'

⁂

Within a day or two of the funeral Bram flew down to Cape Town with Joel Joffe to consult with the Rivonia prisoners on the question of an appeal. It was part of his personal morality: Bram, who never admitted emotion in public form, would not allow private grief to interfere with the needs of others or work that had to be done. In Cape Town they were joined by Himie Bernadt, an attorney and old friend of Bram's (who at short notice had given Ilse the money she needed to fly up to Johannesburg), and the three of them set off on the ferry to Robben Island.

Walter Sisulu remembered what happened when they met. Since their sentencing the trialists had been isolated from news, and had no knowledge at all of the accident. Sisulu greeted Bram, and asked him specially how Molly was. Bram just said, 'Walter, Mo– Molly is all right . . . Molly is all right' – but the tone, recalled Sisulu, was that of a devastated man. Bram was adding this inner price to his grief: he did not want to break down in front of others, and so would not share it with his comrades. Towards the end of the meeting, when Nelson Mandela asked him about Molly, Bram just walked away, it seemed almost rudely. But after the lawyers had left, a prison officer took Mandela aside and explained Bram's behaviour. He was allowed to write a letter of condolence, and took the view that it was a sign of Bram's extraordinary character that he had come to consult with them so soon after Molly had died. But the letter was never delivered: the prison authorities did not post it.

On Robben Island the Rivonia men were dressed, as Mandela had been before, in the shambling attire of prison shorts and sandals, but they were all in high spirits and unbowed. After the threat of death sentences, observed Mandela, life sentences meant very little. Support was coming not only from inside the country, but from all around the world: 'We could actually touch it with our hands, so strong it was. When we were sentenced to life imprisonment we felt we were heroes. The feeling was that we couldn't remain in jail for a long time.' The lawyers too shared that feeling.

They all turned down the idea of an appeal. Mandela, Sisulu and Mbeki had already been clear on this, and now they confirmed their decision in discussion with Bram. Not only did they wish to avoid granting the Rivonia Trial any legitimacy by appealing, or ask for leniency when they had run a defence of justification, but there was also the possibility that an Appeal Court might suggest that they were fortunate not to have received the death penalty – which could cause problems for others in future trials. They also felt, as the lawyers discussed it with them, that an appeal might diffuse the clamour for their release that was arising round the world. For the other prisoners it was more difficult: there was some chance for Mhlaba of a reduced sentence, and even more so for Kathrada. But when they tallied up Kathrada's likely sentence for all the offences to which he had admitted his guilt in the trial, it came to anywhere between 100 and 500 years. He felt he would rather take his ten years in jail, after which they all expected a triumphant resolution to the South African struggle, culminating in their release. They had no idea of how long, in the event, it would take, but on the question of appeals there was complete solidarity.

Bram flew back to Johannesburg, and saw Denis Goldberg in Pretoria, where again he showed his emotional mettle. Denis had heard the news, and told Bram how sorry he was about Molly; he saw Bram clench his fists until the knuckles turned white – and then carry on with the consultation. Soon after that, Bram, Ruth, Ilse, Paul and Sholto Cross drove back in Ivan Schermbrucker's car to Cape Town. The idea was to take a family trip, so that they could come to terms with Molly's loss together. They stayed at the

Bernadts, who were away for a while, and there Ruth would sometimes find Bram wandering around the empty house and weeping. To both Ruth and Ilse he spoke of his feelings of guilt, thinking of what he had done to them when Molly had died. At other times he would try to boost them all, insisting on a drive to cheer everyone up.

After a week or so they left for Onrus, near Hermanus, where Jack Simons and Ray Alexander were staying at their beach house. Earlier in Johannesburg Ray had given Molly the keys so that she and Bram could spend some time there after their arrival in Cape Town. At the house Bram told Jack that the Mercedes-Benz in which Molly had drowned would be the last car he would buy. Outside the police kept watch, obtrusive and visible to all. One morning Bram called Ray out – as always to avoid the surveillance devices inside – and told her that he would have to leave soon. The police, perhaps also waiting for the Rivonia Trial to end, were making swoops around the country, and numbers of people had been detained.

According to Ray Alexander, the Fischers left on Friday, 3 July. The intention, in this strange choreography of taking a holiday while avoiding the police, was to travel down the Garden Route, revisiting all the places Bram and Molly had been to with the children at various times. The following morning, Saturday 4th, the police raided the Simonses. Ray told them when Bram had left, but gave no clue as to where he was going. Little did she know that they had tracked him all the way. That afternoon, in the main street of George, the police stopped Bram's car, but his instinctive skills were still intact. Drawing up his charm, and quite naturally, he offered to follow them to the police station, and they allowed him to do so. But on the way he handed over all kinds of papers to Ruth and Ilse. 'God knows where he had them,' recalled Ilse, but there they were, and she and Ruth stuffed everything into their bras. At the station Bram worked his talents once again: 'Ag, the poor children,' he said solicitously to the police. 'They're so tired. Let them go and have a meal; I'll stay with them, and you can search the car.'

Ruth and Ilse found a restaurant where they relieved their overloaded bras, flushing the papers away and nearly stopping up the toilets. Even then, one piece of paper had been left in the car – it was a plan of how to make a bomb, and again there was no indication of how Bram had come by it. But because the car was Ivan Schermbrucker's, and because Sholto had also been with them, there was no conclusive proof it was Bram's, and the police were unable – or unwilling at that stage – to press the matter.

They let him go. Perhaps they had just been trying to scare him. But Bram knew the road he was on.

'Ry met my' – 'Ride with me.'

How many times had Bram spoken about the Fischer luck turning up again, or claimed the Almighty had been with him? He and Molly had joked about it often, from the first days when they had known each other, when he was in Bloemfontein and she in Bethlehem and he had driven out to see her. Bram had liked nothing better in those days than to have her in the car beside him, with her knees drawn up on the front seat, or her head on his shoulder.

He had had an almost certain belief, the sustained inner aura of a child born to something special. As to his doubts, it was these that Molly had salved. Now she, who loved water, had suffered death in a dark pool surrounded by dry land, while his comrades had been sentenced to life on an island surrounded by sea. He had helped save their lives, but could not save hers. They had been sentenced to a living eternity, she to some other kind, and he to a future without them.

CHAPTER 12

A SUPREME DUTY

4 July 1964 – 25 January 1965

R uth and Ilse couldn't remember where else they went on that trip. Later Bram could barely remember what happened for fully six months after Molly died.

In fact after the incident in George they did little further travelling and were soon on the road back to Johannesburg, finding out along the way that numbers of people were being arrested. In Welkom in the Free State, Ilse bought a newspaper, and when Sholto read it he became quite agitated. He and Bram went off for what, deceiving no one, they called a 'walk in the woods'. Sholto had seen in the paper that someone he had worked with closely had been detained.

They arrived home on Wednesday, 8 July, to find police swarming in cars all about in the street. Inside the house they also found Alan Brooks, whom both Sholto and Ilse knew and who had been associated with the ARM; he had come to Johannesburg because things were too hot for him in Cape Town. Now Bram and the others had to smuggle him out of the house without being detected, which with some effort they succeeded in doing. It did Brooks little good, however, for he was arrested in Cape Town two weeks later, and charged in one of the ARM trials.

That night Bram knew very well what to expect. He went through all his papers, deciding what to keep and what to flush away. The next morning, at about 5 a.m., there was a sharp knocking at the front door. Paul, half asleep, went down to open up. The Special Branch men rushed in and were in Bram's room before he or anyone else could do anything. He may have been unsurprised, but no one was ever fully prepared. The police told him that he was being detained under the ninety-day law, and then searched the house for some four hours. After that Bram was taken to the Security Police headquarters at the Grays, and from there to his rooms at Innes Chambers, where the police sealed off the whole floor while they searched his office. It was a rude intrusion into the demure proceedings of everyday chambers life, and in the case of someone as respected as Bram the shock for his colleagues was doubled. Still, some civilities remained: Paul, Ilse and Ruth were allowed in to say goodbye, and at lunchtime food was ordered both for Bram and for the police.

The following morning, Friday 10th, at 6 a.m., Sholto was detained at his house in Bedfordview. That same day Ruth, Ilse and Paul were allowed a contact visit with Bram, during which he managed to shove a note in Ilse's pocket. (The fact of communication was more important than content: no one could remember what it read.) Because of his ulcer they were also allowed to take him food – fruit, cheese, crackers – as they began to settle into the routines of what looked to be a very long haul. In some ways Bram's arrest, looming for so long, was a relief. Friends dropped by in the evenings, and in the release and extremity of the moment the atmosphere was almost convivial. There was a fair amount to drink and, for Ruth, Ilse and Paul, even a certain dark jocosity as – their mother dead, their father in jail – they contemplated the worst that could possibly happen to a family, and a future that must have seemed as unreal as it was absurd.

Obscure messages came from unexpected directions, one of them via Pat Davidson. As Molly's old friend Liefie's daughter, Pat was about the same age as Ruth and Ilse, an energetic and bluff character who liked nothing better than a good game of squash at some school old-boys' club. In 1963 she had come up to Johannesburg from Cape Town on three months' probation as an aspirant public prosecutor and, despite her prospective avocation, had stayed at Beaumont Street because of the family connection. Within about a week of her arrival, however, and under the thoroughly persuasive atmosphere of the house, she had experienced (as she put it) a complete transformation of her previously non-existent political consciousness. She became very close to the Fischers, and that was why Joel Joffe called her when Molly had died. Now, after Bram's arrest, she was contacted by Ann Cavill, a journalist on the *Sunday Express*, who arranged a meeting with her on a street corner. Cavill told Pat that she had been informed by Gordon Winter – also a reporter, and suspected by many of having close connections with the Special Branch – that Bram would need a Bible for only three days. One did not have to be a prophet to interpret the information, but such messages were not always dependable. The night before Bram's detention Joel Joffe had been tipped off by the *Sunday Times* journalist Margaret Smith, whose information and sympathies were extremely reliable, that both he and Bram were to be arrested. In the event Bram was and he wasn't, but that, remarked Joel, did nothing to improve the quality of his sleep in subsequent weeks.

But this message, quite surprisingly, turned out to be accurate. On Saturday 11th, at about midnight, Ruth and Ilse were heading up to bed when they heard something between a whisper and a shout from outside: 'Ru-uth! Ru-uth!' Ruth looked out the window, saw Bram and, in the same kind of stage whisper, asked him what on earth he was doing there. The whole setting was so bizarre she was convinced he must have escaped – but he hadn't. Shortly before, Bram had been taken out of his cell and told that he was being released. Insistent on protocols now long forgotten by the police, he had pointed out that he had no way of getting home, and demanded that he be provided with transport. And so the police had driven him home – though why he had not used a more conventional mode of entry into the house no one could say. Perhaps he suspected a trap; perhaps he was wary of alarming his family with further knocks at the door in the depths of the night.

Bram had been held for just under three days: it was something of a mystery as to why he had been detained and released so quickly. Moreover, during that time he had been interrogated just twice for an hour apiece, and on both occasions the police had been concerned less to question him than to tell him everything they knew. The natural surmise for Bram was that they were trying to scare him, and then give him the opportunity to flee the country. His abrupt departure would have suited them very well, whipping up the scare against communism, legitimising detention, sullying his reputation in every quarter, and demoralising his comrades – and that was how the police tried to use his release in any case, intimating to other detainees that he had been freed because he had talked. No one believed it, not only because of their faith in Bram, but because they all still thought that no one would talk. Still, it was necessary to counter such speculation, and newspaper reports cited an unnamed legal colleague of Bram's (he himself, of course, could not be quoted) suggesting that it was Bram's refusal to answer any questions unless charged that accounted for his early release.

Bram's detention, coming so soon after the Rivonia Trial, made international headlines. In London he was on the front pages, and barristers voiced their shock, saying that detention without trial compromised the normal privileges of professional confidence (at least one privileged document had been taken from Beaumont Street by the police, relating to Alan Paton's testimony at the trial). In Geneva the secretary-general of the International Commission of Jurists, Sean McBride (whose Irish-nationalist father, Major John McBride, had joined an Irish Brigade to fight against the British in the Boer War), expressed his dismay that one of South Africa's leading advocates had been detained under the oppressive ninety-day law, and called for a full report on the circumstances.

In Marshall Square, down the passage from Bram, Dave Kitson, also in detention, had caught a glimpse of him and tried to make contact. He had no doubt that Bram was released because of his eminence – because his grandfather had been Prime Minister of the Orange River Colony and his father Judge-President of the Free State, because of the international flare-up, because the Johannesburg Bar had kicked up a fuss. At any rate, Bram's departure had its minor benefits as the Special Branch men distributed to the other detainees the left-over cheese and crackers Ruth and Ilse had brought. It was clear that he had been given special treatment. Others were by no means so lucky: Sholto Cross was held for four months. Soon the detainees, and those who depended on them, would learn that almost everyone talked, and that some would do so with dismaying abandon.

⁂

It was just over two months before Bram was arrested again.

In public he tried to be his same old self, shoring everything and everyone up, holding things together by force of optimism and will. Privately, though, he had moments of utter distraction. With Ruth back in England and Ilse in Cape Town, Pat Davidson returned to Beaumont Street to take care of the house and provide moral support. People still came to visit, and Bram would talk and laugh, but then suddenly get up and leave, and Pat would find him alone in his room. She was also with him when he went into the jeweller's shop where Molly had ordered an alarm clock for Ilse's twenty-first birthday. The original had gone down with the car in the accident, and Bram wanted an exact replacement with the same engraved message. But faced with the sudden recollections it evoked when he saw it, he broke down, overwhelmed with emotion. Others who encountered him at this time said he tried hard to be cheery and encouraging, but looked shrunken and somehow unkempt.

The known world was falling apart at a rate that was no less unsettling. After the tacit moratorium of the Rivonia Trial, the bombs had exploded everywhere, not only uMkhonto's but also the ARM's, and the police were responding in kind. That Saturday, 4 July, when Bram had been stopped in George was also the day they made their most significant arrest in breaking the ARM, detaining Adrian Leftwich in Cape Town. He – it appeared under some obscure historical impulse – had all but kept an archive of ARM activity, and soon the police were tracking down his comrades and had located a cache of suitcases filled to the brim with dynamite in the garage of a block of flats in Sea Point. The Johannesburg section of the organisation had been equally haphazard: after their first amateurish attempt – which occurred almost by happenstance – at sawing through the legs of an electricity pylon (they returned a week later to finish the job), they had stolen dynamite from a mine near Witbank and kept it under the hot sun in a ceiling, pouring it into plastic bags even as it became damp and dangerous.

Now, as the arrests gathered pace, some in the ARM escaped, but others were taken in – Lynette van der Riet, Eddie Daniels and Spike de Keller in Cape Town, Hugh Lewin and Baruch Hirson in Johannesburg. In Cape Town it soon became clear that Adrian Leftwich was not only answering police questions but was telling them more than they had any reason to expect. In Johannesburg a person on the fringe of the ARM, John Harris, planted a bomb at the railway station, killing a white woman and maiming her granddaughter. Bram was horrified, for this was precisely the sort of disintegration into futile violence he wanted to avoid. Developments such as this indicated how fine a line one walked – if one could – between a policy with its own restrictions and controls, and violence based on retribution and despair.

Yet if the Communist Party was attempting to be more coherent in terms of structure, policy and security, it hardly fared any better. Bram's old friend Ivan Schermbrucker was detained in June, to be followed in July by Esther and Hymie Barsel, as well as Piet Beyleveld – who, when taken in, apparently became perturbed because Bram had not been arrested as well. As others were detained messages began to emerge, among them that Piet Beyleveld was talking and that one Gerald (or 'Gerard', as he soon became known) Ludi was a police informant. The fact that Beyleveld was talking was a shock to everyone. Like Bram, Beyleveld was an Afrikaner with impeccable political credentials, a leader of the Congress of Democrats (he had conferred the *Isitwalandwe* titles at the Congress of the People), who had joined the Communist Party in 1956, and had been appointed to its central committee after the Rivonia raid. Just days before his arrest he had been lecturing other SACP members on how they should respond if detained.

Ludi's violation was of a different order altogether, and the ease of his success indicated just how vulnerable the Party was to infiltration. He had been a student at the University of the Witwatersrand (then and later, both a focal point of political resistance and prone to police spies), and appeared in retrospect to be a slippery character for whom truth and falsity had an equal plausibility at different times of the day. He had befriended – and then perhaps with a certain deliberation become boyfriend to – Hilda and Rusty Bernstein's daughter Toni, with whom he had travelled to the Soviet Union. The Bernsteins, who opened up their hearts to him almost like an adoptive family, found him completely convincing: decades later they insisted that either he wasn't originally a spy but had been 'turned' by the police, or else that he was the most consummate actor they had ever come across. Others had their suspicions, and rumours began to surface, but these – partly because of the Bernstein connection – were never pursued. According to Mollie Anderson there had been a previous case where rumours had provoked the isolation of a Congress of Democrats member who, in depression, committed suicide; there was now a somewhat guilt-ridden reluctance to repeat the same pattern. Where deception was intrinsic to underground life, betrayal could become awfully hard to identify, while paranoia was a temptation to be avoided.

Even before these latest arrests the Communist Party had become much more safety-conscious. In late 1963 and early 1964 an underground document headed 'Time for Reassessment' circulated, discussing new police bugging devices, the dangers of detention, and the seductiveness and reality of betrayal. In response it also outlined a series of safeguards: each cell was now to have a security officer to monitor the safety habits of its members; disguises were recommended as an expedient within the repertoire of underground life; if a member of the SACP were detained, special precautions had to go into imme-diate effect; no one was to be regarded as wholly reliable. But the Party was rel-atively powerless against a surveillance that had been in place for some time, and locations apparently 'safe' were by no means so at all. Jean Middleton, a member of a Johannesburg cell, had a flat in Hillbrow which had long been a regular meeting and drop-off point. But unknown to the Party (and probably on information supplied by Ludi) the police had rented the apartment next door and there installed one of their agents, Klaus Schroeder, together with a tape recorder. Schroeder had also replaced the glass above the front door with a one-way mirror so that he could observe anyone who came along the corridor.

This arrangement had already been responsible for a minor setback for Pat Davidson, although she had no way of understanding it at the time. When she was first staying with Bram and Molly, still in her guise as public prosecu-tor, Pat had been looking for a place of her own. Molly had taken her to see Jean Middleton's flat, which in itself was something of a risk, since she and Middleton were both banned and legally could not communicate with one another. The three had joked about it, Pat remarking that if the case came her way to prosecute, she'd be sure to botch it up. All of this must have gone on tape next door, and soon after Pat lost her job. At the time the ready assump-tion had been that it was merely because she was staying with the Fischers, and on these grounds Helen Suzman asked questions about harassment and intim-idation in parliament. In response the Minister of Justice claimed that he could say nothing in public but would offer Suzman an explanation in private, if she desired. Suzman, expecting the kind of official brush-off with which she was so familiar, had not bothered, but wrote a letter to Pat – which was then mysteriously stolen from Pat's handbag at work. Only later did everything become clear: the Security Police must have been anxious that Suzman, informed by the Minister, had revealed the truth about Middleton's flat, and had stolen the letter to check.

This was becoming more truly a shadow world of blurred outlines and ambiguous presentiments, when to be at liberty from the authorities was only a provisional condition. It was not wholly a surprise, then, to Bram when the police arrested him once again on 23 September 1964, though it came a little earlier than he expected. He was taken in together with Eli Weinberg, and this time they were not held under the ninety-day law but were charged under the Suppression of Communism Act. In this they were joined with ten others who had been detained for varying times and who had already been charged: Jean Middleton, Ann Nicholson, Paul Trewhela, Florence Duncan, Norman Levy, Esther Barsel, Hymie Barsel, Sylvia Neame, Dr Costa Gazides and Pixie Benjamin. All were white; their listed professions ranged from housewife to medical practitioner. The youngest, Paul Trewhela, was twenty-three; Bram and Eli, both fifty-six, were the oldest. Their case, set for mid-November, became known as the Fischer Trial, and Bram was accused number one.

⁂

Even then, fortunately for Bram, it was not so simple. A week after his arrest he explained it to Tom Karis, an American scholar who, together with his colleague Gwendolen Carter, had visited Johannesburg during the Rivonia Trial. (Though neither had any specific sympathies for communism, both had been wholly bowled over by Bram's qualities.) He now told Karis of the un-usual circumstances he faced: 'Since I last wrote to you I have been arrested on a charge under the Suppression of Communism Act, where it is practically unknown to get bail. I was arrested on the 23rd, but two days before, the Minister, after firmly refusing to grant me a passport, did in fact allow one to be issued. It was therefore on this rather extraordinary ground, namely that a passport had been issued to enable me to go to the Privy Council, that I was given bail in order to leave the country.'

It had to do, peculiarly enough, with the Bayer copyright case which Bram had argued successfully in the Federal High Court in Salisbury two years before, and which had gone on appeal to the Privy Council in London. Bram had been retained by the local firm to represent it once again, and the hearing was set for October. It was on this basis that he had applied for a passport to travel to London, but the Minister of the Interior, Senator Jan de Klerk (father of the President who later freed Nelson Mandela), had refused. Then suddenly, surprisingly, he had agreed – just two days before Bram was arrested. Perhaps one hand of the state did not know what the other was doing – or there were other plans in the offing – but that was why Bram had not expected his arrest quite so soon after the Minister's change of heart.

When Bram and Eli Weinberg were produced in the Johannesburg Regional Court on Thursday 24th to be arraigned for trial, they both applied for bail. Eli, represented by Vernon Berrangé, offered a straightforward argument: he was a professional photographer, the sole breadwinner in his family, and consequently needed to work. Though he had been on charges twice before, he had never made any attempt to flee; he said he wanted to stand trial now. Bram was called to the stand by Harold Hanson, and used the occasion not only for the purpose at hand but to define the issues as of right. He spoke of a family history going back to the eighteenth century, and of his grandfather and father. He pointed out that he had been a member of the Johannesburg Bar Council for many years, as well as its chairman, but that legislation in 1962 had prohibited him from continuing as a regional representative. He told the court that he had been harassed by the Special Branch for the previous fourteen or fifteen years, and that he knew the government was anxious to prosecute him both for his political beliefs and under his banning orders. His house and his office had been raided numbers of times, and recently he had been detained under the ninety-day law. He held a tourist passport for his legal work in Rhodesia, yet, knowing he was under police surveillance, had never made any attempt to leave the country. He offered his assurance that if he were allowed to go to London, he would return in good time to stand his trial.

This for Bram was the essence of the matter: 'I have no intention of avoiding a political prosecution. I fully believe I can establish my innocence. I am an Afrikaner. My home is South Africa. I will not leave South Africa because my political beliefs conflict with those of the Government ruling the country.' It was a statement that went to the core of Bram's convictions, presaging many of his actions in the months to come: South Africa was his place, where he was rooted, where both his obligations and his destiny lay. While the government had done its best to narrow and corrupt an Afrikaner identity, it was his responsibility to remain true to an alternative and more redemptive definition. To that extent, for Bram, wider affiliations were intimately connected with a personal sense of belonging, broader liberties with the assiduous discipline of an inner liberation.

The bail applications were opposed by the prosecutor, who read out a police affidavit stating that both Fischer and Weinberg were members of the central committee of the Communist Party, and that many other communists had fled South Africa, some to avoid standing trial. Yet there was also solid support. The attorney in the Bayer case, a man named Peter Ulrich Rissik, took the stand to say that he was prepared to underwrite Bram's bail for any amount: 'I have absolute faith in his integrity. I would accept his word unhesitatingly, confident that he would carry it out.' Harold Hanson suggested that Bram's colleagues at the Bar were also prepared to pay whatever was required. Yet it appeared to be other considerations that swayed the magistrate's mind when he gave his decision the following day. He pointed out, with respect to Bram, that the Minister of Justice and the Minister of the Interior had, after discussion, agreed to allow him to go to London: 'these two eminent authorities, after careful investigation and consideration, have decided that the interests of the State would not be detrimentally affected if Fischer were granted a passport. It would be rather churlish for any court to come to a decision to prevent [him] from complying with the terms of his brief now before the Privy Council.' Yet at the same time he was prepared to recognise Bram's particular authority: 'Fischer', he remarked, 'is a son of our soil and an advocate of standing in this country.'

This must have proved, for Eli Weinberg, the futility of being neither an advocate of standing nor a son of the soil, for his application was turned down. As for Bram, the prosecution called for his bail to be set at R50,000 – a sum which Berrangé called 'ridiculous', suggesting R5000 instead. The magistrate decided on R10,000 (still a sizeable figure), and then, according to newspaper accounts, any number of Bram's colleagues, many of them by no means sympathetic to his political views, all but queued up to pay the amount (one businessman apparently phoned in to offer the full R10,000). In the event the money was paid by Rissik, which caused Bram some qualms and complications later.

On the Thursday that Bram was charged, two brothers, Essop Pahad and Aziz Pahad, also appeared in the Regional Court under the Suppression of Communism Act, but their case had to be postponed because the counsel due to represent them was Bram Fischer – graphically illustrating the increasingly thin line between accused and defence in South Africa. Then on the Friday he was granted bail, Mollie Anderson (Bram's cousin Connie's daughter) came to watch. She had been arrested in January 1963 and sentenced to six months for participating in a Congress of Democrats sortie to distribute ANC pamphlets (Gerard Ludi had been a member of her group; possibly he had informed the police, or else had been discovered and 'turned' at that time). When the Communist Party arrests began Mollie had lain low, because she had been active in the critical period, and among other things had been to meetings at Jean Middleton's flat. Left alone by the police, however, she thought she was safe, and so had come to court. But as she sat there she felt the familiar heavy hand on her shoulder: it was Lieutenant Broodryk of the Special Branch. Mollie was arrested and would stand trial with Bram and the others – his prediction to her of some time before now come true, his inspiration in her life come to this paradoxical fulfilment.

There can be no certainty as to why the South African government let Bram go. It may have been the barely maintained civilities of due deference to the Privy Council in a hostile international climate. Or perhaps this time they really did want him to leave the country. Was it compassion for old time's sake, a last indulgence by the Afrikaner fold to one of their own, a man who had already suffered untold personal tragedy? Or was the government embarrassed by that very association, wishing if at all possible to avoid a prosecution, hoping instead to make easy allegations of cowardice? There was Bram's standing, his stature, his authority, the history and tradition he represented, the appeal he embodied to a different version of Afrikaner identity. What the magistrate had said was true: he was a son of the soil. Perhaps it would be better if he were gone, out of the picture, sidelined in futility for ever.

Before Bram left he spoke to what remained of the Party's central committee – his friends Ivan and Eli particularly – to determine his future plans, and they were also clear that he should return.

✦

When Bram was released on bail from the Fort in Johannesburg he was met and embraced by Ilse, waiting outside. When he arrived in London on 3 October, he was met by Anthony and Ruth, who hugged him in welcome. 'Just see where I am now!' he wrote to Ilse, Paul and Pat Davidson at home. 'I wish you were with me, even though it's all a bit queer and unrealistic.'

It was a sudden change in pace and atmosphere after the precipitate events of the previous weeks and months. Bram did not move in immediately with Ruth and Anthony, wanting first in his Fischer way to be sure that he would be no burden. Instead he stayed for a few days at Grosvenor House, a Park Lane hotel, where he described to Ilse, Paul and Pat an air of genteel decay and coffee 'not wholly unlike the stuff at Marshall Square'. On the first day of his arrival he, Ruth and Anthony went for a mid-afternoon lunch to a restaurant in Hyde Park, and then for a walk around Kensington Gardens where old men still found the time to sail model yachts on the pond. The universe Bram confronted was very different from that which he had encountered when he first saw London in 1931 – but there may, after all, have been certain resonances. Fascism and racism were still astir in the world as they had been then, and now they were his to face directly.

When Bram did move to Ruth's, she found that the accumulated impact of the previous six months had taken their toll. Bram said nothing and showed nothing overtly, but he was forgetful, and Ruth could see he was strained and distraught. Anthony, more forthright, confronted him on the question of his future, saying his career at the Bar would be lost if he returned. 'Fuck my career,' replied Bram, and though the language was uncharacteristically blunt the sentiment was in keeping. Bram may have had doubts about his plans, but not about the proper place of his own desires and needs. Some who knew Bram at this time felt that the trauma he had undergone only galvanised the steeliness within, as he became, if anything, even more resolutely committed to the path of his decisions.

Yet this was not what most were allowed to see. Harold Wolpe, escaped now for about a year, saw Bram at a party given in his honour, and recalled that he was calm and in control, his usual friendly and genial self. In London Bram met eminent political figures, among them Michael Foot (the future leader of the Labour Party) and Lord Caradon, the British ambassador to the United Nations, whom he informed at length about conditions in South African jails – how Hugh Lewin had been beaten up by the police after John Harris's bomb had exploded, how a young activist, Suliman 'Babla' Salojee, had fallen seven storeys to his death while under police interrogation. An article in *The Observer* at the time described Bram as 'a stocky, red-faced man of fifty-six, with white hair and the quiet courtesy of an Afrikaner farmer' – and that too was the pose he adopted sitting on a park bench for the camera, prim hat placed firmly on his head, hand on umbrella, jaw drawn up benignly but firmly, almost as if (remarked Anthony Eastwood) Oom Paul Kruger had come to London. Mary Benson, back in London and present for some of these conversations, wrote a profile for *The Guardian*, and told how one of his questioners had asked him, 'Why go back?' 'Because I said I would,' came the simple reply, and Benson wrote that Bram's interlocutor had been 'struck forcibly by how extraordinarily cool he was, not in the least concerned about his own prospects'.

But, as in his response to Anthony, Bram was under no illusions as to what those prospects would be. A few months later he prepared an article – possibly intended for publication in London – entitled 'The Threat to the Legal Profession in South Africa'. Although his primary concern in writing it was to give an objective account of the dangers facing the profession as a whole, it was equally clear that the threat he would have to face would be personal. In the article Bram detailed the new ethos in which political trials occurred in South Africa, as well as particular assaults planned by the Minister of Justice. Since June 1963, he wrote, over 900 people had been detained in solitary confinement under the ninety-day law; many had been brutally tortured by electric shock treatment or physical assault; three had committed suicide. Probably in no other country in the world were there so many political prisoners who needed to be defended, but that was precisely what government legislation was being designed to prevent. The Admission of Advocates Act of 1964 had for the moment safeguarded the tradition whereby the courts controlled the admission of advocates to the Bar. But Bram also showed how two initial drafts of the law (it was these that dated from March 1962) had established provisions to exclude communists from legal practice, in concert with the Suppression of Communism Act. In fact, the reason these provisions had been postponed had more than a little to do with him. Bram quoted the Minister of Justice, B.J. Vorster, replying to a question on this matter in parliament in June: 'I deliberately did not include this [the prohibition of communists] in the Bill now, and do not intend introducing legislation this year, for the simple reason that . . . the two senior advocates appearing in the Rivonia case are acknowledged communists, and any legislation I introduce now will be construed by malicious persons outside as an attempt to stop those persons from defending the accused . . . ' But the Minister had given his assurance that from 1965 no attorney or advocate who was a communist would be allowed to practise, and that the relevant legislation would be amended accordingly. As Bram pointed out, since the Minister had the power to deem anyone communist virtually by decree, the outlook was depressing not only for the legal profession but also for all those requiring a defence in political trials.

Perhaps it would make Bram's choices easier: he had little prospect of anything, by way of a legal career, to protect. Mary Benson recalled how in talking of the detainees in London – of Lewin and Salojee – Bram could barely contain his 'wrath and terrible grief' (two days before his death Salojee, despite his lack of religious belief, had smuggled out a message to his wife asking her to pray for him). How could he not make common cause with them, if not in the law then by other means?

⁂

The Bayer case was due to begin in the middle of the month. Strictly speaking it was not in itself an appeal, but an application by Farbenfabriken AG for *leave* to appeal to the Privy Council. Three law lords, representing the Privy

Council, would hear argument by both sides and decide the matter. If leave were granted the case would come up in a year (and who knew where Bram would be by that stage); if not, that was where the proceedings would end. Bram was assigned temporary chambers in order to prepare his case (which he hardly needed given the earlier hearings, but took advantage of in his usual meticulous way), and the proceedings began on the morning of Thursday, 15 October, in the office of the Judicial Committee in Whitehall. August portraits of Lord Chancellors gazed down from the walls, and both Bram and his opposing counsel were robed and bewigged – though the three lords wore suits, as befitted their presence as Privy Counsellors rather than judges.

Anthony Eastwood went to watch, possibly the only member of the public in attendance, and recalled that Bram was confident of his case. It turned on a very narrow point (Bram wrote to Ilse that his opposing counsel had confided privately that the whole thing was hopeless, and that he was only doing it for the fee). None the less, when it was Bram's turn to argue, Anthony could see he was tense: despite his customary easy charm – the kind, remarked Anthony, that convinced judges they were on his side – the sweat was trickling down his face. It was something like an exam, with the essential outline of the problem known in advance, and the only question at issue the performance. The three law lords, all immensely learned and experienced, checked references, were sometimes blunt, anticipated exactly what was going to be said. Despite the general informality, one's whole life as a barrister – especially as an outsider in these surroundings – was on trial.

The case wasn't decided that Thursday, but was held over to the following Monday. That weekend Bram, Ruth and Anthony took off for a trip to Wales. It was a huge relief after the various tensions. The autumn weather was magnificent, and Bram described their progress to Ilse, writing in bed before dawn 'in a tiny pub in a tiny village beside the River Dee'. They had stopped off at Warwick where they had taken in the Castle as well as 'Mop Day', replete with a seventy-year-old local who tended an ox on the spit from ten at night until five the following afternoon, as he had for untold years before. They had come across Savignac ruins from the twelfth century at Buildwas Abbey, and Roman ruins at Wroxeter. Now, as Bram wrote, they faced the dazzling prospect of the Welsh mountains and coast before turning east towards London again.

The following Monday the case was decided abruptly. Bram had told Ilse that on the Thursday he had argued for only three-quarters of an hour, but had managed to repair 'quite a lot of damage done by the other side'. On the Monday he spoke for another hour and a half, and then the two opposing counsel left the room while the law lords took four minutes to come to a conclusion. In a judgment of less than a dozen words they ended a case that had lasted nine years, rejecting the application to appeal. Bram then asked that his opponents be ordered to pay costs, which was granted. Newspapers proclaimed Fischer's 'Triumph', and though in public Bram's modesty held sway, in private he confessed himself delighted – not least, as he remarked to Anthony, because Bayer had been associated with the Nazis during the war. In truth it had been a workaday case for him: unhistrionic, civil and polite, it was the kind that suited his legal personality perfectly, the kind that in a different world might have remained his speciality.

In Bram's letter from Wales, he also mentioned Sholto, who had just been handed a second period of ninety days' detention. This had allowed Ilse to return to Cape Town, away from the constant stress of Johannesburg. From that point of view, remarked Bram pragmatically, he did not regret Sholto's extended detention, nor the fact that he had not yet been charged: 'In a sense time is always on our side.' It is unlikely that there was ever a moment when he surrendered that belief.

⁂

Bram still had until the end of the month before the projected date of his return, and had to think seriously about his plans. At some level, despite his public and private assurances, there was still the question of what he ought to do. He discussed it with Ruth and Anthony, rehearsing the various angles and dimensions. Anthony argued that he should stay in London: in South Africa his political life was as good as over, whereas he could achieve much more from outside the country. Bram listened carefully and thoughtfully; perhaps he was just keeping his thoughts to himself.

From Bram's comrades inside the country came other urgings, that those outside should not try to make him remain in England. There was in fact a degree of bitterness among those who had stayed behind about some of those who had left. Not all who had gone into exile had done so with Party permission, and as the number of departures steadily increased it was hard to avoid the dismaying impression of floodgates having been opened. Once there had been an implicit agreement in the political family that they would all stick together, if necessary by going to jail for as long as it took: this at the least would be their expression of solidarity with South Africans for whom there was no other choice. Circumstances had necessarily altered that presumption, but if Bram were now to stay outside – he who was always so insistent on the need to keep rooted, who had given his word he would return and therefore embodied that insistence – it would be an unbearable blow.

Bram had discussed his options with those at home; now he also had to consult his comrades in London. It was difficult to see many people – Bram had given an undertaking to refrain from political activity while overseas, and even in England he could be followed – but in one way and another he took soundings. Later some suspected that Bram's return to South Africa was ordered by the Party, but this appears not to have been the case. The principal impulse among the exiles seems to have been to make him break his promise and remain outside. Towards the end of his stay Bram had the equivalent of a formal meeting with the London collective of the SACP. Given the circumstances the setting wasn't formal – it was held on a bench in a park – but that did not make it any the less intense. Many years later Joe Slovo, who was there with Yusuf Dadoo, Michael Harmel and others, remembered it vividly, as they argued for three or four hours over whether Bram should return to South Africa. 'We tried desperately to get him to stay outside, to break his bail conditions . . . And you know, with Bram, it was a question of just pure personal loyalty, and political judgement, and I don't know which was the more important thing for him at that point.'

Bram explained his feelings to the others. In political terms – choosing for himself if not for anyone else – he felt that the time had come when leaders ought not to leave but be prepared to stake everything. He was under no illusion that this would cause a complete transformation, but it might have an inspirational effect when people had become thoroughly demoralised. On a personal level, he had given his word that he would return, and all of those listening to him – on what was after all a very different kind of 'bench' – were aware of the significance for Bram that he had given his undertaking in a court of law, of which he was an officer. Bram talked of his discussions with his comrades inside the country: on that level alone he felt it would be a betrayal if he did not return. In a way the London exiles felt they had no standing against such authority: the South African group was trying to reconstitute the Party inside the country, and had to have relative pre-eminence. None the less, remarked Slovo, the London collective might still have taken a decision on the basis of 'democratic centralism', and ordered Bram not to return. But that was not what happened. 'He convinced us,' said Slovo. 'He convinced us – that's what happened.'

As it turned out, Bram was talking not just about whether he should return to South Africa, but what action he should take thereafter. The point was not merely to surrender to an inevitable jail sentence, but to find a way of playing a continued political role. In his South African discussions he had already raised the possibility that he would go underground at some stage: given the extremity of the situation this seemed one of the few meaningful ways of maintaining an active as well as symbolic resistance. It was a radical and dramatic suggestion, and the London group wanted him to keep his options open. If the time came when all other forms of activity were shut down, he could jump bail and leave the country – or, if he really thought it necessary, go underground at that stage. As he spoke to the others that day, it became quite clear that Bram's preference was for the latter. Though these choices must have involved specific kinds of anguish, and not merely on the political level – had the inner map of his life ever suggested such possibilities? – Bram had weighed things up and, as Joe Slovo understood, was resolute.

Bram's brothers had no doubt that he would return: 'His place was here,' said Paul. Rusty Bernstein felt that Bram would have broken his word in a revolutionary cause, but that it was a sense of responsibility to others that made him return. Anthony Eastwood saw, in Bram's adherence to the promise he had made, an innocent sense of ethics for a Marxist, and a quaint loyalty to the legal tradition from which he had come. Joe Slovo had a similar impression, speaking of Bram's 'rather touching fidelity' as a revolutionary prepared on one level to sacrifice his life, but on another committed to personal honour and the importance of carrying out a personal undertaking.

As for Bram, after his London meeting on the bench he was still tense, but not about the question of his return. He had wanted the agreement of his comrades, and had received it, and now the thing to do was go home. Before he left England he made a last visit to Oxford, where he saw the Warden of New College and made arrangements for his son Paul to attend the college should it become necessary: Oxford attachments remained, and supplemented the other kind. Perhaps a number of those who knew Bram, or saw him in Johannesburg or England at this time, considered that the truly revolutionary thing about him was that, beneath the mystery and grief of his personal tragedy, he really was prepared to keep his honour.

He left London on 1 November, and reached South Africa the following day.

Ruth, who saw him off at the airport, was stoic in the Fischer manner when it came to matters of emotion. For her the traumatic moment had been when she left South Africa after her wedding and felt that she would never see her parents again – and that had come true for Molly. Now there was an air of inevitability (Bram had somehow intimated to her the possibility that he would go underground), and she understood things in a different dimension. She said that 'Bram was really deeply depressed, but being Bram he'd just keep going, and one would sort of collude with that really'. A gathering sense of inevitability also affected Bram's brother Gus, who began at this time (as he recalled) to have a 'curiously helpless feeling' about the unfolding events of his brother's life.

In Johannesburg Ilse had been having a truly torrid time. Part of it involved doing for Bram what Molly had done, running his political messages, acting now (to some extent) as his confidante, and about this she had no ambiguities. But, since many of her friends were in detention, she also spent much of the six months after Molly died taking food from one jail to another. Sometimes these visits were awful – seeing Sholto after Babla Salojee died – and sometimes they had their bizarrely comic aspects – fending off the advances of a policeman after he had helped arrange a late-night visit to Sholto. In effect Ilse had fairly regular access to Sholto because she claimed that he was her fiancé: there was nothing particularly remarkable about the invention – just a standard strategy to claim a relationship with a detainee.

The chief purpose of these visits was to relay messages in and out, usually in the seams of the clothing that detainees were permitted from outside. Often there was little of significance to say – just words of greeting and comfort – but in return the detainees would sometimes give news, for instance, of who was talking to the police. When Sholto finally made a statement he became deeply depressed, and let Ilse know. Ilse wrote back telling him to blame Molly for everything: a mother's memory became subject to immediate political needs, and that too was understood as a necessity. Later, when Ilse returned to finish her degree in Cape Town, she provided some of the same comforts to Alan Brooks, whom she had the temerity to claim also as a fiancé. (Two of them: one in Johannesburg, one in Cape Town: it seemed conceivable.) In fact there was a time when she thought she really might marry Alan Brooks: subterfuge and true feeling might coincide, but, if so, it couldn't be revealed.

As for Paul, he was also under pressure, though inevitably of a different kind. Each of the Fischer children had had to face some kind of crisis in their final year of school. For Ruth it was the Treason arrests, for Ilse the State of Emergency and Molly's detention. Now Paul too was in his final year and, when Molly died, had been at home to study for his mid-year exams. As the end of the year approached – as Bram was picked up, detained, released, arrested, went to London, and returned to stand trial – Paul had to face his final exams. He switched on his own saline machine, administered his own insulin injections, made sure his sugar balance was right, and achieved a first-class pass with two distinctions – an extraordinary result under any conditions.

Bram and Molly had never forced any kind of political action on their children, but their lives had been fashioned amidst the invasions and gathering circumscription of politics. Each knew the larger reasons, but each had to find their own inner delineation of a response, and it was work that sometimes had to be done alone.

⁂

Towards the end of October 1964, a number of political detainees, including some of Bram's co-trialists, filed affidavits in the Pretoria Supreme Court regarding police torture. John Harris, Adelaide Joseph (petitioning on behalf of her husband Paul), Mary Moodley (who had been released with Molly after the State of Emergency), Norman Levy, Costa Gazides, Ivan Schermbrucker, Paul Trewhela, Ann Nicholson and Hugh Lewin testified to beatings, chalk squares in which they had to stand for up to forty hours at a time, boasts that they would be made mad, Gestapo mottoes cited proudly by interrogators that guilt or innocence was irrelevant so long as a subject confessed.

It was in these circumstances, with the police holding a brutal upper hand and a major trial about to begin, that the Communist Party lurched along in obvious disarray. Earlier, before leaving for London, Bram had held a meeting with Violet Weinberg and Lesley Schermbrucker, in which he told them that they would have to serve on the central committee. There had for some time been a plan that if the husbands were arrested, the wives would take over, but its implementation now meant less the transcendence of an institutional sexism within the Party than the necessity for desperate stopgap measures. Also new on the central committee was a man named Bartholomew Hlapane, who had once been detained at the time of the Rivonia arrests, and who some of his comrades feared had come close to cracking at that time. It was at best a shaky arrangement all round.

The trial opened in the Johannesburg Regional Court on 16 November. To those already arraigned had been added Ivan Schermbrucker and Lewis Baker, while Pixie Benjamin, who had embarked on a long hunger strike, had been dropped. That meant there were fourteen on trial; Bram was still on bail, as was Hymie Barsel, against whom there was very little evidence. Among the defence counsel was Ismail Mahomed, who because of apartheid's laws could not get rooms in chambers (he used Bram's and Berrangé's for consultation). Three charges faced the accused: that they were members of the Communist Party; that they had participated in the activities of the Communist Party; and that they had furthered the aims of the Communist Party. Though the prosecution had spoken rather grandly at the time of Bram's bail hearing of sentences of up to thirty years, in effect the maximum sentence in the

Magistrates' Court was for three years on any single charge. It remained a mystery as to why the case was being tried in this form, and why the charges were relatively mild, given the options. But it may have been, in the aftermath of the Rivonia Trial, that the state wished to show itself as relatively benign and wholly untroubled by the communist irruption.

When Bram and the others first appeared in court the public galleries were filled, and the overflow of people watched through the windows. Police in pairs guarded all the entrances. After the prosecution had outlined its case, it called, as its first witness, Piet Beyleveld. This caused, reported the newspapers, a 'sensation' in the trial, but the fact was that Bram knew all about it, and had been communicating with Beyleveld for some time. One route was through Beyleveld's wife who, because her husband was co-operating with the police, was allowed regular access. She contacted Violet Weinberg, who in turn contacted Bram. According to Violet, Beyleveld had discussed his plans with his wife, insisting that all the accused stood to face more serious charges and ten years in jail each if he refused to testify. His wife felt that a jail sentence was preferable: at least he would be able to emerge after that time with head held high. Bram wrote back, secreting notes through the laundry exchange, telling Beyleveld that the threat of ten years meant nothing, and that he must not give evidence under any circumstances. In this strange negotiation between betrayer and betrayed, Bram sent messages under the noses of the police right up until the day before the trial, hoping that Beyleveld would change his mind. He had told Mary Benson in London that if Beyleveld took the stand and looked him in the eye, he would not give evidence. But Beyleveld never looked him in the eye.

When Beyleveld was called, he spoke of his own history in the Party, incriminating each of the accused in turn. He told of £8000 he had received from the London committee of the SACP, and how this had been distributed. He spoke of codenames in the Party (which he at last revealed as 'the Family'): his own name had been 'Van' and later 'Rick'; Bram's was 'Jan'. In 1962 he had been a member of the same group as Fischer, Middleton and Nicholson; he had served on an area committee with Esther Barsel, Levy, Middleton and Baker. Bram Fischer had attended four of seven central committee meetings since August 1963, and Ivan Schermbrucker five; Fischer, Schermbrucker and Hilda Bernstein were on the secretariat which carried out day-to-day activities. As he went on, Beyleveld gave some insight into the state of the Party and its inner workings in the new state of crisis. His reconstituted district committee, demolished by detentions, had been forced to meet on street corners for five minutes at a time. Prospective members were recommended by the district committees, but had to be approved by the central committee. Gerald Ludi had been accepted, as had Ann Nicholson; Trewhela and Middleton were already members when he joined; Sylvia Neame was drafted into Middleton's group when she arrived in Johannesburg, and later into Levy's. With each account Beyleveld was specific and mentioned names, and each time the jail doors closed a little more solidly on his comrades.

Yet in some respects his behaviour was ambiguous if not contradictory. For Esther Barsel his testimony was critical, because there was no other eyewitness evidence against her; but Beyleveld did protect her husband Hymie, saying that he didn't know him. He also shielded Bram to some extent, talking of his presence on the central committee only after August 1963 (this was after the Rivonia arrests, when Beyleveld himself had come on to the committee), and limiting Bram's involvement to matters of non-violence. There were moments that suggested a man confronting the blank wall of the end of his life. When the prosecutor asked him whether he had been in favour of the social analysis contained in the SACP Programme, Beyleveld replied, 'I was. I still am.' When Berrangé, cross-examining, asked him if he was a perjurer or a traitor, Beyleveld said that he had confronted 'a set of circumstances' and faced 'a decision'. Berrangé, with his usual lack of mercy, pressed the point, raising the ARM trial in which the judge had remarked that Adrian Leftwich was 'an insult to the genus *rattus*'. He wanted to know if Beyleveld fitted that description. Beyleveld said that if Berrangé wanted to put him in that category he wouldn't argue, but that was not where he placed himself. He told Berrangé that he had not been tortured by the police, and had been questioned only for six or seven hours; he had held nothing back at that stage, and was not doing so now. When Berrangé questioned him on the ease with which he had made his statement, Beyleveld said, 'I recognised that the Party had suffered complete defeat . . . The shock to me was that the police knew as much as they did.' Berrangé asked him if he still owed loyalty to the Party (trying to imply that Beyleveld's testimony might be untrustworthy). Beyleveld replied, 'In the circumstances I cannot tell you that.' When Berrangé pursued the issue, Beyleveld said, 'Let's put it then that I've failed.'

Harold Hanson, taking over the cross-examination, tried a different tack, turning the discussion towards Bram, whom he represented. In response to his questions Beyleveld agreed that Bram had been respected by all classes of society, although he had never concealed his political views. When the Communist Party had been legal he was widely known as a member; he was a champion of the poor and of socialism, and his personal advice was constantly sought by all kinds of men. 'He has been widely revered,' remarked Hanson, to which Beyleveld replied, 'Yes, and by me too. He still is.' 'I was interested to hear you say that,' Hanson responded, and then continued, 'I don't like to put this in my client's presence, but he is a man who carries something of an aura of a saint-like quality, does he not?' To which Beyleveld's simple reply was, 'I agree.'

And yet, as Beyleveld admitted to Hanson, he was quite prepared to put Bram in jail. All betrayals have their own story: perhaps there was still a sense of loyalty under it all, stitched both visibly and invisibly into the abjectness of a surrender. In return for Beyleveld's testimony he was given an indemnity from prosecution and released, to be produced later as a witness at other trials; for his performance both then and later he earned the undying contempt and ostracism of his comrades.

The next witness in the trial was Ludi. He had stories to tell that were by turns spectacular and lurid. He was introduced to the world in James Bond fashion (although he said he didn't like James Bond) as Agent Q018, a warrant officer in the Security Police, and he detailed his progress as a student, then as a reporter on the *Rand Daily Mail* and *The Star*, through the Congress of Democrats, various youth movements and discussion groups, until he had finally been recruited into the Communist Party in May 1963. He claimed that over a period of three or four years he had made five or six hundred reports to the police, and gave some account of what they had contained. He had attended cell meetings at Jean Middleton's flat, where among others he had met Bram, whom he described as 'a very friendly person', and who had warned him at their first encounter of the dangers of police infiltration. Bram had given lectures on economics, had encouraged the others to whip up publicity about ninety-day detentions (reporters were especially useful for that), and had even wanted, said Ludi, to harass the Security Police, phoning them up with threats in the night. He spoke of a tremendous shake-up and reorganisation in the Party after the Rivonia arrests, and detailed gossip and schism within what was after all a small and besieged grouping – to which he had made his own contribution by fomenting rumours that Marius Schoon was a spy.

Some of his evidence showed just how badly unravelled the Communist Party had become. When his cell's post office box had become inaccessible, Ludi was asked to arrange a new one. It was a convenient opportunity: he referred the matter directly to the police, who opened up a new box under a false name, and thereafter any Party mail was first read by the Special Branch before being handed on to Ludi for his group. He spoke in court of a top-secret document – this was 'Time for Reassessment', warning specifically of the dangers of betrayal and police surveillance – which his group was supposed to read collectively and then destroy. But Jean Middleton, against all Party regulations, had lent it to him, and he had passed it on to a Sergeant Kleingeld, who had made a photocopy before returning the original. At various times Ludi had made tapes of meetings, and recorded one meeting in his car. He had tipped off the police on even the slightest activity, such as slogan painting, which they then watched mildly from a few feet away. Added to all this was evidence from Lieutenant Broodryk regarding the flat next door to Middleton's, which he had rented in the name of Frans Rheeder for Klaus Schroeder (identified now as Agent Q043). What Beyleveld had said may well have been correct: there was very little the police did not know.

Some of Ludi's revelations both in his testimony and under cross-examination sank into the sleazier dimensions of invention. Letters he had written to a woman identified alternately as Malay and Indian were produced in court, tawdry evidence of a rather neurotic and self-obsessed love. Ludi had signed them 'Lover Man', 'Turk', and 'L. Geraldo, the Great Bullfighter'. They were full of thoughts of leaving the country for Madagascar (a 'racially harmonious place') and of hatred and frustration in South Africa. He freely admitted that he had tried to seduce women 'as part of my duties', and that these included women who weren't white, in order to prove his multi-racial credentials. He described a party at the Fischers' house where guests had plunged into the swimming pool. Berrangé commented, 'Naked of course,' and Ludi replied, 'Of course' – at which there was general laughter in court.

When Denis Kuny, for the defence, asked Ludi if he enjoyed being a spy, he replied that it was 'far better than being a professional lawyer'. But neither his slipperiness nor his occasional desultory humour could conceal the damage he was doing, and the blank cynicism of his actions. The Communist Party was being dragged through the mud – some real, some invented for the occasion – and there was little they could do about it. Nor could they hide the fact that the Party was to all intents and purposes smashed. As the evidence went on through December, Bram listening to it day by day was faced with the second aspect of the choice he had made in London.

⁂

True courage engages not the possible but the impossible.

Perhaps it had something to do with Piet Beyleveld after all. Joel Joffe, one of the attorneys in the trial, recalled that Bram was hurt deeply by Beyleveld's evidence – not just politically but personally. He hadn't believed that anyone would crack so easily, let alone a leader, someone he had worked with and trusted for so long. Moreover, the fact that Beyleveld was an Afrikaner was shattering, especially in contrast with the courage of others. Just before the case opened, Bram had written to Mary Benson about Vuyisile Mini, once in the Treason Trial, and now executed for his political activities. The execution, wrote Bram, had been 'a terrible blow', but he also described how Mini, a few days before his death, had been offered commutation of his sentence if he would agree to testify against Wilton Mkwayi. Mini, in the most extreme of circumstances, had refused, and nothing could define loyalty more clearly. But Beyleveld, under little threat, had caved in as if supported by nothing more than air, in apparent complicity with an Afrikaner government. Bram was always reluctant to judge individuals, remarking that one had to understand the special pressures that faced them, but this hurt more than he was able to say. Surely it was now up to at least one Afrikaner to prove his good faith.

It was when he saw that Beyleveld and Ludi were giving evidence that Bram called the reconstituted central committee together to outline his proposal for going underground. He had already discussed this with Ivan and Eli before leaving for London, but to those gathered around now it came as a surprise, if not wholly as a shock. Issy Heymann, an older member of the Party in the Bolshevik tradition, now newly on the committee, remembered that Bram wouldn't give his opinion at first, but wanted to hear what the others would say: three were for the idea, and two were hesitant. Violet Weinberg was more emphatic – she said they told Bram he was crazy, and that no possible good could come of his plan. If he were sentenced now, it would be for a limited term, after which life (including political life) could resume; but if he went underground and were recaptured, no one could tell what would happen. Mixed into the political calculations of Violet and the others was their personal affection and admiration for Bram, their unwillingness, after the trauma of the previous few months, to see him placed in even greater jeopardy simply because of his own inherent integrity and goodness. But – just as in London – Violet remembered that Bram persuaded them, insisting that escaping for even three months would constitute a victory. It was only when he received the assent of his comrades that he told them he had already begun making preparations.

As always, family matters needed attention. During the court recess for Christmas, Bram journeyed around Johannesburg with Ilse, who had just completed her degree in Cape Town. Now her aim was to be articled as an attorney, and so she and Bram called in at various firms. None would take her: the Fischer name – stretching from Oupa Abraham through Percy to Bram – apparently counted for nothing. The general paranoia about communism, fuelled by the trial and combined with the threats of the Minister of Justice, had created an atmosphere of prevarication and fear. A profession that had revered Bram refused the most straightforward of jobs to his daughter. Some asked whether, if Bram were jailed, Ilse would make appeals to have him freed. She – with some knowledge now of his real intentions (she said her inter-viewers didn't know the half of it) – was not prepared to give any consoling assurance. Finally a firm was prepared to employ her: they paid her R30 a month to type, and immediately put her on to debt collecting.

During that recess Bram worked hard at his plans. He had met a couple who were set designers for PACT (the Performing Arts Council of the Transvaal), who advised him on disguises. He discussed the practicalities with Violet and Lesley: safe houses had to be arranged and contact routines established, as well as codes for communicating with London (Bram may have brought some of these with him when he returned). Ilse was involved to a certain extent, of necessity now a co-conspirator. Bram was also, at this time, seeing Mary Benson, in Johannesburg to witness the trial, and she persuaded him to draw up a statement to be published overseas, presumably after his sentencing. The article, which Bram duly produced, contained in equal proportions his fears for a civil war in South Africa, and his optimism regarding its prospects if libera-ted. Stability could not be based on oppression, he wrote: 'As we know from history – including the history of South Africa – if the struggle for freedom is smothered in one place or for the time being, it flares up again before long.' The real danger, as always, was that South Africans would be driven 'by the terrorist methods of the State into a violent and chaotic form of struggle'. The long-term interests of whites lay not in maintaining white supremacy, but in extending human rights to all. But a peaceful transition could only be brought about if the government agreed to negotiate with all sections of the people, 'in particular, with the non-white leaders at present gaoled on Robben Island or in exile'. As events transpired, it was something of a prophetic account.

When the trial resumed in January there were further appearances by Ludi, and by Professor Murray who, dredged up by yet another prosecution, re-iterated in a weak parody of his Treason Trial performance that there could be no communism without violence. It must have been galling for Bram, having to listen to the worn-out ramblings of a man whose credibility had been demolished so comprehensively by his defence team just four years before. Bram had gone from an advocate to an accused; and now his life was to under-go yet a further transformation.

On 15 January 1965, following a defence application, the court adjourned for ten days. During the following week Bram finalised his article in collaboration with Mary Benson. Though hardly a revolutionary document it required clandestine arrangements of its own, and she duly posted it off to the London *Observer*, to await the go-ahead to be published. (Ultimately when it appeared, in circumstances Mary did not quite expect, it was excised from South African editions, and the South African papers hardly mentioned it.) On Friday 22nd, Bram saw her one last time, and asked her to be sure to be present when the court reconvened the following week. But when she arrived in court on the Monday, Bram was not there, and never arrived.

By the time this reaches you I shall be a long way from Johannesburg and shall absent myself from the remainder of the trial. But I shall still be in the country to which I said I would return when I was granted bail.

At first there was nothing untoward when Bram did not appear on Monday 25th, even after the magistrate had made his entrance. But then Harold Hanson rose to say that a letter had been delivered to him that morning which he would like to read out to the court. It had been addressed to him by Bram, and this was the letter he was reading out now.

I wish you to inform the Court that my absence, though deliberate, is not intended in any way to be disrespectful. Nor is it prompted by any fear of the punishment which might be inflicted on me. Indeed I realise fully that my eventual punishment may be increased by my present conduct.

I have not taken this step lightly. As you will no doubt understand, I have experienced great conflict between my desire to stay with my fellow accused and, on the other hand, to try to continue the political work I believe to be essential. My decision was made only because I believe that it is the duty of every true opponent of this Government to remain in this country and to oppose its monstrous policy of apartheid with every means in his power. That is what I shall do for as long as I can.

In brief, the reasons which have compelled me to take this step and which I wish you to communicate to the Court are the following:

There are already over 2,500 political prisoners in our prisons. These men and women are not criminals but the staunchest opponents of apartheid.

Cruel, discriminatory laws multiply each year, bitterness and hatred of the Government and its laws are growing daily. No outlet for this hatred is permitted because political rights have been removed, National organisations have been outlawed and leaders, not in gaol, have been banned from speaking and meeting. People are hounded by Pass Laws and by Group Area controls. Torture by solitary confinement, and worse, has been legalised by an elected Parliament – surely an event unique in history.

It is no answer to all this to say that Bantustans will be created nor that the country is prosperous. The vast majority of the people are prevented from sharing in the country's wealth by the Colour Bar in industry and mining and by the prohibition against owning land save in relatively small and grossly over-crowded parts of the country where, in any case, there exist no mines or indus-tries. The idea that Bantustans will provide any solution would deceive no-one but a White South African.

What is needed is for White South Africans to shake themselves out of their complacency, a complacency intensified by the present economic boom built upon racial discrimination.

Unless this whole intolerable system is changed radically and rapidly, disaster must follow. Appalling bloodshed and civil war will become inevitable because, as long as there is oppression of a majority, such oppression will be fought with increasing hatred.

To try to avoid this becomes a supreme duty, particularly for an Afrikaner, because it is largely the representatives of my fellow Afrikaners who have been responsible for the worst of these discriminatory laws.

These are my reasons for absenting myself from Court. If by my fight I can encourage even some people to think about, to understand and to abandon the policies they now so blindly follow, I shall not regret any punishment I may incur.

I can no longer serve justice in the way I have attempted to do during the past thirty years. I can do it only in the way I have now chosen.

Finally, I would like you to urge upon the Court to bear in mind that if it does have to punish any of my fellow accused, it will be punishing them for holding the ideas today that will be universally accepted tomorrow.

With his characteristic thoughtfulness Bram had added a final paragraph for Hanson: 'Please accept my deepest thanks for handling my case as you have. I do hope that my conduct will not embarrass you in any way.'

It was a defining and crystallising moment.

Those who heard Hanson read Bram's letter that day took it in varying ways. Among the accused, recalled Mollie Anderson, there was an inner feeling of delight, and smiles they could hardly contain. Later they heard that Bram was concerned they would think he had deserted them; but rather than abandonment, they felt the solidarity he had expressed. The Security Police, truculent, demanded the envelope the letter had come in from Hanson, who remained quite cool throughout the proceedings. The prosecutor, Liebenberg, was shrill in his denunciation: 'It is the desperate act of a desperate man and the action of a coward,' he told the court. 'He makes a political speech through his Counsel and tells us that bloodshed will follow in this country. It is a disgraceful act.' Most likely he, too, did not know the half of it.

Ruth and Ilse's view was that Bram would never have gone underground if Molly had been alive. Now it did not matter what happened to him. Ruth and Ilse could look after themselves, and as for Paul, Bram had made special provision: in January, before he went underground, Paul left for London, to stay with Ruth and Anthony. This was not only to protect him from the coming trauma of Bram's disappearance, or from detention, which Paul would surely not survive; pragmatically as always, Bram sent him off with lists of clandestine addresses to deliver in London. Paul, aware of Bram's plans, took his brief of secrecy seriously, not even mentioning a word to Ruth until the day set for Bram's vanishing.

Before the Christmas adjournment, and while Ilse was still in Cape Town, Pat Davidson had been alone in the house with Bram and Paul, and became close to Bram at that time. She remembered that when he returned from London he was more positive and calm about things. But she also said he was in no state to decide anything. Bram worked, concentrated on the case, and for the most part was under control. But she also remembered that he still cried about Molly, and drank more than he should. Pat, who had some intimation of his plans, never thought he wasn't equipped to carry them out, but looking back she felt that he was on the edge of a breakdown. Molly was dead, he was on trial, his career was over, his Party smashed, his friends in jail or exile. It was an end, she said, and he saw it; going underground was like 'committing suicide'.

Liz Lewin, who had been in the car during the accident, also saw him then, just before she left for overseas. Bram told her he was going underground. She said he felt his solitude very badly, and was missing Molly. 'I think he missed her enormously. I do know he was very lonely, because just before I left he talked to me about that – about how lonely he was.' Years later, when he was in prison, she wrote to Bram and quoted the first two lines of the Afrikaans poem 'Eensaamheid' [Solitude]. He replied that the coincidence was extraordinary, because as a boy he had carried that poem around with him everywhere.

Perhaps Molly's death both condemned him to, and allowed him to find, a certain freedom, confronting with recognition and acceptance as much as dread the solitude he had first known as a child when he had felt singled out to be special. Now he was radically alone. Yet, though the outer shape of his life had been wholly transformed, this did not mean that his innermost impulses had been utterly extinguished. As long as he lived he could hold on to those, define them in this negative moment as he had hoped to more positively, call into being a future that might never be his in the present. The path to transcendence may lie through despair as much as through glory, but either way it is one before which we can only stand in awe.

That Christmas Bram went to see Issy Maisels, back in Johannesburg after his term on the bench in Rhodesia. Issy and his wife were renting a house until they could find something more permanent, and Bram came to say that the house in Beaumont Street would be vacant, if they wanted to take it. But Issy felt that he couldn't. The prospect of living in Bram and Molly's home after she had died and while he was on trial or in jail was just too sad to imagine. When Bram said goodbye, Issy felt that he would never see him again – and he didn't.

❧

Rissik was paid out in full for the bail money, as Ruth had known he would be when Bram first suggested he might go underground. There were also others he had to address.

Early on the Saturday morning before the court reconvened, Bram sat down to write a number of letters. One of them was to Mary Benson, whom he had seen the previous day but whom he had given no inkling of his plans. In his letter he assured her this was not because he didn't trust her, but because he dared not run the risk of allowing her to be considered even remotely as an accessory. He wrote that what he was about to do might in some ways appear 'crazy', but it was necessary for someone among the whites to demonstrate a spirit of real revolt. That was why he had returned from London, and it was guiding his actions now: 'I have left the trial because I also want to demonstrate that no one should meekly submit to our barbaric laws.' As he looked out at the garden, his thoughts were on Molly who had created it. 'It is very early in the morning and a glow is touching the garden that Molly & I tended for more than 25 years. I have wondered and wondered what she would have advised in the present circumstances. I think she would have approved.'

He also wrote to Ilse. With Paul and Ruth both in London she was the one now literally closest to him; perhaps in his mind she had in some way replaced Molly because of his belief in her political future. Bram may have been in emotional extremity, but that did not prevent his customary care. In fact, he wrote Ilse two letters, the first for the police to find, so that she too would not be considered a collaborator.

23rd Jan. 1965.

Ilse my darling,

I wish I could be with you when you open this – just to steady you a bit when you find out I've left home and am going to try and carry on my political work in hiding.

Apart from the difficulty of making the decision to leave the accused and possibly be accused myself of running away, I have been haunted by the idea of leaving you with everything to handle – the house, chambers &c – and doing so without even saying goodbye.

But it could not have been otherwise. This was the one occasion on which I simply could not consult you about a major decision.

So this will have to be my goodbye to you. I have written some details to Pat & have enclosed in her envelope a copy of a letter I am sending to Harold [Hanson]. That will explain something of what I feel.

Hold thumbs for me as I shall hold mine for you. Don't worry. We shall be again together in happier times.

All my love,
Bram.

The second letter was more personal.

Strictly private & confidential.
Ilse my darling,

I've written you a note – a bit formal – because it may fall into the hands of the police. Even this may, but you can read it and tear it up if you wish.

The sun is pouring into our garden, and presently I shall wake you up and we shall go out for what shall be one of our last swims. We shall look around at what has become a lovely place and both our hearts will be breaking because we shall know that inevitably and quite apart from my decision, explained in my other letter, we had to leave it all.

Ours has been a lovely home with a beautiful garden. Many, many years ago when old man Hutton & I used to catch the bus together, he said to me that our garden would one day become a showpiece, and that came true. But to me the garden and home have always been much more than a showpiece. They have been a sort of epitome of all that Molly was and what she stood for: Friendliness and warmth, strength and love. God, what a terrible thing I did when I had that accident. At times I could nearly go mad with remorse & despair.

I would have done so, I think, but for the help which you & Ruth & Paul gave me. You've all been wonderful, but I want to say something about you personally: some of the things one finds it difficult to speak. You must believe me.

You are a beautiful creature with a very quick mind and a strong personality. I'm sure you are a born leader. You have in you more of Molly than either of the others. People will turn to you for comfort or, in a crisis, for a lead. You must recognize this. You must use it to *lead*.

Bless you, when I started out I did not mean to moralize. I was going to talk about our home and Molly.

I suppose if you look at it as a whole one should not allow oneself to be broken by a death. Death must come, sooner or later. The vital thing is that it should not be drawn out, with suffering. Therefore one must turn to life and away from death, however deeply one loved the dead. Of the past we must think only of the magnificent years we had with Molly, despite all our tribulations. It was a life that was real and glowing.

I'm sure the future will bring you the same sort of life. We shall all get past the stage where the main sensation is one of a great vacuum; where daily one wants to turn to a person who is not there.

Sholto spoke to me last night. He said if anything happened to me, he'd be able to look after you. It was good of him to speak at this moment. I have no doubt that if you two marry you can make a magnificent life together. He has all the qualities that match yours. I'm sure you two will not only live to see the S.A. we all want but will play a major part in achieving it.

Bram.

When a father writes to a daughter in such circumstances, whole worlds swim into and out of focus. Yet, amidst the emotion and inexpressible feeling, the two letters showed that Bram had established alibis for everyone – for Ilse, Pat, and even for Hanson. There was a meticulous and tender grace in such care.

Bram had discussed the first letter with Ilse; in fact, he gave it to her directly before he went. But the second he left for her to find after he was gone, hinting in its opening lines that the police might find it too: perhaps the first might not sound like a real goodbye. In the event the police did find it when they searched the house, for Ilse was as sentimental as Bram, and had tucked it away in her underclothes. She felt the second letter was one reason why she was not prosecuted later.

As for Bram, it was clear: within the law or without, his life was given to the cause of justice – a supreme duty, as he had written.

CHAPTER 13

UNDERGROUND

23 January – 11 November 1965

'ADV. FISCHER VERMIS'; 'GROOT SOEKTOG NA FISCHER'. Three-quarter-inch headlines in the *Vaderland* and *Transvaler* told their story: Advocate Fischer had disappeared, and a countrywide search was under way. Ilse was interviewed by the papers: 'Father fled as I slept,' reported the *Rand Daily Mail*, recounting how, when Ilse and Pat Davidson realised Bram was not up in time for court, they had knocked on his door and received no reply. Entering his room they had found it empty, save for a pile of letters alongside the bed to friends and legal advisers. 'I was shocked when I saw my father had gone,' was Ilse's comment.

Of course that was not how it happened, and if Ilse was shocked it was not in that way.

Ilse had to be involved, because it was she who had to help Bram escape. During the months after Molly died, and especially in those last few weeks of preparation, there was an emotional proximity between father and daughter that had not existed in quite the same way before. Ilse was now not only daughter but collaborator, affiliated through sympathy and personal outrage to the cause of her father, and all the untold ambiguities of familial loyalty could be channelled and harnessed in this form. Through what had happened to Molly, through her own experience, the detention of Sholto, Alan Brooks and others, Bram's world was now also hers. They talked and planned in her room, tucked away upstairs at the back of the house, using the Rivonia Trial technique of keywords on paper – the harsh training of the last few years now a way of life – or they went out into the garden, the setting of a family's identity now given a starker utilitarian value. All the time they knew how closely they were being watched. Evening strolls to walk the dog revealed odd cars parked about the neighbourhood, some empty, some bearing blank-faced figures in suits. They also had to gather the clothing and equipment Bram would need for his disappearance. Observing a middle-aged trousseau accumulating under his bed, Pat asked in her straightforward way what was up. So she was brought into it too – or perhaps that was Bram's way of engineering a suitable form for Ilse to accept Pat's participation.

The departure was set for the Saturday before the court reconvened. Early that morning Bram wrote his final letters, among them his two letters to Ilse, one of which he gave her, one of which he secreted behind. Then, at about nine, he, Ilse and Pat went via the kitchen through a connecting door into the garage, to avoid being seen from the street. Bram squeezed on to the floor of their small Volkswagen Beetle, between the front and back seats. One of the others opened the garage doors: Ilse was to drive, Pat was in the front passenger seat. And so it was that they left the house, Ilse's first task to shake the inevitable police tail following her. Uncertainty and daring kept adrenalin in ready supply, eyes attuned to the slightest element amiss on the road, ears expectant for the police siren's wail. To add to matters, the car was prone to stalling, and whenever they stopped Ilse would have to manage quick switches between clutch and brake, pumping the accelerator with growling roars. Some time later she received an obscure message from Bram about the car and 'pink heels', and went through the Volkswagen with a fine toothcomb, sure it must mean something significant. But Ilse had been barefoot during the escape, and Bram was referring only to her heels – all he could see working away at the pedals from his observation point on the floor. It was his little joke.

They took him to the suburb of Killarney, just off Riviera Road, where one of apartheid's munificent shopping complexes later arose, but then just a patch of veld. That was where Ilse and Pat dropped him off. Bram walked across to a nearby block of flats which had a row of garages at the back. There – as Violet Weinberg had arranged – he was met by a young man who opened one of the garage doors as he came over. Bram had not said much to Ilse and Pat before he left, just that he would be in contact at some stage. They had no idea of how near or how far he was going. He was driven off by the young man.

When Ilse and Pat returned to Beaumont Street, they had to enact an elaborate charade, creating the impression that all was normal and Bram was still at home. They did this even for Tias – though in his case it wasn't too difficult, as he spent most of his time in the garden, and Bram was usually upstairs in his study – but there was a less well-disposed audience to convince. So every now and then Pat and Ilse would stand where they thought the police bugs might pick up their conversation, and complain rather loudly about how hard Bram was working, and how it was high time that he came down. That evening when Tias cooked dinner, they made a show of calling Bram, took a third plate, put food on it and ate it, to keep all the appearances alive. Every night Bram had a set routine of parting the curtains and checking all the windows; so one of them put on his pyjamas and did exactly the same, then climbed into his bed and rumpled it as if he had slept there. The following night they did it all over again. It was of necessity an amateurish performance, using only what skills and resources were available. Yet amidst the taut anxiety of the moment there was a certain element of fun, and somewhat miraculously everything worked.

On the Sunday the doorbell rang: there was a man whom neither Ilse nor Pat had seen before, asking for Bram. Pat was afraid to say he was busy, thinking the man might insist on waiting; so she said Bram was out doing some work, and that the best thing would be to try him at chambers the following day. At that the unknown caller left, but both then and later Pat suspected he may have been a visitor from the Special Branch. The same day there was an expected guest, this time Harold Hanson, there to collect the letter he was to read out in court the following day. He neither asked for Bram nor did he read the letter, and it was Pat's impression that he knew exactly what was in it. In fact when Bram told Hanson what he planned to do, Hanson had said he would do anything to help him. The only hitch over the letter was that initially Pat lost it, so anxious about secrecy that she forgot where she had hidden it. She had put it in her squash raquet cover, and there was inner and outer turmoil until she found it.

On the Monday – the day the trial reconvened – Pat went to court, ostensibly to hand Bram's letter to Hanson. Ilse couldn't bear to go with her, and stayed home, though at some stage during the day she phoned Sholto in panic because, although Bram was gone and the news must have broken, the Security Police had not arrived, and the tension of waiting was terrible. It was that call too, she felt, that kept the police from arresting her, because of her genuine alarm at her father's disappearance. For the next day or two still there was nothing: the Special Branch, perhaps in some shock of their own, stayed away. And then finally they raided, taking whatever they could find, including Bram's second letter to Ilse, and a document in his handwriting they had been searching for since the Rivonia case. After that there was only one further search – when Ilse and Pat, having a drink one evening in the twilight, remarked sardonically for the benefit of the listening devices that the flowers at the bottom of the garden appeared to be moving and that it must be time to go and feed Bram. The next morning the police came in and dug up the daisies.

While speculation ran rife as to where in the world Bram was, or the plastic surgery he would most likely undergo in order to change his appearance, in fact he had not gone very far, and his methods of disguise were more modest. From Killarney he had been driven off to Rustenburg, about sixty miles northwest of Johannesburg, to a small cottage on a secluded farm owned by a Mrs

Milindton (she was the mother-in-law of Stanley Uys, the journalist who had visited Bram and Molly during the Rivonia Trial). There Mrs Milindton (who may or may not have known who Bram was, and who had something of a reputation as a health-food enthusiast) put him on a diet; for his purposes this was not only to change his shape, but to lessen the floridity caused by his high blood pressure. For the rest, he had learned well from his theatre designers. The object was not to become, dramatically, someone else, but to alter the characteristics that identified him as who he was. He shaved the hair back on the front of his head, to make it look as if he were going bald, and dyed what remained of it auburn – not only for the overt disguise, but once again to make his face look less florid by contrast. He grew a goatee beard which, along with his eyebrows, he also dyed auburn, and took to a pipe, which, if kept in his mouth while he spoke, altered the quality of his voice. He exchanged the thick black rims of his glasses for a lighter, rimless pair – and that knee of his, which had swung out when he walked ever since his rugby accident in Oxford, he learned to keep in check. To add to the effect Bram used a walking stick, taking quicker and lighter steps, altogether more prim. He altered the mannerisms of his face and the gestures of his hands, the essential instincts and revelations of the body.

Advocate, accused, and now actor: Bram changed from the solid Afrikaner lawyer and instantly recognisable figure at the centre of his world to a slight and strange, miasmic fellow on the fringes of society who, though diffident and polite, looked as if he never knew the time. He took advantage of the mental after-image of who he had been to become someone whom no one would suspect. He became the negative in the camera, the translation whose inner reality negotiates with outer difference, the being whose edges are blurred. He was the ghost who manages to walk the streets in the places where once he had lived.

It was some six weeks before he resurfaced, taking the name 'Mr Douglas Black' – beyond the practical issues of gaining an identity, a felicitous identification with the majority of South Africa's people. Nelson Mandela too had gone underground, but for him the mere anonymity of being black in South Africa constituted in large part a sufficient disguise. For Bram it was different: he was both himself and disguised into 'black'. And yet the contradictions of the name for a white fugitive suggested the absurdity of racial assignations.

The structures of a new existence had to be set in place. Primarily, Bram needed somewhere to live, and this was duly arranged with pragmatic economy and success. A young woman named Gabrielle Veglio de Castelleto was the girlfriend of a Portuguese man connected with Bram's underground group. She was due to go overseas, and just before she left she rented a house at 57 Knox Street in Waverley, under the name of Ann Getliffe. She stayed at the house for all of three days, and then informed the servant she had hired that she had to leave because her mother was ill, and that her uncle would be arriving. That was what, after a while, Bram as 'Mr Black' did. Knox Street – just a mile or two from Beaumont Street in the leafiest environs of Johannesburg – was where he lived for the following six months.

All those who saw him in his new appearance had a story of their first meeting. When Violet Weinberg came to the Knox Street house, the door was opened by a man wearing a Father Christmas beard, though brown instead of white. Aghast, Violet remonstrated with Bram, saying that he couldn't walk around like that – but it was just a joke, and after tagging her along for a while, he chuckled and took the beard off. Ilse was taken by Issy Rosenberg (the Rosenbergs were near-neighbours of the Fischers and, besides being good friends, were members of the Party) to a deserted warehouse in the industrial area of Selby. There she was left alone – until, after a while, an odd little man walked in. Ilse's first instinct was to think she'd been followed, and that Bram either had been or was about to be arrested. But then she saw it was him: it was his eyes, she said, you couldn't disguise his eyes, and the smile in her voice as she remembered mirrored what she must have seen in his eyes when they met.

The core of Bram's fragile group remained the same, though there were some new additions. Violet Weinberg and Lesley Schermbrucker, still on the central committee in the absence of their husbands, saw him regularly. There were also Ralph and Minnie Sepel who, from their home in Mons Road, Observatory, managed to remain quite deeply underground. They had first met Bram in 1961, when he came to address a small group at their house. Later they attended discussions he led on the theory of Marxism, where they found his own convictions mixed with a personal tolerance that was all, remarked Minnie, that could have won her over. Minnie became an underground librarian, collecting communist literature which had been posted from England and redistributing it to various addresses in Johannesburg. Her sister was one of the Kreels who owned the house and cottage in Mountain View where Denis Goldberg had concealed his car, and Goldreich and Wolpe themselves during their escape. Ralph was a lawyer who had had some dealings with the purchase of Lilliesleaf Farm; yet, though he had been detained for a while, and had given evidence (under instruction from Bram) when subpoenaed in the Rivonia Trial, neither he nor his wife was under obvious suspicion. When

Bram returned from Rustenburg to Johannesburg, it was Ralph who went to meet him at the Marymount Nursing Home, though at first he too did not recognise him. Bram stayed with the Sepels in Mons Road until the Knox Street house was ready; their children called him Professor Calculus, from the *Tintin* books, because that was who, in his eccentric guise, he resembled.

Later Bram's group arranged for him to see Mary Benson, because they felt that he needed the company, and so she too had her first sighting. Improbably, she was called to a meeting with Violet and Lesley, who against all the written and unwritten rules of underground life drew her a map of how to get to Knox Street. She went there directly the following day, with scarcely a check for the police tail. When she was shown into the house Bram again was all but unrecognisable. To Mary, on reflection, he looked with his goatee and rimless glasses more like Lenin or Trotsky than Calculus, but apparently the disguise was already working. Bram had been to a doctor who had no suspicions of his real identity, and was appearing at odd events – quite appropriately, given his play with images – as a photographer.

Disguises may work on many levels, and some of Bram's subterfuges had to do with his own group as much as the police. Soon after his disappearance Pat Davidson began pestering Lesley Schermbrucker and Violet Weinberg to find out if there was some way she could see him. Their consensus was that it would be too dangerous, though other lapses suggested that security was not as tight as it should be. It was not only the matter of Mary Benson's map. Soon after Bram's reappearance Violet remarked to Pat that she had not been able to resist driving past his new house – a fault in the telling as well as the doing, for it gave Pat her first clue that Bram was in Johannesburg. Then Lesley delivered a couple of notes to Pat from Bram, just in greeting. One day, when Pat arrived in her office there was a parcel waiting for her, with Bram's handwriting on it. It was a beautiful vase, a present from him, but no one could remember who had delivered it. Then Pat felt for sure that he was in Johannesburg.

One morning, when she arrived at work and was taking the lift up to her office from the basement parking lot, a man slipped in beside her and spoke to her – some small pleasantry about the weather. She remembered thinking how odd he looked, small, peculiar and even ugly, but she was polite in reply, and he stepped out at the ground floor. Later Bram told her it was him, that he'd been testing his disguise, and knew then that it was 'bloody good'. He told her this when at last they met by arrangement. First Bram sent her some longer letters, via Lesley; then he appointed a time and place, just outside Pat's squash courts at the Old Johannians' Club. One night, at about eight o'clock, after a game Pat had specially arranged for the purpose, she went through a gate at the back – and there, waiting in a car, was the same little man. He tried to insist that he was merely taking her to Bram, but as soon as Pat climbed in beside him she knew who he was, and that was when Bram reminded her about the figure in the lift. He took her to Knox Street, so that she too now knew where it was. But Bram swore her to absolute secrecy: she was not even to tell Ilse she had seen him, because of the prohibition on any contact. He evidently had a need to see people.

⁂

It was at this stage that Bram was faced with an attack from a completely unexpected direction.

In writing his article on 'The Threat to the Legal Profession in South Africa', Bram had been at pains to clarify exactly from which quarter that threat originated. Communists, whether so in reality or deemed as such by the Minister of Justice, had never disqualified themselves as lawyers by their political actions or beliefs: 'In fact there has been no case', Bram had written, 'in which lawyers affected by the [Suppression of Communism] Act have in any way abused their position as officers of the Courts. No such charge has ever been made before a Law Society or Bar Council.' Yet just as Bram was gearing up to continue his political struggle underground, he was about to prove the first counter-example to his own proposition. In a shocking move, just two days after he went underground, the Johannesburg Bar Council decided to institute proceedings in the Supreme Court to have his name removed from the roll of advocates, on the ground that 'in its opinion, [Bram Fischer's] recent conduct is unbefitting that of an advocate'. For Bram it was an unjustified and utterly dismaying betrayal that outdid any he had experienced so far in the witness box.

On one level the move had a certain plausibility: there was the troubling image of a trusted and revered member of the profession breaking his obligation and explicit undertaking as an officer of the court to stand trial. Also, in a context in which the Minister of Justice had fixed his sights firmly on all but the most obsequious sectors of the legal profession, the official application to have Bram disbarred had a certain defensive, if not pre-emptive, quality. But on closer inspection the Bar Council decision was based on grounds that were both shaky and cowardly. Disbarment was designed specifically as an instrument of protection for the public against unscrupulous lawyers who abused their authority for personal gain. One would be hard put to see Bram's actions in this light: everything he had done had been, in the widest sense, for the public good, and no one could imagine that his motive had been personal reward. It hurt Bram deeply that his colleagues, a good number of them close associates whom he himself had represented on the Bar Council for so many years, were unwilling to understand this or trust him. The unseemly haste with which the decision was made by the leadership of the Council only added to the injury. The chairman of the Council, Melville Festenstein – who in the 1940s had worked with Bram in the left-wing ethos of the time – had been in Cape Town for a meeting of the General Council of the Bar of South Africa, and released a short statement to the press from there. Also attending that meeting had been the Minister of Justice, and it was easy for Bram to surmise that Vorster had either participated in the discussion on his case, or else applied direct pressure. As became clear later, any opposition to the decision within the Bar Council had been unceremoniously overridden.

It was in these circumstances that, just when Bram should have been calming his mind in preparation for his new life, he had to defend himself once again in a public arena. Once again he had to write to Harold Hanson, this time from an unspecified location barely a week after he went underground, asking Hanson to represent him if the disbarment case went ahead. He had thought at first, Bram remarked in his letter, of ignoring the whole matter, as it was clear that the Minister of Justice intended ending his legal career in any event before the year was out. But there was a vital principle involved: 'Whether I am to be struck off the roll because I disagree radically with the Nationalist racial policy (and am prepared to fight for my point of view), or whether I am to be struck off, after 30 years of practice, for dishonourable conduct.' That the Fischer legal tradition should end in this way must have been a galling and horrifying prospect for Bram.

His letter to Hanson laid out at length the grounds for his defence in as clear a form as might be assembled, first (in true lawyer's manner) on the principles and then on the facts. On the question of his conduct, the foundation Bram relied on was firmly established in the South African legal tradition: that offences committed because of an overriding belief in the moral validity of a political principle did not constitute grounds for dismissal. This was presumably, wrote Bram, because such actions had no bearing on the professional integrity of an individual, and he was able to cite precedents, dating back to the Boer War and the Rebellion, of people – for the most part Afrikaners – whose political commitment had placed them on the wrong side of the law but whom the Bar Council had not abandoned. In his own case his view was impassioned: 'When an advocate does what I have done,' Bram wrote, 'his conduct is not determined by any disrespect for the law nor because he hopes personally to benefit by any "offence" he may commit. On the contrary, it requires an act of will to overcome his deeply rooted respect of legality, and he takes the step only when he feels that, whatever the consequences to himself, his political conscience no longer permits him to do otherwise. He does it not because of a desire to be immoral, but because to act otherwise would, for him, be immoral.'

Bram of course had no direct information about exact allegations against him, but had gleaned them as well as he could from newspaper reports. On each of these 'facts' as purported, he inveighed as well to Hanson. It was quite untrue, as accounts had suggested, that any member of the Bar Council had given, or been asked to give, any assurance to the Minister of Justice that he would comply with the conditions of his bail. The only time he had asked anyone to act on his behalf was at the time of his passport application, when he had conveyed a message to the Minister via the chairman of the Council that he would refrain from political activity in England – a matter which had nothing to do with his bail. Nor had any officer of the Council given evidence at his bail application. As to his own undertaking, he was prepared to assume, Bram told Hanson, that he had promised to stand his trial until its conclusion (it was a somewhat generous assumption, as this had not in fact been an explicit part of his original assurance). That at any rate had been his initial intention, and Bram mentioned how he had returned to South Africa despite the efforts of many to persuade him to remain overseas. But it was while the trial was in process that his mind had changed, and this for two particular reasons. In the first place, he suggested, no prosecution that relied on evidence extracted from witnesses subjected to extended periods of solitary confinement could by any standards be regarded as fair. Secondly, he was no longer facing an independent judiciary – and here Bram introduced an intriguing point relating to the so-called Sobukwe clause under which Robert Sobukwe, leader of the PAC, was being detained after the conclusion of his sentence at the discretion of the Minister of Justice. The detention was by special legislative enactment, and was to be reviewed annually, but in effect was indefinite. Bram wrote that he had reason to believe, based on a confidential conversation with a colleague who had discussed the matter with the Minister, that he faced a similar fate.

Bram's argument to Hanson suggested strongly that when he had returned to South Africa he did so still with an open mind on the question of going underground. It made his defiance not only a political but also a judicial issue, against a process of overt ministerial and legislative manipulation: 'I cannot believe that any genuine protest made against this system which has been constructed solely to further apartheid can be regarded as immoral or as justifying the disbarment of a member of our profession.' Bram wanted Hanson to take up the matter with the Bar Council, and give them an opportunity to reconsider. His emotion, barely restrained, was palpable. Why had such a drastic decision been taken so hastily? Had any attempt been made to find out from him or his counsel the reasons for his actions, or to warn him of the consequences? Had the fundamental legal principle of *audi alteram partem* (hearing the other side) been regarded as inapplicable? 'My contention', wrote Bram, 'is that if in the year 1965 I have to be removed from the roll of practising advocates, the Minister himself and not the Bar Council should do the dirty work.'

There was some support from his fellow advocates, not least from Hanson, who was prepared to aver in due course that it was he who had passed on (from another colleague) the original message to Bram regarding the Sobukwe clause and the Minister's intentions. And there was other, unexpected reinforcement, freely given and therefore quite special. In an article in the *Sunday Times*, Leslie Blackwell, QC, former judge of the Supreme Court, who had joined the Johannesburg Bar in 1910, underlined the historical precedents Bram had noted. He detailed the celebrated case of F.E.T. Krause, who had been convicted of nothing less than incitement to murder during the Boer War, but who had later been readmitted to the Bar, and then became a judge, and finally Judge-President of the Free State. He also mentioned no less distinguished a personage than B.J. Vorster, the current Minister of Justice, who himself had been 'under detention during World War II as a member of the Ossewa Brandwag', but whose pro-Nazi activities had never produced his disbarment. Bram's offences had been so much milder than those of many of his predecessors: 'Cannot I now make an appeal to my former brethren in Johannesburg', wrote Blackwell, 'to let the matter rest where it is at present as between Fischer and the authorities of this Republic?'

Given the historical precedents both he and Blackwell mentioned, Bram had offered the hope in his letter to Hanson that his Afrikaner colleagues would evince a special understanding of his actions, and given their history they should have. But it was an optimistic and idealised hope. The past had been seized, like so much else, by the government, and those who had once felt themselves oppressed had no memory or mercy in triumph. If Bram felt the meaning of his protest would vibrate lucently in the air from which he had so suddenly vanished, he did not realise that South Africa was under the sway of illusions deeper and more bemusing than any he could muster, and an acquiescence to power that distorted any message he could transmit.

Leslie Blackwell's former brethren at the Bar Council wouldn't listen, and the proceedings against Bram went ahead. By June the court was placing notices in the newspapers advising 'ABRAM FISCHER, male, Queen's Counsel, formerly residing at Beaumont Street, Oaklands, Johannesburg, but whose present whereabouts are unknown' of the case he had to answer, and Bram was mailing replies to attorneys, affirming his intention to oppose.

⚜

As much as Bram wished to protect his professional standing, it was the thought that those close to him might misunderstand his intentions that especially mortified him. Or even worse, that he might genuinely have fallen in their esteem. In a letter to the attorney William Aronsohn written on the same day as his letter to Hanson, Bram asked Aronsohn to let Issy Maisels and others read the latter – of which he enclosed a copy, to make sure it got through: 'It's strange, William, how in times like this one can really feel who are one's friends . . . I feel perfectly clear about them, but I'm always afraid of having a blind spot when I'm personally affected.' Most of all Bram wanted copies to be made available to his children as well as to other members of the family, and he told Aronsohn that he should feel free to express his views quite frankly to Ilse and Pat: 'Perhaps they'll be able to let me know when I'm recaptured!'

But there was no hint of that for a long time, though under the spotlight of the newspapers and the intense public interest rumours and sightings flared from the first. On the day of the first police raid at Beaumont Street, reported the *Rand Daily Mail*, the house was observed by peering housewives relieved to find that the besuited men roving the grounds were not estate agents (there was apparently a housing shortage in Johannesburg, and the women were looking to pick up a bargain). Ilse had to deny to the press that her father had committed suicide. In a column in the *Cape Argus* Bram was compared with Bonnie Prince Charlie, who had evaded his enemies disguised as a Highland lass. 'Could Fischer be a typist at police headquarters', the columnist asked, 'or a wardress at Pretoria Central jail?'

Within days of his disappearance Bram was reported crossing with eleven others into Bechuanaland; but this, it turned out, had been Lionel Gay, making an escape of his own. Exiles in Lusaka said they had seen Fischer walking down Cairo Road with Duma Nokwe, the ANC lawyer and leader whom Bram had defended in the Treason Trial. Later in the year reports placed him on Kenneth Kaunda's farm – which the President of Zambia roundly denied. General surmise held that Bram was organising a new underground Rivonia; he was located in the Que Que area of Rhodesia; a sighting in the Etosha Pan led to police roadblocks in South West Africa. By April it was rumoured that he was living in Soweto, and that Helen Suzman had full knowledge of his whereabouts. General Keevy, the Commissioner of Police, announced a 'substantial reward' for Bram's recapture, and commented that at least *he* knew where he was: 'somewhere between the South Pole and North Pole'. Bram was glimpsed in Cape Town, and the police were put on alert. An anonymous call reported that he was at a house in the Johannesburg suburb of Greenside – yet when the police raided, they found it to be the home of Barney Yutar, brother of Percy, who had led the Rivonia prosecution. Barney was deeply upset at the embarrassment: 'My brother is one thousand percent with the government,' he announced, as if the point required reinforcement.

Bram added actively to the illusion of his ubiquity by mailing letters to people from diverse places in South Africa, which the press, when they got wind of them, publicised. Some he posted himself, on drives into Natal or the Free State, but given his support group it was not difficult to have others mailed for him. As in the case of his comments on the Bar Council decision, each new communication caused a stir. Nelson Mandela had become known as the 'Black Pimpernel' during his period underground, and Bram was now the 'Red' equivalent, the reference quite obvious. By mid-April an article by Margaret Smith headlined '75 Days – Fischer Is Still Free' put it that Bram could be 'anywhere from Malmesbury to Moscow'. Rumours abounded that he was disguised as a priest (a throwback to the Goldreich and Wolpe escape), or that he was passing as an Indian, but Margaret Smith suggested another possibility: 'It has also been put forward that, with some change in the style of his clothes, he is openly walking the streets of some South African city, under [a] new assumed identity.'

That of course was much closer to the truth, and the city in question was Johannesburg, not far from where Bram had lived for the last quarter of a century. In general, his success with his disguise, his feeling of visible invisibility, caused a certain gleeful delight, even after the close shaves that inevitably came his way. On one occasion, crossing Commissioner Street in the city centre, Bram saw a security policeman who knew him well coming directly towards him, but the man showed no sign of recognition, and Bram went on his way. Violet Weinberg took Bram to see a doctor for his blood pressure, and the doctor – who Violet suspected knew there was something on the go – recommended a specialist. There, just as Bram stepped into the lift, he saw one of his chambers colleagues at the back. He simply turned around, he later told Violet, and when he got out 'put on my little steps'. Once he even went back to chambers, and took the lift up and down in the closest proximity to advocates whom he knew well: they would not have dreamed that he was the peculiar little man. Other encounters were more poignant: Bram was next to Marius Schoon's first wife, Diana, in another lift, and later regretted that he had said nothing, for he would never have the opportunity of speaking to her again.

Yet his success gave him confidence, as did the routines of contact and evasion. Every day one or other of Bram's group would phone him from a call box; if meeting points were being arranged, the times would be out by an hour or two, as agreed. One regular stratagem involved Bram parking his car (he had a Volkswagen with two sets of plates) and then walking directly through a house to another car parked on the other side. When Ilse set out to see Bram she travelled on the back of a friend's motor-bike (both Sholto Cross and John Kalk helped her out); it was the best form of transport for losing the police before being dropped off near some point where Bram would pick her up. All this required fairly impeccable timing, but without too many scares it seemed to work. And it all contributed to one of Bram's main objectives: every day at large, every day the police could not find him, was a triumph in itself which kept the meaning of his actions alive. There was a poem by Nazim Hikmet to that effect, on the daily victory of enduring detention, which Bram used to quote to Ilse when Sholto was in prison:

> It may not be a pleasure exactly,
> But it's your solemn duty
> To live one more day
>   To spite the enemy.

Ilse was sure it was what underlay his resilience and purpose now, the determination most simply not to give up.

Beyond the more passive obligation of sustaining an escape, there was serious political work to be done, the most important element of which had to be an attempt to revive the Communist Party in some form. The idea was to establish an entirely new core of cadres, while those who were known to the police (including some in Bram's own underground group) would fall away after a while. Older connections were re-established: a young man named Jeffrey Rudin acted as courier between Bram and Rowley Arenstein in Natal (and then later turned state witness); Fred Carneson, banned and restricted in the most comprehensive manner in Cape Town, received letters from Bram in his flat. Longer-term projections were that Bram could remain underground for extensive periods, then resurface in London or New York in his own identity, to return to South Africa in disguise – all of which would have added immeasurably to the aura of his daring and resistance. His group estimated that at best this would continue for three years, at which point he would have to leave the country for good – if all were successful, with a new and independent structure behind him.

Yet, though a certain amount of activity continued while Bram was underground – duplicating flyers, putting out messages, making contacts – the notion of reconstructing the Communist Party inside the country was in the short term all but impossible. Given the circumstances, it was extremely difficult for him to meet people, organise, recruit and establish an impermeable underground network and, in the absence of more practical options, his role devolved more centrally to the inspirational. In early April, when Beyers Naudé, minister in the Dutch Reformed Church, showed his first signs of questioning the scriptural authority of apartheid, and was prevented from delivering an address, Bram sent him a letter of solidarity and encouragement. Naudé might be surprised, Bram wrote, to receive support from a Marxist, but the concept of brotherhood among men was one that Christians and Marxists shared, 'although we seek it by different paths'. In recalling the original lesson of Christ, he continued, Naudé had a significant role to play: 'How could Christ ever have approved of a policy that allowed people to be disdained, humiliated, insulted and hurt, utimately on the grounds of their colour – but that is something which our so-called Christian leaders invite daily.' His own influence now, suggested Bram, lay chiefly among blacks, but only an Afrikaner could persuade Afrikaners, and this was vital to the survival of their people. 'And that is why I wish to express my fullest support, and my hope that your work will be crowned with success. However strange it might sound today, it is not impossible that one day we may work for the Afrikaner people together.'

Bram, who had been referred to in court as saint-like, was unembarrassed to write to an Afrikaner *dominee* about Christ's original message: for him, it was all part of the unfolding history of the human spirit. In his inclusive approach Christianity and communism were not in their essential aspects adversaries but lay along a continuous spectrum of brotherhood and justice. This may have revealed his sentimentalism, but there was also a specific respect, tolerance and enlightenment – as well as, in the most oblique of forms, once again a prophetic component. For Beyers Naudé in his own time also became an inspirational figure, not only to Afrikaners but also to South African blacks. One letter may not change much; yet the communist and the Christian had found an area of commonality and, though Bram was not there to see the results, in some way they had 'worked together'.

In this time, and in the nature of things, Bram's greatest effects were symbolic rather than practical. Yet symbolism is not unreal, and has practical ramifications. On Robben Island Nelson Mandela and his colleagues came to hear that Bram was underground: though it reflected the kind of commitment they expected from him, they were elated, and it lifted their spirits. Michael Dingake, himself an uMkhonto activist on the run from the police, took the time to meditate on Bram's living solidarity with the oppressed, despite all the opportunities and temptations of the world to which he was heir. Ilse Fischer, meeting Africans of all descriptions, was told time and again how much her father was revered. As much as Bram represented political anathema to confirmed Afrikaner nationalists, or a reproachful conscience to liberal whites, to blacks he was becoming a nearly mythic figure, the one white man prepared to signal his devotion to justice with his life.

In Bram's own mind the central meaning of his action was clear: that not only blacks in South Africa should make sacrifices or risk everything for the cause of freedom. His choice emphasised the nature of the struggle and even helped define it: that it was by all and for all, for a whole society rather than a racially demarcated one. Bram cast himself among the unseen and invisible world, in the way that blacks were normally unseen and invisible to whites. In that sense his action was what he called it, a protest, a refusal to participate in iniquity; but it was also a positive search, in a displaced identity for an alternative identification, a radical statement of the possibility and necessity of a new and undivided world. So long as he remained at large, these meanings remained at large within him. In a form that went beyond the forged names on his driver's licence and bank accounts, Bram became coextensive with his new life.

In the meantime he saw Violet and Lesley and the Sepels, he met Ilse and Sholto and Pat Davidson and Mary Benson. Separately, with Ilse or Pat or Mary, he would set off on picnics, a strange freedom from the everyday world. With Mary he discussed the Afrikaner past – its lost opportunities in the 1920s to take a more radical and democratic direction, his one-time lunch with Verwoerd when he failed to make him a socialist, the poetries of which his language was capable – 'n ligte motreën for the softest of rains, his always-favoured phrase which Molly had loved. He showed Mary a wood where an underground Communist Party conference was once held. With Ilse and Sholto in the Magaliesberg, or with Pat, it was like the days of old – with Molly, or with the children, or his parents – criss-crossing the veld, identifying its plants and birds which he was certain he would never leave. He wrote to his cousin Connie, remembering the farm in their youth, and she was thrilled to get his letter. There were anxious moments: once he and Mary ended up in the middle of some army manoeuvres, which Bram fobbed off by greeting the soldiers in Afrikaans. There he was, ranging over the land, both himself and someone else, present and in a sense absent, where he belonged and did not belong.

⋙⊚⋘

Eli Weinberg told his story in court, as the Fischer Trial continued without Bram. He had been born in Latvia in 1908, he recounted, and was separated from his family by the war. He had become a waif and a stray, a mascot of Cossack soldiers who took him around. 'War made it terrible for me. I saw mud and blood and bodies and bombardments. It made a lasting impression . . . I hate war and I also hate violence.' Later he had become attracted to communism, and as a Jew he was opposed to all kinds of racism. 'My mother and my sister and other members of my family were murdered in a Nazi concentration camp.'

When sentence was passed on 13 April 1965, he and Ivan Schermbrucker were both given five years (one year of two three-year sentences to run concurrently); the others – except for Hymie Barsel, who had been found not guilty – were sentenced to terms ranging from one to three years. That day Bram had been out driving with Mary Benson to Natal, and returned to hear the news of the five years he would most likely have received; the magistrate, Mr S.C. Allen, said he had 'admitted his guilt by becoming a fugitive'. It was a dreadfully cold and rainy Easter. In court to hear the sentences, and then standing outside in solidarity for a last glimpse of the accused, was Ilse Fischer. Photographs showed her without hat or umbrella, somewhat worn and haunted, an indomitable look summoned up through the fatigue in her eyes.

After Bram disappeared, Ilse stayed on at Beaumont Street for approximately a month, the beginning of an extremely difficult time. Pat Davidson had been advised by Lesley Schermbrucker that if she wished to see Bram, she should cut any obvious ties with the family until she was in the clear. So Pat took to her old, pre-Fischer regime of boyfriends, country clubs and squash (the cover for her later meeting with Bram), and only stopped by occasionally. Ilse had to deal with the wake of her father's life and her mother's death alone. She cleaned out the house, finding all Molly's and Bram's old letters – most of which Bram wanted destroyed, but Ilse kept them. There was a host of other mementoes: a paperweight bearing fragments of the last republican Free State flag ever to fly, the wooden chameleon Bram had been given by the rebel prisoner when he was six, the letter from Ouma Steyn to him when he turned twenty-one: 'I know that Bram Fischer is going to play an honourable role in the history of South Africa.' Then Ilse did the same at Bram's rooms in chambers, packing up Oupa Abraham's seventeenth-century copy of the *Institutes of Justinian*, as well as other rare legal texts annotated by the hands of scholars long gone, and by three successive Fischers. She spoke proudly to reporters of this history, but later told Pat she had been nearly suicidal during these weeks. When everything was cleared, she moved out to a small flat in Cavendish Street, Bellevue.

Bram wrote to her, not only because he wanted to, but quite likely because the police would have been mightily suspicious if he hadn't. That did not prevent him – despite the successes of his disguise and concealment – from revealing intimately and quietly that his mood was sometimes no better than hers. 'Ilse darling,' he wrote the week after his comrades were sentenced, 'It's nearly three months since I last saw you. I have had no news except that I have at last managed to get hold of your address and so you can imagine how I'm feeling. I did not realise quite how lonely this would be, and in particular how difficult life would become when one is without the companionship of people with whom one can discuss things. I think I would be prepared to give almost anything to be able to sit down with you this afternoon to hear all the news, how you are getting on, and how you have managed the mountainous task which I left in your hands by just disappearing – closing up the house, finding a job and, I suppose, doing a thousand and one other things. That in fact is what has preyed on my mind most during the whole of this period. It has hurt as much as Molly's death last year did.' It was a letter that might have fallen into the hands of the police; Bram's words spoke the truth through the deception.

For Ilse there was, at the least, ambiguity. As the duration of Bram's period underground extended there was a certain exhilaration, dodging the police on motor-bikes and implementing the other manoeuvres of evasion. Once Bram took her to see his theatre designers so that they could fashion a disguise for her too. They made a false nose, but when Bram as 'Mr Black' took pictures and developed them, the nose was so clearly false that they threw both it and the pictures away. At the same time there was also a certain amount of dread, especially when Ilse went to see Bram at the Knox Street house. It was bleak and sparsely furnished, too big for one person, and only accentuated the echoing space around him. He, with little experience in such matters, would cook and make everything as pretty as possible, but these could feel almost like duty visits – somewhat like seeing him in later years in jail, where each would feel obliged to cheer the other up and find things to talk about. The psychology of the situation meant that there were complications all round. When Bram took Ilse to the house, he made her close her eyes, for security reasons. Yet when she and Pat at last went together no eyes were closed, and Ilse was hurt to see that Pat, on what was meant to be her 'first' visit, was exempt from the rule to which she had been subjected. Pat Davidson and Mary Benson also seemed to have, at a distance, a niggling relationship, each a little jealous in her claim to Bram. He, with his personal magnetism, was surrounded by women, each in her own way devoted; but it was an odd set-up in the attempt to reconstitute a Communist Party.

That was precisely what he was unable to do, and that was what made life most difficult for Bram. In his first letter to Ilse when his comrades were sentenced, he assured her that he was safe 'at the moment and, I hope, for a long time to come, even though it's frustrating when one can achieve nothing'. In truth it was an exceptionally demanding transition: Bram had to make the shift from a fluently gregarious life, whether at home with his family, or prominent and instantly recognised in the world beyond. He had been busy sixteen hours out of any given twenty-four, in the doubled intensities of a legal and political career. Now time and space stretched in every direction, and at fifty-seven (turning fifty-eight) most of his days were spent in solitude, in an identity that wasn't altogether his. He recited the lamentable facts to Pat: 'There isn't anybody. They're all known. Or they're all in jail.' Bram cooked, cleaned, and listened to music, made notes and lists about everything, yet Ralph and Minnie Sepel found him uncustomarily testy and even intolerant at this time, fatalistic where his optimism had been incurable. He became dependent in a new way: Pat Davidson phoned him every day, but if she missed a call she felt he would nearly go desperate. She thought his prolonged solitude was making him careless, and later Bram admitted that he found his period underground taxing in the extreme – on his personality, his state of mind, and his discipline.

The question of discipline drove the Sepels quite spare with anxiety and subdued resentment. With two young children at home they were especially sensitive on the matter, but still could scarcely credit how slack things were. The original plan had been that they would work with Violet Weinberg and Lesley Schermbrucker only for the briefest of periods. Then, as soon as Bram moved into his first house, they would take over and find him a new one, to separate him from obvious points of contact. Everyone agreed to this, but it never occurred: instead, it seemed that Bram was seeing all the most dangerous (because the most traceable) people – Lesley and Violet, Mary, Ilse, Sholto and Pat. Any one of these could be watched, and any lapse would put a number of others at serious risk. Ilse *knew* that she was under surveillance much of the time, and wondered only about the tails she didn't see. Lesley Scherm-brucker used to visit regularly to make arrangements. In this the Sepels felt there was a gap between themselves and what they thought of as the 'old guard' – Bram's circle from what seemed almost a previous era, closely knit friends as much as they were comrades. That was what made Bram testy, if they voiced any criticism, but it was hardly a way to run a revolutionary underground.

Others, at a greater distance, felt the same. Ben Turok, just out of prison for his role in the first wave of uMkhonto activities, was confined to house arrest. One day, as he leaned over his gate, he was approached from the street by someone he knew well who asked if he would rejoin Bram's network under-ground. Willing as Turok was, he could not believe that things were being done in such an unguarded and hazardous way. Still, when he contacted the underground group for permission to leave the country (he and his wife Mary had received information that she was about to be arrested, and they had three small children at home), he discovered that in other respects Bram's discipline was undiminished. It would be better if the Turoks did not leave, came the rigorous reply, but if they did so it could be only on three conditions: that they would not take exit permits; that they would jump the border; and that Ben would undergo plastic surgery and return to South Africa in disguise. In cir-cumstances where too many people had gone overseas Bram was determined to stop the seepage. The conditions he stipulated were no more demanding than those he was living up to himself. Turok had once thought him rather old-worldly and quaint, but now it seemed he had become more absolute in his resolve than anyone else. It was, felt Turok, as if in stripping away the outer layers of his old identity an irreducible essence had emerged at the core.

Three months turned into five, and then six. Improbably Bram remained at large from the police, still a thorn in the flesh by his absence, still an elusive spirit of resistance within the country. On 18 July at least part of the original plan was implemented: he moved from Knox Street into a new house, at 215 Corlett Drive in Bramley, near a busy intersection with Louis Botha Avenue on the north-eastern edge of Johannesburg (on the way to Alexandra Town-ship, where Bram had served nearly thirty years before). The house was sub-divided, though still quite large, and Bram had neighbours – a young immigrant couple from England. One reason for the move was that the lease at Knox Street was expiring and the property was being sold, but this was also an opportunity to improve security, and to some extent Bram succeeded. Once again Ilse had to shut her eyes going to the new house, as did Mary. But Pat did not, and Violet even had a key, which infuriated the Sepels when they found out. Bram kept up his letters, tried to work on reorganisation, and once or

BRAM FISCHER

twice a week communicated with the exile group in London. Some of his letters overseas appeared normal, but had a 'counter-message' written in invisible ink between the lines. More frequently he wrote in code, taking an agreed segment from a book or magazine to provide the key to the encryption he was using. Bram wanted leaders of the Communist Party to return, like himself, to South Africa; chiefly he wrote about money, to run his operations underground, and provide the rent as well as other necessities.

But London was not as forthcoming as he might have expected. One of the reasons Bram took houses too large for just himself was that he was awaiting company to be sent out from England. Everyone was aware that his extended solitude was a problem: the Sepels had discovered from a psychiatrist in Cape Town that Bram's situation was the equivalent of solitary confinement – and they all knew by now how dangerous *that* was, akin to a form of mental torture. It was why his contact habits with his group were so dangerously elastic, to provide him with the necessary social interaction, but this could only be an inadequate solution. Accordingly, the South African group wrote again and again to London, begging for someone to be sent out more permanently, perhaps a working-class couple with the necessary ideological credentials. Company had been promised, and Bram was apt to tell anyone who enquired that he was expecting his daughter and her husband. That too would have been good for neighbours to see, so that Bram would appear less reclusive and conspicuous; but no one ever arrived. The South African group felt some bitterness over this, as they did over the fact that London took an inordinately long time to respond to their letters. Even on questions of money the overseas group appeared to be dilatory and carping, asking for receipts and accounts on the smallest matters from their comrade underground.

From the outside the life of a clandestine figure may appear exotic and romantic, but it consists of an endless array of daily details made all the more difficult because the regular props and struts – the invisible exoskeleton of one's normal existence – have fallen away. Bram's sense of isolation only increased, and as time went on it became clear that he would need to go 'on leave'. He had read up on underground movements, and knew that everyone working alone needed a rest; there was always the idea of his sudden appearance in New York or London. However, for that he needed a passport. Yet once again, although the London group had promised one, it seemed to take forever to arrive. Bram became more and more agitated, not least on the question of his safety: what if the police were on his track, and he needed to leave the country urgently? Eventually he became so anguished that he wrote numbers of letters to Ruth in London asking her to explore the intolerable delay.

For Ruth this was a disillusioning experience. She found that for many of those who had left South Africa the dynamics of an exile life had taken over – the posturing, the politicking, even a kind of lethargy and lack of urgency. When she asked members of the London group why Bram had not received replies to his letters, the response was that writing in code took time. When she asked again and again about the passport, she was told that no one was in London in August – when she knew that at that very moment some of the exiles were enjoying their summer holidays in Italy. It outraged her that the London comrades could not at least stagger their vacations, to man a postbox and take care of Bram's needs. A photograph of him as 'Mr Black' had arrived in London after the first six weeks of his disappearance, and Ruth simply did not believe it could take so long to make a passport. If Soviet bureaucracy was the problem, she was sure there must be London forgers who could do it in twenty-four hours. She knew that Bram, whose first thought was always for the individual, would have worked round the clock to support others in his situation.

Quite possibly Bram's London comrades did not, or could not, imagine what his circumstances were on the ground; nothing like this had ever been attempted before, and there was some dispute as to what exactly had been promised. In their own way they too faced difficulties, whereas for someone in his position it might have been easy for each apparent slight to seem exaggerated. Yet in South Africa there was no doubt that Bram felt abandoned: the Sepels too remembered messages returning that nothing could be done because people were on holiday. It added to the air of fatalism, sapping both energy and will. When Bram's passport finally arrived in October, it was a magnificently convincing piece of work – it would have fooled anyone, in Ilse's view – but by then it was almost too late. One ceases to plan because there appears to be no point. Bram's whole sense of the future had shifted, and perhaps he felt there would be no purpose in using the passport after all, to join the exiles who appeared to be living so carelessly in a distant and different world from the one that had now taken his whole life.

In that first underground letter to Ilse, Bram had written of his decision: 'I suppose it was worth doing – at any rate, I felt I just had to, and that was that.' June came around, with it Ilse's twenty-second birthday, and the first anniversary of Molly's death. Bram wrote again, mainly in Afrikaans, but with the odd sentence in English:

10/6/65

Ilse my skat [Ilse my treasure],

Ek dink hierdie brief sal heelwat te vroeg vir jou verjaarsdag aankom – tensy die pos heeltemal normaal funksioneer! Maar dit kan nie gehelp word nie. Eerder te vroeg. [I think this letter will come much too early for your birthday – unless the post functions completely normally! But that can't be helped. Better too early.]

I shall be thinking of you all day on Wednesday. Maar dit doen ek meeste dae; dus sal jy nie iets besonders oplet nie. [But that I do most days; so you won't sense anything unusual.]

Ek sal ook Sondag heeldag by jou wees – in my gedagtes in ieder geval. Hou moed. Ons sal weer lang dae by mekaar deurbring. Hierdie kranksinnige fasciesme kan nie lank duur nie. [I shall also be with you the whole day on Sunday – in my thoughts in any event. Keep your spirits up. We shall spend long days together again. This demented fascism can't last long.]

Ek skryf nie meer nie. Ek is seker dit word deur anders gelees. Jy weet jy het altyd my liefde. [I won't write any more letters. I am sure that they are read by others. You know you have my love always.]
Bram.

In early October Bram wrote to wish Ilse luck in her law exams, and could not resist giving her advice, in his usual manner, on how to study and prepare herself. How he wished he could be with her, he told her, and Paul when he returned. 'All right,' he instructed, 'don't worry. Our turn is *bound* to come.' His first wedding anniversary without Molly had come and gone: 'The 18th Sept was very quiet. I thought a good deal of you children and of Molly and of all the lovely things we did together . . . All my love – I think in future you must assume that no news is good news.'

While the newspapers revelled in stories of the elusive pimpernel, a year after Molly's death Bram was still in mourning, surviving in isolation. How long could he persist, in another identity, alone? If asked, he might have insisted that his suffering was nothing compared with that of millions of South African blacks, many of them removed from their families as an irremediable fact of existence. Bram had chosen, and that choice had set him on the path of this destiny. Through his grief, through his solitude, he would find the inner depth to meet it. That was a freedom that could not be removed.

On 30 October 1965, Mr Noel Glen, aged 55, was stopped and held by the police while travelling through Warmbaths, in the Transvaal. They were convinced he was Bram Fischer, although Mr Glen, who had met Bram once, didn't think he looked anything like him. Later that same month the

Afrikaans newspaper *Dagbreek* announced that it was offering the sum of R2000 as a reward for Fischer's capture. 'Catch this undermining communist, wherever he hides – in the Republic, in the territories around our borders, elsewhere in Africa, or overseas . . . ' The paper explained that the offer resulted from interest in its fiction series, entitled (somewhat peculiarly) 'Miss Bram Fischer', in which the master spy, Olaf Bouwer, tracked the devious communist down.

In the public world there was an urgent need to interpret his life. Joel Mervis, his schoolboy friend, wrote in the *Sunday Times* of the 'tragedy' of Bram's story, in mollifying tones for a readership that required it: 'However much one may disagree with Bram Fischer, however much one may condemn him, what we are witnessing here is the picture of a man who has deliberately sacrificed the richest rewards that life can offer for his beliefs and ideals.' To Bram such a definition, while well-meaning, may not have signified: how could it be tragic to offer one's life for the highest ideals? Others offered more trivial if not directly malicious views. Piet Beukes, who had been a student with Bram both in Bloemfontein and at Oxford, wrote that Bram had been one of the few students wealthy enough at the time to go to Russia, and his stories on his return had earned him a certain fame. But Bram was small, and must have had an 'inferiority complex'. This was the deeper reason for his attachment, because the Russian trip had made him feel important: 'From that time forward Bram was a dedicated communist.'

The police explored every method they could, including suborning prisoners. Dave Kitson, recently sentenced to twenty years, played a cat-and-mouse game in Pretoria Local Prison with the Special Branch. They came to him because they had discovered that he had been meeting Bram during the Rivonia period, and wanted to find out Bram's habitual venues; meanwhile, Kitson kept on talking to them to find out what *they* knew. He had arrived in prison with a miniature radio taped to his testicles – and, even as they spoke, had it sewn in a pocket under the arm of his prison jacket – but there was nothing like getting information from an authentic source, and so as much as they probed him he tapped them. The Branch men hinted broadly that he already had access to a radio (one of the political prisoners was widely suspected of being an informant), but Kitson demurred: that was at Pretoria Central, he told them, where a public address system relayed the news. The police tried to offer him a deal, suggesting he might soon be together with his wife, like Adrian Leftwich. But Kitson knew they had nothing to offer, since he had already been sentenced. He had only twenty years, he told them, but Leftwich had a life sentence, because he could never hold up his head again. Finally the police left Kitson alone.

Later they were to claim that they had been tracking Bram for six months, using him as a decoy to lead them to others. There were serious reasons to disbelieve this, but there were moments, remarked Pat Davidson, when she had her doubts. After all, was it possible that she was never followed successfully? She met Bram at least once a week, apart from telephoning him every day. Once they went together to the game reserve for a whole week: could they really have got away with that? No matter how methodical and systematic the precautions, there must be inevitable mistakes. Early on, when Pat was meeting Bram in the usual manner, parking her car to jump into his as he drove up to the rendezvous point, another vehicle arrived, and the man inside 'sort of looked at me', she recalled. She turned away immediately, and dawdled into a block of flats, before venturing out again to rejoin Bram, but the incident left an unsettling feeling. On two other, separate occasions, her car was stolen when she left it overnight at an assigned location for Bram to collect – though both times it was later recovered. Pat was observed at a squash game by a man who then appeared in the company of the Security Police; she was chased by two Studebaker Larks (police cars of choice) down the road. Once, on a picnic with Bram, she looked up to see the silhouette of a man on a faraway ridge – though when she pointed it out, Bram was unconcerned. Later that day, when they moved on to another spot, a car stopped at the side of the road, and a man emerged, unfolded a canvas chair, and sat there reading in the otherwise deserted landscape, not a hundred yards away.

In such circumstances it is easy to imagine presences where there may be none, but it was all capped for Pat as October wound into early November. By that stage Bram was running desperately short of money, and Pat had been roped in, probably by Ilse, to drop a package off for him. As arranged, she went to a telephone booth on the corner of Corlett Drive and Louis Botha Avenue, just outside a café nearby his house, and rang him twice, putting the phone down each time as he answered. That was the signal for Bram to come. Pat left the money inside the telephone book in the booth, but then Bram seemed to take forever to arrive. She knew this, recalled Pat, because she went into the café to wait, and while she was fiddling around buying some sweets, a man came in who also proceeded to waste his time, buy cigarettes, and loiter. 'After a while you get the feel,' said Pat. 'I was never paranoid, [but] I was really scared.' Finally Bram arrived, but when he went into the phone booth he couldn't find the package. He scrabbled around, searched, and came out again, and all the while the man was in the store. By that stage Pat was walking towards her car, refusing to look at Bram for fear of the slightest betrayal of a glimpse between them. As she drove off she saw to her relief that he had gone into the phone booth again and found the money. But the incident resonated in her mind.

Later she felt this episode may have been what gave Bram away, although no one could ever be sure. It is possible that the police were indeed following him – and not only through Pat – but did not know who he was. Perhaps they were hoping that the mysterious little man everyone seemed to be meeting might lead them to some other Bram. But even on this there have to be doubts, and it seems their route to him was a different one.

⁂

On Thursday, 10 September 1965, a furore exploded over the arrest of South Africa's first 180-day detainee, Issy Heymann. It was not his first experience of this nature. At the very end of December 1964 he had been detained with the aim of making him testify in the Fischer Trial, but Heymann refused. Still, after he was released, he thought it unwise to have any contact with Bram underground, and even declined to help him escape; he therefore had no knowledge of his whereabouts. But the police, investigating the underground uMkhonto network involving Michael Dingake – with which Issy did have contact – detained him again. That Thursday Heymann's wife Anne obtained a court order for her husband's release, on the ground that the 180-day detention laws had not been properly promulgated. Heymann was duly freed, but immediately rearrested for 'investigation'. The next day Anne Heymann obtained a habeas corpus ruling, ordering that her husband be produced in court by 2 p.m. But at 1.30 p.m. he was arrested yet again under a separate clause of the 180-day law, now promulgated with specific regulations to allow his continued detention. Under the terms of the Act the courts had no jurisdiction in the matter, and throughout the whole procedure no one had so much as seen Heymann.

Once the police had him in their control, they resorted to their now customary methods, and in due course grilled him sleeplessly and continuously for two days and nights. Heymann collapsed three times and had to be taken to the district surgeon. Later – as one version of the story emerged to Rowley Arenstein – tea and cigarettes did what torture could not do, and he made a statement. After that Heymann, with his deeply held Bolshevik principles, felt like a traitor. One night, down the corridor from Dave Kitson and the other prisoners at Pretoria Local, he cut his wrists and ankles with a razor blade, and started to bleed away slowly. When the adjutant on duty, a man called Schnepel – whom Bram came to know only too well – came round at midnight, he asked Issy how he was, and Issy said he was thirsty. Schnepel had enough sense to recognise this as an immediate sign of a suicide attempt (because the body, under stress, draws liquids and salts to the brain), and whipped off the blankets. Heymann was taken to hospital and stitched up.

When his wife came to see him, she was obviously deeply concerned. But Issy managed to say, past the ears of the guards, 'Never mind about me. I'm very worried about my *chaverte*, my *tante chaverte* – and you must see that she goes overseas for treatment. My aunt's in a very bad condition.' His wife knew what and who he was referring to. *Chaverte* was Yiddish for a (female) 'friend' or in this instance 'comrade' and, with the prefix of 'aunt', was an obvious reference to Violet Weinberg. So soon afterwards Anne and Violet met for an hour in the ladies' cloakroom of John Orr's department store in the centre of Johannesburg, and discussed what Violet ought to do. Anne reported back to Issy: she told him that his aunt was a very obstinate old woman, and had simply refused to go. Later when Violet was arrested, the police wanted to know what she and Anne had talked about for so long in the cloakroom.

The exact sequence in these events – even the nature of the events themselves – is necessarily unclear. Afterwards, when Bram was arrested, Issy confessed to him that he felt like a Judas because he had made a statement. As he told it to Bram, the police had pressured him for names, and he had held out, giving only those who were dead or in exile. They had insisted he knew where Bram was, but he revealed nothing, until finally all he said was, 'You have arrested Violet. I am sure she told you.' That would have placed Issy's clue to the police as occurring *after* Violet's detention, with his warning to her coming earlier and his attempted suicide perhaps later. Bram's response was to reassure him, citing his refusal to give evidence as testimony of his courage, and suggesting that Issy's remark about Violet was not how the police tracked him down. He may well have believed it. Marius Schoon remembered discussions in jail in which Bram mentioned that two young white comrades had been arrested round about that time, but were never charged and just disappeared; there was some thought that one of them had been turned.

In any event it made no difference, for there was a strict rule in the underground – any underground – and this underground knew it well, that if someone were detained by the police, any and every contact had to take evasive action. They knew enough now about torture and its effects, and beyond Party policy on the matter Bram's group had something of an implicit agreement. Those who were arrested would attempt to hold out for twenty-four hours or, if they could manage it, forty-eight, but this was all that could be guaranteed, and that time had to be used. The Sepels felt all along that Violet Weinberg should have cut her ties with Bram; now, after Heymann's detention, it was a matter of absolute urgency. There was some discussion about whether she herself should go underground or leave the country; the Sepels were insistent on the latter course, and apparently this was agreed. But then it never occurred: according to the Sepels, Violet decided that she would simply attempt to withstand the pressures of arrest. And so she stayed, perhaps with Bram's private agreement. Among this small circle of the old guard an emotional need to stick together, not to leave the country, to remain loyal and hold out, overrode rational sense.

Bram asked Mary Benson if she knew of a place for a woman to stay. According to later evidence, Lesley Schermbrucker asked a contact named Doreen Tucker, who had been helping to channel funds for the underground group, whether she could arrange something. She found a friend who was prepared to let Violet stay in her house. Bram himself made plans for her to move in with him in Corlett Drive. But none of it was of use in the end, because on 8 November Violet was arrested. Two policemen arrived at her workplace at noon – with Eli in prison, she had a small job at a wholesaler's shop – and told her to come along. They took her to the Grays in Johannesburg where, deceiving a woman detective for a few minutes, Violet flushed some letters she had on her down the toilet. Then she was taken to Compol, the police headquarters in Pretoria.

That day Violet had an arrangement for Lesley Schermbrucker to meet her in her office at one. When Lesley arrived and asked for Violet, the husband and wife who owned the small place told her tremulously that two men had taken her away. Lesley went directly downstairs and phoned Bram from a call box to tell him that Violet had been arrested. Ilse also phoned him later that evening: Violet's son Mark had come round with the news of his mother's detention, and so Ilse got in touch urgently. Bram asked her if she thought Violet could hold out. Ilse said that she was tough, but that there was no point in laying odds. Bram asked her what he should do, and Ilse replied that she didn't know. Bram commented that Violet was strong, and that there was no need to worry.

Perhaps he was trying, one more time, to lift her spirits, though for years afterwards Ilse felt guilty that she had not told him to clear out at once. But the very fact that he had asked *her* – when critical decisions had become the essence of his life – as well as the reality that she did not know what to say was an indication. A different mood had taken them over, and they were, to some extent, paralysed.

On 2 November, just six days before Violet was arrested, judgment was delivered in the Bar Council case for the disbarment of Bram. Sydney Kentridge (now elevated to the status of State Counsel) had appeared for him, assisted by Arthur Chaskalson as junior, presenting as convincing an argument as could be mustered. They pointed to all the precedents – all those Afrikaner commandos, convicts and internees who had later risen to eminence and prestige – and the legal tradition in South Africa that disbarment did not apply in matters of political conscience. They indicated that the present case had nothing whatsoever to do with Bram's guilt or innocence in his trial, but merely with his actions in absconding. For that he had already suffered, forfeiting his R10,000 bail, and living the life of a fugitive who faced the prospect of an increased sentence if recaptured. The central issue, Kentridge argued, was that it was not this court's responsibility to punish Bram, but merely to decide if the public required protection from him should he once again wish to practise law. Nowhere had it been suggested that he was dishonest or dishonourable. If he were ever again in a position to practise, there was no reason to believe that he would not do so in the manner to which he had been accustomed for so long. There was no one who needed to be protected, and no one who would be prejudiced if Fischer stayed on the roll. It was doubtful, commented Kentridge, if there were any member of the Bar that had known Bram who would be prepared to stand up and say, 'He is a less honourable man than I am.'

Hearing the case was none other than Quartus de Wet, Judge-President of the Transvaal, who had presided when Bram appeared before him as leader of the defence at the Rivonia Trial, and now had to judge him in his absence. Quite possibly he felt he had been duped on that earlier occasion; when Kentridge remarked that only Bram's political convictions had caused his disappearance, De Wet interjected that a man who felt as Bram did should resign as an advocate, so that he could 'indulge in illegal activities to his heart's content'. Now, after hearing the case, he spoke of the 'unpleasant duty' of the court in handing down a decision regarding someone who was so well known, both as colleague and as senior advocate. He went through Bram's letters to Hanson in some detail, and the arguments he had offered in his own defence, but at key points was insistent in offering his own misreadings of Bram's explanations, not seeing the essential quality of protest in what he had done. Bram's anxiety about the Sobukwe clause, he remarked, was inconsistent with his avowals that he did not abscond through any fear of punishment. De Wet said that Bram had made full use of his status as Senior Counsel to obtain bail; breaching it was 'dishonest conduct', which in this case meant the same as 'dishonourable'. If such things were to be permitted, the effect on the adminis-tration of justice would, in his view, be 'deplorable'.

Bram's letters, along with his actions, observed De Wet, indicated that he was engaged in subversive activities and fully intended to continue. In effect he had admitted that he was not prepared to conform to the laws of the coun-try, which it was the duty of the court to uphold. The court could not allow an advocate to remain on the roll when he was defying those laws and inciting others to do the same. In considering Bram's position, De Wet allowed only the slightest glimmer of a possible reversal: it was quite true, he remarked, that there were historical precedents for those once disbarred to be readmitted, and perhaps the same might apply one day in Bram's case. 'If the respondent were to apply for readmission at some future time, similar considerations may apply. It is impossible for this Court to foresee what will happen in the future. We are concerned with the laws in force at the present time and with the structure of the society as it exists in this country at the present time.'

Implicit in De Wet's comments was the concession that law and justice were not identical, and that a future legal and political dispensation might view Bram's actions in a different light. There was even the smallest suggestion – though one would have had to push hard to make the point – that future laws might define the present ones as illegal. But in taking the issue to be one of transgression and retribution rather than of morality and justice, De Wet was unable, almost by definition, to comprehend the forms in which both he and his court were implicated in the larger questions Bram had been raising. What, then, of all the soul-searching in Germany after the Second World War concerning judges who had been just as content to administer the law? There may have been some irony in this for Bram, a sense of history repeating itself, as well as some hope for the future whose possibility the Judge-President had admitted. But for now there was little enough to hold on to. 'It is ordered', De Wet had concluded, and his two co-judges concurred, 'that the name of the respondent be removed from the Roll of Advocates, and the respondent is ordered to pay the costs of the applicant.'

Nothing hurt Bram, recalled George Bizos, more than this case and this decision, for he had acted from the highest of principles, and yet had been considered unworthy and dishonourable by his colleagues. Was it inevitable that he had to be persecuted by his peers as much as the police? It was a day that seemed a day of judgment on his life.

That night Bram met Mary Benson, and they went to a hotel for a drink in his sheer disconsolation. He simply could not credit this unwillingness of his colleagues to understand. It was no wonder that, given all the other circumstances confronting him, he was in little state to act when Violet was arrested.

⁂

Violet Weinberg arrived with her captors in Pretoria at 5 p.m. on Monday, 8 November. She was taken to a small room, where the windows were closed and shuttered against the light. There she was interrogated non-stop for seventy hours, until the Thursday evening. She stood almost all of the time, though she managed occasionally to sit on the floor or the radiator. The Special Branch worked on her in relays, as many as three at a time. If she drifted off to sleep they banged on the table and threatened to douse her with water. When she went to the toilet she was accompanied by a policewoman. They told her she would end up in Weskoppies Mental Asylum. They told her, 'We will crack you.' They told her that she had been followed for two months, and that every person she had been in contact with would be arrested. They told her they would have her daughter's bail withdrawn (she had been arrested for slogan painting), and that they would arrest her son Mark, notwithstanding the fact that he was deaf. As time went on Violet could not tell night from day. Her ankles were hanging over her shoes, and her eyes were swollen to mere slits. She told them, 'You are like a group of sadistic schoolboys pulling the wings off a fly, and I feel like the fly.' On the Thursday evening, 11 November, she gave them the information they wanted.

⁂

Violet was held for 179 days in detention, most of them incommunicado. Later she told Ilse that when the police questioned her, they asked her who the little man was with the beard, and if he was her contact with Bram. This was Ilse's reason for thinking they did not know who he was, even though they may have seen him.

⁂

The disjunction between private reality – whether of disguise, concealment or interrogation – and what appeared in the public domain was all but absolute. But private and public worlds were approaching their own rendezvous for Bram.

On Tuesday 9th, as Violet stood in her shuttered room, he made a simple call. When he moved from the Knox Street house in July, he had left R20 with a Mr Mason, the agent dealing with the rental of the house, to cover any remaining expenses on the water, electricity and telephone. Bram, as 'Mr Black', had told Mason he was leaving for Cape Town. When the small amount owing had been paid off, Mason found there was a balance of R18 left; also, a cheque had come in for a Mr Symon, in whose (false) name the lights and water had been registered. Since then he had been trying without success to contact Mr Black in order to return the money; and so when Bram phoned him on the 9th, he invited him in for the next morning. Bram met Mason on the 10th, collected the R18 and the Symon cheque, and then left. He was short of money and must have felt he would need every cent.

On that Wednesday, he made another call, this time in the name of Peter West, which he had been adopting for some time in order to cover his tracks even more effectively. The previous day (after speaking to Mason) he had visited Mrs Mary Lorna James, who had advertised in the newspapers that she had a three-roomed house with a pleasant, secluded garden to rent in the suburb of Dunkeld from mid-December to the end of January, at R100 a month. Bram had looked over the house, telling Mrs James that his invalid sister and his married daughter and her husband would be joining him. She found him affable and charming, and suggested he call the next day to make a decision. That was what Bram now did, and Mrs James invited him to return on Friday 12th to settle the arrangements. But Mr West never kept that appointment, and she was rather surprised later in the day to see a large picture of him in *The Star*.

When the Sepels heard that Violet had been detained, they were desperate that Bram should disappear. Ralph met him on the evening of the 10th in the Craighall Park Hotel, and was vehement. He told Bram he could not spend another night in his house, and at most had another twenty-four hours. He must cut all connection with them, abandon the house and everything in it, and go and live in a hotel if necessary. Then in a few months he could make contact, but in the meantime they should not know where he was. (There was some chance that Violet would talk about the Sepels rather than Bram, to protect him as long as possible.) Bram agreed; in fact he was very agreeable. The following day he phoned the Sepels from a call box. It was 11 November, the day that Ian Smith, Prime Minister of Rhodesia, announced his country's unilateral declaration of independence from Britain. Bram was delighted, saying it was the beginning of the end: Britain would settle Smith's rebellion within days, there would be a revolution in Rhodesia within weeks, and that had to lead to revolution in South Africa. Minnie Sepel asked him if he had moved. Bram said not yet, that he had one more letter to write.

He spoke to Mary Benson on that day as well, for the wife of Canon John Collins (the driving force behind the Defence and Aid Fund in London) was visiting Johannesburg, and Bram was intent on arranging to meet her. When he spoke, he sounded quite cheerful; Mary had already offered to lend him R100 for the deposit on the new house, and now they set up an appointment for Mrs Collins on the Saturday. But this was another appointment that Bram, still looking for revolutionary signs and portents, did not keep.

⁂

'I saw them. I actually saw them because I was meeting him that night. He was going to move . . . He was in the process of moving some stuff in the car – driving down the road when they stopped him.' Pat Davidson witnessed the aftermath of Bram's arrest.

It was 11 November, the day of Rhodesia's UDI, and Pat was due to meet Bram. But when she arrived at the designated pick-up spot, he wasn't there. She hadn't seen him since Violet's arrest, but knew all about it and the emergency it meant. In some panic, she drove off to tell Ilse; both of them thought that something might have occurred. After a while Pat returned to the meeting point, just in case Bram had appeared, borrowing Ilse's car because her own had been stalling. But still he hadn't arrived, and so she decided to drive past the house in Corlett Drive to see if everything looked normal. As she approached she saw a buzz of activity in the driveway, and recognised the Special Branch cars. There was a stream of traffic coming to a stop ahead of her, and she was just abreast of the house. One of the Special Branch men was looking down under his car at a tyre, while the others were standing around chatting. Pat pulled her scarf up around her head for concealment, but that did not make her feel any safer. Then, just as she was pulling off alongside the house, the policeman looked up from his tyre, and recognised Ilse's Volkswagen.

He shouted, and two cars came after her, chasing her up Corlett Drive, into Louis Botha Avenue towards town. She put her foot flat on the accelerator, tearing up the road, weaving in and out of the traffic, not knowing what she was doing or was going to do, the one thought in her head that she had to get away. She saw a gap and whipped into the right-hand lane; the car went onto two wheels, tipped up and then landed again on all fours with a resounding bang. After that the police stopped chasing her: perhaps they did not want to kill the woman they thought was Ilse on the evening they arrested her father. In any case, they already had what they wanted.

Pat drove on to the Old Johannians' Club, her refuge on many an occasion, and watched the squash games. A friend greeted her, remarking that she didn't look very well. She was fearful of returning to Ilse, but finally did so, telling her what she had seen. When Ilse heard the news she felt – as she said – 'pretty lousy', especially since neither she nor Pat could say a word to anyone. As to exactly what had occurred, illusions survived on every side. When Bram was questioned by the police they told him that his daughter had driven past the house as he was being arrested. He in turn wrote Ilse an angry letter, asking her how she could have been so naive. It was only later that he found out it wasn't her.

But Pat was sure she did notice something significant as she drove past. She saw that there was a huge force of security policemen at the house, as if they had been called out on a sudden emergency. Some of them (she said) were in the gathering summer even barefoot; they must have been doing other things when the urgent summons came. It was most likely that the police had not been tracking Bram for six months and then simply decided to pick him up. Violet broke on the Thursday evening after her seventy hours of torture, and as soon as the police got the news they raced with every possible speed to get Bram.

✳✳✳

The police had their own version of these events, as they recounted it later in court.

At about 6 p.m. on 11 November, Lieutenant Van Rensburg of the Special Branch had taken up surveillance duty near 215 Corlett Drive, Bramley. There he saw a white man get into a Volkswagen, registration number TJ 136-212, and leave the property. The lieutenant was in radio contact with other police cars, and they all began to converge on the Volkswagen, now driving in the direction of Oaklands. On the corner of Beaumont (Bram was so near home) and Stella streets, they brought the car to a stop. Van Rensburg walked over, and saw that the driver had a bald patch on the front of his head, a dark goatee and moustache, thin-rimmed glasses, and a pipe in his mouth. He addressed him as Abram Fischer, but the man rejected the appellation. He claimed to be Douglas Black, adding that the police had on a number of occasions accused individuals of being Fischer, only to acknowledge their mistake later. But Van Rensburg had no doubt, and got in touch with Captain Broodryk by radio.

Broodryk, who had been waiting at the Doll's House drive-in-diner in Louis Botha Avenue, was already on his way, and arrived about three minutes later, along with other police cars merging from different directions. Bram was still in the Volkswagen, sitting behind the wheel, now refusing to say a word. Then he put out his hand to Broodryk in greeting, and Broodryk, taking it, yanked him out of the car. They searched him, as well as the car, and then drove back to the house in Corlett Drive. Bram gave Broodryk the keys, and the house was opened up. It must have been then that Pat Davidson drove past.

᠊᠊᠊᠊᠊᠊

Inside they found an identity card and driver's licence in the name of Douglas Black. There was an exercise book and a writing pad containing notes and the practice signatures of 'P. West' and 'Peter West'. There were two envelopes containing cash in the sums of R250 and R160, as well as a copy of the SACP journal *African Communist,* and documents that should not have been left lying around: 'Draft Discussion Statement'; 'Notes on the Experience of Our Portuguese Branch'; 'A Note on Discipline and Training'; 'Rally and Unite Anti-Imperialist Forces – An Appeal from the Central Committee of the Communist Party'; 'Problems and Prospectus: Discussion Statement'. In the boot of Bram's car they had found a list in his handwriting of books from 'The Little Lenin Library', and scattered throughout the house were other relics of his spare life: cheque books, building society statements, deposit slips, two typewriters of different kinds and different typefaces, a skipping-rope, weights, a moustache, false eyebrows, two beards, a wig, a corset, tins of 'Tan-in-a Minute', mascara, Innoxa Foundation 41, Guerlain-Paris cream, wool and knitting needles, a woman's blue hat, a white blouse and green skirt, two pairs of panties, women's shoes, a hand-mirror, spare number plates for the car, a copy of *General De Wet* by Eric Rosenthal, and a Bible.

The Bible had not been for consolation but for code: two letters were discovered in the house, as well as encryption passages for each (one of these had been found in Bram's pocket when he was stopped). The first was from I Samuel, chapter ix, verse 11: 'And when they went up the hill they found young maidens going out to draw water.' The second was from Exodus, chapter xiii, verses 1–3: 'And the Lord spake unto Moses, saying, "Sanctify unto me all the firstborn, whatsoever openeth the womb among the children of Israel, both of man and of beast: it is mine." And Moses said unto the people, "Remember this day in which ye came from Egypt, out of the house of bondage; for by strength of hand the Lord brought you out from this place: there shall no leavened bread be eaten."'

According to these keys to the landscape of heaven as well as the content of underground letters, Bram had written to London in the decoy language of business, as later decoded by the police. Some of it was proud news about Issy Heymann: 'Issy (a) This company was called upon earlier this week to produce evidence in the trial of young Africans. It flatly refused to do so.' But Bram also wrote with some alarm about 'Nancy' (Violet or someone else?):

'I have now ascertained that the losses caused by this accident may be more far-reaching than I anticipated. Of course I do not doubt his constitutional strength, and I remain sure he will recover. What is disturbing, however, is that on the evening before the accident he was handed your latest balance sheet.'

He also wrote about people leaving the country: 'There is an extraordinary phenomenon which I have again encountered here. As soon as an item leaves the country it immediately loses its head. It was especially stipulated that those who helped him over should not be thanked. Despite this a wire arrived to express gratitude not only to the driver, but also to the resident near the border . . . Were it not impossible one would believe the whole thing to be deliberate. There must be some discipline.' And funds: 'This item is now very urgent. I'm afraid I cannot understand your attitude . . . I sit here unable to do anything until I know what the trouble is. I have explained my obligations to you in great detail, and will not repeat this.' And again on money, not only for himself but for others: 'I assume that you have been unable to do anything more than you have during the past few months. If you have and you have failed to do so, this would be absolutely unforgivable.'

Bram wrote, 'Hooray for UDI announced an hour ago. Good old Smithy.' He used the pseudonym 'Paulus'. These were his last letters to London, and they told of miscommunication, danger, hope, persistence and distress. Of course they never arrived.

※◎◎※

Who did arrive, back in Johannesburg from London, and just before Bram was arrested, was Paul Fischer.

His year in England had now run its course, and he was due to return. Ilse, whose flat would have been too cramped for the two of them, had taken a small house in the suburb of Fellside, where they both could live. It had not been an easy matter, for no one wanted to rent accommodation to a member of the Fischer family, but finally Ilse found someone who had known Bram and was prepared to take the risk. But Paul's journey had been far from smooth. In London, with its ever-present damp, he had been sick at regular intervals, becoming more familiar with the Great Ormond Street Children's Hospital than he might have wished. Still, in his independent way he had taken courses, travelled with Ruth, and had even gone on his own to Russia (this last trip ended unceremoniously: though Paul was only touring on holiday, those with Party connections had to undergo rigorous health checks, and Paul was sent back to London).

Now he, Ruth and Anthony were all due to return at more or less the same time. Anthony had completed his studies in law, and accepted a post at the University of Natal to be taken up in Durban in January. He had been reluctant to go back to South Africa, expecting retribution from the government for his own political activities as a student, but Ruth had been determined to come home. The obvious plan was for all three of them to travel together, but Paul wanted to venture out at least part of the way alone. So he left for Italy, where Ruth and Anthony met up with him, and they did the same in journeying on to Greece. After that they left for Cairo, but there Paul became dreadfully ill, with one of his chronic coughing infections eating away at his lungs. He took all the medicines he was carrying with him, but a doctor was nowhere to be found. It became imperative to get him back to Johannesburg, and to do so with all possible speed.

But Ruth could not get him on a plane. The difficulty was that flights from Cairo went as far as Nairobi, but Kenya – now independent and boycotting South Africa – would allow people with South African passports to land only if they were in transit for a connecting flight. But it was precisely this that Ruth could not arrange. Finally she found a plane with two available seats to Nairobi, and simply booked them for herself and Paul. As they were landing, she heard an announcement of a departure for Johannesburg and, frantically latching hold of an official, pleaded with him to stop the plane and allow Paul on because he was so ill. And so Paul travelled on by himself.

He arrived in Johannesburg just before Violet was detained, too sick even to think of a visit to Bram. Then Violet was arrested, and then his father. Ilse, expecting her own imminent arrest – Bram, in the midst of everything, had brought her on to the central committee of the Communist Party – had to sleep away from the Fellside house, and so there was no one to take care of Paul. By Christmas he was in hospital: and no one expected him to live out the year. It was one more item to weigh by default on Ilse's conscience.

As for Ruth, she waited in Nairobi for Anthony to arrive, and they went on to Bulawayo together, reaching it on 10 November. The next day was Rhodesia's unilateral declaration of independence, followed immediately by news of Bram's arrest.

꧁꧂

Almost the first thing the UDI regime did when it took power was to abolish the right of appeal to the Privy Council in London. It was a change with respect to South Africa that Bram had campaigned for as NUSAS prime minister in 1929, but its availability in Rhodesia had permitted his trip to London just a year before, and facilitated his preparations to go underground.

On the night of Thursday 11th, the Sepels were in bed when they turned on the radio for a time-check, and heard a news flash that Bram Fischer had been arrested. They talked it over: should they leave the country or stay? Then another news item came: Bram had been captured with an incriminating document in his possession. That decided them: they would leave, not only for their own safety and that of the children, but also so that they could take all the heat and blame when they were gone. They went to talk with Lesley Schermbrucker, to see what she advised. Her view was that they should make up their own minds, but she was going to stay: her husband was in jail.

On Saturday, 13 November the Sepels left, abandoning their house with everything in it for neighbours to wonder at agog. The police arrived only the following Wednesday, to find them already gone. This was one final reason for believing that the Security Police had not been following Bram for six months: if they had, they would surely have known about the Sepels and arrested them before they escaped. Prior to leaving, Ralph warned a friend whose postbox the underground group had been using to say that Ralph had told him he wanted it to receive pornography. The police did not get to this friend before the Monday.

The day after Bram's arrest, Pat Davidson had a visit from two strange men, early in the morning. She was living to the side of a house, not an obvious place for an enquiry, but they informed her that they were looking for someone who was a friend of the owner of the house. Pat had the distinct impression that they knew exactly who she was, and where to find her. When she went to court later that morning to see Bram charged, one Special Branch man pointed her out to another, remarking for her to hear, in Afrikaans, that she must have had a huge fright.

Ilse dealt with the lugubrious enquiries of reporters, who came with their fake sympathies and search for titillating details. Pretty soon she was taking her own evasive action, thinking she herself might have to leave the country. Bram's photograph was in the papers, arm clasped in the voluminous grip of a security policeman as he was arrested, eyes staring in some shock, stuck open in the spotlights. The Sepels believed he ought never to have been captured, that if only disciplined procedures had been followed he could have escaped even after Violet was arrested. He had a passport, and could have disappeared again, whether inside or outside the country.

Why didn't he go, just pack up and get out? Violet Weinberg said that they all urged him to – to use his passport and leave, even for a while. Lesley

Schermbrucker resisted the idea that Bram was depressed at the end, saying that it was always on the cards that he would be recaptured.

Part of it was loyalty to his comrades in the country, whether inside or still out of prison. It was also an ultimate statement of identification with the majority of South Africans who had no alternative but to remain, whether through suffering or redemption. Even in defeat it was an assertion of belonging, particularly for an Afrikaner whose roots went back into the past, who could not imagine a future elsewhere. Bram had given his word that he would remain in South Africa, and he was not at liberty to leave. Perhaps going overseas now, even temporarily, meant very little to him. He may have just been tired, after everything that had happened in the last year and a half. He could have escaped, and told people he would do so; he was in the process of moving, but was inordinately slow.

What would it mean to begin all over again? In some ways it might have been a relief to have it end. Ilse said, 'It was enough. It was enough for all of us by that stage.'

CHAPTER 14

INTO THE LIGHT

❦

11 November 1965 – 12 May 1975

On the Monday after Bram's recapture he was taken to the Johannesburg Regional Court to be charged, sitting on the front seat of a police car between two Special Branch men, while the newspaper photographers took their pictures. He had emerged into the light, wearing his old glasses again, familiar lenses to see the world. The auburn dye was still in his hair, though his beard had been shaved off, and the bald patch above his forehead was just beginning to be stubbly. On the car seat Bram looked resolutely ahead, mouth turned down at the corners above a strong jaw, gaze lofted just above the horizon.

The newspapers, exercised as much by normality under the unimaginable as they might be by the reverse, tracked the secret life of Mr Black. Local shop-keepers declared their surprise that the mild-mannered man who had appeared so harmless and endearing turned out to be South Africa's most wanted com-munist. The owner of the café where Pat had waited while Bram searched about in the phone booth for money commented that Mr Black had always seemed so polite; there had been something in him that set him apart from other customers. Two women who ran a small bookstore described a well-spoken and pleasant little man who had ordered a copy of *For Whom the Bell Tolls* and returned to collect it. An expert in plastic surgery observed that Bram's disguise showed all the signs of treatment by a skilled surgeon. The English couple who had shared his subdivided house paid tribute to 'an ideal neighbour and a real gentleman'. For much of this time Bram may have been *in extremis* and in disguise, but evidently his inner personality had never left him. It may after all have been a better way to trace him.

A heavily armed guard of forty-five policemen surrounded him as he was led into the court. Watching inside, and overflowing into the corridors, was a crowd of some one hundred and fifty people. Bram appeared composed, wear-ing a blue suit with a plain monogrammed red tie; as he glanced about the court the flicker of a smile crossed his face. When the magistrate remanded him for a week, he responded, 'Thank you, sir.' Paul, Ruth and Anthony were there; Ilse, expecting the worst, kept away. Before the brief hearing Paul, ill as he was, was called out by a security policeman and taken downstairs to the cells to his father; afterwards Ruth was allowed the same privilege.

Bram, hoping to last for at least three months, had been underground for 294 days. On his arrest the police claimed that he was 'a broken man – with little of the spirit of Bram Fischer', but reporters observing his behaviour in court saw, despite the strain, 'the same alert twinkle' in his eyes.

⁂

On the night of Bram's arrest he had been taken to Pretoria Central Prison and then, the day after, to Pretoria Local Prison, where the Jameson raiders had been held in 1896 and Jopie Fourie executed after the 1914 Rebellion. For Bram the historic associations, contrasts and continuities would have been readily apparent.

It was Pat Davidson who had the most immediate and greatest access to him, on the ground that she was his attorney and had to arrange his personal and financial affairs. At that stage Bram hardly had any financial affairs worth considering, but Pat's special status meant that she was admitted once a week and allowed contact visits in an office set aside for the purpose, with a guard keeping watch across the passage. Pat would sit at a desk next to Bram and discuss tax (about which she knew almost nothing), and then, making a show of working out calculations, the two would write copious notes to one another. In fact Pat was acting as a courier, arriving with letters interleaved among her papers, and taking messages from Bram out again. She said that at this time, in the immediate aftermath of his arrest, Bram was considering the possibility of an escape, although there couldn't have been any serious plans; it was more in the way of holding on to something positive to think about. Bram felt that he had achieved very little, recalled Pat, and now he faced the prospect of an extremely long jail sentence. He was in virtual isolation in prison.

George Bizos found that Bram could be bristly when he saw him to prepare his defence. When Bram asked for news of Paul after he had been hospitalised, George reported that the doctor had said he'd been neglected. To this Bram bridled in anger: 'What does he know', he objected, 'of what Molly and all of us did?' The very first time they met, George embraced Bram affectionately, and then asked him if it had all been worth it. He had had his nine and a half months underground: had it been worth sacrificing his family, his profession, and everything else? Bram's response was again angry and clear-cut. He wanted to know if George had asked Nelson Mandela that question: didn't Nelson have a practice and a family? George confessed that he had not asked Mandela. 'Well then, don't ask me,' Bram replied.

It must have been painful that the essential character of his actions and his protest still required translation, even to his friends. It had to be no more unnatural for a white man to make sacrifices for a new and free world in South Africa than it was for a black. This was the definition of his engagement, what he needed to have understood, and it was what he would have to clarify.

⚜

After the first brief remand, there was another short hearing on 22 December at which the prosecution applied to have the case against Bram converted into a preparatory examination, so that new and extended charges could be framed. In this way, through November, December and January, Bram awaited his trial, doing his best as time passed to lift his own mood and remain a rallying point for others, whether family, friends, comrades or merely odd acquaintances. His brothers came to visit, and remarked on how Bram was intent on cheering them up, rather than the other way round. A Johannesburg man awaiting trial on insurance fraud (something of a scapegoat in a larger scandal) later paid tribute to him for keeping him sane at that time.

Every day he was locked up for twenty-three out of twenty-four hours, and had to do everything he could to fill the time. He exercised during the period he was allowed out, walking a mile in thirty-yard lengths of the prison court-yard, and consulted syllabuses for correspondence courses from the University of South Africa. For fourteen hours a day he read all the books he had never had time for – everything from Perry Mason to *Anna Karenina*, Faulkner, Salinger and Jack London, as well as the Afrikaans 'Sestiger' writers who made the language both new and strange, and sometimes frustrating. He told Ilse that he would like his copy of General De Wet's book on the Boer War that he had left at Corlett Drive, remembering how as a boy he and his cousin Theunie Fichardt had played the Boer leaders in their games. (Theunie had always taken the role of President Steyn, while Bram had been De Wet, some-what ashamed that his Oupa Abraham had not taken any active part in the fighting.) For Bram there was a direct line between those old days and these. '*Send me as much political news as you have,*' he wrote to Ilse and, as Christmas approached, told her and Sholto to 'celebrate doubly – for yourselves and for all of us who will be joining you one of these days again'. He sent out detailed lists of matters requiring attention to Ruth and Ilse. 'Destroy old letters,' he ordered, but they disobeyed.

He corresponded with Liz Lewin, who had been in the car when Molly died. Now remarried in America, she wrote of the impending birth of her child, whom, if it was a boy, she was planning to call Abram. 'Perhaps he & I will meet one day,' he replied (after suggesting the folly of naming a child after him – not least because most Americans would think 'that you illiterate S. Africans don't know how to spell Lincoln's first name'), but it was not to be: Liz's child Bram died in a tragic accident some years later. To the Buntings in London Bram wrote that although their children were growing up overseas, they must 'remain South Africans'. As for himself, he told them that he was 'acclimatising myself to my future life . . . how to accept, without kicking, what is inevitable, how to keep myself fit and concentrate on work in prison'. By 'work' Bram meant, among other things, political work, for it was a crucial aspect of the self-definition of any revolutionary that one's arrival behind bars did not mark the end of one's struggle. This was what had happened to Beyleveld and others, but for that reason Bram was all the more determined to resist.

For now, as an awaiting-trial prisoner, his conditions, though unaccustomed, were still relatively privileged: he had visits twice a week, fresh clothing when he wanted, even food that he could keep in his cell. Yet his tasks were already beginning, not least preparing the case he had to fight, the speech from the dock he would present, which he already knew would have to be his lasting testament. George Bizos was collaborating with him on this, and in due course had to jog Bram along, because like all prisoners with time on their hands he was concerned and anxious about everything – his family, his friends, all the possible distractions of his situation. George had observed this during the Rivonia Trial, and now he saw it again.

Yet slowly Bram began to focus. As he returned to the sources he would need, he advised Ilse that if she wanted a tonic she should 'study Uncle Karl's manifesto again', as he had just done. The political polemic in Section III was out of date, he wrote, 'but for the rest – what a superb document'. Later he sent Ruth, Ilse and Paul to Church Square in Pretoria to check the inscription on the statue of Paul Kruger for a certain quotation he wanted to use.

The preparatory examination opened in the Johannesburg Regional Court on 26 January 1966 before Mr S.C. Allen, the same magistrate who had presided in the trial from which Bram had absconded. It was exactly a year and a day since he had disappeared.

The state offered its evidence for a trial, presenting more than two hundred exhibits, including all the letters and encryption codes the police had discovered, the typewriters, tins of cream, driver's licence, passport, the women's clothing. Mrs Milindton appeared, and was rather ingeniously vague on

Bram's initial stay at her farm in Rustenburg. He had called himself Charles Thompson, she remembered, and was upset because his wife had died in an accident; he had said he needed to be away for a while. But in court she couldn't identify the man she had met, and claimed she had never heard of Bram Fischer. She insisted that Mr Thompson had stayed in an outbuilding on her farm, but this was contradicted by her servant, who testified that he had stayed in a back room of the main house. But he too could not identify Bram. After repeated promptings the prosecutor wanted him to step out of the witness box and walk around the court to see if that would help, but George Bizos objected in one of those amusing legal moments in which he specialised: 'Your Worship, there comes a time when a person leading a witness has to give up.'

The flow of evidence – some of it gratuitous in the circumstances – was overwhelming: a stream of bank and building society tellers and managers who testified about accounts in the name of Douglas Black and Peter West, testimony on the role of Ann Getliffe in renting the Knox Street house, codes and encryptions for underground correspondence. Policemen gave their detailed descriptions of exactly how Bram Fischer was arrested. Sholto Cross was called as a witness, and expressed his reluctance, saying he had been introduced merely to embarrass him as Ilse Fischer's fiancé, and concerned too about incriminating himself. Informed that he was being named as an accomplice, after which he would be granted an indemnity from prosecution, he was no less spirited for the concession. When the prosecutor asked him why Bram had gone underground, he replied, 'Well, if you are asking me for my opinion . . . I would say that he felt it was a service to his country to do so.' When questioned as to why he had not reported Bram to the police, he responded that 'it was not morally right, even though it might have been legally right to do so'. Lesley Schermbrucker was also called. After taking legal advice, she refused outright to testify, saying that she was prepared to face the consequences: 'I don't wish to be disrespectful and I don't want to go to jail, but it is a question of principle.' Her husband was already in prison, and the younger of her two children was fifteen: she was sentenced to 300 days for her refusal.

If Sholto and Lesley raised the banner of loyalty in their insistent but unassuming way, the state depended once again, as it had in the previous Fischer trial, on Communist Party members who had abandoned and were now betraying their comrades. Bartholomew Hlapane was called. As with Beyleveld before, this was something of a personal rebuke to Bram. Hlapane had been a member of the Communist Party since 1955, and on the central committee since the end of 1962. Bram had had high hopes for him: when Hlapane was detained, Issy Heymann remembered how Bram had pulled money out of his wallet to be given to his wife. Now he spoke at length (testimony on which he would elaborate in the trial proper) as to how both the ANC and uMkhonto weSizwe were under the control of the Communist Party. He offered vivid accounts indicating that Bram was in favour of violence, and 'wanted action. Positive action.' He described Bram pounding the table, walking up and down, cursing. 'He swore. That is all I remember, your Worship.'

Such was the intricate mesh of truth and lies Hlapane rendered, that Bram felt obliged to refer to the matter when he was asked to plead at the end of the proceedings. 'Regarding my defence,' he told the magistrate, 'I wish to say this: if some of the evidence led is correct, then at my trial I shall not seek to deny that evidence; on the other hand, important evidence has been given which is either grossly distorted or which I shall maintain is untruthful, and this evidence will be denied. At this stage, however, the truthful and the false evidence is so inextricably interwoven that it is not possible, by means of a plea, to unravel the one from the other . . . In these circumstances, therefore, I plead not guilty to all the charges.'

At the same time Bram took the trouble to defend some of the organisations and individuals which the prosecution had roped into the case during its presentation of the evidence – the Christian Institute, Defence and Aid, the South African Institute of Race Relations (for which Bram had once worked, though that wasn't the reason it was mentioned now), the Rev. Beyers Naudé, to whom he had sent his underground letter – in order to paint the threatening picture of a wholesale communist conspiracy to which willing liberal lackeys gave succour. The only sin of these organisations, remarked Bram, was their 'unpopularity with the present government'. And if he had written to Beyers Naudé (Bram's letter had been stolen by the police, photocopied, and then replaced, but the original was now nowhere to be found), 'it is hardly his fault that I hold the same views as he does about the dignity of man.'

The preparatory examination closed on 2 February: there was no question that Bram would be committed for a trial. He elected to be tried by a judge; a jury would not have been helpful in the prevailing climate. Besides, he had issues to explain which he might have hoped a judge would understand.

The trial opened on Wednesday, 23 March 1966 in the central court of the Palace of Justice in Pretoria, with its lofty colonial ceilings and windows, pink-tinged colorations, and fans revolving unhurriedly overhead. Police guards took up their posts at the doors some two hours before the trial started, as spectators arrived to pack the public gallery. Hearing the case was Mr Justice Boshoff. Observers were present from three foreign countries, and security policemen occupied the well of the court. Bram sat alone in the twelve-man dock that had been constructed specially for the Rivonia Trial, accustomed now to the irony – or continuity – which had seen him on both sides of the legal proceedings in that same venue as defence and accused. Once again he appeared serene as he came into court, settling himself carefully before turning to smile at Ruth and Ilse in the gallery. Then, in his characteristic manner – it implied a philosophy as well as instinctive habit – he smiled and spoke with members of the Security Police, and laughed with Sydney Kentridge, leading his defence. Even here, aged and thinner, he had that engaging aura about him which attracted others and put them at their ease.

The charges against him were now manifold. Before, in the trial from which Bram had disappeared, the allegations had been that he was a member of the Communist Party, had participated in its activities, and had furthered its aims. Now there were six detailed charges on that score, but to these still others had been added, of which the most serious (and now the first count) was one of sabotage. At Rivonia and elsewhere, it was the state's contention, Bram had conspired with others to cause 'a violent revolution' in South Africa; it was the same charge that the Rivonia trialists had faced. Compared with this the remainder of the fifteen counts against him appeared almost frivolous: there were six charges of fraud (Bram's pseudonymous dealings with banks and building societies), or alternatively of contravening the Aliens Act of 1937 through the use of false names; and two counts of forgery and uttering, in respect of his false driver's licence and passport. All this showed that the state was pursuing its case with a litigious and demeaning literalism, even though there were aspects that were mildly amusing: Bram's grandfather had granted Barclays Bank its charter in the Orange Free State; now he was being charged with defrauding it. But there was no escaping the seriousness of the main allegation. Before, Bram would have been sentenced to five years' imprisonment; now, on the Rivonia precedent, he stood to get life.

Bram rose to attention in the capacious dock to hear the charges and to plead not guilty. In his own mind his aim was not to conceal what he had done, but only to clarify it. After the staggeringly long years of defending others at the Treason and Rivonia trials (counting the proceedings of the Fischer trial the previous year and the mineworkers' strike trial of 1946, it was the fifth major political case of his career), the substance of it would be over within a week.

On that first day of the trial Bram heard Hlapane again, now the state's prime and most significant witness. In answer to questions put to him by the prosecutor, Mr J.H. Liebenberg, he spoke of a Communist Party underground conference towards the end of 1962 at which uMkhonto's projection for a 'second stage' – what Hlapane explained as guerrilla warfare – had been presented by Joe Slovo. He claimed that he first saw the plan of 'Operation Mayibuye' (the document on which the Rivonia Trial had turned) at a central committee meeting where it had been approved, and that the National High Command of uMkhonto weSizwe was 'responsible to' the Communist Party. He testified that Bram was treasurer of the Communist Party, and was under instruction to make funds available for Operation Mayibuye; he himself had received R4900 from Bram to pay uMkhonto functionaries. At meetings at Rivonia Bram had been chairman of the proceedings whenever he was present, and on one occasion had suggested burning mealie and sugar-cane fields. When Hlapane had acted as a contact with Wilton Mkwayi (codename 'Bri-Bri') in uMkhonto, Bram had given advice on *ad hoc* methods of sabotage, in the absence of dynamite, which was in short supply: to throw ropes over telephone cables and bring them down; to short-circuit railway lines by setting wires across them. Questioned again by Liebenberg on the role of the Communist Party in relation to the liberation movement as a whole, Hlapane replied that it was 'the head of them all'.

It was a serious train of connections, implicating Bram and the Communist Party as ultimately responsible for an ambitious and, in some respects, vicious campaign of sabotage and revolutionary manipulation. Yet Sydney Kentridge pursued Hlapane in cross-examination, pointing out the discrepancies in his evidence. Hlapane, he indicated, had not told the magistrate at the preparatory examination that the central committee had given instructions to uMkhonto weSizwe. At the preparatory there had been no suggestion that a 'second phase' of action meant anything more than further acts of sabotage, or that guerrilla warfare had been approved. Nor had Hlapane mentioned originally that Bram Fischer was to raise money for Operation Mayibuye; in fact, remarked Kentridge, his client had instructed him that he personally, like many others, thought Operation Mayibuye 'a most impractical and ridiculous plan'. When Hlapane testified that Fischer had given him R4900 in 'five pound notes' which he had concealed on his body, did he know, enquired Kentridge, what such a sum in notes would look like? He pointed out that Hlapane claimed to have reported to the central committee on certain acts of sabotage at a time when he had already been in detention for two weeks. In response Hlapane blamed an inadequate interpreter at the preparatory examination, or maintained that certain questions had simply not come up. Kentridge argued the obvious, that subsequent to his initial testimony Hlapane had been coached by the police, tailoring his account to fit the specific charges against Bram.

After Hlapane it was Beyleveld's turn, and although his appearance by now was predictable it was also useful, as in cross-examination Kentridge probed him quietly on Hlapane's key allegations – most of which Beyleveld straightforwardly refuted. On issues of organisation and hierarchy, he stated that there was 'no formal link between the Communist Party and *Umkhonto weSizwe*'. Though sabotage had been discussed as it occurred, there had been no official reports to the central committee; nor had the central committee given instructions to uMkhonto or funded it. On the question of the Communist Party controlling ANC policy, he was blunt: 'Well, we would not have been able to decide its policy. How are we going to get them to agree with it?' His only significant point of agreement with Hlapane was that the campaign of sabotage had been intended to guard against loss of life, his only apparent area of disagreement with Bram (revealed under Liebenberg's re-examination) was that after the Rivonia Trial he had believed the Party should become dormant, whereas Bram had regarded its continued existence as imperative. It may have been a small clue: perhaps it had been that view – one that had already conceded defeat and wanted cessation – that underlay Beyleveld's depression and collapse when arrested.

Then the police infiltrator Ludi appeared once again, to tell of meetings, of chats with Bram Fischer, of front organisations, of Bram's insistence on the need for people to remain in the country, of disputes between the Soviet Union and China. It was gratuitous evidence and a sideshow, and Kentridge indicated that he would decline to cross-examine Ludi because, even where his testimony had been incorrect, it was of no material relevance to the case. Then came the succession of accountants and managers of building societies and banks, each of whom agreed, under Kentridge's questioning, that Bram had in no way defrauded their institutions financially, despite the fact that he had used assumed names. The Receiver of Revenue even acknowledged that Bram had, on the expectation that he might be imprisoned, overpaid what he owed the government in tax, and showed a credit to his account of nearly R2000. So much for fraud, and forgery and uttering.

Other witnesses told their stories: Mrs Mary Lorna James, who had nearly rented her house to Bram; Mr Mason, the agent who had done so indirectly at Knox Street; a black worker at the Rivonia farm; an uMkhonto member who had undergone military training overseas and been sentenced to ten years;

Sergeant Dirker, who had raided Rivonia; the policemen who had arrested Bram. All the evidence had taken just over two days, and on Monday, 28 March, after the prosecution formally closed its case, Sydney Kentridge announced that the defence would not call any witnesses: 'The accused, who is of course well aware of his legal rights, wishes to make a statement from the dock.'

From Bram's first days as an advocate in court he had given many addresses – opening, closing, and in argument. He had also, in his political life, presented lectures, made speeches, written documents. But this was to be a different kind of offering as well as culmination, in which law, justice, politics, autobiography and advocacy were most intricately meshed. Short of historic triumph, a speech from the dock may be a revolutionary's definitive moment: Bram was there to give nothing less than an explanation of his life and what he stood for. In both the form of his presentation and the content of his account, his task was to establish the principles to which he was committed, and further the cause for which he was about to be sentenced. It was to be an address not only to the court, but also, as a South African, to the past with which he remained linked, the present to which he remained answerable, and the future to which his conscience and hopes were still turned. Bram began at ten o'clock in the morning, and it was some five hours before he ended, reading from his notes all the while.

⁂

I am on trial, my Lord, for my political beliefs and for the conduct which those beliefs drove me to. My Lord, whatever labels may have been attached to the fifteen charges brought against me, they all arise from my having been a member of the Communist Party and from my activities as a member. I engaged upon those activities because I believed that, in the dangerous circumstances which have been created in South Africa, it was my duty to do so.

My Lord, when a man is on trial for his political beliefs and actions, two courses are open to him. He can either confess to his transgressions and plead for mercy, or he can justify his beliefs and explain why he has acted as he did. Were I to ask for forgiveness today, I would betray my cause. That course, my Lord, is not open to me. I believe that what I did was right, and I must therefore explain to your Lordship what my motives were; why I hold the beliefs that I do, and why I was compelled to act in accordance with them.

My belief, moreover, my Lord, is one reason why I have pleaded not guilty to all the charges brought against me. Though I shall deny a number of important allegations, this Court is aware of the fact that there is much in the State case which has not been contested. Yet, if I am to explain my motives and actions as clearly as I am able, then this Court was entitled to have had before it the witnesses who testified in chief and in cross-examination against me. Some of these, my Lord, I believe were fine and loyal persons who have now turned traitor to their cause, and to their country, because of the methods used against them by the State. Their evidence, my Lord, therefore may in important respects be very unreliable.

My Lord, there is another reason, and a more compelling reason for my plea and why even now I persist in it. I accept, my Lord, the general rule that for the protection of a society laws should be obeyed. But when the laws themselves become immoral, and require the citizen to take part in an organised system of oppression – if only by his silence and apathy – then I believe that a higher duty arises. This compels one to refuse to recognise such laws.

The law, my Lord, under which I have been prosecuted, was enacted by a wholly unrepresentative body, a body in which three-quarters of the people of this country have no voice whatever. This and other laws were enacted not to prevent the spread of Communism, but, my Lord, for the purpose of silencing the opposition of the large majority of our citizens to a government intent upon depriving them, solely on account of their colour, of the most elementary human rights: of the right to freedom and happiness, the right to live together with their families wherever they might choose, to earn their livelihoods to the best of their abilities, and to rear and educate their children in a civilized fashion; to take part in the administration of their country and to obtain a fair share of the wealth they produce; in short, my Lord, to live as human beings.

My conscience, my Lord, does not permit me to afford these laws such recognition as even a plea of guilty would involve. Hence, though I shall be convicted by this Court, I cannot plead guilty. I believe that the future may well say that I acted correctly.

⁂

Ruth, Ilse and Paul were there to listen, as they had been the previous week to the evidence. It had not been a pleasant experience, especially for Ilse, who had already sat through the major part of the original Fischer Trial. Now they watched Bram speak quietly, undramatically, in his characteristic legal manner, almost as if he were presenting argument to a judge on behalf of a client. Bram was no Nelson Mandela, who had spoken from the dock in this same court just two years before, and there was no obvious drama or passion; but the effect none the less was transfixing. *The Times* of London described the 'rapt attention as in quiet, unemotional tones the slight, silver-haired man explained the standpoint from which his actions had flowed'.

Bram clarified why he had not entered the witness box. This had been, he indicated, because he was not prepared to prevaricate or lie, nor was he prepared to implicate or inform on anyone, whether by his words or silence in answer to questions. If the court drew adverse inferences from his unwillingness to be cross-examined, then that was something he could not avoid. He told of what had moved him to join the Communist Party. In the first instance it had not been Marxism as a social theory, 'just as little, presumably, as a doctor would say he was originally drawn to his field of science by its demonstrable truths'. More immediately he had been compelled, on the one hand, by the glaring injustice which had existed for so long in South Africa, and, on the other, by example: 'It was always the members of the Communist Party who seemed prepared, regardless of cost, to sacrifice most; to give of their best, to face the greatest dangers, in the struggle against poverty and discrimination.'

But injustice by itself did not explain his conduct; it was there for all white South Africans to see, and most regarded it unmoved. It was then that Bram cast his mind back to the experience that, though forty years past, had unleashed everything for him, when at his first meeting of the Joint Council of Europeans and Africans in Bloemfontein he had been obliged to shake a black man's hand and found that it required an enormous act of will. He recalled for the court (as he had already done for Leo Marquard, thinking about these matters after his arrest) the contrast with his youth on the farm, when he had played with his black friends so freely and without prejudice. 'Like many young Afrikaners I grew up on a farm. Between the ages of eight and twelve my daily companions were two young Africans of my own age. I can still remember their names. For four years we were, when I was not at school, always in each other's company. We roamed the farm together, we hunted and played together, swam together and made clay oxen together. And never can I remember a single occasion that the colour of our skins affected our fun or our quarrels, or our close friendship in any way.' He described the crisis of conscience the handshake had precipitated, his consequent understanding that it was he who had changed and not the black man. This, as he put it then, had been his first lesson on the way to the Communist Party, a party that had sustained its firm belief in the eventual brotherhood of all men. Both at that time and for many years afterwards it had been the only political party which stood for an extension of the franchise; to this day its chief objective remained the elimination of discrimination and the granting of all normal human rights. 'My Lord, this is the objective for which the Communist Party has stood, and it is the objective for which I have lived and worked for nearly thirty years.'

Yet he had to explain not only why he had joined the Communist Party, but also why he had continued to remain a member once it had become illegal. It was in this context that Bram took the opportunity – so rare in any public forum in South Africa – to outline, at some length, the philosophy to which he was committed. In preparing his case he had directed his lawyers to read the communist standards – Marx, Engels, Lenin and Stalin ('the old man was probably the clearest writer of them all,' he had suggested in his notes) – and now he offered the court his version of history in the most orthodox of Marxist terms. He described the rise and fall of successive societies, the relationship between economic and political organisation, and how inevitable transformation depended on changes in the methods and modes of production. Marxist theory explained, he suggested, why in different historical periods different kinds of society had existed: 'It also explains why one type of society must of necessity give way to a new and higher form.' History became something that could be rationally understood, and modern society itself assumed a meaning: 'It has not appeared on the stage by chance, nor . . . is it final or immutable, and in its South African form it contains its own contradictions which must irresistibly lead to its change.'

To Bram these truths were, as he put it, 'self-evident'. They may have been less than that to his audience, but his confiding as well as quietly assertive manner suggested he would never relinquish the possibility of persuasion. Marxism, he insisted, was not evil or violent or subversive, having already been accepted as a way of life by more than a thousand million people in the world. South African legislation could not abolish its scientific approach, nor could it abolish 'those four years when the Soviet Union, then the only socialist State, stood as one of the main bastions between civilisation and the Nazi army'. The vast majority of South Africans were governed by a system based upon fear, both of unemployment and of poverty, accentuated by the colour bar – a similar fear that had led Hitler to propagate his monstrous theory of race superiority, leading to the extermination of 'five million Jews'. Communism, far from aiming at a form of despotic government, was the only system which in the long run could make such fears obsolete. A weakening imperialist sector was incapable of catering to the wants of colonial peoples, and in that sense a new era of democracy and independence was inevitable. This was something that Afrikaners, of all people, should understand, for it was they who had once been in the vanguard of the liberation movement in Africa, taking on the greatest empire of all time, to fail in war but succeed ultimately by peace, because 'We knew we could not be resisted.'

And this for him was the ultimate issue: 'the sole question for the future, for the future of everyone, is not whether change will come, but whether [it] can be brought about peacefully, and without bloodshed.' Nothing exercised Bram more, recalled George Bizos, than the danger of impending violence in South Africa and the need to avoid it. If there was passion in his speech, it was here. All that the police state could achieve, Bram warned, would be a short-term period of quiet, and long-term hatred. South Africa was set on the path of civil war, though it was one that the whites could not win. Yet win or lose, the consequences would be 'horrifying and permanent . . . Clearly it is imperative that an alternative solution be found, for in truth, civil war is no solution at all.'

And that, explained Bram, was why he had been a member of the illegal Communist Party, for it was only the Communist Party and the Congress movements that preached racial co-operation and not conflict. If white leaders had followed the same model, South Africa might already have reached a position of safety. 'My Lord, I speak from personal experience. I have worked with every Congress leader in South Africa. With these beliefs I had no alternative but to break the law.'

❧

Bram turned to the issue of why he had estreated bail. It was not to save himself, he pointed out to the court: had he wished to do that, he could have remained in England in 1964. But by 1965 all the imperatives he had laid out were magnified a hundredfold. Moreover, there was a responsibility he felt particularly as an Afrikaner, for it was Afrikaners who were identified with all the evils and humiliations of apartheid. This boded ill for the future, and would require all the wisdom of the Congress leaders now imprisoned to counteract, but it also demanded something more: that Afrikaners themselves should protest openly and clearly against discrimination. That was the mantle Bram had assumed: 'Surely, my Lord, in these circumstances, there was an additional duty cast upon me, that at least one Afrikaner should make this protest actively and positively, even though as a result I now face fifteen charges instead of four.'

'My Lord,' Bram said, 'it was to keep faith with all those dispossessed by apartheid that I broke my undertaking to the Court, that I separated myself from my family, pretended I was someone else, and accepted the life of a fugitive. I owed it to the political prisoners, to the banished, to the silenced and to those under house arrest not to remain a spectator, but to act. I knew what they expected of me, and I did it. I felt responsible, not to those who are indifferent to the sufferings of others, but to those who are concerned. I knew, my Lord, that by valuing above all their judgement, I would be condemned by people who are content to see themselves as respectable and loyal citizens. I cannot regret any such condemnation that may follow me.'

There had been a tea break, there was a lunch break, and through it all Bram continued. Weaving his own story against the backdrop of a broader political history, he dealt with the evidence against him, separating fact from fiction. He had been acting chairman of the Communist Party, but not its treasurer. UMkhonto had from its inception remained a separate organisation from the Congresses and SACP. He himself had become aware of the existence of uMkhonto after it was formed, 'and I did not disapprove'. But the central committee of the Communist Party had exercised no control over uMkhonto, nor instructed it on sabotage or received official reports; nor did Bram have any knowledge of its financial sources. On the question of Operation Mayibuye, this had come up for discussion at a central committee meeting, but the committee had expressed only its 'complete disapproval'. Bram himself had been totally opposed to the whole idea: 'It seemed to me . . . wholly unsuited to the situation in South Africa as it then existed. It was, in addition, totally impracticable. If ever . . . there was a plan which a Marxist could not approve in the then prevailing conditions, this was such a plan.'

Bram flatly denied ever advocating the burning of mealie fields. He had never given Bartholomew Hlapane R4900, nor had such a large sum in his possession. He had never intended to defraud anyone, nor had he used his forged documents until the police arrested him. As for the idea that the Communist Party controlled the ANC, this was the most ancient of canards, thoroughly demolished during the Treason Trial. Bram gave a short disquisition on the nature of torture and solitary confinement (as to the latter, 'every South African voter should try it on himself'), and the way in which they distorted both justice and the personalities of men such as Hlapane and Beyleveld, making their evidence wholly unreliable.

And then he turned again to matters more personal, recalling how he had been a nationalist 'by the age of six, if not before'. He had first seen violence sitting on his father's shoulders when business premises with German names were burned to the ground in Bloemfontein, including those of some of his own family. He remembered his father leaving with an ambulance unit to join the rebel forces. He had remained a nationalist for over twenty years, and had become first Nationalist prime minister of a student parliament. In all those years he had never doubted the policy of segregation until Hitler's theory of race superiority threatened the world with genocide and disaster, and a conversation with an old ANC leader had convinced him that racial separation, far from lessening friction, could lead only to suspicion and hatred. As it approached three o'clock in the afternoon, Bram's speech was coming to an end, and he spoke from his heart.

⁂

All the conduct, my Lord, with which I have been charged, has been directed towards maintaining contact and understanding between the races of this country. If one day it may help to establish a bridge across which white leaders and the real leaders of the non-whites can meet to settle the destinies of all of us by negotiation, and not by force of arms, I shall be able to bear with fortitude any sentence which this Court may impose on me. It will be a fortitude, my Lord, strengthened by this knowledge at least, that for the past twenty-five years I have taken no part, not even by passive acceptance, in that hideous system of discrimination which we have erected in this country, and which has become a by-word in the civilized world.

My Lord, in prophetic words, in February 1881 one of the great Afrikaner leaders addressed the President and the Volksraad of the Free State.

His words are inscribed on the base of the statue of President Kruger in the square in front of this Court. After great agony and suffering, after two wars, they were eventually fulfilled without violence. President Kruger's words were:

Met vertrouwen leggen wy onze zaak open voor de geheele wêreld. Het zy wy overwinnen, het zy wy sterven: de vryheid zal in Afrika ryzen als de zon uit de môrewolken. [With confidence we lay our case open before the whole world. Whether we conquer or whether we die: freedom shall rise in Africa like the sun from the morning clouds.]

In the meaning which those words bear in the context today, they are as truly prophetic as they were in 1881. My motive in all that I have done has been to prevent a repetition of that unnecessary and futile anguish which has already been suffered in one struggle for freedom.

⁂

Bram ended as quietly as he had begun; it was the inscription on Kruger's statue that he had sent Ruth, Ilse and Paul to verify. The South African newspapers, given the right of judicial access, summarised and excerpted his speech at some length. Yet as soon as the trial was over his words became restricted by virtue of his banning, as deeply illicit as any in South Africa. His address from the dock became unavailable, left resonating only in the silence. Yet one day there would be a bridge across which white leaders and the leaders of the South African majority would meet to settle the destinies of all by negotiation and not force of arms. Though Bram would not be there to see it, perhaps his life and affirmation of solidarity here had helped fashion that bridge.

⚜

The proceedings had been brief, but the judge decided, surprisingly, that he needed time to read through all the documents and consider the evidence, and so the court was adjourned for six weeks. On Wednesday, 4 May 1966, Bram was convicted, and on Monday, 9 May, sentence was delivered. Bram was conducted into court after Mr Justice Boshoff had entered – entirely unusual, but most likely to prevent demonstrations – and stood alert for the twenty-five minutes it took Boshoff to speak. The judge accepted the evidence of Hlapane and Beyleveld (notwithstanding their mutual contradiction), and found in the face of everything Bram had maintained that the Communist Party had authorised the activities of uMkhonto weSizwe. Remarking that the deterrent and preventive aspects of punishment called for emphasis in this case, he sentenced Bram to life imprisonment on the count of sabotage; to twenty-four years on the six charges under the Suppression of Communism Act; to fines totalling R120 (or six months' imprisonment) for six contraventions of the Aliens Act; and to three months on the two counts of forgery. All the terms were to run concurrently, but it made no difference: in South Africa, life meant life.

After the judge had concluded, Bram turned round to where Ilse and Paul sat in the front row of the crowded gallery and smiled. Then he raised his right fist with thumb extended in the ANC salute: *Afrika! Mayibuye!* Africa! May It Come Back! As he was taken down to the cells, a throng of supporters remained to talk to the Fischer children until the police cleared the gallery. Then Ilse and Paul left by a back door into the street behind the court.

The night before, Bram had written to them, as he had to a good number of friends and comrades, a letter to arrive after his sentence. 'My darlings,' he wrote, 'This is farewell – I think. We seem to have said it so often that I am growing somewhat sceptical about its ever happening. Goodness, we seem to have been through several lifetimes in the past two years, don't we. [But] . . . just as there is a "last night" as an awaiting trial prisoner, so there will come a "last night" for me as a prisoner. Just think what a night that will be.'

He thanked them for the new birthday shirt which he would wear on his final day in court. 'All my love – Good luck,' wrote Bram.

⚜

The speech and sentence were reported worldwide, and letters and telegrams flowed in – not only from communist parties (Hungary, Italy, Austria, New Zealand, Bulgaria, British Guiana, Britain, Romania, Israel, Canada, Australia, Cyprus), but also from a range of student and other organisations in Scandinavia, England and elsewhere. Paul Fischer received a letter signed by a number of people from his old school, St John's, assuring him of 'sympathy, understanding, and friendship', and in the circumstances it was a courageous gesture.

Lesley Schermbrucker was sentenced to 300 days for her refusal to testify against Bram, and Violet Weinberg to three months when she declined similarly in the trial of Issy Heymann and Michael Dingake. Ultimately both were charged in a new Communist Party trial, and pleaded guilty after some of the counts against them had been dropped. They – two women with husbands in jail and children at home – had kept faith, whereas men like Beyleveld and Hlapane had not. Hlapane, who testified against them as well, had almost certainly been driven unstable by successive detentions; later, after being dragged around for some years as a peripatetic witness, he, like Patrick Mthembu, was assassinated. The capacity not only for heroism but for destruction seemed an implacable part of the South African situation, and it was the looming threat of destruction that Bram most of all regretted and feared.

It was a destruction that still hovered over his family. A week after the trial Ilse Fischer and Sholto Cross were listed as communists. Paul was still desperately ill, having emerged from successive bouts in hospital. As for Ruth, the reason she was not in court to hear Bram sentenced was that she had in effect been banished from the country. First Anthony had been expelled, declared a prohibited immigrant just weeks before he was due to take up his post in Natal. At that point he returned to Rhodesia, while Ruth commuted back and forth between her father on trial and her husband. Then on the evening Bram's case was adjourned prior to judgment, she tried unsuccessfully to get on a plane to Rhodesia. The next morning she phoned the railways to make a reservation; no one knew of her plans, but when she arrived on the platform at eleven o'clock, the Security Police were waiting and confiscated her passport. So Ruth was stuck in South Africa, and Anthony in Rhodesia. Later she was able to obtain a British passport and moved to join him, living under another renegade government and permitted to see her father once a year.

꧁꧂

When Bram was first brought into Pretoria Local Prison after his arrest, Issy Heymann was in his cell, more or less in solitary confinement following his suicide attempt, counting (as he recalled in a private memoir written years later) the number of bolts on the metal door over and over. He heard people walking up the stairs, past the door, and someone say, 'Look here, Fischer.' In the unsparing confines of prison it was a careless remark, followed by a hushed silence. A door was unlocked, something said, too far away to hear properly; but Issy knew he would never forget that moment.

Prisoners awaiting trial were kept separately from those who had been convicted, and so there was no contact. But one night Issy heard Fred Carneson's voice (he had also been arrested) talking to Bram a few doors away. He called out, 'Hello Fred!', but then Bram said, 'We'd better leave it, somebody heard us.' Later Issy discovered that he could communicate by placing a stool on his table and talking into the meshed-wire fanlight. He would whistle the first line of 'The Red Flag', and because it was so out of tune Bram would complete the rest; it became a regular routine during his trial. Issy told Bram about the sentimental novels he had been reading, and Bram confided for companionship that he too was sentimental. Yet the night after his sentence he did not climb on his table to speak to Issy. From the floor he told him that he had been given a life sentence, and was not going to appeal. There was a sob in his voice which he quickly suppressed, and then he changed the subject.

❧

> The problem is not falling a captive,
> it's how to avoid surrender.

Bram, who had quoted Nazim Hikmet to Ilse, might also have known these lines written from a Turkish prison by a poet who had been sentenced to twenty-eight years: they captured the new contours of his struggle. At the age of fifty-eight Bram slept on mats, who had once lived with Molly lofted among the trees at Beaumont Street. His drinking water was balanced unlidded on top of his toilet pot, which every morning he had to clear out. There was a head warder who controlled the limits of his existence, who hated him and did everything he could to humiliate him. No one would have said from the letters that he wrote while his trial was proceeding that already his life was conforming to this inordinate shape, because he did all he could to flood every word with brightness and encouragement. After his sentence there were those who said that he never expected that 'life' would mean life. The revolution was coming, Rhodesia would fall, those who had been imprisoned would be liberated, they would never see out their terms. But day by day, as time stretches out, there is another world that closes in. New prisoners come, old prisoners go; in this world within the world one day comes after another, and it is hard to believe that it is not the same day. Here the task is to transform from within, to wage the struggle for dignity even here, a politics inside the prison, inside the self, not to succumb to the ultimate sentence which is acquiescence. And slowly this begins to happen: with one's friends and comrades a new life is made, meanings found, landmarks established in the indeterminate expanse. Prison, the most radical expression of confinement, can also create the most radical dimensions and moments of liberty. Words cannot mirror this time within another time, except to suggest its fragile truth: that even here there was an inner light that struggled to push back at the darkness. As the poet Hikmet suggested, there was always a horizon to follow.

> Some people are free, their minds barred,
> some people behind bars, feel free.

The warder who hated Bram was called Du Preez. Under-educated as most warders were, he was exceptional in the explosive temper and incorruptible literalism that made every prison regulation a matter for the voluble exercise of personal power. Like Bram he was an Afrikaner, and perhaps there was a degree of vengeance in the way he made this traitor to the *volk*, this eminent ex-QC who consorted with *kaffirs* and Jews and communists, live through daily degradation.

At that time there were only three political prisoners in Pretoria Local: Bram, Issy Heymann and Harold ('Jock') Strachan. Strachan was a cheerfully irreverent type who had first been sentenced to three years along with Ben Turok in 1962. Upon his release he had authored a series of articles (published heroically by the *Rand Daily Mail*) setting out the barbaric conditions in place for political prisoners. For Strachan's trouble the state charged him with perjury, and suborned Raymond Thoms, an unstable man and their only ready collaborator, to testify against him. Soon Strachan was back inside Local, and conditions, which had improved, rapidly worsened again.

Bram was alone with Strachan and Heymann through an accident of timing. In March 1966 the bulk of the political prisoners were moved from Pretoria Local to Pretoria Central in an effort to eradicate the distinction (which the South African government disallowed) between political and common criminals. (The fact that at Pretoria Central they might become subject to the corruptions and therefore surveillance of 'normal' prison life would only be an added advantage.) Meanwhile, back at Local (as it was termed), Du Preez lavished his attention on the three who came into his charge in the interim. In the courtyard was an edifice known to the prisoners as the 'Potemkin', in sardonic honour of the revolutionary battleship whose superstructure it parodically suggested. It was an ablution block with urinals, two toilets and two showers, surrounded by a four-foot wall, but open to sight on every side. Du Preez took his pleasure standing in the middle while he made Bram and the others – but particularly Bram – wash the toilets and urinals by hand with rags. They swept the floors of corridors with brooms worn down to the wood. They were subject to rules of silence and Du Preez's regular screaming outbursts. Du Preez handed out clothes to Bram, especially finding the baggiest and most lopsided and denaturing. He gave Bram a greasy old hat that was too big, which Bram washed in boiling water until it resembled a muddy-looking rag. But humiliation could be turned inside out. Bram kept on to that hat until it became part of his identity in prison. Jock Strachan sewed on a bow with green and red checks, and the whole became an appendage of character and distinction which Bram regarded with complete and personal affection.

Yet when the other political prisoners returned from Pretoria Central in November, they were shocked to see Bram's appearance – dishevelled, ragged and somewhat depressed. As for them, the experiment of sending them away had failed completely. Not only had they not become indistinguishable from the regular run of common prisoners, but from the latter they had picked up 'boop-craft' – the wiles of survival, barter and smuggling in jail – and some of the mental attitudes to go with it. Yet here were Bram and the others living under the terror and trauma of Du Preez's regime, to which they too were being returned: they would have to work their way out of that.

⁂

Issy cheered up Bram with his humour. 'Let the shithouse see it's clean,' he would say while they were working on the Potemkin under Du Preez's obsessive regard. Jock, who had all the wiles anyway, showed them his resilient tricks – how to get the enamel toilet pots meticulously clean and then disinfected by standing them in the sun, how to hose down the yard, how to take an interest in the smallest insect they might find at work. When the others returned from Central, they gathered round Bram, and Ivan Schermbrucker especially took him into his care. One day Issy saw Bram with his shirt off at labour in the yard and realised he was getting into his stride. In December 1968 they all moved again, now to what was called the 'New Section' of Local, constructed specially for them. Issy Heymann remembered an old Russian song: 'Return my comrade to me, and nothing more do I want.' As time went on, Issy recalled, Bram was happy among his comrades.

⁂

On May Day, 1967, just short of a year after he had been sentenced, Bram was summoned suddenly and told to prepare for a visitor. To be called out in this way was always a matter of some dread, because no one knew what it portended, and Bram was kept waiting for an hour in the sun in his heavy corduroy prison jacket. When he returned, though, he looked as if there were something special about him. The others questioned him, but he would say nothing. Finally he relented: he had been awarded the Lenin Peace Prize, he told them quietly, and had known for some time it was coming. The formal announcement was made that same day in Moscow, and among the other recipients that year was Pastor Niemöller, who had resisted the Nazis, who too had held himself personally accountable.

Bram may have been characteristically modest towards the others, but inside he was beaming, recalled Ilse. His co-prisoners wrote him a poem on a card (later confiscated), which read in part:

> . . . This
> is your fight
> That other men might have the right to peace.
>
> For this belief in man . . .
> men have honoured you.
> We too.

Bram sent out an announcement in a letter to Ilse that this was an award he could accept 'only as a representative of people who are far braver than I and who have given far more'. He also wrote that he couldn't imagine not sharing it with Molly, without whom it would have been unthinkable. Probably Bram was the only Rhodes Scholar ever to be awarded the Lenin Peace Prize; no wonder he was beaming inside.

⁂

They were called *bandiete* by the warders, the warders were called *boere* by the prisoners, and Bram used the term like everyone else.

In the 'New Section' of Local they were faced with unprecedented luxury: single cells, bunk beds with real mattresses, basins with hot and cold water, and flushable toilets. More significantly, they left Du Preez and his regime of outright terror behind. Their new commanding officer was Captain Schnepel, a man who confessed to being an admirer of Hitler, and whose brother-in-law, Colonel Aucamp, was the Security Police liaison for political prisoners. But though Schnepel attempted at first to tame the prisoners, in time he came to realise that a policy of relative accommodation provided a certain stability. For the *bandiete* it was always a matter of working through Schnepel's combination of profound certainty and equally profound incomprehension – in his over-large proportions they called him 'Heffalump' – to make him feel in charge and achieve what they wanted. There were roles to play, and if on occasion a measure of obsequy produced success, these hyper-educated, congenitally strategising political prisoners were not above making the drama work in their favour.

It was their task as political prisoners, as well as instinct as a community, to take every opportunity to enrich the surrounding barrenness of their lives. At first there were plays at Christmas, until the prospect of *The Tempest* in 1968 – with its easily allegorised figure of the slave Caliban – produced their whole-sale cancellation. The prisoners' early lectures to one another – each from his own area of expertise – were supplemented by permission to study through the University of South Africa, of which they took full advantage. For, abysmal as the Unisa courses often were, they allowed one to read any book that was listed or referred to, and even an ideologically unpromising offering such as 'Native Administration' provided riches of the latest writings on Africa. The *bandiete* were also allowed to buy books the prison library didn't have; later they were permitted paperbacks for 'light reading'. So they ordered directly from booksellers and, along with the thrillers and science fiction, received Amilcar Cabral, Frantz Fanon and Bobby Seale before the South African censors had seen them. Yet even the thrillers and science fiction were crucial, for cut off from news in any form as the prisoners were, every slightest clue as to the changing shape of society was seized upon, analysed and then rearticu-lated in a thoroughgoing discipline of prison hermeneutics to re-create the world. It was like seeing the universe through the thinnest sliver of a window, and then attempting to imagine it whole.

After a while they were allowed music, at first with records and speakers provided by Helen Suzman, and then later as the prisoners purchased their own slowly accumulating collection. Variations in preference produced the odd conflict. Once there was nearly a conflagration because one of Issy Heymann's children had recommended Jimi Hendrix, and the *boere* refused to turn off the *kaffir*-music so that the *bandiete* might suffer from their bizarre predilections as much as possible. As to Bram's own tastes, he was strictly traditional and conservative: in music he stuck to the classics, and hated jazz and rock; in fiction and film (movies came once a fortnight after 1969) his allegiance was to realism. He liked *Pride and Prejudice* with Greer Garson, and could not resist anything with Sophia Loren or Audrey Hepburn; documentaries were his favourite, or a film like *Z* which had a political message. But when he saw *Blow-Up* with its absurdist final scene of an imaginary tennis game, he could not contain his disgust, and flashbacks bothered him immensely. In a continuing courtyard debate on linguistics he was insistent that conceptual terms could have only one meaning: that, after all, was how he had lived his whole life.

In the exercise periods and on weekends there were sports, on the concrete slab in the middle of the courtyard. There was 'boop-squash' and volleyball and tennis, and Bram took to his old game, played now with reinforced beach bats. At the age of sixty he still had a vicious kick-spin serve and the disingenuous wiles of his youth. An opponent would hit a drop-shot over the net, and Bram, his knee still gammy from that rugby accident at Oxford so many years before, would anticipate and go clomping up to angle the ball gently away – and then stand there with the most seraphic smile on his face. Denis Goldberg remembered a game of 'bucket-ball' – a variant of basketball – when Hugh Lewin, instead of bouncing the tennis ball, suddenly started running with it. Bram, all his old rugby instincts suddenly alive, went after to tackle him, avoided Hugh's hand-off, got his feet up towards Hugh's chest, and yanked him over in a kind of judo throw.

Even under Du Preez's regime these white prisoners in Pretoria were not treated anything like as badly as the black prisoners on Robben Island. When they sewed mailbags in silence in the freezing courtyard of Pretoria Local it was not the same as breaking rocks in the lime quarry of the Island. Yet for them, as on the Island, it was imperative to continue the political struggle in whatever manner possible, and to this end they formed an organisation called Recce – officially the Recreation Committee – to direct the tenor of their lives. As an elected committee Recce determined objectives and tactics, and, most importantly, was in charge of news, the most valuable commodity for political prisoners. All information, down to the smallest snippet, whether gathered from some stray view of a magazine in a doctor's or dentist's surgery or from a coded message during a visit, was centralised, assessed by a chief co-ordinator, and then channelled back via news disseminators to all.

During those years the prisoners averaged about fifteen to twenty in number and, though ideologically diverse, stuck together in self-definition against a common enemy. Only once, early on, was there the serious threat of an internal split, revolving around the issue of peaceful coexistence with the West (advocated by Khrushchev), which then divided China and the Soviet Union. Rowley Arenstein was an admirer of Mao, and, when he first came to Local, began to argue the issues with a phenomenal memory for documents and finely honed debating skills. He won a convert, Paul Trewhela: this outraged Bram (he was 'particularly furious' about this, recalled Baruch Hirson), who felt there should be no attempt at recruitment, no factional proselytisation, no division among those who by and large held the same beliefs. In later years Paul Trewhela commented that Bram was responsible for excluding Arenstein, and that this was typical both of his Stalinist tactics and of the intellectual rigidity of the Communist Party. It is true that Bram would brook little criticism of the Soviet Union (only one army had prevented the Nazis from controlling the world, was his answer of last resort), and was nothing if not steadfast in his allegiances; but his heart was in the matter in another way, and it does not appear that he ostracised anyone. Arenstein himself remarked that Bram was 'magnificent' in jail, and a peacemaker. All that he could not bear was division in the family.

Proximity among prisoners could cause friction: they were all in their present surroundings precisely because they were headstrong and prepared to hold firm views against any odds. Yet by and large among these liberals, (one) Trotskyist and communists there was a solidarity in their dealings with one another, a resolute morality that became the definition of their daily struggle for human dignity – their equivalent, inside prison, of the political struggle for liberation outside. Though they were – oddly – more isolated than the black prisoners on Robben Island, because their numbers were neither so large nor replenished so regularly, it was a matter of absolute commitment to maintain in every way the principles for which they had been incarcerated. It was only Raymond Thoms, who had testified against Strachan, who was ostracised – and then only because he was evidently dangerous, lashing out at his co-prisoners, alternately betraying them and trying to win their confidence. But even here Bram was insistent. They could not be responsible for driving a man into madness, he argued, and he and Baruch Hirson set up a limited if difficult contact. Later, after Thoms was released from prison, he did in fact commit suicide.

Bram was almost always elected to Recce, and by common consent was the presiding and guiding figure in prison. Everyone came to him with their needs and their troubles, and no decision of any import was ever taken without hearing his views. Whenever requests or complaints had to be made – on the regular abuse suffered by the prisoners on raids in the cells or through punitive regulations – it was invariably Bram Fischer who was their representative. One night Brigadier Nel, the Deputy Commissioner of Prisons, arrived in a semi-drunken stupor to berate the *bandiete* for being Jews or communists or (in some cases) both, and he had particular words of scorn for Bram, telling him he was a fool and asking him how he, as an Afrikaner, could betray his people. Yet in the aftermath Bram was the figure through whom the matter was settled – standing up to Colonel Aucamp with the prisoners' demands for restitution – and though the affair ended in something of a stalemate, Nel never visited the prison again. Even across the borderlines of prison enmity Bram managed to make the kinds of connection that defined him. Warders came to him for advice, whether on family problems, legal difficulties or water rights (his old speciality). Whereas they called all the other prisoners by their surnames, he was always 'Bram' or (with diminutive affection) 'Braampie'. 'Kyk die stasiemeester' [Look at the stationmaster], Schnepel once remarked of Bram as he stood in the yard with his hat, and there was a particular intimacy about it. Hugh Lewin told the classic story of Bram out of time in a Unisa exam: his invigilator, a warder with whom he had earlier been discussing his old days as a Free State scrum-half, looked at his watch and said, 'Ag, Bram, vat maar nog 'n paar minute, so te sê, beseeringstyd' [Take another couple of minutes', so to speak, injury time]. The idiom could not have been more exact.

The only difficulty with Bram, reflected the others, was that he would not talk himself, would not confide or take any help. ('He had the broadest shoulders I ever knew,' remarked Baruch Hirson.) He shared out the extra eggs and milk he was allocated because of his ulcer; he worked as hard as everyone else, though they tried to protect him because of his health and his age. He polished his cell floor as they did on his 'taxis' (folded rags or blankets) under his feet and the corridors with round rubber 'tits' under his knees.

Yet among it all, there were tasks he enjoyed. By day, when the others went off to the prison workshop, Bram was assigned with Ivan Schermbrucker and Baruch Hirson to the garden, which they had laid out in beds around the concrete recreation block in the middle of the courtyard. There Bram tended and watched the revolving cycle of flowers through the seasons. Molly had had her plants at Beaumont Street, and Oupa Abraham his trees at Bergendal. Bram, who had said that come the revolution he wanted to work as a gardener at the Wilds in Johannesburg, and who had gone out to be a farmer in the Cape in his youth, became at last a gardener in prison, bringing life and beauty out of the soil.

In the evening, after lock-up, they watched the birds who came as their guests to eat the seeds and crumbs they had left among the flowers. Bram still woke early, at about 4.30 a.m. as was his habit, reading on his bed by the spotlight that came through his window. At midnight they heard the changing of the guards, and the killer Alsatian dogs outside that shrieked and tore up the flower beds.

⁂

Prisoners were graded from 'D' to 'A', and for the politicals there was the long slow wait – much slower than for common criminals – to be upgraded and allowed extra privileges. At first they were rationed to two letters a year both in and out, then four, and then more, but everything still passed through the censors. Bram, who had written to Molly at such length, now had to confine himself to the regulation 500 words a time, condensing thoughts telegraphically, abandoning articles, prepositions, conjunctions. His words had to fight against space, and letters spawned only letters as matters inadequately conveyed had to be explained, interpreted, redressed.

Visits, the highlights of a prisoner's life, were a matter of delicate and sometimes rough anguish. In advance one prepared for weeks, making lists of everything to be discussed (family matters only were permitted). Then, finally ushered in to the small cubicle – where prisoner and visitor could see one another only from the waist up through cloudy perspex with perforated boards on either side for sound, and warders stood behind monitoring each word – everyone rushed through, trying to get everything said and always failing, trying on top of that to formulate an impromptu allegoric code to receive or impart some news of the world. And then afterwards, when everything was suddenly cut off by the warders, one felt either elated or terrible. Visits were a crucial and yet wholly unsatisfactory mirror in which prisoners searched for signs of their own continued existence and meaning. Their lives went from unexplained euphoria to despair, and everyone took to themselves from time to time.

Bram wrote to Ilse and Paul, orchestrating the order of their communications and visits. He was keeping well, though a bit stiff despite squash, he wrote in May 1967, and put that down to old age. He described what he was reading – Hobson's *Imperialism* and De Wet's history of the Boer War yet again, Meintjies's life of Olive Schreiner, *Lear* and Fanon ('what a strange fellow he must have been,' wrote Bram). He too became euphoric when he was upgraded to 'B' group in June 1969 ('that means two letters per month and one double visit'), but knew the other kind of experience as well: 'Isolated, we sometimes panic.' He encouraged Paul and Ilse to follow their own pursuits:

Paul, when in 1969 the regime of studying medicine in Johannesburg became too taxing, and he decided to go down to Cape Town for an Honours degree in economics instead; Ilse, when turmoil in her private life tempted her to leave the country, if necessary on an exit permit, meaning that she might not see him again. Never mentioning the pain her departure might cause, he thrilled to the possibility of her visiting places he and Molly had seen thirty years before, and told her to ignore anyone who criticised her for not staying with her menfolk: 'we *know* (not merely believe) we'll all be together again sooner than they could possibly expect.'

Chiefly, he could not bear the idea of his children sacrificing their lives out of loyalty to him. He told Ilse she could not give up her life even for Paul: 'If only for our sakes he'll just have to look after himself – as he has, always? mostly? – and take all precautions – and write often!' He told Ilse that what mattered most of all was her happiness. He tried to imagine all he could about his children's lives, and said that one day they would have to explain everything to him, patiently. He wrote of his roses, sweet peas, 'mesems' and poppies, and birds. 'Thinking of taking up birds again since two of us have induced large flocks of sparrows and doves (even Rockpigeons) to come & feed here & also watch Ibis "V's" wend their way across sky in early mornings . . . '

He wrote: 'Evenings about 7 turn deep violet.' And: 'Lovely evenings – no real rain – but large clouds floating over Silverton and beyond.'

⁂

During the second half of 1969 Paul went down to Cape Town with Ilse to begin an Honours degree at UCT, which he completed towards the end of the following year. He still had to work on his body and lungs for three hours a day in order to keep going, and would return from lectures exhausted. None the less, he managed to become a tutor, teaching others as well as learning, and for him it was an extremely happy time. Ilse looked after him: for her it was a combination of the dreadful, as in Paul's declining health he would go through inevitable crises, and of an experience that remained inviolably special. When Paul received a second class for his Honours, Bram was upbeat at this less than perfect result: 'For three generations we seem to have got along nicely that way!' It turned out to be his last letter to Paul.

For on 27 January 1971 Paul died. Ilse was away at the time, on a trip to Hogsback in the Eastern Cape with Tim Wilson, whom she later married. Paul, for whom stays at Groote Schuur Hospital had become a regular feature of life, had checked himself in unexpectedly. Friends who had seen him there left him cheerful; but during the night there was a collapse and his breathing stopped quietly and suddenly. Ruth felt afterwards that having achieved what he wanted to – the Honours degree he had set his heart on – he simply allowed himself to slip away; and he did it without troubling anyone. Paul was twenty-three years old.

The hospital managed to contact Bram's brother Paul in Bloemfontein, he reached Gus, and it was Gus who came to see Bram, permitted a special visit. He arrived just after the prisoners had already been locked up for the night, and Bram was called out of his cell. They were separated by the perspex as usual, and Gus told Bram that he had bad news. Bram asked if it was Paul, and Gus told him the little he knew. After that Bram was returned to his cell, and the only gesture that was offered was when Schnepel came up to enquire through the locked grille if he was all right. Later Gus remarked that during the visit Bram had been extraordinarily steadfast, whereas he had been the one closer to breakdown. But when the other prisoners asked Bram what had happened, he refused to say, and spent that night alone.

The prison authorities would not allow Bram to attend Paul's funeral. When Ilse and Ruth came to see him, they were not allowed a contact visit.

It was Arthur Chaskalson who spoke at the funeral. Paul's life, he remarked, was dominated by his illness, but the triumph of his life was that he was able to acknowledge it, to come to terms with it, and to surmount it with a grandeur that defied description. Paul had the same integrity and commitment 'which made Bram the great man that he is', but he was not simply Bram Fischer's son: 'He was Paul Fischer; a boy who grew into a young man, who lived fully, and was loved by all who knew him . . . He would not have wanted us to gather here today to pay tribute to him; but that is our right and he is not here to prevent it, not to prevent our saying that we are glad that he lived and that we knew him.'

Later Bram wrote to Ilse to console her: 'My darling, I understand all the time what you are feeling – the deep depressions and the pain which is as if physical. For you it is worse than for anyone since, for over five years, he was your constant companion and care. Yet, as your pain is greatest, your consolation too should be greatest. We all did what we could, given the initial tragedy of genes that went wrong, to make his life as full and happy as possible. But no one succeeded as much as you did . . . For that Ruth and I owe you a debt we can never repay . . . Bless you. Someone, some day in our new world will reward you. For the time you have only our love.'

For a long time after that, recalled Hugh Lewin, Bram would barely talk about Paul. Hugh had become very close to Bram because after Ivan Schermbrucker left prison in 1970, he had taken over as his general caregiver and caretaker. Hugh was not in the Communist Party, and as there was no question of political hierarchy or responsibility they ranged freely and widely in their discussions. Yet the only time Bram ever mentioned Paul it was about the medical nature of his condition, a catch in his voice the sole indication of what he was going through inside.

Yet he was the person, remarked Hugh, who took care of others, who listened to their troubles, who took individuals sometimes badly broken down and brought them up into the community of all. As always, in Bram's case, it was a direct and personal kind of communism. Once when Hugh was raving deliriously with the flu, Bram held his hand and saw him through it. Once, when Hugh sensed that Bram was in a particularly bad way, he smuggled a note in through the outside window of his cell, saying the things one normally couldn't because of Bram's privacy and modesty. In the stripped-down world of prison where the emotions are correspondingly heightened and the vulnerabilities raw, the essentials are also clarified. 'You know, you talk of closeness, you talk of love, and you talk of all those things,' remarked Hugh Lewin. 'Certainly I was fortunate to be in that position with Bram. Possibly it was one of the most rewarding things of my life.' For prisoners such as Hugh, Marius Schoon and others, Bram's was a presence that had an utterly transforming effect on their lives.

Paul had died; but when Ruth adopted a baby girl, Bram showed off her picture with abundant pleasure and pride. He was a grandfather like his Oupa and father before him, and this was evidence that his life continued outside, even if obliquely. When Ilse and Tim Wilson were married in 1971, they wanted the ceremony to be held in prison during a special visit with Bram. Yet, though visits by two people were permitted, a minister would make a third, and so the request was turned down. For her wedding Bram wrote to Ilse: 'Mind will be wandering . . . to a tiny toddler at Umzumbe, with tiny flaxen curls . . . To an active little girl, with golden curls, who used to run ahead of her parents – as she did on the way to the lotus lilies in Maritzburg park, so that after he'd passed her, on his way out, an old gentleman was heard to mutter: "Who said there were no fairies." . . . And, to jump over many years, to the pink heels that are still entirely vivid to me. We've seen life, haven't we?'

Hugh Lewin was released in November 1971, having served seven years; Baruch Hirson left in 1973 after nine. The goodbyes were always sudden and incomplete. Bram told Denis Goldberg, the other life-prisoner who saw one day cycle endlessly into another, that if his life was going to be spent in prison, then that was the way it had to be. He was not going to show any doubt.

⁂

Soon after Paul died, the Beaumont Street house was at last sold. Bram, who had cherished the idea that one day they might all live there again, wrote to Ilse in pride and sadness that the trees were not to be moved, at peril that he would return to haunt the new owners. One day, he wrote, 'in the new city of Johannesburg', the tree at the swimming pool would be the centre of a children's playground the size of two blocks.

⁂

Mary Benson wrote to him from her travels in America, camping out in the Nevada desert. Bram was stirred by the image of satellites winking through the night sky overhead. 'Is this one of the ways in which the world has changed?' he asked.

⁂

During these years in prison, Bram wrote to his old mentor Leo Marquard, opening up intimately, despite political differences, to someone who could remember the whole past with him, who knew the world Bram had emerged from, who had prompted Bram's early changes. It was when Bram was still awaiting trial (and perhaps thinking towards his speech from the dock) that he ran through some of that past with Leo – the adult literacy classes in Waaihoek, the Joint Council and his handshake, the fact that he had not undertaken 'this last adventure out of euphoria or sheer cussedness'. In 1966 when Leo published the letters of his mother, Margaret Marquard – which told, in passing, of her encounters in Winburg with Abraham Fischer – Bram wrote of a lost world of 'kindliness and understanding and even of intellectual advancement', in contrast with which much of the contemporary Free State struck him as a 'harsh and mentally blacked out civilisation'. It always amazed him, wrote Bram, that in the 1870s his great-grandfather, Dr Robertson, had run a Shakespeare reading circle in Fauresmith. Yet, while he was prepared to concede that there were many kindly and understanding people in the Free State, he was still enough of an orthodox communist to describe the general lack of awareness (in 'my jargon', as he put it to Leo) as indicative of a '"kulak" civilisation'.

Then in March 1974 Leo died, and Bram wrote to Nell, circling once again through that past, the Joint Council, Waaihoek classes in the cold and dust, the

NUSAS parliament, tennis, Oxford, his entry into the Marquards' 'magic circle'. He mentioned Leo's 'outstanding characteristic: his ability to guide without ever asserting his views', and he might have been describing himself: clearly he had learned well from his teacher. He wrote: 'And you, Nell? I know what I feel. Hence I know your desolation, to which only time can accustom you.'

Bram's letters revealed, as well as empathy, a sustained spirit and determined humour, and perhaps something else. He had written to Leo as 'your disbarred & incarcerated Bram', and told him that he looked forward to leisurely discussions when he left prison as a 'retired gentleman'. He wrote to Nell after Leo had died: 'My love to you & all the family – both of us here join in this.' Nell may well have wondered if by that, in a letter full of reverie, he meant Molly.

⚜

Ruth's marriage was failing because Anthony had had an affair, and she visited Bram to discuss it. Upset as Bram was, he advised Ruth that she and Anthony should not let the matter get in the way of the continuing significance of their relationship. He suggested that many marriages underwent such things: in this he included his parents as well as himself and Molly, although he gave no details. This in turn was another surprise for Ruth: so all had not been what it seemed between her parents, and it remained an area of mystery. When Bram and Molly were young they had argued the point (Bram more in theory then) that both were passionate creatures, and that the arrival of others should not affect the essence of what lay between them. For now Anthony (to whom Bram wrote) argued that it was odd for a communist to be defending the bourgeois institution of marriage. But most likely that was not what underlay Bram's point at all. It had more to do with deeper fidelities, what he and Molly had conceived of when they imagined 'Ruth' in the first place – and strangely, even, with the sustaining undercurrents of loyalty that had now brought him to prison.

Ultimately Ruth and Anthony separated, and she returned with her daughter Gretel to Johannesburg.

⚜

First in 1970, and then again in 1973, when Bram turned sixty-five, there were campaigns for his release. In the first campaign Louis Babrow, doctor and ex-Springbok rugby player, who had been junior to Bram at school, made the case that he had once appealed for clemency for the ex-Grey pupil Robey

Leibbrandt, condemned to death as a Nazi agent. Leibbrandt's sentence had been commuted, and the Nationalist government had later released him: couldn't they now do the same for Bram Fischer? Leo Marquard, to whom remained the dubious honour of having taught both Leibbrandt and Fischer, took up the theme in 1973, and there were others who joined: Lesley Blackwell, Helen Suzman, Archbishop Hurley, Dr Christiaan Barnard (recently the world's first successful heart-transplant surgeon), among others.

During the 1973 campaign Ruth and Ilse wrote to the State President, the Prime Minister, the Minister of Justice, and every judge they could think of. Reciting family history, they invoked the South African tradition of compassion towards people who had broken the law for political principles. Bram could be released under any conditions the government stipulated, they suggested; he had little time to enjoy whatever pleasures of old age with his family remained. But it was clear from the replies which returned that this was a plea that would not be countenanced. The State President passed his letter on to the relevant Ministers, and Ruth and Ilse received a missive indicating that although the Minister of Justice had 'sympathy with you, he cannot accede to your request'. The Judge-President of the Transvaal indicated that members of the judiciary had no knowledge of whether Bram would resume the activities for which he was incarcerated: 'In the circumstances we regret that we are not in a position to support the request officially.'

⚜

And then came the news that Bram himself was ill.

In 1969 he underwent a cataract operation, for he had been having trouble seeing – bending low over the flowers in his garden, missing the ball at tennis, experiencing difficulties with his reading. After that he was fitted with a contact lens, which helped a good deal – except when, as Bram described it to Paul, he thought he had lost it, and a whole crowd of prisoners washing a corridor would end up searching through the soap and rags and water until he discovered it – under his eyelid. At that time too Bram went on a diet – 'you have no idea how necessary it is,' he told Ilse – measuring his waist with a length of knotted string. He began to suffer from arthritis in his left hip, exacerbated by the Pretoria winter cold, and would stand in the shower with the water boiling hot until his buttock was red for the only relief he could get. His brothers remembered seeing him during visits squirming around on that hip, but politely insisting that he was all right.

In May 1974 – now eight years into his sentence – Bram was admitted to hospital because of internal haemorrhaging from a bleeding ulcer; then in July he had his prostate removed. On neither occasion was his family informed until afterwards. When the prostate was removed it showed signs of cancer, and tests were done; but the only remark in Bram's file indicated that the prostate was negative for cancer, and the laboratory reports went missing. This last fact became apparent when a doctor from the International Red Cross (there was a yearly inspection of the political prisoners) examined the file, and asked Marius Schoon to translate some of the Afrikaans. Later it was established that Bram did indeed have cancer, and that the prostate was the primary site, but in the meantime he had been returned to prison.

During September of that year the pain in his hip became acute, and Bram asked for a crutch. The response was that there was nothing available, and so his comrades found him a broom of the right length to use; only then did his jailers provide him with a pair of crutches. During October he was sent for X-rays, following which the specialist warned him of the danger of falling, because the neck of his femur appeared fragile. This in itself might have been a sign, because one effect of prostate cancer is to spread secondary sites to the hip; but in the nature of prison medicine – and possibly given the missing reports – one doctor did not know what another had seen.

On Wednesday, 6 November, Bram slipped and fell while struggling into the shower on his crutches. The pain was almost unbearable. On the following day he asked for a doctor because he suspected a fracture, but no one was sent. There was only a medical orderly, and he had precious little training; his response was to do some basic physical tests which showed, he assured Bram, that everything was fine. Aside from one sympathetic warder who found him a wheelchair, Bram was getting absolutely no help from the authorities; it took thirteen days before he was admitted to hospital. During that time he was becoming aphasic, and it was immensely distressing to his co-prisoners. Once, when Dave Kitson was in the shower with Bram alongside him, Bram suddenly took off on his crutches down the passage. Kitson, realising something was wrong, rushed after him, only just managing to reach him at the top of the stairs. When Denis Goldberg asked Bram who he – Denis – was, Bram said he was someone he knew named Shorty Levy.

When Bram was finally taken to hospital on the 19th, his femur was pinned because there was a fracture after all. His brother Gus, reflecting on this afterwards in his capacity as an orthopaedic surgeon, considered that the fracture may well have been pathological – meaning that the bone had been so weak that the break preceded the fall that was its apparent cause. Either way, there can be no doubt that for nearly two weeks Bram was kept needlessly in the most excruciating pain and the most alarming mental distress because of methodical negligence. Nor did the tale of brutality end there, because two weeks later, on 4 December, Bram was returned once again to prison, despite being in no condition to go back. When he arrived the other prisoners found him alone at one o'clock in the dining room, confused and unable to speak.

By mid-afternoon on that day he was running a high temperature, and was unable to help himself. Denis Goldberg proposed to Schnepel that he stay with Bram in his cell, to see him through the night, but at first Schnepel refused, citing the regulations forbidding two men in a cell (this was to prevent homosexual activity, though strangely three cellmates were allowed). At last, however, Schnepel relented, and so Denis stayed with Bram. For two nights he put Bram to bed, lifted him to the toilet, caught him when in his fevered delirium he tried to get up by himself. After the second night Bram was readmitted to hospital; he was unable to speak or do the simplest things for himself.

At some point during this time Dave Kitson remembered finding Bram outside in the sun and offering him some cream cake he had bought. (Since they had all been upgraded to 'A' status, they were now allowed such privileges.) When Bram looked at him in a daze, Kitson began feeding him with a spoon – and then, as Bram ate ravenously, realised how hungry he was, because he had been forgetting to eat.

Dave Kitson and Denis Goldberg used to carry him up and down stairs in a fireman's seat. Denis said Bram was so light he could carry him anywhere. They carried him into the sun, and into the shade.

❧❧

Later Denis wrote it up on a leaf of tissue paper smuggled out of prison by Marius Schoon when he was released. The tissue paper measured 7.1 cm by 16.1 cm, about the same area as an average postcard, with five ruled columns running down lengthwise, each slightly narrower than 1.5 cm in width. It was in those columns that Denis wrote microscopically, using a pencil sharpened to the finest and most exacting point. Meticulously he told the whole story, day by day as it developed. He raised the obvious questions, that Bram had suffered from malpractice at the least, and purposeful cruelty at worst. He described how he had cried when he first discovered that Bram had cancer, how he had taken care of him in the night. In that most limited of spaces he told what would have taken numbers of pages in normal writing. No monk in his medieval cell attended to his task with greater scribal devotion.

❧❧

This was how Denis's columns began:

What follows on AF's
medical treatment has
to be used with great
care (1) because ostensibly
there could not be
access to his medical
file; (2) because there
might be simple (!?)
medical reasons for
what happened – but
I doubt it.

12 (?) May '74 AF to
Hospital after ulcer
had haemorrhaged.
Some days in Hosp., then
in Central Prison Hosp for
few days. No op,
but transfusion etc.
July '74 On own
request & with Doctor's
recommendation AF

has prostatectomy.
Surgeon did a section
in theatre. Report in
file says that it
was negative for
cancer but showed
all signs of being
cancerous, & ∴
gland sent to path.
lab for thorough
histology & path
lab report to be
sent to prison. This
report apparently
not on file.
Was path lab work
done? Was it re-
ported? Was report
sent to the prison?
Did prison Dr. press
path lab for report?
&/or for histology to
be done? . . .

There was in addition another document Denis transcribed which was later smuggled out – a copy of a submission, by the prisoners, to a Commission of Enquiry into the Penal System of South Africa, in which they recorded at length their detailed objections to the punitive conditions they had to endure under the jurisdiction of the Security Division of the Prisons Department. It was signed on 9 December 1974, and Bram was one of the signatories; although he was barely functioning by that date, it was his original draft that had been followed. But the account was not even accepted for submission by the commission; and as for the fact that Bram had signed, that was one more reason for the government's anxiety about him and vindictiveness towards him, even at this late stage.

Tim Wilson, who was also a doctor, later investigated the whole history of Bram's illness and determined that there was probably not malicious neglect, though Bram could have been saved unnecessary suffering if his fractured thigh and the cancer that had caused it had been detected earlier. As for the cancer itself, it was unlikely that anything could have prevented it or stopped it once it was under way.

By 11 December in hospital Bram was reported in a 'critical condition', and soon fell into a coma. Yet it also happened that the radiographer who attended to him was none other than Dr Theunie Fichardt – his cousin and friend from his youth, with whom Bram had played rugby at school, and whose Dingaan's Day celebration in London he had once addressed. Without any hope of a cure Theunie decided to treat him with radiotherapy, solely so that he might regain his faculties and have some time with his family. On the ward at H.F. Verwoerd Hospital in Pretoria were prison guards; as Bram began to recover they took care of him tenderly like a baby. He pulled out of the coma, and Ruth and Ilse came to visit him every day. Ruth brought her daughter Gretel – it was the first time Bram was able to see and touch his granddaughter. As his condition improved he read her *The Hungry Caterpillar*.

The campaign for his release escalated, now taking on an international dimension. In London Mary Benson contacted Michael Foot (who remembered Bram as 'one of the most impressive people I have heard in my life'), Lord Goodman, Neil Kinnock, James Callaghan, and (in the United States) Congressman Donald Fraser and Senator George McGovern. Yet letters from these people to the South African ambassadors in both countries met only with bland references to all of Bram's criminal transgressions, and the need for his continued medical care – in short, polite but very firm rejection. In New York Ivor Richard, British ambassador to the United Nations, took up Bram's case behind the scenes, and Secretary-General Kurt Waldheim (with a number of his own skeletons in the cupboard) petitioned Prime Minister Vorster for clemency. In South Africa André Brink, the Afrikaner novelist, paid tribute to Bram in a moving address at the University of the Witwatersrand. Helen Suzman visited Bram in hospital and – her tongue as sharp as ever – commented to the newspapers that when so many millions were being spent on security, she had no idea why the government remained afraid of one bedridden and incapacitated man.

Ruth and Ilse telephoned for an interview with the Minister of Justice, Jimmy Kruger, and met him in his cavernous office in the Union Buildings in Pretoria; General Van den Bergh of the Security Police joined them for the discussion. But prevarication was the order of the day. When Ruth and Ilse raised the issue of Bram's cancer, Kruger (who later oversaw the fracas of Steve Biko's murder in prison) responded that Helen Joseph had also suffered from cancer, but had recovered; in any event, he insisted, it wasn't certain that it was cancer Bram had. And yet he hedged: if Bram were to be released, he suggested, it could not be to Johannesburg, insinuating that Ruth and Ilse should think of another location. As Helen Suzman had intimated, it was clear that the might of the South African government still feared that Bram, cancer-ridden as he was, would somehow remain a rallying point. And so things were left hanging.

Then one day out of the blue, Kruger phoned Ruth at eight in the morning, embarking on a rambling conversation. He remarked that if the situation were reversed, he hoped that his children would do the same for him as Ruth and Ilse were doing for Bram, and he reminisced about the days when he and Joe Slovo used to catch the train into university together. But nothing concrete emerged from the discussion. In January 1975 Ruth flew down to Cape Town and met Kruger and Van den Bergh again. Kruger pointed to a portrait of Vorster on the wall, calling him 'my Leader', and proclaimed that if his leader were dying he would want to stand in the doorway just to gain strength from looking at him. And yet in some odd way he was friendly. Ruth left with a distinct impression of the unreality of it all.

By February 1975 Kruger was requesting Ruth and Ilse through the press to give unspecified 'undertakings' if Bram were to be released. To this they responded that such an approach was ridiculous, since Kruger had every power at his command and could stipulate any conditions he desired. In early March Helen Suzman visited Bram once again, and found him 'skeletal . . . gaunt and very frail'; she commented that he could not be a rallying point for communism or anything else. Then suddenly on 10 March it was announced that on the recommendation of Dr Fichardt, Bram Fischer was being released to his brother Paul in Bloemfontein. He was partially paralysed in both legs and could not walk, and though he had recovered sufficiently to travel there was no point in any further treatment.

<hr />

It was on a Friday at midday that Paul Fischer received a telephone call at work from a general in the Prisons Department in Cape Town who said, 'You are taking your brother', and Paul could not tell whether it was a statement or a question, but said, yes, that he would. The general told him that Bram would arrive at three o' clock on the Monday, and that Paul had to arrange all nursing and medical supervision. Paul asked for more time, but the general refused; the only concession was that the Prisons Department would pay for everything, since Bram was still a prisoner.

That weekend Paul spent in frenzied preparation. Then, on the Monday, about twenty minutes before he was about to leave for the military airfield to meet Bram's plane, there was another call, this time from the local head of the Prisons Department, to say that he needed to see Paul right away. He arrived at Paul's house a few minutes later, and there made him sign all sorts of under-takings as to Bram's confinement as a prisoner – chief among them that he could receive no visitors outside of family without permission. Paul felt he had been bamboozled and blackmailed, and barely suppressed an outright refusal, but by then Bram was already on the plane from Pretoria, and it was impossible to say no.

Ilse and Tim accompanied Bram down on the plane, having sought permis-sion so that he would not become disorientated if he travelled alone – as had happened when Percy Fischer was ill. When they arrived at the airport at Voortrekkerhoogte in Pretoria that morning, they found that Bram had also been forced to sign undertakings, and all the way down to Bloemfontein he was as angry as anything about that. But when they took him out of his stretcher in the aeroplane and put him on a seat, Bram became tremendously excited to see Johannesburg laid out below, the new city highway gleaming snakily along. Tim and Ilse had brought along a picnic basket with some wine, and half-seriously contemplated knocking the guards out with the bottle and hijacking the plane to Mozambique.

In Bloemfontein Paul had been instructed that he should make Bram's arrival as quiet and discreet as possible, but when he arrived at the airfield he found a full-blown cavalcade. There were traffic policemen on motor-cycles, the ambulance Paul had ordered, his own car, and two cars full of security policemen. When Bram arrived they all took off at high speed – seventy miles an hour, police and ambulance sirens wailing all round, the motor-bike out-riders halting the traffic to let them pass. At one point Paul, alarmed by the pace, slowed down, and a security car swooped in front of him to make sure he was properly surrounded. In the ambulance Bram was amused, and turned to Ilse to say, 'Pretend nothing untoward is happening'; it could have been his mother speaking. Finally, still at breakneck speed, they swerved up in front of Paul's house, and by then the entire neighbourhood, drawn out by the frenzied wailing, was watching.

That was Bram Fischer's discreet arrival at home. The Security Police wanted him to sign some papers yet again, but by then he was prepared, telling them they could go to hell, he wasn't signing anything.

At first he was determined to walk again, shuffling up and down, and terribly pleased with himself. To weigh him, Tim would pick him up and hold him on the scale.

Ruth reflected later that it was, after all, a very peaceful time. They would sit and have tea, while Bram would read *Time* magazine, sometimes a whole morning for an article. Ruth and Ilse knitted; Gretel played with a neighbour's child. The ordinary people of Bloemfontein took to them, and treated them with great affection and consideration. Visitors arrived, among them Nick de Villiers, with whom Bram had once gone off driving to Bethlehem to see Molly; now he was Judge-President of the Free State, Percy's old position and the one that at the least Bram could have had. Later the Red Cross came, and were very distressed when they gave Bram a newspaper and he folded it up in his blankets to hide it, the prison training ingrained. There was the predictable South African confrontation when the Security Police discovered that Bram had a coloured night-nurse, and demanded that she be dismissed. Paul, furious, responded that he had undertaken all the medical responsibilities, and that if they didn't approve they could do what they liked. A white nurse was sent in her place.

Virtually every day, at about the same time, a car would pass the house, with four men in open-necked shirts inside: surveillance continued. Yet the local chief of prisons, Colonel Scheffer, turned out to be a humane and decent man. He would visit apologetically once or twice a week, and sit with everyone else on the veranda. When Bram needed radiotherapy again and had to be transported, Scheffer insisted that he take him, on the ground that Ilse's Volkswagen was too small. He would lift Bram into his car, and sometimes, on the return journey, would drive him around Bloemfontein. He asked Bram where he wanted to go, and once Bram replied that he wanted to see the jail where as a child he had been taken to see the rebel prisoners and had been given his toy chameleon. Now he was the prisoner, nearly free.

In these quiet circumstances Bram and his family discussed politics very little: though he conceded that mistakes had been made, he believed what he had always believed.

It came to Ruth that when someone is in that condition, it is his essence as a person that emerges. For Bram it was his gentleness. To his nurse, Mrs Van der Merwe, a poor Afrikaner woman with four sons on the railways, he was always courteous and polite, and she, appreciating the dignity and consideration he extended, treated him with the same care she would have one of her sons.

And then it became harder to talk to Bram; he was on morphine and in intense pain. On 23 April, his sixty-seventh birthday, his condition became critical, and soon after that he lapsed once more into unconsciousness. On 8 May, at about seven in the morning, in the interval between the night-nurse's departure and the arrival of the day-nurse, Paul heard him make some choking sounds, and went into his room. He could have cleared Bram's throat, but decided not to, and stayed with his brother. Then at about half past seven he came to Ruth and Ilse to tell them that Bram had died. Ruth remembered that when they went in to see him he looked so extraordinarily peaceful that the moment felt surprisingly uplifting. There was a general feeling of peace.

It was one day less than nine years since Bram had been sentenced to life imprisonment. The date was Thursday, 8 May 1975: Ascension Day.

Mrs Van der Merwe said that the only gift she could offer was that they should not pay her for her services that day.

Bram was cremated the following Monday. The chief of prisons attended in a suit and tie, and made a point of mentioning that he had come to pay his respects in his private capacity. A number of Indian mourners and comrades came up from Natal, but were not allowed to spend the night in the Free State – it was the old legislation that Oupa Abraham had supported. There were a few lawyers from the Johannesburg Bar, among them Arthur Chaskalson, George Bizos and Issy Maisels, all three Bram's companions from the great political trials. A bouquet of red roses adorned Bram's casket. Arthur Chaskalson read messages from Lilian Ngoyi of the ANC, Fikile Bam (recently released from Robben Island), Hugh Lewin, André Brink, and Ruth and Ilse, and gave a short speech himself. In addition there were telegrams from Yusuf Dadoo, Moses Kotane and Oliver Tambo that could not be read because the senders were banned. Afterwards, they all returned home to Paul's house, and that was where they sang 'Nkosi Sikelel' iAfrika': God Bless Africa.

When Issy Maisels was at the airport returning to Johannesburg, he happened to meet old Mr Justice Rumpff, who had presided during those long years at the Treason Trial. Rumpff asked Maisels where he had been, and Issy told him. Rumpff thought for a bit, and then spoke: 'You know,' he said, 'he'll be remembered long after you and I are forgotten.'

As soon as Ruth and Ilse phoned the Security Police with the news that Bram had died, they arrived at the house with a letter. It stipulated that the family could have Bram's body for a funeral, provided that it was held in Bloemfontein, that it was held within a week, and that his ashes, if there were a cremation, would be returned to the Department of Prisons. When the newspapers discovered the information and a furore ensued, Jimmy Kruger let it be known through the press that if the family applied to him he might reconsider the matter. But Ruth and Ilse refused, saying it was not a matter to be negotiated.

So Bram's ashes returned to the Prisons Department. But he was light and had gone into air, and they couldn't touch him again.

ON THE MOUNTAIN

⌒◯◯⌒

12 May 1975 – 10 May 1994

'Do not weep for Bram. He would not have you weep on his behalf.' Hugh Lewin wrote from London, the message that was read by Arthur Chaskalson at Bram's cremation.

'And do not weep for the recent long years in jail. That especially he would not like. For though they were long painful years away from his family and friends outside, for Bram inside they were not lost years. They meant for Bram, in a very real sense, a rounding and a completion. However full the man who first went to jail – however distinguished the lawyer, however fine the father, husband, friend, adviser – however full the man before, jail encompassed the fullness and enlarged it.' Hugh Lewin told how in the beginning prison had stripped Bram bare, only to reveal his essential greatness. He spoke of the humiliation, the curious affection Bram had won even from warders, the story of his 'injury time', how he had never complained except on behalf of others, how he had kept his fellow prisoners attuned to the continuing commitments of the outside world. The Lenin Prize had honoured him, and so had his companions inside. Wherever people thought of Bram Fischer, wrote Hugh, they would 'think also of a free South Africa'.

Lilian Ngoyi, Treason trialist whom Bram had defended, and inspirational figure within the ANC Women's League, made it clear in her funeral tribute that the meaning of Bram's life extended much farther than the walls of Pretoria Local Prison or the white world from which he had come. 'We the blacks of South Africa', she wrote, 'mourn the death of a statesman, a hero of the liberation struggle . . .

'With the change that will come in the years ahead, our children will know that South Africa bore a son like you.

'Blacks everywhere dedicate themselves to carry on from where you have left off.

'We bear in mind today the men on Robben Island and all political prisoners.

'Bram, we will always remember you.'

Fikile Bam's thoughts pursued a similar theme: 'Bram's dedication and his complete sacrifice for equality and justice is an inspiration and example such as no other white South African has imparted to his black compatriots. Africa has lost one of its great men.'

André Brink, who in the last months of Bram's life had come to regard him as a spiritual father figure – and who had written privately to him moved by that feeling even as Bram approached his very last days – sent a message considering his significance as an Afrikaner. From that point of view, Brink suggested, the injunction laid upon those Bram had left behind was the same as that set upon Horatio by Hamlet: to 'report me and my cause aright'. It was not the case that Bram had alienated himself from his people by deviating from their traditions and prescripts; on the contrary, he had 'enlarged and deepened the concept of Afrikanerdom . . . If Afrikanerdom is to survive, as I think it will, it may well be as a result of the broadening and liberating influence of men like Bram Fischer.' Brink also took pains to separate Bram's commitment from his communism – to him yet another oppressive system, foreign in its essence to Bram Fischer's thought – yet he argued that an unwavering dedication to liberty, justice, compassion, trust, mercy and dignity represented 'the real Bram Fischer'; and it was these ideals that those who remained behind had the responsibility to keep alive.

The South African Communist Party had no doubt that Bram's ideals had been inseparable from communism. Its journal, the *African Communist*, offered a statement in tribute by the central committee: 'The death of comrade Bram Fischer has removed from the political scene one of the greatest figures in the South African revolutionary movement. A member of our Central Committee since 1945, comrade Fischer was a communist in the truest mould. Those who knew him, worked with him, and shared cells with him in South Africa's prisons, will mourn the loss, not only of an outstanding revolutionary, but also of a man whose comradeship and warmth earned him the affection of all liberation fighters. Comrade Fischer died as he lived: an example of the highest dedication to the cause of freedom and social emancipation regardless of personal cost.'

Friend, mentor, prisoner, South African, Afrikaner, comrade, symbol: these tributes applied to the dead, but they also applied to the living. Bram would be claimed, reclaimed, disclaimed, invoked, and forgotten – all the penalties of those who can no longer speak for themselves or answer back. He had emptied out of the lives of those who had known him, except as memory and reiteration, an impression on the mind of image, gesture and attitude. He had emptied out of the present into the past. But in the shadowed afterlife of echo and interpretation, perhaps there was some influence on the future, whether seen or unseen. As at any death those left behind peered after and towards him, as if into the bright and light-scattering haze at the dissolving edge of the sea.

❧

Letters and telegrams poured in to Ilse and Ruth, registering in their varied ways loss, sadness, love, honour and awe. A telegram arrived from Winnie Mandela, on behalf of her husband and his comrades: 'Deepest sympathy from Robben Island. Farewell, people's hero. His spirit will live forever. Our salute, great son of Africa.' Other messages came from the Kotane family; from Edwin Ogebe Ogbu, chairman of the United Nations Special Committee on Apartheid, with whom Ilse had been in contact, and who had worked tire-lessly on Bram's behalf during his illness; from Archie Gumede, ANC stalwart; from Theunie Fichardt, Bram's cousin, close at the beginning and end of his life; from the Natal Indian Congress; from the students at the University of Durban-Westville; from the Students' Representative Council of Natal Uni-versity; from Helen Suzman; even from Bram's old school, Grey College; and from Melville Festenstein, who had overseen the moves to have Bram dis-barred. From exile in Zambia, Jack Simons and Ray Alexander wrote with tender feeling: 'Dears, We have just received the sad news that Bram is dead. We are sorry beyond description . . . ' Nell Marquard wrote as well, of the man her husband had taught: 'His brave and noble spirit is at rest; and one gives thanks that his body too could find the rest and contentment of being with those he loved . . . I think Bram's life was a triumph . . . '

Memorial services were held elsewhere, in London and New York. At Pretoria Local the group of white prisoners held a small memorial of their own, recalling Bram's life and all that he had meant to them and the cause they supported. In due course a letter arrived for Ruth and Ilse describing at length and in detail a ceremony on Robben Island for Bram and three others who had died in the course of the struggle. Nelson Mandela had presided, Walter Sisulu (among others) had spoken. 'When we learnt of your pa's ill-ness,' the anonymous correspondent wrote, 'we tried to contact him in hospi-tal through official channels, and even made representations in this regard at the highest level, without success. We did so in the hope that the knowledge that he was constantly in our thoughts at such a critical moment would inspire and comfort him, and even improve his health.' Beyond cement walls and the cold currents of the Atlantic Ocean there were sympathies of the heart and mind that no apartheid government could imprison.

Bram's presence had evidently touched many, in many different ways, as he had been touched. When he was ill he had received a letter out of the past, from the man who had been his 'moral tutor' when he was at Oxford: 'We were lucky enough', wrote Christopher Cox, still, in 1975, an honorary fellow in residence at Bram's old college, 'to have many splendid people in . . . New College in those active tutorial years of mine in the late twenties and thirties; but none whom I think of, if I may say so, with more respect and regard than yourself.' The letter had been written just before Bram's last birthday, and must have arrived after he had lapsed into his final unconsciousness. But did that matter in the case of such a thought? There was something about a person's spirit living on across time and space irrespective of his actual presence and consciousness, and even Bram in his atheism might have credited that form of endurance.

⚜

If Bram had lived another twenty years, what would he have seen?

When he died in 1975 he had already witnessed the beginnings of change, although some of it was inevitably misleading. On 25 April 1974, just two days after Bram's sixty-sixth birthday, an army officers' coup in Lisbon brought down the Caetano regime, heralding Portugal's withdrawal from Africa, and the independence of Guinea-Bissau, Angola and Mozambique. By April 1975 Saigon had fallen to the communist forces of Ho Chi Minh, a shattering blow (as Bram would have understood it) to American imperialism in Indochina. Tim Wilson remembered how, in the last months of his life, these events had registered in Bram's mind so that he felt – as always – that the world, and particularly southern Africa, was on the brink of revolutionary change. His optimism was irrepressible, even then.

If he had lived just over another year he would have seen, on 16 June 1976 – Ilse's birthday, yet again – the explosive resistance of the young in Soweto that became the Soweto Revolt. What those who participated in and led it would have thought of him may have been another matter, for they were infused not with loyalty to communism or even the ANC, but rather by the precepts of Black Consciousness, which sought solidarity on racial rather than trans-racial grounds. To some of the Black Consciousness proponents a person such as Bram would have been one of their more insidious enemies, precisely because he presumed to cross racial boundaries and to speak on behalf of black freedom, diverting blacks from freeing themselves. (And yet when the Black Consciousness leader Steve Biko was asked whether blacks had any heroes among the whites, his reply was simple: 'Yes. Bram Fischer.') Bram for his part might have been fascinated and inspired by the innate rebelliousness of the youth; he would certainly have marvelled at their extraordinary courage as unarmed children sustained the revolt nation-wide for more than a year; yet the racial exclusiveness would have alarmed him, and he may have seen it as the harbinger of the civil war he had dedicated his life to avoid. By 1977 the brutality of such a war would have been confirmed, not only by severe repression across the country, but by the murder in police confinement of Steve Biko himself, kept naked and manacled in a nightmare trip from Port Elizabeth to Johannesburg, his head finally smashed against a prison wall.

State repression under Prime Minister Vorster and his successor, P.W. Botha, succeeded for a time, and rebellion inside the country was tamped down once again, while the ANC in exile languished relatively ineffectively for all its efforts. Yet, as Bram would have prophesied: not for ever. The early 1980s saw the rise of the United Democratic Front, which linked the revolt of the youth with the renewed popular legitimacy of the ANC, as a plethora of political and community groups joined in a nearly uncontrollable grassroots expansion, growing as if by cellular division. By 1980 Zimbabwe had achieved its independence; inside South Africa the black trade-union movement was on the rise; South African control in South West Africa, under attack by SWAPO and at the United Nations, was becoming an unacceptable drain on the government's resources.

The apartheid regime did what it could: two States of Emergency in the 1980s, neo-colonial adventures of conquest and disruption in Angola and Mozambique, destabilisation and wanton destruction in the region in general, the murder of opponents inside the country and in neighbouring territories. Ruth First was killed by a bomb, as were Marius Schoon's wife Jenny Curtis and their child. Matthew Goniwe, Griffiths and Victoria Mxenge, and David Webster were assassinated, just some among the untold numbers of local activists inside South Africa who suffered from the savage butchery of a power which had lost all sense of morality, a police force which was a state within a state. And yet there was that other story: of the fall of P.W. Botha, and the installation of F.W. de Klerk; of writing on the wall which the latter became somewhat adept at reading; of conscience, and hope, and devotion; of secret negotiations initiated from prison by Nelson Mandela; of the long walk towards an historic miracle.

At the end of 1987 Govan Mbeki was released from prison, to be followed in October 1989 by Walter Sisulu, Ahmed Kathrada, Andrew Mlangeni, Raymond Mhlaba and Elias Motsoaledi – the men Bram had defended at the Rivonia Trial so many years before. There were rapturous gatherings in Soweto and elsewhere, all of which preceded the main event, as on 11 February 1990

Nelson Mandela (just over an hour late after all this time) took that short walk out of the gates of Victor Verster Prison in Paarl, raised his right fist in victory, and moved towards the crowds who had gathered to see him as the world watched via satellite in wonder. Later that day, as the sun dipped into the Atlantic Ocean he had gazed on for so many years from Robben Island, Mandela spoke to a tumultuous crowd from the mayor's balcony in Cape Town, paying tribute to all those who had kept the hope of liberty alive, and some of whom had paid the ultimate price. Among these were Moses Kotane, Yusuf Dadoo and Bram Fischer, whose memory, declared Mandela, would be 'cherished for generations to come'.

Then those other years: of tense negotiations, confrontations, threats of withdrawal. Chris Hani was assassinated; the neo-fascist Afrikaner right paraded under facsimile swastikas and threatened armageddon; in Natal the ANC and the Inkatha Freedom Party were locked in murderous battle; the security forces, still far from neutral in the conflict, promoted train attacks, massacres, more butchery. Yet resolute through it all, as if fixed to its only guiding star, Nelson Mandela and the ANC remained loyal to a vision of non-racial democracy which no disruption or resistance could counter. Until finally, towards the end of April 1994, the impossible happened, and in a peaceful drama played out before the world South Africa's first free and full elections were held, electing a Government of National Unity, and Nelson Mandela as President.

It was reconciliation that Mandela had preached: it was a vision that came out of the years of his past, and the movement of which he had been a part; out of his own wisdom, and that of the people with whom he had been at one. When he was first released, he too spoke to multitudinous crowds. At Soccer City in Soweto he flew in by helicopter to speak to 100,000 people; Mzwakhe Mbuli, 'the people's poet', paid him tribute. On the stage along with Mandela were Arthur Chaskalson and George Bizos, the junior members from the Rivonia team, as well as the other Rivonia accused; if Bram had been alive he would have been there. On 10 May 1994 Nelson Mandela was sworn in as President at the Union Buildings in Pretoria while South African Air Force jets swooped overhead and the highest-ranking generals of the defence force and the police pledged their loyalty. It was a scene that Bram had played over and over again in his mind. When everyone knew that they would never live to see it, that South Africa would never emerge from a world frozen into morbid immobility, he always knew it could happen. If he had been alive, he would have been there.

What else would Bram have seen if he had lived another twenty years?

He would have been witness to certain ironies, for not everything played to the script he had prepared. Those socialist governments inaugurated in Mozambique and Angola were fifteen years later in ruins. Much of that could be attributed to the predations of the South African state, its overt and covert support for rebel movements, joined in this – in Angola at least – by the United States of America. But what of the era of African independence, initiated with such hope in the early 1960s, just as the South African opposition to apartheid faced its darkest years? By the 1980s and 1990s many African countries were in crisis, in seemingly irrevocable debt to the First World, but also ravaged by the corruptions of power, internal divisions of wealth, and ethnic and regional conflict. By 1994 South Africa, whose freedom had been so long delayed, was emerging as the hope of a continent where once before it had embodied its woes. For Bram, whose eye was always on the bigger picture, the inversion would have been more than simply ironic but less than entirely pleasing; he might have hoped that the South African renaissance would galvanise a continental resurrection.

What, more particularly, of the belief that had infused some forty years of his life, in the rightness and goodness of communism? If he had lived, he would have had to live with this as well. When Bram was young his journey to the Soviet Union appeared (as he looked back) to offer a model: South Africa too could be another country, and one could travel into that future as one could across distance. But in 1989, as the walls of oppression came tumbling down, they were not only the walls of apartheid. Across the globe, in Berlin, crowds of a different, though equally tumultuous, kind broke through the Berlin Wall towards their own vision of freedom. In the USSR Mikhail Gorbachev, much like F.W. de Klerk in South Africa, attempted to contain breakdown through reform, but the changes that he initiated only accelerated the demand and necessity for wholesale transformation.

The aftermath produced ironies of its own: not only freedom but also disruption and corruption; not only new national identities but also disintegration, regional conflict, secession and ethnic cleansing – the abysmal future which Bram had believed only communism could neutralise for ever through its fulfilments and equalities. Yet if he had lived he would have had to concede that the more morbid of these developments occurred not only despite but because of the communist record. Winning or losing (in this case the Cold War) proves nothing about morality in and of itself; but Bram would have faced an historic correction and a certain verdict. As oppression had yielded to liberty in South Africa, so he would have had to recognise that the form of liberty he believed in had contained its own systematic oppression. Communism had failed, and if socialism in any aspect was to survive it would have to be in reconfigured, if not wholly transfigured, shape. And yet those other terms and ingredients of his life – non-racialism, humanisation, reconciliation – had been fulfilled: the moment would have been unutterably bitter-sweet.

The future is another country: it arrives, but not exactly in the form we foresee. South Africa became the land Bram had hoped for, but not wholly in the terms he had anticipated or desired. For those of us looking on at century's end – a hundred years after this story began – the conjunction of these two equally unheralded events at disparate ends of the globe provides a certain perspective: the drama of which Bram was a part is thrown into relief by the simultaneous falls of apartheid and communism. But if these two events are like contrasting spotlights on either side of a single stage – suggesting the extent to which Bram was both right and wrong – they also provide a recognisable illumination of human experience. In that sense the future is another country for us all: in such a form all our commitments face uncertainty, all our rights contain shadows of wrong, all our visions of what is to come remain a matter both of responsibility and of opacity.

But as for Bram, understanding that the future was both known and unknown, he had staked his all on creating it, in fulfilment of the imperative to make humanity meaningful and available to everyone. That was the existential component of his commitment, the moral dimension of his politics, the integrity in his ideology, and he had followed it wherever it led. That he could do so with such conviction and courage still creates a sense of mystery, as we look on across our own time and distance.

⁂

Which does not answer the question of tragedy.

When Bram went underground, Joel Mervis had first raised the idea, and now in the aftermath of his death it was a hard one to avoid. In the image of a man of such honour, promise and prestige laid low, it was difficult to suppress the sense of something gone tragically wrong. Where Bram had been born for success and achievement, where he had offered so much to his society, all this had apparently come to nothing. Could he not have found some way to negotiate with power in something less than an absolute form? Or, conversely, could his society not have found some more flexible way to accommodate and accept the exceptional gifts that he had tendered? André Brink, in his funeral address, objected that to call Bram's life a tragic waste, as some were doing, was to ignore the meaning of his commitment and actions. And yet his remarks, although apposite, could not settle the question entirely: it seemed such a desperate loss.

When George Bizos approached Bram after his recapture, Bram had been clear that an evaluation of his actions could not be based on outcome, and the same must be true in any larger assessment. If Nelson Mandela entered prison for twenty-seven years and then emerged to lead his country to freedom, could that be considered a 'tragedy' or 'waste'? Perhaps it was a necessity or precondition, in ways that are hard to understand. When Mandela was sentenced to life imprisonment, he was prepared, as he announced, for death, yet if he had died the commitment that produced a wholly different outcome would have been exactly the same. To measure tragedy by result is to abandon significance to the unpredictable dispositions of fate, but for a fuller meaning other dimensions must come into consideration.

If we are thinking about such issues it is worth returning to the authorities, and it was this last point that Aristotle, in lending tragedy its classic definition, understood so clearly. If the tragic lay merely in the decisions of the gods, that would have little to do with human significance. Hence the essential feature of his account: tragedy involves the actions of a great individual who contributes to his fall through some crucial error or flaw. In that light, tragedy lies at the intersection of the internal and external, where both combine ineluctably towards some inevitable and doom-laden result. For some this would have been a definition that suited Bram Fischer exactly, and in his case the error was communism. Thus Laurens van der Post, responding many years later to my general enquiry on his knowledge of Bram, found himself unable, because of the emotional complication of such recollections, to write of much besides this overwhelming aspect: 'I was devoted to Bram, and yet could not have differed more openly from him in his extraordinary allegiance to the unreality of communism, joined to his own unreality about the unreality of communism. It was a tragic Greek entanglement . . . ' In this view, if Bram's vision had not been fixed on the communist mirage, his talents and gifts might have found their appropriate expression, changing both him and his world.

In absorbing such a point, we have to be clear in determining the grounds on which it stands. If the judgment is purely historical – that Bram was wrong because communism failed – it will be contingent and superficial: change the result and we would have to change the verdict. A more telling version is the moral one: Bram's flaw was that he was swayed by a morally compromised ideology, and the specific absolutism it induced produced his particular tragedy. After all, moral blindness is one consequence of the classic tragic flaw, and given the Soviet show trials, the gulag, the invasions of Hungary and

Czechoslovakia, perhaps it captures Bram's one failing. Or perhaps, with somewhat greater nuance, Bram's flaw was one of *understanding*, in that he did not fully comprehend the wider resonances and implications – the essential fatalism – involved in his choices.

Yet none of this entailed that he had to suffer from cancer in prison as a consequence, and in every one of these respects there can be no easy rush to judgment. For one thing, a commitment that – to take the strongest formulation – may have become immoral some time after the revolution in the Soviet Union could appear quite different in another setting. As Bram pointed out in his speech from the dock, when he joined the Communist Party there were precious few other avenues for inter-racial politics in South Africa. Also, on that score, it was clear that Bram's allegiance to communism was never altogether 'blind': his characteristic assessment, as he expressed it to others, was that 'mistakes had been made', and that these were to be avoided in future; he would not have supported the gulag. Most tellingly, in his case there was evidently no personal immorality, but quite the reverse: in that light, how could moral means have immoral ends? If Bram had a flaw (that is to say), it could not have been one of *virtue*, if questions of intention or purpose have any meaning. For Aristotle, tragedy in its true form inspires pity and fear: pity aroused 'by unmerited misfortune', fear by 'the misfortune of a man like ourselves'. But in this respect Bram parted company from the model, for in his essential aspect he was a man quite *unlike* most of the rest of us. Indeed, one might say that if he had a fault it was nothing more or less than *identical* with his virtue: the very element – perhaps loyalty – that spurred him to an absolutely demanding morality. For that reason, if his last days prompted any characteristic emotions among those who knew him, they were not so much pity and fear as regret balanced by admiration and awe: an awe of the truly resplendent.

There are of course other definitions of the tragic. Georg Lukács once defined tragedy as 'the clash of two necessities' – an account that has some obvious resonance for Bram. In such a version an unregenerate force of apartheid had to be met by uncompromising resistance, and the individual who took a stand (and paid the price) was of course the tragic one. Like Antigone (although he would not have understood it this way), Bram obeyed the moral laws of the gods and not of men, and though his mortal fate was sealed, that was where true nobility lay. In such a setting, one might say, choice of this kind becomes the definition of *identity* – and so we might develop a third definition of tragedy: the tragic figure is one who sustains identity in circumstances which make that no longer possible. This is a definition that would fit Bram

Fischer absolutely, and in it we see not only the humbling but also the ennobling and clarifying aspects of tragedy, the dimensions that establish transcendence, in which we encounter not only outcome but stature. By these measures, Bram Fischer was a tragic figure indeed; but his story had the right ending.

⁂

In the week after Bram's death, each newspaper in South Africa was permitted to publish one photograph of him, with the proviso that the picture had been taken before his period underground. *Die Burger*, which missed the deadline, printed a whited-out silhouette, presenting a ghostly and vacant image, replete with hat. An editorial in the newspaper, regretting that Bram had been 'a lost son who did not return', suggested that a nation that wished to retain the loyalties of its questing children would require wisdom and love to preserve the bonds of affection. Only then would it be able to escape the terrible self-reproach implicit in David's grief: 'O Absolom, my son, my son . . . would God I had died for thee.'

Bram's life migrated into fiction, suggesting the extent to which his legacy both required and invited sustained meditation. In Mary Benson's *At the Still Point*, he entered into the novel most overtly as the character of Jakob Versfeld, a lawyer who goes underground and is eventually recaptured. André Brink, who had been so affected during those last months, wrote *Rumours of Rain*, in which the lawyer Bernard Franken was very much modelled on Bram Fischer. Nadine Gordimer, who had long been interested in Bram, and had observed and written on his trials in the 1960s, finally turned to him in the figure of Lionel Burger in *Burger's Daughter*. There, in measuring what remains of her father's legacy in the aftermath of the Soweto Revolt, Rosa Burger's innermost feeling is, 'I don't know the ideology./ It's about suffering./ How to end suffering.' But she is also quite prepared to recognise what she terms Lionel's 'sublimity'.

There may have been something prescient in that, for it was a recognition that spread further afield. In February 1994, when Joe Slovo spoke with Arthur Chaskalson, he was prepared to talk of Bram as being a different kind of communist: 'he wasn't a communist in the sense that we used to understand the way a communist operated. And in that sense he laid the basis for the future . . . In his personal relationships with people he had a sort of humanistic approach to the way people should operate in a political party.' There was a particular echo to his words, for Joe Slovo had been deeply affected by the fall of the Soviet Union – not only as a failure and as a fact, but also as a rebuke to those such as himself who had been unwilling or unable to see certain truths. When I spoke with him in December 1991, his voice seemed to say it in indirect ways: he knew he had something to learn. At that time he was confronting his own mortality, already suffering from the cancer that would ultimately cause his death – and he was also engaged in the negotiations which produced the constitutional settlement of 1994. Mandela had said that Slovo had drive, but now he showed a crucial flexibility, becoming responsible, more than anyone else, for the compromises and agreements that were reached as the non-racial and inclusive visions of the future prevailed. In particular, it was he who suggested the idea of a government of national unity – a form of temporary power-sharing between the ANC and the National Party – that provided the crucial formula.

It was just at that time that he had been thinking of Bram as a different kind of communist. Could there have been a connection, in the vision that Slovo was able to draft as if in the air for the eyes of others? There is no need to detract from Slovo himself, and no one can ever know, but it is tempting to think that in this way something of Bram passed – in the best way – into history, infusing the humanising and peacemaking gestures of his being into those he left behind. As for the rapprochement that Slovo suggested, between blacks and Afrikaners in South Africa, it would have meant everything in the world to Bram.

⁂

And what of his actual family?

Bram's beloved sister Ada died before he did, also of cancer. His brother Piet – always the exception among the siblings – continued his life as a Jehovah's Witness and Afrikaner nationalist, embarrassed by Bram's politics but not by his presence as he, too, on occasion visited him in jail. Paul and Gus – the two doctors – moved to Plettenberg Bay, where Gus called his house 'Klein Bottelary', after the original Fischer farm which had belonged to Oupa Abraham's family (and which is still owned by a branch of the Fischers). Paul, too, later died of cancer, but it was in Gus's house that he told me how in Bloemfontein, every year on 23 April, the servant who had been with him when Bram was ill would come to remind him that it was Bram's birthday. 'I think he is happiest', Paul had remarked of his brother as if he were simply sitting in the next room, 'in the way that things turned out.' Talking of Bram's capacity to win people over, he said, 'It was extraordinary how he did, how he did sort of . . . catch on.'

Ruth and Ilse were there to see the birth of the country their father helped create and, at the least, have found that pleasure among many others. Ruth, whose focus was always more personal, continued her profession as a clinical psychologist and, during the Emergencies of the 1980s, was among a group of therapists who worked with young black detainees, helping them recover from the trauma of their isolation and torture in prison. Ilse, whose reflexes were always more overtly political, had to live through other traumas of her own, finding for instance that St John's College – which her brother Paul had attended – could not afford the political risk of her employment as a librarian at the time when Bram was ill. Both Ruth, in her first and second marriages (the latter to the educationist Michael Rice), and Ilse have children, whom they adopted. Neither had biological children, and in the darkest years after Bram's death one might have said that in this way too the Fischer line had come to a halt, as if brought to a stop by the encompassing malevolence that ended his life.

But that is not the reality, and perhaps the larger change in South Africa helps us to see things in a different light. For there *are* children indeed, and it makes no difference whether they are of a strict biological line. In this way, as in others, Bram's continuities are not literal and direct but metaphoric and oblique, sustained across the disruptions of biology and history by an essential movement of life and meaning. In the widest perspective, one may suggest that many born as if for a second time into the new South Africa could consider themselves the 'children' of Bram Fischer and those like him.

Something similar may be said of his heritage as a lawyer.

Bram was never reinstated, even posthumously, on the roll of advocates by the Johannesburg Bar Council, and this for an inevitably technical and legalistic reason. Only practising advocates may appear on the roll; someone who is no longer alive can no longer practise; therefore Bram could not be reinstated. And yet, as in other areas of his life, there are continuities which suggest that his presence, in some way, survives. Each of those junior members of the Rivonia defence team, Arthur Chaskalson, George Bizos and Joel Joffe, has in his own way sustained the principles of justice for which Bram stood, through an active involvement in South African affairs. More significantly, the tradition of which Bram was a part – rightly he would not have taken credit for this – of a resolute resistance to apartheid in the courts, continued both while he was in prison and after his death. In that forum, in many a political trial through the 1960s, 1970s and 1980s, those lawyers who had worked with Bram, or who came to work with others who had worked with him, or who had never known him but took up the mantle of that tradition, maintained a remarkable record of courageous, patient and often decisive intervention in an otherwise unpromising setting. The law – with some redemptive irony – became one of the primary sites of resistance in South Africa to an otherwise rampant apartheid.

In 1978 – three years after Bram died – Arthur Chaskalson took leave as a full-time practising advocate to co-found the Legal Resources Centre, an organisation whose purpose was to chip away, through the courts, at the legal underpinnings of apartheid. There Ilse Fischer was employed as a librarian, and had the pleasure of seeing, on a daily basis, her father's law library, housed at the Centre at a time when so little of Bram's life had any public legitimacy. Yet that aspect changed as well: in June 1995 Nelson Mandela gave the first Bram Fischer Memorial Lecture in Johannesburg, and one year later the Bram Fischer Memorial Library was formally opened at the Legal Resources Centre, again by President Mandela.

George Bizos became a confidant of Nelson Mandela, both through the prison years and after. In 1997 Ismail Mahomed, who could not get rooms in chambers during the first Fischer trial, became Chief Justice – one of the two highest judicial posts in the country. The other was occupied by Arthur Chaskalson, who in 1994 was appointed President of South Africa's newly created Constitutional Court. Here there was a further, if oblique, connection. After Bram had gone to prison, he gave his advocate's gown to Arthur Chaskalson when the latter took silk in 1971 – though he wrote to Ilse that perhaps Arthur should reconsider accepting it: 'look where it landed previous wearer.' There was something slightly comic in the gift, for Bram had been short, and Arthur was over six feet tall, so that he never wore it. Yet Arthur kept the gown as one of his most prized possessions; he did not share Bram's ideological beliefs, but his feel for justice was passionately the same. Bram had also given him his desk, which Arthur took with him to the Legal Resources Centre and then to the Constitutional Court.

And so one may say now, in a manner of speaking, that Bram Fischer's gifts – gown and desk – have come to preside over the Constitution in South Africa, the foundation of justice in the land.

❧

Beyond questions of tragedy, however, beyond irony, reversal or transcendence, we may still ask whether it was worth it: whether, in particular, it was worth it for Bram to go underground and spend the rest of his life in captivity. What, in reality, did he achieve?

It is now a question surprisingly easy to answer. There may be those who would say that what Bram achieved was purely symbolic – that he became a symbol of resistance, but that nothing practical was gained. This is a mistake in itself – to think that symbols have no effect on the real. The *idea*, in such a setting, that sacrifice was not colour-bound, that solidarity was not limited by race, that there was a moral commitment and continuity that transcended death – these were immensely powerful thoughts, incarnate in the life and experience of one man. In this respect symbols live longer than people.

Moreover, it is hard not to feel that the question of *sacrifice* has quasi-mythic overtones, as if Bram were the one who had to die for the regeneration of the community. From that point of view he presented the reverse image of a Nelson Mandela. Mandela was the towering figure who lived to enter the promised land. He was the hero resurrected from the underworld, the voyager escaped from the cold island of entrapment to return to the land of the sun, bringing life and joy back to the world as well as to his people. Mandela was the embodiment of renewal combining youth and age, in whom the cycle of rebirth came through to its redemptive fulfilment. Bram, in contrast, was the one who had to succumb, as if taking the burdens of his people upon him, paying for their sins as an Afrikaner, dying because there was no place for him except in some non-existent future. His life, which had begun so full of light, ended on the dark side of the circle of regeneration.

And yet – in the deepest sense of the word – Bram was a prototype. He came out of Afrikaner nationalism; he died belonging to the whole of South Africa. He never saw this as a betrayal of Afrikaner identity, but rather as its fulfilment, its extension towards a true meaning of the name 'African'. He was a white man able to undertake, in the course of his own life, the personal transformation that must accompany, if not herald, the political. At a time when it would have been almost unimaginable to say so, instinctively and by conviction he understood that if whites were to have a meaning and future in South Africa, this was the kind of change they would have to undergo. And so he took it on – a story of identity, its retention and extension, into the marrow of his own life.

How difficult this is to do is evidenced in the lives of every one of us in our different places on the earth. Yet in the context of Bosnia and Rwanda, of ethnic cleansing, of sectarian and other hatreds, of oppression and exploitation in so many settings and versions, nothing could be more important. There may be other changes in our identities and relationships – beyond race, class, religion, gender or nationalism – which will become equally if not more crucial, even if they are now only dimly apprehended on our horizon in a time when both the prospect of venturing into space and the necessity of redeeming an impending ecological disaster on our planet seem equally likely. For any and all of this we will have to change our lives within; and that was what Bram Fischer, in his own way, did.

Who can ask if that was 'worth it'? Bram Fischer's is a life not only for South Africa, not only for a world recovering and attempting to move forward from a history of colonialism and racial supremacy, but it is also, in ways we can barely imagine, a life for the twentieth century and the century to come. It most certainly was 'worth it'.

⁂

Bram's ashes were never recovered. When the new democratic parliament first met, official questions were asked, but the answers were obscure. The most likely suggestion was that a chaplain had scattered his ashes in the Garden of Remembrance in Bloemfontein in the presence of a prison official. For the first time Ruth and Ilse also learned that in that same garden a plaque for Bram had been installed, among the rows of many such items. It was the simplest of tablets, marking the date of his birth with a star and that of his death with a cross. There was no other memorial.

⁂

A life begins long before it starts; it endures long after it ends.

This story began in the deserts of Namibia; it ends in the mountains of Lesotho: across a century and across the landscape of South Africa.

In March 1986 I was travelling with two historians, Bob Edgar and Jim Campbell, northwards from Maseru to Butha Buthe, the small village from which, in the 1820s, Moshoeshoe had moved his fledgeling nation, the Basotho, to the stronghold of Thaba Bosiu, the Mountain at Night. We were on our way to visit Edwin Mofutsanyana, one of the old-time Communist Party members, who had travelled to Moscow in the early 1930s, and worked with Bram Fischer during the second half of that decade and after. Bob Edgar had 'discovered' Mofutsanyana after he had dropped from sight for many years, and was now recovering his story to the intense fascination of all those interested in a previously suppressed South African history.

We found Edwin Mofutsanyana in his hut in the village. He was an extra-ordinary man, as ancient and angular, it seemed, as the mountain sides that surrounded him. His eyes – so strangely for an African – were a piercing blue. Mofutsanyana was deaf, and told us matter-of-factly that he had been hearing voices, sometimes emanating from the roof of his hut. I wrote out my questions

on index cards, and he answered in a meandering but transfixing way, sometimes hard to follow, but with an unexpected strength and decision in his
voice. He told stories – of bringing James Majoro, secretary of the
Mineworkers' Union, to meet and work with Bram in the period before the
mineworkers' strike of 1946, and of sundry encounters with the police.
Mofutsanyana recalled complaining at one point to Bram that the Communist
Party was becoming too respectable – to which Bram had jokingly responded
that that was because the Party had the best lawyers.

Mofutsanyana also returned to the distant past. He told of a longstanding
family connection with the Fischers which had existed many years before he
met Bram; indeed, one of his elder brother's sons was called 'Fischer'. The
origins of this had been in the Boer War, when the Mofutsanyanas lived in
Witzieshoek, on the border of Basutoland and the Free State. At that time,
although Africans were not officially involved in the hostilities, there was
something of a hidden campaign in the area to take advantage of the Boers
and steal their cattle. Yet Edwin's father was among the five or six men who
opposed this policy, regarding it as a contravention of official agreements with
the Free State. Soon it was reported to the British that the men were spying for
the Boers; the others escaped into Basutoland, but Mofutsanyana's father
refused to leave, and spent some three years in prison in Pietermaritzburg for
his pains. Later, during the Rebellion of 1914, Mofutsanyana's father had
again been close to the Afrikaners – so much so, recalled Edwin, that he had
spent time coming and going 'for weeks on horses that I didn't know'. In these
circumstances the name of Fischer had clearly had some resonance: 'So that's
why that name of Fischer crept into the family, and we had a son called
Fischer.'

An alliance from the turn of the century had turned into a different kind
of comradeship between Edwin and Bram – an emblem, perhaps, of the kind
of affiliation between blacks and Afrikaners in the universal claims of the
Communist Party that Bram had believed was so natural. 'He was no pre-
tender,' remarked Edwin of Bram. 'He wholeheartedly believed what he had
undertaken to be . . . I think of all the Afrikaners I have known, Bram Fischer
was always the best.' Edwin said, 'I think naturally, not politically, he was
naturally a kind man.'

During the repression of the 1960s, Mofutsanyana had escaped back into
Basutoland, where with the instincts of a survivor he had held out in the
Drakensberg for a number of years, living on his own, seeing no one, getting
no news. These were the same mountains Bram and Molly had taken such
delight in from Lusthof, just across the way in the Free State. When I showed

him my last question his eyes were getting tired, and he couldn't make it out; he asked me to read it. I repeated it a number of times: 'Do you ever think of Bram Fischer?' As soon as he heard, Edwin responded without hesitation, 'I think more than anyone else.' And then after some moments he told me how, when he was alone on the mountain, somehow he had known that Bram was out of prison, but ill, just before he died. 'So much that even when I was on top of the mountain I knew that he was out, but sick. He was always in . . . in my mind. As I say, he was a very good . . . person.'

That was the last thing Edwin said to me. He had paused as he spoke, choosing his words carefully, but though his voice had lingered and lowered as he remembered, his last sentence had a quiet gentleness about it.

Outside there were sounds – a mother's voice, a baby crying, men speaking together.

Inside there was a silence, then thank-yous. We went out into the bright and angled sunshine.

NOTES

What follows here is a brief summary of my major sources as I have used them in each chapter, with commentary where necessary or of interest. Unfortunately, space does not permit anything more detailed. For that reason too, I cannot do anything like full justice to my major and most consistent source in this biography, the collection of family correspondence and related material entrusted to me by Ruth and Ilse Fischer. All I can do here is pay tribute to the wealth and substance of those letters to, from and among Bram and Molly, Percy and Ella, and the Fischer children; I believe they have enriched this book in innumerable ways.

Only the most significant letters, therefore, will be cited individually; readers will have to assume that they underlie much of what is told in this account. Similar economies will be followed with other sources, which are given only in the most general form. Wherever correspondence is cited, it will take the form 'B/M' for Bram to Molly, 'B/Ella', and so on. Dates have been abbreviated in the South African and British format (dd/mm/yy), except that for the nineteenth century the full year is given. For interviews, refer to the list in the Bibliography for dates and locations, though again only general references will be made here. For those who have a specific interest on particular matters, I shall be happy – as long as I am able and available! – to provide the more detailed notations, references and directions at my disposal.

Prologue

The Rev. F. Bernsmann's journey comes from my interview with Pauline Jenisch, and excerpts (typed and handwritten) from the *Tagebuch* of Friedrich Bernsmann (1845–1920) as well as the text of an obituary ('Zum Gedächtnis') for Bernsmann by Missionspräses J. Olpp. Thanks to Anne Halley and Robert Moeller for assistance with translation.

Chapter 1

A Mother Aunt's letter comes from the Abraham Fischer Collection (FSA A59) 59/7/3, H. Denyssen/Abraham Fischer 27/11/07. This collection too, in its various parts, has been my major source for this chapter – in particular the extensive and quite remarkable correspondence of Abraham Fischer to Percy Fischer 22/12/1888–1/1/03 in FSA A59 59/8/1 (my thanks to Drs Paul and Gus Fischer for granting me access to this restricted part of the Fischer Collection).

My major interview sources both for Abraham and Percy, and also for Ella Fichardt and her family (as well as Nakie Smith), have been those with Drs Paul and Gus

Fischer, Ruth and Ilse Fischer, and Connie Anderson. (On the matter of Abraham's early life there is a small mystery: Bram's brothers believed that their grandfather had studied overseas after SACS, and Ruth Fischer was sure that like Bram he had been to Oxford, but this is not in other sources I have consulted, and has been impossible to confirm in any records at Oxford.)

For Abraham as Prime Minister: Prime Minister's Office (FSA PMF 2), selected correspondence 14/1/08–27/2/08; also Papers of Lt. Governor, ORC (FSA G 110), particularly 444/5, Minute 933/3, 18/2/09, drafted and signed by A. Fischer, and other views expressed to Percy Fischer. For Abraham's cabinet appointment, accounts from London (on Harry's difficulties and other matters), and the cabinet crisis, selected correspondence in the Fischer Collection to, from and among the following individuals: Abraham Fischer, Louis Botha, Percy Fischer, Ada Fischer, President Steyn, General Hertzog. The vote of no confidence comes from FSA A59 59/7/6 v. 2, Resolution passed at District Committee Meeting, Bethlehem 13/6/13; and Abraham's death from *Imvo Zabantsundu*, n.d.

Other particular accounts and observations, whether on Abraham and Percy or the times they lived through, emerge from the following: David Jacobs, 'Abraham Fischer in sy Tydperk (1850–1913)'; Leo Marquard (ed.), *Letters from a Boer Parsonage*; J.A. Venn (ed.), *Alumni Cantabrigienses*, Pt II; Phyllis Lewsen (ed.), *Selections from the Correspondence of John X. Merriman 1899–1905* and *Selections from the Correspondence of John X. Merriman 1905–1924*; Sol T. Plaatje, *Native Life in South Africa*; and *Indian Opinion*, Golden Number, 1914.

CHAPTER 2

For Percy's role in the Rebellion, Bram's home and family life on the farm, early schooling and experiences, I have depended on extensive descriptions in interviews with Drs Paul and Gus Fischer, Ruth and Ilse Fischer, and Connie Anderson. Other information and perspectives come from Maude Bidwell, *Breath of the Veld*, and comments by George Bizos, in Bizos/Chaskalson conversation. Bram's correspondence with his parents begins in 1916, and in this early sequence continues until September 1920; also, miscellaneous letters to Ella Fischer from Luise and 'Pinkie', Sept.–Oct. 1917.

The family's return to Bloemfontein, and Bram at Grey: in addition to the interviews mentioned above, those with Gladys Walker and Joel Mervis. Information on Leo Marquard comes, in particular, from the Marquard Papers (UCT BC 587), and Bram's views on the 'magic circle' from his correspondence in that collection: B/Leo Marquard 4/12/65, and B/Nell Marquard 3/4/74; supplementary accounts from interviews with Drs Paul and Gus Fischer, Ruth and Ilse Fischer, Joel Mervis.

Bram's cadet story, his nationalism, and the 1924 election come again from interviews with Drs Paul and Gus Fischer, Ruth and Ilse Fischer, Connie Anderson, and Joel Mervis; the Prince's visit from B/Parents 18/5/25–25/5/25. Bram on the farm: interviews, again, with his brothers and daughters as well as cousin Connie; his (self)-revelations on race from B/Parents 3/2/26–7/3/26, and Ella/B 2/2/26–19/2/26.

For Bram's life at UCT: B/Parents 10/3/26–10/12/26; also Connie Anderson/ 'Maggie' 16/9/76, and B/Paul Fischer 6/6/26. The decision on Grey: correspondence from this time, as well as interviews with Drs Paul and Gus Fischer, and Ruth and Ilse Fischer; also B/Mollie Anderson 26/4/54. Back with the Marquards, and lasting effects: B/Leo Marquard 4/12/65, B/Nell Marquard 3/4/74; '*State* vs *Abram Fischer*', Record of Proceedings, pp. 207–8.

CHAPTER 3

For Bram's work in association with NUSAS, and the parliament of 1929, the following sources, among others: *The NUSAS*, June 1928 and Sept. 1928; Records of the South African Institute of Race Relations, Part I (UWL AD843/B) 98.1 (on the ISS); UCT BC 587 B/Leo Marquard 4/12/65, 6/3/66; Bram Fischer, speech notes for the parliament; reports from *Rand Daily Mail* and *Star* 22/7/29–26/7/29 inclusive (there was some discrepancy between these accounts and Bram's recollections to Leo Marquard in his correspondence); Bram's correspondence with his parents; and interviews with Drs Paul and Gus Fischer.

Bram on the Bloemfontein Joint Council, and his work on the Native Economic Commission: Records of the Joint Council of Europeans and Africans (UWL AD1433), Bloemfontein; UWL AD843/B 34.4.1, 'Memorandum of Evidence'; Native Economic Commission (UWL AD1438), Minutes of Evidence, Bloemfontein 23/2/31. Dr Xuma's appreciation: 'Bridging the Gap between White and Black South Africa', in Thomas Karis and Gwendolen M. Carter (eds.), *From Protest to Challenge*, vol. 1, p. 226. Bram's private sentiments: B/M 16/8/31.

For Bram and Molly's relationship, and his life up to and including his departure for England, my major source has necessarily been the correspondence between Bram and Molly for these and later years. Notable moments include Molly's 'leap': B/M 26/1/31, 28/1/[32] (misdated, by a slip back in time, 1931); the 'electric shock': B/M 29/4/37; and the text of Ruth: B/M 5/7/31, 27/11/33. Supplementary information from interviews with Drs Paul and Gus Fischer, Ruth and Ilse Fischer, Pauline Jenisch, Herleve Yates, Dr Beck de Villiers. Molly's early life and family background come from interviews with Ruth and Ilse Fischer, Pauline Jenisch, Herleve Yates.

Bram's rugby exploits against the All Blacks: *Friend* 16/7/28, 30/7/28, and *Star* 30/7/28. His twenty-first: programme and notebook, kept by Ella Fischer (it was when I saw that programme that I realised that Bram Fischer and I have the same birthday). Mrs Steyn's message: article by Margaret Smith, n.d. [*Sunday Times*, Feb. 1965].

In addition to these sources, other aspects of Bram's life (his apprenticeship to 'Oeffie, J.P.', his father's judgeship) come from his correspondence with Ella Fischer. Specific perspectives on the Rhodes, and Bram's last letters on departure: Leo Marquard/Ella 24/11/30; Nell Marquard/Ella 21/11/1930; B/Ella 17/12/31; B/M 17/12/31; Ella/B 17/12/31.

CHAPTER 4

For Bram's stay in Oxford in its entirety, as well as his travels in the Soviet Union and Europe, I have used the large store of letters between Bram and Molly, and Bram and his parents, 1932–34 (only Molly's letters from 1934 are missing). Supplementary information is from interviews with Drs Paul and Gus Fischer. For England in the 1930s I used with particular pleasure Samuel Hynes's excellent *The Auden Generation*, and Valentine Cunningham, *British Writers of the Thirties*; Spender's lines on 'the shadow of a war' are quoted by Hynes, p. 38. Bram's pursuit of the news is recalled in Mary Benson, memoir, p. 23.

On the Ralegh Club, I am indebted to Arthur Keppel-Jones, in interview and personal correspondence 2/5/84, and to notes on the Ralegh kindly given to me by David Everatt. (Nakie Smith's response on Bram's success is in Ella/B 31/5/33.)

Bram's major description of the Soviet Union is in B/Percy 19/8/32, with additional political perspectives in B/Piet Fischer 22/7/32. Recollections by one of his companions have been especially helpful: personal correspondence from Sir Geoffrey Cox 17/8/92 and 30/8/92, with Note on an Intourist Tour of the Soviet Union in July 1932. Also, Malcolm Muggeridge, 'When Stalin Organised a Famine', *Manchester Guardian Weekly*, 26/3/89, reprinted from the *Manchester Guardian*, March 1933. Rudzutak's fate is mentioned in Isaac Deutscher, *The Prophet Outcast*, p. 387.

Bram's letters from Europe, July–September 1932, both to Molly and to his parents, come from The Hague, Riga, Prague, Berlin, Vienna, Grundlsee. For Ada Fischer and her studies in London: interviews with Drs Paul and Gus Fischer, and Dr Beck de Villiers. Bram on Nazism and nationalism in 1933: B/Percy 4/7/33, 4/8/33, 29/8/33 (all these letters in Afrikaans). The Vienna Uprising of 1934: B/Parents 19/2/34; John Costello and Oleg Tsarev, *Deadly Illusions*, pp. 127ff; G.E.R. Gedye, *Fallen Bastions*, chs. 7–8; Stephen Spender, 'Returning to Vienna 1947', in *The Edge of Being*; also, Spender, *Vienna*. Bram remembered: Marianne Mahler/B 26/12/65.

As always, there are particular letters of note between Bram and Molly: on children and 'Ruth': M/B 19/4/32; B/M 5/5/32, 9/5/32; Molly on 'socialism': M/B 22/6/32; sex and philosophy: B/M 22/9/32, 17/11/32; M/B 12/10/32, 26/10/32; Molly out of love with Bram: M/B 30/5/33, 6/6/33, and B/M 10/7/33 (both Molly's letter announcing that she was back in love, and Bram's first response to her lack of it, are missing). The Book of Ruth: M/B 5/4/33; B/M 10/7/33.

Bram's Dingaan's Day speech comes mainly from the Programme, Restaurant Frascati, London 16/12/33, and his speech notes. Items of interest regarding Bram's final exams in 1933 include Christopher Cox/B 1/8/33; Leo Marquard/Ella 12/9/33; C.K. Allen/Percy 17/8/33; also, confidential report on Orange Free State Rhodes Scholars, apparently appended to Allen's letter. Allen's final word on Bram's Oxford years: Confidential Report for 1933–34 on Rhodes Scholars from Orange Free State.

CHAPTER 5

For Bram's life in Johannesburg, including his law and continuing relationship with Molly, I have again relied heavily on volumes of correspondence. The year that Molly was away in Windhoek may suffice as an example of activity at its most intense: during this time she and Bram wrote to one another on average three to four times a week each, both by rail and the newly initiated airmail; they also spoke – breathlessly – by long-distance telephone. In addition, and as usual, Bram was writing to his parents, they were writing to him, Molly was writing to them, and they wrote a few letters to her. Lives may be more detailed when people are apart; my accounts are drawn from all these sources – except the telephone calls!

Supplementary information on Bram's return to Johannesburg, including his legal and social life, comes from interviews with Drs Paul and Gus Fischer, Jack and Phyllis Lewsen, Joel Mervis, I.A. Maisels, Arthur Chaskalson, and Raymond Dart. Bram's first murder case is from B/Parents 14/2/35; his acceptance in his new surroundings from Programme of Johannesburg Bar dinner 29/11/35; his Thaba Nchu advice: B/Parents 30/11/36, 29/1/37; B/M 8/11/36, 15/11/36. Particular references for the three vignettes from Bram's life: Oliver Schreiner/Percy 21/2/37; Walter Nhlapo/B 4/6/37; Villiam K. Motsepe [signed thus]/B 11/5/36.

The progress of Bram and Molly's relationship is too detailed in their letters even to gesture at here. But among the items on their engagement, Bram is not to ask permission: M/B 8/6/36. Also Auntie Maggie/B 15/5/36; M/Percy n.d.; M/Ella n.d., 13/8/36; notice, *Volksblad*, 8/7/36.

Molly's confessional letter on leaving Windhoek: M/B 3–16/4/37. Her travels in Europe, and Bram in Johannesburg: M/B 17/4/37–26/7/37 inclusive; B/M 4/6/37–2/7/37 inclusive; and B/Parents 3/6/37–14/7/37 inclusive; also, 'Jock'/M 7/9/37, 12/9/37, 3/12/37.

Molly's last attempt to postpone the wedding, and Bram's response: B/M 10/5/37. Final negotiations, and the wedding script: B/Parents 30/8/37–15/9/37 inclusive; M/B's Parents 30/8/37; Ella's wedding notebook. The actual ceremony: interviews with Drs Paul and Gus Fischer; Herleve Yates; Pauline Jenisch; also, B/Parents 27/8/37, and *Friend* 20/9/37. Bram's final unmarried letter: B/M 15/9/37.

Birth of Ruth Fischer: B/Ella n.d. [14/8/39]; newspaper notice, n.d. [15/8/39].

CHAPTER 6

For the War on War League and the origins of the CPSA I have drawn on Jack and Ray Simons (hereafter Simons and Simons), *Class and Colour in South Africa 1850–1950*, Edward Roux's *Time Longer Than Rope*, and *Fifty Fighting Years* by A. Lerumo [Michael Harmel]. These same sources – used with some care because of their interested and (in Lerumo's case) official nature – have supplied the background for much of the political history of this chapter. Additional sources include: 'Keeping the Red Flag Flying: An Address to the S.A. Labour Party', War on War League (S.A.), March 1915, in *South African Communists Speak*, p. 4 (supplemented by full version seen in Yale MSSA); UWL AD843/B 41.2.8, extract from *Ons Vaderland* 20/11/19 for Hertzog on Bolshevism, quoted in a pamphlet issued by the Friends of the Soviet Union; interviews with Willie Kalk, and Rowley Arenstein. Simons and Simons comment on the Trotsky/Bunting parallel in *Class and Colour*, p. 450.

On the rise of the Broederbond, and Afrikaner intellectuals, see T. Dunbar Moodie, *The Rise of Afrikanerdom*, chs. 6, 8; Diederichs is quoted on pp. 168–9. The lunch with

Verwoerd: interview, Walter Sisulu; Bram told Mary Benson that he had lunch with Verwoerd when the latter was trying to make up his mind whether to be a Nationalist or a socialist (memoir, p. 24). Also Issy Heymann, prison memoir of Bram Fischer, p. 55.

For the Joint Council movement in general, Bram's role within it, and his appointment to the Executive Council of the South African Institute of Race Relations, my account comes from the Records of the Joint Council of Europeans and Africans (UWL AD1433), minutes and Annual Reports 1935–41, and related correspondence and documents; also material on the 1921 Constitution of the Joint Council, and correspondence on Sidney Bunting's application. Supplementary material on the 1936 Bills in particular comes from UWL AD843/B, including *Race Relations* vol. 2 no. 4 (Aug. 1935), and Advocate Fischer's notes on Thaba Nchu [n.d.]. For the SAIRR in general I have used UWL AD843/B, selected boxes and documents 1931–40; the Communist Party view is found in UWL AD1433 Cj 2.1.16, *Umsebenzi* 8/2/36. For Oliver Tambo on the Joint Council: AD1433 Cj 2.3, Annual Reports 1946–47, 1947–48, 1948–49.

On the rise of fascism and anti-Semitism, UWL AD843/B 88.6.1–4 for correspondence between Hoernlé, Sauerländer, and others, as well as documents collected by the SAIRR. Also Yale MSSA 605 (African Collection) B25 F480, for the Constitution of the South African National Party (Greyshirts). Supplementary material and perspectives from the South African Jewish Board of Deputies Archive, and Brian Bunting, *The Rise of the South African Reich*, ch. 4. For the Society of Jews and Christians, and Bram's membership: UWL AD843/B 88.5, assorted material including Executive Committee's Reports; also SAJBD F607A, Executive Committee Reports 1940–43; and my own correspondence and long conversation with the wonderful Amelia Levy.

Bram and Molly's honeymoon and home life is from the correspondence between Bram, Molly and his parents 1937–9. The *Loutering* translation: B/Parents 29/1/39; M/Ella n.d. [31/1/39]. Molly's pregnancy: particularly M/B's parents 21/6/39. The Beaumont Street house: virtually every letter from February 1938 to June 1939; also interviews, Ruth and Ilse Fischer.

Global events, and Percy and Ella's trip: Bram and Molly to Percy and Ella, January–July 1939, inclusive. Stalin's speech at the eighteenth Party congress is quoted in Alan Bullock, *Hitler and Stalin*, pp. 597–8; and the whole of his ch. 14 on events in Europe and the Nazi–Soviet Pact. Bram's absorption of this argument: Benson, memoir, p. 23. Percy's aloe: interviews, Drs Paul and Gus Fischer.

When Bram joined the Party: personal correspondence from Arthur Keppel-Jones 2/5/84 and 11/6/84; from Errol Harris 29/7/84; from Sir Geoffrey Cox 17/8/92. Also, interviews with Drs Paul and Gus Fischer; I.A. Maisels; Hilda and Lionel Bernstein; E.J. Burford; Edwin Mofutsanyana; George Bizos; Issy Heymann (and Heymann memoir); Ray Alexander (Simons); Rowley Arenstein; Sonia Bunting; Joe Slovo; Joel Mervis; Ruth and Ilse Fischer, among others. The world progressing by contraries is from Blake rather than Hegel or Marx.

Photograph of the Johannesburg District Committee: 'Democracy in Action':

Proceedings of the Johannesburg District Annual Conference of the Communist Party, 17–25/3/45, p. 14.

CHAPTER 7

For Bram's response to the German invasion: B/Parents 29/6/41, 2/8/41; his radio talk: B/Parents 29/6/41; M/B's Parents 23/[6/41], 7/7/41.

In this chapter I have used a plethora of documents for the political history of the period, the culture of the left during the war, and the social and political campaigns of the CPSA throughout. My major archival sources have been the Records of the South African Institute of Race Relations, Political Collection (UWL AD2182) A.I–III, and the Communist Party of South Africa Papers (Yale MSSA Film 701). Notable items (among the many) from the first include J. Morkel, 'The War and South Africa'; 'The Nationalist Party: The Truth Behind the Split'; 'Internment of Anti-Fascists'; 'Smash the Black Market'; 'Everything for the Front'; 'Away with Passes'. And from the second: 'A Complex Situation', *Freedom*, Feb. 1940; 'Cape Town Salutes Stalingrad'; 'The Debt We Owe Them'; Souvenir Programme, Civic Week for Medical Aid for Russia; Programme, 26th Anniversary Celebration of the Soviet Union Committee; 'Programme for Victory'. There are also a number of memoranda and pamphlets put forward by the CPSA in UWL AD843/B, on beer, rationing and the Alexandra bus boycott. Descriptions of the war and its progress, including telegrams to Stalin and related phenomena, come from the *Guardian* 1941–3. Additional information on all these topics is from Bullock, *Hitler and Stalin*; Simons and Simons, *Class and Colour*; Catherine Burns, 'An Historical Study of the Friends of the Soviet Union and the South African Peace Council'; and interviews with Bessie Greenstein, E.J. Burford, Baruch Hirson, Joe Slovo.

Smuts is quoted on the Japanese threat in Simons and Simons, *Class and Colour*, pp. 540–1; the Communist world-view *c*. 1943, is a rendition from Yale MSSA 605 B25 F476, 'Meet the Communists', Cape Town, n.d.

For Bram's life during the war across a broad range – his law, health, political activity at the Left Club and elsewhere – I have used a number of sources: primarily, the usual steady flow of correspondence (Bram and Molly, Percy and Ella); but also interviews with Drs Paul and Gus Fischer, Ruth and Ilse Fischer, Violet Weinberg, Hilda and Lionel Bernstein, Joe Slovo; and reports in the *Guardian*, *Vaderland*, and *Volksblad*. Bram's election to and service on the Bar Council: W.M. Furze, Secretary, Society of Advocates (Witwatersrand Division)/B 19/2/64.

Bram in Maseru and the Copper Belt are from B/M 12/2/43–25/3/43, and 9/7/43–23/7/43. Ilse's birth: M/B's Parents 30/6/43. For household details and home life during this period there is a dense supply of information throughout the letters, supplemented by detailed accounts in interviews with Ruth and Ilse Fischer. These interviews too for Nora's arrival, and related issues.

For the section on Alexandra Township and the Alexandra Health Committee, I have used stores of documents in UWL AD843/B. Notable items include North Eastern Districts Protection League, 'Alexandra'; S.L. Kark, 'Alexandra Township: A

Study of a Pocket of Ill-Health'; Statement on the Future of Alexandra Township, submitted by the Alexandra Township Health Committee; and Alexandra Anti-Expropriation Committee Memorandum. There is also a wealth of correspondence, on Bram's appointment to the AHC but also on many other matters, between Bram, Hoernlé, and numbers of others. In addition to all this: minutes of meetings 1942–3; Medical Officer's Reports; Abridged Minutes of Conference, Union Buildings, Pretoria 23/10/42. For more personal recollections: correspondence from C.J. Johnson, 15/4/87; this too for Bram and the squatters.

The Alexandra bus boycott: B/Parents 10/12/44; also UCT BC 587, Leo Marquard/Nell Marquard 20/11/44. The 1943 ANC Constitution: interview, Mary Benson; also Karis and Carter (eds.), *From Protest to Challenge*, vol. 2, pp. 84–5 (though the latter note that there is some dispute as to whether or not Bram played a role in drawing up the Constitution).

For Molly's Council campaign: B/Parents 23/9/45, with copy of flyer, 'Safeguard their Future', as well as newspaper reports. Molly's defeat, and VJ Day: *Star* 1/11/45; M/B's Parents 21/8/45, 20/11/45. 1945 for Bram, and new moods post-war: a range of documents from Yale MSSA Film 701, and UWL AD2182, including posters, pamphlets and programmes. Also reports from the *Guardian, Times* 6/3/46 (text of Churchill's Fulton speech), and *Fighting Talk*; South African House of Assembly Debates 13/3/46, cols. 3473–82; interviews with Jack Simons, and Joe Slovo. For Bram's expectations: B/Parents 6/2/46.

The AMU strike, the trial, Bram's involvement, and the aftermath come again from a range of sources, including the following: Simons and Simons, *Class and Colour*; Roux, *Time Longer Than Rope*; Mary Benson, *South Africa: The Struggle for a Birthright*; UWL AD843/B 36.4.1, Memorandum of the Johannesburg District Committee, CPSA, to the Witwatersrand Mine Natives Wages (Lansdown) Commission; Danie du Plessis, 'When You're Awaiting Trial', *Guardian* 12/9/46; reports on the trial in *Star* 16/8/46–4/10/46, *Rand Daily Mail* 27/8/46–20/9/46, and *Guardian* 29/8/46–10/10/46. For personal comments and recollections: Leo Marquard/B 4/9/46; and interviews with Drs Paul and Gus Fischer, Ruth and Ilse Fischer, Marius Schoon, Edwin Mofutsanyana, Joe Slovo, Jack Simons, Nelson Mandela.

The day in a million: B/Parents 18/12/47. National Party victory 1948: *Vaderland* 28/5/48 (thanks, again, to Stanley Trapido for remembering that cartoon); *Argus* 28/5/48 for full results. The Suppression of Communism Act: drawn from Simons and Simons, *Class and Colour*, and Kahn's announcement of dissolution, p. 608.

CHAPTER 8

The general political history in this chapter – comprising everything from further details on the dissolution of the CPSA, through to the regeneration of the ANC, the Defiance Campaign, the Liberal Party, the COD, the reconstitution of the SACP, and (later in the chapter) its underground habits – comes from a variety of published sources: Simons and Simons, *Class and Colour*; Lerumo, *Fifty Fighting Years; South African Communists Speak*; the enormously helpful documents and discussion in Karis and Carter (eds.), *From Protest to Challenge*, vol. 2; Mary Benson, *Nelson Mandela*; Peter Walshe, *The Rise of African Nationalism in South Africa*; Janet Robertson, *Liberalism in South Africa 1948–63*; Tom Lodge, *Black Politics in South Africa since 1945*. More personal recollections and observations are from interviews with Jack Simons, Hilda and Lionel Bernstein, Joe Slovo, Edwin Mofutsanyana, Nelson Mandela, Walter Sisulu, Myrtle Berman, Violet Weinberg, Ben Turok, and David Everatt's interview with Ben Turok. Bram and the founding of SACOD is from Treason Trial Exhibits (UWL AD1812) Ef 3.3.1, 'The Road to Liberty', and Ef 3.2, SACOD Press Release 22/10/53. The liquidation and listing of communists was widely reported in the press. Perspectives on the code of multi-racialism from my *The Novels of Nadine Gordimer*, ch. 2.

Bram is KC: cuttings from *Star*, *Friend*, and *Rand Daily Mail* 19–20/11/51. Also, C.R. Swart/B 20/11/51, Leo Marquard/B 20/11/51, and good wishes from numbers of other correspondents, including Helen [Suzman], who asks, 'Can I still argue with you now?' Bram's reply to 'Oom Blackie' is in two undated handwritten drafts, one of which is clearly more 'final' than the other. Bram's ensuing political cases from a range of sources, but particularly my interview with Nelson Mandela. His response to the Defiance Campaign trial: B/M 4/12/52.

Bram's journey to Europe and the Vienna Peace Congress: primarily, B/M 28/11/52–4/1/53; also letters to children, and Percy and Ella at this time. In addition, among other sources, *New York Times* 12/13/52; and 'Congress of the Peoples for Peace', no. 11, 20/12/52, Report of the 15th, 16th, 17th and Closing Sessions, including statement by Abram Fischer, and poem, 'War and Peace' by Kazim-As-Samavi.

Molly in Europe and China, 1954, comes in the main from her correspondence, M/B 21/7/54–8/11/[54], and Bram's letters to her during this time. Other material: UWL AD1812, Ex 2.2, M/Rev. D.C. Thompson 15/7/54; 'South African Woman Delegate Leaves for Home', mimeo 30/10/[54]. Joe Slovo's views: B/M 11/11/54.

The social and cultural life of Sophiatown has been widely celebrated, particularly by its black writers, most of whom are listed in my Bibliography.

For Bram at Peace venues, his banning and Molly's, reports in *Advance*, *Friend*, and selected documents from the Treason Trial Exhibits. Soviet bloc anti-Semitism, and the South African (including Bram's) response: reports in *Advance* 29/1/53, 5/2/53; also UWL AD1812, Ex 2.3.1, 'For Peace and Friendship', April 1953. Stalin's death, revelations, and Hungary: selected articles in *Advance* and *New Age*; interviews with Hilda and Lionel Bernstein, Joe Slovo, Myrtle Berman, Miriam Hepner. Particular views from Bram, Sam Kahn, and Molly: B/Parents 20/3/56; *Advance* 12/3/53, 4/3/54. The Rosenberg execution: *Advance* 4/6/53, 25/6/53; *New York Times* 20/6/53, 21/6/53.

Bram and Mollie Anderson: interviews with Mollie Anderson, and Connie Anderson; B/Mollie Anderson 16/6/53, 26/4/54.

Home life while Molly was away: Paul/M 17/7/54, and Bram's letters to Molly during her journey. On Paul Fischer: nearly every one of Molly's letters to Bram's parents and very many of Bram's have news of Paul's health during these years. Additional views and information on his condition, Paul's character, and the way Bram and Molly cared for him: interviews with Drs Paul and Gus Fischer, Drs Mervyn Susser and Zena Stein, Ruth and Ilse Fischer, Mary Benson, Violet Weinberg, Jack and Phyllis Lewsen,

Hilda and Lionel Bernstein; and Arthur Chaskalson, text of address at Paul Fischer's funeral.

The swimming pool: apart from the correspondence, and the glowing remembrances of everyone I spoke to who had been there, the pool has received its most famous treatment in fiction, in Nadine Gordimer's *Burger's Daughter*. Ruth and Ilse's home life, *Guardian* dances, etc., come mainly from extensive information in interviews with them.

Percy Fischer's retirement: 'Die Vrystaatse Regbank', *Volksblad* March 1948; supplementary information from interviews with Drs Paul and Gus Fischer. His death: Ella/B 16/6/56, 17/6/57. Molly's father's death: B/Ella 10/7/56; M/Ella 15/7/56. Concluding views of Bram, and what it all meant: interviews with Nelson Mandela, and Walter Sisulu.

CHAPTER 9

The Alexander Principle, and Trial: F. Matthias Alexander/B, postmarked 6/6/49 (with Hanson's name misspelled in the original); also, Wilfred Barlow, *Alexander Principle*, for a full account of the philosophy; Frank Pierce Jones, *Body Awareness in Action*, ch. 10; *British Medical Journal* 20/3/48 and 8/5/48; interviews with Raymond Dart, and Drs Paul and Gus Fisher. My thanks to Stephen Cooper for personal insights into the Alexander Principle.

Details on Ludorf, the *Star* libel case, and *ITC* vs *UTC* are from reports, variously, in *Rand Daily Mail*, *Star*, *Friend*, and *Volksblad*, as well as Bram and Molly's correspondence with Percy and Ella. The Congress of the People, march on Pretoria, and treason arrests have received celebrated published accounts, among them in Anthony Sampson, *The Treason Cage*, and Helen Joseph, *Side by Side* and *Tomorrow's Sun*. My major source on the first event was from UWL AD1812, E9 3.2.4.3, R.F. 36 ('R.F.' almost certainly stood for Ruth First). Also interviews with Ruth and Ilse Fischer, Hilda and Lionel Bernstein.

The Treason Trial, being so huge, has had entire books devoted to it, in effect divided into those on the Preparatory Examination (Sampson, *The Treason Cage*, and Lionel Forman and E.S. Sachs, *The South African Treason Trial*), and the wonderful 'inside' work on the Trial proper, Helen Joseph's *If This Be Treason*. There is also Tom Karis's invaluable *The Treason Trial in South Africa: A Guide to the Microfilm Record of the Trial* – an obligatory resource for anyone interested in the topic.

In the main I have used the Preparatory Examination, the Record of Proceedings of the Trial, and the Exhibits, not from microfilm, but in the collection at UWL AD1812 [Political Trials] Treason Trial. The full Record of the Trial runs to some 9,500,000 words bound in 180 volumes of 200 pages each. Perhaps mercifully, the Johannesburg version is not complete, so where necessary, because of gaps, or else for the sake of sanity, I have also used the *Treason Trial Bulletin* (AD1812 C3, nos. 1–13) and the Treason Trial Defence Fund (TTDF) Press Summary (AD1812 C.2, nos. 1–58), for the most part compiled from Helen Joseph's original notes. Supplementary information has come from those who were involved, either in the defence team, or as accused:

interviews with I.A. Maisels, Sydney Kentridge, Paul and Adelaide Joseph, Ben Turok, Hilda and Lionel Bernstein.

As to details, only the barest essentials can be mentioned here. Bram's cross-examination of Truter comes at UWL AD1812 F7 vol. 19, pp. 3744–6, and his examination of Resha at F25 vol. 78, pp.16571–3; his application for Rumpff's recusal is at F25 vol. 79, pp. 16620–9 (on this see also Joseph, *Side by Side*, p. 94). Regarding Murray, his role has been the subject of rueful fascination for a number of writers; but as to his ironic significance in the case see AD1812 A12, Judgment as Read Out to Court by the Presiding Judge, Mr Justice F.L.H. Rumpff: 'That the issue of Communism is relevant in this case to the issue of violence, and that on the evidence as a whole the Prosecution has failed to prove that the accused had personal knowledge of the Communist doctrine of violent revolution, or that the accused propagated this doctrine as such'; and AD1812 A13, Reasons for Judgment, Rumpff, J: 'In the present case the evidence of Professor Murray as to what constitutes Marxism–Leninism stood unchallenged.' The two-witness rule is from John Henry Wigmore, *Evidence in Trials at Common Law*, vol. 7, pp. 348–59, §§ 2036–9, and its South African application in L. H. Hoffmann, *The South African Law of Evidence*, pp. 403–4 (thanks to David Rosettenstein for these sources).

My account of the Sharpeville massacre is from reports and photographs in *Golden City Post, Star, Rand Daily Mail, Sunday Express, Sunday Times*, variously 24/3/60–31/3/60. See also Ambrose Reeves, *Shooting at Sharpeville*, and Lodge, *Black Politics in South Africa since 1945*, ch. 9.

Sources on the final stages of the trial are also worth mentioning. Bram's argument: interview, I.A. Maisels, and TTDF Press Summary no. 58, 20–29/3/61. Judgment and celebrations: AD1812 A12, Judgment as Read Out to Court; 'Treason Trial Accused Acquitted' and other accounts, *Star* 29/3/61. Molly's letter: M/B 22/3/[61]. Bram's account, and party at Beaumont St: B/Ruth and Ilse 1/4/61; *Treason Trial Bulletin*, Final Issue, no. 13, May 1961. Luthuli's view: *Treason Trial Bulletin*, no. 13, pp. 1–2. SACP announcement: *South African Communists Speak*, p. 218.

CHAPTER 10

Books on the State of Emergency – most notably as it affected the women – include Joseph, *If This Be Treason* and *Side by Side*, and Hannah Stanton, *Go Well, Stay Well*. My account of the general circumstances of Molly's detention, the possible reasons for it, her life inside, the household at home, and visits comes from a number of sources: Extraordinary Government Gazette, vol. 199 no. 6403, 30/3/60, with amendments; '10020 vs Col. le Roux N.O.', in the Supreme Court of South Africa, with depositions and Judgment; reports, primarily in *Rand Daily Mail*; interviews with Ruth and Ilse Fischer, Ben Turok, Myrtle Berman, Hilda and Lionel Bernstein; and correspondence between Molly, her family, and Ella. For Paul in particular: Paul/M 28/4/60, and n.d.; M/Paul 25/5/60.

The children's demonstration, and delegation in Cape Town: interviews, Ruth and Ilse Fischer, and newspaper reports from *Sunday Express, Sunday Times, Star, Rand Daily*

Mail, and *Cape Times*. 'Dawie's' response is from *Burger* 21/5/65 (cutting with note from Bernard Sachs). Molly's home life after her return comes from her correspondence with Ruth and Ilse.

Contexts for the early 1960s: a range of published sources of which the most useful, as always, are the documents in Karis and Carter (eds.), *From Protest to Challenge*, vol. 3. Macmillan's 'wind of change' comments are well known, Verwoerd's less so: Yale MSSA 605 B33 F599, 'The Price of Appeasement in Africa', speech in the House of Assembly, 10/3/60. Also UWL AD2182 C, the final issue of *Spark* 6/12/62–28/3/63, and a number of intriguing novels of the period, ranging from Nadine Gordimer's *The Late Bourgeois World*, to Richard Rive's *Emergency*, and C.J. Driver's *Elegy for a Revolutionary*, as well as Gordimer's 'Censored, Banned, Gagged' (1963), in *The Essential Gesture*. The police narrative of the Rivonia Raid is in Lauritz Strydom, *Rivonia Unmasked*, chs. 1–2. Anti-communism, later in the chapter, is from Yale MSSA 605 B34 F621, Dr J.D. Vorster, *Kommunisme die Vuurrooi Draak*.

For the SACP underground, Bram's role, and 'The Road to South African Freedom', interviews with Ben Turok, Joe Slovo, Fred and Sarah Carneson, Esther Barsel, Violet Weinberg, Drs Paul and Gus Fischer, George Bizos and Arthur Chaskalson. At Bram's trial, in commenting with pride on the fact that the SACP had been the only party to stand for a full extension of the franchise, Bram remarked: 'this appears from my own draft, a very rough draft, of an introduction to the Programme, which has been admitted to be in my handwriting' ('*The State* vs *Abram Fischer*', Record of Proceedings, p. 210).

On the question of violence, to the above interviews add those with Jack Simons, Rowley Arenstein, Denis Goldberg, Walter Sisulu, Nelson Mandela, Ruth and Ilse Fischer. For Mandela's views on Bram's choices, see *Long Walk to Freedom*, pp. 340, 411.

On Rivonia, its origins, transactions, Bram's presence, and the raid, a number of sources including the following: Yale MSSA 605 B94, '*State* vs *Nelson Mandela and Others*', State's Concluding Address, Pt. 2; interviews with Hilda and Lionel Bernstein, Joe Slovo, Ben Turok, Harold Wolpe, Nelson Mandela, Walter Sisulu, and Denis Goldberg (particularly for the account of his arrest). Also, '*State* vs *Abram Fischer*', Record of Proceedings, p. 237; Hilda Bernstein, *The World That Was Ours*; Ruth First, *117 Days*.

For the Kariba Arbitration and Bayer case: correspondence between Bram and Molly, but particularly '*Farbenfabriken Bayer Aktiengesellschaft* vs *Bayer Pharma (Pty) Ltd*', *South African Law Reports* 1963 (1) Jan.–Mar. (Decisions of the Supreme Courts), pp. 699–714. For Bram and Molly's home life, their rebanning, and Paul: again, correspondence, but also interviews with Ruth and Ilse Fischer, and Mary Benson. Bram's personal touch in difficult times: interviews with Denis Goldberg (Kathrada story), Harold Wolpe, Mollie Anderson, Marius Schoon. See also AnnMarie Wolpe, *The Long Way Home*, p. 96.

On the aftermath of Rivonia it is worth saying that because events occurred so rapidly, and any individual's knowledge was of necessity limited, recollections of these developments may vary or have somewhat blurred outlines. I have depended particularly on interviews with Ruth and Ilse Fischer, Denis Goldberg, Dave Kitson, and

Harold Wolpe; the most complete account of the Wolpe escape is in AnnMarie Wolpe, *The Long Way Home*, with other versions in Bernstein, *The World That Was Ours*, and First, *117 Days*. For the Connolly cartoon: *Rand Daily Mail* 30/8/63.

Views on Bram's new capacity to take risks: interviews, Joe Slovo, and Hilda and Lionel Bernstein. Ella's death, and funeral: interview Ruth and Ilse Fischer (the last letter of Ella's that I have is Ella/M 8/7/63). Molly's world in 1963: in particular, M/Ilse 7/10/63.

CHAPTER 11

Bram's opening address at the Rivonia Trial is from '*The State* vs *Nelson Mandela and Others*', Record of Proceedings (UWL AD1844), Box 3, vol. 19, Defence Opening Address and Nelson Mandela's statement, pp. 1–4. Also, Joel Joffe's memoir of the trial: J.G. Joffe and M. Koff, 'The Rivonia Trial', manuscript (Yale MSSA Film 899), here pp. 222–5. The Court Record and the memoir have been my major sources for the trial throughout (though Joel Joffe has since published his account of the trial as *The Rivonia Story*, all references here are to the manuscript). Supplementary informa-tion and personal perspectives come from other members of the defence team, some of the accused, and others who were involved: Arthur Chaskalson, George Bizos, Joel Joffe, Hilda and Lionel Bernstein, Jean and Himie Bernadt, Nelson Mandela, Walter Sisulu, Denis Goldberg, Ruth and Ilse Fischer. In addition – as might be expected – newspaper reports, and published accounts, including Bernstein, *The World That Was Ours*.

Just a few of the many notable moments in and aspects of the trial are as follows. On Percy Yutar and his role, Joffe and Koff provide a veritable disquisition throughout. Application to quash the first indictment: Joffe and Koff, 'Rivonia Trial', pp. 71–84. Operation Mayibuye: Rivonia Trial, Exhibit R71. Bram's attitude to it: '*State* vs *Abram Fischer*', Record of Proceedings, pp. 249–50 (and see also Mandela, *Long Walk to Freedom*, p. 313). Bernstein and Dirker – a celebrated account; I have relied on Joffe and Koff, 'Rivonia Trial', pp. 205–6. Strategy on Mandela's statement and questions of giving evidence: interviews with all the lawyers, and in particular George Bizos for the 'Socratic' definition. Mandela's speech from the dock: UWL AD1844, Box 3, vol. 19, pp. 4–55. For the effect in court, and the judge's gentle response, Joffe and Koff, 'Rivonia Trial', pp. 226–30. Bram's reluctance on the final paragraph: Mandela, *Long Walk to Freedom*, p. 316. Mitigation testimony: Alan Paton, *Journey Continued*, pp. 249–52; interview, Elizabeth Franklin (Lewin); and Benson, memoir, p. 32. Waiting for sentence, the sentence itself, and scenes in the immediate aftermath: interviews with Nelson Mandela, Walter Sisulu, Denis Goldberg, Arthur Chaskalson, George Bizos, Mollie Anderson; UWL AD1844 Box 4, vol. 31, Judge's Remarks in Passing Sentence; Bernstein, *The World That Was Ours*, pp. 184–7; *Star* 11/6/64.

Other aspects of this account: a day in Molly's life, and her circumstances come from M/Ilse 24/11/63; also interviews with Anthony Eastwood, and Pat Lewin (Davidson). Bram's activities underground: interviews with Dave Kitson, and Ruth and Ilse Fischer.

Liz Lewin's story in its entirety: interview with Elizabeth Franklin. (Confusion can be eliminated here by pointing out that Liz Lewin became Elizabeth Franklin, whereas Pat Davidson later married Hugh Lewin, and was Pat Lewin when I interviewed her.) Her account of the accident and its aftermath supplemented by interviews with Drs Paul and Gus Fischer, Ruth and Ilse Fischer, Pat Lewin, Hilda and Lionel Bernstein, Violet Weinberg. Snow in Johannesburg: *Rand Daily Mail* 18/6/64, 19/6/64.

On Robben Island: interviews Joel Joffe, Walter Sisulu, Nelson Mandela; also, Mandela, *Long Walk to Freedom*, pp. 339–40. Denis in Pretoria: interview, Denis Goldberg. The question of appeals: interviews, Joel Joffe, Nelson Mandela, and comments by Arthur Chaskalson; also Joffe and Koff, 'Rivonia Trial', pp. 366–71.

The exact chronology of the succeeding events is understandably blurred in the memories of those for whom this was a traumatic time, although the incidents they retell are clear. I have worked out the most likely sequence I can. Information around and about the family trip to Cape Town is from Joffe and Koff, 'The Rivonia Trial', and interviews with Ruth and Ilse Fischer, Jean and Himie Bernadt, and Jack Simons and Ray Alexander.

There is some dispute about the exact date when Bram was picked up in George. The newspapers are quite clear it was Saturday, 4 July (*Sunday Times* 5/7/64, *Argus* 9/7/64), but Ray Alexander said that he was stopped the previous day, Friday 3rd, and that when the police came to question her on the Saturday they were trying to tease out Bram's contacts and destination. I have kept by the newspaper accounts, although Ray Alexander's account would also make perfect sense, and I have noted elsewhere her remarkable memory. For details of the event: interviews, Ruth and Ilse Fischer.

CHAPTER 12

Bram's return to Johannesburg, his detention, and release are from newspaper reports in *Sunday Times* and *Argus*, as well as a number of interviews: Ruth and Ilse Fischer, Pat Lewin, Dave Kitson, Elizabeth Franklin, Jack and Phyllis Lewsen. For political contexts (ARM, Harris, SACP arrests, Beyleveld, Ludi), add the following interviews: Hugh Lewin, Drs Paul and Gus Fischer, Esther Barsel, Hilda and Lionel Bernstein, Mollie Anderson; also Miles Brokensha and Robert Knowles, *The Fourth of July Raids*. 'Time for Reassessment' is quoted at length in 'We Must Learn Lessons from the Past', *Sunday Times* cutting, n.d. The story of Pat Davidson's job: interview, Pat Lewin.

Bram arrested and charged, and bail proceedings: interviews, Ruth and Ilse Fischer; B/Tom Karis 30/9/64; cuttings, *Argus*, *Friend*, and *Sunday Times* 24–27/9/64; interview, Mollie Anderson (since she was married at the time she was referred to in court proceedings as Mollie Doyle, but I have retained her original name for clarity).

Bram in London, and the Privy Council case, from a range of sources apart from his letters to Ilse, Paul and Pat Davidson: Mary Benson, 'From the Bar to the Dock', *Guardian* 14/11/64; Benson, memoir, and 'A True Afrikaner'; sundry newspaper reports in South Africa and London; 'The Threat to the Legal Profession' (typescript copy marked 'Bram Fischer, early 1965', in Benson private papers); B/Tom Karis 28/8/64; interviews with Ruth and Ilse Fischer, Anthony Eastwood, Harold Wolpe, Mary

Benson. For the political and personal aspects of his decision on whether to return, add interviews with Drs Paul and Gus Fischer, Hilda and Lionel Bernstein, Lesley Schermbrucker, Rowley Arenstein, Violet Weinberg, Issy Heymann, Ben Turok, Joe Slovo, and Chaskalson interview with Slovo (the one detail that differs between the two Slovo accounts was whether the 'park-bench' meeting was in Regent's or Hyde Park; sadly, I can't say which).

Contexts at home – Ilse and Paul, torture affidavits, new central committee: interviews, Ruth and Ilse Fischer, Violet Weinberg interviewed by Hugh Lewin, Myrtle Berman; 'They Talked of Making Me Mad!', *Post* 25/10/64. Also, Michael Dingake, *My Fight Against Apartheid*, pp. 73–5.

The 'first Fischer Trial' (as it came to be known), including Beyleveld and Ludi's evidence and its effects on Bram, is from a variety of sources: interviews with Joel Joffe, Violet Weinberg, Ruth and Ilse Fischer, Esther Barsel, Dave Kitson, Drs Paul and Gus Fischer; also, Benson, memoir, 'A True Afrikaner', 'Notes on the Fischer Trial' (in Benson private papers), and B/Mary Benson, postmarked 15/11/64; cuttings throughout the trial from *Star*, *Argus*, *Rand Daily Mail*, *Sunday Times*; John D'Oliviera, *Vorster: The Man*, pp. 166–7. Ludi gave varying accounts of his actions on 'Time for Reassessment'; for the later version, see '*State* vs *Abram Fischer*', Record of Proceedings, p. 130.

Bram calls central committee together, and preparations for going underground: interviews with Violet Weinberg, Lesley Schermbrucker, Issy Heymann, Ruth and Ilse Fischer. Also Benson, memoir; and typescript of article by Bram marked 'Not to be published until all clear given' (Benson papers), printed in abbreviated form, *Observer* 13/2/65, and later in *African Communist*, vol. 21 (April–June 1965), pp. 78–82.

Events of 25 January 1965, Bram's attitude, and immediate aftermath, again from a range of sources: typescript copies of Bram's letter to Harold Hanson (n.d., 4 pp.); interviews with Esther Barsel, Norman Levy, Mollie Anderson, Ruth and Ilse Fischer, Anthony Eastwood, Pat Lewin, Elizabeth Franklin, I.A. Maisels; reports in *Star* and *Argus* 25/1/65.

Bram, on leaving the house: B/Mary Benson 23/1/65; B/Ilse, first letter dated 23/1/65, the other n.d. Also, interviews with Ruth and Ilse Fischer.

CHAPTER 13

Headlines on Bram's disappearance are from *Vaderland* 25/1/65, and *Transvaler* 26/1/65; Ilse's newspaper story from *Rand Daily Mail* 26/1/65. For the details of Bram's escape I've obviously depended on interviews with Ruth and Ilse Fischer, and Pat Lewin.

For Bram's life underground in its entirety – from the details of his disguise, to his activities and escapades, contact with others, and concerns – I have used a large swathe of sources, and should mention them in some order here. Interview accounts, both for the South African and London sides, are from Ruth and Ilse Fischer, Pat Lewin, Lesley Schermbrucker, Violet Weinberg, Mary Benson, Ralph and Minnie Sepel, Norman Levy, Fred and Sarah Carneson, Rowley Arenstein, Hilda and Lionel Bernstein, Nelson Mandela, Walter Sisulu, Joe Slovo. For sightings etc.: tracts of newspaper reports from the *Argus*, *Rand Daily Mail*, *Cape Times*, *Burger*, *Star*, *Sunday Times*,

Sunday Chronicle, Golden City Post, Sunday Express, Dagbreek, Landstem and others. Throughout, for details as they were later revealed, I have used '*State* vs *Abram Fischer*', both the Record of Evidence from the Preparatory Examination, and the Record of Proceedings from the trial proper. Other sources included Benson, memoir, for Mary Benson's detailed recollections; and Michael Dingake, *My Fight Against Apartheid*, which gives moving testimony on pp. 89–90. The Nazim Hikmet lines are from 'Some Advice to Those Who Will Serve Time in Prison' (1949), in *Selected Poetry: Nazim Hikmet*, p. 12 (thanks to Agha Shahid Ali for the clue).

The Bar Council case: initial newspaper report [*Star* 29/1/65], and interviews variously with Arthur Chaskalson, George Bizos, Anthony Eastwood and Mary Benson. For Bram's exposition of his position, and concerns: B/Harold Hanson 4/2/65; B/Andrew Brown at Bell, Dewar and Hall 9/7/65; B/W. Aronsohn 4/2/65. Significant documents relating to the proceedings include a copy of Affidavit by Melville Henry Sydney Festenstein, 10/6/65, and related correspondence; also, Notice of Motion, Society of Advocates 14/6/65; Court Order 29/6/65; B/Messrs Edward Nathan, Friedland, Mansell and Lewis 9/7/65; text of notice placed in *Sunday Times* 4/7/64. Blackwell's intervention: *Sunday Times* 7/2/65. The decision: '*The Society of Advocates of South Africa (Witwatersrand Division)* vs *Abram Fischer*', Judgment, 2/11/65, De Wet, JP, with Hill and Boshoff concurring. Bram's feelings particularly from accounts by George Bizos and Mary Benson.

The first Fischer Trial as it continued is from reports in *Rand Daily Mail* and *Star*; also Benson, memoir, and 'A True Afrikaner'. Ilse's solitude comes particularly from interview with Pat Lewin; also *Sunday Chronicle* 14/2/65, and article by Margaret Smith, n.d. [*Sunday Times* Feb. 1965]. Bram's solitude is from a number of the interviews with those who saw him, and B/Ilse 11/4/65.

The Heymann story comes from reports in *Eastern Province Herald* 10/9/65 and *Rand Daily Mail* 11/9/65, as well as interviews with Issy Heymann, Ralph and Minnie Sepel, Rowley Arenstein, Lesley Schermbrucker, Marius Schoon, Violet Weinberg. As a number of the interview accounts were based on hearsay, and all of them on memory, it is worth saying that the exact sequence of events is particularly difficult to reconstruct.

The story of police activity, and the drift towards Bram's arrest, comes from many of the interviews, including Pat Lewin, Dave Kitson, Ralph and Minnie Sepel, Ruth and Ilse Fischer, and Lesley Schermbrucker. Violet's detention and interrogation is from her testimony at her trial for refusing to give evidence against Michael Dingake and Issy Heymann, as reported in the *Star* 18/5/66, and *Rand Daily Mail* 19/5/66. The question of the man with the beard is from Ilse Fischer's recollection of what Violet Weinberg had told her at the time. The exact and particular sequence of Bram's arrest comes from a number of sources: interviews with Pat Lewin, Ilse Fischer, Mary Benson, Ralph and Minnie Sepel; Benson, memoir; and detailed police accounts, evidence and exhibits in '*State* vs *Abram Fischer*', both Preparatory Examination and Record of Proceedings.

In the midst of everything, Paul Fischer's return (and Ruth's) are from interviews with Ruth and Ilse Fischer. The key newspaper reports of Bram's arrest are from *Rand*

Daily Mail 12/11/65, where the main headline was 'Rhodesia Under Sanctions', but tucked in, at the centre of the page, was a short column, 'Disguised Bram Fischer Arrested'; and *Transvaler* 12/11/65 (including photograph). As for the Sepels' suddenly empty house, the artist Cecil Skotnes, who lived over the road – and down Mons Road from us – mentioned this.

CHAPTER 14

Bram appears in court to be charged, first sightings by his friends and colleagues, and his life awaiting trial, from a number of sources: the many frenzied newspaper reports; interviews with Pat Lewin, George Bizos, Ruth and Ilse Fischer, Drs Paul and Gus Fischer; Bram's letters to his family, Elizabeth Franklin, and Brian and Sonia Bunting.

The Preparatory Examination is from '*State* vs *Abram Fischer*', Record of Evidence, with Bram's plea and statement on the evidence at pp. 244–7. The trial proper is from '*State* vs *Abram Fischer*', Record of Proceedings, with Bram's speech from the dock at pp. 202–65 (for the final sentence of Bram's speech I have relied on a text circulated by Mary Benson to the United Nations Special Committee on Apartheid, which is more intelligible in context). In addition, newspaper reports; Nadine Gordimer, 'Why Did Bram Fischer Choose Jail?' (1966), in *The Essential Gesture;* interviews with George Bizos, Arthur Chaskalson, Ruth and Ilse Fischer. Bram's last letters prior to sentence: B/Elizabeth Franklin 30/4/66; B/Ilse and Paul 8/5/66; also a collection of letters from individuals and organisations around the world addressed (in the main) to Paul Fischer. Surrounding contexts and experiences as they affected those who had refused to testify, as well as persecution of Ruth, Ilse and Sholto Cross: newspaper accounts; and interviews with Violet Weinberg, Lesley Schermbrucker, Ruth and Ilse Fischer.

Bram's arrival in Pretoria Local: interview, Issy Heymann, and Heymann, prison memoir of Bram Fischer (this latter a quite remarkable document). As for the section on Bram's life in prison together with his comrades, it depends on so many stories told by so many people that it is hard to separate them. A whole book could be written on this period, and there are some, including Hugh Lewin's *Bandiet* and sections of Baruch Hirson's *Revolutions in my Life*. I cannot match these for first-hand authenticity, nor is it appropriate to try. My thanks for their time and willingness to remember to the following: Rowley Arenstein, Fred Carneson, Denis Goldberg, Issy Heymann, Baruch Hirson, Dave Kitson, Norman Levy, Marius Schoon, and Paul Trewhela. In addition, I have obviously used Bram's regular, though constricted, correspondence throughout, as well as interviews with Ruth and Ilse Fischer. Though not all aspects of Bram's experience can be annotated here, a few particular references follow.

For the Hikmet poems: first excerpt from 'That's How It Goes', Bursa Prison (1948), in *Selected Poems: Nazim Hikmet*, p. 82; the second from 'The Moscow Symphony' (1952), in *The Moscow Symphony and Other Poems*, p. 40. Text of poem on the Lenin Prize: Dave Ernst (who wrote it) to Paul Fischer 10/1/70. *Beseeringstyd*: Hugh Lewin, memorial tribute for Bram Fischer. Birds, garden and evenings, and Bram's last letter to Paul: B/Paul 21/1/70, 16/2/70, 21/12/70. Circumstances of and around Paul's death, both inside and outside prison: interviews with Ruth and Ilse Fischer, and Drs

Paul and Gus Fischer, as well as a number of those cited above; Hugh Lewin, *Bandiet*, pp. 223–5; Arthur Chaskalson, text of memorial tribute at Paul Fischer's funeral. Bram's consolation: B/Ilse 29/3/71. Ilse's marriage: B/Ilse 21/10/71 (Bram's last letter in the family collection that I have seen is B/Ilse 24/4/72, the day after his sixty-fourth birthday). Contact with Leo Marquard, and Leo's death: UCT BC 587, B/Leo Marquard 4/12/65, 1/5/66; B/Nell Marquard 3/4/74. Anthony's affair, and Bram's response: interviews Anthony Eastwood, and Ruth and Ilse Fischer.

The campaigns for Bram's release were reported in all the major South African newspapers. In addition, Ruth and Ilse Fischer, letters to State President, Prime Minister, and Minister of Justice (all 6/4/73), and draft letters to judges throughout the country; and replies indirectly or directly from some of the above. Further information on this continuing theme: interviews Ruth and Ilse Fischer. On the international campaign: notes, correspondence in Benson papers to and from Donald Fraser, George McGovern, Neil Kinnock, James Callaghan, Ivor Richard, Carel de Wet, Pik Botha.

On Bram's declining health and accelerating illness, I have again drawn on a number of accounts, including descriptions and recollections by Denis Goldberg, Dave Kitson, Marius Schoon, Drs Paul and Gus Fischer, and Ruth and Ilse Fischer. Also, and primarily, document relating to the illness of Bram Fischer [written by Denis Goldberg] (pencil on tissue paper, 7.1 cm x 16.1 cm, 5 cols.), Institute of Commonwealth Studies Library. This, reproduced in small part in the text, was perhaps the most startling document of all that I have seen in researching this book; my thanks to Dr Baruch Hirson for telling me about it, and gaining me access. Also at the ICS, two Memoranda (similarly reduced) submitted to the Commission of Enquiry into the Penal System of the Republic of South Africa, the first (9/12/74) signed by Bram and eight others, the second (a supplementary memorandum 16/2/75) when Bram was incapable of signing.

The story of Bram's release is, in the main, from interviews with Drs Paul and Gus Fischer, and Ruth and Ilse Fischer, along with swathes of newspaper reports. Bram's death, cremation, and ashes scandal are also from interviews with his brothers and daughters, with supplementary recollections by I.A. Maisels, and reports in newspapers nation-wide and internationally, 8/5/75–13/5/75.

EPILOGUE

Eulogies for Bram: typescripts of memorials from Hugh Lewin, Lilian Ngoyi, and André Brink; also *South African Outlook* (May 1975), pp. 66-70 for other messages; 'Death of Bram Fischer', and Peter Mackintosh, 'A Communist in the Truest Mould', *African Communist*, no. 62 (Third Quarter) 1975, pp. 24–5, 27–33. Letters and telegrams from multitudes of others were collected by Ruth and Ilse Fischer. Other memorials: interview, Denis Goldberg (Pretoria Local); *International Defence and Aid Fund News* n.d. (London); partial text of letter to Ruth and Ilse Fischer n.d. (Robben Island). Bram's moral tutor: Christopher Cox/B 18/4/75.

In the section on what Bram would have seen, the view from Steve Biko is from Bernard Zylstra, 'An Interview with Steve Biko', *The Reformed Journal*, vol. 27 no. 12 (December 1977), p. 18. Other accounts of the period from Mandela, *Long Walk to*

Freedom (for the text of Mandela's Cape Town speech, electronic thanks to Irwin Manoim). Bram had a sustained belief that he would be taken directly from prison to government: recollection by Justice Ludorf, as reported in *Sunday Tribune*, 11/5/75.

On tragedy: correspondence from Sir Laurens van der Post 15/1/92; the definition by Georg Lukács is from *Studies in European Realism*, p. 33.

Reflections of and on Bram: *Burger*, editorial 9/5/75, and silhouette photograph with Himie Bernadt and Joel Joffe, 17/5/75; also, Mary Benson, *At the Still Point* (see the Afterword in the 1991 edn); André Brink, *Rumours of Rain*; Gordimer, *Burger's Daughter*, quote p. 332. Joe Slovo's quoted comments are from the interview with Arthur Chaskalson; additional perspectives from my interview with Slovo. His role in the constitutional negotiations: Mandela, *Long Walk to Freedom*, pp. 510, 518.

Sections on legacies of various kinds: interviews, Drs Paul and Gus Fischer; Aelred Stubbs, CR/Bishop of Johannesburg 15/3/75 (resignation in protest from St John's School Council), and Stubbs/Ilse 18/3/75; text of first Bram Fischer Memorial Lecture, by President Nelson R. Mandela, Market Theatre 9/6/95. Bram's gown, and desk: B/Ilse 12/8/71; and e-mail confirmation from Arthur Chaskalson 27/5/97 and 28/5/97.

Bram's ashes: in particular, e-mail correspondence from Ruth Fischer 20/5/97 (it turns out that Bram's sister Ada's ashes had also been scattered in that same Garden of Remembrance). Final views and recollections: interview with Edwin Mofutsanyana.

BIBLIOGRAPHY

ARCHIVAL

Free State Archives Depot (FSA)
  Abraham Fischer Collection
  Prime Minister's Office (Orange River Colony)
  Miscellaneous: Colonial Office; Municipality of Bloemfontein; Governor's Office;
    Provincial Secretary's Office

Grey College School
  Grey College School Magazine

Institute of Commonwealth Studies Library, London University (ICS)
  Document relating to the illness in prison of Bram Fischer
  Memoranda to the Commission of Enquiry into the Penal System of South Africa,
    December 1974 and February 1975

South African Jewish Board of Deputies Archive, Johannesburg (SAJBD)

University of Cape Town Libraries, Manuscripts and Archives Department (UCT)
  Leo Marquard Papers

University of the Witwatersrand Library, Historical Papers (UWL)
  Native Economic Commission
  Records of the Joint Council of Europeans and Africans
  Records of the South African Institute of Race Relations
  Records of the South African Institute of Race Relations, Political Collection

Yale University Library, Manuscripts and Archives (Yale MSSA)
  African Collection
  Communist Party of South Africa Papers 1932–48 (Microfilm: Hoover Institution)

COURT RECORDS AND TRIAL MATERIALS

'The Society of Advocates of South Africa (Witwatersrand Division) vs Abram Fischer', In
    the Supreme Court of South Africa (Transvaal Provincial Division), Judgment
'The State vs Abram Fischer', Preparatory Examination, Case No. G375/64, List of

Exhibits, Offences Charged, Record of Evidence
'*The State* vs *Abram Fischer*', In the Supreme Court of South Africa (Transvaal Provincial Division), Record of Proceedings
University of Witwatersrand Library, Historical Papers (UWL)
  'Preparatory Examination in the matter of *Regina* vs *153 Individuals on an allegation of high treason*', In the Magistrates' Court for the District of Johannesburg
  '*Regina* vs *F. Adams and Others*' (Treason Trial), In the Supreme Court of South Africa (Special Criminal Court constituted in terms of Section 112 of Act 56 of 1955, as amended), Record of Proceedings
  Treason Trial Exhibits
  Treason Trial Bulletin
  Treason Trial Defence Fund Press Summary
  '*The State* vs *Nelson Mandela and Others*', In the Supreme Court of South Africa (Transvaal Provincial Division), Record of Proceedings
Yale University Library, Manuscripts and Archives (Yale MSSA)
  '*The State* vs *Nelson Mandela and Others*', In the Supreme Court of South Africa (Transvaal Provincial Division), Indictment and State's Concluding Address
  J.G. Joffe and M. Koff, 'The Rivonia Trial' (Microfilm, University of Chicago Library)

LETTERS

From Ruth and Ilse Fischer, and Joel Joffe: correspondence and associated papers to and from
  Bram Fischer and Percy and Ella Fischer
  Bram Fischer and Molly Krige/Fischer
  Molly Krige/Fischer and Percy and Ella Fischer
  Bram and Molly Fischer and Children
  Percy and Ella Fischer and Grandchildren
  Bram Fischer and Siblings
Correspondence given by the following: Connie Anderson, Mollie Anderson, Mary Benson, Brian and Sonia Bunting, Elizabeth Franklin, Tom Karis

PRIVATE COLLECTIONS / PAPERS

Mary Benson, including memoir of Bram Fischer (typescript), and 'Notes on the Fischer Trial'
Arthur Chaskalson, including material relating to '*The Society of Advocates* vs *Abram Fischer*', '*10020* vs *Colonel le Roux*', memorial tribute for Paul Fischer
Elizabeth Franklin, including copies of memorial tributes for Bram Fischer by Hugh Lewin and others
Issy Heymann, prison memoirs of Bram Fischer and Eli Weinberg
Pauline Jenisch, material on the Rev. F. Bernsmann

Lesley Schermbrucker, including prison memoir by Issy Heymann of Ivan Schermbrucker, and copies of memorial tributes for Bram Fischer by Hugh Lewin and
others

INTERVIEWS AND CORRESPONDENCE

Taped Interviews

Connie Anderson, 'Koppiesrus', Bloemfontein 10/2/86
Mollie Anderson, 'Koppiesrus', Bloemfontein 10/2/86
Mary Benson, London 8/8/83
Hilda and Lionel Bernstein, Dorstone, Herefordshire 4/9/84 (2 tapes)
E.J. Burford, London 20/9/84
Adv. Arthur Chaskalson, SC, Johannesburg 8/3/86 (2 tapes)
Anthony Eastwood, Harare 16/5/87
Drs Paul and Gustav Fischer, 'Klein Bottelary', Plettenberg Bay

    Tape 1   1/2/86
    Tape 2   1–3/2/86
    Tape 3   3/2/86
    Tape 4   3–4/2/86
    Tape 5   4/2/86

Ruth and Ilse Fischer, Johannesburg

    Tape 1   27/2/86
    Tape 2   6/3/86
    Tape 3   22/5/86
    Tape 4   22/5/86–7/8/86
    Tape 5   7/8/86–28/8/86
    Tape 6   28/8/86
    Tape 7   11/9/86
    Tape 8   1/10/86
    Tape 9   5/11/86
    Tape 10 20/11/86 (Ilse Fischer)
    Tape 11 12/12/86 (Ruth Fischer)
    Tape 12 9/6/87–24/6/87
    Tape 13 24/6/87

Elizabeth Franklin (Lewin), Cleveland, Ohio 15/5/88
Denis Goldberg, London 4/8/87 (2 tapes)
Baruch Hirson, London 17/8/84 (3 tapes)
Joel Joffe, Liddington, Wiltshire 9/8/87
Paul Joseph, London 15/8/87
Willie Kalk, Johannesburg 23/7/86
Adv. Sydney Kentridge, SC, Johannesburg 8/12/88
Dave Kitson, London 17/8/87
Hugh Lewin, Harare 16–17/5/87 (2 tapes)
Pat Lewin (Davidson), Harare 17/5/87 (2 tapes)
Jack and Dr Phyllis Lewsen, Johannesburg 10/12/84

Adv. I.A. Maisels, SC, Johannesburg 23/4/85
President Nelson Mandela, Johannesburg 28/12/91 (accompanied by George Bizos)
Joel Mervis, Johannesburg 3/4/87
Edwin Mofutsanyana, Butha Buthe 15/3/86 (accompanied by Robert Edgar and James Campbell)
Marius Schoon, Johannesburg 7/12/91
Jack Simons and Ray Alexander (Simons), Cape Town 13/12/91 (interviewed separately)
Walter Sisulu, Johannesburg 6/12/91
Joe Slovo, Johannesburg 23/12/91
Drs Mervyn Susser and Zena Stein, Hastings-on-Hudson, New York 28/2/88
Paul Trewhela, London 11/8/87
Ben Turok, London 6/8/87
Gladys and Peter Walker, Buxton, Derbyshire 19/9/84
Violet Weinberg, Johannesburg 29/11/91 (accompanied by Ilse Fischer)
Harold Wolpe, Cape Town 19/12/91

Interviews: Notebooks
Connie and Mollie Anderson, 'Koppiesrus', Bloemfontein 10/3/86
Connie Anderson, 'Koppiesrus', Bloemfontein 13/3/86
Rowley Arenstein, Durban 4/5/87
Esther Barsel, Johannesburg 26/6/87
Myrtle Berman, London 23/9/84
Jean and Himie Bernadt, Cape Town, Jan. 1985
Adv. George Bizos, SC, Johannesburg 27/6/87
Adv. George Bizos, SC, and Adv. Arthur Chaskalson, S.C., noted conversation, n.d.
Sonia Bunting, London 18/8/87
Fred and Sarah Carneson, London 13/8/87
Adv. Arthur Chaskalson, noted conversation, Johannesburg 3/12/91
Prof. Raymond Dart, Johannesburg 7/2/85
Dr Beck de Villiers, Bloemfontein 12/3/86
Johan de Villiers, Johannesburg 22/11/85
Bessie Greenstein, London 27/9/84
Miriam and Bill Hepner, Johannesburg 15/4/87
Issy Heymann, Johannesburg 30/6/87
Rica Hodgson, Johannesburg 6/12/91
Pauline Jenisch, Johannesburg 12/11/85
Prof. Arthur Keppel-Jones, Johannesburg 5/3/86
Freda Levson, London 1984
Norman Levy, London 7/8/87
Dr Phyllis Lewsen, Johannesburg 10/12/84
Lesley (and Jill) Schermbrucker, Johannesburg 29/6/87
Ralph and Minnie Sepel, London 6/9/84

Sir Edgar Williams, telephone interview, Oxford 3/9/84
Herleve Yates, Cape Town, Jan. 1985

Interviews by others
Joe Slovo, interviewed by Arthur Chaskalson, Johannesburg 17/2/94
Ben Turok, interviewed by David Everatt, London 1988, Tape 2, transcript
Violet Weinberg, interviewed by Hugh Lewin, Harare, Zimbabwe c. Oct. 1985

Correspondence
Personal correspondence from Sir Geoffrey Cox, Errol Harris, C.J. Johnson, Arthur
    Keppel-Jones, Sir Laurens van der Post

NEWSPAPERS, PERIODICALS, JOURNALS

Cuttings, archival and other research from the following, with place of publication
where known or relevant:
Advance
African Communist (London)
Argus (Cape Town)
Beeld (Johannesburg)
British Medical Journal
Burger (Cape Town)
Cape Times (Cape Town)
Daily Dispatch (East London)
Eastern Province Herald (Port Elizabeth)
Fighting Talk (Johannesburg)
Freedom
Friend (Bloemfontein)
Golden City Post (Johannesburg)
Guardian (Cape Town)
Imvo Zabantsundu (King William's Town)
Indian Opinion (Durban)
Landstem (Cape Town)
Manchester Guardian Weekly (Manchester)
New York Times (New York)
Nkululeko [sic]
The NUSAS (Cape Town)
Political Science Quarterly
Post (Johannesburg)
Race Relations (Johannesburg)
Rand Daily Mail (Johannesburg)
Die Rapport (Aberdeen)
Rapport (Johannesburg)

The Reformed Journal
South African Law Reports
Spotlight on South Africa (ANC, Dar es Salaam)
Star (Johannesburg)
Sunday Chronicle (Johannesburg)
Sunday Express (Johannesburg)
Sunday Times (Johannesburg)
Sunday Tribune (Durban)
The Times (London)
Transvaal Communist
Transvaler (Johannesburg)
Umsebenzi (Johannesburg)
Vaderland (Johannesburg)
Volksblad (Bloemfontein)

PUBLISHED AND OTHER SOURCES

Aristotle. *The Poetics of Aristotle*, ed. S.H. Butcher, 3rd edn. rev. London and New York: Macmillan, 1902.

Barlow, Wilfred. *The Alexander Principle*. London: Arrow, 1975.

Benson, Mary. *South Africa: The Struggle for a Birthright*. Harmondsworth: Penguin, 1966.

Benson, Mary. *At the Still Point*. Gambit: Boston, 1969; London: Chatto and Windus, 1970. Rpt: Harmondsworth: Penguin, 1991.

Benson, Mary. 'A True Afrikaner', *Granta* 19, 1986, pp. 198–223.

Benson, Mary. *Nelson Mandela: The Man and the Movement*. London and New York: Norton, 1986.

Benson, Mary (ed.). *The Sun Will Rise: Statements from the Dock by Southern African Political Prisoners*. London: IDAF, 1981.

Bernstein, Hilda. *The World That Was Ours*. London: Heinemann, 1967.

Bidwell, Maude. *Breath of the Veld*. Cape Town: Juta, 1923.

Brink, André. *Rumours of Rain*. London: W.H. Allen, 1978.

Brokensha, Miles and Knowles, Robert. *The Fourth of July Raids*. Cape Town: Simondium, 1965.

Bullock, Alan. *Hitler and Stalin: Parallel Lives*. New York: Vintage, 1993.

Bunting, Brian. *The Rise of the South African Reich*. London: IDAF, 1986.

Burns, Catherine. 'An Historical Study of the Friends of the Soviet Union and the South African Peace Council,' B.A. Hons. Dissertation. University of the Witwatersrand, 1987.

Clingman, Stephen. *The Novels of Nadine Gordimer: History from the Inside*. (Johannesburg: Ravan, 1986; 2nd edn Amherst: University of Massachusetts Press, 1992; London: Bloomsbury, 1993).

Costello, John and Tsarev, Oleg. *Deadly Illusions*. New York: Crown, 1993.

Crossman, Richard (ed.). *The God That Failed*. New York: Harper, 1950.

Cunningham, Valentine. *British Writers of the Thirties*. Oxford: Oxford University

Press, 1988.

Davenport, T.R.H. *South Africa: A Modern History*. London: Macmillan, 1977.

Desmond, Cosmas. *The Discarded People*. Harmondsworth: Penguin, 1971.

Deutscher, Isaac. *The Prophet Outcast: Trotsky 1929–1940*. 1963; London and New York: Oxford University Press, 1970.

Dingake, Michael. *My Fight Against Apartheid*. London: Kliptown Books, 1987.

D'Oliviera, John. *Vorster: The Man*. Johannesburg: Ernest Stanton, 1977.

Driver, C. J. *Elegy for a Revolutionary*. London: Faber and Faber, 1969.

First, Ruth. *117 Days*. 1965; New York: Monthly Review Press, 1989.

Forman, Lionel and Sachs, E.S. *The South African Treason Trial*. London: Calder, 1957.

Foster, R. F. *Modern Ireland 1600–1972*. Harmondsworth: Penguin, 1989.

Gedye, G.E.R. *Fallen Bastions: The Central European Tragedy*. London: Gollancz, 1939.

Gordimer, Nadine. *The Lying Days*. London: Gollancz; New York: Simon and Schuster; 1953.

Gordimer, Nadine. *The Late Bourgeois World*. London: Cape; New York: Viking; 1966.

Gordimer, Nadine. *No Place Like: Selected Stories*. London: Cape, 1975; New York: Viking, 1976.

Gordimer, Nadine. *Burger's Daughter*. London: Cape, 1979.

Gordimer, Nadine. *The Essential Gesture: Writing, Politics and Places,* ed. Stephen Clingman. Cape Town: Philip; London: Cape; New York: Knopf; 1988.

Hikmet, Nazim. *Selected Poems: Nazim Hikmet*. Translated Taner Baybars. London: Cape, 1967.

Hikmet, Nazim. *The Moscow Symphony and Other Poems*. Translated Taner Baybars. London: Deutsch, 1970.

Hikmet, Nazim. *Selected Poetry: Nazim Hikmet*. Translated by Randy Blasing and Mutlu Konik. New York: Persea, 1986.

Hirson, Baruch. *Revolutions in my Life*. Johannesburg: Witwatersrand University Press, 1995.

Hoffmann, L. H. *The South African Law of Evidence*. Durban: Butterworths, 1970.

Huddleston, Fr Trevor. *Naught for your Comfort*. London: Collins, 1956.

Hutchinson, Alfred. *The Road to Ghana*. New York: John Day, 1960.

Hynes, Samuel. *The Auden Generation*. Princeton: Princeton University Press, 1972.

Jacobs, David Stephanus. 'Abraham Fischer in sy Tydperk (1850–1913)'. D.Phil. Thesis. University of the Orange Free State, 1960.

Joffe, Joel. *The Rivonia Story*. Bellville: Mayibuye, 1995.

Jones, Frank Pierce. *Body Awareness in Action*. New York: Schocken, 1976.

Joseph, Helen. *Tomorrow's Sun*. London: Hutchinson, 1966.

Joseph, Helen. *If This Be Treason*. London: Deutsch, 1963.

Karis, Thomas. *The Treason Trial in South Africa: A Guide to the Microfilm Record of the Trial*. Stanford: Hoover Institution, 1965.

Karis, Thomas and Carter, Gwendolen M. (eds.). *From Protest to Challenge: A Documentary History of African Politics in South Africa 1882–1964,* 4 vols. Stanford: Hoover Institution Press, 1972–77.

Lerumo, A. [Michael Harmel]. *Fifty Fighting Years: The Communist Party of South Africa*

1921–1971. London: Inkululeko, c. 1971.

Lewin. Hugh. *Bandiet*. London: Barrie and Jenkins, 1974; Heinemann, 1981.

Lewsen, Phyllis (ed.). *Selections from the Correspondence of John X. Merriman 1899–1905*. Cape Town: Van Riebeeck Society, 1966.

Lewsen, Phyllis (ed.). *Selections from the Correspondence of John X. Merriman 1905–1924*. Cape Town: Van Riebeeck Society, 1969.

Lloyd, T.O. *Empire to Welfare State*. 3rd edn. Oxford: Oxford University Press, 1989.

Lodge, Tom. *Black Politics in South Africa since 1945*. London: Longman, 1983.

Ludi, Gerard and Grobbelaar, Blaar. *The Amazing Mr Fischer*. Cape Town: Nasionale Boekhandel, 1966.

Lukács, Georg. *Studies in European Realism*. London: Merlin, 1978.

Mandela, Nelson. *Long Walk to Freedom: The Autobiography of Nelson Mandela*. Boston, New York, Toronto, London: Little, Brown, 1994.

Marquard, Leo (ed.). *Letters from a Boer Parsonage*. Cape Town: Purnell, 1967.

Matshikiza, Todd. *Chocolates for my Wife*. London: Hodder and Stoughton, 1961.

Millin, Sarah Gertrude. *God's Step-Children*. London: Constable, 1924; Johannesburg: Ad Donker, 1986.

Mitchison, Naomi. *A Life for Africa: The Story of Bram Fischer*. London: Merlin, 1973.

Modisane, Bloke. *Blame Me on History*. London: Thames and Hudson, 1963.

Moodie, T. Dunbar. *The Rise of Afrikanerdom: Power, Apartheid, and the Afrikaner Civil Religion*. Berkeley and Los Angeles: University of California Press, 1975.

Nakasa, Nat. *The World of Nat Nakasa*. Johannesburg: Ravan and Bateleur, 1975.

Nkosi, Lewis. *Home and Exile*. London: Longman, 1965.

Paton, Alan. *Journey Continued*. New York: Scribner, 1988.

Pirow, Oswald. *Shangani*. Johannesburg: Dagbreek, n.d.

Plaatje, Sol T. *Native Life in South Africa*. 1916; Johannesburg: Ravan Press, 1982.

Reeves, Ambrose. *Shooting at Sharpeville*. London: Gollancz, 1960.

Rive, Richard. *Emergency*. London: Faber and Faber, 1964.

'The Road to South African Freedom', The Programme of the South African Communist Party. London: Ellis Bowles, n.d. [c. 1962]), 53 pp.

Robertson, Janet. *Liberalism in South Africa 1948–63*. Oxford: Clarendon Press, 1971.

Roux, Edward. *Time Longer Than Rope: A History of the Black Man's Struggle for Freedom in South Africa*. Madison: University of Wisconsin Press, 1964.

Sampson, Anthony. *Drum: A Venture into the New Africa*. London: Collins, 1956.

Sampson, Anthony. *The Treason Cage: The Opposition on Trial in South Africa*. London: Heinemann, 1958.

Sarakinsky, Mike. 'From "Freehold Township" to "Model Township": A Political History of Alexandra, 1905–1983.' B.A. Hons. Dissertation. University of the Witwatersrand, 1984.

Simons, Jack and Ray. *Class and Colour in South Africa 1850–1950*. London: IDAF, 1983.

South African Communists Speak. London: Inkululeko, 1981.

Spender, Stephen. *Vienna*. London: Faber and Faber, 1934.

Spender, Stephen. *The Edge of Being*. London: Faber and Faber, 1947.

Stanton, Hannah. *Go Well, Stay Well*. London: Hodder and Stoughton, 1961.

Strydom, Lauritz. *Rivonia Unmasked*. Johannesburg: Voortrekkerpers, 1965.

A Survey of Race Relations in South Africa. Johannesburg: South African Institute of Race Relations, annually.

Swan, Maureen. *Gandhi: The South African Experience*. Johannesburg: Ravan Press, 1985.

Themba, Can. *The Will to Die*. London: Heinemann, 1972.

Van de Velde, Theodoor H. *Ideal Marriage*. 1930; New York: Random House, 1965.

Venn, J.A. (ed.). *Alumni Cantabrigienses*. Pt II, 6 vols., 1752–1900. Cambridge: Cambridge University Press, 1940.

Vermaak, Chris. *Braam Fischer: The Man with Two Faces*. Johannesburg: Afrikaanse Pers, 1966.

Walsh, Peter. *The Rise of African Nationalism in South Africa*. London: Hurst, 1970.

Warwick, Peter (ed.). *The South African War*. London: Longman, 1980.

Weinberg, Eli. *Portrait of a People*. London: IDAF, 1981.

Wigmore, John Henry. *Evidence in Trials at Common Law*, vol. 7. Boston: Little, Brown, 1978.

Wilson, Monica and Thompson, Leonard (eds.). *The Oxford History of South Africa*. 2 vols. Oxford: Clarendon Press, 1969–71.

Wolpe, AnnMarie. *The Long Way Home*. Cape Town: Philip, 1994.

INDEX